Also by Ashley D. Farmer

Remaking Black Power:
How Black Women Transformed an Era

New Perspectives on the Black Intellectual Tradition
(coedited with Keisha N. Blain and Christopher Cameron)

Queen Mother

Queen Mother

Black Nationalism, Reparations,
and the
Untold Story of Audley Moore

Ashley D. Farmer

Pantheon 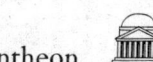 New York

FIRST HARDCOVER EDITION
PUBLISHED BY PANTHEON BOOKS 2025

Published by Pantheon Books, a division of
Penguin Random House LLC, 1745 Broadway, New York, NY 10019.

Pantheon Books and the colophon are registered trademarks of
Penguin Random House LLC.

Grateful acknowledgment is made to the following: Taylor & Francis Ltd. for permission to reprint "The Enigmatic Eloise" by Audley Moore, from "Poetry," *The Black Scholar* 1, no. 8 (1970): 50–52, copyright © 1970 The Robert Chrisman Foundation, reprinted by permission of Taylor & Francis Ltd., https://www.tandfonline.com on behalf of The Robert Chrisman Foundation; and the Warner family for permission to reprint "The Twain Has Met," "School Board Protest Poem," and "The Princely Malcolm X" by Audley Moore, courtesy of the Warner family.

Library of Congress Cataloging-in-Publication Data
Names: Farmer, Ashley D., author
Title: Queen Mother : Black nationalism, reparations, and the untold story of Audley Moore / Ashley D. Farmer.
Description: First hardcover edition. | New York, New York : Pantheon Books, 2025. | Includes bibliographical references and index.
Identifiers: LCCN 2025000263 (print) | LCCN 2025000264 (ebook) | ISBN 9780593701546 (hardcover) | ISBN 9780593701553 (ebook)
Subjects: LCSH: Moore, Audley, 1898–1997. | African American women political activists—Biography. | African American political activists—Biography. | African American women—Biography. | Black nationalism—United States—History—20th century. | African Americans—Reparations. | African Americans—Politics and government—20th century. | United States—Race relations—History—20th century. | LCGFT: Biographies.
Classification: LCC E185.97.M75 F37 2025 (print) | LCC E185.97.M75 (ebook) | DDC 323.168092 [B]—dc23/eng/20250813
LC record available at https://lccn.loc.gov/2025000263
LC ebook record available at https://lccn.loc.gov/2025000264

Book design by Betty Lew

penguinrandomhouse.com | pantheonbooks.com

Printed in the United States of America
1st Printing

The authorized representative in the EU for product safety and compliance is
Penguin Random House Ireland, Morrison Chambers, 32 Nassau Street,
Dublin D02 YH68, Ireland, https://eu-contact.penguin.ie.

*For Ade—who co-writes our long history together
with love, grace, and patience*

Contents

Introduction

When I was nine years old, my mother, Madeline Farmer, sat me down on our living room couch in Nashville and unfolded *I Dream a World: Portraits of Black Women Who Changed America* between us. My feet kicked excitedly as I watched her carefully turn the glossy pages. The nearly two-and-a-half-pound, eleven-and-a-half-inch-tall book felt massive on my little lap. But I ignored the impressions it made in my skin as I traced my fingers over large black-and-white photos of civil rights icon Rosa Parks and Olympic sprinter Wilma Rudolph, all while my mother regaled me with stories about epic boycotts and hard-won footraces.

This was what Pulitzer Prize–winning photographer Brian Lanker hoped for when he curated the exhibit of the same name in 1989. When *I Dream a World* debuted, it was an instant hit. People piled into galleries from Chicago to Washington, D.C., to view his seventy-five giant black-and-white portraits of Black women activists, entertainers, politicians, and thinkers.[1] The photographs were a quiet testament to Black women's pride, character, and even glamour. After two hundred years of being the mules of the world, as writer Zora Neale Hurston famously put it, Black women activists, political leaders, and cultural workers were finally getting their due.[2]

"These were the women who took a mighty step across the stage of America," Lanker wrote in his preface to the book. "I felt the need to prevent these historical lives from being forgotten."[3] Throughout the 1990s, Black people across America put the oversized book on display in their homes and offices as a way to keep vigil with Lanker—a way to keep these women's memories alive. Many of the women featured in *I Dream a World* are household names today. And yet others, giants in their own right, are still missing from the history books. This is the story of one of those forgotten heroes: Audley Moore, one of the most consequential Black Nationalists of the twentieth century.

Lanker's photo is the most popular published image of Moore today. It radiates regality. In it, she sits in her Harlem apartment facing the camera, in an old striped armchair, both hands flat on her lap and chest open so her African-print kaftan and headdress are in full view. Strands of beads encircle her neck. Her left wrist rattles with bangles. Her eyes are cast to the side as if she is waiting for us to genuflect before she meets our gaze.

Behind Moore are bookshelves full of tomes on everything from ancient Africa to the modern Black liberation struggle. Papers, petitions, and posters spill out from behind her. Propped up on the shelves are pictures of her family, fellow activists, and intellectual interlocutors. There's a portrait of her sister Eloise, and photographs and paintings of Malcolm X and Winnie Mandela, wife of South African anti-apartheid leader Nelson Mandela.[4] It's an assortment of ephemera that would rival any archival collection today, and an incredible record of the radical Black Freedom Struggle. Yet almost all the items pictured—from the bangles Moore wears to the books behind her—are lost. Moore's artifacts have met the same fate as the woman who amassed them.

Stories abound about where Audley Moore's belongings might be today. Some say a fire destroyed the books and papers. Moore endured her share of natural disasters; her Brooklyn apartment, for example, went up in a blaze. And yet her only son has the portrait of her sister Eloise pictured behind her. Clearly, some keepsakes escaped the flames. Other accounts contend that at her own request Moore's most prized possessions were buried in New Iberia, Louisiana, the small town about 130 miles west of New Orleans where she was born. A few others claim friends and foes alike raided her apartment when Moore moved into a nursing home at the end of her life, pillaging the activist's belongings piece by piece.[5] If you were to stop by a community event or protest in Harlem today, you very well might come across activists who claim to be wearing one of Moore's headdresses or bracelets.

No one can say for certain where these items are today, or why a woman who meticulously collected all of this memorabilia from the

Black Freedom Struggle has no formal archival collection to speak of. The only certainty is this: what we know of Audley Moore, one of the most important activists and theorists of the twentieth century, remains largely confined to a handful of photos—a seven-decade history of struggle distilled down to a few still shots. Until now.

"Queen Mother Moore has dedicated her life to active struggle on behalf of all people of African heritage," Lanker offers on the page accompanying her portrait as a succinct summation of Moore's life. Moore makes a more convincing argument for her importance in her autobiographical account. Here, she recounts major moments of her life, from meeting Marcus Garvey—the most famous Black Nationalist the world has ever known—in the 1920s to becoming friends with Malcolm X after a rally in Harlem in the 1950s. She explains that she began fighting for reparations in the 1950s, well before anyone had truly heard of or championed the idea of repayment, and she summarizes her numerous visits to Africa as the special guest of its liberation leaders.[6] By the end of her narrative, one thing is clear: if Rosa Parks was the mother of the Civil Rights Movement, then Queen Mother Audley Moore midwifed modern Black Nationalism.

This was no small feat. Black Nationalism conjures up poignant images in the American psyche: Malcolm X peering out from behind a window, brandishing a rifle; the Black Panthers, clad in their black leather jackets and black berets, with raised fists, exclaiming, "Fight the Power!" But few speak of the substance behind the symbolism. Most see Black Nationalism—both a political philosophy and a movement—as the violent, incoherent, and nihilistic inverse of the Civil Rights Movement. Integration's "evil twin."[7]

Nothing could be further from the truth. Civil rights and Black Nationalist organizers had the same goal: they wanted Black people to live free, happy, and self-fulfilled lives, even if they differed on how to achieve that. Civil rights activists believed this goal was best attained through full integration, for Black people to assimilate into American life, culture, and politics. Black Nationalists like Moore argued that physical, political, cultural, and economic separation from white people was the only plausible answer to Black people's centuries-long suffering. Civil rights organizers fought for the end of legal and cultural segregation, voting rights, and Black political power using largely nonviolent tactics. Black Nationalists advocated for the Black folk's right to govern themselves and to defend themselves—from attacks against their reputations, their bodies, and their communities. For many nationalists, taking up arms was a necessary resort.

Yet strict observance of ideological lines was nearly impossible in the heat of day-to-day struggles. Throughout the twentieth century, these two strands of the Black Freedom Movement were constantly intertwined. Activists crisscrossed these ideological borders, simultaneously joining organizations on both sides of the alleged divide and sharing protest stages and grassroots strategies. They often locked arms with each other at boycotts and marches.

Whether they were well-known leaders or rank-and-file organizers, throughout the twentieth century nationalists and integrationists spurred each other on, transforming debates about racial justice and pushing the American government to make good on its call for liberty and justice for all.

Remarkably, Audley Moore was a witness to nearly all of it. Born in 1898 and living until 1997, Moore joined, nurtured, and led radical Black organizations and protests for nearly eighty years. Moore knew her life was history in the making, even if others didn't. Anyone who stepped inside the apartment captured in Lanker's photo found it "cluttered with memorabilia and photographs, plaques and books."[8] If we were able to riffle through the papers behind her, we might find newspapers and pamphlets from her days as a member of Marcus Garvey's Universal Negro Improvement Association (UNIA), the largest Black Nationalist organization in history. Moore became a lifelong devotee of the UNIA after Garvey's 1922 visit to New Orleans, where she first encountered Black Nationalism as an idea and a practice. She kept Garvey's teachings alive through various organizations and celebrations for the better part of a century, cajoling everyone from baby boomers to Gen Xers to support Black pride, self-determination, and control over their communities' schools, housing, institutions, and culture.

Thumbing along her bookshelf, we would likely find volumes about the Communist Party. Perhaps she dog-eared the pages featuring her old comrades or herself. Moore, like many Black folk who moved to Harlem in the early twentieth century, joined the Communist Party

USA. She worked nonstop for the organization for more than fifteen years, captivated by its adoption of Garvey's ideals and its stalwart support of the Black working class during the Great Depression. But she left the organization on bad terms in the 1950s when the leadership renounced its commitment to radical Black liberation. Much to Moore's chagrin, her communist comrades and historians alike often erased her from this period of radical organizing because of her Black Nationalist beliefs.

If we turned the corner that led to her bedroom and opened the closet door, we would likely find plenty of African-print fabric dating back to the 1960s and 1970s, when Black women adopted African dress and hairstyles as a political act.[9] Moore, who was in her sixties by then, began to dress in traditional West African headdresses (sometimes called *geles*) and vibrantly colored robes and kaftans to assert her pride in and connection to the African continent.

On a 1972 trip to Ghana, she formalized this relationship. Elders there anointed her a "Queen Mother" of the Asante tribe, the highest position bestowed on a woman in that culture, and a title that garnered reverence across the African Diaspora. Moore embraced this title and style of dress at a moment when Black people were embracing Black Power in the United States. Her status as an African-anointed Queen Mother crystallized her leadership in a time when Black organizing was largely a young man's game.

Moore's status as a respected elder of the Black Liberation Movement brought luminaries like Malcolm X to learn at her feet. She mentored Malcolm before and after he renounced his spiritual and political teacher, Elijah Muhammad, and left the Nation of Islam. Moore believed Malcolm to be one of the best and brightest soldiers in the nationalist fight, and she pushed him to broaden his thinking about reparations and African liberation.[10] Perhaps this is why she kept a photo of Malcolm prominently displayed in her living room—a personal vigil for a freedom fighter cut down in his prime.

Malcolm wasn't alone. Numerous other Black activists and leaders sought Moore's counsel throughout the 1960s and 1970s. They visited her often, seeking everything from organizing advice to a place to hide out from the FBI, tasked with surveilling and stamping out Black activism. Moore herself had an extensive file. The FBI spied on her for nearly fifty years. Buried in the stacks of papers in her living room, we might find drafts of Moore's letters to young activists, exhorting them to keep their eyes trained on global Black liberation and offering practical advice for evading the feds.

If there was any lesson that young activists took from Moore, it was that Black people are owed reparations for enduring slavery and its aftermath. The ex-slave turned activist Callie House first popularized the idea of restitution for the formally enslaved in the late nineteenth century. But Moore single-handedly revitalized this call in the late 1950s when she founded the modern reparations movement. She developed repayment plans, formed grassroots organizations, and disseminated her 1963 treatise, *Why Reparations?* We'd likely find copies of the pamphlet shoved between the books on the shelves in her Harlem apartment. Anyone who met Moore found she often had one on hand.

In the late 1970s, Moore took her call for reparations abroad. As a Garveyite, she was always committed to his idea of "Africa for the Africans," and she championed decolonization struggles across the continent. Perusing her bookshelves, we would find more than a few wood carvings and statues, artifacts from her visits to eight different African countries as the honored guest of presidents and dignitaries. Julius Nyerere and Sékou Touré—the presidents of Tanzania and Guinea, respectively—treated Moore like royalty. To them, she was the queen of Black America.

Moore also knew the political was always personal. Nothing reminded her of this more than the portrait of her younger sister Eloise, which sits just behind her left shoulder in Lanker's photo. Audley was the oldest of the three Moore sisters. And she, Eloise, and Loretta all dedicated their lives to the Black Liberation Movement. Audley credited Eloise with encouraging her to participate in her first protest. She also claimed Eloise was the trio's true leader and theorist. The eldest Moore sister spoke fondly of their days together on picket lines and attributed her shrewd political analysis to their numerous late-night debates. Audley even went so far as to pen and publish a poem as a testament to Eloise's life and the unrecognized genius of everyday Black women. We would undoubtedly find a copy of "The Enigmatic Eloise Moore's Philosophy and Works" wedged between books on the shelves behind Moore. It's no wonder, then, that she placed Eloise's portrait next to Malcolm X's in her living room.

It stands to reason that anyone of Moore's experience and stature would be immortalized in some kind of archive. Her papers should be neatly compiled and cataloged, and her art, clothing, and jewelry stored in boxes in a temperature-controlled room. And yet so much of Moore's remarkable life has been lost. It's disappointing, but not surprising.

After all, archives have nationalist origins of their own. In their earliest iterations, archives were a tool for political leaders to collect and compile records of governance and administration. They established nations and fortified their power. Thus, the archive became a repository for a nation's "official" history and values.[11] To be sure, the archive is a tool for safekeeping, for preserving a wealth of important historical ephemera. But before long, "important" becomes "dominant." A pile of ephemera from those in power becomes a wealth, whereas ephemera from the oppressed remains just that—a pile, flotsam and jetsam.

Black people in America have rarely been granted inclusion in these archives. For much of this nation's history, it was illegal for them to read and write, or formally collect their histories and stories. Thus, these typical methods of historical preservation were never meant to and could not possibly collect, catalog, or contain the capacious and complicated contours of Black life—let alone preserve the works of a Black woman who dedicated her life to toppling Western domination.[12]

The result is tacit erasure. Writers and scholars have largely ignored Moore, claiming there is inadequate source material to substantively write about her life.[13] More often than not, Moore is altogether missing from accounts of the watershed historical moments she helped spark. To conjure the life of an American pariah, you have to look beyond the institutions that barred her entry.

Over the last decade, I have assembled the most complete collection of records on Queen Mother Audley Moore to date, chronicling her life with the rigor it deserves. I have found that evidence of Moore's life and legacy was not destroyed, as some have argued. Rather, it was scattered across the globe, preserved by those who still carry on her work, or hidden away by those who would rather see it buried. With the help and encouragement of her family, I have spent months living and researching in Moore's childhood hometowns of New Iberia and New Orleans. I have uncovered land deeds, baptismal records, and photos from her early life—artifacts that others claimed did not exist. Her girlhood in Louisiana, once deemed undiscoverable, has now been unearthed.

Once Moore became an activist, the federal government surveilled her for decades, first through the House Un-American Activities Committee (HUAC) and then through the FBI's Counterintelligence Program (COINTELPRO). I have combed through thousands of pages of government surveillance and cross-referenced these documents with local newspapers and archival artifacts to produce the most complete picture of Moore's political work to date. Moreover, I've tracked down former organizers, writers, and journalists who have long recognized Moore's genius, even when other writers and archivists did not. Many of them have stacks of pictures, newspaper articles, and drafts of her speeches in their possession. I interviewed Moore's friends and family and spent days upon days sifting through their attics, file cabinets, and personal collections to discover the hidden truths of Moore's life.

Like her protégé Malcolm X, Moore was the kind of political philosopher who was always "thinking in motion." She formulated her ideas about nationalism and liberation on the go. And she articulated these ideas in a wide range of mediums: poetry, pamphlets, spontaneous speeches, and more. She developed and deployed her political philosophy on street corners, on stepladders, and in secret meetings rather than within the "strictures of a carefully edited writing project."[14]

But this doesn't mean Moore didn't leave a written record. I have found donation rolls that demonstrate her commitment to Marcus Garvey's UNIA and poems scribbled on the back of scratch paper that she penned on the fly. I have sifted through basements in New York and file cabinets in Los Angeles to find drafts of her speeches about the direction of the Black Nationalist Movement, filled with Moore's handwritten insertions and ad-libs. I found documents detailing the founding of her organizations, such as the Universal Association of Ethiopian Women, at rare book auctions and legal pads with her handwritten notes in London.

Taken together, these sources reveal a master of "tactical flexibility."[15] Moore's ideological compass was always pointed toward Black Nationalism. But she had a malleable approach to organizing that led her to join groups, protests, and causes that were pro-Black even if they were not explicitly nationalist. Audley Moore believed organizations were "vehicles" through which to express her politics.[16] She did not demand that fellow activists subscribe to her politics to join forces with them. Moore saw opportunities to collaborate and convert people to nationalism all around her and was open to almost any place or space that would give her a platform.

The evidence shows that while Audley Moore did not birth Black Nationalism, she did mother its modern manifestations. Audley Moore believed in Black Nationalism not just as a viable path to Black liberation but also as a way to free us *all* from our servitude to a nation that doesn't serve our interests. Moore desperately wanted Black people in America to have a separate nation where we could live, work, and grow beyond the grasp and gaze of white supremacy. But more broadly, she wanted to set a precedent. Black people's political, cultural, and economic independence was critical to a free and just world.

Many of the ideas she championed were on the fringe then, as they are now. Others, like reparations for slavery and its aftermath, have become commonplace—some form of reparations legislation exists in many statehouses across the country today. Whether or not her ideas gained traction, one thing is clear: Moore kept her eye trained toward liberation. She was doggedly committed to helping communities— past and present—address racism, cultural erasure, and economic degradation. Her life was a master class in striving for a dream she knew would likely never come true.

Today, a better and freer world feels far away, just as it did for Queen Mother Moore. Countries like Uganda and Nigeria, which Moore championed as they threw off their colonial chains, still suffer the consequences of Western economic rule. Women's reproductive rights, as sure a right to self-determination as any, are evaporating. The southeastern United States, where Moore wanted to build her Black nation, is deteriorating due to climate change. And, if the possibility of America ever truly reckoning with its treatment of Black people seemed proximate during the 2020 uprisings, that hope is now receding as we regress into the most virulently repressive laws and racial violence that America has seen since Reconstruction.

Like many of us today, Moore had few resources and even fewer reasons to believe her emancipatory dreams would come true. But she never wavered. That is, after all, what it is to be a mother. It is to always see potential. It is to offer unwavering support. But most important, it is to relentlessly, interminably, and some might say foolishly work toward the world we want for those we love with little surety that we will ever see it.

Who better, then, to show us how to keep our hearts full of hope, our political imaginations broad, and our eyes trained on freedom than Queen Mother Audley Moore—a woman who remained committed to the simple but seemingly impossible dream of complete and total Black liberation for nearly one hundred years?

Queen Mother

CHAPTER 1

My People Had Pride in Themselves

The sound of a horse-drawn wagon along the dirt road was nothing new for Audley Moore. But there was something off about the familiar rhythm. Audley's family always urged her and her two sisters, Eloise and Loretta, to be models of propriety. They were never to gawk or stare. But the eldest Moore girl couldn't resist. She ran to the window to see what was coming down their street. Excitement quickly turned to horror when the spectacle came into view: white men on horses "hollered like wolves" as they dragged a Black man by his feet off the back of a wagon. Another gaggle of them followed close behind, yelling and screaming with animalistic fervor. Audley would soon come to recognize the screams of a lynch mob and what it meant for any Black person caught in its path.

Moore's grandmother was all too familiar with what the young girls were witnessing. She quickly shut the windows and hissed at them to get down. "I remember Grandma allowing us to look through the shutter," Audley later said, so long as they were careful not to be seen. Crouched down low with her sisters, Audley tried to be still and quiet her breathing as she peered through a small opening in the blinds. Her eyes widened and her mouth fell open as she watched the man's head "bumping up and down on the clay, the hard, crusty road." Moments like this—witnessing the horrors of white supremacy from the safety and protection of her household—defined Audley Moore's early life.[1]

The eldest child of St. Cyr and Ella Moore, Audley was born in New Iberia, Louisiana, on July 27, 1898. Her well-to-do family taught Audley the value of Black empowerment and the price many would pay to get it.[2] With their twenty-year age difference, St. Cyr, born in slavery, and Ella, who came from a free Black community, made for an unlikely union. They were brought together by their families, who had willed themselves forward during Reconstruction, desperate to take advantage of all the possibilities that emancipation had to offer. As they stepped out of the shadows of slavery, both sides of Audley Moore's family pushed against the constraints of southern racism, took pride in their ability to obtain an education and property, and defended their rights at the ballot box, all in an effort to secure a piece of the American pie.

Still, the idea that Black people could and should forge a separate nation of their own would have been anathema to St. Cyr Moore. Born in the early 1850s to Arsene and Anderson Moore, Audley's father likely spent the first years of his life enslaved in what is now known as Iberia Parish but at the time was part of St. Mary and St. Martin Parish.[3] Though St. Cyr could hardly imagine Black people claiming Louisiana as their own nation, plenty others already had. The land he and his family worked on first belonged to the Indigenous Ishak or Atakapa people. The French and Spanish crowns alternately claimed it as part of their empires from the sixteenth to the nineteenth centuries, each seeking to control its rich soil, large mineral salt deposits, and proximity to the Bayou Teche—a 125-mile-long waterway that snaked through southern Louisiana's remote interior, connecting the sole of the Louisiana boot to the Mississippi River.[4]

By 1850, plantations lined the bayou all across the parish, and sugar production governed the Moores' lives. Rising early and dressing in master-issued plain cotton sleeveless shirts and pants, they would have trudged from their slave cabins to the fields with knives in hand and spent hours in ankle-deep mud, slicing cane at the stalk and loading it onto mule-drawn wagons. When it was time to grind, they'd feed the cane into horse-powered mills, unless they worked for a master who had purchased a steam mill and a vacuum pan, which more quickly produced sugar that was whiter and of higher quality.[5] No matter how they worked, the systematized violence of slavery made one thing clear to the Moores: they were the true engine that powered America's sugar seat.

"My father's father was a white man. His mother had been raped, you see, on the plantation," Audley explained.[6] His parentage could have brought St. Cyr either security or scrutiny. As the master's child, St. Cyr might have lived in the "big house"—a multistory brick structure that was a unique commingling of French colonial architecture and Greek flourishes with a row of windows, a veranda on the top floor, and several large doors on the bottom. Then again, he and his mother could have been the bane of the mistress's existence. The master's wife would have banished them to the far corners of the plantation, where "rectilinear rows of whitewashed slave cabins seemed to stretch into the distance."[7]

If he was favored, then his master might have sent St. Cyr on errands to Jeanerette, a smaller town about twelve miles south of New Iberia. Down a dirt road lined with large, looming oak trees, the town took its name from the tutor turned plantation owner John W. Jeanerette.[8] Lining the bank of the Bayou Teche, the area quickly gained the nickname Sugar City because of all the sugar plantations nearby. By the 1840s, Jeanerette attracted more young white men looking to make their fortunes on the backs of slaves like the Moores. On the eve of the Civil War, St. Cyr would have found himself surrounded by plantations in the New Iberia–Jeanerette area—the Weeks, Richardson, and Loisel estates the most "prized" among them.[9]

Thus, it came as no surprise when these planters grabbed their guns as war broke out. Louisiana, and especially New Orleans, was a geographical and financial stronghold for the Confederacy, and slaveholders in the Bayou Teche joined their southern brethren in building an army to defend their state and their way of life.[10] Some of them signed up when, on January 26, 1861, delegates from across Louisiana convened in Baton Rouge and voted to leave the Union. Nearly eight weeks later, on March 21, 1861, even more cheered as Louisiana joined the Confederate States of America.[11]

Lincoln expressly excluded St. Cyr, his parents, and any enslaved person living in Teche country when he signed the Emancipation Proclamation in January 1863. The president intended to free only those in Confederate regions, and he, somewhat optimistically, believed the Teche to be under Union control.[12] His soldiers had indeed made a battleground of the bayou. On April 15, 1863, federal troops stormed through Jeanerette, confiscating animals, sugar, and other staple crops.[13] They also captured New Iberia and seized the Weeks family plantation as their headquarters.[14] St. Cyr, now about ten years old, might have heard rumors of the Union soldiers' imminent arrival. Perhaps he prepared to leave with them, like the hundreds of thousands of other self-emancipated men and women who set up camps near Union forces for protection and sustenance.[15] It is also possible that the Moores changed their minds about fleeing to Union lines when the rebels recaptured the town and held it from June to October 1863. But Jeanerette was soon under Union control again, and the Moore family stayed put.[16] With the Union army's presence as strong as it was, they gambled on waiting to see what would become of the Teche after the war.

Many in the Moore family's shoes turned to the Freedmen's Bureau, the federal agency created in 1865 to help the newly emancipated integrate into the American polity. Bureau leaders established its Louisiana headquarters in New Orleans and sent Union soldiers turned agents throughout the parishes to negotiate labor contracts, establish schools, issue marriage certificates, locate family members, and keep the peace. But the bureau offered spotty protection at best. Its promise of paid labor often meant apprenticing Black children as young as four to white planters, and quelling violence often meant putting down ex-slave "insurrections" as opposed to challenging white mobs. But most important, the bureau lacked the funds, infrastructure, and progressive personnel to truly assist the millions of freed men and women who came calling.[17]

Where the government failed families like the Moores, Black people in the bayou stepped in. St. James Methodist Church, the oldest Black congregation in New Iberia, supported residents as they transitioned to freedom, offering worship services, community programs, and material aid, while Young Union and Solid Rock benevolent societies, among others, helped them care for the sick and bury the dead. Now a teenager, St. Cyr could have made the journey from Jeanerette to New Iberia for annual "turn outs," citywide social gatherings in which the Black community dressed in white suits, church hats, and dresses and paraded through town to collect money for their social and cultural institutions.[18] Or perhaps he enjoyed Easter Sunday traditions, where he could get some food and admire the local women dressed in their Sunday best as they came out to sell "gumbo, cakes, pralines, and coffee at tables or booths immediately in front of St. Peter's Catholic Church."[19] This kind of community building made Jeanerette and New Iberia vibrant, albeit precarious, spaces for St. Cyr to make a life.

St. Cyr likely saw his hometown as a place of potential prosperity. Postwar rebuilding had brought new industries to Jeanerette and New Iberia, including lumber factories, sawmills, and, most notably, a Tabasco sauce factory, made possible by Edmund McIlhenny's "discovery" of pepper plants.[20] In fact, many New Iberians, both Black and white, believed their area was on the rise but that parish officials were trying to keep them down. Despite dutifully paying their taxes, white folk in the area grew tired of what they saw as a lack of infrastructure—the roads, bridges, and ferries needed to expand industry. And so, they did what many people often do when they want to take control of their futures: they seceded. Residents separated and formed Iberia Parish in 1868.[21]

Perhaps St. Cyr was hopeful when he got wind of the split. Although his hometown was still largely segregated, Iberia Parish was a Republican stronghold. Thirteen years after the end of the Civil War, Republicans were still known as the party of Lincoln, and white lawmakers carried this liberatory spirit into the 1870s, allowing for a bevy of Black men across the South to gain a foothold in American politics through the party. Not only did the county separation portend more potential opportunities for entrepreneurial men like St. Cyr, but he likely felt an added sense of security given the party's track record on Black rights.[22]

Radical Reconstruction bolstered St. Cyr's belief in a prosperous future. After the Civil War and Lincoln's assassination, Vice President Andrew Johnson assumed the presidency and attempted to resume business as usual. Under Presidential Reconstruction, Johnson forced Confederate states to abolish slavery. But he required only 10 percent of the voters in these rebelling states to swear allegiance to the Union before reentering and reconstructing their state governments. This left the door open for former white Confederates turned politicians to enshrine racism in state laws and courts. Aghast at their leaders' leniency, the radical wing of the Republican Party tried to seize control of Congress in the 1866 election. They were successful, and a faction of Black and white Republicans spent the next decade passing legislation that propelled America toward its founding ideals with unparalleled fervor. The Thirteenth, Fourteenth, and Fifteenth Amendments outlawed slavery, granted Black citizenship, and extended the franchise to Black men. Radical Republicans also passed the Reconstruction Acts of 1867–68 and divided the former Confederacy into five Union army–patrolled military districts to enforce these amendments and other measures, including the Enforcement Act of 1871, also known as the Ku Klux Klan Act, designed to combat white hate groups.[23]

St. Cyr certainly took advantage of the opportunities available to newly freed and enfranchised Black men. Now in his twenties, he was considered among Jeanerette's finest Black men. Many classified St. Cyr as a Creole of Color, a mixed-race group that occupied the middle social, political, and cultural ground in a socially stratified society that included the formally enslaved, white and European land-owners, and everyone in between.[24] Some white people saw him as a "respectable-looking colored man" because of his fair skin, tailored clothes, and fine hair that he kept short on the sides with a coiffed swoop in front and a bushy but well-groomed mustache. Still others described him as "powerfully built," forceful, and "uppity" because he refused to accept his "place" in society—a trait he would pass along to his daughter Audley.[25]

St. Cyr began earning a living by working in the growing local lumber business. He also tried his hand at being a constable in New Iberia, a position that allowed him to command respect from his white counterparts and, at least in theory, protect his Black ones. His position would become a source of pride for young Audley, who continually pointed to St. Cyr's time on the force as evidence of his commitment to armed Black self-defense.[26]

The Moore patriarch married his first wife, Rebecca Keller, in the late 1870s and began building a life as New Iberians built their new town.[27] The first iteration of the Moore family lived in Jeanerette, where St. Cyr worked as a carpenter and Rebecca as a seamstress while raising three children. Their first son, Henry, was born in 1880. A daughter, Mattie, followed three years later, and little Clarence came as the decade closed in 1889.[28] Perhaps because St. Cyr had waited to wade into parenthood until he was in his thirties, his first set of children enjoyed some privilege. He was able to put a roof over their heads, albeit with the help of a wife who worked, too, in a racially mixed neighborhood. Henry, Mattie, and Clarence might have had some schooling. Perhaps they played with the Childresses, a Creole family on the block, or talked about the latest news they heard in town with the Porters and the Browns, two large Black families down the street who survived the transition from slavery to freedom by working as washerwomen, farmworkers, and carpenters in town.[29] Audley's half-siblings were ten to twenty years older than her, and they inhabited a racially fluid world that she could never have imagined. But it wouldn't last.

As St. Cyr was climbing out of the shadows of slavery, so too was Ella's family. On her mother's side, Audley came from a line of determined women who hailed from St. Landry Parish, an area known for its French settlers turned plantation owners, Creoles, and free Black people.[30] Like New Iberia, St. Landry, and its parish seat, Opelousas, was under the dominion of Indigenous peoples, the Spanish, and the French before the land became part of the American Cotton Kingdom.[31] Audley's maternal great-grandmother, Pelagie, came into the world around 1820, when cotton took hold and the city of Opelousas, about sixty miles northwest of New Iberia, was formally incorporated. She had a daughter, Honora, around 1845.[32] If Pelagie had other children, their names have been lost to history. But mother and daughter stuck together as scrapes over slavery ratcheted up in the 1850s.[33] They were likely free before the war, but the fall of slavery still portended a shift for them. On the eve of the Civil War, Nora (as Honora sometimes called herself) and Pelagie weren't sure if the fighting was going to bring them fortune or strife.

After all, their antebellum life was not without its advantages. While St. Cyr descended from Africans whom French and Spanish soldiers had enslaved, Pelagie and Nora's ancestors had likely been freed at least one generation before. Some of the enslaved in their region gained their freedom after wartime service. Others came into it as mistresses or illegitimate children. However their ancestors made the transition, by the time Pelagie and Nora were a part of Opelousas, they joined a stratified but not completely separated society that included French immigrants turned American plantation owners, Creoles of Color, free Black people, and the enslaved.[34]

White planters quickly tried to enshrine this racial hierarchy into law. Back in 1724, they had created the *Code Noir* (Black Code), which established a three-tier system of masters, slaves, and a free Black population in between that could lay claim to the legal rights and privileges of whiteness but would never occupy the same cultural or social plane. But this was easier said than done in rural areas like Opelousas. While free Black people and Creoles of Color worked hard to distance themselves from the enslaved and the horrors they endured, they took a different approach with their white neighbors. By the early nineteenth century, an increasing number of them chipped away at this social order by establishing personal and political relationships with the white elite. In the decades leading up to the Civil War, interracial alliances and relationships—and the social and familial spaces that such liaisons created—remained a fixture in the region despite laws prohibiting interracial marriages and many formal business contracts.[35]

By the time Honora was born, Creoles of Color had developed a thriving community in the city and the wider parish. She grew up in a community of children whose parents abandoned African names for French ones, sent children to schools taught in French and English, and went to Catholic churches on Sundays. As soon as they got wind that a battle over slavery was brewing, Creoles of Color scrambled to hold on to their social status by consolidating their land and businesses, suing to solidify their property and civil rights, and marrying into white society.[36]

When the war made its way to Louisiana, Pelagie and Nora's hometown was more of a government seat than a battleground. Once Lincoln's army captured Baton Rouge, state officials relocated to Opelousas, bringing an influx of Confederate officials into the area and making it a tenuous place for enslaved and free Black people alike. The rebels moved the government to Shreveport soon thereafter, creating some breathing room and perhaps even allowing the light of freedom to shine through the cracks.[37] But Nora and Pelagie weren't sure what would be left once slavery fully crumbled.

They were right to be worried. Their world looked very different in the aftermath of the Confederacy. Creoles of Color found their ability to move freely about the city, buy property, get an education, and build wealth had evaporated during wartime. With no hope of returning to their old way of life, they had to pinch pennies. Some even had to apprentice their children to white families to make ends meet. Audley's mother, Ella, might have eventually met such a fate. Growing up, she heard stories about when her mother "lived with a very rich family who wanted a little Black girl" as a companion to their daughter.[38]

Emancipation poured salt in their yet open wounds. Without the economic and legal lines that slavery provided, it was harder for women like Pelagie and Nora to set themselves apart as romantic matches. It wouldn't be long, they feared, before white people began to group them together with the formally enslaved and redraw the power lines firmly around race rather than class or social status.[39]

Amid this upheaval, Nora met and married Alphonse Dubourdieu, a free man of color in Opelousas. They had three children between 1864 and 1869: daughters Evelina and Alphonsine, and a son, Amile.[40] Through this relationship, Nora further solidified her status within the Creole community and perhaps found a sense of security that only patriarchy could provide. After all, the Union army did not actively patrol St. Landry Parish, and white supremacists could and did pillage with impunity after the war. Violence was uncoordinated but common. The largest and bloodiest massacre of the Reconstruction era occurred in their backyard.[41]

On a cool day in September 1868, all hell broke loose when word spread that a white mob had attacked local Black Republican leader Emerson Bentley. Bentley had escaped with his life, and a small group of Black men assembled to avenge him. White vigilantes took this as a sign that the Black uprising they constantly feared was imminent. On the first night, the white mob killed 27 Black men and set the office of Bentley's newspaper, *The St. Landry Progress*, on fire. They continued on their racial rampage for two weeks, during which "most able-bodied white Democrats were involved in one way or another." By the end, nearly 250 people had died.[42]

Alphonse survived what would later be known as the Opelousas Massacre, only to die a month later. He left Nora with a small plot of land and a large amount of debt.[43] She and her children moved back in with her mother, Pelagie, and Phillip Johnson, whom Pelagie now claimed as her husband. Perhaps in an attempt to flee the violence, the Johnsons left St. Landry and moved south to St. Martinville, a mere ten miles north of New Iberia.[44] The good life in St. Landry was long gone. Once likely considered among the Creole elite, the multigenerational Johnson household now made a living as sharecroppers, growing cotton and crops on land that belonged to Oneziphore Delahoussaye Jr., a descendant of a slaveholding family.

The Johnsons might have fled their home, but they didn't desert their convictions. In September 1871, Phillip Johnson took Delahoussaye to court for violating their tenancy agreement, seizing their crops, and kicking his family off the land. Standing up for his family, Phillip demanded the court compel Delahoussaye to pay him for the loss of his food, capital, and labor. Delahoussaye countered the suit, and the parish judge dismissed the case when Phillip failed to appear in court.[45]

The legal documents may conceal the case's violent underpinnings. According to Moore family legend, local white men lynched Phillip for standing up to Delahoussaye's land grab. Audley often told of how "they ran [her] grandmother off the land," forcing her to "flee for her life with the things [she and the children] had on their back, nothing else."[46] The story of Phillip's courage always loomed large in Audley's mind. She would come to see it as proof that both sides of her family were willing to stand up for themselves no matter the cost.

In the aftermath of Phillip's murder, Pelagie, Nora, and her three children moved farther south to New Iberia, where they would eventually cross paths with the Moores. Nora found her next partner around 1871 and gave birth to a daughter, Ella Mary Johnson, the following year.[47] Unlike Nora's other children, Ella had darker skin, tightly curled hair, a short mouth, and smiling eyes. There is no record of Ella's father, and unlike Nora's other children, Ella retained her mother's new surname, Johnson. It's possible the relationship was troubled, short, or even scandalous.

For love, or perhaps to regain her respectability, Nora then married William Henry in St. Peter's Catholic Church in December 1878.[48] A Louisiana native, Henry was a landowning farmer who accepted Nora with all her baggage, moving her mother and four children into his home.[49] The pair welcomed a son, Narceas Joseph Henry, within a year of tying the knot. As his family grew, William Henry looked to expand his landholdings by taking out a mortgage to build a bigger home in 1880.[50]

That same year, St. Cyr Moore entered the landowning class nearby, purchasing an acre of dirt running parallel to the Bayou Teche.[51] By the 1890s, St. Cyr's landholdings rivaled William's—no small feat given the continual threat to Black men's lives and livelihoods at the end of the nineteenth century.[52] St. Cyr spent the final years of the century building wealth by amassing property and honing his carpentry skills, while William focused on farming.[53] Fifteen years after the Civil War, both sides of Audley's family had survived unimaginable violence, buoyed by the belief that a more prosperous future was within reach.

The Henry and the Moore families likely encountered each other in Jeanerette and New Iberia. Both matriarchs would have gone into town often, and Rebecca and Nora might have greeted each other politely when they visited Cheap Jack's Dry Goods Store or Mr. Monnot's General Store in Jeanerette.[54] The patriarchs probably also crossed paths at E. Provost or D. Mallet's shops, the best harness makers in town.[55] Both William and St. Cyr mixed with local, unpropertied Black men who found work in the new, modern sugar mills and local lumberyards.[56] Perhaps they took in a baseball game when the Jeanerette Pelicans faced off against the New Iberia Quicksteps or nodded to each other as they stopped to get a sweet treat from LeJeune's Bakery.[57] If St. Cyr and Ella ever met during this period, they couldn't have imagined they would one day be joined together in marriage. St. Cyr, now in his thirties and married, was focused on raising his family and securing their future. Ella, just a teenager, was figuring out what life had to offer a young girl in small-town Louisiana.

Both sides of Audley's family gained a foothold in New Iberia as the door to opportunity was closing. The previous decade brought considerable gains in every aspect of Black life. Black men held local and national political and judicial offices, and Black literacy and landownership rates rose during Reconstruction.[58] But after the Compromise of 1877, a gentleman's agreement that resolved the stalemated 1876 election by withdrawing federal troops from the South, any hopes that Black Americans might finally enjoy the full spoils of citizenship began to evaporate. White Republicans abandoned the cause of freed people, and Democrats began to reclaim their states with the express purpose of excluding Black Americans from politics, society, and economic advancement. Former slave owners and white workers joined forces to institute a nationwide wave of lynchings, political murders, rapes, and arsons.[59] The Moores and the Henrys surely thought they were witnessing the end of Republican rule and that violence would only worsen as it crept closer to New Iberia.

They were right. If Ella or St. Cyr walked down Main Street in January 1889, they would have seen a crowd huddled around a posted notice:

> To Adolphe Wakefield, Jim Rosemond, Reason Barns, and son, Joe Francis (ex-convict), Eugene and Louis Dantryve (keepers of a negro den), J. J. McGaffey and son, Yellow Sam (gambler) and Dan Richardson: For the good of this community you are hereby notified to leave the place on or before Sunday noon, the 27th instant. If you fail to comply, you will be dealt with summarily.—Whites.

A few days later, Captain C. T. Cade, the deputy sheriff and leader of a local militia known as the Iberia Guards, led white draymen, farmers, laborers, and the editor in chief of the *New Iberia Enterprise* in a brazen attack on these men and their families.[60] Adolphe took heed and got out of town. His brother Sam's arrest and lynching for allegedly killing the white man he worked for was enough for Adolphe to not think twice about it. That same Sunday evening, the mob lynched Jim Rosemond on a bridge over the Bayou Teche. His only crime was his alleged association with Sam Wakefield. Reports indicated "not a single man in New Iberia, officer or citizen, could give any tangible reasons" why the mob of nearly two hundred white men targeted, attacked, and killed Rosemond and Wakefield.[61] But Ella Johnson and St. Cyr Moore knew why. By 1890, they both understood that the mere thought of Black people trying to claim even the smallest piece of the American Dream was enough to set white men on a rampage.

St. Cyr tried to shield his family from the violence, but he couldn't stop death from knocking on their door. Rebecca passed away in August 1890 at the age of forty.[62] A widower with three children, he looked to marry again quickly. This time, nineteen-year-old Rose Edgar, a fair-skinned Creole of Color and Jeanerette native, became Mrs. St. Cyr Moore. The two joined their lives in St. John the Evangelist Church on April 18, 1892, in the presence of her parents and other well-to-do Black and Creole families of New Iberia.[63]

Rose soon learned just how willing St. Cyr was to defend himself and his family. Audley would often tell an old family story in which one of St. Cyr's sons, likely Clarence, came home one day agitated and breathless after an incident with a white playmate. Although segregation was slowly creeping into society, the custom had not yet reached all the playgrounds of the South. Clarence claimed that while they were playing, the white boy "got angry and went into the house and told his mother." When the white boy's father came home, he took it upon himself to horsewhip Clarence. St. Cyr wouldn't stand for such a brazen show of disrespect aimed at his boys or himself. "Papa called the white man to the door," Audley recalled, having heard this story many times throughout her childhood, "and took his horsewhip and horsewhipped him."[64] If true, this was a stunning display of self-defense on the part of St. Cyr—and one that, in turn-of-the-century Louisiana, could easily have gotten him killed. Audley acknowledged as much, recalling that both Black and white folk told St. Cyr it was time to get out of town. Around 1895, he moved his family to New Orleans in hopes of starting a new life and a new business as the century closed.[65]

He soon found the Big Easy to be anything but what the name implied. Within a year, Rose had left him—and in scandalous fashion. New Orleanians packed into a police board meeting on August 26, 1896, where they learned of Rose's extramarital affair with Germaine Cenance, a married white patrolman.[66] Any affair would have gone against the social mores of the city. But the fact that Rose Moore was a "negress" and Cenance a white cop made it a bona fide scene. Cenance claimed St. Cyr was a husband in title only, that he never really cared for Rose and her true desire was to be with him instead. He might have been right, but because they were both married, it was a moral taboo. The board removed him from the force.[67]

St. Cyr may have taken solace in the fact that Cenance's reputation was tarnished, but so too was his own. Not only had he lost his wife to another man, but to a white and working-class one at that. For a man who fancied himself still among the well-off Creoles of Color in the city, this was a particular affront to his manhood and gentlemanly reputation. St. Cyr had to take action to defend himself, even if it meant going against the mores of the Catholic Church, which regarded marriage as an insoluble bond.[68]

Audley's father filed for divorce, asserting that he had "conducted himself as a dutiful husband" while Rose had "neglected her marital duties" for months. He hired a white lawyer to litigate his case, a sign that the strictures of segregation had not yet fully tied off Creole men from the resources available to their white counterparts. By March 1897, the court decided in St. Cyr's favor, not only granting him a divorce, but also saddling Rose with the legal costs of their failed marriage.[69] St. Cyr had lost another wife but had salvaged his reputation.

If news of the scandal made its way back to New Iberia, Nora Henry didn't let on. Instead, she was hard at work securing her daughters' futures as the sun set on what few freedoms they had left. She married her first two girls off to established men. The eldest, Evelina, married Baptiste Senegal, a twenty-five-year-old widower and native of the neighboring Lafayette Parish.[70] Her second, Alphonsine, wed John M. Springfield in 1887.[71] The Senegals and the Springfields initially made their homes in Jeanerette with the help of William and Nora, who gave both young families loans to buy land.[72] With that settled, Nora then turned her attention to Ella.

Nora must have known that property ownership, more than anything, could help ward off any questions about Ella's paternity. In 1896, she helped Ella buy a tract of land in New Iberia.[73] A twenty-five-year-old landowner from an affluent family, Ella was a sound marriage prospect. Perhaps this was what caught the attention of St. Cyr, who by the end of the 1890s was looking to marry a third time.

CHAPTER 2

Little Bourgeois Stinker

Still reeling from his split, St. Cyr returned to Jeanerette. After all, he still had a modest home in the Louisiana countryside, and the fresh air and change of pace would have been a welcome respite after the tumultuous few months of divorce drama he'd just endured. Local girls likely lingered a little longer when they greeted the middle-aged man as he meandered about town. News of his divorce had no doubt reached New Iberia, thanks to his willingness to publicly denounce Rose and tout the court's decision in his favor. Many a mother in the countryside still found him to be an upstanding and principled man—not to mention a moneyed one—and would have been eager to marry their daughter off to him. Nora Henry was the one who ultimately succeeded.

Ella Johnson and St. Cyr Moore were engaged after a quick courtship, despite their considerable age difference. As a young girl, Ella surely dreamed of marrying in front of her local congregation at St. Peter's Church in New Iberia. But St. Cyr's newly inked divorce probably kept them from sealing their union at a Catholic house of worship. Instead, Reverend Joseph Johnson, leader of the Tabernacle Baptist Church in New Orleans, bound them together before God on June 22, 1897.[1]

Ella was a true beauty, with chocolate-brown skin, thick curly hair, and a petite frame. That she came from a property-owning family made her even more attractive. Still, it was a risk for Audley's father to marry her. By looks alone, St. Cyr clearly belonged to the Creole class, his fair skin and fine hair a sign of his mixed-race ancestry and proximity to whiteness. Ella offered no such assurances at first glance. But her good looks coupled with her good family were enough to make St. Cyr commit what Audley would later call a "cardinal sin" of the time: marrying a woman who was darker-skinned than him.[2]

Eager to solidify her status as St. Cyr's new wife, Ella quickly bore children. Audley arrived in July 1898.[3] A boy, Charles St. Cyr, was born in 1899 but survived for less than a year.[4] Eloise arrived in March 1901, and little Loretta came along in June 1902.[5] This third iteration of the Moore family, along with St. Cyr's older sons, Clarence and Henry, from his first marriage, lived at the intersection of Howard and Perdido Streets in New Orleans's Third Ward.[6]

When Ella set out on her daily calls and errands, she passed by Irish and German immigrants living, working, and doing business with Black people from all walks of life. Ella would have nodded politely as she passed her neighbors but probably would not have stopped to speak. After all, these women worked as domestics, seamstresses, and shopkeepers. They were out in the waterlogged, foul-smelling streets because they had to make ends meet.[7] She was a housewife, and well-off by comparison, owing to St. Cyr's business acumen.

Yet her husband's money couldn't shield her from all the harsh realities of life. The Moore family home was situated on the edge of the predominantly Black "back of town," a neighborhood that was decidedly working class and less classy than what St. Cyr and Ella were used to as Creoles from the countryside. In the first decade after the Civil War, freed men and women flocked to the city propelled by promises of better jobs, housing, and cultural and social outlets. But with no money and only basic agricultural skills to rely on, the newly emancipated could usually find housing only in the low-lying area of the city, a neighborhood near the cypress swamps that was prone to flooding.[8]

As Creoles of Color, St. Cyr and Ella were far better off socially and economically than the freedmen nearby, though still a world away in wealth from their white counterparts. But the postbellum influx of people like the Moores stretched the geographical and racial bounds of the Crescent City. By the early twentieth century, new drainage technology coupled with a need for more housing prompted city officials to open up even more low-lying areas of the city for housing, and Creoles of Color soon moved in. Although lawmakers relegated them to the lower part of the city, Creoles of Color used street names, social institutions, and schools to try to distance themselves from the

Black lower class.[9] Audley's parents settled in a neighborhood that served as a spatial buffer between Black and white citizens with the hope that, over time, they could move closer—both physically and socially—to white folk.

After all, New Orleans was a place where Reconstruction *could* have succeeded. Their lives could have been transformed. Although the city had a powerful white elite, before the war it was also home to sizable Black and Creole of Color communities, as well as a white merchant class that had experienced the economic benefits of a multiracial society firsthand. Fearful of how a war would shift this delicate status quo, moderate white New Orleanians "opposed secession and rebellion until shots were fired," and reluctantly joined the rebel cause. Thus, communities of color across the Crescent City were cautiously optimistic once the Confederacy fell. Many hoped that, given their previous success within the city's stratified society, white business owners and their working-class counterparts could be persuaded to put their racial animosity aside as long as supporting Black rights would also propel the postbellum economy.[10] And so Creoles, Black people, and progressive Republicans forged ahead, passing a bevy of civil rights laws that required local businesses to uphold "patronage of all persons without distinction on account of race and color," and began desegregating city parks, bars, restaurants, and other previously "white only" spaces with fervor.

They had help from the top brass: Governor Henry Clay Warmoth and his lieutenant, Oscar Dunn. When the Illinois native's Union army regiment disbanded in the city in 1864, Warmoth decided to put down roots in the South rather than go back home. He set up a law office and, in just a few short years, seized control of the newly reconstituted Louisiana State Republican Party. A multiracial voting bloc carried him to the governor's seat four years later at the age of twenty-six. Although Warmoth was more of a political opportunist than a stalwart civil rights supporter, he saw to it that Reconstruction was somewhat successful across the state. As governor, he supported Black enfranchisement and integrated central aspects of city life—including the New Orleans Police Department—in the hopes of creating a stable Republican regime.[11]

But it was Lieutenant Governor Dunn, one of a handful of Black men to hold official posts during Radical Reconstruction, whom peo-

ple like the Moores saw as their man in the statehouse.[12] Creoles of
Color and freedmen alike appreciated Dunn for his earnest and honest nature and his willingness to champion their rights—particularly
school integration—during this precarious moment in the city's history. Despite a white political majority, with his help Black residents
voted, served on juries, and held local government offices in the years
immediately after the Civil War.[13]

But as Warmoth and Dunn were mobilizing, so too were their enemies. "We have Africans in place all about us, they are jurors, post
office clerks, custom house officers & day by day they barter away their
obligations and duties," U.S. Supreme Court judge and former Confederate John Campbell opined of Republicans' civil rights success in
the city. "The Southern communities will be a desolation until there
is a thorough change of affairs in all the departments of government."[14]

Local white Democrats took Campbell's call for change as a personal challenge. First came an assault on the Black vote. The party
began to push for "ballot reform," a euphemism for Black disenfran-
chisement, during a period of supposed racial reconciliation.[15] Next
came their targeted attack on integration that culminated in the 1890
Separate Car Act, which required railroads operating in the state to
provide "separate railway carriages for the white and colored races."[16]

In September 1881, Creoles and well-to-do Black folk in the Moores'
community created the Comité des Citoyens to fight the Separate Car
Act and take "part in all struggles to secure justice" in the city. The
group hired the white lawyer Albion Tourgée to challenge the act,
and Homer Plessy, a mixed-race shoemaker, volunteered to be the
one who would test the law and become the plaintiff in a lawsuit challenging it, if need be.

On June 7, 1892, the thirty-two-year-old Plessy walked into the
depot at Press and Royal Streets in New Orleans and bought a first-
class ticket for a train bound for Covington, Louisiana. He took a deep
breath, walked by the sign designating the railcar as WHITES ONLY,
and sat down. A conductor and private detective arrested him when
he refused to move to the "colored car." The incident sparked the
landmark case *Plessy v. Ferguson*, in which the U.S. Supreme Court
affirmed the constitutionality of "separate but equal," or segregated
public accommodations across America, in 1896.[17] An avalanche of Jim
Crow laws soon followed. While St. Cyr's first set of children came

into the world at integration's grand debut, Audley and her sisters were born at its final curtain.

Audley's parents did what they could to shelter themselves and their children from segregated life. St. Cyr opened a stable and livery business, where he rented out horses to draw carriages for the rich and wagons for the working class.[18] This business, along with the family's landhold-ings in Jeanerette, helped St. Cyr keep his family firmly ensconced in Creole society and offered his wife and girls a level of security that few around them could count on at the turn of the century.[19]

"So many times rich white men would come to our door to see Papa," Audley recalled of her days as a young girl in New Orleans. She and her sisters often rushed to open the door. But not St. Cyr. When they announced a caller had come, the patriarch instructed his daughters to "tell them Papa's eating," and that the guest could have a seat and wait until he had finished. Remarkably, Audley remembered, the white men obliged. Her father's defiance was seared into her early memory. "Papa," Audley recalled, would "never run and jump up to no white man."[20]

St. Cyr also had a sensitive side. Every now and then, he took Ella out for nights on the town—a way to spoil his wife and flaunt his wealth. Audley loved watching her mother ready herself for the eve-ning. She tried to stay out of the way as Ella climbed out of her bath, dressed, and sat at her vanity to put on her perfume and makeup. Audley then dutifully followed her mother as she picked up the train of her long, black, hand-beaded brocade dress that she had paired with a golden chain necklace and an ostrich-feathered fan and walked out of the house and into one of St. Cyr's finest carriages that would spirit her off to the Old French Opera House. Audley likely popped up onto her toes and peered through a window as Ella took St. Cyr's outstretched hand and climbed into the coach.[21]

These glossy moments also helped smooth over the less savory aspects of their marriage. The thrice-married St. Cyr had a mistress in the countryside named Lucinda, whom Audley knew as Miss Cindy. When Ella found out about the woman and her two daughters, she sent for them. "As young as I was," Audley recollected, "I can remember Mama going and buying a bolt of gingham ... and making her three little girls and Miss Cindy's two little girls [dresses] all off the same bolt of material. We all had dresses just alike."[22] When St. Cyr came home that day, he was "amazed to find Miss Cindy ... in the house with her two little girls." Ella knew "concubinage was a common thing" in Creole culture, according to Audley, and so she accepted Lucinda's girls just as she had St. Cyr's older boys.[23] St. Cyr provided a good life for her and her girls. In exchange, Ella overlooked her husband's indiscretions.

One particular perk of being St. Cyr's wife was membership in the Société des Jeunes Amis (Society of Young Friends). Creoles of Color founded the organization in 1867 as a social and mutual aid group.[24] By the time Audley's family joined, the Jeunes Amis had around two hundred French-speaking, dues-paying members.[25] Starting in 1901, St. Cyr dutifully paid $2 a month into the collective fund and then drew on it when Audley, Eloise, or Loretta fell ill.[26]

Soon after St. Cyr joined, the Société became more than just a safety net. It was also a way of keeping the Creole community together as Jim Crow and industrialization shifted race and class lines.[27] Headquartered on Dumaine Street in Tremé, the Jeunes Amis quickly gained a reputation for putting on elaborate fundraisers, annual picnics, and dances that rivaled those in white society and confirmed that Creoles of Color still had some wealth and power in the Crescent City.[28]

Nowhere was the Société more on full display than at its balls. The same could be said of the Moores. Whenever these semiannual events came around, Ella put her little girls in their finest dresses. Audley and her sister Eloise accompanied their parents in the carriage to the dance hall. When they arrived, they dashed off to the children's area, where they had a few hours to dance and play games before their nurse escorted them home so the adult revelry could begin. When Audley and her sister peeked into the grand ballroom on their way out, they burst into giggles. St. Cyr was many things, but a good dancer was not one of them. No matter how dashing he was in his suit, he couldn't help bumping into people—and the decorative posts—on the dance floor. "We teased Papa about dancing awkwardly," Audley recalled, when the family reconvened and recounted the events of the night.[29] But St. Cyr was a good sport.

Yet these glamorous nights out couldn't outshine the hard realities of racism in the city. One cold December night, a white watchman, Leonard Schroeder, claimed he chased "a negro carrying away with a sack of oats" and saw him run into a house on Perdido and Howard Streets—the exact location of the Moore family home. Schroeder called other officers to the scene, and they arrested St. Cyr and charged him with breaking and entering as well as petty larceny, claiming they found three sacks of oats at the scene.[30] Neither the community nor Société members believed he was guilty.[31] St. Cyr Moore didn't steal food from white men. He made them wait in the drawing room while he ate.

St. Cyr was no stranger to hiring legal help. He engaged a lawyer named Paul Lasalle to defend him and his reputation when the case went to trial. Lasalle littered the trial with witnesses who attested to his client's innocence, but it ended in a conviction.[32] Lasalle immediately filed a motion for a new trial, but the second one ended like the first, with the jury convicting St. Cyr and sentencing him to two months in the parish prison based on the watchman's word and his alleged possession of stolen oats.[33] Audley never discovered the true story behind her father's arrest, but she took it as a sign that by the turn of the century even respectable men like him couldn't escape the long arm of Jim Crow laws.

St. Cyr's savings, along with his membership in the Jeunes Amis, meant that his daughters still had the means to explore the city even if their father was behind bars. Perhaps they begged their half brothers, Henry and Clarence, to take them along when they went about town conducting business. Or maybe they warmly greeted the women of the Phillis Wheatley Club, an organization that established the Wheatley Sanitarium for Black patients and a training school for Black nurses, as they filed into their local meeting hall.[34] They might have nodded politely at the children who attended the Fisk Colored School, a nearby vocational institution, or chatted with the longshoremen on their way home from unloading cargo on the docks.[35] The Moores' neighborhood was also home to the Mount Zion Baptist Church and the United Sons of Honor Hall, where many a Black funeral procession would start. Perhaps Audley found herself swaying in unison with the blaring brass band as it followed the coffin and mourners. She may have even been tempted to join the women twirling colorful parasols and waving handkerchiefs in the second line, a distinctly New Orleans tradition where locals drop into the procession behind the band at celebrations, weddings, and funerals.[36]

But then again, Audley would have known better. Ella and St. Cyr deemed such public displays of emotion inappropriate for young Creole Catholic girls and would have cautioned them against letting anyone from their local congregation see them step out of line. When they first came to New Orleans, the couple worshipped at St. Joseph's Church on Tulane Avenue. An interracial congregation, St. Joseph's exemplified the Catholic Church's tenuous efforts at fostering faith across the color line after the *Plessy* decision, especially in cities like New Orleans where class, not color, had long been the primary demarcation among the pews.[37]

In the early twentieth century, St. Cyr and Ella Moore proudly led their trio of girls down the nave of St. Joseph's to their pew. Audley, now around five, tried her best to sit still and stare straight as her mother instructed. But the little girl's eyes often wandered as the service wore on, especially to the shiny silver plaque bearing her family's name in recognition of the fact that they had purchased the pew—a common way Creoles of Color displayed their wealth.[38]

Such was their Sunday ritual until, one week, Ella and her girls walked into the church and found a FOR COLORED ONLY sign next to the rows of pews in the back. This gave Audley's mother pause. But Ella was Creole, not colored. So she regained her composure and proudly led her girls to their usual seats. Audley's mother was mortified when church leaders came over, spoke to her in hushed tones, and then ushered her "away from her pew to the back of the church." Audley watched her mother kneel down to pray, staring at the heads of white parishioners she had once sat beside. She was embarrassed and confused. But she knew better than to cause a scene.

Ella tried to stay stoic in the face of this public embarrassment, but she couldn't hold it together. "I saw my mother cry," Audley remembered. "My mother, who had taught me [to] never show your feeling[s], I saw the tears roll down my mother's cheek."[39] It's possible Ella's rare display of emotion was due to her pride, her discomfit at the public slight. Or maybe she was grieving something deeper: the realization that under this new Jim Crow regime no amount of money or respectability could save her or her girls from the long arm of segregation.

Worried about losing worshippers like the Moores, Francis Janssens, the fifth archbishop of New Orleans, decided to create a Black parish and school funded by Philadelphia heiress turned nun Katharine Drexel.[40] But Ella, St. Cyr, and others saw this for what it was: a Jim Crow measure. A group of self-proclaimed Black and Creole "practical Catholics...emphatically protest[ed]" the "endeavor to establish a church exclusively for colored people."[41] The Comité des Citoyens instigated a public campaign against the creation of St. Katharine's Church, while New Orleans native and writer Alice Dunbar Nelson (then Alice Ruth Moore) spread the news nationally.[42] Writing for the *Women's Era,* the first newspaper by and for Black women, she labeled St. Katharine's a blow to Catholicism. For her, Catholic worship should be "one broad common plane where all might meet and for once forget the petty prejudices of birth or race." If the priest's plan went forward, it would surely be the start of Jim Crow churches in New Orleans and beyond.[43]

Nevertheless, St. Katharine's opened on May 19, 1895. Located just a few blocks from Canal Street, which also served as the "informal boundary between New Orleans's primarily French and Creole downtown population," St. Katharine's had "dazzling white" walls "relieved with a border at top and bottom of pale gold."[44] The pews were all new, as was the organ loft, which was now bigger to accommodate the new, larger all-Black choir. At the opening Mass, Janssens spoke for nearly an hour on the value of the newly minted congregation. He assured them that "it is not intended in opening and dedicating this church to convey the idea that there is a religion for the white people and one for the colored people"; it was simply that "on account of the particular conditions of the south it is almost impossible for white and black to mingle together and freely assist at religious services in the same edifice."[45] St. Katharine's was a Black-serving church, not a segregated one, according to Janssens. But Audley's parents saw the writing on the wall.

Ella and St. Cyr begrudgingly joined the first generation of St. Katharine's parishioners. Perhaps they capitulated because it was a way to hold on to their Catholic roots and Creole culture. Or maybe

St. Cyr saw it as the surest way to secure their social status amid an increasingly segregated landscape. Whatever the reason, St. Katharine's soon became a central part of Moore family life. St. Cyr's eldest son, Henry, married Celeste Houston in the nave as the patriarch looked on with pride. Both Eloise and Loretta were baptized in the church, and Nora served as a sponsor for her granddaughters' sacraments.[46] These moments helped solidify the blended family's stature in local society. They also showed a young Audley that no matter what her parents taught her, Sundays were now unequivocally separate and unequal.

By the time Audley was of school age, St. Katharine's inaugural priest, Father Charles Remillon, had turned his attention to building a Black Catholic school. The institution filled a niche in the city. Before the Civil War, New Orleans had led the way in expanding public education. In the early 1870s, city officials successfully desegregated many public schools, confounding naysayers who suggested Black and white students could never learn together. But the end of Reconstruction ushered in white supremacist politicians who reduced the school budget to reify racial hierarchies. By the time Ella and St. Cyr were ready to educate their girls, local politicians had destroyed one of the most expansive public school systems in the Deep South and only begrudgingly committed to educating Black children up to fifth grade.[47]

St. Katharine's was one of the few options available to Audley and her sisters. The parochial school opened its doors in 1895, and by the turn of the century it was known as "one of the leading colored schools of the city."[48] It expanded steadily, educating at least fifty girls a year by 1900 and enrolling close to one hundred pupils by the time the Moore girls attended a few years later.[49] As segregation spread across the city, St. Katharine's teachers dutifully taught literature lessons and ladylike habits to the daughters of New Orleans's Black elite.[50]

Audley ate it up. "At five years old I was already a stinker," she recalled. "My nurse took me to school and when I got to the door of the school, I took out my little pocket handkerchief and noticed that there was a hole in the hand-crocheted lace, and [I] made her bring me all the way back home to get another handkerchief.... I was going to be a little bourgeois stinker."[51]

But Audley's bourgeois training was cut short on February 17, 1904, when Ella died suddenly at only thirty-one years old, an extraordinary loss for young Audley. The cause of death was likely an infection, a common occurrence in the days before antibiotics were widely available.[52] Audley tried to make her mother proud amid her grief. "When she died, I was sitting in the little rocking chair and ashamed to let anybody see me cry," she recalled. "Mama had taught me that, never show your feelings. So I put my head down in my hands and did my crying like that."[53] As young as she was, Ella's eldest daughter had absorbed her mother's paramount lesson in propriety.

When Audley looked up, she found her father's mistress, Lucinda, among the mourners. Nora Henry was indignant at such a blatant display of disrespect for her deceased daughter. She had doubts about Lucinda's ability to care for Ella's girls alongside her own, for one. But more likely, she also chafed at Lucinda making such a quick play at becoming the new Mrs. Moore. She promptly gathered Audley, Eloise, and Loretta, and took her granddaughters back to New Iberia.[54]

Contrite and in mourning, St. Cyr Moore initially obliged his mother-in-law. Audley and her sisters got their first real taste of Black life in the Louisiana countryside, a slower, more socially confining existence with little schooling or supervision.[55] Yet life for St. Cyr, again a widower and without his girls, was lonely. After a few years, St. Cyr brought the trio back to New Orleans and their old way of life. He reenrolled his daughters in St. Katharine's, which had come under the control of the Sisters of the Holy Family, an order of Afro-Creole and Black nuns. Audley, now an adolescent, was delighted to be back in school and enthusiastically threw herself into catching up on her lessons.[56]

While his girls were gone, St. Cyr sold their house on Howard Street where Ella had died and bought a home on South Hagan Avenue, in the city's Second Ward.[57] When Ella's daughters came back, so too did her stepsister Alphonsine. She and her husband, John Springfield, moved in next door. Still concerned with St. Cyr's ability to care for the girls, Nora followed soon after, as did Ella's youngest half-sibling, Narceas.[58]

Ella's extended family guided Audley and her sisters through their gilded adolescent years. Perhaps Audley took piano lessons from Mrs.

Margaret M. Maurice, a concert pianist and teacher, or stopped by Vic Barrios's Penny Store on Lapeyrouse Street to buy herself a trinket after her lesson. On a nice night out, St. Cyr might have taken his daughters to the Astoria Hotel and Café, known for hosting the "best" of Black New Orleans, or spoiled the girls with a treat from Orleans Ice Cream Works. When Audley and her sisters could steal away from the watchful eyes of their father and family, they would run off and get "a half a nickel's worth of beans and half a nickel of rice" to devour, careful not to incriminate themselves by spilling it on their nice dresses.[59]

As Audley got older, her aunts could have hired Mrs. Cora to come and fit her for a new corset or taken her to Mrs. W. A. Jackson's parlor to get a dress made in the latest style for a Jeunes Amis ball. Or maybe the Moore girls needed something to wear to an event at the Pythian Temple, the six-story "fireproof, majestic" hall "built and operated by people of African descent" in downtown New Orleans, with business offices, a banquet hall, and meeting rooms for clubs and political organizations.[60] Whenever she stepped into this building, it was clear to Audley that Black people could not just survive but thrive in the segregated city.

If the Moore sisters overheard men and women in the temple talking, they must have realized that Black political organizing was a nationwide trend. In response to the rise in segregation laws, racist violence, and the election of white supremacist Woodrow Wilson to the presidency, leaders including W. E. B. Du Bois and Booker T. Washington worked to protect and advance Black life. As Audley reached adolescence, the National Association for the Advancement of Colored People (NAACP) gained a reputation as the Black elite's response to Jim Crow, organizing the wealthiest and most educated Black Americans to support its antisegregation lawsuits, voting registration drives, and antilynching legislation. Some saw this as an alternative to Booker T. Washington's call for "self-help," or what he termed the more material, "progressive, constructive work" of building Black people's craft, farming, and industrial skills so they would be able to integrate into the South's slowly industrializing economy.[61] Black New Orleanians took up both men's visions.

Not to be outdone, Black women added their voices to discussions about Black liberation. Perhaps the Moore girls came across writer and educator Anna Julia Cooper's pivotal 1892 text, *A Voice from the South*, in which the slave turned Sorbonne graduate championed Black women's education, intellectual acumen, and suffrage. Or maybe they longed to be old enough to join the Black Women's Club Movement, a collection of charity and social clubs across the country that comprised middle- and upper-class Black women invested in racial uplift. They would have been well aware of the National Association of Colored Women (NACW), the big-tent organization founded in 1896 that sought to bring club women together and channel their collective efforts toward their motto of "Lifting as we climb." During the first two decades of the twentieth century alone, the NACW built schools, created childcare and retirement centers, and held countless events all aimed at "bettering the race" by improving Black women's lives and opportunities. Members also advocated for antilynching legislation and led the fight for Black women's suffrage.[62] Ella's side of the family taught Audley that these women were the best the Black community had to offer.

Unfortunately for Audley, *les bons temps* turned to bad times just as she was old enough to enter society. In the fall of 1917, St. Cyr was ailing. His health had most likely been declining for years before his children rushed him to Charity Hospital, one of the only medical clinics that would take Black patients.[63]

Audley kept vigil by his bedside, desperately hoping he would recover. But as the days wore on, the realization that he might not make it started to creep in. All her life, she had relied on St. Cyr and her half brothers to keep her housed and well-heeled. But her father had kept all his business dealings between him and his two older sons, and Audley had only cursory knowledge of how their family made ends meet.

Sitting by his bedside, the eldest Moore girl took stock of her current financial standing. She knew St. Cyr and Henry had purchased a building at 2725 South Rampart Street (later Danneel Street) and used it as a headquarters for his livery, wood, and coal businesses.[64] She also recognized that "every Monday...Brother Henry would come and he'd take away bags of [money], big bags...and go put it in the bank." Her father had always seen to it that Audley and her sisters had never wanted for anything. But she feared that once he was gone, the trio would be left to fend for themselves.

"What will we do?" she asked her father when it was clear the end was near.

"Brother Henry will give [to] you rather than take from you," the ailing St. Cyr croaked. But Audley wasn't so sure. Her fears were confirmed only a few weeks later, on October 25, 1917, when St. Cyr Moore left this world.[65]

His body wasn't even in the ground before Henry kicked Audley and her sisters out of their house. It's not clear where exactly St. Cyr miscalculated. Audley's father could have thought that there would be more money left for the girls after Henry had settled his debts. Or maybe Henry saw himself as the rightful heir to the Moore family fortune and never intended to help his half sisters in the first place. Either way, as the daughters of St. Cyr's late third wife, the Moore girls had little recourse. Audley had to figure things out, and fast. Smart and resourceful, she snuck into the family stables one day while Henry was gone. She took three of St. Cyr's mules and quickly sold them at a local auction. With the bit of money in hand, she rented an apartment for her and her sisters.[66]

Whatever dreams Audley had of joining the Black elite had vanished overnight. She was a young woman with little education, no job, and no prospects for protection. Her days of being a self-proclaimed little bourgeois stinker were gone.

CHAPTER 3

Wartime Disruptions

Now both orphan and caregiver, Audley Moore found herself in a New Orleans completely unlike the one she had always known. Gone were the days spent learning manners and math at St. Katharine's and evenings at Jeunes Amis balls. Audley was nineteen years old and the sole provider for her two young sisters, just as America was entering World War I.

Audley turned to the only reliable employment for Black women at the time: domestic work. The eldest Moore girl now spent her days in white women's homes, "cooking, serving the meals, scrubbing the floors, making the beds, running errands . . . and waving [a] big palmetto fan over the dinner table to shoo away flies" for "75 cents a week."[1] Just a few years before, she could have never imagined cleaning her own house, let alone someone else's. Now, at the end of every day, she sat in the cramped room she shared with her sisters and surveyed the calluses on her hands and the bruises on her knees.

Audley was determined to be both mother and father to her two sisters. In the years immediately following St. Cyr's death, she desperately tried to keep a roof over their heads and their school fees paid so Eloise and Loretta still had a shot at becoming the respectable young women that their parents wanted them to be. But it came at a personal cost. Between "washing [her sisters'] clothes and ironing them, getting them ready for school and so on," she lamented, "I found myself going to school late and finally I just dropped out."[2] Audley now spent her early twenties living and working as if she were a single mother of two.

Help was hard to find as Ella's family dispersed. Her grandmother Nora, now in her eighties, headed back to New Iberia, likely to live close to her daughter Evelina. She had few other options, after all. Her other daughter, Alphonsine, had moved to Texas with her husband, and thanks to the 1917 Selective Service Act, which forced all men between the ages of twenty-one and thirty to register for the armed forces, her son and Audley's step-uncle, Narceas, could be drafted at any moment.[3] Neither Audley nor Nora was sure they could depend on his support. Times were so tough that Audley considered going back to the countryside as well. But she found it lacking in opportunity. Even with all its challenges, Audley believed "New Orleans was heaven compared with Iberia."[4]

If the backbreaking labor of domestic work didn't put her new class status in sharp relief, then the constant sexual harassment did. When she was younger, Audley had counted on her father and half brothers to defend her when white men tried to violate her body or her reputation. Spending all day cleaning and cooking in their homes meant that she had to face the fact that there was "no peace from white men." Although she changed jobs frequently to try to shield herself from harassment, Audley found that in one way or another the man of the house's eyes and hands always wandered onto her.[5] She got by daydreaming about her younger days, when she could luxuriate in claw-foot tubs rather than clean them. One day, she succumbed to the fantasy.

Audley was busy scrubbing the bathroom floors when she noticed the house was eerily quiet. She stopped and stilled, making sure she was indeed alone. And then, trembling with both fear and excitement, she "filled the bathtub with warm water and emptied into it nearly a bottle of cologne water and bath salts from the bathroom shelf." She nervously peeled off her cleaning uniform and set it to the side before climbing in. It was pure bliss. She took a deep breath, leaned back, and rested her arms on the sides of the tub, giving in to a fleeting moment of ease. Then, just as she exhaled and sank deeper into the water, the lady of the house walked in.

Audley shot straight up and began clawing her way out of the bath amid the woman's earsplitting screams. At first she tried flattery: she only took a bath because she wanted to smell just like her employer, she nervously explained. "So clean and cool . . . as nice as the flowers."

"Oh, you want to be a lady, do you?" the white woman screeched as Audley frantically dressed. "Well, you don't eat off the same dishes as my family, do you? You are not allowed to sit on my chairs, are you?

Yet you think you can bathe in my tub! Get out of this house!"[6] As she scurried out, Audley tried to remember her mother's mantra: a lady never shows her feelings. But she must have fought back the prick of tears from the humiliation, and the fear—and the devastating realization that she might never be considered a lady again.

It would take thirty years and a nationwide Civil Rights Movement before Black women were able to move out of domestic work en masse. Until then, they had to depend on white housewives "to buy their strength and energy for an hour, two hours, or even a day."[7] Once hired, they navigated the unique precariousness of the position: white women expected them to perform intimate acts of personal care such as raising their children and cleaning their clothes, even as they reviled them as unclean and unfit caregivers.[8] Domestic work provided Audley with swift lessons about racial hierarchies, sexual politics, and class relationships, ones that the adults around her had largely shielded her from when she was a part of upper-class Creole society. It didn't take long to realize she needed to find another way to survive, and fast.

Tough times called for unorthodox methods. "I had to take up a course in hairdressing and lied about my age," Audley recalled. "I was supposed to be twenty-one." She likely attended Crescent Hairdressing College on Dryades Street in New Orleans, a local institution where Black women could take hairdressing, manicuring, and massage courses.[9] The beauty industry offered Audley greater personal autonomy, more control of her time, increased mobility, and most important, the ability to avoid abusive white women and their husbands' roaming hands. By the time she was in her early twenties, Audley, like many other poor and working-class Black women across America, was able to supplement her income by pressing hair.[10]

Hairdressing offered more safety and stability, but not the kind that marriage could provide. As wartime rationing ratcheted up, Audley and her sisters kept an eye out for eligible bachelors who might offer security in exchange for companionship.[11] The youngest Moore girl, Loretta, soon became enthralled with one Charles "Charlie" Bazile, a slender eighteen-year-old with black hair, brown eyes, and a light complexion reminiscent of her father's. He was handsome and held a steady job as a chauffeur, quite the catch for a young, uneducated woman with few job prospects.[12]

If Loretta wanted to keep him, she had to act fast. Charlie could be called up to serve at any moment. In April 1918, her elder sisters looked on as Loretta, all of fifteen years old, stood at the altar staring into her young husband's eyes.[13] The newlyweds had little time to make their house a home. A few months after they moved in together, Charlie shipped off to World War I.

While Bazile was headed to battle, Audley and her sisters seized their freedom. Although they were self-sufficient, the Moore girls—now nineteen, seventeen, and fifteen—were all technically minors. Louisiana law set the age of maturity at twenty-one. Loretta had been emancipated by marriage, but this alone would not allow her to lay claim to any of her family's property or estate. And, in an interesting twist of fate, her two older sisters, whom the state considered under-age, became Charlie's legal dependents when she wed.

Louisiana law allowed anyone over the age of eighteen to peti-tion the court for emancipation.[14] And so, in May 1918, only a month after Loretta married, all three girls filed emancipation claims with the New Orleans City Clerk of Court. The sisters had navigated the world as best they could in the seven months since St. Cyr died. But they found themselves stymied from obtaining housing, schooling, and the ability to lay claim to any money he might have left behind. Aud-ley and Loretta filed a joint petition. Eloise filed a separate petition to claim any remaining funds owed to them from their father's member-ship in the Jeunes Amis. Judges approved both petitions, marking a rare moment when the southern courts sided in favor of young Black girls.[15]

By the time the Moore sisters gained their legal independence, Black Americans were feeling the confines of war. Black boys boarded box-cars to be shipped off to foreign and domestic bases, and women rationed their food while giving their time and energy to wartime causes. Of the 3.7 million men who served at home and abroad during World War I, 400,000 were Black soldiers, although most were con-signed to segregated support roles rather than combat. A Black man in uniform was a dangerous precedent, after all. Lawmakers and army generals alike knew it wouldn't be long before equal rights proponents asserted the "link between military service and civic status." If Black soldiers could fight and die alongside white ones, why couldn't Black civilians live alongside white folk?[16]

These crosscurrents of racism and patriotism were on full display in New Orleans. As Audley moved around the city cleaning homes and pressing hair, she likely stopped to marvel at the Liberty Bond parades, soldiers running drills at Camp Nicholls and Camp Martin—hastily thrown-together training sites in public parks and on local fairgrounds—and women on street corners cajoling the public to provide medical supplies and chocolate bars for soldiers.[17] Even still, civilians' expressions of wartime patriotism were segregated.

On the home front, white women often joined their state chapter of the War Department's Woman's Committee or worked with the Red Cross and the YMCA. Black women were eager to engage in war work in New Orleans, writer Alice Dunbar Nelson reported, yet government employment bureaus saw them only as "a potential scrub woman, no matter how educated and refined the girl may be."[18] Federal agencies and private companies segregated Black women in jobs and charity work if they allowed them to participate at all.[19] Frustrated but not deterred, Black women across the country created their own wartime networks.

Audley surely heard about the National Association of Colored Women's focus on how the war affected Black men and their families.[20] President Mary Burnett Talbert urged Black women to ration their food, fundraise, and send material goods to Black troops. Black club women also overlapped in membership and advocacy with groups like the NAACP, linking their support of Black soldiers with their demands for women's suffrage.[21] Audley likely longed to join them. But she had neither the time nor the money nor the status to be a wartime suffragette.

Instead, the Moore girls' entry into wartime activism was more personal. Eloise was infatuated with a boy who was soon to ship off. The middle Moore sister was surely afraid of losing her beau in battle. But she was also worried about how he would be treated on the army base. She was right to be concerned. When they went down to the train tracks to say goodbye, Eloise and her sisters noticed the Red Cross was handing out coffee and doughnuts only to white soldiers. They had nothing for their Black counterparts. In response, the Moore sisters went door to door asking their neighbors to whip up coffee and baked goods. They then cajoled local Black women to come and hand it all out to the Black soldiers waiting to depart.[22]

"If they [are] treating our boys like that here, what will they do over there?" Eloise worried out loud as her boyfriend left. On a whim, she decided to hop on a train and follow him and the other Black soldiers to Anniston, Alabama. She was certainly willing to go alone, but she hoped her sisters would come with her.[23] As she packed up, she begged them to do the same. Audley considered her options. She had never been outside Louisiana, and she had no idea what awaited them in Alabama. What's more, she had no idea how they would survive once they got there. But if she was being honest with herself, their life in New Orleans wasn't exactly easygoing. Following the soldiers would be, at the very least, a break from the daily drudgery of domestic work and destitution. It was risky. But her motherly instincts ultimately won out. "I couldn't let her go by herself," Audley recalled. "She was younger than me. So, we all went."[24]

The sisters quickly realized Jim Crow had followed them across state lines. Audley observed that the army base, Camp McClellan, "had a place for white boys . . . to play cards and everything. They really had nothing for black ones."[25] Although Black soldiers at Camp McClellan fared better than those on other bases across the country, most of them still never saw combat. Instead, they became part of a coerced labor regime, working ten to fifteen hours a day digging trenches and stacking up supplies for white soldiers, only to come back to substandard housing and racist commanding officers.[26] By 1918, when the war was winding down, these same officers forced Black soldiers to work nine to ten hours a day without a clear sense of why they were still enlisted while their white counterparts got to go home.[27] It was only at this late point in the war that auxiliary organizations like the YMCA and the Red Cross stepped in to offer social support and medical aid to Black troops.[28]

Audley and her sisters were appalled. But if the government refused to step in, then they would step up. The sisters found an old, abandoned church and pleaded with the locals to let them use it. Then they scrounged up an old phonograph and some scratched-up records, a few tables and chairs, and some cards and games for the Black soldiers to play. Before they opened their doors, Eloise repurposed a standard-issue army jacket and found an old pair of military-issue khakis that she sewed into a skirt. When Black soldiers walked into the old church, they found the Moore sisters, one in uniform, sashaying around serving coffee and doughnuts while soldiers relaxed, talked, and enjoyed the music. "We consider ourselves having the first U.S.O. among Blacks," Audley recalled of this venture.[29]

They were onto something. Reports emanating from War Camp Community Service indicated that "as many as 40,000 black soldiers had no comfort stations or canteens, no movie theatres," or other recreational means. "Not even a place where a colored soldier might sit down and write a letter."[30] Audley later joked that her sister Eloise was the "first WAC," a reference to the Women's Army Corps, a World War II–era women's auxiliary unit.[31] But Eloise was more likely guided by the local Hostess Houses, YMCA-supported facilities that housed soldiers' families and provided recreational activities on military bases. Billed as a "home away from home" during wartime, Hostess Houses had kitchens to prepare and serve quality meals and dining rooms and recreational spaces in which to enjoy them.[32] But just like the rest of the war effort, they were segregated, and most of the "colored" Hostess Houses weren't finished until October 1918, a month before the war ended.[33] The Moore sisters' makeshift community space in Anniston filled a pressing need.

Eloise was the undisputed mastermind of the sisters' wartime activism, and perhaps for the first time since their father died, Audley found she could step back and take on a more supportive role. She quickly took stock of the growing number of women hanging around the army base. And they all needed their hair done. So Audley began charging the local Black women sixty cents to shampoo and press their hair and seventy-five cents to curl it. She joined a bevy of Black women who created an informal economy around the war effort, through beauty culture, sex work, and other cultural and recreational activities.[34] For Audley, it was a welcome change from domestic work in New Orleans. Moreover, living and working around the army base showed her that she didn't have to choose between helping her community and helping herself.[35]

In more ways than one, World War I "supplied a new theater" for debates about nation making, race, power, class, and equal rights.[36] Audley and her sisters were keen spectators. They looked on as America made its grand debut on the world stage as a great emancipator—

a masterful public performance as liberty's beacon shining from the West, all while extending white supremacy's tendrils across the globe. Audley was intimately familiar with Louisiana's brand of racism. But traveling to Anniston and witnessing the derision of Black soldiers was a revelation. As she worked around the base, Audley heard stories about how Black soldiers—from Great Britain to France to the Caribbean—endured the same racist treatment as the boys at home. White supremacy was global in its scope and relentless in its furor. Perhaps even more distressing for the eldest Moore sister was the realization that Black women were even worse off. While the American government was using Black soldiers as pawns in its geopolitical games, Black women were not even on the chessboard.

Audley had always been resourceful and headstrong. But she wasn't necessarily protest-minded. Witnessing Eloise challenge the mistreatment of Black soldiers and meet their material needs had a profound effect on her. Eloise was a natural intellectual. Although she only had an elementary school education, the middle Moore sister innately understood the power dynamics around her and had a will to tip the scales. Eloise had cajoled Audley out of her comfort zone in New Orleans. She had also helped her big sister develop an eye for injustice and a confidence that she could do something about it.[37]

Although World War I ended on November 11, 1918, Black folk in America didn't have the luxury of laying down their arms. The Moore sisters returned to a New Orleans that buzzed with parades heralding Black veterans one day and then held funeral processions for victims of vigilante violence the next. Meanwhile, wartime had shifted the city's demographics, jumbling people across neighborhoods, political affiliations, and sometimes even classes. Some of the Moore sisters' old haunts were still standing. Black people were still a substantial portion of the city's population, and many of them still held on to their French, Spanish, and Creole roots. But they now had to contend with another wave of German, Irish, and Italian immigrants who further fortified their neighborhoods and political strongholds after the war.[38]

Black people had some help of their own, too. The city saw an influx of Black workers and Caribbean immigrants after the war, bolstering and diversifying the long-standing fight for civil rights across the city. But even put together, they were no match for the white elite. No matter how gallantly Black people had fought during the war, Jim Crow was a different battle entirely.[39]

The sight of Black veterans in uniform enraged white Americans, and peacetime brought a resurgence of lynchings across the country, with monstrous murders occurring frequently between March and December 1919.[40] When picking off Black people one by one wasn't enough, some white citizens turned to full-blown race riots.

The Red Summer of 1919 kicked off on a hot Saturday night in May in Charleston, South Carolina, when five white sailors gathered in a Black part of town called the Tenderloin. "We are looking for a damn nigger whom we gave $8 to get us bug juice," one sailor announced by way of an explanation for why they were there.[41] Furious that the bootlegger cheated them out of booze on their weekend off, the sailors started a fight with any Black man they could find. A shot rang out from somewhere. This was the white sailors' cue to attack. Within the hour, word got back to the Charleston Navy Yard that a fight was brewing, and white sailors rode into the Tenderloin by the carload. They began attacking Black folk indiscriminately until 3:00 a.m., when the mayor used the U.S. Marines to restore order.[42] When the dust settled, six people—four Black men and two white sailors—were dead and scores of others were injured.[43] Washington, D.C.; Omaha, Nebraska; and Longview, Texas, were next, each riot set ablaze by claims of a Black man's affront to white manhood or womanhood.

If race riots in the nation's capital astounded Black Americans, then the violence in Chicago decimated their hope of racial progress. Nicknamed the Promised Land, Chicago was the exemplar of Black urban life and a go-to destination for those looking to leave the Jim Crow South. But the reports coming out of the Windy City during July 1919 tempered Black folk's enthusiasm. Looking for some relief from the brutal summer heat, Black and white kids flocked to Lake Michigan to cool off. On July 27, seventeen-year-old Eugene Williams and his friends inadvertently drifted across the invisible color line that segregated Black swimmers from white ones in the water. Outraged by this affront, white swimmers started throwing stones at them, striking Williams and causing him to drown. Enraged at Williams's murder, Black people took to the streets. White people responded in kind. The violence soon spilled out of the beach and into Chicago's South Side.

Seven days later, fifteen white and twenty-three Black Chicagoans were dead.[44]

Audley read about the riot, and about the Red Summer violence writ large, in the New Orleans newspapers. She soon learned any perceived affront to white men or claim of rape by a white woman could lead to deadly race riots and lynchings. Amid this treacherous landscape, a growing push for women's suffrage was coming to a head, and Audley hoped that the vote would give her a potent weapon against white violence. Yet she found local and national organizations often encouraged Black women to support Black men above their own interests. Civil rights and women's suffrage divided rank-and-file organizers, so these groups claimed, and there wasn't enough oxygen for both.[45] Nevertheless, generations of women's organizing culminated in the ratification of the Nineteenth Amendment in August 1920. When Moore came home from the war effort, she could finally head to the ballot box. But she barely set foot across the suffrage threshold before southern states began to shut the door to enfranchisement.[46]

Meanwhile, Loretta's husband came home from Fort Stotsenburg in the Philippines, where the army kept Black soldiers stationed, but out of combat, until the end of the war.[47] Soon after he returned, the youngest Moore sister gave birth to a daughter in early 1920 and named her Audley, an homage to the woman who had been her mother, sister, provider, and friend for the past three years.[48] Against all odds, the Moore sisters had survived being orphaned and the turmoil of war. They were now hurtling toward the tumultuous 1920s with the next generation of Moore girls in tow.

CHAPTER 4

Following Garvey

As the Moore sisters resettled in the city, so did a number of West Indian soldiers whom the winds of war had brought to New Orleans. Josiah Leopold Spraggs had dark skin, a slender frame, a hard jawline, and a scar over his right eye—every bit the sailor archetype. He was born in 1890 in Savanna-la-Mar, Jamaica.[1] Tucked under the southwest ledge of the island and known more for its endurance of pirates and hurricanes than anything else, Sav (as the locals call it) was a major port for sugar exports. The town offered little by way of schooling or employment, and at the end of the nineteenth century hurricanes had wiped out the island's sugar and banana plantations. If young men like Spraggs wanted a better life, they would have to set sail for other lands. Sail Spraggs did. He spent his early twenties working on ships owned by the United Fruit Company (UFCO), an American-owned corporation that exploited Caribbean and Latin American land and labor to bring tropical fruits to the States.[2]

Spraggs reached adulthood as the banana industry matured. In the late nineteenth century, the fruit was considered a bourgeois treat. But by the 1910s it had become "positively proletarian." The banana trade spiked, as did the demand for laborers to keep it churning. For many Jamaicans, it was an opportunity to seek new fortunes beyond the island's depressed economy.[3] United Fruit was known as *El Pulpo*, or the octopus, because it had "tentacles everywhere." Between 1916 and 1919, he worked on United Fruit's "Great White Fleet," a name it borrowed from U.S. Navy battleships and a sign of the company's close ties with American imperialism.[4]

UFCO's money-hungry executives soon realized they could make even more money ferrying people as well as fruit. Their long, angular white ships became the precursors to the modern cruise ship industry, whisking white and white-clad men and women from the United States to company-owned hotels on tropical islands like Jamaica.[5] Spraggs rose in the morning and donned his impeccably pressed black-buttoned white waiter's coat and black pants to serve these passengers as they lounged on sprawling promenade decks and in well-ventilated salons.[6] Serving tourists aboard ships like the SS *Atenas,* the SS *Saramacca,* and the SS *Jamaica* was thankless and sometimes degrading work. But being a ship waiter paid better wages than harvesting bananas on UFCO's plantations. The job also gave Spraggs a chance to see a bit more of his small corner of the world. In just a few short years, the young Jamaican had sailed around the Caribbean: from Cuba to Panama, Costa Rica to Puerto Rico and Guatemala.[7]

In many of the places where Spraggs stopped, young Jamaicans were a large and vulnerable portion of the labor force. United Fruit plantation workers had flimsy contracts, endured perpetual labor rights violations, and were subjected to anti-Black animosity from locals and local governments alike. If that weren't enough, the company often pitted members of their multinational, multiethnic, and multiracial workforce against one another to stymie collective organizing.[8] Little did the banana bosses know that these labor conditions would catalyze Black Nationalist organizing.

In the fall of 1910, a dark-skinned man with a round face and stocky build stepped off a steamboat and into a heated labor dispute between UFCO bosses and workers in Costa Rica. A Jamaica-born man who, like Spraggs, sought economic security by working for United Fruit, Marcus Garvey hardly stood out amid the thousands of workers who passed through the company's various banana republics in the early 1910s. But he soon made his mark—on UFCO and on history—when he landed in the coastal city of Limón.[9]

Using the skills he had learned as a printer's apprentice in his hometown of St. Ann's Bay, in the spring of 1911, Garvey founded a bilingual newspaper to promote workers' rights and cross-national solidarity. He provocatively called it *La Nación,* or *The Nation.* Garvey wasted no time publishing articles assailing company bosses and the local West Indian elite. The young editor spared no one who he believed was harming workers, a tack that got him rounded up and roughed up by the local police. Garvey made so many enemies in just a few years that when his printing press broke down, he could find no one willing to provide the parts or labor to fix it. His need to reboot his publishing operation, along with UFCO bosses, finally ran him out of town.[10]

Garvey hopped from one UFCO enclave to another. He spent the next few years in Nicaragua, Honduras, Colombia, Ecuador, and Venezuela gaining a reputation for stirring up trouble—read: Black people's political consciousness—wherever he went. Visiting these different banana republics, the young Jamaican saw that no matter where he was, the problems "the Black race" faced were the same. He began to ponder how to harness their collective experiences and jump-start a liberation movement.[11]

When Garvey returned to Kingston in 1914, he met Amy Ashwood, a smart seventeen-year-old woman with radiant brown skin, round eyes, and a short bob. Ashwood was taken with Garvey's political ambition; he with her intellect. They soon married and founded the Universal Negro Improvement Association (UNIA), an organization meant to foster race pride and Black political and economic independence, all in service of eventually creating "a central nation for black people" back in Africa.[12]

Much to the chagrin of UFCO officials, Garvey's new organization stirred up the Afro-Caribbean workforce just as much as his previous ventures had. His countrymen, Spraggs among them, carried word of the new nationalist group across the high seas. News of an organization promoting political and economic autonomy for Black people crisscrossed the Caribbean, fomenting resistance as it went.[13] It didn't take long for UNIA chapters to pop up in Cuba, Panama, Trinidad, Costa Rica, Guatemala, Honduras, and Jamaica as the world went to war.[14]

When America joined the fight, the War Department requisitioned United Fruit's Great White Fleet. Banana boats became battleships, and the crew aboard became soldiers. Josiah Spraggs registered with the British West Indian Regiment.[15] However, his stint in the army was short, perhaps owing to Great Britain's resistance to arming Black men in its colonies, or because he was one of the nearly fourteen thousand Jamaican volunteers whom the British army discharged on medical grounds.[16] Whatever the case, Spraggs was spared combat but afforded a new level of mobility. His time in the army helped clear his way to enter the United States and settle in the Big Easy.[17]

Perhaps the young sailor caught Audley's eye when she stopped by the lunch house he worked at on North Villere Street for a quick bite between hairdressing clients.[18] Or maybe they locked eyes at the Longshoremen's Hall, the dockworker union's meetinghouse that doubled as a community organizing space. However they first encountered each other, it's easy to imagine Audley was taken with his sharp looks and political savvy; Spraggs by her worldliness and independence. With Loretta married and Eloise recovering from following a young soldier to Anniston, it was Audley's turn to try her hand at love. She could certainly do worse than Spraggs, who held down a steady job and had seen some of the world.

They tied the knot in the heat of the New Orleans summer. With little money to her name, any dreams Audley might have had of an elaborate wedding were long gone. But perhaps she was able to hang on to some traditions of her past life. The girls she ran with when she was at St. Katharine's often wore modest, knee- or floor-length wedding dresses with long sleeves and a simple flapper veil or hat when they wed. They donned little jewelry, save maybe a family heirloom, and carried small, simple bouquets.[19] It's possible Moore was able to grab a dress or some small baubles before she and her sisters fled their family home after their father died. If so, she would have pressed and polished the trappings of her old life before marrying Spraggs on July 26, 1920.[20]

It didn't take long for the pair to settle into a comfortable new life together, making their money by opening and operating a small grocery store on Erato Street.[21] Audley soon found that Spraggs had similar values and qualities to St. Cyr's. One day, while Audley was weaving in and around the store shelves, a white man came in to collect their insurance payment for the month. He stepped across the threshold and headed straight toward Spraggs without acknowledging her existence. Spraggs stepped forward, held out his arm, and stopped the man in his tracks. Audley stilled and her eyes widened; she had seen this kind of exchange end badly before. "Don't you see my wife? My wife is in here," Spraggs said, and gestured to Audley. She was due the same respect this man would have given any white woman, and her husband wasn't afraid to say so. Audley nodded politely after the man begged her pardon.[22] In moments like this, Audley found that she was finally able to reclaim some of the respectability and social status she had lost after her father died. But everything she thought she wanted changed when Marcus Garvey came to town.[23]

On a muggy summer evening in 1922, Audley Moore made her way toward the Longshoremen's Hall on the corner of Jackson Avenue and Franklin Street. She expected the night air to be hot, but she was sweating even more than usual this evening. Audley was packing some heat of her own. She had a .45-caliber pistol stashed in her bra and another in her purse. She also had a briefcase full of extra bullets at her side. If it was a fight the New Orleans police wanted, then she was ready to give it to them.

Audley rounded the corner and came upon the building that had served as a rallying and radicalizing space for Black New Orleanians for decades. It was an iconic building: angular, white, and imposing with darkly painted rectangular windows and wide double doors. But on this night, it stuck out for a different reason. A crowd had already gathered outside—domestic workers, store owners, homemakers, and longshoremen were all filing in to hear New Orleans's newest visitor deliver a speech. "He'll speak tonight. Believe me, he'll speak tonight," Audley heard people mutter as she said her hellos. She nodded in agreement and made her way inside.

The air in the hall felt as thick as it did outside. Everyone had heard what had happened the night before. Marcus Garvey had come to New Orleans. Afraid of his penchant for rousing Black crowds—he had made a name for himself delivering speeches about the storied history of Africa and proclaiming the time had come for Black people around the world to come together and fight white supremacy—the police blocked Garvey from speaking by issuing an injunction against the meeting. His followers had contested the move, and word was they had won. Audley hoped the rumors were true.

She watched nervously as "the police came in the Longshoremen's Hall. They filed in, down through the center aisle, and lined themselves up, each man on a row of benches." Audley exchanged knowing looks with others in the audience and shifted in her seat. Everyone was anxiously waiting to see who was going to make the next move, Garvey or the police. Cheers rang out as the Black Nationalist entered, walked down the center aisle, and took to the stage. "My friends, I want to apologize to you for not speaking last night. But the Mayor of New Orleans permitted himself to be used as a stooge by the chief of police," he said to cheers.[24]

The police jumped up. They were poised to attack. The Black New Orleanians—who, like others across the Deep South, had been bearing arms for self-defense since slavery—responded in kind.[25] Like a wave, their guns went up. Audley joined, drawing a "little pearl-handled gun" from her pocketbook and a smaller one from inside her dress and hoisting them high in the air.

"Speak, Garvey, speak! Speak, Garvey, speak!" the crowd chanted in unison.

Audley watched in astonishment as the "police filed out of there like little puppy dogs wagging their tails."[26] She stashed her guns and settled in to hear the speech that would transform her life.

Or at least that's how Audley would always tell it—the mostly true story of her birth as a Black Nationalist. Garvey did indeed arrive in New Orleans with plans to speak at the Longshoremen's Hall. As soon as Mayor Andrew McShane heard the nationalist had come to town, he tried to thwart the leader by denying the UNIA a permit for the event. McShane won the battle but lost the war. The next day, local UNIA members hired a lawyer from one of the "best firms" in the city to challenge the injunction. They succeeded, and Garvey took to the podium the following night and spoke to a crowd of thousands.[27]

In Garvey's telling of the event, captains of several different local police precincts as well as "several dozen Secret Service men and detectives lined up at the front of the platform" in the Longshoremen's Hall that night. "Things got so hot," the UNIA leader continued, "that the police chief rose and said: 'If you say one word about the police force I'll lock you up.'"

"Sit down there! Sit down!" Garvey shot back in his booming voice.

In his version of the story, it was Garvey's chastening of the cops that ran them out of the union hall, not the hoisted handguns of his devoted followers.[28] Wherever the truth lies, the effect that night had on young Audley is unquestionable. Garvey and his UNIA had repelled white supremacy and taken back her community. She became a lifelong Garveyite right then and there.[29]

That night in 1922 was actually Garvey's third visit to New Orleans. The city was the linchpin in his strategy to mobilize the American South, and he had been watering seeds of nationalism there for years. Black Louisianans' had a long history of nationalistic thought, dating back to slavery, when imported Africans revolted and immigrated to Haiti guided by a collective sense of sovereignty. The self-deterministic current continued well into the twentieth century, when some Black folk in Iberia Parish had tried but failed to declare themselves a separate nation "in exile," and institutions like the Tulane Baptist Church in New Orleans championed African liberation and emigration during Jim Crow.[30] The separatist spirit had been widespread in the state before Garvey rose to fame. It blossomed even more once he arrived on the scene.[31]

Louisiana quickly became home to the greatest number of UNIA chapters in the South, and the New Orleans Division (NOD) was, by far, the largest and most successful.[32] It began when fifteen Black locals gathered in Alaida and Sylvester Robertson's home on October 12, 1920, to discuss Garvey's teachings. Alaida was a well-known community activist, and Sylvester a bank porter. The Robertsons were considered upstanding members of the Black community who could be trusted to build local support around Garvey's teachings. It didn't take long for this handful of nationalists to grow into a group of hundreds, each prepared to fight for Black autonomy.[33]

Spraggs, Audley, and her sisters joined them after Garvey's infamous visit. At the end of each week, the family would make their way to the Longshoremen's Hall, the new meeting space for the rapidly growing New Orleans Division, and take their seats in the neatly ordered rows of chairs. When Audley looked out across the sea of people, she saw Black women sprinkled through the audience, clad in all-white dresses emblazoned with a black cross. These were members of the Black Cross Nurses, a women's auxiliary modeled after the Red Cross. Also present were the men of the Universal African Legion, a paramilitary group that protected Black folk around the city against state-sanctioned and vigilante violence. They donned uniforms of dark blue pants, blue jackets, and blue peaked caps, with Black Nationalist iconography pinned in the place of traditional military honors. While the indignities of segregation, large and small, chipped away at Black folk from all walks of life, the UNIA and its auxiliaries were spaces where they could command honor and respect.

Audley never had an ear for pitch or tone. But this didn't stop her from standing and singing, loud and off-key, UNIA hymns praising "Afric's sunny fountains" and "golden sand," and calling for flags to be "unfurled beneath the glittering lights while eager eyes mirrored the dream of Africa redeemed" as the meeting opened.[34] Business soon followed the pageantry. Audley and the other members took their seats and settled in to hear the speaker of the week, whose lengthy lectures covered everything from international events, such as the Rif War raging in Morocco, to the manifold meanings of nationhood, diasporic politics, and Black pride.[35]

Being a Garveyite demanded education—a willingness to learn about global Black history and contemporary struggles for liberation. "In the Garvey movement," Audley recollected, "there wasn't this round-the-clock activity. There wasn't this day-to-day struggle.... We learned, and we talked about our history."[36]

Learning under Garvey was both freeing and disorienting for Audley. "It was Garvey who brought the consciousness to me," she recalled of her time in these meetings. "You can experience a thing without being conscious of yourself.... [You can] see the brutality of the police all against us ... the fact that jobs are denied [to] our people, housing is denied to us and so on, and yet a consciousness is not aroused."[37] During the first twenty years of her life, Audley had witnessed the daily injustices that segregation, unequal schooling, and racial violence had wrought upon Black people. But the relative security she enjoyed, as a child in a middle-class family and then as the wife of a small business owner, had exempted her from some of the injuries many faced.

The UNIA helped her develop an awareness of Black people's plight beyond her own circumstances and hometown. When Audley came of age in New Orleans, her understanding of the African Diaspora was largely rooted in the Afro-Caribbean community's experiences. Her wartime travel into the heart of Alabama certainly broadened her worldview. However, it was only after she became a Garveyite that she began to see herself as part of a global Black community, united with people of African descent around the world regardless of their station in life.

"Garvey brought us a message the likes of which I had never heard," she remarked. "He told us about the splendors of our ancient history and culture, of the great kings and queens that we had been, of the riches of Africa, and of the kind of people that we were."[38] Nowhere did this ring more true than when these lessons touched on the history of Ethiopia. Ethiopia was central to Garvey's brand of Black Nationalism—both the real East African country and the mythologized idea of it.[39] In the late nineteenth century, Black religious and political leaders alike invoked Psalm 68:31—"Princes shall come out of Egypt and Ethiopia shall stretch forth her hands unto God"—as evidence of divine providence that Black people would be delivered from their hardships. Garvey seized upon this scripture in the early twentieth century, using it in the masthead of the UNIA's newspaper, *The Negro World,* and as the basis for his claims that with the Diaspora's help Africa could be liberated and redeemed.[40] As the sole African nation (with the unique exception of Liberia) to never be colonized, Ethiopia became the idealized site of Garvey's Pan-African redemption project.[41] Audley had always been proud of her family history. But becoming a Garveyite helped her develop a more capacious vision of racial pride and African heritage.

"Prior to that time, I used to feel that, oh, to be white would be wonderful," Audley remarked. "Not poor white. I want that very clear. To be rich, rich white." Garvey blew that worldview to pieces. Like many of her fellow followers, Audley found that as she embraced Africa, she began to reject her internalized racism. "All of us wanted to be Black then," she recalled, "jet black."[42]

Garvey had just as much of an impact on her class politics. Growing up, Audley and her sisters had been taught that money was what distinguished them from those who lived in New Orleans's struggling neighborhoods. But Garvey had a different message. In the UNIA, members rose through the ranks "not by clothes, or money, or birthright, but by service to the race."[43] The genius in this approach was that it allowed his mostly working-class base—from domestics to dock loaders—to lay claim to leadership roles and respectability just by adopting Black Nationalist ideals. This was especially impactful for Audley, whose fluctuating family fortunes had caused her to slide down the economic ladder in her late teens. Garvey had shown her that through having racial pride, she could garner respect no matter her station in life.

When the NOD welcomed female speakers to the Longshoremen's Hall, Audley learned that Garvey believed that Black women earned respect by following his mandates about sex, sexuality, and reproduction. He championed gender politics that felt like an awkward combination of Victorian gender ideals, modern eugenics, and Black Nationalist philosophy, claiming the "Negro [was] dying out" and thus it was the Black woman's job to birth children and raise them with nationalist values.[44] Black women were meant to tend to the people of the sovereign Black nation, while the men were meant to rule it.[45]

Audley's local division upheld these ideals. Black women founded, sustained, and propelled the New Orleans Division, which by 1922 was estimated to be nearly four thousand strong.[46] However, they weren't considered *true* leaders. Mirroring nineteenth-century Black fraternal and religious organizations, the UNIA had a hierarchical, gender-segregated structure. Each chapter had a "lady president" who oversaw the women's auxiliaries such as the Black Cross Nurses and Ladies of the Royal Court of Ethiopia, the UNIA's social networking wing.[47] This separate sphere did offer Garveyite women some autonomy and power. However, they lacked full equality within the organization they helped build.[48]

The paradox was that Garveyism, as both a philosophy and a movement, would never have thrived without the women who defied its patriarchal mandates. The UNIA owed its early success to Amy Ashwood Garvey, who helped found the organization and organize its inaugural events in Jamaica. And Marcus Garvey would have never been as renowned if not for his second wife, Amy Jacques Garvey, who published and popularized his speeches and ideas.[49] Charismatic UNIA organizers like Maymie de Mena were responsible for growing his movement in and out of the United States. Hailing from St. Martin Parish, de Mena was a gifted orator. She worked closely with other leading Garveyite women, including Baltimore-born actress and activist Henrietta Vinton Davis, on speaking tours and membership drives that brought thousands across the Americas into the movement.[50] These and other women defied the idea that they could only be subordinate, stalwart supporters of Black men. They became board members, field officers, and committee leaders in UNIA chapters around the world.[51]

In fact, Audley became a Garveyite as the debate about women's roles in the organization came to the fore at the UNIA's 1922 convention in New York City. The excitement was palpable as the New Orleans Division made plans to attend. They surely hoped the meeting would recapture the spectacle of the previous two, when hundreds had paraded through the city streets decked out in their Black Cross Nurse and African Legion uniforms flanked by a line of members riding in cars. They got their wish. That year, the procession began at the UNIA headquarters on West 135th Street and wound its way through Harlem. Passersby cheered as UNIA members walked through the late August heat waving red-green-and-black-striped flags—the Pan-African colors. Others held signs that read, WE WANT A BLACK CIVILIZATION and THE NEGRO SHALL TRIUMPH.[52]

The tone shifted from spectacle to substance once the meeting began. Hundreds crowded into the single-level, low-ceilinged meeting hall to debate the direction of the organization. For several days, male delegates droned on about business, parsing through committee reports and debating high-ranking officials' salaries while never ceding the floor to a woman to speak. Eventually the women had had enough. A small group of lady delegates interrupted the afternoon session to voice their concerns about the gender dynamics of the organization. They had prepared a list of demands, and St. Louis member Victoria Turner read them aloud.

The "women of the UNIA know that no race can rise higher than its women," went her opening salvo. A woman, not a man, should lead the Black Cross Nurses at the national level, she continued, and women should be allowed to serve on national committees and hold critical offices. They wanted a clearer path to leadership within the UNIA, and they called for leading female organizer Henrietta Vinton Davis to "be empowered to formulate plans . . . so that Negro women all over the world can function without restriction from the men."[53]

In what reports later described as a clever maneuver, the women presented these recommendations when Garvey was out of the room. When he returned, he was unenthused. Garvey "didn't see any reason for the resolutions." If a UNIA woman felt stonewalled in her political organizing, she should take it up with her local leaders.[54]

Garvey had a point. Despite his deep investment in male-led nationalist liberation, he had devised a structure that offered Black women more formal positions than other contemporaneous Black organizations. Black women were not the primary leaders of the organization, to be sure. But Garvey believed UNIA women's frustrations largely stemmed from their daily interactions with the men in their divisions.[55] And Audley's New Orleans Division was a mixed bag. Although the division leader, Alaida Robertson, was a charismatic and skilled organizer, she still subscribed to conventional ideas about how Audley and her fellow female Garveyites should organize.

Robertson had no problem asserting this position at the convention as factions formed over the role of women. Some women, like Mrs. Morgan from Chicago, proclaimed that the women of the UNIA "were not willing to sit silently by and let men take all the glory while they gave the advice." Robertson countered by pointing out that she had, for a short moment, served in a leadership role akin to the ones they were demanding, and she believed it put her and other women in compromising and immoral positions. For her, Black men's respect for and approval of their women were paramount for the movement's success. Placing women in public, high-ranking positions undermined this goal.[56]

Ultimately, UNIA women left the convention with some concessions but no real immediate changes. Garvey saw no harm in supporting women who wanted to broaden their involvement in the organization. But he resisted the suggestion that Henrietta Vinton Davis be charged with creating autonomous roles for women. There would be no "severance of the women from the men in the work of the organization" while he was in charge.[57]

In her early twenties and at the beginning of her political awakening, Audley was very much a student of the Alaida Robertson school of thought. She was enamored with all things Garvey, and she trusted his mandates for women and their roles in his movement. After all, he had already been battle hardened by the time she came into the movement, and she was determined to uphold his ideals no matter what came next.

After hearing Garvey speak at the Longshoremen's Hall, Audley learned he was a wanted man for more reasons than one. Several months earlier, on January 12, 1922, federal authorities had charged into Garvey's West 130th Street apartment in New York City and carried him out in cuffs. When Harlemites asked why the nationalist was carted off, the answer they got was astounding: the feds accused Garvey of defrauding investors of the Black Star Line (BSL).[58]

Founded in 1919 and inspired by a luxury British ship company called the White Star Line, the UNIA-owned steamship company was Garvey's ambitious attempt to foster Black economic independence across the African Diaspora. With funds raised from the rank and file, Garvey planned to purchase ships to ferry goods from Africa to the Americas. All the while, the BSL would also carry Black people back to Africa to establish a new nation-state there.[59]

In the first year alone, the UNIA raised $800,000, much of it coming from everyday folk like Audley Moore, who saved up and sent in their money to buy stock in one of the BSL ships and, perhaps, a piece of history. Looking to capitalize on this momentum, Garvey hastily purchased vessels, which were beset with problems—to say nothing of the staff members he hired, some of whom tried to sabotage his venture.[60] Garvey's business practices were dubious, to be sure. But his missteps were largely a product of his misplaced trust in workers, insufficient business acumen, and legal technicalities rather than a genuine attempt to extort his followers. Yet, when FBI Assistant Director J. Edgar Hoover suspected that Garvey was hemorrhaging money—and thus via mail selling stock in ships he had not yet purchased—he saw his opportunity. Hoover pushed the federal government to charge Garvey with fraud.[61]

The majority of the New Orleans Division, including Audley, saw the charges for what they really were: an attempt to discredit Garvey and disband the UNIA. Hence, they came out by the thousands to hear Garvey speak at the Longshoremen's Hall in 1922 as he toured while out on bond. Publicly, Spraggs, Audley, and thousands of other division members stood firmly by the steamship company, which they still believed was a symbol of "the ambition and aspiration of the New

Negro."[62] Privately, however, they must have started to wonder if this would be their beloved leader's undoing.

In addition to his fraud case, Garvey was fighting his share of interorganizational battles against prominent UNIA members like Reverend James Eason. A former NAACP leader, philanderer, and blowhard, Eason was once one of Garvey's most devoted followers—until his missteps became too much for the preacher to take. Eason was outraged at Garvey's mishandling of the Black Star Line.[63] Even more egregious was Garvey's decision to secretly meet with Edward Young Clarke, an imperial wizard of the Ku Klux Klan, seeking to forge an alliance based on the idea that the UNIA and the KKK both believed that America was the white man's country and that Black people should have a country of their own in Africa.[64] For Eason, this was the final straw. No self-respecting Black Nationalist could align with a white hate group to reach his liberatory goals.

Garvey took offense at Eason's public criticism, not to mention his rising popularity in places like New Orleans. He put Eason on trial for conspiring to undermine the UNIA and for his alleged lewd behavior with female members. Some of the women in Audley's division served as witnesses in the case. In the end, Garveyites remained loyal to their leader and voted to expel Eason.[65]

Riled up and out for revenge, Eason created a rival organization: the Negro Improvement Alliance (NIA). Hardly disguising his enmity for the organization that had cast him out, he set about recruiting disaffected Garveyites by claiming the NIA, while still nationalist in its aims, was more decentralized and democratic than the UNIA.[66] He, like Garvey, understood that the New Orleans Division, because of its size and influence, was key to any nationalist movement's success. And so Eason spent considerable time trying to recruit locals like Audley.[67] Put off by the fact that Eason, who had once said that he wanted "his bones to be taken to Africa to rest in the soil of his motherland," was now claiming Garvey's Back to Africa movement was a "wild scheme," Audley stayed with Garvey.[68] Many in New Orleans did the same, but a few defected to Eason's side.

It didn't take long for the duel to dismantle the division. The paranoia among UNIA members was so great, in fact, that leaders established an intelligence unit to spy on Eason, identify his supporters, and undermine his agenda.[69] On January 1, 1923, those who had been watching Eason from the shadows moved into the light. They gunned him down as he was finishing up a speech at St. John's Baptist Church in New Orleans. He survived for a few days in Charity Hospital before succumbing to his injuries.[70]

Eason used his dying breaths to claim Garvey was behind the violence. But when Audley conferred with her fellow members on street corners or in weekly meetings, word was that Eason was killed over one of his alleged affairs, not his dispute with the UNIA leader. Whatever the truth, the rivalry had been conveniently resolved, and there was now a murder to be investigated. Still, division leaders were stunned when the police arrested William Shakespeare and Constantine Dyer for the crime. Although they were certainly part of an anti-Eason faction of the UNIA, there were serious questions as to whether the two men were responsible for Eason's death.[71]

All this confusion and violence gave local law enforcement an opening to suppress one of the UNIA's largest and most successful divisions. On January 18, 1923, the police broke into a meeting, arrested nine of the most prominent members, and seized the group's membership rolls. Twenty police officers charged into the Longshoremen's Hall again on February 11, this time with guns and tear gas in hand, and ordered members to vacate the building while seizing even more UNIA paraphernalia.[72]

News of the raids spread almost as quickly as that of Eason's murder. In *The Negro World*, UNIA leaders decried these blatant attempts to pin Eason's murder on the organization and called on "every member throughout the world to rally to the defense of the New Orleans Division."[73] Garveyites from New York, Florida, Pittsburgh, Cuba, and Haiti, among others, gave ten, twenty, and fifty cents apiece to help what Garvey heralded as "the strongest division of the U.N.I.A."[74] Meanwhile, on March 23, 1923, the jury found Dyer and Shakespeare guilty of manslaughter and sentenced them to eighteen to twenty years in prison.[75] Three months later, the feds convicted Garvey of mail fraud and sentenced him to five years in prison.[76] Despite all the tumult, Audley and Spraggs remained steadfast and loyal to his nationalist cause.

Three months later, Garvey was out on bail while he appealed his conviction. Looking to reassure and galvanize the masses, he announced the incorporation of another maritime business modeled after the now-defunct BSL: the Black Cross Navigation and Trading Company. These new ships would help with the next phase of his Back to Africa plan: a large-scale relocation of UNIA members to Liberia that he had first announced in 1920.[77]

Liberia had loomed large in the Black American's consciousness for more than a century. It started in January 1820, when Daniel Coker, a Black man from Baltimore, set sail on the *Elizabeth* with nearly ninety other Black Americans and two agents of the American Colonization Society (ACS) for Liberia—a small strip of land bordering Sierra Leone. The ACS had one goal: to send free Black people back to Africa rather than incorporate them into the American polity. Coker and his compatriots were unsuccessful in their first attempt, but subsequent ACS ventures led to the establishment of Liberia as an independent state in 1847. It limped along, and by the end of the nineteenth century Liberia boasted a modest population of around twenty thousand emigrants. After the American Civil War, emigration and colonization were a tougher sell for Black Americans. Their interest in African repatriation ebbed and flowed as the tide of Jim Crow crested and fell. By the time Garvey endorsed the idea in the early twentieth century, Black Americans had engaged in at least a dozen different efforts to immigrate to the small African nation.[78]

Garvey announced he was moving the headquarters of the UNIA to Monrovia, the capital of Liberia, to begin one of the most popular iterations of the Back to Africa movement in American history. Supporters and detractors alike thought that this was an ambitious move. But Garvey never intended to relocate Black America to Africa all at once. Rather, he planned to send a group of skilled Black Americans first to set up schools, roads, and infrastructure in Liberia. After this initial building phase, the masses—people like Audley and Spraggs—would join, helping to populate the free Black nation and spread the gospel of "Africa for the Africans" across the then largely colonized continent.[79]

Over the next few years, Garvey courted the Liberian government. Liberian officials had been engaged in protracted negotiations with American officials for a $5 million loan with little success as their coffers dwindled. Here, Garvey saw an opportunity. He offered a loan from the UNIA as a solution to Liberia's money problems and a way

to get his foot in the door. With few other options, the Liberian government, at least initially, was willing to entertain Garvey and his
emissaries.[80]

Audley and Spraggs were more convinced. At division meetings,
they learned the UNIA was sending a delegation to Africa in the hope
of securing means for Black Americans to emigrate. They, along with
many other rank-and-file members, were excited by the prospect of
being on the front lines of realizing a free and united Africa. And so,
when UNIA leaders called on members to start pinching pennies to
save up for a "repatriation boom" to Africa, the two took heed.[81]

The couple sold their store, packed their trunks, and prepared to
leave New Orleans behind. That is, until Audley's aunt—perhaps on
a visit from New Iberia—came bursting into their home crying. "You
can't go to Africa. Why, those people will eat you up," she pleaded with
her niece. Surely, the trip across the Atlantic would be the death of
the young couple.[82] As Audley listened, she likely realized becoming a
Garveyite had opened a chasm between her and her extended family.
She had come to view Africa as a place of redemption and freedom;
they still viewed the continent as backward, primitive, and dark.

Exactly what came next isn't clear. Perhaps her aunt showed Audley press releases from the Liberian U.S. consulate, which indicated
Liberian officials' efforts to distance themselves from Garvey after
it was clear he lacked the promised funds. Or maybe the trip simply
wasn't as feasible as they first thought. Whatever the case, the couple
changed their minds about emigrating. And the New Orleans Division
gave them a good reason to stay.

After the dust from the Eason scandal settled, it reclaimed its status as one of the largest and most influential UNIA divisions in the
country. Members rallied behind Garvey with a new fervor amid his
appeal for his fraud conviction and his impending deportation.[83] In
parades akin to those held in Harlem, they marched through the New
Orleans streets in full force, carrying signs that read, MARCUS GARVEY
WE ARE BEHIND YOU 400,000 STRONG and STONE WALLS DO NOT A PRISON
MAKE, NOR IRON BARS A CAGE.[84] Meanwhile, a wave of lecturers—
everyone from Amy Jacques Garvey to the UNIA's interim president,
William Sherrill—came through the Crescent City. This rich tapestry
of lectures and events, coupled with visits from neighboring divi-

sions, resulted in a spike in recruitment and the restoration of Audley's division to some of its old splendor, even as its leader remained
embattled.[85]

But this local nationalist renaissance couldn't gloss over the daily
indignities of Jim Crow in the Crescent City. Even if they couldn't go
back to the motherland, there was still the gleam of greater freedoms
outside the Deep South. So, with the money in hand from selling
their store, Audley and Spraggs packed their bags again. This time,
they headed west.

CHAPTER 5

From Migrant to Militant

When Moore and Spraggs left New Orleans in the early 1920s, they followed a winding path. They were part of the Great Migration, a mass exodus of Black Americans from the South in search of opportunity and refuge from segregation.

Their first stop was Los Angeles, a fairly safe bet for two young Black folk from the Crescent City.[1] Whether at UNIA meetings or while working in their store, Audley and Spraggs were always hearing about locals who had decided to go to California. In fact, some even called Los Angeles "New Orleans West" because so many Black Louisianans had migrated there in search of better job and housing prospects.[2] When Audley and Spraggs said their goodbyes and struck out on their own, they did so with the hope they would find friends or even some kinfolk out there.

While Los Angeles was hardly Liberia, traveling across the country in the 1920s was no simple feat for a young Black couple. They had a few options: go by car, train, or bus. But no matter how they chose to travel, every step of the way was segregated, from train stops and gas stations to hotels and restaurants. Nearly a decade later, postal worker and travel writer Victor Hugo Green would publish the *Green Book,* a critical guide for Black travelers that listed safe places for them to eat and sleep.[3] But in the 1920s, the couple had no such guide. They had to rely on their gut and a little bit of luck to make it.

If they went by car, Audley and Spraggs would have had to pass through many a sundown town: all-white, segregated areas with posted signs warning Black people to leave by dusk or risk death. The couple would have tried to keep their eyes on the road as they passed through, rather than make contact with the local white folk leering at them from the sidewalks, while they struggled to figure out where they could safely stretch their legs or stop for a bite to eat. Their safest bet would have been to keep driving, each taking turns sleeping while the other was behind the wheel.[4]

Train and bus travel might have offered slightly more safety but no less humiliation. Black rail and road travelers had to endure over-crowded and filthy segregated cars and bus stations, often located in the messiest and noisiest parts of town. What's more, the couple would have had to navigate byzantine segregation laws that varied from one state to the next. It was not uncommon for a bus or train conductor to stop before crossing state lines and demand Black passengers reshuffle their seating to meet the shifting mandates.[5] While there's no record of how the pair made the trip, it's safe to assume it was exhausting. When they finally made it, Audley must have wondered if it was worth the trouble.

Los Angeles certainly had its charms. Audley had left the muggy Louisiana air behind and, for the first time, experienced perpetually arid and warm Southern California days. As she drove the wide city streets, she passed through neighborhoods like Boyle Heights and Temple Street, thriving Black enclaves with palm trees and manicured lawns the likes of which she had only ever seen in picture shows. Here, she could stop, stretch her legs, and take in the sun as it warmed her caramel-brown skin.

Central Avenue, the "Black belt of the city," was the main draw for new migrants. As Audley walked down the street, she took in the sights and sounds of smartly dressed Black people wandering in and out of small businesses, offices, and hotels.[6] Black people here were making three to four times more than they had as southern farmers and now had some money to spend.[7] The Sidney P. Dones Company, a Central Avenue staple, was the go-to office for real estate, insurance, and legal services for many of them. They got their news right next door at the *California Eagle* newspaper offices, owned and edited by activist Charlotta Bass, a leader in the local NAACP and UNIA.[8]

Eagle articles clued Audley into Central Avenue's nightlife. Jazz had come west with the wave of New Orleanians, and there was no short-age of clubs, dance halls, and cafés that catered to migrants like her and Spraggs, people who had a little bit of money and were looking for a lot of fun. The pair might have frequented the Cadillac Café, where Jelly Roll Morton played in the early 1920s. Or if they were in the mood for smoother sounds, they could have swung by Murray's to hear singer Ada "Bricktop" Smith.[9] Whenever they stepped out on the town, they found just what the *Eagle* had described: dizzying lights in dazzling clubs full of laughter, flowing cups, and women in colorful gowns fluttering around like "tropical butterflies."[10]

Yet nights spent on Central Avenue couldn't cover up the affronts that took place in broad daylight. Audley was disappointed, if not entirely shocked, to find that even in Los Angeles city leaders confined Black people to the lowest-paying jobs, forcing them to compete with other marginalized groups in the labor and housing markets. Local white residents further entrenched these patterns. They refused housing loans to creditworthy Black residents to bar them from certain neighborhoods, a practice that would later come to be known as redlining. Worse still were the threats of violence. An increase in Black and Mexican American migrants to the area led to the rise of the Ku Klux Klan in the West, particularly in Southern California.[11]

Yet it was the smaller, daily insults that soured Audley on the city the most. She recalled that whenever a Black person wanted to grab a drink to cool off from the sweltering sun, white businesses charged them $5 for a five-cent bottle of soda. And even then, they wouldn't let them drink it in the store. Incidents like these left her "disillusioned and disgusted with California." The spite that Audley had experienced in the Golden State only worsened as more migrants from the South poured in. In time, Los Angeles would simmer into a hotbed for Black Nationalist organizing. But Audley didn't wait around for it. She and Spraggs stayed in the City of Angels for only a few months before setting out again.[12]

When Audley stepped off the New York City subway at 125th and Lenox Avenue in the mid-1920s, it felt both brand-new and oddly familiar. After all, she was no stranger to bustling city streets and skyscrapers. On their way from California, Audley and Spraggs had stopped in Chicago to see if it might be their new home. Black Los Angelenos had told Audley that Chicago was the ideal city for them, and southerners were relocating there just as quickly. In fact, by the

end of the Great Migration in the 1970s, more Black people lived in
Chicago than in the entire state of Mississippi.[13] Still, it was a tough
choice, trading the California sun for midwestern snow.

The pair donned their big coats and hats as they navigated the city
streets, taking in everything from the Stroll—a strip of State Street
lined with Black-owned restaurants, dance halls, and businesses—to
the rhythmic sounds of workers putting the finishing touches on the
Wrigley Building and the rumbling of the L train overhead. But, just
like in Los Angeles, she found the realities of racism impossible to
unsee.[14]

"I went to Chicago and I found all the black people shuttled into
one little district," Audley explained, "and the condition there was
worse than we had in New Orleans."[15] Jobs were hard to come by, and
health care was limited. Most Black migrants had little money, food,
or clothing and lived stacked on top of one another in dilapidated
buildings where landlords had turned basements and kitchenettes into
makeshift living quarters with no electricity or heat. Southsiders had
ways of taking care of one another. They created Black banks, life
insurance companies, churches, and mutual aid programs to support
their beleaguered community.[16] Still, Audley found she had no taste
for the Windy City.

St. Cyr's daughter had high standards, after all. Black and white
folk alike loved to paint Black migrants as backward and uneducated
country folk who unwittingly abandoned their southern homes without considering how they would navigate city life. But Audley, like
many others who migrated, was nothing of the sort. She was a literate,
politically engaged Black woman who had spent most of her life in
a bustling city filled with Black culture. The eldest Moore girl was
savvy and street-smart, and she had a little bit of money thanks to
marrying Spraggs.[17]

Audley was searching for a way forward, but Chicago felt like a
step back. "It's not here, it's Harlem, this is where you needed to go,"
Southsiders told her.[18] And so, she and Spraggs headed even farther
east, hoping Harlem would live up to its reputation as the Black
Mecca of America.

As they exited the train station and headed uptown, the couple
scanned Harlem's main avenues. At first glance, the neighborhood
delivered. Black women dressed in colorful flapper jackets, cloches,

and long pearl necklaces walked arm in arm with men adorned in tailored silk or wool suits, passing by panhandlers and street peddlers seeking spare change.[19]

When they crossed over to 135th Street, Audley had to push her way through the crowds. They had reached Speakers' Corner, the go-to spot for preachers, politicians, and protesters to shout from their soapboxes. Some lectured about the politics of the day, race relations in the city, or getting right with God.[20] Others proselytized about socialism and separatism. Hearing the echoes of Garveyism as they passed, the pair might have stopped and set down their suitcases for a moment to listen to what the street-corner spokesmen had to say. But they couldn't linger long. The newly minted New Yorkers had to get moving if they were going to find a place to stay. They eventually turned off Lenox Avenue and onto quieter, brownstone-lined streets in search of a walk-up with a room to rent. It was at this point that Audley realized "Harlem, too, was Jim Crow." She was stunned to find "FOR WHITE" signs hanging on the doors of buildings as she passed and, just like in Chicago, Black people packed so densely into makeshift, shoddy apartments they had to sleep in shifts.[21]

Sugar Hill, home to the Black elite and those who aspired to join them, was where they made their first home.[22] Residential segregation made it so Sugar Hill's elite lived cheek by jowl with newcomers and transplants. Virtually every Black luminary lived within a stone's throw of one another in the neighborhood: Langston Hughes, Duke Ellington, W. E. B. Du Bois, and many others.[23] For young migrants like her, however, the neighborhood was far from glamorous. Rent was so high Audley often joked that the neighborhood was called Sugar Hill because it was "the place where the white man got all the sugar."[24]

To make rent, Audley joined the masses of Black women who did domestic and factory work. When she wasn't toiling in white households, she was working as a garment presser or a tobacco factory worker.[25] The daily drudgery of clocking in and out wasn't her speed. She longed for the mobility and autonomy that she once had as a hairdresser and small business operator in New Orleans. Audley eventually enrolled in Poro College, a cosmetology school founded by Illinois-born Black entrepreneur Annie Malone. Poro was a nationally recognized brand with colleges across the country, and it later served as the model for Poro alumna turned beauty entrepreneur Madam

C. J. Walker's career. When she graduated from the school, Audley proudly received her degree from Malone herself.[26]

Home life, too, had shifted. Soon after they settled in Harlem, she and Spraggs went their separate ways. By the end of the decade, they were still legally married but living apart.[27] It wasn't uncommon for migrants to divorce—moving around a lot with few resources put a strain on relationships. It's also possible Audley felt she had started to outgrow Spraggs once she saw more of the world. Whatever caused the rift, Audley never spoke on it. She simply closed the door on that chapter of her life and opened herself up to new possibilities in New York.

Now in her early thirties, Audley was far from lonely. She had sent word about her marriage troubles, the toils of factory work, and the triumphs of Harlem to Eloise and Loretta back in New Orleans. In no time at all, Eloise had migrated north to join Audley, and the two eldest Moore sisters moved in and out of upper Manhattan apartments together, eking out a living and supporting each other. Though they had little, they knew that by banding together in the Big Apple, a better life was within reach.[28]

Living on the margins left little time for political engagement, but Moore tried her best to stay connected to Garvey's movement. She had kept an eye on the latest developments in his conviction and appeal as she bounced around the country. Garvey had been out of jail for two years while he appealed the verdict. In early 1925, however, the U.S. Circuit Court of Appeals upheld his original conviction, and he was rearrested and incarcerated in the Atlanta Federal Penitentiary. Moore joined with other UNIA members in "petition[ing] every possible authority to have him freed" for good. "We all knew that Garvey was innocent and the charges against him were false," she explained, "but we also knew that Garvey could not win because of his teachings."[29] She was devastated when she first got word that he'd lost the legal battle, but to the relief of her and her fellow Garveyites, President Coolidge commuted the nationalist's jail sentence. On December 2, 1927, dressed in a light brown derby hat and three-piece suit, Garvey delivered his farewell address in New Orleans aboard the SS *Saramacca*. He was deported back to Jamaica on the same ship Spraggs had sailed on.[30]

Garvey might have left, but Garveyism was there to stay. He continued to galvanize Black people from Jamaica and London, while the U.S.-based UNIA hosted meetings, held fundraisers, and organized protests to keep his dream of Black Nationalist liberation alive. Predictably, however, Garvey's physical absence cleared the way for organizational infighting. Audley would have surely caught wind of UNIA members' dissatisfaction with Fred Toote, who served as acting president during Garvey's incarceration. Factions and rival organizations soon cropped up, and the UNIA's influence across the country began to weaken even as Garvey continued to orchestrate the movement from abroad.[31]

Audley is noticeably absent from the UNIA's membership rolls from this time. It's possible these internal disputes discouraged her from formally affiliating with the Harlem Division—though not likely. She was no less devoted to Garvey's cause in the late 1920s. She followed his movements and teachings with great interest, and she stayed abreast of UNIA activities when she could. More likely, she would have struggled to pay her membership dues, given that she was living hand to mouth in New York. Audley was wise to hang on to what little money she had. The tumult inside the Garvey movement would soon pale in comparison to the maelstrom that awaited Black people in the 1930s.

The Great Depression was disproportionately devastating for Black Americans. As the poorest segment of the population, they fared far worse than most of the nation.[32] After the stock market crash of 1929, overproduction in factories skyrocketed while consumption plummeted. Any American who managed to hold on to their job had their wages severely cut.[33] In New York, the few decent jobs available to Black people evaporated overnight. By 1932, one in four people in Harlem were unemployed, leading to rampant homelessness, hunger, and child neglect. Audley must have been shocked to find that amid record joblessness and a severe housing crisis Black folk still flocked to Manhattan's upper blocks.[34]

Many decided to take up New York's governor, Franklin D. Roosevelt, on the New Deal he offered during his 1932 presidential run. Until then, Black people like Audley rightfully saw Roosevelt, and the Democrats more broadly, as the party of slavery and the primary perpetrators of anti-Black violence since Reconstruction.[35] But in an effort to salvage the destitute nation, the party swung the other way and began to court the Black vote.

New Deal programs had the potential to provide relief to Black people, but they were not without flaws. State agents distributed benefits and jobs unevenly, giving more aid to white farmers and workers than to their Black counterparts. Still, programs like the Works Progress Administration provided unprecedented employment and creative opportunities for Black writers like Claude McKay and sculptors like Augusta Savage.[36] Some Black women also made modest gains by acquiring steady, better-paying government jobs.[37] In New York City, for example, state employment services offered more secure employment opportunities for Black domestics by formally placing them in white women's homes.[38]

Audley wasn't so lucky. Unable to get government support, she instead joined the masses of Black women standing on street corners, waiting for white women to "come and—almost just like slavery days—feel their muscles, look at their knees to see if they had crust on their knees." The ones who had bruises and calluses would get hired: "It meant that they would get on their knees to wax their floors." Audley likened it to standing on the "auction block."[39]

Harlemites told Audley the best thing she could do to help "change these conditions" was "to get into politics." They pointed her toward the Democratic Party. She was skeptical at first. St. Cyr's stories of all the "Democrats did to overthrow the Republicans" during Reconstruction reverberated in her mind. Instead, she volunteered for the Republicans, joining J. Dalmus Steele's 1933 campaign for the New York State Assembly.[40]

Hailed as the "Mayor of Harlem," Steele was a savvy politician and an advocate for everything from tenants' rights to health care.[41] If elected, the chocolate-brown, cherub-faced politician promised to create a congressional district in Harlem that would be majority Black and therefore force "both major parties to nominate a Negro to run for Congress." He also vowed to reform and equalize public education, incorporate Black history into local curricula, and reduce taxes and basic utility rates.[42] Even if Steele's goals were lofty, his campaign was grounded. He supported Depression relief efforts and Harlem-based unemployment programs, many of them also backed by the local UNIA.[43] Steele was the neighborhood favorite, and most thought he would be victorious over his Democratic opponent. But much to the chagrin of Harlemites, he couldn't eke out a victory.[44]

Steele might have lost, but the Republicans won big overall in New York City. When it was time to celebrate, a white campaign worker told Audley that white Republicans were planning a "victory dinner on Broadway" and that the "colored" campaign staff should go ahead and plan their own, separate gathering.[45] Audley was stunned. Despite all the work she and others had done on behalf of the party, segregationist attitudes still carried the day. It was a wake-up call for the budding activist. The party of Lincoln had used Black voters to advance its own interests but had little interest, she realized, in advancing Black life. Audley surmised that she "may as well have been a Democrat" if she was going to endure this kind of treatment.[46]

She wasn't alone in her disillusionment, either. The resentment Audley felt for New York's Republican Party mirrored a nationwide trend, as the party once known for at least token Black representation reversed course. The Republican Party began ousting Black candidates and supporters alike, remaking itself in the image of its "lily-white" Democratic opponents. It was just the beginning of a mass defection of Black voters, one that still defines America's political landscape today.[47] For Audley, it wasn't so much a beginning as an end. From the mid-1930s onward, she refused to be a pawn on the two-party politics board.

Audley was still reeling from the aftermath of the election when Eloise burst through the door of their Harlem apartment one day. Audley paused from washing clothes as Eloise explained, between deep gulping breaths, that "Harlem [was] ablaze." A huge demonstration had erupted in the streets in support of the Scottsboro Boys.[48]

On March 25, 1931, about two dozen white and Black teens surreptitiously hopped onto a train headed from Chattanooga to Memphis. As they jumped from car to car, some of the white kids spotted eighteen-year-old Haywood Patterson, a Black teen, hiding out. The train was for whites only, they declared—even if they, too, were stowaways—and they tried to push him off. The other Black boys soon came to Patterson's defense. They booted Patterson's white attackers from the train and then settled in for the rest of the trip. But when the train rolled into Jackson County, Alabama, trouble was waiting for them. The humiliated white kids had run to the police and said they had been attacked by a gang of Black men.

Officers stopped the train at the next depot to arrest the suspects. As they combed through the cars, however, authorities also found two white women illegally riding the train: seventeen-year-old Ruby Bates and twenty-one-year-old Victoria Price. Afraid police would arrest them for vagrancy and who knew what else, Bates and Price deployed an all-too-common strategy for white women in a pinch: they claimed the Black boys had raped them. Police arrested nine Black kids in total—aged thirteen to nineteen, some of whom had just met each other that day—and took them to the neighboring town of Scottsboro to await trial. Poor and without counsel, the boys were convicted of rape by an all-white jury based on Price and Bates's accusations. They sentenced eight to death. The youngest, thirteen-year-old Roy Wright, was initially spared by a hung jury when eleven jurors voted for the death penalty rather than a life sentence.[49]

Audley, who now thought of herself as part of the Harlem activist community, had read about the Scottsboro Boys but had heard nothing about the protest.

"Who's having a demonstration?" she asked her sister.

"The Reds are having it," Eloise replied.[50]

Audley had likely heard of the Communist Party but didn't know much about it. Before the Depression, the organization had a negligible presence in Harlem; it was no match for the NAACP or the UNIA.[51] The party first found its footing in the United States in 1919, and by the early 1920s communists had managed to woo a handful of Black intellectuals and organizers. Thinkers and activists like Grace Campbell, Richard B. Moore, and Cyril Briggs were among their earliest Black recruits. They formed the African Blood Brotherhood, a militant liberation group that, by combining Black Nationalist and communist ideas, slowly popularized party ideals in Audley's neighborhood.[52]

As early as 1922, other early Black recruits, including Claude McKay and Otto Huiswoud, had called upon communist leadership to address what they called the "Negro problem," or the issue of Black oppression in the United States.[53] In response, the Communist

International (Comintern) began discussing racism, colonialism, and the revolutionary potential of the Black proletariat at its annual congresses. While Audley was caught up in Garvey's whirlwind, a "steady stream" of Black Americans began visiting the Soviet Union to study communist thought and suss out the party's commitment to antiracist revolution. Many liked what they saw, and they came back determined to organize a communist movement at home.[54]

By the end of the decade, the Comintern had given these early Black organizers a boost. In 1928, officials adopted the "Resolution on the Negro Question in the United States," or what many called the Black Belt Thesis. Communist leaders argued that Black Americans represented an oppressed nation set apart from other Americans by their "prominent racial distinctions," "considerable social antagonism," rampant economic subjugation, political exclusion, and geographical segregation. True freedom for this nation within a nation required nothing short of secession.[55] Many interpreted this declaration as an indication that the Communist Party had embraced Black Nationalism and the Black proletariat who championed it.[56]

Audley Moore was oblivious to the party's shifting position on the plight of Black folk like her. But she was intrigued to hear of the group's support of the Scottsboro Boys. And so, she left her clothes in the suds and bolted out the door to join her sister at the massive protest.

"When I got there, I'd never in my life seen such an outpouring of people," she recalled. "There was thousands of people, there was banners, red banners, the hammer and sickle, things I'd never seen." Audley stood on the sidewalk, mouth agape, unsure what to do next. Just then, she saw a white woman walk past holding a sign with DEATH TO THE LYNCHERS scrawled across it.

"No, you give me that sign," Audley said, snatching it from the woman as she passed by. "You can walk beside me, but I must carry the sign. I am the Black woman, I must carry that sign." Moore then fell in lockstep with the other protesters, holding the sign over her head and chanting that the "Scottsboro Boys shall not die!" as she followed them to their rallying point to hear party leader James Ford speak. Audley was stunned to find "a black man, talking about imperialism in Africa" and championing a "movement with the working class organized throughout the world." It was a script that could have been ripped straight from a *Negro World* column.[57]

The turnout that day caused Audley to look inward. Her love for Garvey and his principles was unfailing. But she could no longer deny his movement had weakened in the years since his deportation. She had now witnessed local communists galvanize a cross section of Black and white New Yorkers and integrate Garveyite principles into their work. "If they've got a movement like that and they're conscious of this thing that Garvey had been speaking about, then this may be a good thing for me to get in to help free my people," Audley reasoned, reflecting on the march.[58] In the early 1930s, Audley decided to give the Reds a try.

Around 1933, she joined the International Labor Defense (ILD), a prisoners' defense organization founded in 1925 that had an open membership policy and embraced Marxist tenets.[59] Due to the massive overlap in membership between the ILD and the party, it took Audley months to realize that she had not, in fact, become a card-carrying communist; rather, she was working with one of the party's affiliates.[60] Their Scottsboro Boys protests drew her in, but the ILD's organizational agenda made her stay. Her local chapter supported government relief for hungry Harlemites and tenants' rights. It defended Black and white political prisoners and called for the end of the poll tax that barred most Black people from voting.[61] Nationally, it backed Angelo Herndon, a nineteen-year-old Black activist arrested for organizing Black and white industrial workers in Atlanta, and defended the rights of sharecroppers, farmers, and workers like Tom Mooney, a white West Coast labor organizer who was convicted of murder after a suitcase he was asked to carry exploded, killing ten people in San Francisco.[62]

Flipping through the ILD's newspaper, the *Labor Defender,* Audley learned about working-class struggles taking place all over the country. She probably paused when she came across articles like DENMARK VESEY—A LESSON IN SELF DEFENSE, which offered a compelling portrait of the formerly enslaved South Carolinian who had planned one of the most extensive slave insurrections in the United States. This and other articles offered Audley historical primers on Black history and armed self-defense.[63] Whether it was in its literature or its litigation, the ILD made one thing clear: this was an organization through which she could keep the hope of Black liberation alive.

Audley's work with the group came to a head when "Harlem witnessed the coordination of all her forces" to organize demonstrations and aid for Ethiopia. In 1935, the burgeoning activist watched in horror as Benito Mussolini attempted to annex the free African nation by military force. For Black people around the world, this was an atrocity: a blatant act of imperial aggression and an affront to Black sovereignty.[64] Audley joined the Medical Committee for the Defense of Ethiopia, which collected supplies for the Ethiopian army. At an October 1935 rally featuring Black church leaders and communist-backed organizers, she delivered a rousing speech on how the white supremacist oppression that Black people faced in Harlem was connected to those suffering under the weight of imperialist aggression in Ethiopia. So moved was her audience that many agreed to donate funds and medical supplies then and there.[65] Only a few years after joining the communist cause, Audley found herself at the epicenter of Black protests in Harlem, articulating an anti-imperialist, pro-Black agenda.

While Audley was working, the Communist Party was watching. "They didn't just recruit anybody," she later noted. "They let you be tested first."[66] For months, local comrades observed Audley as she relentlessly sold copies of their newspaper, *The Daily Worker,* and pushed party pamphlets into the hands of passersby. They liked what they saw. Audley's astute politics and work ethic earned her an invitation to join the organization. By 1936, she was a full-fledged member and on her way to becoming one of the most influential organizers and recruiters in the Upper Harlem Branch.[67]

When Audley Moore formally filled out her membership card, she joined a dynamic group of organizers that had more than doubled in size since the early 1920s, thanks in no small part to the sizable number of Black women who joined the organization.[68] The communists were a relatively egalitarian group compared with other major civil rights organizations like the NAACP, which was still largely middle class and male led.[69] Audley became part of a group of Black women, along with other activists like Bonita Williams, Louise Thompson Patterson, Williana Burroughs, and Maude White, who rose to prominence in Harlem. She found this cohort to be "a serious group of women who wanted more than what the Democrats or Republicans had to offer."[70] Like Audley, they saw the party as a viable third path, a shift away from the pitfalls of two-party politics.

As a new member, Audley devoted herself to what many called "Jimmie Higgins work," a term lifted from Upton Sinclair's 1919 book of the same name, featuring a socialist who undertakes the mundane work needed to build a movement.[71] She made a name for herself as part of the party's Unemployed Council, a group that organized workers and had a particular knack for throwing together rapid-response demonstrations. When organizers got word that a white-owned butcher shop was price gouging Black customers, for example, she and her comrades rushed down to the store. As soon as they saw Black customers come out, they "would go in and weigh the people's food after they bought it" to see if the shop owner had cheated them. If so, Audley recalled, they would shame the butcher and demand that he give them what they paid for.[72]

Other protests hit closer to home. By the time Audley had joined the communists, Loretta had joined her sisters in Harlem. She brought along her daughter, Audley Marie, now a teenager, but left her first husband, Charlie Bazile, behind. Loretta had taken up with one of Spraggs's former shipmates, Rudolph Langley. Just shy of six feet, tattooed, and missing the tip of his third finger, Langley could easily look the part of a menacing sailor. But he preferred to play the well-dressed gentleman, often sporting a suit, bow tie, and charming demeanor.[73] Four years older than Loretta, Langley had visited all the corners of the Caribbean working as a ship cook. He must have seemed positively cosmopolitan to the youngest Moore girl, who until then had been to only Alabama and New York City.[74] Langley lived with Loretta, her daughter, Audley, her new son-in-law, Crawford Burns, and three other lodgers in a walk-up on 123rd Street in Harlem. The elder Audley lived on the same street, scrunched into an apartment with other families and boarders all contributing what they could. Eloise stayed about ten blocks downtown on 114th Street.[75]

When the Moore sisters faced housing struggles, they turned to Audley, now a seasoned veteran at navigating shoddy housing and labyrinthine tenants' rights laws. By the late 1930s, she had earned a reputation as a rabble-rouser among Manhattan's landlords, thanks to her political organizing. Back when she too lived on 114th Street, she had hauled her building owner to court for refusing to provide heat. This power play got her evicted and blacklisted by local realty companies. But Audley wasn't deterred. With the backing of the Consolidated Tenants League, a group that developed out of rent strikes on Sugar Hill, Audley and her sisters fought for the right to safe housing.[76] They garnered local media attention in November 1936 when Audley, Loretta, and eight other tenants braved the cold to picket on 135th Street, carrying signs that read, PROTECT YOURSELF FROM RENT ROBBERS. The women were protesting a rent increase of $25 per month, a hike made even more outrageous by the fact that residents reported "wires dangling from walls" and "a leaking roof," and that one tenant had "fall[en] through a splintered floor."[77] Audley's early housing protests had limited success, but they stoked a fire in her. Through them, she gained a more sophisticated "understanding of capitalism," and she always credited her early tenants' rights organizing as the space where she "really learned to struggle."[78]

When she wasn't on the picket line, locals could find Audley in the Harlem People's Bookshop on West 135th Street. She served as the manager of the shop for a short while and made it her mission to keep it stocked with titles like W. E. B. Du Bois's *Black Reconstruction,* Booker T. Washington's *Up from Slavery,* and Carter G. Woodson's *A Century of Negro Migration.* For her, the store was more than a place for Harlemites to "get books about Negroes." It was a way to engage in political education. Her time in the Communist Party and out on picket lines had shown her that many Black people intrinsically understood injustice but sometimes overlooked its systemic roots. "That is one way in which this bookshop is going to play an important part in the lives of people in Harlem," she explained to those who passed by. "It will show them where to put the blame."[79]

Audley's tenure here marked a key shift in her life. Instead of spending her days scrubbing white women's floors, she now sparred with Harlemites about the state of Black America. The job helped refine her idiosyncratic political consciousness, one that was still steadfastly nationalist but now infused with Marxism. It also amplified her reputation as an organizer and a political educator. But it was her ongoing activism in defense of the Scottsboro Boys that solidified her place as a leader in the community.

By October 1937, the ILD had won the release of four of the nine boys and joined forces with the NAACP and other groups to exonerate the remaining five. The roster for the initial meeting of the committee was a who's who of Black activism. Famed communist organizer

Richard B. Moore (no relation) and renowned community builder Reverend Adam Clayton Powell Sr. headed the group, now called the Harlem Scottsboro Defense Committee. The list of sponsors included A. Philip Randolph, a socialist and head of the Brotherhood of Sleeping Car Porters, one of the largest Black labor unions in the country; Louise Thompson Patterson, a radical labor organizer; Ada Wright, mother of one of the Scottsboro Boys; former political prisoner Angelo Herndon; and Claudia Cumberbatch (later Jones), a leading communist theorist. Audley was elected treasurer of the committee, a sign of her popularity among Harlem's activist circles.[80] Also in attendance was a handsome man named Frank Warner, a dry cleaner and member of the International Ladies' Garment Workers' Union, who happened to catch the still-single Audley's eye.[81]

If Audley had taken stock of her life then, she would have marveled at how much had changed over the last decade. She had left the only home she had ever known, made dangerous treks across the country and back again, and found a home in one of the biggest, most bustling cities in the United States. She was thriving in Harlem. She had left her husband, reunited with her sisters, and found her place among radical Black communists. Most important, Audley had learned an organization need not be explicitly Black Nationalist in its mission for it to advance the cause. She used this realization to her advantage over the next decade, championing Black sovereignty and self-determination wherever she went.

CHAPTER 6

Pulling Weight in the Popular Front

On any given day in the late 1930s, Audley Moore dressed herself in one of her few simple cotton print dresses, fixed her hair into an updo with a slight marcel wave on the front right side, and balanced her wire-frame glasses on her nose.[1] She had a light breakfast, perhaps half an apple and a slice of old bread, before smoothing out her dress in the mirror, trudging down the stairs of her walk-up, and heading out into the Harlem air.[2]

A quick scan of her neighborhood showed there was much work to do on behalf of Harlem's Black citizens. Making her way to the street corner, Moore saw men and women out of work, gathered on steps and sidewalks, looking for ways to pass the time. Some congregated near the local grocery store, canned goods stacked into careful pyramids in one window and a sign in the other signaling that it still sold milk, sugar, bacon, and starch. They might have hoped a paying customer could spare enough change to help them buy some food. Almost half the Black population in New York was out of work and on the brink of starvation.[3]

Moore must have marveled at how the men and women, homeless and sleeping in the streets, could get any shut-eye with the subway rumbling below and cars honking as they blazed by. Equally distressing was the number of abandoned young Black children, out of school and roaming the streets. Perhaps they gathered around her when she stopped at the corner, holding out their hands in hopes she could spare a dime for them to get a parcel of meat scraps to share. But Moore was barely hanging on herself. All she could do was direct them to the breadlines and soup kitchens, where hungry Harlemites waited for hours hoping a local church or charity could give them their one

meal of the day.[4] Moore knew these lines well. Although she was more
fortunate than others during the Depression—she had a place to live
and a meager salary as a Communist Party worker—she and her sisters also relied on the generosity of others to make ends meet.

Still, survival wasn't the average Harlemite's only worry. As they
stood in breadlines and packed into soup kitchens, Black people talked
in hushed tones about the news coming out of Europe. If the papers
were to be believed, fascism was advancing and America was on the
brink of another war. Fresh off defending Ethiopia against Mussolini
in 1935, Harlemites had seen how quickly one nation could invade
another and subjugate its people. As they followed news of Hitler's
rise to power in Germany and his plans to take over Europe, Moore,
her neighbors, and Black folk all across the country worried about who
and what was coming next.

Moore pondered this on her way to Lenox Avenue and 125th Street,
where she opened the door to the Communist Party's Harlem office
to start her day as the head of the Upper Harlem Branch's Women's
Commission.

The commission signaled a shift in strategy for both the party and
for Moore. The looming threat of fascism had birthed the Popular
Front, an ideologically diverse coalition of communists, socialists,
and liberals who declared a ceasefire in their leftist squabbles to fight
against fascism. As the decade wore on, party leaders instructed members to jettison their critique of the American government and capitalism, champion FDR's New Deal programs, and widen their outreach
to appeal to labor activists, intellectuals, artists, writers, and women.
To Moore's surprise, the party also backed away from its attacks on
moderate Black middle-class organizations, instead partnering with
progressive groups to create an interracial, anti-imperialist organizing
front.[5] The Women's Commission was a key site of this work, designed
to bring women from all walks of life into the party and the Popular
Front. More a practical ally than a bona fide red ideologue, Audley
Moore fit right into this political landscape. As the Popular Front grew,
so too did her reputation as a capable organizer among a range of civil
rights, tenants' rights, and women's rights groups.[6]

No two days looked the same now that Moore was charged with
bringing women into the party fold. Some days she visited clubs,
unions, and neighborhood associations to stump for the Communist

Party, assuring audiences it had the answers to their worries about high unemployment rates and food prices. On others, she extolled the party as the vanguard for women's unemployment insurance and government-sponsored relief programs. Wherever she went, Moore assured women of all backgrounds that "democratic rights, equal rights, courage, and honesty" were at the core of the party. Communists, she added, were in favor of "any organization that honestly supports the fight against fascism."[7]

But she wasn't all talk. As Moore became more entrenched in women's organizing, she realized women from all walks of life had one universal concern: in the thick of the Great Depression, none of them could afford milk for their babies. Now a more experienced organizer, Moore knew a galvanizing cause when she saw one. In October 1937, she called on "churches, lodges, and civic groups to send contingents of women" in Harlem to join a protest against the high prices of milk for children. Three weeks later, on November 20, Black women, dressed in their overcoats, pushing baby carriages and dragging along small, groggy kids, gathered in the early hours of the morning to join a "baby carriage parade" through Manhattan.

As it started to rain, Moore passed out signs with slogans admonishing the mayor for allowing the "milk monopoly" to form across the city as companies drove up prices while New York's young went hungry. The women formed a line and began their march downtown to city hall. When New Yorkers peered out their water-streaked windows, they saw a long chain of baby carriages and children filing down the street. The march grew in size as Moore's group linked up with other contingents of mothers and caregivers from Little Italy, the Lower East Side, and other neighborhoods along the way. When Mayor Fiorello La Guardia looked out his window around 11:00 a.m., he was likely stunned to see more than three hundred women, children, and baby strollers headed toward his office. "Give us milk prices we can afford to pay," the marchers chanted as they circled their carriages out front. Meanwhile, Moore ushered some inside in the hopes of presenting the mayor with the group's demands. Chief among them: that he establish free milk stations for women and children throughout the five boroughs.[8] Officials heard the women out but ultimately made no promises.

Moore's Women's Commission work wasn't always so dramatic. In

December 1937, a fire roared through a Seventh Avenue apartment building. Hearing the gut-wrenching screams from those trapped inside, two men—one white and one Black—risked their lives and ran into the burning building to pull men, women, and children out. The white man, William Campbell, succumbed to his injuries. Moore, who knew all too well the piercing pain of losing a patriarch unexpectedly, visited Campbell's wife more than once. As she sat in the forlorn woman's living room, Moore offered her condolences and announced local communists' plans to raise funds to help her survive the first months of widowhood.[9] From baby-wailing protests to these quieter moments, Moore proved she would show up when her community needed her and cross ideological and racial lines for the collective good.

Moore frequently shared the stage with like-minded white women, in fact. She welcomed legendary Communist Party leader Ella Reeve Bloor, affectionately known as Mother Bloor, to her neighborhood more than once. Like Moore, Bloor was born into an affluent family and an unlikely advocate for the working class. Yet she too had been radicalized by the loss of her parents and the drudgery of caring for her younger siblings. She became a lifelong communist, celebrated for her support of women's rights and suffrage.[10] If Bloor was the mother of the communist women's movement, Elizabeth Gurley Flynn was its energetic daughter. The child of working-class socialists, Flynn was active in the multiracial Industrial Workers of the World as a girl and served as the chair of the International Labor Defense as an adult. She joined the party in 1937, just as Moore was rising in prominence in Harlem, and became a tireless advocate of working women's rights.[11]

With the threat of another world war rising, Moore, Bloor, and Flynn embodied the party's Popular Front ethos. They united their constituencies in support of women's rights and peace. Astute and engaging, the trio capitalized on events like International Women's Day—a global celebration of women's activism and rights that took place each March—to hold multiracial demonstrations in support of women and families.[12] They also galvanized "Catholic Women, Jewish Women, and Negro Women" to "protest the Nazi terror against Jewish women and children" by boycotting German goods in 1938.[13] These collaborations caught the attention of party leaders, who praised Moore for coordinating "the fight for jobs, security, peace, and democracy for all."[14]

Building interracial women's alliances didn't occlude Moore's focus on securing Black rights. She fought alongside Reverend Adam Clayton Powell Jr.—a local Baptist preacher turned politician and the head of Harlem's Abyssinian Baptist Church—to force local utility companies to hire Black workers, and with her sister Loretta tested the Minkoff Rent Law, a rule that forbade rent increases for buildings that failed to comply with the housing code. She led a twenty-four-hour protest in front of the Empire State Building against the impending World's Fair, because organizers refused to hire Black people to work the event, which was set to take place in Queens in 1939.[15] And she advocated for aid to Black women who had turned to sex work out of desperation during the Depression. Moore publicly declared it was out of a need to survive, not some inherent lewdness, that Black women had to become "love girls" during hard times.[16]

Yet this broad-strokes approach also came at a cost. As the Communist Party moved toward the political center, it backed away from some of its Black-focused initiatives. Of particular concern for organizers like Moore was its dissolution of the League of Struggle for Negro Rights, a group charged with actualizing the Black Belt Thesis and advocating for the Scottsboro Boys, antilynching legislation, and an end to Jim Crow laws.[17] This shift was one of the first signs of trouble for Moore, who had found her footing in the party precisely because it allowed her to express her Garveyite principles of race pride and self-determination through everyday struggles for the Black working class. As she rose in the party ranks during the late 1930s, Moore started to get a sinking feeling that the organization was abandoning Black folk.

Still, she put on a good show at the New York State Communist Party's annual convention in May 1938. Moore likely fidgeted with her dress and papers as she sat among the hundreds of party members who had made their annual pilgrimage to settle the organization's agenda for the year. Although she was no stranger to taking the stage at neighborhood rallies and protests, speaking before hundreds of mostly white delegates from across the state was a different matter. Moore had prepared her remarks ahead of time. She wrote a speech that highlighted her committee's successes while still making it clear there was much more work to be done to reach gender parity—in the party and in society. She sat through several days of speeches before she was finally called up to give the Women's Commission Report. Amid light applause, Moore stood, strode to the lectern, unfolded her glasses, and began to speak in her unmistakable Louisiana drawl.

"Comrades, the fact that 39 per cent of our Party members are women, the fact that there is least fluctuation among women, is an indication as to what great possibilities there are to build the Party among the masses of women looking for a way out of the miseries that the monopolies have forced upon them," Moore said to open her speech. She enumerated what this steady group of women had accomplished during her tenure on the Women's Commission, everything from "Mother's Peace Day celebrations in the neighborhoods" to "women's pickets around the Italian consulate in support of Ethiopia." She highlighted their stand against the high cost of living during the Depression and foregrounded the Black women in Harlem who created women's and children's health clinics when the government would not. These efforts, Moore asserted, showed that "women have taken their place in the developing progressive movement."[18]

It was precisely because of these successes that the party should devote even more time, attention, and resources to women's social and political needs. Moore called on delegates to support legislation that mattered to working-class women: a measure that would end legal discrimination against women and establish "a state law for maternity insurance, for free education from day nursery to college, and for the child labor amendment" to limit, regulate, or prohibit labor for minors. Ever the advocate for Black people and their interests, Moore noted that any legislation had to include "special provisions" to work toward "equal rights for Negro women."

Now more than ever, Moore was convinced that women were the key to the Popular Front's success. She wanted party leadership to see this, too. "Comrades, women are not only half the population," she offered by way of a conclusion, "but we must now add—they are nearly half of the voters in the State of New York. Women hate war and fascism. They want peace and democracy. They want jobs and security. They want some little degree of family life."

"Win the Women," she proclaimed as a call to action, and the party would be successful in 1938 and beyond.[19]

The speech was a watershed moment in Moore's communist career. As a Garveyite, she had learned to subsume women's work under the larger goal of Black liberation. The UNIA's women, ultimately, worked to restore Black men as the leaders of Black nations. But the more she engaged in Women's Commission work, the more she came to see that women did, in fact, face a different and unique set of political and social challenges. She found that bettering women's lives could in turn better entire communities. In just a few short years, Moore had developed a more nuanced understanding of organizing. While Black liberation was still her priority, she had come to see Black women's struggles as a cornerstone of this cause.

These changing ideas about women's roles shaped Moore's home life, too. As the Popular Front ramped up, Moore got serious with Frank Warner. She had a type. Warner, like her first husband, Spraggs, was a skilled and entrepreneurial West Indian immigrant who had first settled in Louisiana.[20] He was also active in the labor movement and campaigns for racial justice. Although Warner was six years younger than her, Moore likely enjoyed that they could talk about everything from life in the urban South to their shared struggles as migrants and workers.[21] Or maybe Moore liked that Frank was both an activist and an avid antique furniture collector—a man who took pride in his race and in his home.[22] However they came together, by the mid-1930s, they lived together in an apartment on West 123rd Street. Frank supported them as a tailor and owner of his own dry cleaning business in Harlem.[23]

With a steady home and a man who supported her activism, Moore became more open to family life. Until then, she had opted for organizing rather than child-rearing. It's impossible to know exactly why. Her perpetual economic instability might have been the cause, or perhaps the thought of motherhood was too much to bear after she had suffered a miscarriage in her twenties.[24] Frank helped change her mind. By the end of the decade, they had welcomed a new addition to the family, a son named Thomas.[25] But homemaking time was short-lived. When World War II began in Europe in 1939, Moore redoubled her commitment to the Popular Front. She now had one foot in her home and one foot in the movement. Straddling this line was harder than she could have imagined.

No group drew more public ire during wartime than the communists. In August 1939, the Soviet Union signed a nonaggression pact with

Hitler's Germany. Each side would refrain from taking military action against the other. The agreement put American communists like Moore in an impossible situation. Supporting the Soviet Union, which was directly exposed to potential German military aggression, meant they were at odds with U.S. organizations that supported the American cause. But rejecting the Soviets' pact meant defying direct orders from the Comintern and running afoul of the global communist movement. While the American wing of the party publicly declared that the pact was a "wonderful contribution to peace," its leaders privately hoped that the agreement could buy the Soviet Union enough time to build a force to defend itself against Hitler. When Moore talked with her comrades at party meetings and social events, she found they had mixed reactions. Many, like her, did not agree with American intervention in the war. Other, more ardent members left the organization altogether over its unpatriotic position.[26]

History tends to remember the Communist Party's stance as a singular, dark stain in a time of coalescing patriotism. But it was hardly alone. Antiwar sentiment simmered across the Black American Left. Veterans and civilians alike were still smarting from the sting of racism in the armed forces during World War I. Organizers such as labor leader A. Philip Randolph advocated against American intervention, forming the laboriously named Greater New York Committee to Keep America Out of War. Some NAACP chapters initially adopted an antiwar position. Other notables, including the famed Harlem writer, journalist, and socialist activist George Schuyler, joined the Negroes Against War Committee.[27] Many activists were not yet aware of the scope and scale of the Holocaust when the war first broke out. Instead, they pointed to the many atrocities the United States had previously committed against Black citizens as a primary reason to refrain from fighting.

Moore incorporated this antiwar sentiment in her unsuccessful 1940 campaign for a seat in the New York State Assembly representing the Nineteenth District. The Harlem Branch put Moore forward as a candidate because she was now a well-known organizer in Manhattan, and many poor and working-class people regarded her as a "leader in the struggle for jobs for Negroes." Moore was astute enough to know she wouldn't win. Despite its Popular Front participation, the party was still on the political fringe in Harlem—and across the entire United States, for that matter. Its candidates rarely triumphed over the entrenched two-party system. Moore likely agreed to go along with the campaign because it could serve as a platform to promote Black people governing their own communities.

She had a simple but effective platform: "Jobs, Security, Civil Rights, and Peace."[28] On the campaign trail, Moore connected the discrimination Harlem mothers and workers faced due to the government's mishandling of New Deal aid and defunding of domestic programs to amplify military spending as the country ramped up for war. Whether she was stumping at a women's club or a civil rights group, Moore's message was the same: "The battle as [Harlemites] see it is for jobs, with decent pay and an American standard of living for the parents of our children. The fathers and mothers of Harlem are unalterably opposed to the sacrifice of the welfare and future of their children on the altar of the enormous appropriations for war materials."[29]

Moore's campaign pillars dovetailed with the next organization she joined: the National Negro Congress (NNC), founded in 1936.[30] In its heyday, the NNC brought together communists, the labor movement, Black leftists and intellectuals, and white and Black progressives under one organizing umbrella. The group cut its teeth on a platform of anti-lynching legislation and labor organizing while protesting employment discrimination and police brutality.[31]

Moore found the NNC to be a useful vehicle to advocate for Black rights. What's more, she could do it in the company of like-minded Black women—trained organizers who shared her commitment to using the party's class analysis in service of Black liberation. She worked alongside other proven communists and labor organizers like Louise Thompson Patterson and Thelma Dale, who amplified the group's civil and labor rights initiatives from New York. Moore also joined forces with Esther Cooper Jackson, another vibrant theoretician and organizer who led the NNC's youth wing—the Southern Negro Youth Congress—in fighting for voting rights across the South.[32] These organizing spaces became political and racial safe havens for Moore as the greater Communist Party began to abandon its commitment to Black Nationalist principles in its move toward the political center.

Moore and her fellow organizers did their best to keep Popular Front organizations like the NNC skewing left. But with war now raging in Europe, they realized that it was only a matter of time before the United States got involved. An ardent antiwar activist, Moore preferred that government dollars go to housing and food rather than tanks and ships. But if America was going to spend its way out of the Depression, she didn't want Black people to be left with empty pockets. As an NNC member, Moore lobbied the Roosevelt administration to integrate defense industry jobs, establish fair employment practices, and ensure that Black defense workers had access to equal housing and wages. Always looking to push for Black control over Black communities, she also advocated for "Negroes [to be] placed on all policy and planning committees of local defense councils" so that Black people could have a say in wartime plans like public victory gardens or the building of bomb shelters in Harlem.[33]

But her greatest impact within the group was securing jobs for Black workers. Moore and other NNC members argued that if Black men and women did not forcefully advocate for jobs and fair employment practices, segregation across all sectors would become "even more firmly established as a result of the government's headlong drive toward war."[34]

With this in mind, she set her sights on the segregated transportation sector.[35] In March 1941, a collective of NNC members, communists, and other Black leftists launched a strike against the Fifth Avenue Coach Company and the New York City Omnibus Corporation to open up jobs for Black New Yorkers.[36] For four weeks straight, Moore, Adam Clayton Powell Jr., and others arrived at six bus stops in Harlem at 9:00 a.m. carrying signs and chanting "Don't ride where you can't work" all day. It worked. Black people avoided the buses, and the companies had to concede. The collective won 170 jobs for Black New Yorkers—a significant increase.[37] In his victory speech, Powell likened the win against racist companies to a victory against fascism, noting that Harlemites triumphed because "this is New York, not Berlin."[38] Moore was proud of these on-the-ground successes. But she knew there was much more work to do. She remained obstinate: the American government should keep out of the war and focus on bettering conditions within its own country. And she vowed to do what she could to stymie America's wartime climb.

———

"We will not be drawn into any war in Europe ... to make profits for Wall Street," proclaimed New York labor leader Michael J. Quill at an "emergency peace mobilization" meeting in Chicago in September 1940. The audience, speckled with NNC members, the American Youth Congress—a Black youth group "organized around issues of war, conscription, and employment"—communists, artists, and civil rights organizers, erupted in cheers.[39] When this motley group convened at the hastily planned meeting in the Windy City, they weren't sure what to expect. But they were grateful to find that so many around them shared their concerns about America's impending entry into World War II.

Energized by their numbers and convictions, attendees voted to set up a permanent organization to address these concerns. The American Peace Mobilization (APM) was born then and there with the express goals of keeping America out of the war and ensuring the rights of all its citizens. Scholar, singer, and communist political activist Paul Robeson became a vice-chairman of the organization, and Black writers like Richard Wright and Langston Hughes peppered the membership rolls.[40] While Moore was organizing with the NNC, newly minted APM members fanned out across the United States and set up chapters in their hometowns to unite civil rights organizers, teachers, trade unionists, and antipoverty advocates.[41]

By early 1941, the APM had momentum, but it was still on the political margins. If members were going to successfully stymie war preparations, then they needed the support of seasoned activists. The New York chapter began courting Moore.[42] Members piqued her interest with a platform connecting pacifism and civil rights. Moreover, New York organizers were especially active in day-to-day struggles. They held mass meetings, planned antiwar parades, and hosted forums to educate the public on the pitfalls of wartime spending and defense department discrimination. She joined the APM's Women's Division and served as Director of Negro Women's Work in April 1941.[43] Despite her title, Moore was never one to be pigeonholed into traditionally female spaces.

In May 1941, Moore made the trek from New York to Washington, D.C., to participate in the APM's most high-profile protest: a contentious, 24/7 peace vigil in front of the White House. For forty straight days, APM picketers held strong in the nation's capital. Dressed in sensible shoes, a shin-length dress, and a straw hat to block the sun, Moore spent several full days marching back and forth on the sidewalk in front of 1600 Pennsylvania Avenue. At times she stood ramrod straight, holding a red, white, and blue APM banner in her right hand, purse in her left. Other times, her banner slumped with fatigue from hours of marching and shunning the bystanders and soldiers who heckled her.[44] Yet whenever a reporter passed by, Moore would perk up and pipe up, poised to explain the importance of the protest. She asserted the APM platform: that Roosevelt should reinvest in the New Deal, stop Black conscription into the racist armed forces, and desegregate the military units that were already assembling for war. When journalists asked Moore when the protest would end, she was resolute: she hoped "it would keep going forever."[45]

Such bold antiwar proclamations didn't make Moore or the APM any friends across the Popular Front, which was coalescing around the war effort. But it soon faced a far more serious threat than the American Left. Started in 1938 and chaired by Texas congressman Martin Dies Jr., the House Un-American Activities Committee (HUAC) was the latest iteration of Washington-backed investigations of "subversives," people and organizations the government suspected of having communist or fascist ties.[46] Armed with the Smith Act, a 1940 law that criminalized anyone advocating the overthrow of the American government by force, HUAC took aim at leftists.[47]

HUAC quickly branded the APM as a communist front.[48] Terrified of prosecution under the Smith Act, some APM members capitulated and turned over their records and turned on each other in exchange for immunity.[49] To make matters worse, at times Dies partnered with J. Edgar Hoover, now FBI director, to entrap and compel members to supply information to the bureau. Dies made quick work of unraveling the group, which had political ties to far bigger organizations across the Popular Front. But the APM and other groups like it were low-hanging fruit. The true target was the Communist Party.

When Dies learned that ten years earlier the party's white current executive secretary, Earl Browder, might have traveled abroad under assumed names and with false documents, he found his opening. HUAC subpoenaed Browder and eventually indicted him on the felony charge of passport fraud.[50] In March 1941, Browder began his four-year prison sentence in a federal penitentiary in Atlanta—just like Garvey had.[51]

Moore immediately recognized the parallels between Garvey's and Browder's captures, despite their racial differences. She believed "the persecution of any individual or minority for political beliefs represent[ed] a danger for all minority groups and especially for the Negro People," and she quickly became the National Negro Representative for the Citizens' Committee to Free Earl Browder.[52] Her ideological commitments, protest prowess, and outspoken rejection of the government's Red-baiting—officials' attempts to harass or persecute Americans due to their known or suspected communist sympathies—made her a target of Hoover's growing surveillance apparatus. His special agents started submitting regular reports on Moore in late 1941.

Undeterred, Moore joined New York communists the next month as they began an ambitious campaign to free Browder. Since she was now a well-known organizer across the state thanks to her "Win the Women" speech, the party charged Moore with organizing Black people to free the embattled communist leader. From a small office on West 125th Street, she cajoled Black organizations across the nation to back Browder's release.[53] She planned rallies featuring communist celebrities and placed ads and articles in newspapers like Adam Clayton Powell Jr.'s *People's Voice* to alert Harlemites to Browder's plight—and to how quickly it could become their own. Soon, anyone who supported progressive organizing would be deemed a "subversive" if the Black community didn't denounce Red-baiting, Moore warned.[54] She had moderate success. Browder remained behind bars for fourteen months. In his absence, Moore knitted together a Black-centered, antifascist front.

Leftist activists heralded the tireless Moore as "another Sojourner Truth."[55] But like Truth, she quickly learned the more one fought for freedom, the more one faced repression. Being pro-Black and pro-Red with ties to multiple "subversive" groups came at a price. As America entered World War II, Moore found her reputation as a "Negro Woman Leader" would soon bring her both fame and regret.

CHAPTER 7

Negro Woman Leader

I never did lose all my nationalism," Moore once said of her war-time organizing.[1] In the early 1940s, holding on to it wasn't easy. As the fighting crept ever closer to American soil, Moore had to wrap her activism in the trappings of patriotism or risk being called subversive or seditious. She moved toward the political center to survive, diving headlong into Black-centered organizing and making political connections that would have once seemed preposterous. Her successes made her a household name. But as the 1940s wore on, Moore wondered if this newfound fame came at too steep a political cost.

Once America's entry into the war seemed imminent, Moore became one of the millions of Black Americans who adopted the "Double Victory" wartime strategy, proposed by a Black cafeteria worker, James G. Thompson, in a letter to *The Pittsburgh Courier*. "I suggest that while we keep defense and victory in the forefront that we do not lose sight of our fight for true democracy at home," Thompson wrote. If Black people were going to join the war effort, he argued, then they should "adopt the double VV.... The first V for victory over our enemies from without, the second V for victory over our enemies from within."[2] It was a simple but poignant approach, tying the fight against racism to the fight against fascism. And it caught on like wildfire. Black people across the nation embraced "Double V" as both a slogan and a call to action.[3]

Nothing epitomized this approach better than the A. Philip Randolph–led March on Washington Movement. Shortly after resigning the presidency of the National Negro Congress, Randolph created the blueprint for what became one of the most successful civil rights strategies of the twentieth century: massive marches in the nation's capital to force the federal government's hand. Frustrated by Roosevelt's resistance to desegregating the military, Randolph called for tens of thousands of Black Americans to converge on the nation's capital on July 1, 1941, to demand equal rights for civilians and soldiers alike. Black labor activists, civil rights organizers, and factory workers threw their weight behind the march.[4] Once it was clear to Roosevelt—thanks in no small part to Hoover's surveillance—that Randolph could and would bring Black people to his doorstep in droves, he signed Executive Order 8802. Starting in June 1941, federal agencies, unions, and companies engaged in war-related work had to desegregate. The newly founded Fair Employment Practices Committee would monitor and enforce the new policy.[5] Satisfied with the response, Randolph put his March on Washington plans on hold. In two decades, President Kennedy's inaction on civil rights legislation would jump-start the movement once more.

At first, Moore's various activist networks operated parallel to the March on Washington Movement. They neither endorsed it nor criticized it.[6] However, Germany's June 1941 invasion of Russia obliterated the nonaggression pact the Soviets had previously supported, and Japan's attack on Pearl Harbor six months later crushed any hope of America keeping its hands clean. The growing sense of patriotic fervor, coupled with the ongoing Dies Committee investigations, made it nearly impossible to oppose the war effort. And so, in an ideological reversal that must have felt like whiplash to Moore, the Communist Party issued a full-throated endorsement of the war.

She was stunned by how sharp a turn the party's rhetoric took. Communist leaders now proclaimed that if Americans did not "jointly fight to destroy the Axis" powers, "there [would] be neither the old American capitalism nor a new American socialism—there [would] only be slavery to the Axis." The organization now advocated for victory at all ideological and personal costs.[7] Maintaining a hardline antiwar stance was political suicide, it was plain to see. But this abrupt shift in the party line—and especially the invocation of slavery all while siphoning attention from Black liberation—made Moore uncomfortable. "I realized [they] were no longer moving in our best interests," she said wearily. And that "there were certain forces within the Communist Party that was racist."[8]

Not yet ready to cut the mooring line, she buoyed herself by clinging to her fellow Black comrades. She found a kindred spirit in Claudia Jones, a young Trinidadian organizer with almond eyes and a toothy smile. Like Moore, Jones first caught wind of the party after its support of the Scottsboro Boys in the 1930s. Seventeen years younger than Moore, Jones joined the party's youth organization, the Young Communist League, rather than becoming a full-fledged member. But she quickly rose in the ranks. By wartime, Jones was a leading Marxist theoretician, known for her regular column, "Half the World," which ran in the party's newspaper, *The Daily Worker*.[9] In her articles, Jones explained how she came to view "Hitler's attack on the Soviet Union as a bid for world conquest," one that "endangered the continued independence and existence of all nations and people," including Black and Brown people everywhere.[10] Moore discussed these ideas with Jones and other Black party leaders such as Benjamin Davis Jr., Bonita Williams, and Abner Berry. Small but mighty, the party's Harlem branches continued to cast segregation during war as an affront to Black civil rights at home. Promoting global democracy in opposition to fascism, for them, was a way to achieve Black sovereignty abroad.[11]

If there was a silver lining for Moore, it was that being a Soviet sympathizer was no longer the scarlet letter it had been just a few years earlier.[12] Moreover, the communists' support of the Allied powers and the war effort, coupled with the widespread military enlistment of their men, opened up opportunities for women like Moore to step into leadership roles and shape the party to fit their political needs.[13] Always one to rise to the occasion, Moore threw herself deeper into the party and other like-minded leftist groups. Along the way, she would make some new friends—and some strange bedfellows.

Moore was now a permanent fixture at wartime events in Harlem. The place was still packed. Of the approximately 485,000 Black people who lived in New York City, more than 60 percent of them lived in the upper Manhattan neighborhood.[14] The Great Depression was over, but it left lasting devastation in its wake. Moore still passed by dilapidated apartment buildings and men and women out of work on her block. Her body stiffened and her stomach hollowed when she walked by policemen hassling Harlemites. Police brutality was often the spark that ignited urban rebellion in cities like New York, and she had witnessed the "first modern race riot" just a few years before, when Harlem broke out into violence after police detained a young Afro–Puerto Rican kid accused of stealing a penknife from the local Kress department store in 1935.[15] Even still, she had reason to hope the winds of change could snuff out such fires. The Popular Front protests she had participated in had already brought some jobs and better housing conditions to Harlem.

Wartime Harlem was a unique, precarious mixture of racial tension and reconciliation. In the early 1940s, Moore engaged in a dizzying array of protests, committees, and councils aimed at stabilizing unrest. Under cold, gray January skies, she huddled with other Black leftist leaders at the Harlem Defense Conference to talk about programs for Black civilians while most Americans were focused on supporting the troops. The group concluded that Harlem would participate in the war effort but also keep pushing for solutions to its unique problems: the lack of air-raid shelters, the need for jobs, and "freedom [for] those persecuted by the Dies Committee."[16]

The next month, she spoke on behalf of "the millions of Negroes who still need better housing" to government officials in Washington, D.C., who were siphoning federal dollars from domestic infrastructure to fund the military.[17] Two weeks later, she was part of a communist-sponsored, citywide speaking tour in support of party leader Earl Browder.[18] And, as the icy winter melted into spring, Moore called upon large crowds to "smash Hitler," including in front of hundreds at a rally in Harlem.[19]

By the time the nip in the air gave way to hot summer days, Moore was serving as the co-chair of New York's National Negro Achievement Day, an annual event honoring Black leaders and veterans. Flanked by Black sailors, labor leaders, and civil rights advocates, Moore led a procession down Lenox Avenue from 145th to 111th Street before turning west to head back up to Colonial Park. As the marchers gathered in the park, Moore joined Henrietta Miller, mother of Black war hero Dorie Miller, in front of the crowd. Dorie had risen to national acclaim when, without any prior combat training, he manned guns to defend the naval base during the attack on Pearl Harbor.[20] Later, Moore accompanied Mrs. Miller to the local Golden Gate Ballroom, where they honored boxer Joe Louis and actor and activist Paul Robeson, as well as civil rights organizers W. E. B. Du Bois and Mary

McLeod Bethune (in absentia). The festivities ended with a dance that lasted into the wee hours of the morning.[21]

As orange and red seeped once more into Central Park's leaves, Moore protested price gouging alongside Elizabeth Gurley Flynn, worked on the Citizens Committee for Lower Rents in Harlem, and served on the executive board of the Coordinating Committee for Employment, an Adam Clayton Powell Jr.–led group that advocated for defense jobs for Black Americans.[22] She spent what little downtime she had writing directly to Roosevelt about the Black experience in wartime. In her letters, she beseeched him to "consider seriously the plight of the Negro people" who were suffering during wartime from the lack of decent places to live.[23] While New Yorkers were stringing up lights and trimming Christmas trees in December, Moore was pressuring local officials to create more childcare centers for working parents in Harlem, or taking the four-and-a-half-hour train ride to Boston to speak to the Communist Party of Massachusetts about Browder's court case.[24] Hardly a week went by that Moore wasn't out at a protest, a rally, or a community meeting aimed at keeping America's eyes on Black rights amid the war.

Moore's wartime advocacy also pulled her into the Black Women's Club Movement—an unlikely place for a Black Nationalist and communist. An invitation from National Council of Negro Women (NCNW) leader Mary McLeod Bethune brought her into the fold. Like Moore, Bethune was born in the South in the late nineteenth century and came of age amid the rise of Jim Crow. While Moore went the radical route, Bethune pursued mainstream education with fervor. She started a school for Black girls in Daytona Beach, Florida, what is today Bethune-Cookman University. Bethune used that success to launch herself into the upper echelons of Black life, joining civil rights groups like the NAACP and garnering a national reputation as an activist and educator. Her uncompromising vision of racial equality, combined with her practicality, made her a shoo-in for FDR's Black Cabinet, an Eleanor Roosevelt–supported group of Black leaders who advised the president from 1933 to 1945. For Moore, Bethune was more than just a celebrity. Her life was a glimpse into what Moore's could have been like, had she not been orphaned at a young age and cast out of the Black upper class.[25]

While Moore was delving into communism, Bethune joined the National Association of Colored Women and pushed for suffrage, wage equity, jobs, and justice for Black people at the ballot box. But she also recognized that the group was riddled with classism and colorism. Leaders like Mary Church Terrell and Josephine St. Pierre Ruffin looked and acted like the moneyed world that had made them, always dressed in the finest lace and exuding ladylike poise. They often viewed poor and working-class Black women as lesser—lacking in "proper" social, cultural, and moral schooling. From Moore's vantage point, these women's attitudes smacked of condescension.[26]

Bethune took issue with the NACW's culture.[27] In 1935, she created her own Black women's organization: the National Council of Negro Women. Bethune envisioned her group as a sort of conglomerate, drawing in an array of Black women to form one main lobbying mechanism for the country. This was Moore's kind of group. To be sure, Bethune still exuded that high-class respectability. She was always dressed conservatively and perfectly coiffed, a stark contrast to Moore, who spent most days pounding the pavement at party and Popular Front protests for an activist's meager salary. But Bethune recruited women from all walks of life. She was intent on advocating for Black women's entry into wartime defense jobs, voter registration, and antilynching legislation, and she knew that she needed brainy, energetic women to take up her cause.[28]

Moore fit the bill, no question. And so, in hopes of forging friendly ties, Bethune invited the communist firebrand to speak at the NCNW's "Negro Woman's Committee for Democracy in National Defense" conference at Howard University.[29]

Moore demurred when asked to give a speech. She worried that having slipped out of the world of the Black elite, she had lost the respect of high society. "Mrs. Bethune, I've never been to school," Moore said. "I can't talk to those women. They're professors, and doctors, and intellectuals." But Bethune was sure Moore was the right woman to rouse a moderate, measured, middle-class crowd to action. "Get out there," she replied. "You got more in your little finger than they got in their whole hands, you get out there and talk to them. They need what you got to say."[30] And get out there Moore did. Her speech was electric; it confirmed, for Bethune, that Moore was an asset. And as word of Moore's activism spread, members repeatedly invited her back to the club's meetings.

It didn't take long for the NACW, Bethune's former club, to covet Moore as well. These women invited her to address the group at its biennial convention in Oklahoma City. There, she shared her expertise on "successful efforts in opening new job opportunities for Negroes" and extolled joining forces across political, organizational, and class lines.[31] By the convention's end, the NACW had selected Moore to join its newly minted Committee on Women in Industry. The club women lauded her ability to bring Black women from different organizations and political affiliations across the Black Left together.[32]

The feeling was mutual. Moore had discounted the Black upper class ever since she left it. But as she walked through their convention halls and sat in their meetings, she came to see there might be more to these women than met the eye. They could be conduits through which Moore could help Black women find jobs and gain political autonomy—key steps in achieving Black self-determination.

By 1943, Bethune and Moore were established wartime allies. Bethune needed women like Moore to reach the Black masses, and Moore benefited from Bethune's power and political connections. Bethune invited Moore to join her club's executive committee and to become the honorary president of its news arm: *The Aframerican Woman's Journal.* Moore agreed to take on the role—and the others that Black club women offered her—with gusto.[33] The Popular Front ethos of the times was her guiding light: join forces across ideological lines, but cling to your radical roots.

Against all odds, Moore was part of a pivotal moment in Black women's club history. Bethune recognized that if the NCNW was going to be a serious player in national politics, it needed a brick-and-mortar headquarters in Washington, D.C. She set her sights on a house in Dupont Circle, but local white owners balked at the idea of a Black woman buying in their neighborhood. Undeterred, Bethune found another house on Vermont Avenue. Moore was among the women who approved their leader's purchase of the sixteen-room building, no small feat for a Black women's organization during World War II, when resources were scarce.[34] When word of the celebrated purchase peppered the pages of the Black press, there was Audley Moore, seated in the front row of the photo op and just to the left of America's foremost female race leader.[35]

Soon, Moore was helping Black New Yorkers make history of their own through another keen political partnership, this time with Black Communist Party leader Benjamin Davis Jr. A Harvard Law School graduate, Davis was tall, with expressive eyes and a thin mustache that shot straight across his upper lip. He was the son of Ben Davis Sr., a Georgia newspaper owner and Republican politician. Davis Jr.'s legal career was off to an auspicious start in the early 1930s, until he defended communist and labor organizer Angelo Herndon against charges of inciting an insurrection among white and Black laborers during the Depression. Herndon and his communist compatriots' courage in the face of the recalcitrant racism radicalized Davis, who joined the party during the trial. He relocated from Atlanta to Harlem soon after, in part because he was a marked man for supporting a Black communist in the South.[36] By the early 1940s, many viewed Davis as a fearless fighter for the Black community.[37]

Together, Moore and Davis gained a citywide reputation. In 1943, they persuaded Macy's to stop selling what the company called a "mugging night stick." When the department store's white clientele peered into the display window at Herald Square, they'd see the latest handbags and gloves on display, alongside a billy club complete with a silk wristband and an ad that read, "Carry a Bully Stick and Be Safe at Night."[38] The implication was clear: for the white woman who has it all, this ladylike weapon could protect her from the Black man out to take it. Davis declared such products "made 'mugging' and 'Negro' synonymous," and "that possession of the stick by any woman would give her the right to use it." Moore took it a step further. She told store executives and journalists alike that "only a person with a fascist outlook" could have cooked up such a crass luxury item. She asked, "What could prevent a fascist group from buying up quantities of them and using them on Negroes?"[39] The pair's public protests—and their linking the billy club with fascism, during wartime, no less— chastened the company. Macy's removed the sticks from its shelves.[40]

With showy, successful protests like this one under his belt, Davis

announced his candidacy for city council in 1943. He had big shoes
to fill. Two years earlier, Moore's friend and fellow activist Adam
Clayton Powell Jr. set his sights on becoming the first Black New
York City Council member, an ambitious goal during Jim Crow. New
Yorkers picked their council members in citywide elections, and as
Powell observed, that meant "no Negro could be elected without the
complete unity of all of Harlem, plus considerable support in white
areas."[41] Powell formed the People's Committee, a conglomeration
of organizers and community members inside and outside Harlem,
to get elected. This collective, Moore among it, was the boost Powell
needed to win. He became New York City's first Black city council
member in 1941.[42]

In 1944, Powell decided to run for Congress. He endorsed Davis
as his successor, as did a slew of progressive groups, including Black
churches, Black fraternal organizations, and the two massive labor
unions: the American Federation of Labor and the Congress of Industrial Organizations. The young lawyer turned communist ran on a
capacious wartime platform, calling for an end to all racial bias in
civilian and military life, lower goods prices and rents, and the "speedy
victory over Hitlerism at home and abroad."[43]

Davis had the pedigree to get elected, but Moore had the political
chops. Communist Party leadership knew it, too. They gave her $500
and free rein to organize the campaign. With the seed money in hand,
she made history.[44] Throughout 1943, Moore called on every constituency she had ever come in contact with to bring prominent club
women, famous musicians, politicians, doctors, lawyers, neighborhood organizers, and labor activists to Davis's cause.[45] With catchy
songs and a ground game that papered the island from Harlem to
Hell's Kitchen with pro-Davis literature, Moore waged a landmark
campaign.[46] Yet there were plenty of skeptics. After all, when had an
interracial constituency of voters ever elected a communist?

"Ben himself called me in his office and told me to cool it because
I was arousing too much enthusiasm around his campaign," Moore
recalled. "There was a danger that he would not be elected and then
the Party would be terribly let down." Davis was right to be worried.
His communist past didn't bode well for his political future. But the
campaign "caught on like wildfire" as it stretched into the summer
months. According to Moore, the "Communist Party didn't know

what was happening out there amongst the people."[47] She was sure her guy had it.

Still, nerves crept in as she huddled under an umbrella outside the Harlem Armory, a brown art deco building and frequent meeting-house for Harlemites, as the count came in on the evening of November 9, 1943. "He's in! We've won!" New York State Party Secretary Gil Green exclaimed as he came running out of the building and into the rain. Moore swept him off his feet and, in her excitement, "planted dozens of kisses on his face." Moments later, Davis joined his campaign manager outside, and they whooped and hollered. Supporters honked wildly as they drove by.[48] At ten minutes past nine o'clock, Davis's drenched Democratic challenger, Samuel DiFalco, made his way inside the armory to concede the election.[49] The room erupted in deafening cheers as Davis took the stage to give his victory speech.

For any grassroots challenger in New York City, winning a citywide seat was impressive. But for Davis, a Black communist running for public office in the United States, the victory was historic. Leaders and organizers across the Left hailed his win as the beginning of a national transformation. It was a sign that the Popular Front alliances forged in wartime just might last into peacetime, with organized labor, communists, and civil rights organizations working together to achieve lasting freedom.[50]

Moore took her own victory lap in the pages of *The Daily Worker* and Powell's *People's Voice*. She told New Yorkers the campaign's "strength has come from people like yourself...giving their time, energy, and money behind a candidate that stands for all the things that [you] hold dear."[51] They returned the accolades. Articles celebrating Moore peppered local newspapers, with journalists proclaiming she had far exceeded everyone's expectations and running headlines like DAVIS SUPPORTERS WILL LONG TELL OF AUDLEY MOORE'S WORK.[52]

Publicly, Moore played the part of the dutiful public servant. But privately, she was beginning to have doubts about the cause. For the past few years, she had grown increasingly troubled by the party's shifting political positions on Black self-determination and wartime militarization. The Davis campaign, for all its good, added to her concerns. She was especially upset at how party leadership handled the star-studded "Victory Show" for Davis in the weeks leading up to the election. In October 1943, Black film celebrities, theater and nightclub stars, and radio personalities all descended on Harlem's Golden Gate Ballroom to rally voters in support of Davis. With a lineup that included Coleman Hawkins, Billie Holiday, Ella Fitzgerald, Art Tatum, and Duke Ellington, the Davis campaign had put on a fundraiser the likes of which neither the party nor Harlem had ever seen.[53]

But immediately following the event, "the Communists came and took all the Gate receipts," Moore recalled. She claimed they absconded with the official records and attendance rolls, too, making it impossible to reach out and thank those who had donated their time or money to the campaign.[54] For Moore, this was just the latest instance of the party undermining its Black members' ability to organize fundraisers, campaigns, and protests in their communities as they saw fit.[55] If the party couldn't even let Black people run a fundraiser on their own, how could they claim to support a sovereign Black nation?

These personal and political betrayals mattered to Moore. She "loved the Party to death," and she was devoted to her comrades.[56] But the more she branched out from them, the more she started to see the party's pitfalls. As she took stock of the world around her, Moore wondered if the Popular Front—which had made room for the Black Nationalist during the desperate days of war—would still welcome her once it was all over.

Burning Questions

On a crisp spring day in April 1944, Audley Moore walked down Main Street in Springfield, Massachusetts. She took in the rows of contiguous mid-rise brick buildings, the colorful awnings advertising bookstores, soda shops, and banks. She followed the directions to a meeting hall where a reception was set to take place in her honor.[1] Moore was moderately pleased when she stepped into the small room and saw that twenty-five people—some party members and some locals—had come to hear a "Negro woman Communist leader" from New York speak. Sure, she usually drew bigger crowds than this. Moore had spent the last few years packing parks, music halls, and meetinghouses with men and women from all walks of life. But she was seasoned enough to know that in the battle for the hearts and minds of Black Americans it wasn't the size of the crowd but their capacity for change that mattered. She greeted a sprinkling of labor leaders and politicians and chatted with domestic workers and students who had made time despite their hectic days. When the room quieted down and settled in, Moore cleared her throat and launched into an impassioned speech about the Communist Party.[2]

Now was the time to fight the "reactionary" Republicans, who she claimed were seeking to undo all the progress Black Americans had made during wartime. There was no better place to do this, Moore told them, than from within the Communist Party, which was fighting to ensure Black rights weren't rolled back while America focused on winning the war. She made a convincing case; nine people joined the party on the spot. Among those new recruits was a ninety-four-year-old man who had hobbled over to Moore after her speech. He was interested but hesitant to join, he explained, because he thought he was too old. "There is no age limit 'upwards,'" Moore told him, and he signed his membership card then and there.[3]

This was precisely why the party sent Moore out on membership missions during wartime. She could work a room. But her sterling recruiting record was only possible because the party had fallen in lockstep with Roosevelt and the Allied forces' agenda. Its members were enlisting in the military and supporting workers who agreed not to strike during wartime. They had even acquiesced to the forced relocation of Japanese Americans into domestic detention camps after Japan bombed Pearl Harbor.[4] Moore championed the party's patriotism at receptions and meeting halls across the Northeast. But in quieter moments, when she returned home from rallies, she questioned whether she should still be toeing the party line. Was it right to keep recruiting her brethren to an organization wavering in its commitment to their rights? Had she compromised her ideals, using the party's reach to foster Black Nationalist sympathies? Or was the party, in fact, using her?

Politicking from within the party further stirred her doubts. Just two months before she visited Springfield, party leader Earl Browder made a stunning announcement that transformed the organization as she knew it. On January 7, 1944, delegates from across the country converged on New York City for their annual three-day conference. This meeting was typically a closed-door session—National Committee members only. Thus, many were stunned to find Browder had packed the hall with more than two hundred interlopers, known Browder loyalists at that, to witness the proceedings. Browder's game was obvious. The next day, he took to the stage and said the party now faced "an unprecedented situation within the world and within our country." The November 1943 Tehran Conference—when Allied leaders Joseph Stalin, Franklin Roosevelt, and Winston Churchill met in the Soviet embassy in Iran and made plans to invade western Europe in May 1944—was a tectonic shift in the world order.[5] Though the war was still raging, Browder predicted a "long period of world peace and orderly post-war reconstruction" was just on the horizon. The task before the party was to champion Allied victory and solidify a place of power in this postwar world order.

The delegates listened intently, braced by Browder's surety. The party would support the "restoration of universal suffrage to the

Southern people, the elimination of anti-Negro and all other undem-
ocratic restrictions in the primary elections, and the total removal of
all anti-labor laws."[6] Few objections there. But then Browder changed
tack. To achieve this agenda, the party would need to disband. At this,
the audience was stunned. A new organization would then rise in
its place, Browder continued. The Communist Political Association
(CPA) would still be a left-wing organization. But it would be more
lenient in its ideological commitments. Namely, its members would
need to make peace with coexisting alongside capitalism.[7]

Those in attendance were swept up in Browder's vision. After all,
recent events seemed to confirm his claim that a new world order
was coming. Ben Davis's recent election was the prima facie omen.
But New York wasn't the only place where liberties were being won.
By 1944, more Black people were able to vote thanks to *Smith v. All-
wright,* a landmark Supreme Court decision that outlawed excluding
Black folk from primary elections. Poll taxes had become increasingly
unpopular, and the military was desegregating too, albeit more slowly
than most Black people would have liked.[8] Change, it seemed, was in
the wind.

At first, Moore had few qualms about the shift in party name and
approach. She fancied herself more a grassroots agitator than a true
communist demagogue. She was interested in the daily work of bettering Black life, not the party's theoretical twists and turns.[9] Moore
chose to focus on Browder's dreams of eliminating anti-Black laws and
rallying behind civil rights. Even better, in Moore's eyes, this new iteration of the party would shed its Russian trappings and instead wrap
itself in red, white, and blue, invoking the symbols of patriotism to
protect it from persecution. For a woman like Moore, whom J. Edgar
Hoover's special agents now trailed daily, it was a welcome rebrand.

But then came the gut punch. In his January 1944 article, "On the
Negroes and the Right of Self-Determination," Browder concluded
that Black people had "ma[d]e their decision once and for all. Their
decision is for their complete integration into the American nation as
a whole, and not for separation." Moore was taken aback. The sheer
audacity of it—a white leftist claiming on behalf of all Black people
that Black Nationalism was dead and that assimilation was the path
forward. And she was outright stunned when Browder implicated her
in his decision, arguing it was precipitated by the party's years of

organized labor victories, voting rights fights, and most notably "when Benjamin J. Davis, Jr., was elected to the New York City Council by a combined vote of Negroes, trade unionists and progressive white people." Black people, according to Browder, now saw gaining the "position of equal citizens in America" as their "immediate political task."[10] Moore had sniffed out the party's wavering commitment to the Black Belt Thesis during wartime. But Browder's article was an outright rebuke, a repudiation of the separate Black nation—real or imagined—that had once been so integral to communist thought.

In the wake of the article, Moore found that, in Harlem at least, Browder's bombshell did little to change her day-to-day work. She still toiled alongside the same comrades, in the same spaces, and for the good of the same people that she always had. So, she soldiered on. Instead of rebuking Browder and the new direction of the CPA, she kept her eye trained on local struggles throughout the spring of 1944, fighting for the rights of Harlem tenants whose homes were destroyed in a fire and advocating for the passage of labor laws that benefited Black women.[11] But when the party announced Browder would formally usher in the new organization at a May 1944 national meeting, Moore wanted to hear what he had to say firsthand.

On the moderately warm morning of May 20, Moore sidled into the ballroom of the Riverside Plaza Hotel on West Seventy-Third Street. She took her seat and looked up at the stage, where a large poster of Stalin, Roosevelt, and Churchill loomed—a sign Browder was deeply invested in the Allied forces and the promise of the Tehran Conference. Her eyes then moved to a podium draped in a white service flag with a red border. The flag sported a gold star, representing families with sons killed in action, and a blue star for families with sons in the service. Organizers emblazoned "9,250" across it—the number of communist boys currently enlisted.[12] These accoutrements sent a clear message: the CPA was America's answer to the Soviets' communism. It was in league *with* global capitalism, not against it. Browder strode to the podium and presented the official resolution to dissolve the American Communist Party. Gone was the rhetoric of the Comintern; Browder addressed the crowd as "ladies and gentlemen" rather than "comrades." Here to stay was American patriotism. Any who looked to "weaken or overthrow" American democracy would be expelled from the organization.[13] Half an hour later, the American Communist Party was dead, and the CPA was born.[14]

A new organization meant a new set of officers. First on the docket was electing a leader. Naturally, Browder was put forth as the potential president. But what began as a decorous sea of hands in favor of the longtime communist leader evolved into a mob. Cries of "We want Browder!" rang out, and Moore watched, perhaps stunned at the staging, as hundreds burst into song, singing "Browder is our leader, we will not be moved" to the tune of "The Battle Hymn of the Republic" before confetti rained down from the galleries.[15]

As the euphoria died down, a cross section of Moore's longtime friends—including Elizabeth Gurley Flynn, Mother Bloor, and Black members James Ford and Ben Davis—were all elected to the CPA's National Committee.[16] Her comrades chose her as one of the twenty alternates who would serve if someone had to step down. Leadership maintained that her alternate status was a testament to her popularity.[17] Moore read it differently. It was certainly a personal slight, given all the years she had given to the party. She also believed it was a sign that her fellow members had started to look "upon [her] with suspicion," because she publicly questioned Browder's new position on Black nationhood. Leadership, she claimed, didn't trust her enough to toe the line as an elected official.[18] Moore added this rebuff to the list of insults she faced from the party during wartime. But even as the slights accumulated, she still loved the day-to-day work, and the comrades she toiled with, enough to stay.

Her loyalty backfired. The CPA's top brass reassigned Moore, sending her off to Detroit—"one of the hardest districts" for political organizing, she later explained—to develop the local CPA chapter and recruit Black workers into its newly reconstituted rank and file.[19] Leadership gave her this assignment, they claimed, because she was one of their most capable recruiters. But Moore wasn't fooled. Detroit was "the graveyard of all the black communists," the place the party sent members "whenever they wanted to get rid of them."[20] Harlemites met her reassignment with equal dismay. "One woman told me it was like uprooting a big old tree," she recalled.[21]

Moore's pending departure was met with just as much disquiet at home. Frank was frustrated with her unwillingness to cover her share of the household responsibilities. And the prospect of uprooting their lives in Harlem only deepened Tom's resentment toward his mother, who always seemed to choose work over family. If his mother was hardly at home, even when she was in New York, then she would be virtually nonexistent in his life if she moved to the Midwest.[22] Moore was in a tough spot. If she wanted to keep her career alive, she needed to follow party orders. But she also needed to appease Tom and Frank if she had any hope of maintaining a home life when she came back. So she compromised—kind of. When Moore went to the Midwest, she took Tom with her.[23]

Moore's characterization of Detroit as a communist graveyard was unfair. The Motor City had its challenges, but it also had a lot of life. When she and Tom arrived in June 1944, they found a unique commingling of people, all living amid a wartime industry boom and a city bursting at the seams from the influx of Black folk looking for better jobs and a respite from southern racial terror. If they had stepped off the train at Michigan Central Station, Moore and Tom would have witnessed wartime Detroit in all its glory. A three-story train depot connected to an eighteen-story brick tower, it was the tallest depot in the country and the fourth-tallest building in Detroit—impressive, even to a pair of New Yorkers.[24]

If they gathered their bags and followed signs to the exit, they must have marveled at the huge bronze chandeliers hanging from the soaring, fifty-plus-foot ceilings and the dizzying array of travelers whose shoes click-clacked across the marble floors. They would have passed soldiers shipping out, workers heading home from a long day in the factories, and well-heeled white ladies dressed in the latest fashions and holding bags from the local Crowley, Milner department store. On toward the large bronze doors with mahogany trim they would go, until they stepped into Michigan's glistening city on the river.[25]

Detroit was a simmering city. Roosevelt had requisitioned auto factories for the war effort, and by 1941, Chrysler, Ford, and Hudson Motor plants had become ship, gun, and artillery factories. For many Black Americans, nothing sounded better than a northern city with tons of new jobs. But as production demands increased, so too did racial tensions. Black workers found their dreams of stable work and a better life difficult to realize. By day they were shut out of war-time factory and government jobs. And they had few places to lay their heads at night, thanks to inadequate housing and residential segregation.[26]

But they fought back. Like Harlem, Detroit had an established working class and an active Communist Party that had made inroads in the Black community since the Great Depression.[27] The 1932 Ford Hunger March, when three thousand workers marched from Detroit to a Ford Motor plant in Dearborn to deliver a list of demands to Henry Ford, put the party on the map. Members had worked with other progressive groups to organize the demonstration, and the International Labor Defense backed protesters after their violent arrest. After police killed Curtis Williams, a Black organizer, during the melee, it was the Communist Party that held a funeral for him.[28]

Detroit communists joined a vibrant, interracial, progressive front that included the NNC and the NAACP during wartime. And yet party members found it difficult to counter the fierce competition among the city's laborers for scarce resources—namely housing. The Detroit Housing Commission recognized the city as a hotbed for racial tension. In 1941, it announced the creation of the Sojourner Truth Housing Project: forty-six two-story redbrick row houses to be built in Detroit's 7 Mile–Fenelon neighborhood to house impoverished Black residents. White families vehemently opposed the housing development, as did middle-class Black folk in the area, each group fearing it would devalue their property and social status. Bending to white pressure, the Housing Commission instead promised the houses to white residents. The decision sparked two weeks of protest from working-class Black folk. Ultimately, officials split the difference, designating the housing project specifically for Black workers contributing to the war effort. This proved just as disastrous.

At 7:30 a.m. on February 28, 1942, several Black families driving "moving vans, laden with furniture," headed toward the newly built homes. They came to an abrupt stop when they saw "a picket line of 700 whites" surrounding the project on one side, several hundred Black folk facing off against them on the other, and a "thin line" of nervous police trying to keep the peace. Both sides had brought "clubs, brick bats, guns, and knives." And as soon as one of the moving vans started to nose its way through the throng of people, white men attacked. Bedlam ensued, and Detroit soon had a race riot to quell. Police arrested more than two hundred people by the end of the night, and forty more were injured.[29]

Still, the party soldiered on. Before Moore arrived, the Michigan Communist Party, under the leadership of a seasoned white organizer named Pat Toohey, unanimously voted to join the CPA. Toohey led Midwestern members in pledging their allegiance to the Allied cause and fighting for Browder's vision of a postwar future. Not long after, they got word that their newest member was on her way from Harlem. As soon as Moore set her luggage down in her new home, locals elected her as one of two Michigan CPA vice presidents.[30]

Toohey knew his communists had a "problem of development" when it came to Black leaders. So he begrudgingly obliged when the national office sent Moore to grow Detroit's network of Black activists. Her task was to re-create her Harlem successes, pulling in Black organizers from the host of other progressive organizations in town.[31] But both Moore and Toohey had their doubts about how well this partnership would work.

From June to November 1944, Moore dutifully did her part. She spoke at local CPA meetings and YMCA gatherings, attended picnics to drum up support for *The Daily Worker,* feted Black organizers when they came to town, and visited every Black church, women's club, and community organization that would open its doors to a Black woman communist.[32] She focused on the progressive movement's most patriotic projects: increasing the Black vote and desegregating wartime industries. At rallies and on the radio, she reminded Black Detroiters the key to their freedom and prosperity was reelecting President Roosevelt and supporting the CPA's host of progressive causes.[33]

These one-off shots at recruiting were useful, but Moore knew if she truly wanted to increase Black membership, she had to mount a full-court press. Four months earlier in New York, her compatriots had put on a Negro Freedom Rally to honor Black civilian and military contributions and reinvigorate the fight for Double Victory. It was a huge success, with tens of thousands packed into Madison Square Garden. Moore hoped to replicate it in the Midwest.

With the help of several local communist and progressive groups, Moore drew a multiracial and multiethnic crowd of twenty-three thousand, all packed into Detroit's Olympia Stadium on Friday,

October 27. Another ten thousand waited outside the arena, hoping there'd be space for them just to get through the doors. Vice President Henry Wallace opened the rally. But most Black Detroiters came to hear luminaries Paul Robeson, Adam Clayton Powell Jr., and Mary McLeod Bethune speak.[34] If there were any doubts as to why the national office had sent Moore to the Midwest, the massive Rally to Re-elect Roosevelt put them to rest.

Despite these successes, Moore's tenure in Michigan was short-lived and poorly received. FBI agents listening in to communists' conversations via wiretapped phones reported "persons who had lived in Detroit for a long time resented being pushed around" by Moore, "whom they considered an outsider." Locals likely took offense to anyone—but especially an older Black woman—coming into their community to take over operations. It didn't help that Moore was as headstrong as she was, and particularly opinionated. Some started to complain that she took an "un-democratic position" toward leading the group "and ha[d] practically everyone in the negro communities in Detroit antagonized."[35] Detroit's communists disliked the "old tree" from New York putting down new roots in their city.

The feeling was mutual. Both Moore and her son were miserable in their new home. Letters and newspaper reports from back home reminded Moore how much she missed her sisters, who were thriving in New York. Tom, now fourteen, fared no better. His mother had taken him away from his friends and father. He felt like a fish out of water. A few comrades overheard Moore saying that "she had a great many personal difficulties since coming to Detroit and she felt it would be best to be sent back to New York City." Leadership agreed. After all, she had achieved what she had been sent to do, dutifully raising the CPA's profile among Black Detroiters. Better to send her back home before she wore out her welcome. Moore and her son boarded a train bound for New York on November 8, 1944.[36] After just a brief stay in Black communism's graveyard, Moore now faced the task of resurrecting her old life.

Reviving her New York life was second nature for Moore. Perhaps to make amends for leaving in the first place, she agreed to marry Frank. They wed on January 22, 1945, and settled into their home on

Barker Avenue in the Bronx, part of the United Workers' Cooperative Colony that many called the Allerton Coops.[37] Home had never
looked so good. The Coops were the nicest place Moore had ever
lived. She now came home to a three-bedroom apartment in a sprawling Tudor Revival–style complex built in the 1920s: brown brick with
half-timbered gables, sloping roofs, and quaint chimneys. It felt worlds
away from the noisy, cramped Harlem walk-ups she was used to.

The two-block-long housing development on Bronx Park East
was considered a triumph for the working class. The United Workers' Association, which largely comprised communist-leaning Jews,
had pooled its money to build the complex and escape the cramped
quarters of downtown Manhattan and the first wave of government
Red-baiting in the 1910s. By the 1940s, the apartments were home to
mostly Jewish and Italian immigrants. But there were a handful of
Black leftist families who lived there as well—Moore, Frank, and Tom
among them. Although many claimed the different ethnic groups lived
in harmony, Black families were often relegated to the top-floor apartments, perhaps hinting the housing development wasn't as cooperative
as its name implied.[38]

Nevertheless, Moore was enchanted with her new home. The
newlyweds and their son lived in a top-floor apartment with freshly
painted white walls. Moore stuffed the small space with artifacts of
racial terror and resistance—everything from large lynching photos that she'd bring to protests to memorabilia from the Ben Davis
campaign.[39] Frank kept the place chock-full of antique furniture that
would have rivaled any store showroom.[40]

Tom was happier, too. Not only did their apartment sport beautiful
views of the Bronx Park, but the Coops also had a library, recreation
rooms, and a large playground with a basketball court. By day, he
went to Evander Childs High School with his lifelong friend, Charles
Turner, another Coops kid. In the evening, Charles and Tom gathered
with other kids in the Carmen Jones Club, a Black social organization
they'd fought for after they saw that the Jewish kids had one of their
own.[41] As Tom roamed in and out of their building, he often found his
mother "standing on the marble step stoops or on top of soap boxes
chatting with 'the people.'" Even on her days off, she loved to "cajole,
ignite and unite" neighbors and passersby with her straight-talking
screeds about Black liberation and class politics.[42]

But a new marriage couldn't keep Moore homebound for long. She jumped back into organizing in early 1945, continuing her work for the CPA. For Moore, the Popular Front ethos had never really died. She was still celebrating war workers, working with women's clubs, promoting FDR—who had just won an unprecedented fourth term—and supporting local club women and Black fraternal institutions like Harlem's Elks Lodge. In February 1945, she was a featured speaker at the lodge alongside Marcus Garvey's first wife, Amy Ashwood Garvey. Moore feted Amy again at a reception in August of that same year. Still a Garveyite at heart, she relished these moments when she could let her nationalist flag fly without anyone questioning her commitment to communism.[43]

A multiday March 1945 trip to Baltimore and Washington, D.C., epitomized Moore's commitment to the CPA as World War II wound down. Communist leaders sent her to Baltimore as an emissary, but the work she did there extended to all corners of the capital's Black community. Moore met with local NAACP members, Black Methodist ministers, cooperative leagues, and club women.[44] Drawing crowds by the hundreds, she lived up to her reputation as a master orator. During speeches like "Have Communists Abandoned the Fight for Negro Rights?," Moore reassured the crowds that the CPA hadn't lost its leftist thrust, and she visited the Cafeteria Workers Local 471 to reaffirm communists' commitment to labor unions and workers' rights.[45]

On the train ride home, Moore must have wondered whether she put up a good enough front, or if her audiences could see through the facade. Publicly, she epitomized the CPA's wartime ideals. But privately, she knew the organization was falling apart. There had always been a section of the party, spearheaded by longtime labor leader William Foster, that questioned Browder's postwar prognostications and his call to collude with capitalists.[46] Nearly a year into the CPA's tumultuous creation, more and more members had started to wonder if the widespread prosperity and racial harmony Browder prophesied would ever truly materialize.

These concerns came to a head in April 1945, when Jacques Duclos, leader of the French Communist Party, published a scathing critique of Browder's CPA known as the Duclos article.[47] Surprised but not deterred by the public rebuke, Browder doubled down on his post-

war vision. But many in the CPA agreed with Duclos, and they began
to more vocally denounce Browder's leadership. Private conversations spilled into the press as members chose sides. Debates over
party direction raged in *The Daily Worker* and even in the mainstream
papers.[48]

Moore was caught in the tumult. Whereas once she would joy-
fully bound into party meetings, spaces of camaraderie and collegial
debate, she now found these gatherings taking on a dark, even hys-
terical tone. The blood drained from her face and her stomach did
backflips as she watched her comrades turn on each other.[49] And with
all the infighting, Moore found she couldn't get a word in about her
primary concern: the party's disavowal of Black Nationalism.

In quieter moments, Moore began to wonder how and why she
had so easily capitulated to the CPA, and whether her lack of formal
education meant that she was not sophisticated enough to understand
the ramifications of its creation. The organizer had lost her sense of
belonging in the group. But more crucially, she had lost confidence in
her own voice and political compass. She was scared to speak up about
her concerns for fear of her comrades' wrath.[50] Moore was starting
to question whether the party was still the place for her, and yet she
feared she'd have no community to turn to if she left.

It wasn't as if she hadn't tried to voice her concerns. About a year
before, she'd asked for a meeting with party leaders to discuss their
treatment of Black members. She explained to Browder that after the
CPA's abandonment of Black Nationalism she was "no longer able to
see [her] own role in the Communist movement." She felt that she
and other like-minded Black members no longer had a place in the
organization.

Just a few months after Duclos's indictment of the party, the
National Committee called a three-day meeting to debate and vote
on a response. On the morning of June 18, Moore solemnly filed into
the New York District's old, dank party headquarters, where leadership hoped to hash out their new position and codify it in a draft
resolution. Browder, sensing the end was near, refused to attend. He
brooded in his office, just four floors above.[51] Moore watched as her
comrades stood up, one by one, and walked back their support of
Browder and the CPA.

The CPA had "abandoned the basic principle of a Leninist revolutionary organization" in broadening its political scope, said Peter Cacchione, an Italian American immigrant turned local political leader.[52] Browderism was a "complete departure from anything Marxist," Moore's friend and comrade Israel Amter asserted. They had all been too blinded by Browder's optimism to see that following him down this road "was bound to lead our Party and workers to disaster."[53] The room nodded in agreement.

It was all well and good for them to see the error of their ways. But as the meeting wore on, Moore wondered if anyone would address her concerns about the treatment of Black communists. She let out a sigh of relief when Harlem activist Rose Gaulden finally took the floor. Gaulden agreed that the Duclos article had correctly diagnosed CPA's missteps, and the blame they all shared. But this wasn't her primary concern. In Gaulden's estimation, "Negro working-class comrades felt in many respects as second-class members of the CPA." Gaulden questioned how her comrades could so easily accept Browder's claim that *all* Black people had opted for "their complete integration into the American nation as a whole . . . and not for separation." Such an approach, in her eyes, alienated Black party members and bolstered white racism.[54]

Browder had "allowed his faith in progressive capitalists" to blind him to racism against Black Americans, former ILD head William Patterson said, piling on. He cut through Browder's disavowal of the Black Belt Thesis, asking how Black people "under the conditions of extreme political, economic, and cultural exploitation and oppression" could be asked to reject self-determination in favor of integration. "The Negro remains an oppressed nation," he concluded, "despite our dropping of this issue."[55]

The next day, it was finally Moore's turn. She had read and reread her remarks ahead of time. But as her comrades quieted and looked to her, a rush of anxiety came over her. In a moment of pure candor, she admitted to the crowd that this dispute, and her attempts to soldier through it, had taken a toll on her. She took responsibility for her part in it. "Our opportunist line led us to work from the top," she offered shakily. "We neglected the little people who constitute the basic mass of all organizations." What gains they had made for Black folk, Moore said as she steadied herself, were in danger of evaporating as soon as the fighting ended.

If Black people were going to hold on to their wartime wins, then the party needed to return to its roots. Moore called on her comrades to reinvigorate the working-class consciousness they had developed among Black and white workers before the war and to always bolster this consciousness with a vigorous critique of racism. "Where we speak of Negro rights, we should explain and challenge white supremacy," Moore continued, now addressing the language of the draft resolution itself. "Too long, we have just said 'white supremacy' and let it go at that." But the party, and in particular its white members, had an obligation to practice the antiracism they often preached—to "root out white supremacy" and bring real, material change to Black lives. Moore cautioned against letting white members lead this fight. The Communist Party could not afford to keep up this paternalistic treatment of Black workers—not with the threat of fascism still looming large. It needed to recognize that Black people were their own best advocates in their fight for freedom.

Moore's rebuke was clear. But, perhaps to appease her comrades, she concluded on an oddly optimistic note: "I think we are going to come out of this in the whole," she reassured them. "I am sure that all of our comrades will go along with the correct position."[56]

This was a moment of much-needed reflection for Moore. She had been so entrenched in the Popular Front's struggles, in the day-by-day labor of fighting for the Black working class, that she had hardly popped her head up long enough to second-guess the party's wavering values. She now realized that what she had hoped was a minor tremor—a shake-up needed to mollify the Red-baiters and bring more members into the fold—was actually a full-blown earthquake. It had nearly swallowed up her life and the causes she cared about most.

She felt the tremors deeply. Until this point, Moore believed that taking a capacious approach to activism—collaborating with groups whose values were not always explicitly nationalistic—was the surest path to liberation. Being a Communist Party and Popular Front member had not only offered her a wide berth to work for "her people" but also granted her entry into social circles and closed-door meetings she would have once thought far out of reach as a young Black woman scrubbing floors and setting curls. She had seen firsthand how eschewing ideological purity had helped her promote Black liberation while building a broader leftist front. But the party's flip-flopping forced her to reckon with the possibility that, maybe, she had ceded too much ground.

She wasn't the only one facing the music. With an Allied victory on the horizon, America was preparing to shift back to peacetime, and the patriotic fervor that had ushered the CPA into existence was turning into despair. The postwar period would likely not bring the progress Browder had prophesied. Many began to suspect the "end of hostilities would bring depression, domestic political reaction, imperialist expansion, and the threat of war between the United States and the Soviet Union" instead.[57] As a result, rank-and-file party members began to question leadership or abandon it altogether. Membership plummeted, recruitment was down, and *The Daily Worker*'s circulation dropped. Something had to change.

In July 1945, the National Committee gathered for another three-day emergency meeting to vote on the previous month's draft resolution and the future of the party. Browder saw the writing on the wall and agreed not to oppose the adoption of the document. This time, there would be no balloons or singing, just a short discussion and a vote. In a matter of minutes, the CPA was dead and the Communist Party was reborn. Browder was out, and his main political opponent, William Foster, was the new chairman.[58] As Moore took stock of the personal and political wreckage, she questioned whether the organization had the wherewithal to regain its ideological footing, or whether it was lost forever.

Under this new leadership, the party returned to its Marxist-Leninist roots. It elected new delegates and attempted to recapture its working-class base.[59] But it didn't take long for Moore to realize that despite their proclamation of support for the Black Belt Thesis behind closed doors, many of her comrades were not interested in making it a central concern of the newly reconstituted party. A cloud of anxiety now hovered over Moore as she carried on with her party work. She found herself increasingly at odds with comrades whom she had once admired, and she was growing more and more impatient with her white counterparts' refusal to recommit to the Black masses. She was beginning to sound like a broken record when she broached the subject at meetings. The exasperation was mutual. "When I talked with the whites, they said I made sense," Moore recalled. "When I went to the Negro comrades, they wouldn't touch it."[60] Fresh off the Duclos debacle, fear of being attacked by party loyalists had quelled all opposition.

Moore understood her Black comrades' trepidation. Even when the party had officially supported the Black Belt Thesis, white leaders had ousted those they felt embraced it too fervently. Trinidad-born organizer and theorist George Padmore, for example, joined the party when he moved to the United States in 1924 and became one of its foremost Black organizers. He worked diligently for the international communist organization until he became disillusioned with the Comintern's slumping support for Black and anticolonial struggles in the 1930s. When Padmore formally resigned from his post, Comintern officials responded in kind. They expelled him from the party in 1934, accusing Padmore of making "deviations from the program of the Communist Party" and adopting "petty bourgeois nationalism." In other words, Padmore had drifted too close to Garveyism.[61] Moore's friend and comrade Richard B. Moore met the same fate nearly a decade later, expelled for openly supporting a Black Nationalist agenda.[62] Moore had made no secret of her Garveyite political groundings and her unwavering support of Black nationhood. She began to wonder when she might meet a similar fate.

Now, whenever she walked into a meeting or an event, she felt a "coldness and aloofness" settle over the room. People whom she once considered friends shot her sideways glances and moved out of her earshot.[63] Moore started to suspect that Hoover's agents weren't the only ones talking about her. She was right.

The FBI recorded phone calls between Ben Davis and Gil Green in which they wondered if Moore was in an "indefinite state of suspension with the National Office" for her recalcitrance. The activist was at "loose ends" with the party, and everyone could see it.[64] It wasn't as if Davis and Green didn't sympathize with Moore. They too had issued mea culpas for going along with Browder's plans, and they too believed the party should recommit to supporting Black rights.[65] Moreover, Davis and Green noted that Moore was still well regarded among Harlemites, who had little knowledge of the party's internecine squabbles. If they wanted to keep their community connections and postwar gains, they needed to keep Moore on the payroll.

She still had the organizing chops, the grassroots networks, and the fundraising savvy to run successful protests and campaigns. So the New York leadership put her back on the payroll as manager of Davis's 1945 reelection campaign.

Getting a Black communist elected at the dawn of the Cold War would be no easy task. During his first term, Davis had enjoyed widespread support from Republicans, Democrats, and labor leaders. And in an unprecedented move, Tammany Hall, the city's Democratic machine, stepped out on a limb and endorsed the communist for a second term.[66] This kind of cross-party coalition might have flown during the war. But now that the communists had doubled down on their Marxist principles, they were back to being outcasts. Stories of "Tammany and its communist allies working hand in hand to take over the city government" spread, and the Democrats revoked their support. Undeterred, Moore assured voters that Davis was "in the race to stay."[67] She intended to resurrect her old playbook: make Davis the face of the struggle against Jim Crow by day, and fete him at star-studded galas at the Golden Gate Ballroom by night.[68]

This time, she got a boost from an unlikely place: the baseball field. The fight against fascism had brought renewed pressure to end segregation in all aspects of life, including in America's greatest game. Activists had been calling for the league to desegregate baseball since the 1930s. The Congress of Racial Equality (CORE), a national, non-violent civil rights group, picked the fight back up after the war, picketing at Yankee Stadium during the spring of 1945.[69] Ever the political strategist, Moore made sure the Davis campaign was front and center at these demonstrations. As fans packed stadiums in the summer of 1945, she was on the street corners extolling the virtues of an integrated diamond. Moore admittedly didn't "know one base from the next." But that didn't stop her from attending "End Jimcro[w] Baseball" rallies, where she and Davis asserted that if Black "troops fought for the Four Freedoms overseas," then they deserved to enjoy those "freedoms in America's National Pastime."[70]

The plan worked. New Yorkers reelected Davis by a substantial margin that November, with more than a 40 percent increase in votes from the previous election.[71] What's more, the racial causes Moore cared about benefited from Davis's victory. Not only did she help desegregate baseball, but Moore had also used the campaign to fight against police brutality in Harlem.[72] Still, the second Davis campaign was, in many ways, Moore's communist swan song.

By the fall of 1945, both the campaign and the war were over, and Moore paused her party work. During the past year and a half, she had witnessed the rise and fall of the CPA, been planted and uprooted in Detroit, and carried Davis to victory yet again. With all this hard work, she hadn't had time to address the questions that kept her up at night: Could she be a communist *and* a Black Nationalist? And if not, what should she be at all?

CHAPTER 9

Postwar Blues

Wartime had made strange bedfellows of the United States and the Soviet Union, all in hopes of stamping out the threat of fascism. But the two countries never fully trusted each other. And any chance of continuing this uneasy postwar truce was shattered when beleaguered and tyrannical Soviet leader Joseph Stalin began marching into Eastern Europe to regain the territory his country had ceded during the war.[1] Harry S. Truman, now president after Roosevelt's April 1945 death, made it his mission to stop communist expansion at home and abroad, and he gave Hoover and the FBI free rein to terrorize communists and their associates, all in the name of protecting democracy. Whereas Roosevelt's New Deal had shown Moore how the government could create a safety net for its citizens, Truman's crackdown revealed how these same powers could be used as a dragnet.[2] She was afraid of getting caught up. She needed a break—some fresh air and a fresh start.

And so, when Moore got word from a friend at the National Maritime Union (NMU) that the Coast Guard was looking for workers, she hastily applied for a job. Moore became one of the few female members of the NMU, a group co-founded in 1937 by Jamaica-born labor activist Ferdinand Smith, who grew up in Sav-la-Mar just like Moore's first husband, Spraggs. The NMU and the Communist Party maintained close ties throughout the 1940s, bound together by their shared anti-imperialist sentiment and commitment to international working-class solidarity.[3] Now the NMU needed civilians to help escort "war brides," foreign women who had married American GIs while they were off fighting, to the United States. For the next year and a half, Moore sailed to and from France and England, spiriting "brides of every nationality (except German), to America."[4]

Some of these women were married to Black GIs, and some even had small children. Moore's official job was to reunite the families on American soil. Unofficially, she used the job to put some literal and ideological distance between her and the Communist Party she had once championed—and the FBI detail that had followed her because of it.

For weeks at a time, the forty-eight-year-old activist would come on deck, listen to the rhythmic slapping of the waves against the ship, and look out over the endless expanse. On sunnier days, she might have felt some clarity about her life. She knew it in her heart before she could ever say it out loud: her belief in Black Nationalist liberation was incompatible with the Communist Party. Though the party had talked a good game about Black rights and self-determination, they never truly practiced what they preached.[5] She had finally voiced her disillusionment out loud. And as the sun glistened off the water and warmed her face, it must have felt as if a weight had been lifted.

But on days when the cloud cover dimmed the Atlantic, Moore must have felt rudderless. To keep on as a card-carrying communist seemed impossible. But even still, she found it hard to cut the cord. Moore had given more than a decade of her life to the party, and she had neglected Frank and Tom in the process. While the rest of the country settled into postwar life, Moore felt as if she had been left adrift.

Black soldiers were feeling the postwar pangs, too. They had returned home to find themselves excluded from the figurative and material rewards for their sacrifices. But it was the uneven distribution of wartime benefits—most notably the GI Bill—that stung the most. The Servicemen's Readjustment Act, as it was formally known, provided college tuition and mortgage assistance, among much more. But what good was college tuition remission or mortgage loans when higher education was still segregated, and white folk still banded together to bar Black vets from buying houses in their neighborhoods? While white veterans climbed up to the middle class, their Black counterparts remained on the lowest rung. They were undereducated and lived in substandard housing, and many wondered what postwar white supremacy would bring to their doorsteps.[6]

Meanwhile, Moore found America's unique brand of racism had

followed her across the Atlantic. When Moore went ashore, English hotels barred her and the few other Black stewardesses from entering. White workers could stay, but Moore and her compatriots had to look elsewhere. Ever the organizer, Moore whipped her fellow steward- esses into action right then and there. She denounced their segregated accommodations and chastised the English for their role in slavery and colonialism. Her impromptu protest didn't get her a hotel key. But it did garner her a Scotland Yard detail. "They began to follow me everywhere I went in England after that," she later recalled. And they reported on Moore to her fans in the FBI.[7]

When her ship docked back home, Moore marched down the gang- way and toward a gaggle of reporters, where she gave portside inter- views about the racial dynamics on and off the ship. As a young blond woman from Yugoslavia made her way to the pier, Moore pointed at her and noted, "She has married a Brooklyn GI and already she knows that the Statue of Liberty means more to her than it did to me, a colored woman, who brought her here." Moore had used her spare time at sea to educate these would-be Americans about lynching, Jim Crow, and the racism at the root of American life.[8]

Moore put on a good show in front of the cameras, but behind closed doors her personal life was falling apart. While she was help- ing unite newlyweds, she was neglecting her own marriage. Sure, she spent some time at home in between her ten trips to Europe. But she knew every time she walked out the door and onto a ship, she was putting more than just physical space between her and Frank. Just two years after they tied the knot, their marriage was severely strained. She and Frank now parented Tom separately, if at all.

At sixteen, their son had become fiercely independent. Moore did her best to prepare him for her long absences. A steady paycheck from the Coast Guard meant she could leave him with money to pay the rent, buy food, and keep the telephone line and lights on whether Frank contributed or not. By her own account, she had raised an "hon- est, beautiful boy" who could take care of himself. For an absentee mother, Moore knew her son. Tom was truthful to a fault. He never lied about his whereabouts or how he spent the money she left him; he even confessed to dipping into the emergency fund to buy a new tire for his bike. But deep down, Moore knew every time she left for a protest, a parade, or a stint overseas, she was causing irreparable damage. "My son has paid the price," she later said about her commitment to the work. Though understated, it pointed to what would become one of her life's greatest regrets.[9]

Tom and Frank weren't the only ones moving on without her. The Communist Party's debates about race raged on while she was gone. Her old comrades, including Claudia Jones, Benjamin Davis, and Doxey Wilkerson, continued to discuss if and how Black separation and self-determination could be reconciled with the newly reconstituted organization. Some, like Wilkerson, now rejected the idea of a separate Black nation. He believed the Black Belt region of the South was diminishing in economic and cultural importance in the postwar era, and he felt the thesis was no longer appealing to Black folk in the party. Others, like Jones, argued that Black people's wartime civil rights gains could not "be considered a substitute for the right to self-determination," and that Black Nationalist liberation was not mutually exclusive with integration. Just like Moore, Jones still believed Black people's piecemeal acceptance of integration did not mean they couldn't still strive to build a separate Black nation-state.[10]

But it was the Communist Party's 1947 publication "Resolution on the Question of Negro Rights and Self-Determination" that ultimately confirmed where the organization stood. Regardless of what leaders and rank-and-file members felt about Black self-determination and separation, the organization had once and for all pulled the plug on it. Sensing this would ruffle feathers, leadership walked a thin line.[11] In the pamphlet, William Foster and others affirmed the importance of Black people's "struggle for full nationhood." Yet they asserted it could somehow be "achieved" in their current circumstances. Moore saw racism and capitalism as mutually constitutive; you couldn't eliminate one without the other. To make matters worse, her once-beloved organization now claimed it would not propose any specific theoretical solution to Black people's right to a Black nation, nor would it "raise self-determination as an immediate slogan of action."[12] For a tried-and-true Black Nationalist, this was indefensible. Any hope Moore had that the party might return to its nationalist roots after the war was gone for good. And she needed to go, too.

But uncoupling herself from her life's work was costly. Moore couldn't bear to pay the price all at once. Instead, she threw herself into working for Black-focused, communist-affiliated organizations like the National Negro Congress. After the war, the group was withering under the weight of reinvigorated Red-baiting, and hemorrhaging members and funds. But its Manhattan Council was still an active, militant collective and as good a place as any for Moore to camp out while she plotted her next steps.[13] She joined its executive board in 1947 as the organization made its last stand.

Moore found a congenial organizing partner in Victoria "Vicki" Garvin, seventeen years Moore's junior and the NNC's executive secretary.[14] Together they helped organize the massive "Death Blow to Jim Crow" protest in March 1947, successfully packing thousands into the Golden Gate Ballroom by connecting the event to the political scandal of the moment: claims that Mississippi senator Theodore Bilbo was also a known Klansman. Once they had a captive audience, they made another big push for Black voter registration. While some members gave rousing speeches in favor of enfranchisement, others fanned through the crowd with clipboards and pencils to sign up new voters, all while trying to rally the audience to support the NNC's renewed fight for desegregation in the private and public employment sectors.[15]

These mass gatherings made headlines, but Moore still garnered respect for her more quotidian protests, too. In the first half of 1947 alone, the Manhattan Council fought the Bronx Division of the IRS, which had engaged in discriminatory labor practices. They "declared war on negligent landlords," who were raising rents and evicting Harlemites. Alongside longtime labor activist and NNC member Bonita Williams, Moore led nearly a thousand tenants to the state capital in Albany to protest housing discrimination, only to be turned away at the capitol due to claims the group was sponsored by communists—a sign that the Red Scare was seeping deeper into leftist activism.[16] Still, Moore stayed the course. She spearheaded the group's picketing of Disney's *Song of the South*, a patronizing film depicting plantation life and Black workers. She called for a national boycott of the movie's "attempts to stereotype . . . the Negro people as subservient Uncle Remus ignoramuses."[17]

Yet it was the NNC's international work that kept Moore tethered to the embattled group. World War II transformed Black Americans' relationship with the African Diaspora. Many African and Caribbean countries had spent the first half of the twentieth century struggling under the weight of European colonialism. But the war had ravaged once seemingly indestructible countries like England, forcing them to focus on rebuilding their own communities rather than dominating others.[18] Black organizers across the globe spotted this chink in the colonial armor, and they exploited it. The late 1940s saw an explosion of anticolonial organizing led by a new generation of young African activists such as Kenyan leader Jomo Kenyatta and Ghanaian teacher turned political leader Kwame Nkrumah, who laid the groundwork for future nationalist independence struggles.

More than simply lifting the colonial veil, wartime had also opened national borders, making it easier for ordinary Black people to forge community across national lines and, for the first time, travel abroad. Soon enough, Kenyatta, Nkrumah, and many others had reinvigorated the Pan-African Congresses, a series of international meetings first convened in the early twentieth century. Trinidadian lawyer and activist Henry Sylvester Williams organized the First Pan-African Congress in 1900, during which attendees including W. E. B. Du Bois pushed for the independence and self-determination of peoples of African descent. Indeed, Black people had long conceived of themselves as part of a global nation, bound together by an oppressive past and a shared path to future liberation. But when Kenyatta, Nkrumah, and others—including Garvey's first wife, Amy Ashwood—began reconvening these global meetings after the war, they felt they were at a turning point.[19]

They weren't alone. An increasing number of Black Americans now recognized the similarities between their oppression and that of Black people suffering around the world.[20] NNC members, in particular, declared it a "new day" in which Black people the world over were "inextricably linked" in their struggle for civil and human rights.[21]

Meanwhile, Western nations were hard at work creating a federation of their own. After years of meetings, backroom deals, and formal alliances, a conglomerate of countries formally ratified the United Nations Charter on October 24, 1945. A new, international organization was born, and its inaugural members boldly declared their commitment to global peace, upholding international law, and protecting human rights.[22] "What an opportunity," wrote an

editorialist in *The Pittsburgh Courier.* Here was a chance for Black
Americans to "persuade, embarrass, compel and shame" the American government "into a more enlightened attitude toward a tenth
of its people!"[23]

In 1946, the NNC petitioned the UN to investigate the United
States' denial of constitutional rights to thirteen million Black people.
This strategy placed the NNC at the vanguard of what soon became
the defining mid-century organizing tactic adopted by Black Ameri-
cans: appealing to international governing bodies abroad to force
America to live up to its democratic ideals at home.[24]

The organization commissioned Herbert Aptheker, a bespectacled
white historian, Communist Party member, and dedicated student
of African American history, to draft an eight-page report on Black
people's ongoing systemic oppression, which they would submit to
the UN secretary-general. UN officials rejected it immediately on
submission. The interim head of the UN Secretariat of Human Rights,
Petrus Schmidt, claimed the NNC needed to provide clear proof the
United States was violating Black Americans' rights if they wanted
their petition to be considered. And even then, he warned the international organization had no power to intervene in domestic affairs.
Still, the NNC accepted Schmidt's challenge.[25]

Moore joined the fight in February 1947 as a member of the NNC's
Continuations Committee on the Problems of Minorities and the
United Nations.[26] Along with a small collective of historians and organizers, she set out to document the United States' human rights abuses
against Black people and gain signatures in support of the NNC's
petition to the UN. Moore must have felt the committee's goal was
promising, even as it seemed impossible. She also knew the odds were
stacked against the NNC—an underdog story of David and Goliath
proportions. But there was momentum, at the very least. Just two years
after the world had marshaled to end a genocide in Europe, the UN
was wary of allowing another. If there was ever a time for Black people
to shine a light on theirs, this was it.

Over the next few months, Moore worked with the NNC to hold
"People's Tribunals" in Chicago, Detroit, Los Angeles, Birmingham,
and a handful of other cities to gather firsthand accounts of oppression
from Black folk. She was optimistic at first. The collective found that
their Black brethren were eager to document their experiences, and

they even collected several thousand signatures in support of their petition. But the campaign soon stalled. Red-baiting had taken such a toll on the NNC that its network of nationwide chapters had atrophied. Members had left the organization in droves for fear of being branded communists. Without a large network of organizers across the country, remaining members like Moore had little hope of carrying out such an ambitious campaign.[27]

The NNC had one more trick up its sleeve: it could try to get other, more mainstream organizations to support its cause. Moore joined remaining NNC members in reaching deep into their networks, hoping to get the old Popular Front band back together for one last song. But fears about the group's communist ties caused many Black leaders, including Moore's old friend Mary McLeod Bethune, to withhold their support. The NNC ultimately failed in the face of anticommunist repression and, ironically, lack of support from the Communist Party itself, which was mired in its own struggles against the state. By the end of 1947, the HUAC had effectively ended the NNC's efforts to deal a "Death Blow to Jim Crow."[28]

Even amid this defeat, all was not lost for Moore. Sticking with the NNC during its last stand gave her a quick lesson in geopolitics. Although the campaign had failed, NAACP leader Walter White recognized that the petition had "captured the imagination" of Black Americans across the country, and he endorsed the NNC's strategy.[29] Moore took note. She had a hunch she would need to deploy the tactic again.

While the NNC was attempting to sway international politics, the United States was developing a new foreign policy of its own. On March 12, 1947, the president debuted the Truman Doctrine. Communism was on the move, Truman claimed, most immediately in Greece, where it purportedly threatened to take over the country amid civil war. In response, America would take its rightful place as the new world superpower by supporting democratic foreign governments that, like Greece, were "under attack" from "authoritarian" forces— all dog whistles the Truman administration used for communism.[30]

Nine days later, Truman issued Executive Order 9835, which established the first-ever loyalty program in the United States to root out communist influence in the American government. Although the goal was to keep communists out, it didn't take long for the widespread panic over subversive infiltration to creep in. In the end, very few government employees would be found to be actively engaging in subversive activity.[31] Yet fears of communist cavorting in the United States, coupled with Hoover's zeal for ferreting it out, resulted in the screening of more than five million federal workers and the end of many employees' careers—especially if they were Black or gay.[32]

Within a week, Moore had joined her fellow Harlemites and party members to formulate a rapid response. Alongside her comrades Claudia Jones and Ben Davis, she asserted "the civil liberties of the Negro people are gravely threatened by the Truman Plan for worldwide intervention and by the 'anti-Communist' witch-hunt accompanying" it. They interpreted America's new foreign policy as a "smokescreen to destroy democracy at home" and a way to ensure that "any Negro or white person who fights against Jim-crow status quo can be ruled 'subversive' and legally barred from employment."[33]

Moore then took the extraordinary risk of going public with her critique amid the government crackdown. She joined local activists and community leaders in insisting on the legal rights of communists, and any other group, for that matter, to function as an organization and a political party. "It is clear to us that if the government can suppress the Communists," the collective noted, "even organizations of the Negro people, fighting for Negro democratic rights, can be called 'Communist' and forced to disband."[34] By this point, Moore no longer counted herself among the party faithful. Yet she knew defending it against Red-baiting was the best way to guard Black people—herself included—from facing a similar fate.

As postwar Red-baiting ramped up, Moore doubled down on supporting progressive and communist-associated groups. In 1947, she became a member of the Congress of American Women (CAW), an organization born out of women's postwar frustrations with their second-class status inside and outside the Communist Party. CAW members "valued women's roles as housewives and mothers, challenged the social and cultural structures that excluded them from work and politics, and insisted that women could be different but still equal to men."[35]

Here, Moore found she could put her head down and work with a diverse group of women around CAW's three-pronged platform: child welfare, international peace, and the status of women.[36] The group's Brooklyn chapter was an especially familiar and welcoming place.

It comprised mostly Black women advocating for better access to employment and childcare.[37] But for Moore, the political was also personal. It was no secret she had always struggled to meet the demands of being a full-time organizer, a wife, and a mother. CAW was filled with women who faced these same challenges. Moore found comfort and some community among like-minded women, who saw her unique melding of her personal and her political life as a strength, not a shortcoming.

Perhaps this was why Moore had few qualms about putting herself squarely in HUAC's crosshairs as a CAW member. When the feds went looking for Moore in April 1947, they found her in Washington, D.C., marching alongside other CAW members, holding a sign exclaiming ONE WORLD—NOT TWO! It was her way of rejecting world leaders' efforts to carve up the globe into communists and capitalists.[38] When passersby asked Moore why she was protesting, she expertly explained, "I think that the State Department has embarked upon an imperialistic expansion policy. Representatives find it necessary to try to stifle the democratic voices of the people by trying to frighten them." Moore stated that she had met people from the European countries Truman claimed were under siege. It was clear to her the U.S. government didn't have their welfare in mind. It was simply "anxious to go to war with Russia."[39]

Yet standing with CAW was costly. The group never hid its communist associations.[40] It was a principled stance, but it served CAW members up on a silver platter to a hungry HUAC as the Red Scare ramped up. In its *Report on the Congress of American Women,* the anticommunist committee identified Moore as a "leader of the CAW delegation to Washington D.C." and published a detailed account of her work with the group and the party at large. Investigators were especially disturbed by the 1947 May Day celebration in Harlem, where Moore led thousands of marchers in demanding jobs, higher wages, and better housing.[41] Moore wasn't afraid of a little HUAC heat. But she also had a son and two sisters to protect. She decided to lie low for the rest of that year, and she did it well. Neither the feds nor the press could draw a bead on Moore, and her exploits during the latter half of 1947 remain a mystery.

In January 1948, Moore returned to the public eye ready to fight. Her focus was twofold: defending Black women's rights and dignity and organizing with one of the last remaining vestiges of the Popular Front. First on the docket was protecting her comrade Claudia Jones. When she got word the FBI had stormed into Jones's home and arrested her in the dead of night, Moore mobilized. Agents charged Jones with violating the Smith Act, another draconian attempt to root out sedition. Everyone could see the feds intended to use a particular Smith Act statute allowing for the deportation of "dangerous, disloyal, or subversive" persons to oust Jones, a Trinidadian immigrant. In a matter of days, Moore and her comrades started the Save Claudia Jones Committee to stave off this next wave of government repression.[42]

The Communist Party was caving under the pressure of it all. But Moore knew there were still a few stalwarts she could count on. She wasted no time calling on her old friends Mother Bloor and Elizabeth Gurley Flynn to help rally the club women, churches, and community centers across New York City to Jones's defense.[43] Under the watchful eye of Red-baiters, the trio pieced together a patchwork quilt of support by galvanizing thousands of Black, white, and immigrant women in New York, appealing to them on the grounds that many were "mothers of useful American citizens, some of whom died defending our country against fascism." With a diverse collective behind her, Moore led the defiant women's committee in issuing a rebuke, declaring they would "never permit ... the Truman Administration to put its clammy, and cowardly hands upon Claudia Jones, one of the highest flowers of Negro American womanhood."[44] Even those party leaders who were no longer fans of Moore had to admit they were impressed. National Chairman William Foster noted that the "women's committee for Claudia, headed by Audley Moore in Harlem, is getting a good start" in the defense campaign and lauded Moore for helping women "recognize the attack on Claudia as an attack on each of themselves."[45]

But women's work was dangerous work. To publicly defend a self-professed communist and Black immigrant like Jones could be costly

for anyone. To do so after the FBI and HUAC had already been tailing her for years put Moore's freedom on the line. Still, Moore never
wavered in her support of Jones or the many other communists eventually charged with treason and subversion. Moore always valued people over party politics and never tried to save herself by disowning her
past work and personal connections. That said, she also realized if she
was going to keep putting herself at risk, she needed to better armor
herself. The Civil Rights Congress (CRC), established in Detroit in
April 1946, was a space where Moore could build her citadel.[46]

CRC leadership comprised leftist activists still willing to take a
stand during the height of mid-century government repression. NNC
head Max Yergan, Harlem activist Adam Clayton Powell Jr., women's
rights activist Susan B. Anthony II, and *California Eagle* editor Charlotta Bass put their lives and livelihoods on the line to support the
CRC, while fearless leftist lawyer and former ILD leader William
Patterson headed the organization.[47]

Headquartered in New York, the CRC had a network of mostly
women organizers spread across forty to seventy chapters dotting the
country.[48] The NNC was gone. But this small collective was determined to pick up where it left off.

Organizers followed a playbook that the Popular Front had per-
fected: "skillful legal strategy inside the courtroom and 'mass pressure'
outside it."[49] Their first major success was the "Oust Bilbo" campaign,
in which they rallied white and Black luminaries, including physicist
Albert Einstein and dancer Katherine Dunham, to get Mississippi
senator Theodore Bilbo expelled from the Senate.[50] The CRC also
conducted a "Lobby to End Lynching" campaign, fought for school
desegregation, and pushed for an end to employment discrimination
across numerous sectors in the United States.[51]

This advocacy was all well and good for Moore, but she was especially interested in the CRC's defense of everyday Black folk—
especially Black women.[52] In the early months of 1948, every Black
newspaper she picked up in the Bronx reported the latest on Rosa Lee
Ingram, a Black woman, widow, and mother of twelve who eked out
a living as a sharecropper in rural Georgia.

November 4, 1947, had started like any other cold day on the farm
for Ingram, until John Stratford, a sixty-four-year-old white sharecropper whose farm abutted hers, came barreling toward her, rifle

in hand, admonishing her for allowing her animals to roam onto his parcel. The livestock and the land were not hers, Ingram reminded him—both of them were just tenants on the farm. If Stratford had an issue, he should take it up with their landlord. Enraged at Ingram's recalcitrance, Stratford got aggressive. The sound of the squabble sent seventeen-year-old Charles, sixteen-year-old Wallace, fourteen-year-old Sammie Lee, and twelve-year-old James racing to their mother's defense. They fought back, and the scuffle that ensued left Stratford dead from several blows to the head.[53] Local police arrested Ingram and her sons on the spot. Prosecutors initially charged Rosa Lee, as well as Charles, Wallace, Sammie Lee, and James, with Stratford's murder. The court eventually released the youngest, James. Rosa Lee and her other three boys endured a one-day trial in January 1948. Black people like Moore were hardly surprised—yet still appalled—when an all-white jury sentenced them to death.[54]

By this time, Moore was no stranger to defending Black women from the brunt of the law. She quickly pulled together an array of women across organizations in support of Ingram and her kids.[55] Moore also used the CRC to bolster the United Women and Youth to Save Mrs. Ingram in Harlem. This small, New York–based women's collective kept tabs on the trial, publicized the case, and formed a delegation to push the president to intervene on Ingram's behalf. As one member explained, the group "thought the least we could do was to help our Georgi[a] sister in her hour of need. Sojourner Truth went often to see President Lincoln about the rights of her people.... We are going to see President Truman about enforcing freedom and doing something about his own civil rights program."[56]

Audley Moore led this women's delegation to Washington, D.C., on March 18, 1948. The collective left Penn Station on a crisp, fifty-degree morning at 7:30 and checked in with the local chapter of the CRC upon arrival. When they tried to obtain an audience with President Truman, he instead sent Philleo Nash, a round-faced white anthropologist turned government official and special assistant to the president for minority problems, to meet with them. Nash toed the line, telling the group, "Presidential action is impossible." He tried to placate them with claims that the Department of Justice was monitoring the case.[57]

"Sir, the history of the State of Georgia merits our fears for Mrs.

Ingram and her children," Moore said, amid dissatisfied murmurs from her peers. "We are here for an answer from our President. What will he do for this Negro mother and her child?" Nash demurred, drumming his fingers on the table. Moore continued: "I'd like to know, sir, whether our government which is now appropriating billions of dollars to fight the Greek people . . . couldn't find one dollar somewhere for the eight small children of Mrs. Ingram now without any means of support?" The room grew tense, but no satisfactory response would come. Nash ended the session with a sheepish promise to convey Moore's message to Truman, then left.[58]

Moore didn't wait for Truman's reply. Instead, she joined with another group, the Negro Youth Builders, to support Ingram and her other children. She pushed Harlemites to donate funds for medical supplies, clothing, and food for the younger ones.[59] She allegedly even took one of Ingram's boys into her own home, fed him, and sent him to school for a short time.[60]

Like in the past, Moore's tendency to take matters into her own hands sparked controversy. The NAACP was hard at work supporting the Ingrams, joining the legal fight to repeal their convictions while also raising money for the family. But Moore questioned their effectiveness. She published a letter, said to be "written to her by Mrs. Geneva Rushin, daughter of Mrs. Ingram, stating that the Ingram children were suffering from influenza, that a doctor had said the younger children were ill from eating too much of the same kind of food, and that she herself needed a coat." In response, Moore claimed, she and the Youth Builders sent food, money, and clothes. The subtext was clear: although the civil rights organization had raised thousands of dollars to support Ingram, Moore believed the money wasn't making it to Ingram's kids. The NAACP fired back, publishing their own set of letters and claiming they had proof they were financially supporting Ingram. But when Moore still refused to back down, they resorted to Red-baiting. The NAACP publicly claimed Moore and her fellow activists all belonged to "left-wing" organizations—a dog whistle meant to highlight Moore's communist membership, which until now had not factored into this fight.[61]

Moore had seen the civil rights group deploy this strategy against the CRC before, and with some success. In a time when even mainstream organizations like the NAACP were under investigation for communist activity, smaller groups like the CRC made easy scapegoats to draw HUAC off their trail.

Still, the material gains for Black folk were why Moore stayed with the CRC, and the communist-leaning Left more broadly, even as the walls were closing in.[62] But as her fellow member Thelma Dale put it, "There's a limit to human endurance."[63] By the late 1940s, Moore had reached it.

A lot had changed in the few short years since the war's end. Moore had joined the Communist Party when it offered a radical vision of Black self-determination, not capitulation to racial capitalism. She endured the party's ideological twists and turns in the hopes that it might return to the nationalist ideals she knew and loved. But she could no longer deny the truth: it had relegated Black people, their rights, and their beliefs to the margins. It was time to cut the cord.

CHAPTER 10

Heartbreak

Wisconsin senator Joseph McCarthy detonated the blast that reduced the Communist Party to rubble. When he came into office in 1947, the obscure Midwestern politician deduced there must be at least a few communist-supporting spies in his midst. He soon found he could make a name for himself by ferreting them out of their clubs, government posts, and political organizations.[1]

Moore could see why McCarthy chose this plan of attack. By the late 1940s, every morning millions of Americans opened newspapers like the *Chicago Tribune* and the *Washington Times-Herald* and read salacious stories of men and women caught allegedly scheming for the Soviet cause. After dinner, they switched on their radios to hear HUAC's research director, Ben Mandel, explain how communists "recruited" young children. Families quieted as Mandel recounted stories of "young men and women who had left comfortable homes to follow the Communist will-o-the-wisp, with tragic results."[2] And after parents tucked their kids into bed, some settled in to read *Modern Woman: The Lost Sex,* a 1947 bestseller that analyzed life for American women after World War II. In it, sociologist Ferdinand Lundberg and psychologist Marynia Farnham claimed "the political agents of the Kremlin" were "beat[ing] the feminist drums in full awareness of its disruptive influence among potential enemies of the Soviet Union," a not-so-subtle nod to the Communist Party's support of women's equality.[3]

As McCarthy rose to fame, Moore watched the party become a pariah across the Left.[4] Whatever hope the communists had of restoring the organization to its Popular Front–era prowess was gone. McCarthy's offensive, it was clear, was the death knell. Whereas once Moore had packed banquet halls with athletes, Hollywood actors and directors, and labor leaders in support of a communist city council candidate, nowadays it was rare to find a celebrity or a construction worker brave enough to even acknowledge the party.[5]

By the summer of 1948, Moore's old comrades Ben Davis and Gil Green were at the epicenter of the anticommunist hysteria. When they stepped out of their car and into Manhattan's Foley Square, they found that the typically calm cul-de-sac of federal buildings had become a circus. Hundreds of officers corralled an equally large crowd of supporters carrying signs that decried the unfair jury selection and Wall Street influence in the trial of eleven members of the Communist Party's national board, known as the CP-11. Amid cheers—and jeers from counterprotesters—the eleven defendants walked up the wide granite steps of the newly finished courthouse. This would be Davis and Green's ritual for nearly a year: each day, they and the nine others watched their defense attorneys duke it out with state prosecutors over whether membership in the Communist Party made one complicit in the organization's alleged aim to overthrow the U.S. government by force. After enduring what was at the time the longest criminal trial in U.S. history, the jury convicted and sentenced ten of the CP-11 to five years in federal prison in October 1949.[6]

Moore's other comrades didn't fare much better. Claudia Jones's fight reached its disappointing but inevitable end when the Immigration and Naturalization Service convicted her for violating the Smith Act in 1953.[7] Those who weren't imprisoned or deported still buckled under the weight of government repression. Some, like Moore's fellow NNC organizer Esther Cooper Jackson, became "Smith Act Wives," women who had to shoulder both child-rearing and breadwinning responsibilities while the government targeted or imprisoned their husbands for "subversive activity." Moore rallied to support Cooper Jackson when her husband and fellow party member, James Jackson, went underground to escape the feds after his Smith Act conviction.[8] She found that even Black elders and luminaries were not spared. Although he wasn't a party member at the time, the federal government put W. E. B. Du Bois on trial for circulating a petition in support of the Stockholm Appeal, which called for a ban on nuclear weapons—a "treasonous" position for a citizen of a country continually on the brink of nuclear war with the Soviet Union.[9]

The writing was on the wall for Moore. "I think I'm about the only one in the party that resigned. They didn't expel me. I resigned," she offered as an epitaph to her Communist Party career.[10] Moore formally renounced her membership in late 1950, an agonizing decision for a woman who had worked "twenty-five hours a day" and "eight days a week" for the group, as she described it.[11] "I couldn't go any further the way I was going. I knew I was going wrong, absolutely wrong and detrimental to my own interest[s]," she finally realized.[12]

Moore had never been afraid of HUAC's hunters. For years, she had put her life and livelihood on the line to support those ensnared in Dies's and McCarthy's schemes. She was among the most stalwart supporters of the party's Harlem branches and its embattled Black members like Davis Jr., Jones, and Green. The threat of indictment or jail time alone was not enough to scare her away. But the thought of standing up for the organization when it had abandoned her people was too much to bear.

When asked about her time with the party, Moore would later say that while she did a lot of good work there, she was in "no position" to truly transform it. In her more sobering moments of reflection, she'd claim she had not done enough to develop herself—personally and politically—before joining the group. And this had led her to be too trusting of party leaders, even while they openly turned their backs on the Black Nationalist cause.[13] As heartbreaking as it was to leave, Moore knew she had to recommit to her nationalist work. But calling for a separate Black nation would be no easy task amid McCarthy's tyrannical reign.

At fifty-two, Moore was on her own in more ways than one. She and Frank were separated and headed toward divorce.[14] And Tom, now in his twenties, was out on his own. But for a workhorse like Moore, the worst of it was having no organizational home. For the first time in her life, she had to completely rethink the meaning of family and community and what it meant to be a Black Nationalist without an organization behind her.

Her sisters helped ease the pain. The Moore women weren't far from one another; Eloise and Loretta still lived in Harlem, even after Moore had married and moved to the Bronx, and they were a balm to her broken spirit. Moore visited with them often as she plotted her next move. But as she passed by old haunts and ran into former comrades on the street, she felt pangs of anxiety and regret. Giving up on the work that had defined her life was nauseating. She struggled to reconcile how the very same people who had defended the idea of Black nationhood alongside her for so many years could now abandon it, and all for favor with a political party on the edge of collapse. Even more heartbreaking was their reaction when she refused to make the same bargain. "They began to look upon me as an enemy," Moore recalled. "You're not supposed to think out of their realms."[15]

The one thing Moore seemed to retain from her past life was her FBI detail. The activist often stole a few sideways glances at the pair of white men, dressed in black business suits, thin black ties, and white starched shirts, who followed her at a distance from sunup to sundown. "Name your price," one of the agents murmured after closing the gap between them one day.[16] Hoover's boys had gotten wind of her heavyhearted resignation, and they hoped to grease her palms in exchange for names.

Tired of their incessant tailing and clandestine calls to her home, Moore decided to speak to the FBI directly. On a cold December day, she and Eloise marched down to the New York office on East Sixty-Ninth Street to be interviewed. Hoover's men brought the Moore sisters in, paraded them past a gaggle of white agents, and shut them in a bare room with bright lights and a couple chairs.

Once everyone was seated, the agents opened with their typical first question: Was Moore currently, or had she ever been, a member of the Communist Party? Moore didn't mince words. She readily admitted to once being among the party faithful, but explained she was gone for good. She refused to give them the satisfaction of thinking she had left on the government's account, though. Moore said her departure was "no sudden decision, that as early as 1945 she had begun to suspect that the CP was not sincerely interested in Negro equality, and was merely using the issue to promote their own interest[s]."

The agents must have started salivating at Moore's candor. Maybe she could be recruited to help hunt down her former comrades. They kept pushing. What were the "specific nature and dates of your CP activity"? Moore redirected. "The Negro was oppressed by the White man," she lectured. "Any activity in which I have been engaged was motivated only by [my] desire to improve the lot of the Negro."

Were you part of the New York State Communist Party? "I don't know if I should answer that question," Moore replied initially. Perhaps realizing that she had already admitted as much, she added that it didn't matter, as she had "never held a position of actual leadership with the party because [she] had not been trusted."

What about communist espionage? She had "never participated in such activities, had no knowledge of such activities, and at no time in the past would have acquiesced to suggestions or demands."

Moore was tough to crack. She wasn't being blatantly uncooperative, but she wasn't giving her interrogators what they wanted, either. Having spoken her piece, Moore took it upon herself to wrap up the interview. She would "not be a witness against Communists or Communism," and she did "not wish to be interviewed again." She and Eloise stood up and strode out of the room. The agents concluded Moore was "extremely bitter with regard to the race problem" in the party and the nation at large, and that she was "interested only in denouncing 'white men.'" They let Moore leave, but they didn't let her out of their sights. Hoover would continue to receive reports on her for decades to come.[17]

If Moore wasn't going to be a paid operative, then she needed to find another way to survive. She had to return to the only tried-and-true job available to a Black woman without a formal education: domestic work. In her quieter moments, Moore must have marveled at life's cyclical nature. Now in her early fifties, she was back to where she had been in New Orleans nearly thirty years before: no family save her sisters, little money, and no political home to call her own.

She kept one eye on the fight for Black rights while she scrubbed floors to make rent. She was especially attuned to the aftereffects of *To Secure These Rights,* the President's Committee on Civil Rights' 1947 report on the legal and judicial obstacles Black Americans faced in the United States. Unsurprisingly, the committee found America had much work to do in securing liberty and justice for all. The following year, to improve America's reputation on the global stage and road test later civil rights reform, President Truman issued Executive Order 9981, which outlawed racial, national, and religious discrimination in the armed services.[18] Moore might have initially thought the order was too little, too late, coming three years after the end of World War II.

But when she got word of a fight breaking out on the Korean Peninsula, she knew the order would soon be put to the test.

When Truman declared America's support for South Korea in June 1950, Moore's stomach sank. Under Truman's new order, if Tom was drafted, he would likely see combat in Korea. She feared her boy wouldn't get to experience any life before he was forced to face death overseas. And so, with the help of a white employer, Moore paid for Tom to enroll in Mexico City College for a while. It wouldn't keep him out of the war forever. But it would let him see some of the world first. "I sent him to Mexico so he could at least experience a little bit of freedom," Moore later said. "Whether he was going to come back alive or not, I wanted him to feel what it was like to walk in the street without fear ... [fear] that he was going to be mowed down."[19]

Tom stayed abroad until he was called home to join Truman's newly integrated armed forces in 1951. While Moore was enduring the iciest front of the Cold War, shut out from friends, family, and former activist networks, Tom had been thrown into the heat.

Moore's new priority in life was to do what she could to bring her son home alive. She joined the American Peace Crusade (APC) as soon as Tom shipped out. The APC opposed the Korean War out of reasonable fear it could lead to nuclear war between the United States and the Soviet Union. The group advocated for an end to nuclear armament and the removal of General Douglas MacArthur, whom they believed to be the architect of the ill-advised war. The collective also called for the complete withdrawal of U.S. troops from Korea.[20]

The APC was no Communist Party, but it had some familiar faces. Moore joined the New York chapter and worked alongside other Black activists and comrades including W. E. B. Du Bois and Paul Robeson. She made the March 1951 pilgrimage to Washington, D.C., where APC supporters from across the nation protested and demanded an audience with State Department officials.[21] Four months later, she joined other Black mothers for a peace protest and picnic, during which they presented a petition to the UN calling for "a successful and immediate conclusion of ceasefire negotiation in Korea." Moore later called the APC a "great opportunity for the Negro women in the Harlem community to express their deep desire for a ceasefire ... and for a permanent peace." She also tied the fighting abroad to injustice at home, remarking that "our women are indignant over the treatment of our Negro troops at the front, who are... forced to fight for a democracy which neither they nor their loved one[s] enjoy in the United States."[22]

Predictably, Red-baiting took a toll on the APC before it could truly get off the ground. The group's antiwar stance was considered unpatriotic at best and proof of communist infiltration at worst.[23] The group limped along until the late 1950s, fending off multiple HUAC attacks. Meanwhile, Moore's public involvement in the organization made her even more of a political pariah.[24]

Tom returned from the war two years later, wounded, with two Purple Hearts and a different outlook on life.[25] In yet another heartbreak for Moore, she found the war had not radicalized Tom as she had hoped. Her only child was not interested in joining the struggle for a separate Black nation. Instead, he was set on using his GI Bill benefits as most were: to buy a house, get a college education, and settle down.[26] The world opened up for Tom postwar as he entered the middle class. Meanwhile, his mother's world continued to shrink.

When Black actress Beulah "Beah" Richards published her wildly popular 1951 poem "A Black Woman Speaks of White Womanhood, of White Supremacy, of Peace," it electrified Louise Thompson Patterson, a friend of Moore's and a fellow activist. The poem eloquently captured the horrifying experiences of being a Black woman amid mid-century racism and sexism, and it got Patterson thinking about the need for an organization focused solely on Black women's struggles. But she needed a co-organizer; she couldn't marshal the atrophying leftist forces all on her own. And so Patterson approached Richards, and after a few all-night planning sessions in Patterson's Harlem apartment, the pair established the Sojourners for Truth and Justice.[27]

Even amid political repression, the duo pulled together a starstudded group in a matter of weeks. It took a little convincing. But Patterson's fellow Communist Party and Popular Front members— among them, Paul Robeson's and W. E. B. Du Bois's wives, Eslanda Robeson and Shirley Graham Du Bois; newspaper editor Charlotta Bass; and young, up-and-coming playwright Alice Childress— soon joined the Initiating Committee and issued "A Call to Negro Women."[28]

"The time has come for us Negro women of these United States to personally address this government for the absolute, immediate, and unconditional redress of grievances," the committee proclaimed. "We cannot, must not, and will no longer in the sight of God or man sit by and watch our lives [be] destroyed by unreasonable and unreasoning hate.... We have watched our husbands and fathers burned, quartered, hanged and electrocuted by hooded and unhooded mobs.... We have seen our sons rotting in prison, we've seen them poured into foreign wars in defense of a government that denies them equality back home.... We have seen our daughters raped and degraded, and when one dares rise in defense of her honor she is jailed for life." It was as strong a rebuke of American brutality as had ever been heard from the Black Left.

"We therefore, issue this call. Negro women of the United States, dry your tears, and in the spirit of Harriet Tubman and Sojourner Truth, ARISE... come to Washington and speak your mind."[29]

The plan was to bring hundreds of Black women to the nation's capital during the final days of September 1951 to demand justice from the Truman administration.[30] As soon as Moore read the call, she was in. Here was a group of Black women bold enough to denounce the American government and carry the banner of Black women's self-defense and self-determination. In other words: her kind of people.

In the early hours of September 29, Moore gathered excitedly with other women from across New York on the platform at Penn Station. After greetings and introductions, they fastened Sojourners buttons to their overcoats and boarded the noon train to the nation's capital.[31] Once in D.C., they climbed onto a bus that took them to the Cafeteria Workers Union building to rendezvous with other Sojourners from across the country. Moore found herself among a dynamic, intergenerational group of Black women nearly one hundred strong: activists, domestic workers, factory employees, mothers, and housewives, all ready to mobilize against injustice.[32]

Moore took her seat for a late lunch, pausing between bites to get up and greet old leftist comrades like Patterson, Robeson, and Du Bois. As the plates were cleared, she settled in to listen to introductions and well-wishes from the group's founders and organizers, including an exhilarating speech by the eighty-eight-year-old National Association of Colored Women leader and suffragist Mary Church Terrell.[33]

The mood then shifted as several women made their way to the front of the room to testify. The chatter stopped and clanking forks stilled as Mrs. Emma Westray of Portsmouth, Virginia, told the heartbreaking story of how a New York policeman had gunned down her son. Dorothy Hunton and Eslanda Robeson shared how the government had targeted their husbands, Alphaeus Hunton and Paul Robeson, revoking their passports and sentencing them to prison for their Communist Party and Civil Rights Congress activism.[34]

The next day, Moore woke up ready for a fight. The Sojourners planned to divide and conquer. Leadership tasked attendees with fanning out across the city to demand audiences with Washington leaders. Moore was among the Sojourners who went to the Pentagon to meet with Secretary of the Army Frank Pace. The Defense Department was on notice; a few weeks before, Beah Richards had sent a letter warning them the Sojourners were on their way to demand answers about the department's treatment of Black people at home and abroad. When the Sojourners showed up on October 1, officials agreed to let six representatives into the building, largely to avoid a public kerfuffle in front of the press.[35] Moore was one of the handful who slipped past the door.

Once inside, the delegation marched in a phalanx toward Pace's office—until Major General Frank Shaw intercepted them. Shaw corralled the Sojourners into his office as others questioned why a gaggle of Black women had stormed the building. He shut the door and turned to face the group, and Moore seized her chance.

She pulled out a Black Sambo doll, a childlike, racist caricature of the Black slave who dances for and entertains the masses. Shaw and the other Sojourners sat in silence as she wound up the "black as coal" doll, outfitted in "loud clothes and vest and little derby," and set it down so it would dance across his desk. Once the toy had finished its stilted routine, Moore picked it up and turned it over to reveal a label: "Made in Japan."

Moore excoriated the general, who sat there, stunned: "Is this what the army is exporting to Japan? Where did they get the stereotype if it was not from you?" Shaw called the meeting to an abrupt end, and the other Sojourners, equally stunned, filed out of the room.[36]

At the end of the day, Moore returned to the Cafeteria Workers Union's hall to hear how the other delegations had fared. Unable to obtain an audience with Attorney General Howard McGrath, sixty Sojourners met instead with Maceo Hubbard, assistant to the director of the civil rights section of the Justice Department, and demanded to know why the federal government refused to protect Black southerners against white mobs. Five Sojourners called upon Representative William L. Dawson, a Black lawyer and Democrat from Chicago, and demanded that he "take a stand on Cicero," a Chicago suburb where thousands of whites had attacked Harvey Clark, a Black veteran who rented an apartment in the otherwise all-white neighborhood. The rest of the Sojourners held a silent vigil on the White House lawn to protest President Truman's refusal to meet with them.[37]

For many of the women, the protest was "the most inspiring experience in their lives." They declared then and there the organization "must fan out to every corner of the country to arouse Negro women." And fan out they did. By the end of 1951, organizers had established chapters across the country, from Los Angeles to North Carolina.[38]

Moore became an active member in the New York City branch. This new political home gave her a renewed sense of hope and purpose. Some days she could be found helping members raise awareness about Harriette and Harry Moore (no relation), leaders of the Florida NAACP who were killed on Christmas night, 1951, when the Klan planted a bomb under their bed.[39] In "Our Cup Runneth Over," their press release about the tragedy, the Sojourners reminded Americans that "Black women the world over know far too well the tearless grief of Mrs. Rosa Moore, whose 71 years of sacrifice gave to the world a fighting son of the Negro People, Harry T. Moore." The Sojourners spread the word of Harriette's mother's anguish, how she "sat by the bedside of her dying daughter," and how her loss "pierced the side of every Negro mother."[40]

On other occasions, Moore's work with the Sojourners hit closer to home. In early 1952, she came bounding into the Harriet Tubman Center on Lenox Avenue, where the local chapter was meeting, and exclaimed, "You know what they have on at the Apollo Theatre? They have a white man down there with a little dummy, he is a ventriloquist, and he has an act about coming up to Harlem cause that's where black women are a dime a dozen." At Moore's behest, the women bolted down the street to the theater, bought tickets to the show, and scattered themselves among the audience. One by one, each Sojourner stood up and screamed when the ventriloquist began his racist routine: "Stop that man! He's defaming our women." So disruptive were the Sojourners the comedian ended his performance then and there.[41]

Moore loved the Sojourners' radical politics and protest style. But others on the Black Left did not. NAACP leaders rejected the Sojourners' attempts to collaborate for fear their communist affiliations would sink the civil rights group.[42] Other organizations—both white and Black—grew suspicious of the Sojourners, believing they had taken a "nationalistic turn."[43] Leftists feared the group's exclusive focus on Black women's liberation would undermine progressive organizing. The Sojourners were disappointed by the lack of support. But they soon had bigger problems.

The Sojourners had hoped that by staying laser focused on Black women's rights, they could divert attention from their communist associations and weather the Red-baiting era. But they made the wrong gamble. FBI agents began surveilling the group in September 1951, anticipating that initial sojourn to Washington, D.C., to confront the government. Quick-fire reports among agents chronicled a growing concern that "prominent women" such as "Mrs. Paul Robeson, Mrs. Willie McGee, Mrs. Shirley Du Bois, and Mrs. William Patterson" would attract hundreds of Black women to D.C.[44]

The FBI grew concerned the Sojourners were attempting to "disguise" the "true Communist character" of their organization by duping everyday women who were just interested in civil rights and indoctrinating them into communism. The bureau's biggest concern, though, was the Sojourners' broad appeal—their ability to rally large numbers of Black women at a moment's notice. The Sojourners' roster of activists certainly didn't help their cause. Agents who infiltrated the organization reported that almost every member of the New York City chapter, including Moore, was already on the bureau's list of "subversives."[45]

With the Washington, D.C., demonstration wrapped, the FBI's next big worry was the Sojourners' proposed March on Georgia, where they allegedly planned to gather hundreds of Black women in support of Rosa Lee Ingram, who was still imprisoned. Agents claimed the Sojourners were wrangling "a thousand or more colored women to protest the imprisonment of Rosa Lee Ingram and her sons," and to "forcibly take 'Mother Ingram' from prison" in "ho[pes] of provoking an incident that will cause bloodshed and 'spark a revolution throughout the South.'" They alleged that the D.C. demonstration the year before was just a "test movement" for a full-on prison break in Georgia.[46]

Some of that intel was correct, but the FBI grossly exaggerated the scope of the Sojourners' plans. At their Eastern Seaboard Conference in March 1952, activists had developed a "plan of action" that included organizing a mass demonstration in Georgia.[47] The Sojourners never intended to forcibly free Ingram. Nevertheless, the FBI worked with Georgia's governor, Herman Eugene Talmadge, to thwart the group.[48] In the days leading up to the alleged march, Talmadge positioned eighty state troopers at the prison and deputized them to "take over all guard activity outside the prison walls and conduct active patrols 24 hours per day."[49]

If it was a standoff the officers wanted, they were sorely disappointed. Unable to organize a large protest in such a short time, the Sojourners instead sent a small delegation to visit Ingram in prison. When the group arrived, armed state patrolmen turned them away, claiming that a local judge had issued an injunction against their entering the building.[50]

According to Moore, the group largely disbanded after the "Ingram affair."[51] The lack of support from other leftist movements amid FBI surveillance and rampant Red-baiting was a lethal combination. Many of the Sojourners kept organizing on their own. Louise Thompson Patterson and Esther Cooper Jackson focused their energy on freeing their husbands, both of whom were either jailed or underground due to McCarthyite repression.[52] Others, like Claudia Jones, kept organizing for Black rights even after the government deported her to London.[53]

Although Moore had made it clear to the FBI that she was done with the Communist Party, HUAC still hounded her.[54] In the years to come, prosecutors would even start using Moore's name to ensnare others in alleged acts of treason. Questions like "Do you know Audley Moore?" and "Have you ever been present at a meeting in which Audley Moore spoke?" are strewn across HUAC and Subversive Activities Control Board transcripts from the 1950s.[55] One thing was now clear: it was becoming increasingly dangerous both to be Moore and to know her.

CHAPTER 11

Not Your Negro

In the early 1950s, friends, neighbors, and old comrades who passed Moore on the streets of Harlem or the Bronx found a shell of the woman they once knew. She was devastated, disoriented. It's "very, very hard, when you're seeking and you're searching and you can't explain yourself," she said of this period in her life. "You don't have the development enough, the educational background, to be able to put into words how you feel." Commiserating with her closest confidants, Moore confessed to feeling as if, somehow, she had wandered astray from a once-clear political purpose. She just couldn't see the next step forward.[1]

At her core, Moore still believed that Black Nationalism was the only political ideology radical enough to meet the repression of the moment. It was something she felt, deep within her, as much as it was something she understood. But with the Cold War raging, her activist networks destroyed, and the Civil Rights Movement gaining steam in its fight for integration, the future of a thriving Black nation-state felt tenuous. Riding the train, wandering the city streets, and cleaning white women's floors, Moore pondered if or how she might find a new political purpose and home.

If there was any place that might have the answer, it was Harlem. Moore's old neighborhood was very much still Garvey country. Some remained dedicated to his Back to Africa push, and others had picked up the baton, envisioning a Black nation here on American soil. The sheer number of Black people in the upper Manhattan neighborhood ensured that its separatist enclaves survived, even as civil rights leaders encouraged Black people to integrate into the American promised land.

In search of inspiration, Moore started returning to the street corners she had frequented during her first days in New York. There,
towering above the thrum of 135th Street, she found Carlos Cooks, a
slender young man with deep-set eyes and a black pencil mustache,
shouting from a stepladder he had set up on the corner. Born in 1913
in the Dominican Republic, Cooks was the child of Garveyite parents
who immigrated to New York in 1929, just a few years after Moore
had settled in the city herself.[2] Cooks arrived on American soil just
after Garvey had shipped out from New Orleans for good, never to
return to the States, and they stayed true to the UNIA leader even as
he was forced to run his movement from abroad for the next decade.

During the 1930s, Cooks enthusiastically joined the UNIA's enduring subsidiaries such as the Universal African Legion and championed nationalist causes including defending Ethiopia against Italy's
invasion in 1935.[3] His commitment to African liberation so impressed
Garvey that the UNIA leader chose Cooks to head the organization's
New York Division in 1938. Cooks took on the role with aplomb.
He donned military dress, just as his idol Garvey had done before
him, and marched around Harlem proselytizing for the famed Black
Nationalist until Garvey died in 1940.

Cooks then took it upon himself to fill the leadership void. Within
a year of Garvey's death, Cooks started the African Nationalist Pioneer Movement (ANPM), a group "composed of people desirous of
bringing about a progressive, dignified, cultural, fraternal and racial
confraternity among the African peoples of the world."[4] Every week,
Cooks marched out into the Harlem streets, sometimes adorned in
a silver-buttoned, high-necked black suit and a leopard-print fez,
unfolded a stepladder, climbed atop it, and extolled the virtues of
Black self-determination for hours on end. Potential converts weren't
the only ones eagerly watching from the crowd. Hoover's agents were
there, too. Cooks's radical message earned him a swift draft into the
military during World War II to keep him quiet—the government's
preferred way of dealing with dissidents when possible.[5] But much to
their chagrin, Cooks survived the war and returned to Harlem, ready
to dedicate his life to cultivating Black Nationalism.

The young speaker first caught Moore's attention when he reen-
ergized two key trademarks of her old days in the nationalist movement. The first was Garvey's penchant for elaborate parades through

the Harlem streets. Cooks organized short yet showy processions featuring members dressed in full regalia, waving red, black, and green flags, and carrying signs that boldly proclaimed, BUY BLACK, AFRICA MUST BE FREE, and WE ARE AFRICANS, NOT NEGROES. This last sign was a sticking point for Cooks. The use of the word "Negroes" was something he often debated in the second prewar tradition he had revitalized: the *Street Speaker* newspaper.[6] Articles in it declared, "We are against all caste names whether Negro, Colored, Sepia, Tan, or 'what have you.' We prefer to be called what we are, Black Men and Women."[7]

Of course, Cooks was hardly a pioneer in these sorts of debates. He was one in a long line of Black activists who had been interrogating the use of these words for decades. In 1919, Black socialist W. A. Domingo asked readers of his newspaper, *The Messenger,* "What are we, Negroes or colored people?" In response, Domingo didn't call for the outright eradication of the Negro moniker. But he did argue for its capitalization. Most crucially, he sparked debate about when, if ever, white people should use the word.[8] Moore was likely introduced to the issue when she was first settling into Chicago's South Side. Like most Black migrants, she dutifully read *The Chicago Defender* during the 1920s and 1930s when its editor Robert Abbott published editorials calling for "the term 'Negro' [to] be completely eliminated and the word 'African'" to replace it. The former term psychologically alienated Black people, or so the argument went.[9] The Garveyites Moore was still in touch with back then were also thinking through the terminology; some had suggested the UNIA reconsider using "Negro" in its name because "African people violently reject the term."[10] The debate over the pros and cons of the word raged in the Black press and at the pulpit. Readers and reverends alike discussed the issue well into the mid-century.[11]

In the early 1950s, Cooks took the issue to the streets of Harlem. Moore would stop and listen to the ANPM leader shout from his stepladder. "It is the devout policy of white supremacists to make Negroes out of every Black man, woman, and child," he preached in a Garvey-like cadence. "The word, Negro, is a weapon and a scheme of whites to disassociate Black people from the human family and their homeland, Africa." He called upon Harlemites to "be rid of that word, Negro, as a racial classification of the African people" as they passed him, and to embrace their "true racial identity—Black people or Africans."[12]

Now Moore was intrigued. The climbing population of Harlem had reached its zenith in the 1950s.[13] But even still, the material realities of daily life were at a nadir. Overcrowding and high unemployment were mainstays for Black folk in New York. Moore felt this acutely, now in her fifties and perpetually on the brink of financial destitution. Black activists across the country were starting to successfully integrate schools, parks, restaurants, and movie theaters, but it often felt as though the spoils of democracy and opportunity never spread to Harlem. Moore's people were still segregated, still unequal, still unemployed, and still fighting.

White folk would go to great lengths to make Black people believe they were inferior, this much she knew. But until this point, Moore had never truly considered how white people used language to debase Black people—how a word like "Negro" and the ideas of vileness, backwardness, and ugliness associated with it had acculturated Black people to their own oppression.

Moore ruminated on this as she walked downtown to the Frederick Douglass Book Center, run by her former comrade Richard B. Moore, a slender man with rich brown skin, a square face, and discerning eyes. The center was on 125th Street between Seventh and Lenox Avenues. Richard named the small outfit, no more than twelve feet wide, with a slim storefront window featuring a few bestsellers, after his favorite Black thinker and orator.[14] Born in Barbados in 1893, Richard immigrated to New York in 1909, arriving in the harbor amid spectacular fireworks on July 4—an auspicious start to his life of "freedom" in America. But daily racism at school, at church, and in Christian groups like the YMCA quickly taught the young Caribbean migrant that the right to life, liberty, and the pursuit of happiness didn't apply to him.[15]

Like Audley, Richard found a political home among local communists because of their firm stance on Black self-determination. By 1925, he was part of a cadre of well-known Black organizers who called upon the Comintern to adopt the Black Belt Thesis and support Black-centered, communist-led initiatives.[16] Audley and Richard followed similar activist trajectories. During the Depression, they both served on the Harlem Scottsboro Defense Committee, advocated for Ethiopian independence, and pushed party leaders to center the Black experience.[17] Both were master orators who were known to "keep folks spellbound" on street corners for hours, speaking about "communism in the cadence of Garvey."[18]

By World War II, both had also grown tired of having to build their Black liberation dreams according to communist blueprints. But Richard questioned the party's commitment to Black liberation earlier and more openly than Audley did. It put him on the outs with the organization as the CPA rose to power and Audley buckled down to make peace with the new order.[19] When Audley offered her postmortem on the Communist Party, she said anyone who tried to bring up its commitment to Black self-determination was expelled. She was surely thinking of Richard, who had met such a fate in 1942.

As luck would have it, Richard's break with the party fostered new spaces of inquiry for Audley and her sisters. By the early 1950s, Richard was "hardly ever seen on 125th Street without appendances of brown paper packages neatly wrapped and carefully tied with a cord to be untied and reused" as he walked to his book center. Eloise, Audley, and Loretta were regulars, often stopping by to see what literary or historical work he was going to unwrap and add to his inventory: perhaps Richard Wright's *Black Boy,* or *Life and Times of Frederick Douglass,* the former slave turned abolitionist's third autobiographical account of his life.[20]

Richard purposely called his operation a center rather than a store. It was, in fact, so much more than just a bookshop. It was a place to store his massive collections, a way to disseminate literature, and most important for Audley and her sisters, a gathering spot for Black radicals—especially nationalists.[21] Audley felt at home perusing the narrow shelves, whose order mostly made sense to the center's proprietor. She would scan his holdings, sometimes passing a book over to Loretta or Eloise. The click of the lock and waft of air rushing in alerted the Moore sisters to a newcomer, be it a Black army vet, a group of African students, or just anyone whose curiosity had led them to wander into a known former communist's outfit. As she drifted away from the Communist Party, Audley gravitated toward Richard's center. It was a safe haven to discuss Blackness, nationalism, and the nuances of language that arose from the movement—one of the few left. The space soon gained a reputation as one where patrons exchanged "more arguments than books." And first among the debates of the day was the use of "Negro" and the effect it had on the good people of Harlem.[22]

Conversations on street corners and in book centers forced Moore to take a sobering look inward. She now saw her work for the Communist Party, especially the campaigns she had once touted as successes, in a new light. "When the white folks came to me and asked me to organize a committee to get the Negroes in the Big Leagues," she offered as an example, "I didn't know anything about baseball, but they knew my fervor and that I knew people and could get the people out." She put all her energy into getting one or two Black players into the Major Leagues, and all while she was heading Davis's second city council campaign. But with the clarity of hindsight, she now realized she had made the wrong demand. If she had known better, Moore lamented, she would have fiercely fought to improve the conditions for all players in the Negro Leagues. Not to get a few token Black men into the white man's game.[23]

Reflecting on moments like this made Moore realize maybe she had been more susceptible to white tools of control than she had previously thought. She needed to better understand the world around her. But where and how to start? She found her answer in the first and most faithful activist network she ever had: her two sisters. "With my limited knowledge and education, and my sister Eloise and my other sister, Loretta, we three sisters . . . just had to begin," Moore recalled.[24] The trio sat up day and night, rotating between their various New York apartments. They parsed through stacks of books, from the Bible to Black literature borrowed from Richard's book center, hunting for ways to understand how they had been severed from their African ancestry and history. Central to it all was the word "Negro": where it came from, how Black folk had come to adopt it as their own, and how it pervaded even leftist spaces, like the UNIA and the Communist Party.

When Audley, Eloise, and Loretta heard that a group of Harlem-based Black writers, activists, and academics were coming together to discuss these concerns, they quickly signed up. The Moore sisters brought these and other questions to meetings of the Committee to

Present the Truth About the Name "Negro." Here, they gathered with locals like Richard Moore, Langston Hughes, and historian and fellow Garveyite John Henrik Clarke to work toward one goal: vanquishing the word in the press and popular culture by publishing "the facts about the origin of the term, the purpose of its being, and the nature of its evil use."[25]

The committee began by carefully documenting the history and derogatory use of the term. It was the "Spanish or the Portuguese who coined this term 'Negro' as an adjective meaning black," and the word was then "foisted as a noun, as a designation, as a name, upon those who were unfortunate enough to be caught in the clutches of the slave traders" in the fifteenth and sixteenth centuries.[26] The power of a name is in the impression it makes and the ideas it invokes, they argued, citing the widespread use of "Negro" as a pejorative, from biblical references to Shakespeare's plays to American literary works like *The Negro a Beast*, published in 1900. Its purpose was clear: to mark Black people "by virtue of their color for a special condition of oppression, degradation, exploitation, and annihilation."[27]

Moore's worldview was forever shifted. Language could be a means of control, "an art, a high science"—a weapon wielded by the American project to disintegrate Black thought, culture, and political self-perception.[28] "The White man used everything, all of his lies against us, about Africa," she explained. "His Lil Sambo came onto the scene. His Klan began to rise. His terror opened up on us. All the books, the moving pictures, all the derogatory movies about us, came on the scene to help prepare us psychologically for our own overthrow."[29]

"A Negro follows," Moore continued. "He is incapable of scrutiny, he's incapable of analyzing, and he's incapable of perception. A Negro is functioning with a European mind, a European mentality. So he's not hisself . . . he'll do almost anything."[30] So long as Black people adhered to this kind of mentality, Moore asserted, they could never get truly free. They would fight to carve out a place within a blighted system rather than overturn it. They'd be active participants in their own oppression. "A Negro is his own destruction . . . he doesn't need the white man to destroy him anymore."[31]

As she continued to mull these ideas over, Moore developed a theory, or maybe more a philosophy, she would come to call "de-

Negroization": the process by which a Black person could become aware of the mental, social, and cultural control white people had historically wielded against them, and thus overthrow it.

She wasn't just postulating in a vacuum. Moore's foray into political theory was very much in conversation with the thinkers of her time.[32] "De-Negroization" harkened back to W. E. B. Du Bois's ideas of a bifurcated self-image, what he had once called "double-consciousness." A Black American was "always looking at one's self through the eyes of others," he had argued, "measuring one's soul by the tape of a world that looks on in amused contempt and pity."[33] Moore's emphasis on language as a tool of oppression also dovetailed with Nation of Islam (NOI) leader Elijah Muhammad and his then-rising protégé, Malcolm X, whom Moore would soon befriend. The two had popularized the phrase "the so-called Negro" and pushed back against the word as a form of self-identification.[34] Instead, they preached the importance of reconciling that same twoness Du Bois identified. They believed in creating new, positive associations with Blackness and leaving the old behind.[35]

But it was Martinican psychiatrist Frantz Fanon who most explicitly linked language with the mindset of Black America—albeit to a starkly different conclusion.[36] In his 1952 book, *Black Skin, White Masks,* Fanon argued language was a tool of colonial subjugation, explaining that "all colonized people—in other words, people in whom an inferiority complex has taken root . . . position themselves in relation to the civilizing language."[37] The more Black people adopted the language patterns of white America, by this logic, the more they might come to be seen as "whiter," closer to "a true human being." Moore could not have felt more the opposite. The word "Negro" worked to habituate Black people to the dominant culture, she argued, while depriving them of the recognition of their identity and humanity. Yet she agreed with Fanon on one point: to accept white people's terminology was to adopt their oppressive worldview.[38]

To reject the term "Negro" and all its baggage wasn't simply a matter of semantics for Moore. It meant reexamining every aspect of her life—even her Garveyism. She believed Garvey himself interpreted "Negro" as a derogatory term and that his use of it was, in part, an effort to reappropriate the moniker and promote Black pride. But, for

Moore, it was not enough to simply reclaim the word. Black people needed to eradicate it from their vocabulary, from their self-imagery. Garvey had transformed her life, and she was still very much devoted to his teachings. But the student was now diverging from her teacher. She began to feel, and explain to any who would listen, that Garvey hadn't taken his ideals far enough. "Garvey didn't de-Negroize us," she now remarked.[39]

As the 1950s waned, Moore began advocating for a new terminology: "Africans born in the United States." Looking at other immigrant communities in America, she often wondered aloud "why we [Black Americans] of all the people in the world had to change our names, change our character, change our terminology, our national heritage, our national origin," all to assimilate. Why does "China produc[e] Chinese, Japan Japanese, French the French, [but] Africa produces negroes? Why can't Africa produce Africans?"[40]

Moore found an antidote to the "Negro mentality" in her inseverable bond with Africa. "So I say to my people, who think because they [were] born in the United States they [are] no longer Africans, that if a cat had kittens in the oven, you wouldn't call them biscuits." The activist had finally found clarity about her identity and its political importance at least. "We're Africans, no matter where we [are] born."[41]

CHAPTER 12

Arise, Ethiopian Women!

In February 1956, Audley, Eloise, and Loretta walked into their child-hood house on Danneel Street in New Orleans. They dropped their bags, looked around, and breathed a sigh of relief. Nearly forty years earlier, when their half brother Henry had kicked them out without warning, they thought they would never set foot in the house again. But after his son, heir, and the last remaining Moore man, Henry Jr., took his own life, St. Cyr's girls finally got to come home.[1]

Long out of touch with the Moore side of the family, the sisters learned of their half nephew's death from newspaper reports. New Orleans native Mary Belle Patterson was publicly claiming to be the sole heir to the Moore estate. Patterson had told a local judge that she was Henry Jr.'s common-law wife and that he had left a handwritten will bequeathing his entire estate, including the house on Danneel Street, to her a week before he died.[2] The Moore sisters were skeptical. So they charged into New Orleans in the winter of 1955 to challenge her claim to their father's home and legacy in court.

It took time, but they were victorious. They were "firm believers in the things that our father, the late St. Cyr Moore . . . stood for," Moore told the reporters huddled together on the courthouse steps after they won their suit in early 1956. They planned to stay and "perpetuate the high ideals and principles of right that our father upheld."[3] Moore was devastated when she and her sisters lost their father and their home in one fell swoop some thirty-eight years earlier. Reclaiming his memory and his property in New Orleans brought her a bit of solace. Some past wrongs could indeed be made right, and the Moore sisters decided to stay at the Danneel Street home for a while.

Decades of Black migration and struggle had transformed their hometown. While they were in New York, Moore and her sisters had read reports that the Depression had hit New Orleans hard. But World War II was an about-face. The federal government had pumped millions of dollars into Port of Orleans defense contracts, attracting Black folk eager to exchange their low-paying agricultural work for steady industry jobs. And when the war ended, those jobs stayed. Another wave of migration reshaped the city's social and political landscape, spawned a new network of labor unions, and created a thriving Black professional class—laborers, teachers, physicians, nurses, and clergymen all.[4]

Old and new Black New Orleanians joined forces in a postwar push for civil rights. In the 1940s, the NAACP gained a substantial foothold in the state and won important victories for voting rights. Meanwhile, like-minded civil rights organizations such as the Southern Conference for Human Welfare, an interracial coalition of activists seeking equal rights and electoral equality, gained traction.[5] Soon the number of local Black voters multiplied; Black residents could vote in sixty of the sixty-four parishes in Louisiana; and Acadia Parish elected its first Black official in more than fifty years.[6] Black activists desegregated public libraries and city parks and even formed police forces in several parishes; Black people finally had a chance to control who patrolled their communities and how it was done.[7]

Legal suits soon followed. Civil rights lawyer and New Orleans native A. P. Tureaud teamed up with the NAACP's lead counsel and legal strategist, Thurgood Marshall, to break down the barriers to integration in Louisiana. Segregationists knew they were in for a fight when they saw the old, stocky Tureaud ascend the courthouse stairs next to the younger, taller Marshall. The pair came charging through the state, making national headlines for their ambitious attack on school segregation. Starting in 1952, they filed a series of lawsuits that helped integrate Louisiana State University, marking a substantial victory before the landmark 1954 *Brown v. Board of Education* decision that declared segregated schooling unconstitutional in the United States.[8]

But the backlash to these triumphs was both swift and fierce. White Citizens' Councils, middle- and upper-class segregationist groups, cropped up across the country after *Brown*. In New Orleans, they stalled federally mandated school integration by barring Black children from entering white schools, intimidating Black folk at the ballot box, and attacking local civil rights organizations. They had no qualms about resorting to the Red-baiting of the times, or to outright violence.[9] In 1956, white supremacists scored a substantial victory when they successfully outlawed NAACP meetings in the state.[10] This repression hit Louisiana activists "like a bolt from the blue." Red-baiters routed out civil rights organizations, tarnishing the reputations of their members.[11] And many local NAACP chapters had disbanded by April 1956.[12] Other national civil rights organizations like the National Urban League, a well-established group that had been advocating for Black economic betterment and civil rights since the 1910s, fared no better.[13] By the time the Moore sisters returned to their hometown in 1955, the statewide Civil Rights Movement was gasping for air.

This did little to deter them. Life in Harlem had helped them acclimate to the Cold War climate. Moore knew Black radicals were still organizing in the underground. She just had to ferret them out. It didn't take long for her to find her old people, a small but committed collective of local activists fundraising and recruiting for the glory of Garveyism amid McCarthyite repression. By the mid-1950s, they had reinvigorated the UNIA in the city.[14]

There was just one problem. If there was anything Black New Orleanians knew about Moore, it was that she was a communist. Although she had cut ties with the party, if she wanted to join forces with local nationalists, Moore would need to prove she could be trusted to uphold Garvey's ideals and not to bring Red-baiters to their doorsteps. The best choice was to fall in line as a good nationalist foot soldier. And so she joined the Sons and Daughters of Ethiopia, an auxiliary of the UNIA and a holdover from Garvey's heyday.

Black New Orleanians had created the Sons and Daughters during the Depression to aid the local community where the New Deal had failed to.[15] Decimated by white supremacist pushback, but not completely defunct, by the mid-1950s the group had turned its attention to antilynching legislation and Black prisoners' rights—two causes Moore believed were intimately intertwined.[16] She jumped right into organizing, joining their fight to save John Michel, a Black man sentenced to death for allegedly raping a white girl on February 10, 1953—an age-old false accusation that white folk levied against Black men.

The group of old Garveyites entered the fray as Michel's execution date approached. By day, they held press conferences to alert Louisianans to the case. At night, they gathered and passed a candle from one person to the next while praying that Michel's lawyers would be able to gain a stay of execution. Their prayers went unanswered in the end. Michel thanked them for their advocacy on his way to the electric chair in Angola State Prison.[17] He "became the forty-third Negro to be executed for allegedly raping white women," according to *The Louisiana Weekly*, whereas "the last white man to die for rape in New Orleans" was in 1907.[18]

Despondent but determined, the group next channeled their efforts to freeing Joseph Oliver Jenkins. A white jury convicted Jenkins, dubbed the Mardi Gras Slayer, of fatally shooting a Tulane medical student during the annual celebration in 1957. Questions abounded about his fitness for trial. Anyone who entered the courtroom could see Jenkins wasn't well, sitting next to his lawyer and muttering to himself while anxiously fiddling with the rosary hanging around his neck. Yet the state prosecuted him mercilessly, ignoring those around him, including some medical experts, who declared him insane.[19] Moore, now the co-chair of the group, led the Sons and Daughters in calling for Jenkins to be spared.[20]

To fight for prisoners like Jenkins from the comfort of New Orleans was one thing. But to see them and the brutal realities they and other Black prisoners faced behind bars was another entirely. Moore now regularly packed up food and crammed into a car with other Sons and Daughters organizers and made the two-and-a-half-hour drive down the I-10 to the Louisiana State Penitentiary. When they arrived, Moore stepped out of the car and into another world.

The remnants of slavery lingered at Angola Prison, a former plantation situated on a bend in the east bank of the Mississippi River. Confederate officer Samuel L. James took over the plantation in 1880 and resurrected it as a convict-leasing site. He made a fortune by "lending" out convicted criminals to the state without their consent to perform the grueling labor of rebuilding the South after the Civil War. When state officials wrested the complex from him in 1901, they claimed its existing prisoner population and infrastructure, including a cotton gin and a barracks, made it an ideal site to develop a penitentiary farm, where prisoners would grow crops and raise livestock the state would in turn sell for a profit. It was the same age-old, brutal system of coerced labor, all under the guise of modernization and prisoner rehabilitation.[21] When Moore surveyed the Angola landscape, she saw mostly Black prisoners enduring the backbreaking work of cotton and sugar farming. White guards and their families, ensconced in the surrounding Victorian-style homes, completed the twentieth-century plantation tableau.[22]

Moore sat in the waiting room of the "worst prison in America" for hours, while wardens weighed whether or not to grant the Sons and Daughters visitation privileges.[23] As she slumped down in the cold, hard chairs, Moore started to notice jail officials allowed local clergy to walk right in and speak with prisoners—especially those whom the police had brutalized, or those on death row.[24] She had found her loophole. Moore soon joined the Ethiopian Coptic Church, a religious group making inroads into the United States in the early 1950s. The Diocese of North and South America was slowly gaining traction among Black Americans after it established a headquarters in Harlem during the late 1930s. Priests baptized Moore alongside hundreds of others on a trip back to New York, and she worked quickly to gain the designation of abbess in the faith. Moore always maintained she joined the church because it was a "vehicle" for prisoner advocacy. But she stayed because of its ties to "Mother Africa" and to progressive politics.[25] She was now able to more freely roam the dark halls of Angola, where a whole generation of forgotten Americans desperately needed her.

"Aroused in righteous indignation" over the dozens of Black men who were "executed as a result of the whims of white women," Moore decided it was time to take matters into her own hands. She founded the Universal Association of Ethiopian Women (UAEW) in 1957, which she ran from her family house on Danneel Street. Her organization reflected her continued commitment to Garveyism in both name and principle. Back when the UNIA reigned supreme in the city, so too did talk of a free and powerful Ethiopia, a homeland for the Black Diaspora. Knowing that many in the Crescent City still revered the Jamaican Black Nationalist just as she did, Moore gave her organization a name that would galvanize former Garveyites. She envisioned it as a successor to the UNIA and the Sons and Daughters, with a "de-Negroizing" bent.[26]

In addition to her sisters, the growing roster included prominent local activist and former Garveyite Virginia Collins, whose political trajectory had followed a course similar to Moore's.[27] Other local, like-minded, and middle-aged Black women joined the group: Alma Dawson served as treasurer, Enola Jackson as organizational secretary, and Bessie Phillips as vice president. Moore's nationalistic rhetoric brought the women through the door; her organizing agenda made them stay. They gathered weekly in the Moore sisters' living room to hatch plans to challenge racial injustice.[28]

The UAEW picked up where the Sons and Daughters had left off. Still reeling from the execution of John Michel, they vowed that incarcerated men like Henry Hills and Isaac Peart would not face the same fate. New Orleans police accused Hills of attacking a fifteen-year-old white girl at gunpoint and Peart of raping a white woman even though he had a strong alibi.[29] The collective fought tirelessly on behalf of these men, among others. But it was their effort to stay the executions of Edgar Labat and Clifton Poret that made the group a household name in New Orleans.

On a cool morning in late November 1950, New Orleans native and hospital orderly Edgar Labat was lounging about his home when he heard a loud knock. Thinking it was his sister, who lived a few blocks away, he sauntered over and casually opened the door. "Where is that nigger who raped that white woman last night?" a police officer screamed as he and five others charged in. Before Labat could figure out what was happening, two policemen lunged at him. They tackled him and held him down while the others searched his house. Terrified, the young Black man tried to explain he was home alone and had no idea what they were talking about. Outraged at Labat's outspokenness, the officers snapped a leg off his wooden kitchen table and started beating him mercilessly. After they reduced him to a heap on the floor, they dragged Labat out of the house and stuffed his bleeding body into a squad car.[30]

At the precinct, they admitted Labat was not one of the two men wanted for the robbery of Robert Penedo and the rape of his companion, Helen Rajek, in the early morning hours on November 12. But the couple had said one of the attackers was a Black man with lighter skin. "This is the only light-skin Nigger in that vicinity to our knowing," the arresting officer told his colleagues. No one cared if they had the right suspect. Any Black man would do. And so they forced a battered Labat to limp out into a lineup.

"It was so dark, but that looks like the fellow [w]ho robbed you, huh?" Penedo asked Rajek as Labat stood to face them.

"Yes, it could be," she replied.

"Yes, he is the one," an officer interjected. Police then threw Labat back in a jail cell and beat him again for good measure. They waited a few days for the swelling to go down before taking his mug shot and booking him for the crime.[31]

Labat spent his days in a nine-by-seven-foot jail cell while New Orleans police hunted for his alleged accomplice. Months later, and more than five hundred miles away, police in Tennessee dragged a Black man named Clifton Poret out of his jail cell and drove him to Louisiana without a word of explanation. It was only after he arrived in New Orleans that Poret learned he was being charged as Labat's accomplice after the couple picked out his mug shot from others police showed them. Jailers beat Poret for days until he falsely confessed to the crime to make the pummeling stop.[32]

The two men had never met. But their lives were now inextricably linked as they languished in Angola for two years. When Labat and Poret finally got their day in court in February 1953, an all-white jury convicted and sentenced them to death, due to be doled out in just four days. Days turned to weeks as their legal teams fought to appeal their convictions on grounds that the jury was biased, that witnesses gave false testimony, and that the judge refused to follow the correct trial procedures.[33] Their appeals dragged on for years. In a Hail Mary, lawyers then filed a writ of habeas corpus, claiming constitutional rights had been violated in both Labat's and Poret's arrests and convictions. A judge rejected the application the following day and set their execution date: September 20, 1957.[34]

As soon as she got word, Moore called an "emergency mass meeting" in New Orleans "for the purpose of getting stays of executions" for the two men.[35] Moore harkened back to her street speaking days, rallying community members in support of Labat and Poret by invoking the many other local Black men whom the state had executed without a fair trial. Part vigil, part protest, complete with a dramatically staged roll call for those Black men murdered at the hands of the state, the rally galvanized supporters and raked in money for the defendants' cause.[36]

Still, Moore knew it was going to take more than thoughts and prayers to save the two men. And so she took to the road, going on a hastily arranged speaking tour to raise awareness of their impending executions. Her first stop was New York. Moore reconnected with her former comrades in Harlem and even persuaded her old communist compatriot Abner Berry to publicize the case in *The Daily Worker*, where he shared the men's stories and lauded the UAEW for "manning an important part of the front" against racist violence in the South.[37]

Next Moore looked to the mainstream, writing to the now nationally known civil rights organizer Rosa Parks for help. The thirteen-month boycott of the segregated Montgomery bus system was a massive, masterful grassroots effort. But Parks had become the face of the protest after she had refused to give up her seat to a white passenger on December 1, 1955. Parks was not just a Black woman who happened to spurn segregation laws one day. The then-forty-two-year-old was a veteran activist who had garnered a reputation among moderates and radicals alike for standing up for Black women rape victims and the Scottsboro Boys. Moreover, Parks refused to shun communists during the height of the Red Scare, and she continued to partner with groups the government deemed "subversive" as she gained notoriety.[38]

"My Dear Ms. Parks, I've just returned from NYC to find your most welcome letter," Moore scrawled on the back of a pamphlet detailing the UAEW's latest activism. "As you can see from this document, I am in work up to my neck," she added. But Moore still had the time to answer a few of Parks's questions about the UAEW and its support of Labat and Poret's case. "Life is pushing us so fast with eventful problems," Moore explained, in response to the civil rights organizer's queries about the group's formal structure and incorporation. But "we would welcome your contribution." She had been chasing the now-famous activist for a while, hoping Parks might join or perhaps even help lead the organization. Parks had been coy. She feared the group wasn't prepared for the legal trouble they might face in supporting Black death row inmates. But Moore vowed to keep her in the loop either way. "Love to you for all you've done for us," Moore scribbled quickly, signing off. Her admiration was unconditional.[39]

Moore's correspondence with Parks reignited the FBI's interest in its longtime mark. She had tried to close the door on the government's surveillance when she walked out of her interview at the bureau's offices a few years before. But agents had kept her file open, and they now had even better means to track her. In 1956, Hoover centralized the bureau's surveillance and suppression operations into the Counterintelligence Program (COINTELPRO). The director initially intended the program to disrupt the Communist Party and discredit its members, but it quickly ballooned into something greater and far more nefarious. The FBI was now in the business of wiretapping, harassing, entrapping, imprisoning, and even killing off leftist activists.[40] It wasn't long before the UAEW caught COINTELPRO's attention. Agents started infiltrating its meetings and protests soon after the organization began.[41]

The FBI followed Moore as she made her way back to New Orleans and threw herself into the fight to save the wrongfully accused. On every podium and at every microphone, Moore reiterated that the UAEW "firmly believes in Labat and Poret's innocence" and proclaimed the group would join with any and all forces interested in supporting their "last minute, all out fight to save" the men.[42]

As the clock ticked down to their execution day, Moore started to lose hope. But then a breakthrough hit. The UAEW received a tip that police might have coerced a local Black man, Earl Howard, into providing the false witness statement used to charge the men. They rushed to Howard and pleaded with him until he recanted. With their prodding, he produced a sworn statement admitting he hadn't witnessed the incident, but had claimed Labat and Poret were guilty to avoid his own beating and arrest.[43] Finally, a break in the case.

The UAEW kept digging. Moore's group gathered a "sworn statement by a woman disclosing that she was with Poret in a bar from 11:15 p.m. until 12:20 a.m. and that she later rejoined him at 2 a.m. and stayed until 7 a.m. the night and morning the rape occurred." Labat's girlfriend offered even more proof of their innocence. Moore and her peers discovered the woman had told police that she was with Labat the night of the crime, but the officers refused to record her statement and submit it for evidence.

Moore and the other UAEW members were aghast that she would withhold this information when two men's lives were on the line. When they asked her why, she explained sheepishly that "she feared what her husband might do to her."[44]

This was it, the break they needed. The new evidence persuaded Judge John Minor Wisdom to grant a ten-day stay of execution to determine whether the court had denied Labat and Poret due process and refused to allow their lawyers to exhaust all possible appeals.[45] The case then moved to the Supreme Court, where Justice Hugo L. Black signed a fifteen-day stay of execution.[46]

Labat and Poret picked up publicizing their case. Poret, originally from Los Angeles, placed an ad in the *Los Angeles Times* detailing his wrongful incarceration. A local Black butcher, Nelson Soll, saw the ad in September 1957 and helped create a defense fund to secure his release.[47] As funds and support rolled in, they obtained eight consecutive stays of execution, one coming only three hours before they were set to be killed.[48] Then, in 1963, Labat began corresponding with a Swedish woman, Solveig Johansson, who learned of his incarceration through international news. At Johansson's prompting, the Norwegian newspaper *Dagbladet* collected close to two thousand signatures demanding clemency for Labat.[49] Despite this international attention, Labat and Poret languished on death row throughout the 1960s.[50] Their legal battle finally ended in December 1969, when they agreed to plead guilty to attempted aggravated rape, and the district attorney accepted a sentence equal to the time already served.[51] Although both men had sat in jail for nineteen years before the courts finally released them, *The Louisiana Weekly* proclaimed their lives had been spared "as a direct result of the untiring efforts of the Universal Association of Ethiopian Women."[52]

Before their work on the Labat and Poret case was finished, the UAEW members paused to reflect on their organizing thus far. They realized that while they had devoted much time to righting the injustices inflicted on Black men, they had not worked hard enough to call atten-

tion to the violence Black girls and women faced on the regular—
women who were "raped by white men with impunity."[53] There were
plenty, painful testaments to this truth: men like Theodore B. Snider,
a local white man who had raped an eighteen-year-old Black woman
in July 1958 and then walked free.[54] Moore's group took up the young
woman's cause.

First, the UAEW forced its way into a meeting with District Attorney Richard Dowling to question him about his inaction on the case.
The women scoffed when he disingenuously claimed the case had
"never been called to his particular attention." As they stared each
other down, both the UAEW and Dowling knew he never intended
to charge Snider. "It was only because of the efforts of the Universal
Association of Ethiopian Women," *The Louisiana Weekly* reported, that
the "case even reached the Grand Jury." But in "typical Southern
fashion," the jury refused to indict Snider when he went to court, citing insufficient evidence of the crime. "Dissatisfied with the lack of
concern for Black women," the UAEW met with the district attorney
again to demand Snider be rearrested.[55]

When Dowling didn't respond, the UAEW members took their
charges to the Justice Department. "Injustice inflicted upon our people because of color has been established," they wrote. "This recent
case of aggravated rape upon one of our teenagers by a white man (the
Theodore B. Snider case) who was freed with impunity is evidence
of this fact. We feel there is no hope for us in the South unless the
Department of Justice intervenes immediately."[56] While they awaited
a response, the group held numerous meetings at the Moore home
about the Snider case and Louisiana's one-sided "Rape Law." They
knew that while the state continually executed local Black men on
false charges of raping white women, "no Louisiana white man has
ever paid the death penalty" for assaulting a Black woman.[57] The
UAEW vowed to marshal all its forces to see that the state meted out
the punishment Snider and men like him were due.

In just a few short years of being back in New Orleans, Moore had
tangled with everyone from state governors to Angola prison wardens.
Until now, her focus had largely been on publicly indicting white men
while defending Black men and women. But she had yet to air her
grievances about the white women of Louisiana and the role they so
often played in brutalizing Black folk. Something compelled Moore to

choose poetry as the medium through which to challenge the South's fraught racial and sexual dynamics. Putting pen to paper, she published "The Twain Has Met" in 1959:

> *To Southern white women, we now appeal:*
> *You must know what excruciating pangs we black women feel,*
> *To see our men folk of rape wrongly accused,*
> *While our women, by your men are violated and abused.*
>
> *Not long ago, we won women's suffrage rights,*
> *The very foundation of that struggle, was the slave's freedom fight,*
> *For emancipation from your very own race,*
> *Who held us in bondage while keeping you in your place.*
>
> *When Susan B. Anthony and Lucretia Mott,*
> *Attended London's Anti-Slavery conference, what a lesson they got;*
> *They were shunted to the gallery, just as we are now,*
> *For white women had no more voice, than the slaves, or a sow.*
>
> *In your homes you've suffered, for your husbands have sown,*
> *Seeds that produced mulatto children, resembling your own.*
> *Millions of mulattos, yet no white man has paid,*
> *The penalty for raping us as the law said.*
>
> *The Louisiana Rape Law of 1892 is ignominiously used to only protect you.*
> *Oh white women! Too long you have been silent on this,*
> *Let not history record that you're woefully amiss,*
> *Of your civic duty, now that you have the Vote.*
>
> *While white men violate this law,*
> *Don't be used as a scapegoat.*
> *Let your men explain all those teasing browns, which will expose many*
>   *reasons*
> *For keeping the black man down.*
>
> *Courageous truth must now come out your mouth,*
> *For it is you, destined to save the South,*

From the mire of debauchery for your children's sake,
Who must face the world's challenge, embarrassed by the laws you make.

So, Southern white women, isn't our cause the same
When "half-white children" are produced in white supremacy's name?
There is no doubt, that the twain has met.[58]

In 1960, Moore's group found that white women's lies weren't local Black women's most pressing concern. That honor went to the newly passed Suitable Homes Law. During the Great Depression, New Deal officials had created the Aid to Dependent Children (ADC) program, more commonly known as welfare, to support families headed by widows and divorced, abandoned, or separated mothers. Black folk soon found that, just like most New Deal programs, the ADC was a raw deal. Welfare officials had the power to decide if a woman was "deserving" of public assistance, and it didn't take long for southern states to design laws with discriminatory definitions of a "suitable home" by which to deny benefits.[59]

Louisiana's Suitable Homes Law prohibited women in "common-law marriages" and those who bore children out of wedlock from receiving welfare benefits. Once removed from the aid rolls, these women had to provide the state proof they had entered a "valid marriage" or "ceased their illicit relationship" with a male partner to get benefits again. When it was passed, twenty-three thousand women and children—mostly Black—became ineligible for state aid.[60] Outraged, Moore and her UAEW sprang into action, partnering with the Urban League, the NAACP, and local religious organizations to pressure state officials to repeal the law.[61]

Moore led a delegation of UAEW women to Washington, D.C., to pester the nation's leaders.[62] The small group of Black women contacted officials in the U.S. Department of Health, Education, and Welfare, the Agriculture Department, and the Children's Bureau in hopes of educating them about how the law was racist and pointedly punitive. They even tried to get the White House to take a stand. President Dwight D. Eisenhower's only reply to their telegram was that this was a "state issue."[63]

And so the UAEW went back home. The following month, Virginia Collins, Alma Dawson, and Audley Moore met with the State Welfare Commission in Baton Rouge. According to Moore, "It was clear from the outset... that while the officials were in sympathy with the plight of the hungry mothers and starving babies, they could do very little under the present law."[64] Any solution, she realized, would have to come from the grassroots.

So Moore mobilized the way she knew best. She once again tapped into her old organizing networks and went on a short speaking tour through New York in the latter half of 1960. Moore appealed to groups like the Buffalo Mothers Alliance, tugging on their heartstrings with stories of "Mrs. Mildred Reimoneng and her ten children," who lost welfare benefits at a moment's notice and would never survive without their help. She then made the 145-mile trek to Elmira, where, with the help of local Black clergy, she held an event at the local Masonic Lodge collecting canned food and clothes donations. At each stop, Moore encouraged her audiences to compel the government to step in by letting "Europe, Asia, and Africa know about the predicament of poor mothers in Louisiana."[65] Her tried-and-true Cold War strategy was back on the board.

After stumping for donations for weeks, Moore headed home. In the early hours of January 3, 1961, she stopped at a gas station in Bean Station, Tennessee, fifty miles north of Knoxville, to fill up for the next leg of her journey. Moore stepped out of her car, shivered in the cold January air, and pulled her brown wool coat close as she placed the nozzle in her gas tank. She scanned her surroundings. A Black woman traveling on her own always had to keep her wits about her. Moore froze when she saw them: a group of white men by the station watching her. She needed to get going.

Moore paid for the gas, jumped in the car, and breathed a sigh of relief as she drove off. But a quick look in her rearview mirror, and her stomach dropped. The men were following her. Moore stiffened and gripped the steering wheel. For the next fifteen miles, her eyes darted back and forth between the road and the mirror. If Moore was hoping to spot a safe place to stop off, she was sorely disappointed. There was nothing but flat land and empty road as far as the eye could see. So she kept driving south, perhaps praying she would make it back home to see her sisters again.

The car's driver punched the gas and sped up beside her. While he kept the car steady, the other men rolled down their windows. They had guns. They fired straight into Moore's car, and she swerved to avoid the bullet spray as the men sped off. "I lost control of the vehicle and the car went into a ditch," she later recounted. Rattled but miraculously uninjured, Moore climbed out and surveyed the damage. There were bullet holes through the windshield and windows, yet the car still seemed drivable. She just needed to get it out of the ditch. Moore waited on the roadside for hours until a friendly driver with a trailer pulled her out. She then drove to Knoxville and reported the crime before making the rest of the journey home in her bullet-riddled car. Louisiana journalists reported on the attack, noting that "white supremacists of Fayette and Haywood Counties" had attacked Moore "in an attempt to prevent supplies from reaching the helpless refugees" in Louisiana.[66]

Shaken but still steadfast, Moore picked the fight back up and sparred with state officials to appeal the welfare law. She was stunned when Louisiana's governor, Jimmie Davis, walked into a press conference and proclaimed the Black women kicked off the welfare rolls were nothing more than "prostitutes."

"We resent the insulting remarks of Governor Jimmie H. Davis," the UAEW fired back publicly. "The governor must be reminded that all baseness, vileness, and illicit relationships among our people in the United States of America started through the white slavers' breeding farms where mothers were forced to breed for the slave mart." And the UAEW didn't stop there. "Almost every African woman or girl was raped on her arrival here," it proclaimed. "And the raping continue[s] until this day."[67] The UAEW argued that many of the Black women Davis reviled did not want to be on welfare. Rather, they were forced to seek state aid to feed their children, because the white fathers would not provide for them for fear of being labeled "race traitors."

When Black New Orleanians opened the newspaper, they were stunned to see the UAEW's chastening, its unabashed rebuke of white men's sexual violence. The group soon earned a reputation not only for defending poor and working-class Black women, but also for openly discrediting the twisted sexual politics of the segregationist South—its fears of "race mixing" and its penchant for killing Black men for their alleged defilement of white womanhood as a tool of social and political control. In the early 1960s, playing into the racialized sexual terror of the time was often the price for the modicum of freedom Black women claimed. But Moore and her UAEW were simply unwilling to pay it.

In the end, their scathing indictments moved the needle. The UAEW generated enough negative press that Washington eventually threatened to revoke Louisiana's federal funding unless the state adjusted its Suitable Homes Law.[68] Louisiana legislators amended the law to require state officials to prove the "unsuitability" of a home, rather than simply disqualifying recipients based on their nontraditional families. In 1962, state officials ended the suitable homes requirement altogether. Yet they still clung to "man in the home" laws, which prohibited mothers and children from receiving aid if there was an adult male living with them, until 1968.[69] Eventually, those laws were struck down, too. Just as with Labat and Poret, the UAEW's advocacy sparked a flame that would one day burn a slew of racist policies to the ground.

Moore's return to the streets of her youth had been tumultuous. She had heard the screams of Black men wrongfully locked away in Angola, and those of hungry babies robbed of the safety net meant to keep them fed. As she tangled with everyone from racist white governors to frothing vigilantes, one thing was becoming abundantly clear: "The time has come for our people to realize that we cannot achieve freedom under this white man's system of white supremacy," she declared.[70] As the 1960s dawned, the activist was more determined than ever to liberate those the United States had oppressed the most. Her determination would lead her back to Angola. But this time her mission was personal.

CHAPTER 13

The United Nations and Reparations

The first time Moore laid eyes on Jose Cuevas, she winced at the bruises across his body, the imprints from the shackles guards had used to string him up "with his hands up against the wall like Jesus." As she entered Angola that day in late 1958, the jailers told her there was a man who didn't "speak English too well" but looked as if he needed her help. She nodded and dutifully followed them. Jose was combative at first, prone to outbursts. But it was nothing Moore couldn't handle. He wasn't the first prisoner she had met who was recovering from the abuse Angola guards meted out: solitary confinement, electric shock treatments, and myriad other forms of torture.[1]

Because it was many miles away from any major city, it was rare for any inmate in Angola to get a visitor, let alone Jose: a Puerto Rican man in his late twenties who had been jailed on a marijuana charge since 1953.[2] Far away from his family and with little command of English, Jose had no one to turn to as he endured years of beatings at the hands of prison guards before they threw him in the hole—the dingy, single-person cell with a bucket for a toilet. Moore was the first person he had met in years who treated him with any kindness or respect. For a long time, he had tried to tell people as best he could about his former life in Puerto Rico, and how he had been "maltreated in the South only because he is a Puerto Rican." Moore had worked alongside enough folk from the island during her Communist Party days to know he was right: white people had often treated Puerto Ricans like second-class citizens, too. Surprised by her care and concern for him, Jose began to open up to Moore when she came to minister to him and other inmates as an abbess. She found Jose was the "kindest man in the world when he was pleased," and she was taken with his talk of the Puerto Rican Nationalist Movement surging on the island.[3] And so she began to see Jose regularly when she came to Angola, lingering a bit longer when she stopped by his cell.

Behind the aggression and the trauma, she found a determined man with a strong sense of self whose rage had been deeply politicized by the racial violence he had endured on the mainland. Jose saw Moore for what she was, too: not your typical missionary, but rather a woman on a mission.

While Jose had come around to Moore, Angola's officers didn't. As soon as they sensed Moore and Jose's relationship might be moving beyond the clerical, they stepped in. "The warden don't let me see her" because "they classify me in the white side and [say] that she is colored," Jose later recalled.[4] The U.S. Census and Migration Division did indeed classify Jose as officially white, a common practice for Puerto Ricans both on the island and Stateside.[5] But Angola had its own set of racial rules. Jose's jailers had always treated him like a "colored" man. It wasn't until they saw Jose growing closer to Moore that they started enforcing the color line. But by then, it was too late.

"What do you want with that nigger?" the warden asked Jose one day, nodding to Moore. The two were sitting across from the warden in his office as he questioned them about their relationship. Jose was incensed at the disrespect, and his fuse was short. He lunged at the warden, scraping to get ahold of him from across the desk. Moore, bless her heart, swooned over his bravado.[6] In the back of her mind, she must have wondered if his violent outbursts could one day be aimed at her. But her desire for Jose trumped her fear. She was a sixty-year-old Black woman, curvy with a seamed face. And she was smitten by this slender, thirty-two-year-old Puerto Rican man with a gold tooth.[7]

The age gap between Jose and Moore was wide, and they came from starkly different backgrounds. But their worldviews were closely aligned. Jose was a Puerto Rican Nationalist, invested in the movement to free the island from American colonial rule. Puerto Rico had always been on Moore's radar. The United States invaded the island the same year she was born, establishing a military base and embarking on a colonization project. As she was joining the UNIA, Puerto Ricans were themselves joining the American empire as the United States granted them quasi-citizenship.[8] She had witnessed the hardships that Puerto Ricans experienced as second-class citizens in East

Harlem when she ventured into their enclaves as a Communist Party member to drum up support. It was no wonder, then, that by the time Moore met Jose in the late 1950s, the Puerto Rican Nationalist Movement was growing, and a number of organizations on the mainland called for the island's independence. The two bonded over their belief in total separation from the American nation.[9]

Moore was fed up with the slow pace of integration. The accelerating nationalist movements within and beyond the United States, meanwhile, were galvanizing. By day, Moore and the other UAEW members worked tirelessly on behalf of the Black and Brown people of Louisiana; by night, they heard radio reports of oppressed peoples throwing off the yoke of their colonial oppressors in Africa, Latin America, and Asia, establishing their national independence. This led Moore to proclaim "the problems of Black Americans were so great" that nothing less than total separation would do.[10] Now, when she wasn't working to free Jose from jail, Moore was leading the UAEW in devising a new and bold plan: calling for an independent Black nation funded through reparations.

Her move was well timed. Americans—both Black and white—were thinking about national identity differently now. Locked in a cold war with the Soviet Union, the United States was hard at work trying to contain communism wherever government officials believed it to be festering. The Truman administration was poised to quash the communist threat with American troops, and was further developing the atomic bomb as a last resort. When Dwight D. Eisenhower took over in 1953, his administration had a balancing act to maintain. It had to assert the superiority of the American way of life through consumer culture while assuaging growing fears the United States and the Soviet Union were headed down a path of mutual annihilation.[11]

By the late 1950s, whenever Moore picked up a newspaper or stopped by a store with TVs in the window, she was inundated with ads touting white households with well-stocked pantries, led by an upwardly mobile man and maintained by a devoted wife and mother. Amid a bevy of packaged mixes and modern appliances, suburban life was here to stay. Moore and other Black people saw this messaging for what it was: the American government asserting the primacy of the white middle class and neutralizing the threat of racial, gender, and sexual nonconformity. It was both pervasive and persuasive. The task ahead of the American government was to now export its propaganda abroad, convincing other countries to join its side.

Much to Moore's delight, Black folk of the world, particularly in newly independent African countries, refused to be pawns in this geo-political game. She was among the vocal minority who supported African independence throughout the fraught decade. She had watched with horror as white Afrikaners, building on the racial hierarchy the British colonial empire created, established apartheid rule in South Africa in 1948. And she had been encouraged when the Kikuyu people in Kenya fought British rule during the Mau Mau rebellion of 1952. But Moore also knew it wasn't enough to sit idly by and watch. While she fought for the liberty of Black Louisianans through the UAEW, she also amplified African liberation struggles abroad, joining collectives like the Hearts of Africa Committee, a New York–based group that raised moral and financial support for South Africans and Kenyans.[12] And as a member of the International Committee in Defense of Africa, Moore, along with a small band of Black women organizers (including her sister Eloise), partnered with up-and-coming North Carolina–based Black Nationalist leader Robert F. Williams to "create a better relationship between Africans and the people of African origin and descent throughout the world."[13]

Garvey's calls for "Africa for the Africans" had long seemed like a distant dream to Moore. But by the end of the decade, it was almost clear enough to see. At midnight on March 6, 1957, Kwame Nkrumah declared, "At long last the battle has ended! And thus Ghana, your beloved country, is free forever!"[14] Moore had first heard of the Ghanaian leader when he was a student at Lincoln University in Pennsylvania in the 1930s, and she followed his career as he emerged as a leader in the fight for African liberation at the Fifth Pan-African Congress in Manchester, England, in 1945. She delighted in the reports she heard about what life was like under his administration after he became the first president of the free Black nation in 1960. Some of her old Sojourner comrades such as Vicki Garvin and Shirley Graham Du Bois had visited or even immigrated to Ghana after its independence to continue their work, and their dispatches gave Moore hope that even as the mainstream Civil Rights Movement gained steam, Black Nationalism could still prevail.[15]

These reports also kept a long-held dream alive for Moore: that one day these independent African nations would become a "third force" in geopolitics, one that was politically aligned with all Black people, rather than the United States and Western Europe in the Western Hemisphere or the Soviet Union, China, and their communist allies.[16] So committed was Moore to this vision that she used the UAEW to foster a global alliance. One of the group's go-to strategies was to appeal directly to African liberation leaders to advocate on behalf of Black Americans. When trade unionist and organizer Tom Mboya came to the United States in 1959, for example, the UAEW published a telegram to the Kenyan leader:

> Today we are deprived of our heritage and our proper national name and branded with the ignominous [*sic*] slave term Negro. We long for the day when our people and leaders everywhere will be treated with dignity and respect. We pray for Africa's freedom and for our many innocent black men doomed to die in the barbaric electric chair in the states of Louisiana and Texas on trumped up charges of rape upon white women....Please join us in this prayer for the Freedom of Africans everywhere at home and abroad.[17]

These missives foregrounded the UAEW's grassroots struggles and Moore's "de-Negroizing" imperatives. The UAEW intentionally wrapped its activism in the rhetoric of anticolonialism and human rights, situating the struggles of Black Americans alongside those of Africans shirking colonial rule. The testimony was a clarion call for international leaders, a reminder to challenge U.S. intervention in Africa under the auspices of bringing "liberty" and "justice for all" to the continent.

In fact, Black Americans across the political spectrum were growing increasingly interested in appealing to international governing bodies, especially the United Nations. Now fifteen years old, the acceleration of global decolonization sent shock waves through the intergovernmental organization.[18] By 1960, seventeen newly independent countries had joined the global conglomerate. These nations often worked together to pressure colonial powers to relinquish their strongholds and to persuade the UN to condemn Western countries' political and military abuses. Presidents, prime ministers, and premiers the world over were losing the moral high ground as a new vocabulary coalesced around the atrocities they had inflicted upon Africa, Asia, and Latin America: words like "human rights," "genocide," and "apartheid."[19]

Moore and her fellow UAEW members wrote to Dag Hammarskjöld, Secretary-General of the United Nations, begging him to "intercede [o]n behalf of our people of Ethiopian origin in the United States of America." It was an old ploy she had learned when, as a member of the National Negro Congress, she helped gather support for the group's UN petition in 1947. And in 1951, as a member of the Civil Rights Congress under the leadership of William Patterson, she knew the group had submitted a damning report of America's systemic racist treatment of Black people called *We Charge Genocide* to UN officials in New York and Paris.[20]

Moore told the UN leader that "although we're born here, we're not considered citizens" and that "planned lynch terror and willful destruction of our people, amounting to the crime of genocide, prevail throughout the land and especially in the South." In a headline-grabbing declaration, she proclaimed, "We charge genocide ... and urge that immediate steps be taken to save us from total extermination."[21]

Moore still believed there was something to be gained in appealing to the UN. Sending a telegram to such an esteemed international organization was a surefire way for the UAEW to make national news, and publicizing Black Americans' plight to international leaders made it harder for the United States to claim the moral high ground. Yet past experience had shown her that it was not enough to persuade the international body to act. She had seen firsthand how the UN, still dominated by the United States and wary of alienating its strongest player, circumvented the NNC's and the CRC's previous appeals by claiming that they did not originate from a governing body or a government-sanctioned group.[22]

Now, more than a decade later, Audley Moore took a different tack. Huddled together, the UAEW women penned and published the "Draft Resolution for the Establishment of an Independent Black Republic." In the two-page mimeographed pamphlet, Moore used the format of America's founding documents to undermine the nation's own legitimacy: "We the Black people of the sovereign states of North America, having petitioned for redress in the most humble terms against oppression now realize that the only solution to our problem can be solved through self-determination." The document continued: "Therefore we ordain and present *this Declaration* for our *Independence,* to put an end to the colonial system of tyranny that has prevailed consistently during the period of our captivity until this present day."

The statement listed the "abuses committed against our people since the signing of the Emancipation Proclamation," which included everything from the use of the degrading term "Negro" to the now-famous lynching of fourteen-year-old Emmett Till in Mississippi in 1955. "The prisons are filled with our men and youth," it read, "many who are awaiting execution on trumped-up charges of rape upon white women" while "untold numbers of our women and young girls are raped by law-enforcement officers at gun point."

The group accused the United States of setting up an "arbitrary government...based on white supremacy, wherein a Black man has no right that a white man is bound to respect." Black men were drafted into "wars for a so-called democracy that they do not enjoy." Black children "have been and still are miseducated with distorted history." And all Black people face "the denial of all opportunities for economic development." Under white supremacist rule, "there is a willful anni-hilation of our people through planned acts of destruction, which constitutes the crime of Genocide according to the convention of the United Nations," they concluded.[23]

The only reasonable response was total separation through secession:[24]

> Be it further resolved that the only solution to end the so-called racial conflict in the United States of America and which is in keeping with the Declaration of Human Rights of the United Nations Charter is to form an INDEPENDENT BLACK REPUBLIC, which in truth will be separate and equal.... In keeping with the principles of true liberty... we DECLARE OURSELVES A NATION, and do not feel bound b[y] the laws of this government.[25]

Moore and her peers had done what many across the Black Left were afraid to: reject American citizenship entirely and publicly call for the formation of a Black nation. They were as practical as they were imaginative, wrapping Moore's core ideas in the trappings of Americana to proselytize them to an otherwise hostile audience—an audience that often included other Black Americans.

According to member Virginia Collins, the UAEW sent its declaration to "all the bureaus, the senate, the congress, every bureau where you supposed to be sending stuff."[26] Politicians might not have known what to make of the tract when it slid across their desks. But in the early 1960s, for $1, New Orleanians could pick up a pamphlet at UAEW rallies that offered them a new, bold vision for Black liberation and a Black nation. There was just one question left to answer: How would they pay for it?

Moore and her fellow UAEW organizers were hardly the first to sit down and hammer out a case for reparations. Black women pioneered the movement that was already more than a century in the making. A former slave turned washerwoman named Callie House was among the first to take up the cause. A widowed mother of five, House lived and worked outside Nashville and was part of a vibrant, politically engaged community that had long been debating how to recoup the funds the American government owed former slaves.[27] She found an answer in the 1890s, when activists came to Nashville selling a simple leaflet: "Freedmen's Pension Bill: A Plea for American Freedmen."[28]

House and her compatriots joined a tradition dating back to the founding of America. As early as the 1770s, Quakers called for the manumission and renumeration of slaves. As part of a Christian group known for its belief in the spiritual equality of all people as much as for its pacifism, members called for an end to the slave trade, gradual manumission of slaves, and reparations in the form of land.[29] It didn't take long for the enslaved around them to turn their moral creed into a legal claim. In 1783, an Africa-born woman named Belinda petitioned the Massachusetts legislature for a portion of British Loyalist Isaac Royall's estate after the government had confiscated his holdings at the end of the Revolutionary War. Belinda explained she had been ripped from her African home and survived the Transatlantic Slave Trade, only to be enslaved by Royall for nearly forty years, during which time her labor helped him amass his fortune. Now that he was gone, she found that "by the laws of the land, [she was] denied the enjoyment of one morsel of that immense wealth, a part whereof hath been accumulated by her own industry." Whether moved by Belinda's petition or the desire to further disgrace Royall by dismantling his estate, the legislature agreed to her request for repayment. It awarded her $15 a year in reparations.[30]

Since most petitions of this sort came from Black women and men, House was surprised to learn the pamphlet's author, Walter Raleigh Vaughan, was a white man from Selma, Alabama. Coming of age in the antebellum era, Vaughan had witnessed slavery and the Civil War firsthand, although he was too young to bear arms for the Confederacy as his slave-owning father and brothers had. Instead, he was concerned with the fate of the U.S. economy after the war.[31] In the pamphlet, Vaughan urged lawmakers to pass legislation providing money for the "men and women who have been set free without support, and without the capital necessary to acquire such support."[32] The southerner argued that $15 a month and a lump sum of $500 for every ex-slave over the age of seventy would be "a measure of recognition of the inhumanity practiced by the government in the holding, for a century, of men and women as slaves." But maybe more crucially to Vaughan, it would stimulate economic growth, rebuild the southern market, and make good on the American principles of liberty and justice for all.[33]

Neither white legislators nor the Black elite thought providing for the Black poor, as Vaughan's proposal suggested, was important. But House did. She teamed up with Black educator, minister, and former Vaughan employee Isaiah Dickerson to form the National Ex-Slave Mutual Relief, Bounty, and Pension Association in 1897. As the assistant secretary of the association, House traveled around the nation, encouraging former slaves to petition Congress for pensions. Even if they never saw a dime, House explained, membership in the organization had its perks. The association also offered aid for death and burial expenses, a significant concern for the generation of Black people who were born into slavery and now reaching old age.[34]

A national movement to give pensions to ex-slaves was anathema to white lawmakers. Soon the federal government launched a targeted attack on the association and its leaders, arguing House was using the mail to "wheedle the elusive dollar" from "unsuspecting negroes" who were already struggling to make ends meet.[35] Federal agents imprisoned House in 1916 and a jury convicted her of mail fraud in 1917, sending the organization into disarray. Nevertheless, the National Ex-Slave Mutual Relief, Bounty, and Pension Association carried on, holding conventions for Black New Orleanians well into the 1910s.[36]

A teenager at the time, Moore might have heard of the association's New Orleans chapter and its reparations advocacy. St. Cyr and Ella would have likely taught their eldest daughter to look down on this movement—just working-class folk scraping for an easy leg up.[37] But once Moore slipped out of the Black elite and became a Garveyite, she joined the early-twentieth-century reparations movement. The same year the feds jailed House, Garvey migrated to the United States, and the UNIA attracted a working-class base in many of the same cities where the association was popular.[38] The two groups shared more than membership. Redress was an important component of Garveyism, too. The UNIA leader called for both symbolic and material reparations, demanding European countries "hand back" the land, the riches, and the culture they had stolen from African people and their descendants in the Americas.[39] When Moore and Spraggs threw their support behind the UNIA's plans for state-funded African emigration, they were perhaps unwittingly engaging with a form of reparations.[40]

In time, Moore came to see the two great wars as further models for redress. When warring nations hammered out the 1919 Treaty of Versailles, Germany had to pay reparations for its wartime damages to the Allied and associated powers.[41] And after World War II, international courts again called on Germany to pay reparations for the Nazi regime's crimes against humanity, as well as the other Axis powers to the nations they had brutalized.[42]

And there were plenty smaller, U.S.-based reparations cases, too. In 1946, lawmakers approved the Indian Claims Commission Act, creating a mechanism through which Indigenous peoples could settle previous land and property claims as well as take private parties to court to demand redress.[43] Two years later, President Truman signed the Japanese American Evacuation Claims Act, which allowed Japanese Americans sent to internment camps during World War II to submit claims for their lost property, which many saw as a first step in obtaining reparations for the traumatic experience itself.[44] Although they were hardly adequate, these initiatives proved to Moore the government could be compelled to pay its citizens for past wrongs.

Why then, Moore reasoned, couldn't the American government repay Black people?

Moore and her fellow UAEW members set out to find a way.[45] Each night, after the day's packed schedule of advocacy was done, the UAEW women huddled in the Moore family home and researched. They pored over stacks of old books and papers borrowed from libraries, churches, and old friends, looking for successful examples of Black people getting reparations—or at least a clear justification for why they should. There was no limit as to what the Louisiana women thought might be useful; no source they didn't seek to find some sort of inspiration.

It seemed as if they might never find what they needed until, according to Moore's recollections, a clause in an old Methodist encyclopedia stopped her in her tracks. The eldest Moore sister ran her finger along the page as she read aloud: "Those who find themselves captives and do not place before their captors judicial demand for their liberation within a hundred years are considered satisfied and belonging to their captors."[46] It likely didn't take long for the other women to realize what their leader had already surmised. Here was a passage, based in the Christian faith, that could be interpreted as a directive for Black people to petition for reparations—and soon. This was it. The thing they needed to galvanize their brethren to demand redress.

Moore gathered the other members of the group, and the women quickly mobilized. As Callie House had done long before, they launched a campaign to encourage Black Americans to file formal reparations claims within the next two years, before the centennial anniversary of the Emancipation Proclamation came in January 1963.[47] Even if the basis of their reparations activism was nebulous, the group's mission was clear. This small band of Louisiana Black women had jump-started the modern reparations movement.

CHAPTER 14

Somebody Has to Pay

Anyone who passed by 714 North Thirty-Fourth Street in West Philadelphia could have mistaken it for a meetinghouse or a school. Word had got around that the home belonged to three elderly sisters, old-school organizers who had set up shop in the City of Brotherly Love. Those who took a quick peek inside the front window saw walls lined with bookcases and young Black men strewn about in old, thrifted armchairs, their laps piled high with books. Some of them perused pamphlets that surely raised eyebrows: *The Communist Manifesto,* for one. Others held books with "*Negro Liberation* by Harry Haywood" printed down their spines. One or two sat on the floor, encircled by newspaper articles, glancing back and forth as if trying to decode a message.[1]

Sometimes the living room transformed from a study into a meeting room, and silence gave way to conversation, spirited debate, and laughter. Activists, ministers, and community members came and went, day and night, their booming voices carrying off into the Philadelphia air. "You want to make revolution in a capitalist country," the eldest sister would say, "you got to first understand how capitalism works." She'd shove a book into a young man's hand on his way out the door with a parting warning: "I want you to get this; I don't want this to get you."[2]

Philadelphia was a cradle of nationalist dreams—both Black and white. Although it was ground zero for the founding of the American nation-state, the city was also home to some of the most successful campaigns for Black rights and autonomy in the country.[3] And if the rumors were true, Audley, Eloise, and Loretta Moore had come to radicalize its Black masses. But for Audley in particular, fleeing to Philadelphia was as much a personal endeavor as it was political.

Moore had helped Jose gain parole right before the end of his eight-year sentence. She married him as soon as he was out in 1961, on a balmy May day in Manhattan.[4] But getting out of jail didn't deliver Jose from his demons. By his own account, years of carceral violence had left Jose traumatized, prone to "nightmares of people chasing him and attempting to kill him." When he was awake, he heard voices and saw people from his past who weren't there. The fury and the bravado that had made Moore's heart flutter when the two first met now terrified her.[5] A change of scenery, she hoped, might help ease his mind. And Philadelphia, home to the third-largest Puerto Rican population in the country, seemed as good a place as any.[6]

Moore also hoped to rekindle her relationship with her son. Marrying a man Tom's age hadn't helped matters. Still, she knew the root of the issue wasn't Jose; it was her long track record as an absentee mom. "I left him alone all his life because there was struggles and I had to go," she explained. By Moore's reasoning back then, Tom was just one child, and there were millions of other Black children who needed her just as much. "That was the way I consoled myself, running away, you know, to leave him."[7] Tom was a survivor. But Moore knew that with each passing year her chance to make amends with him shrank. Moving her family and the UAEW headquarters to Philadelphia was her Hail Mary.[8]

Tom's world looked very different from how Moore's had all her adult life. He had gotten married back in New York and had started a family since moving to Philadelphia. And thanks to the GI Bill, he became the first in the Moore family to go to college.[9] For a young, educated Black man, Philadelphia had real promise. Its 1951 charter included the creation of the Commission on Human Relations, a government agency that mandated fair employment practices and banned discrimination in private hiring and housing. This opened up a range of jobs for young Black men across the city. And for some, the possibility of homeownership.[10] Tom was just one among many who had found success in Philadelphia. He moved into the northwest neighborhood of Germantown, and with it, up into the American middle class.

Moore lived close to her son, but looking at her neighborhood, you'd think it was worlds apart.[11] The Moore sisters and Jose settled in West Philadelphia, amid a hodgepodge of single-family homes, apartment buildings, public housing complexes, and abandoned lots, all densely crowded and racially segregated.[12] Though the neighborhood was poor, it still had a rich cultural life. Small businesses, social clubs, Black theaters, and Latin music clubs were all a stone's throw away from the Moores' new home, and there were myriad Black and Puerto Rican neighborhood associations and community groups throughout the city aimed at helping ease the hardships of life.[13]

Moore hoped Jose could find a bit of home here. It was a far cry from San Sebastián, where he was born in 1929. But as the youngest of eight children in a farming family, Jose had always wanted more from life than his little island town could offer.[14] By the time he came into the world, U.S. corporations had turned almost a third of all arable land on the island into sugar plantations and seized control of Puerto Rico's essential infrastructure, including the postal service, railroads, and seaports. Jose's hometown was crumpling under the weight of the sugar monopolies and expensive U.S. imports by the time he was a teenager.[15]

Dreaming of a different life, Jose might have been drawn to the "Generation of 1930," a group of Puerto Rican intellectuals, writers, and artists who were carving out a national identity, and a nationalist consciousness, in the early twentieth century.[16] Jose was too poor to get his hands on their books and poems, and it's possible he couldn't yet read and write anyhow. But if he had hitched a ride to the neighboring city of Arecibo, he would have witnessed these writers' dreams of a free island brought to life. The Cadets of the Republic, the Puerto Rican Nationalist Party's paramilitary group, marched through Arecibo's streets dressed in white pants, black shirts, black ties, and overseas caps, their black boots clicking in unison to announce their arrival.[17] Their cries of "Viva la República" were a call for the island's unconditional and complete independence from the United States. Though Jose had only a seventh-grade education, he was savvy enough to catch the message.[18]

Jose's nationalist sympathies grew as he did, perhaps making him prey for the FBI. In the 1930s, Hoover extended his dragnet to the island through the Carpetas program: a massive surveillance outfit that tracked and suppressed anyone who entertained the idea of a free and independent Puerto Rico.[19] Jose was likely one of many caught in the bureau's crosshairs. Settling into a Puerto Rican community on the mainland would be a fresh start, a chance to lose any agents who had been tailing him on the island. He decided to join the nearly half a million Puerto Ricans who journeyed Stateside after World War II in search of a new life.[20]

If there was anyplace a Black and Puerto Rican Nationalist couple could build a life together, it was Philadelphia. Garvey's UNIA had been particularly popular there. During the two world wars, the city was home to the second-largest UNIA division in the nation, with a broad enough membership base to support a choir, a Black Cross Nurse unit, a UNIA-owned grocery store, and a medical clinic, all of which chugged along until the mid-century.[21] Many locals stayed true to Garvey's mission even as his organization dissolved. Others melded into the Nation of Islam, a religious and nationalist group that Georgia-born Elijah Muhammad now headed and that borrowed both its political principles and its iconography from the UNIA. Malcolm X, who had come from a family of Garveyites and was now a nationalist leader in his own right, became the leader of local Temple No. 12 in 1954. His tenure helped further entrench the NOI in the northern part of Philly.[22]

But the NOI wasn't the only player in town. By the early 1960s, Philadelphia's Black and Brown communities were vibrant and booming, and they brought a newfound militancy to the mainstream civil rights struggles raging nationwide. Jose didn't have to wander far to find collectives like the Puerto Rican Civic Association, which would have seemed politically conservative by his nationalist standards but also could have connected him to more like-minded countrymen such as Roxanne Jones and Juan Ramos, who were making increasingly militant demands for Puerto Rican rights by the early 1960s.[23]

Their organizing mirrored the work of local Black activists like Cecil B. Moore (no relation). Similar to Tom, Cecil was a veteran who had migrated to the city hoping it would live up to its harmonious reputation. However, the daily injustices he experienced as a lawyer defending Black folk like those in Moore's neighborhood quickly dashed his dreams.[24] His clashes with the local white establishment—

namely Frank Rizzo, a white police officer who eventually became the
city's police commissioner and mayor—fomented Cecil's radicalism.
His adoption of Black Nationalist rhetoric and tactics left him with
few friends among the Black liberal elite. But the poor and working-
class Black folk were behind him. The lawyer turned activist quickly
gained the support of a wide swath of Black Philadelphians who
elected him president of the local NAACP, a sign they were ready to
reject high-minded ideals of nonviolence.[25] Even as Cecil alienated
moderate Black movement leaders like Dr. Martin Luther King Jr.
(whom he even discouraged from visiting the city), Black Philadelphians rallied for their charismatic, sharp-dressing firebrand and his
dreams of prosperity.[26]

Philadelphia's students soon caught the rebellious spirit, too. It all
started several hundred miles away on February 1, 1960, when four
Black students at North Carolina A&T wandered into a Woolworth
department store in Greensboro, browsed for a few minutes, and then
sat down at the lunch counter. "We don't serve colored in here," the
white waitress told them as they each asked for a cup of coffee and a
doughnut. Segregated lunch counters were a staple across the South.
Stoic in the face of hecklers—Black and white—the four freshmen
stayed in their seats until the store closed. Their "simple impulsive
act of defiance" caught flame. The following day, they returned with
reinforcements. By the end of the week, some two hundred students
had joined the protest.[27] Black students across the country soon followed suit, taking over movie theaters, restaurants, pool halls, and
department stores, refusing to move until the white owners agreed
to serve them.

The sit-ins were just the start. Soon the sentiment had spread to the
decades-long fight to desegregate interstate travel. On May 4, 1961,
seven Black students and six white ones nervously boarded two New
Orleans–bound buses in Washington, D.C. They weren't breaking any
laws; with its 1960 *Boynton v. Virginia* decision, the Supreme Court had
just added bus terminals, restrooms, and other travel facilities to the
list of public places where segregation was banned. But segregationists
didn't care. The mere sight of Black Americans riding the same buses
or sitting at the same depots as white folk was enough to send racists
into a rage. The students, who were also members of the Congress of

Racial Equality, knew this. They hoped for it, in fact. In provoking an incident, they sought to force the federal government to intervene and defend their rights.

Their ride through Virginia and the Carolinas was relatively peaceful. It was in Alabama where the real battle began. As they entered the Yellowhammer State on May 14, 1961, another Greyhound bus driver signaled to the Freedom Riders' driver to pull over. A white man bolted across the highway and hurriedly told him that there was an "angry and unruly crowd gathered in Anniston" and police had closed the local bus terminal. The kids on the bus went cold hearing the news. But there was no turning back. Hoping the crowd would be little more than a few irate locals, they told the driver to press on. Their bus crept into the station around 1:00 p.m. and all seemed quiet. At first.

Suddenly a mob rushed the coach. About fifty white people holding pipes and pistols, and led by the local Klan chapter, surrounded the Freedom Riders, screaming racial epithets and calling them "dirty Communists." "Duck down, everyone," one rider screamed as the mob started slashing tires and throwing rocks at the windows. The police arrived on the scene belatedly and lackadaisically, chatting with the mob before clearing a path for the Freedom Riders' bus to leave. The driver put the bus into gear and followed the police cars out of the station, leaving a trail of shattered glass in its wake.

The Freedom Riders made it out of Anniston, but the fight wasn't over; it was time for round two. Their police escort turned back and left; the Riders were again at the mercy of a new mob of Klan members and white supremacists, some of whom had arrived on the scene from church and were dressed in their Sunday best. With two flat tires, the bus soon crawled to a stop. "Fry the goddam niggers," the mob yelled as three white men "tossed a flaming bundle of rags through a broken window." A plume of black smoke engulfed the bus as the kids inside frantically searched for a way out. Some crawled headfirst through open windows as the mob members blocked the front door of the bus. It was only after a fuel tank exploded that they retreated and the remaining Freedom Riders were able to escape.[28] The mob took aim at the Riders with bats and bricks as they spilled out of the bus, but with the help of a few local Black and white folk, the student activists made it to local hospitals, nursed their wounds, and again vowed to continue. But no bus company or driver was willing to transport them. It seemed the Freedom Rides were at an end.

"The students have decided that we can't let violence overcome," Nashville sit-in organizer and Fisk University student Diane Nash said. She knew if the young activists stopped riding buses then and there, the racists would win. The Chicago native turned southern organizer gathered a local, interracial group of students, and on May 20, 1961, they decided to continue the Freedom Rides.[29] As Nash and the new group of Freedom Riders boarded a bus to Birmingham, they prepared to face the same fate as their peers from the North: ravening mobs, severe beatings, and arrests all across the South. But the message was getting out. Aghast and embarrassed by the photos of racist violence printed in newspapers around the world, Attorney General Robert F. Kennedy feverishly worked the back channels, procuring buses and police escorts to get the Freedom Riders to New Orleans safely. But he couldn't bring southern governors and police chiefs to heel. The violence continued into the fall, with police arresting hundreds of Freedom Riders all while the Kennedy administration beseeched the Interstate Commerce Commission to uphold the *Boynton* ruling.[30]

The Freedom Riders had galvanized their fellow students back on campuses. At Central State College in Ohio, for example, a group called Challenge began to make waves. An ideologically diverse collective of Black leftists, Challenge sparred with segregationists on and off campus in hopes of fostering Black consciousness and creating a more racially inclusive learning climate.

When Challenge members and Philadelphia natives Muhammad Ahmad (Max Stanford) and Wanda Marshall weren't out protesting their university's paternalistic policies, they were reading revolutionary literature, including writer and cultural critic Harold Cruse's article "Revolutionary Nationalism and the Afro-American," which reiterated many of Moore's long-standing nationalist claims. The more Ahmad, Marshall, and other students studied, the more they became convinced that militant Black activism was the way forward. In the spring of 1962, Challenge evolved into the Revolutionary Action Movement (RAM), a youth-based nationalist group that promoted militant activism and armed self-defense. And when summer break came later that year, Ahmad and Marshall brought the student fight back to their hometown, setting up a RAM chapter in Philadelphia, where the Moore sisters were now settling in.[31]

As the heat of summer took over, RAM was making hard-won progress integrating the City of Brotherly Love. But Ahmad had doubts about the cause. He questioned whether the risk and the debasement of these sit-ins were worth it, just for a seat at a white table where Black people would never, truly, be treated as equals.[32] At the advice of Malcolm X—after a trip to Harlem, where he and Marshall met with the notorious activist in a fluorescent-lit restaurant—Ahmad decided to keep his compass pointed toward nationalism.[33]

The pair decided to reinvest in RAM and in radicalizing Philadelphia's Black working class.[34] The city's old guard on the Black Left was intrigued: here was a group of young activists with a nationalist fire and a keen class analysis. It wasn't long before Ahmad and Marshall caught the eye of a local elder, Ethel Johnson, who was known for nurturing Black radicals and scorching white supremacists. Johnson saw promise in the young leaders, but they still had much to learn. So, she pointed Ahmad and Marshall toward the best local radical ideologue she knew: Audley Moore.[35]

"You, darling, you are the one I want," Moore called to Ahmad, pointing at him as he tried to disappear around a corner in her house one day. Although Moore had just moved to the city, her home was already an epicenter of political activism. She was hosting a "Save Mae Mallory" meeting that afternoon. A Harlem-based Black Nationalist, Mallory had gone to Monroe, North Carolina, to help local organizers Robert and Mabel Williams support another group of Freedom Riders who were set to arrive on August 28, 1961. After white supremacists attacked the nonviolent student organizers, the Black community gathered in front of the Williams home ready to defend themselves and the Freedom Riders. An old white couple, Bruce and Mabel Stegall, drove onto the Williamses' street and into the fray, enraging the Black crowd, who was convinced the Klan had sent them to scout out "what defenses" they had amassed for the night. As the crowd grew irate, Mallory and Williamses offered the couple refuge inside. The Stegalls thanked them for the gesture by later claiming the pair had kidnapped them. Convinced the Klan would soon be out to kill them, Mallory and the Williams family fled. Robert and Mabel escaped to Cuba. Mallory went underground. As part of the Women's Committee to Save Mae Mallory, Moore raised awareness and funds to defend Mallory from prosecution.[36] And according to some, Moore even offered her home as a safe haven for Mallory while she was on the run.[37]

Ahmad didn't know much about Moore, beyond that she supported Mallory and that she had been a member of the Communist Party back in the day. Coming of age in the McCarthy era, Ahmad had been taught that "communists could brainwash you." He was, by his own admission, scared to death of the woman.[38] And so he decided that he would just try to blend in and scope out the scene. In and out.[39]

Moore had also heard of Ahmad and his work organizing students in Philadelphia and Cleveland. When she noticed the young wall-flower, she tried to corner him. It scared the "living daylights" out of him, and Ahmad immediately made for the door. But Moore caught him on his way out. "If you ever want to come by," she told him as he looked around nervously, "the front window of my study is open, just raise it and come on in."[40]

A few weeks later, the young organizer was making his way through the west side when he happened to pass by Moore's house again. He was still wary of the Moore women, but in that moment his curiosity got the best of him. Ahmad cautiously approached the home, climbed up the porch steps, and jiggled the front window. It was open, just as Moore had promised. He stilled and listened for voices. Nothing. He climbed into her first-floor study, and there before him was a world of rare books, newspaper clippings, pamphlets, and flyers, all gathered from Moore's decades of work. Even if she was a Red, Ahmad could see Moore had a life's worth of wisdom to give.

"Oh, what do we have here?" Moore asked when she found Ahmad ensconced in her office. He had been in the study for an hour or two before she had come down the stairs and found him. "Take your time, I'm going upstairs to fix us something to eat," Moore told him. When dinner was ready, Ahmad joined Moore upstairs, where she began to share her experiences from her decades in the struggle. When her lesson was done, she pulled out a cot, washcloth, and towel for the young activist and invited him to stay for the weekend.

Ahmad spent the next few days in deep discussion with Moore, talking about everything from communist class politics to nationalist ideologies. She encouraged him to read James S. Allen's *Reconstruction: The Battle for Democracy* and then move on to W. E. B. Du Bois's *Black Reconstruction* for a more textured understanding of what Black people endured after the Civil War. She distilled Marx and Engels's *Communist Manifesto* and paired it with the leading Black communist Harry Haywood's *Negro Liberation* to show him how European class warfare informed the Black struggle.[41] By Sunday, Ahmad realized Moore "made more sense" than "anyone in life." At the next RAM meeting, he assured the other members Moore was safe; she wasn't a Red, and she was an invaluable educational resource. The group agreed: they would approach the eldest Moore sister and ask her to be RAM's political adviser.[42]

RAM was only one of the many groups that sought out the Moore sisters' teachings. The women had now taken to hosting regular nationalist training sessions in their living room. On any given day, one might walk in to find Jose Cuevas swapping stories with Thomas Harvey, a local Garveyite legend and president of the UNIA, or Eloise chatting with Playthell Benjamin, a radical organizer, RAM member, and radio host who was always ready to spar.[43] Young activists chopped it up with community organizers, local Black preachers, and other nationalist leaders—including Malcolm X.

According to Moore, she first encountered the young nationalist leader in the late 1950s at an open-air meeting in Harlem, where he was living after NOI leader Elijah Muhammad made him head of Harlem's Temple No. 7 in 1954.[44] She liked what she saw. Not since Garvey had she come across a nationalist who could channel their political message in a way that captured the masses so. She made a point to befriend the burgeoning activist before she left that day, and she spread the word about him to her old communist and nationalist comrades when she sat down to catch up on her correspondence at night.[45]

Malcolm kept track of Moore, too. He scribbled down the location of her Danneel Street home in his address book when she left New York City in the late 1950s, in case he found himself in New Orleans on one of his speaking tours.[46] And now that Moore had come back to the Northeast, the pair reunited in her Philadelphia living room from time to time. At this point, Malcolm was no longer an up-and-coming preacher. He was the Elijah Muhammad–appointed representative of the Nation of Islam nationwide and the sagacious leader of the Black Nationalist Movement. But he knew he still had much to learn. If anyone walked into her house expecting to hear the Muslim minister speak, they would have been surprised to find that whenever he shared a space with Moore, Malcolm sat down, shut up, and listened just like everyone else in the room.[47]

Moore was generous with her knowledge, but she had an agenda. She wanted Malcolm, RAM, and the others she mentored to join her reparations fight. The clock was ticking down to January 1963, the deadline for when Black folk could file an official reparations claim. She had less than a year. Moore had been doing what she could to spread the word about her big push for repayment, but experience had taught her one activist alone wasn't enough to spark mass change. She needed a vehicle, an organization that would back her cause and boost her message. Moore soon saw her chance. Newspaper reports indicated that fifty delegates from different social, religious, and civil rights organizations were coming to Philadelphia to plan the citywide festivities celebrating the hundredth anniversary of the Emancipation Proclamation come January. The National Emancipation Proclamation Centennial Observance Committee (NEPCOC), as they called themselves, was a golden opportunity.[48]

The Black press arrived at a church on North Broad Street on a cold day in January 1962 to cover the NEPCOC's first meeting. Reporters expected to find representatives from mainstream groups—everyone from the NAACP and CORE to the Black Greek-letter fraternities and sororities. When they walked in, they were stunned. No civil rights groups or representatives from "orthodox denominations like the African Methodist Episcopal Church, the National Baptist Convention, and other organizations" were there. Instead, reporters found the Black Hebrews, led by a local clergyman named Rabbi Eliezer, Nation of Islam members, Moore and her sisters, and a handful of activists representing smaller Black Nationalist and African liberation groups.[49] From that point on it was clear: the NEPCOC's events would take on a decidedly different tenor.

By all means, the committee should aim to commemorate the freeing of slaves, Moore acknowledged once the nationalists had taken the helm. But the real, urgent work ahead of them was to redeem the losses slavery had wrought. The group agreed to orient the NEPCOC's plans toward a massive reparations drive, including organizing an elaborate parade in Washington, D.C., to commemorate emancipation and commissioning a "ship to tour Africa and to arrange for an equal number of Africans to tour the United States."[50] These events, they told locals and Black reporters, would kick off a national campaign to "mobilize more than 20 million Afro-Americans entitled to 5,000, or more, indemnity payments in the form of reparations for more than 300 years of forced free labor of their foreparents."[51]

The raucous parades and the tour ships were an obvious callback to Garvey's UNIA—to his marches that lit up Harlem's streets, and the Black Star Line that chugged from the Caribbean to the States. Moore looked forward to seeing it all come to life. She started by headlining events like the All-Africans Freedom Day Celebration and Bazaar. On April 12, 1962, Black men, women, and children packed into Philadelphia's Times Auditorium and milled about to the low, rhythmic beating of African drums until the lights dimmed and Moore took the stage. The spotlight followed her as she paced from one end to the other, speaking about Black people's "glorious African Heritage" and the systematic obliteration of their culture.[52]

Their "ancestors were sold as commodities, branded like cattle, not only with irons but with the ignominious term 'negro,'" she said. "Germany was forced by the Nuremberg Courts to pay reparations," and the "United States was forced to pay reparations to Japan." Surely America should pay Black people for its crimes, too. "1962 is the last year in which we may seek our reparations," Moore exhorted. Her urgency was palpable.[53] For many Black Philadelphians, it was the first time they'd ever heard of the concept of reparations. With Moore settled in their city, it certainly wouldn't be the last.

Next, she went to Washington, D.C., where the NEPCOC had hoped the Moore sisters would call on the newly elected president, John F. Kennedy, to consider making reparations a key piece of the upcoming centennial celebrations.[54] Moore suffered no delusions; she knew Kennedy wouldn't meet with the trio. But she also knew the power of a good photo op when she saw one. If anyone questioned the Moore sisters' commitment to the cause, the grainy photos that circulated in the Black press put their doubts to rest: three aged Black women, who had come to their nation's capital seeking an audience, being turned away at the White House gates was a poignant image. Moore and Rabbi Eliezer followed up this visit with an open letter to Kennedy, imploring him to act as the "zero hour of the Centennial approached."[55] But the photograph was the true fuel Moore needed. During her cross-country road trip in the summer of 1962 to drum up support for the reparations drive, it would become her badge of honor.[56]

By the fall, she was back in Philly with her family, headlining the NEPCOC conference. Black Americans were at a critical juncture. They were on the tail end of nearly a decade of sustained, high-profile civil rights action, most of which had angled for an equal seat at the American table for Black folk. The conference was meant to be a kind of gut check. In the great debate between integration and separation, which approach would ultimately bring Black Americans true liberation? For Moore, the answer was clear as day.

"Make no mistake," she opened at her keynote address, "we stand today at the crossroads of our destiny." Down one path was the well-worn road of "accommodation," a path "laden with wrecked hopes, partial victories that change nothing, and ever-recurring frustrations." Down the other, a "road to national independence and dignity, with freedom to determine our own destiny." She followed with two poignant questions: "Have we not traveled too long on the old road? Is it not time to change our objectives?"[57]

Moore understood the appeal of the mainstream Civil Rights Movement. She conceded that nonviolent resistance—the Freedom Rides, the sit-ins, and much more—had "forced the imperialist enemy to retreat" more than once. "We should not scoff at the non-violent resistance movement," she acknowledged. "But neither should we be deceived by the minor concessions to it by the enemy." Moore had hit her stride. "We nationalists reject and abhor the turn-the-other-cheek philosophy of Rev. Martin Luther King," as well as "enemy efforts to dictate and shape our program, policies, and tactics."[58]

"We are a nation within a nation," Moore concluded, quoting visionaries like Martin Delany and Marcus Garvey, nationalists who had come before her. And so it was only right, Moore told her audience, that they "demand" a "national territory in a country developed by our blood and tears and unrequited slave labor" as well as "reparations for the injuries inflicted upon us by the dominant white nation."[59]

Even at sixty-four, Moore still had it. She could move a crowd to action in mere minutes. Inspired and persuaded, conference goers penned the NEPCOC "Resolution on Reparations" then and there. The one-page document opened with a sobering assessment of the Black experience in America: "African People were forcefully transported from their ancestral home" under brutal conditions and "enslaved in what became the United States of America in the fifteenth, sixteenth, seventeenth, and eighteenth centuries." They were "reduced to chattels and their culture and family life completely destroyed."

Then they made their case: "Black victims of this system were ostensibly freed during and after the Civil War with recognition by Congress of their right to reparation" with "forty acres of land for each family as partial reparations."[60]

Moore was thrilled with her newest converts to the cause, even as they questioned her about the logic of her argument. How could a people who abhor the American government, and who deliberately hope to separate from it, demand repayment from it? Moore, as always, had an answer. Petitioning the "oppressor nation . . . in no way compromises our demand for recognition as an independent and sovereign nation," she told them, so long as they were using the government's resources in service to Black separatism and self-determination.[61]

Some of the younger activists in Moore's midst even took it one step further. On the last day of the conference, a handful of organizers created the African Descendants Nationalist Independence Partition Party (AD NIP), with the express aim of founding a separate nation on American soil. Moore spent her final moments at the conference guiding one of those activists, Nassir A. Shabazz, a young man from California, as he put forth the resolution to establish a "provisional government" for a "black republic" in the southeastern United States. Reparations would be the seed money for this venture, and it would require no small sum. Shabazz argued the United States owed its Black citizens $500 trillion total, part of which should be repaid in the land across the South that would become this new Black republic. The remaining balance would be paid directly to Black folk once a year.[62]

AD NIP's founders made quick work of building out their organization. They elected officials; established the Black Guards, a paramilitary wing; wrote a national anthem; and founded a Black Nurse

Corps not unlike what the UNIA had done before them. They dubbed October 14, as good a day as any other, African Descendants Independence Day.[63]

In what must have been a surprise to many, Moore wasn't elected as AD NIP's leader. Instead, she agreed to serve as the organization's minister of foreign relations. The younger organizers who had founded the party hoped her years of experience and deep political connections would lend the group credibility among elder Black Nationalists around the world.[64]

If it angered Moore to play second fiddle, she didn't let on. Although she had inspired and helped found AD NIP, she seemed content to cede leadership to the young men for practical, personal, and political reasons. For one, AD NIP's headquarters was on Fillmore Street in San Francisco, where Shabazz lived. Moore had no plans of uprooting herself yet again. She hoped to stay in Philadelphia with her husband, son, and sisters, and a less central leadership role allowed her to work from afar. It also can't be denied that she was still a Garveyite at heart, and she had come of age in a political world that equated power and leadership with manhood. Although she was well equipped to lead and had been doing so for decades, she was still prone to promoting Black men as the symbolic leaders of the movements she built, whether reparations or Black nationhood.[65] And last of all, she knew this fledgling reparations fight was going to be a long one. By ceding leadership to an energetic man like Shabazz, Moore hoped to bring momentum and vision to the cause that would last long after she was gone. Her instincts were, as ever, on the money.

A few days later, Moore was at home recuperating from the conference when she heard a banging on her door. Startled but not scared, she answered it, thinking it might be Ahmad or some other young organizer in need of help or advice. But when she cracked the door, a group of police shoved past her, flashing a warrant. Moore was stunned. She stayed rooted to the floor as the cops searched the house, handcuffed her husband, Jose, and loaded him into a squad car.

Moore followed them to the police station. There, she learned what had happened. Earlier that morning, Jose had gone to see his friend Rafael Caraquijo. Caraquijo had recently won $50 off Jose in a game of dice, but Jose needed cash. He wanted to borrow back $3. When Caraquijo refused, Jose pulled out his gun and shot the man, then came home to hide out afterward.[66]

It must have felt like déjà vu for Moore, once again fighting to get her husband out of jail, this time citing the lack of due process in his case and the arresting officers' violation of his constitutional rights. She testified on his behalf, but it was no use. A jury convicted him, and, Moore knew, as a repeat offender, Jose was unlikely to escape a harsher sentence. This time, Moore wouldn't be there to help him through it.[67]

Later, Moore would reframe her marriage to Jose much as she had her first two: as a hindrance to her political work. "I had a Puerto Rican husband and I divorced him because he wanted me to be his wife," she once said. "I didn't want to be a wife. I wanna be a queen." Jose, she claimed, found her to be ungovernable. He chafed at the idea that she should be the ruler of their home, of their marriage, and of her own life. To be sure, Moore was often frustrated by Jose's insistence that she take on a more traditional domestic role, and there must have been some sense of relief in her newfound freedom. She was also saving face. Many people in Moore's life had criticized her, questioned her judgment for marrying a convicted felon thirty years her junior. Now, when organizers from RAM, AD NIP, and other groups stopped by her house and asked after Jose, her answer was resolute: "I knocked that brother out of the way."[68]

However she truly felt, Moore was once again a one-woman show. With the mainstream Civil Rights Movement picking up steam around her, and the clock ticking down to her January 1963 deadline, it was time to kick her reparations tour into high gear.

CHAPTER 15

The Reparations Committee Inc.

Moore wasn't the only one ramping up her work ahead of the new year. Coming off a successful student sit-in movement and a wave of high-profile boycotts across the South, A. Philip Randolph dusted off his 1941 plans for a massive march in Washington, D.C.—this time with Dr. Martin Luther King Jr. as the face of the movement. With longtime behind-the-scenes civil and human rights organizer Bayard Rustin at the helm, King, Randolph, and myriad other organizations spent 1962 planning the March on Washington for Jobs and Freedom, all to compel Congress and President Kennedy to pass the Civil Rights Act, a sweeping piece of legislation that would outlaw discrimination based on race, religion, nationality, or sex.

Preparations for the massive protest came together in large part thanks to Black women leaders and organizers who performed much of the intricate, behind-the-scenes work. Women in Black churches, civil organizations, sororities, and clubs fundraised, planned, and provided transportation, food, and lodging for the 250,000 participants.[1] Moore, notably, wasn't one of them. As Black Americans set their sights on Washington for the next year's watershed march, Moore was on a one-woman pilgrimage west, to the city she had left behind decades earlier. She was on a mission to spread the gospel of reparations, and Los Angeles was ready to listen.

When Audley Moore first moved to the City of Angels in the 1920s, the racism she encountered was so intolerable that she left soon after she arrived. Forty years later, she found it had only metastasized in her absence. As she walked the streets, Moore discovered most of her old haunts on Central Avenue had shuttered and many of the city's pockets of Black prosperity were gone. Black life in L.A. had fallen behind the "cotton curtain" of the 1950s, which sought to keep people like Moore from living, working, or just simply *existing* in the surrounding suburbs.[2] Thanks to racist city planning policies and restrictive housing covenants, by 1960 the distinct Black enclaves she and Spraggs had once hopped between were now largely reduced to one packed neighborhood in the southwest part of the city, within the fifteen-mile stretch between Olympic Boulevard to the north and Artesia Boulevard to the south.[3]

Still, there was a silver lining, even if the shimmer was slight. Many mark the start of the city's nationalist reawakening as the spring of 1957, when Malcolm X came through and established Nation of Islam Temple No. 27.[4] By the time Moore returned in late 1962, Malcolm's Temple, as many locals called it, was known for hosting thousands of Black Angelenos for speaker series, night classes, and an Afro-Asian bazaar to foster Black interest in the Diaspora.[5]

But the NOI was only one of many leftist hotbeds. Nationalists and Pan-Africanists huddled together in shops and bookstores across the city, exchanging literature, ideas, and impassioned words. Anyone off the streets curious enough to pop in was welcome to join. Moore likely stopped in to talk to Alfred and Bernice Ligon, owners of the Aquarian Bookshop and Spiritual Center on West Santa Barbara Avenue, which displayed an impressive collection of pamphlets, magazines, newspapers, and paperback books on the Black experience. If Moore had a stack of NEPCOC literature tucked under her arm that day, as she so often did, she undoubtedly would have plopped a few "Resolution on Reparations" pamphlets down next to the other flyers, which read, "After 100 Years: Integration or Separation?" and "The New Africans in the United Nations."[6]

The Ligons were old guard. But if Moore wanted a more youthful take, she could talk to Adele Young, activist, owner, and manager of the Hugh Gordon Bookshop on a deteriorating but still determined Central Avenue. Young had been working since the 1950s to make the shop a hub for Black education.[7]

But it was at Africa House where Moore truly found her tribe. Billed as a space for "Black Americans, Africans, and Blacks of African descent" to "join hands culturally, socially, and economically, and historically," the community center was founded and run by two former Garveyites, Pat and Sanford Alexander, who also owned and edited the popular Black newspaper the *Herald-Dispatch*. When Africa House opened in 1959, the Alexanders hoped to help Black Angelenos better connect with Africa's past and present by hosting markets, lecture series, and even language classes.[8] It was a lofty goal, but it grabbed the attention of like-minded advocates across the country.

The Alexanders, in turn, were keeping their ears to the ground. When they heard about Moore's efforts to drum up support for reparations claims in 1962, they were delighted. They began running articles on the NEPCOC in the *Herald-Dispatch* on the regular. When readers picked up a paper, they learned about Moore's reparations push alongside articles about Africa House, the political landscape of Los Angeles, and the syndicated column "God's Angry Men," written by the Alexanders' personal friend and frequent visitor Malcolm X.[9]

Moore's arrival in Los Angeles sparked a wave of grassroots reparations advocacy across the city. Spurred on by the looming January deadline, the Alexanders joined other local organizers in founding the Reparations Committee for the Descendants of American Slaves—or Reparations Committee Inc. for short.[10] Moore was named both the president and the public face of the group, and the *Herald-Dispatch* offices on Jefferson Boulevard became its makeshift headquarters. The newspaper was the committee's greatest tool in mobilizing Black Angelenos to stake their reparations claims. Full-page advertisements invited them to a weekly slate of activities: everything from teas and luncheons to lectures held at Black businesses and meeting halls.[11]

The Black Left was plenty skeptical. Even *Herald-Dispatch* readers wondered why they should join the reparations cause amid the more widespread push for civil rights legislation. The Reparations Committee Inc. had its answer at the ready. Civil rights legislation alone could never truly level the racial playing field. Such laws sought to ban discrimination today and forevermore. But they didn't account for the centuries of dehumanization and degradation that Black people had already endured. The American government needed to atone monetarily for its racist past before Black people could invest in the country's future.

Reparations Committee Inc. members pressed their literature into the palms of potential recruits on their way out the door at Africa House. Their most popular piece was penned by Moore herself and titled *Why Reparations?* Ever the pragmatist, Moore provided the answer in her subtitle: "Reparations Is the Battle Cry for the Economic and Social Freedom of More Than 25 Million Descendants of American Slaves."[12]

For $1.50, Black Angelenos could snag a pamphlet and find Moore's opening salvo. "After 244 years of free slave labor and the most inhuman, sinister and barbaric atrocities which pass in magnitude any savagery perpetuated against human beings in the history of the planet earth," she wrote, "the Committee [is] seeking Reparations for the descendants of America's Slaves."

Moore called out America's hypocrisy as a self-styled champion of human dignity: "The United States is a *signatory*" of the UN charter and its Universal Declaration of Human Rights, which "prohibit cruel and oppressive treatment of any racial or ethnic group." And yet the United States continued to violate that very same charter, and even its own Constitution, through its flagrant mistreatment of Black citizens.[13]

Moore knew her readers would have their doubts. She had met her fair share who argued reparations, no matter how deserved, were implausible—if not impossible. But this was no pipe dream. Moore had spent sleepless nights studying with her sisters, dredging up precedents from the forgotten corners of history. Her call for recompense was bold, but it was hardly novel.

And what's more, it was methodical. The Reparations Committee Inc. had already filed a claim for money damages on behalf of twenty-five million Black Americans, Moore wrote. She knew her readership was more moderate in its politics, relatively. By and large, they were interested in reparations as a means to better their lives as Americans. The idea of building a sovereign Black nation wasn't even on their radar. It's maybe why Moore's most famous treatise on reparations is steeped in the rhetoric of American uplift. Reparations could help alleviate "the national poverty which the American citizens of African descent suffer as a result of chattel slavery," she explained. And her solutions went beyond just cash dropped into bank accounts. She called for hiring quotas in every level of American industry, with Black Americans entitled to 13.1 percent of all jobs. And she envisioned robust training programs to prepare this new Black workforce for success, to "balance the mal-treatment of which the Negro has been a victim in this country for over [2]44 years." Without these efforts,

Black people would never catch up. They'd never truly "be on equal terms with White America."[14]

It was as strong a claim for repayment as the Black Left had heard to date. History bore witness to Black Americans' right to cash recompense. And they would have it, according to Moore—not in just "a few thousand dollars for one group to control" each year, but in community programs, education, infrastructure—tangible, life-altering, and lasting gains for the atrocities that Black folk had endured.[15]

The Reparations Committee Inc. dutifully echoed Moore's clarion call, expanding the reach and scope of its work. The small but determined nonprofit filed a formal claim on behalf of *all* Black people in America in December 1962—a last-ditch effort in anticipation of the Emancipation Proclamation centennial. While this claim wound its way through the courts, the group made plans to lobby local legislators to introduce reparations legislation in Congress requiring the government to pay "money damages to African slaves' descendants."[16]

A handful of interested Black folk in San Francisco joined the group in hopes of eventually building a chapter in Northern California.[17] But as the committee continued to spread its wings, it veered further away from Moore's nationalist vision. Whereas AD NIP comprised Black Americans and was separatist in its aims, the Reparations Committee Inc. began welcoming "all people regardless of race, religion, and political affiliations" among its ranks. What's more, it shied away from calling for the establishment of a separate Black nation on American soil.[18] Rather, it billed reparations as the best way to usher "25 million step-citizens [into] the American Dream."[19]

Meanwhile, the Kennedy administration had planned a stunt of its own. On Saturday, September 22, 1962—one hundred years to the day after Lincoln had signed the preliminary Emancipation Proclamation—the White House threw the Emancipation Proclamation Centennial Celebration for the nation. It was a hastily cobbled-together affair. Nevertheless, Black Americans gathered around TV sets to watch the festivities taking place on the steps of the Lincoln Memorial. United Nations ambassador and former Illinois governor Adlai Stevenson headlined the event, while New York's governor, Nelson Rockefeller, presented an original draft of the final proclamation, which had gone into effect on January 1, 1863, to the Library of Congress. Black faces were conspicuously absent, save for Thurgood

Marshall—now a federal judge—and famed gospel singer Mahalia Jackson. Also missing was President Kennedy himself.[20] He prerecorded his remarks for the day. Moore likely listened closely, hoping to hear some mention of reparations. Instead, Kennedy noted the "remarkable fact" that "despite humiliation and depravation, the Negro retained his loyalty to the United States and democratic institutions" and "never stopped working toward his own salvation." Moore must have cringed. But on one item, she and the president agreed. "Like the Proclamation we celebrate," he said, "this observance must be regarded not as an end, but a beginning."[21]

Ultimately, the January 1, 1963, deadline Moore had heralded came and went without any meaningful action from the government. Black churches, civic groups, and college communities marked the occasion instead. The congregants of the Sixteenth Street Baptist Church in Birmingham welcomed a pastor from the Tuskegee Institute in Alabama to celebrate the day, while the members of the Sigma Gamma Rho sorority sponsored a three-day celebration in St. Louis, replete with Black history classes and a local pageant.[22] The mayor of Columbia, Missouri, proclaimed January 1 would henceforth be Emancipation Proclamation Centennial Day, and the faculty and staff at Wayne State University in Detroit kicked off a yearlong celebration that included lectures, performances, and granting of honorary degrees to prove how far Black people had come.[23]

Still, Moore took President Kennedy at his word; she treated this first reparations push as the beginning of something greater. Though she vehemently disagreed with what the March on Washington stood for, she also saw it for what it was: an opportunity to boost her message. In the summer of 1963, Moore wrote to her old friend A. Philip Randolph and told him of her efforts over the "last six years to inform our people of the advantages of supporting the move for Reparations," her work establishing the reparations movement, and her desire to spread the word in Washington. She hoped her bona fides on the Black Left would persuade him to let her speak at the march.[24]

Forty years earlier, Moore and Randolph had been on the same side at protests and picket lines. But time had sent them down diverging roads. Randolph rebuffed his old comrade. Moore retaliated publicly, claiming "the Negro Revolution of 1963 with its anti-climax March on Washington on August 28 resulted in little or no gains for the Negro masses." The march was doomed to fail, she argued. True integration was "only possible among equals."[25] And equity in America could not be, not without recompense.

Back in Philadelphia that fall, Moore set out to rally some heavy hitters to her cause. Whether at movement meetings, at protests, or just in her living room library, Moore would corner the young minister Malcolm X whenever and wherever she could. The scion of the Nation of Islam studiously listened to Moore's lectures, as always. But he was slow to take her cause on. It wasn't that he wasn't interested in movement politics. Malcolm believed "wherever black people had committed themselves, in the Little Rocks and Birminghams and other places, militantly disciplined Muslims should also be there—for all the world to see, and respect, and discuss."[26] But Elijah Muhammad forbade his acolytes to get involved in the political struggles of the times. This irked Moore, who, like Malcolm, believed the NOI should take a more active role in radical organizing. She later remarked with no lack of irritation that before Malcolm "could even say the word" "reparations," he'd first need permission from Muhammad.[27]

Now that Malcolm had an international reputation—Muhammad designated him the NOI's official global representative, much to the chagrin of the ailing leader's own sons—Moore trained her sights on the young minister. She believed he could be one of her movement's "bravest and most dedicated soldiers," given the chance.[28]

Malcolm was desperately pushing Muhammad to let the NOI take a stand on racial issues. At the same time, he had to attest to his loyalty to the man whom many called the Messenger and allay fears that he was trying to usurp the organization. But everything changed when rumors began circulating of Muhammad's rampant infidelity. After months of trying to stay the course, Malcolm finally broke ranks. He contacted the women—former NOI secretaries, no less—with whom Muhammad had allegedly committed adultery and fathered children out of wedlock. It was in these closed-door discussions that Malcolm learned Muhammad had branded him as dangerous, "tearing [him] apart behind [his] back."[29]

Though Malcolm was reeling, Moore believed he was coming into his own. She was delighted to see some of herself—her writing, her lectures, bits and pieces from the conversations they had shared—cropping up in his public remarks. In front of a packed house at Michigan State University, Malcolm challenged his audience's antihistorical and degrading beliefs about Africa. "The average American Negro" believes "when he was kidnapped by the white man, he was a savage in the jungle," he said, chastening the crowd. "There were civilizations on the African continent at a time when people in Europe were crawling around in caves."

Africa's stolen riches were a recurring theme for Malcolm. "If I take the wages of everyone here, individually it means nothing," he continued. "But collectively all of the earning power or wages that you earned in one week would make me wealthy. And if I could collect it for a year, I'd be rich beyond dreams." Magnify that by the millions of Black people whose wealth and wages had been stolen for the past 310 years, and "you'll see how this country got so rich so fast."[30] A grave debt was due to the Black victims of American empire.

At the same time, Moore's ideas were gaining purchase closer to the political center. At the close of 1963, Dr. Martin Luther King Jr. had come to a similar conclusion as Malcolm. King noted that at the start of the year "plans were afoot all over the land to celebrate" the "one hundredth birthday of the Negro's liberation from bondage." But all the celebrations and the committees and the pageantry "only served to remind the Negro that he still wasn't free, that he still lived a form of slavery disguised by the niceties of complexity."[31]

King felt America owed a "long-overdue debt" to Black citizens, and they demanded recompense. It couldn't be purely symbolic. King, like Moore, believed preferential treatment for Black Americans was a viable way forward.[32] Of course, their end destinations diverged. King would never come to understand what he deemed a nationalist fantasy, "some imaginary state" either at home or back in Africa. His dream was the American Dream.[33]

Moore's life and work came to a screeching halt later that fall, when on October 10, 1963, her beloved sister, mentor, teacher, and confidante Eloise passed away.[34] The doctors said it was cancer. But Moore insisted Eloise died of a broken heart, shattered by the degradation that her people still endured, even as the Civil Rights Movement gained steam.[35]

Nationalists from Philadelphia and New York turned out to mourn the middle Moore sister that fall. She had an "insatiable desire to learn," her friends and family eulogized. She was "what you call a leader. Eloise was a thinker. Eloise was a philosopher." She "educated herself on every subject."[36] But now she was gone, and far too soon. As they all laid Eloise to rest, a small group of Black Nationalists from across the country vowed to keep her legacy alive through the Eloise Moore Award, a prize for those in the movement who shared Eloise's insatiable thirst for knowledge.[37]

But for Audley, soldiering on without her sister felt impossible. Eloise was everything to her. She was the one who first pushed Moore out of her comfort zone and into a life of activism all those decades earlier in Anniston, Alabama. She was a courageous and principled thinker for whom no idea was too radical. She was the one you could trust to be at any protest at a moment's notice or to stay up into the morning hours poring over political theory. But of course, above and before all, she was Moore's little sister—one third of the Moore women, who had been scraping a life together on their own since they were kids. Audley Moore's world would never be the same.

Moore chose to enshrine her younger sister's legacy a little differently than the other mourners. Though she was hardly a wordsmith, she poured her grief into the rhyming verses of "The Enigmatic Eloise Moore's Philosophy and Works":

> *Eloise, the Enigmatic: Deep as Egypt's Sphinx*
> *We owe a debt to her, as she taught us how to think,*
> *About Nationhood, Reparations, Self-determination and such*
> *To her without fundamentals, life did not mean much . . .*

If there was ever any doubt, this showed that Moore believed she owed her younger sister everything—her political consciousness, her cause, and the future she fought for:

> *Eloise taught the motives and the reasons why,*
> *They not only called us "negroes,"*

But kept us looking in the sky,
For milk and honey, such lies they told,
While they robbed Africa of her streets paved with gold.
The immortal Eloise couldn't accept a name that wasn't a proper noun,
She chided a capital "N" to that misnomer, made us appear as clowns.

A truth is a truth[,] take it as you please,
A major contribution was made by Eloise.[38]

The surviving Moore sisters began circulating the poem as part of a pamphlet meant to raise money for the Eloise Moore Memorial College of African History and Research. They hoped to build the school and research center on Mount Addis Ababa, a plot of land in Parksville, New York, the trio had bought a few years earlier. They named it after Ethiopia's capital city, a beacon of African pride.[39]

A year and a half later, Audley and Loretta had moved back to the Bronx. Still grappling with their grief, on February 21, 1965, they switched on the wireless to news that would shake the whole of the country: Malcolm X was dead. The Moore sisters rushed to Harlem in search of anyone who could confirm it. Amid crying crowds and mass confusion, they learned what had gone down.

"As-salaam alaikum," Malcolm began, offering the typical "peace be with you" greeting of the Muslim faith. It was all he had time to say before two men started tussling in the back of the auditorium in the Audubon Ballroom. As Malcolm and his security turned their attention to the fight, a member of the Newark temple, William 25X, ran up from the fourth row, pointed a sawed-off shotgun at Malcolm, and pulled the trigger. The blast threw Malcolm up and backward and left him lying on the stage and gasping for air. Two more men, Thomas Hayer and Leon Davis, then approached. They drew their pistols and needlessly fired more rounds into him. Malcolm X took his final breaths in front of his pregnant wife, Betty Shabazz, and three of his daughters.[40]

In time, the motive behind the assassination became clearer. Years earlier, Elijah Muhammad had suspended Malcolm from the Nation of Islam indefinitely after a series of high-profile scuffles—most notably, Malcolm's insistence that John F. Kennedy's assassination was a case of "the chickens coming home to roost." Then, in March 1964, Malcolm announced he was starting his own organization, Muslim Mosque Inc., a space that would provide a "religious base" for Black folk to carry out the "political philosophy of Black nationalism."[41] But his five-week tour of the Middle East and Africa months later— during which he made a pilgrimage to Mecca and received a new Islamic name, El-Hajj Malik El-Shabazz—had blessed him with "new insight into the true religion of Islam, and a better understanding of America's entire racial dilemma."[42] When Malcolm returned, he created the Organization of Afro-American Unity (OAAU), a Pan-African group whose foundation was built, in part, on Moore's philosophy of reparations.[43] Modeled after the Organization of African Unity (OAU), a coalition of fifty-three African nations founded in 1963 that worked to unify and free the continent, Malcolm's group hoped to link America's Black Nationalists with those from the motherland. Such a holistic approach to Black liberation coupled with Malcolm's popularity spelled trouble for the separatist and sectarian NOI. Malcolm had to be stopped before he ended them.

Six days later, Moore returned to Harlem to mourn her student. Donning a leopard-print headdress and scarf, and silver earrings that swayed in the frigid February wind, the aged activist walked down barricaded streets lined with mourners and made her way to the Faith Temple Church of God in Christ. At the front of the church lay El-Hajj Malik El-Shabazz, his body shrouded in a simple white cloth, as was the Islamic funeral tradition, and placed in a copper coffin.

Moore lingered after the pallbearers carried the slain leader out of the church and into the silver-blue hearse that would wend its way to his grave site at Ferncliff Cemetery in Hartsdale. She passed crying women clustered together on the sidewalk and students discussing Malcolm's politics on stoops. "That man didn't teach violence like the papers all say. He taught me about myself. He taught me I was more than a Little Black Sambo or Kinky Hair or nigger," one woman said. "He opened my eyes."

Eventually, Moore spoke up. But she didn't strike the same chord as the chorus of mourners there. "I wasn't a follower of Malcolm X," she told the group. "I was his mother. He used to call me his Queen Mother."[44]

CHAPTER 16

Becoming Queen Mother

A year later, almost to the day, Moore awoke to a bitter chill in the air before she donned a dress and a fur-lined, checkered cape and hurried to 110th Street and Lenox Avenue. When she rounded the corner, she hoped to see hundreds if not thousands gathered and ready to begin a procession to mark the first anniversary of Malcolm X's death. But when she got there, Moore found only about seventy-five people willing to brave the cold to honor the slain nationalist. She hid her disappointment as the clock struck 11:30 and a drummer clad in a black leather hat and black boots began to tap out a slow, solemn beat. The crowd arranged themselves "three abreast" behind the percussionist and a row of marchers carrying a fringed red, yellow, and green flag emblazoned with an ankh—the Egyptian symbol of life. The sound of the drum ricocheted off the brick buildings as they paraded through the barren Harlem streets for an hour and fifteen minutes.

Barred from renting the Audubon Ballroom, Moore rallied the small procession at the front entrance of the two-story building and exhorted the crowd to keep Malcolm's ideals alive. "Arise you mighty, captive, non-self-governing nation...because you can move mountains if you dare!" she shouted. It was as if she were conjuring the spirit of her teacher, Garvey, in memory of one of her favorite students, Malcolm. "Uhuru!" Moore called as she finished her speech, reciting the Swahili word for freedom. Her breath fogged in the cold air. "Uhuru!" the crowd responded with upraised fists.[1]

Three months later, Audley and Loretta joined Malcolm's sister Ella Collins, musician Max Roach, and singer Abbey Lincoln for a small commemorative ceremony at the OAAU headquarters in the Hotel Theresa.[2] That the Moore sisters had been invited to such an intimate event was a testament to their relationship with Malcolm and to their deep commitment to the community he had left behind.

Malcolm, Moore still believed, belonged in the pantheon of nationalist greats alongside Garvey and Nkrumah. But she was never one to leave her own praises unsung. In what was quickly becoming a sort of calling card for the aged activist, Moore circulated her latest work of poetry, "The Princely Malcolm X," at memorials like this:

> *The impact of Malcolm upon our struggles were great.*
> *To engage our enemies in verbal combat, he'd not hesitate.*
> *He brought dignity, depth and courage to our cause*
> *Trying to teach our people that there was no Santa Claus.*

However rocky the start, Moore's poem ended on a crescendo:

> *Like Jesus they crucified him, though he knew they would*
> *But he kept on preaching until we understood.*
> *We the elder mothers loved him so,*
> *but we chided him on the phrase "so called Negro."*
> *Tell our people who they are, we used to say*
> *and that's why they're called Afro-Americans today.*

> *But we knew Afro was not our proper name.*
> *To us, the terms Afro and Negro are just the same.*
> *We went to the platform after the meeting was through*
> *And whispered in his ears, "we must talk to you"*
> *"Africans-Americans" [sic] is the proper way to describe*
> *our people and Malcolm said, "OK."*
> *That's the last I remember seeing him alive*
> *Next I heard on the radio just about five*
> *the news that shocked the world, "Malcolm had died."*

> *Like Garvey, Lumumba, and Eloise*
> *Malcolm died to keep our people off their knees.*
> *Not one of them thought us to be meek*
> *Nor to stand abuse and turn the other cheek.*
> *That philosophy to them made no sense.*
> *Their answer to brutality was self defense.*

Their memory will live forever in our hearts
As long as each of us pledge to do our part
To hold up the blood stained banner for which they fell
And send our oppressors, where they belong,
                    IN HELL[3]

Elsewhere across the United States, the Black Left was radicalizing in the wake of Malcolm's martyrdom. Nowhere was this more the case than in Lowndes County, in the heart of Alabama, where Black residents made up 80 percent of the population but only one Black person could vote. Hoping to change this, local Black folk created the Lowndes County Christian Movement for Human Rights the month after Malcolm died and launched a voter registration drive. When the members of the Student Nonviolent Coordinating Committee (SNCC) heard about this enfranchisement effort, they knew they had to support it.

Founded at Shaw University in April 1960, SNCC was an interracial group of students committed to nonviolent direct action to achieve civil rights. Like many other organizations then, SNCC staged sit-ins and boycotts across the country. But it also embedded itself in Black communities to help amplify existing grassroots work. After a few short years of living, working, and organizing in the Deep South and across the country, SNCC had helped propel the passage of the 1964 Civil Rights Act and the 1965 Voting Rights Act. Angered by Malcolm's death, but buoyed by a wave of post-1965 Black voter registration, its members began to wonder how they could help Black people govern their own communities. Lowndes County seemed as good a place as any to start.[4]

Stokely Carmichael was among the SNCC members who went down to Lowndes. A former Howard University student and Freedom Rider, Carmichael had the know-how and the charisma to spark a movement. He and his fellow SNCC workers, including Bob Mantz and Gwen Patton, had been living and working in Lowndes County for about a year when another SNCC researcher discovered a Reconstruction-era statute that allowed voters to form their own political party. An idea was born. Local folk created the Lowndes County Freedom Organization, the first all-Black political party in the South, in April 1966.[5]

By this time, Carmichael was a rising star in SNCC. In May 1966, the group elected him its new chairman. "Mr. Carmichael does not advocate violence but neither does he believe in turning the other cheek," *The New York Times* reported upon his ascent. Anyone could see the clear shift, post-Malcolm. Even the more mainstream groups were getting a wild hair.[6]

The media followed Carmichael when he headed to Greenwood, Mississippi, the following month. The twenty-five-year-old, Trinidad-born activist had come down South to continue activist James Meredith's one-man March Against Fear—or the Meredith March, as some called it. Back in 1962, Meredith had endured a harrowing fight to desegregate the University of Mississippi. Four years later, on June 5, 1966, he decided to take on a solitary march from Memphis, Tennessee, to Jackson, Mississippi, to call attention to the rampant racism and voter discrimination in the South. As soon as he set out, white supremacist Aubrey James Norvell shot him down. Meredith survived, but couldn't complete his trek. So, Dr. King, Carmichael, and the newly elected head of the Congress of Racial Equality, Floyd McKissick, vowed to march in his stead.[7]

They were hounded every step of the way, and Carmichael was particularly agitated on this hot summer night in June—having endured weeks of death threats, arrests, and scuffles with southern police and vigilante racists—as he climbed onto a makeshift stage in Greenwood's Broad Street Park. "This is the twenty-seventh time I've been arrested," he exclaimed, holding the microphone in his left hand, gesticulating with his right, a bright spotlight illuminating his face in the Mississippi night. "The only way we gonna stop them white men from whuppin' us is to take over. What we gonna start sayin' now is Black Power!" Carmichael's intensity electrified Greenwood's Black citizens. News of his "Black Power" speech spread like wildfire.[8]

A hundred miles away, members of the Lowndes County Freedom Organization were making good on Carmichael's clarion call. Envisioning an all-Black political party that could challenge white control over their towns, schools, and lives, they established a democratic caucus ahead of the November 1966 local elections and ran a slate of Black candidates for every office, from the sheriff to the county coroner. They called their caucus the Black Panther Party, pat-

terned after an animal that when pressured, according to SNCC organizer Ruth Howard, "moves back until it is cornered, then it comes
out fighting for life or death." Black people in Lowndes had been
backed into a wall politically, financially, and economically for nearly
a century. It was time for them to fight back.[9]

As they were organizing, a young Black man in Oakland, California,
came upon a pamphlet touting how everyday Black folk in Lowndes
County were trying to take back their communities through their
Black Panther Party. "A few days later," Huey P. Newton recalled,
"Bobby [Seale] and I were rapping and I suggested that we use the
panther as our symbol." The infamous Black Panther Party for Self-
Defense was born.[10]

Four hundred miles south, in Los Angeles, activists still clung to
Malcolm X's calls for a cultural revolution as well. The summer after
Malcolm was gunned down, the predominantly Black south central
neighborhood of Watts went up in flames. The six days of Black civil
unrest that followed, in the summer of 1965, is now known as the
Watts Rebellion. That fall, local organizers Maulana Karenga, Dorothy Jamal, and Brenda Haiba created the US Organization ("US" as
opposed to "them") to help the residents rebuild their decimated city
and embrace Malcolm's call to reclaim Black culture.[11]

Guided by the idea that culture is the "crucible in which Black
liberation takes form," Maulana Karenga developed the Kawaida doctrine, a political ideology to help Black Americans reconnect with
their ancestral African cultures—or to create new, Black-centered
traditions where those ties had long been severed.[12] US encouraged
Black Los Angelenos to adopt West African names, hairstyles, and
dress. They believed that by engaging in cultural and political ceremonies modeled after precolonial African societies, Black Americans
could heal the cultural ruptures that the Middle Passage had wrought
and push Black folk toward political action. One such tradition, and
maybe the most famous of Karenga's creations, was Kwanzaa: the holiday inspired by African harvest festivals and devised as an alternative
to Christmas.[13]

For some young activists, including writer, poet, and award-winning
playwright Amiri Baraka, US-devised celebrations were the "next
stage" of Black organizing. Together with his wife, Amina, Baraka

created the Committee for Unified Newark (CFUN) in their New Jersey city, another Kawaidist organization that used art, poetry, and cooperative projects to transform the lives of Black Americans.[14]

Kawaidists across the country joined in the zeitgeist, and all under the banner of Black Power. Some sought power through politics. The 1965 Voting Rights Act outlawed the grandfather clauses, poll taxes, and literacy tests that had barred Black Americans from voting for generations. Armed with this legislation, student and grassroots activists alike organized massive Black voter registration drives that propelled Black politicians into power in cities like Gary, Newark, and Cleveland in the late 1960s. Men like Richard Hatcher and Carl Stokes became the first Black mayors and representatives since the Reconstruction era, transforming the local and national political landscape, redrawing district lines, and shifting control of federal and state funding for housing and schools to Black communities.[15]

But even with these gains, life was still hard. While the Lyndon B. Johnson administration had worked to better racial conditions in America, its methods were suspect. In January 1964, Johnson introduced his War on Poverty social welfare campaign, only to follow one year later with his War on Crime.

Black people were the connective tissue between these two battles. As Johnson explained, in order to end poverty, the government had to "eliminate the causes of criminal activity whether they lie in the environment around us or deep in the nature of individual men."[16] Rhetorically, Johnson was advocating for poverty eradication as a form of crime reduction. Realistically, he planned to deputize the government to quell crime at all costs. Local police budgets ballooned, and for the first time officers were tasked with not only addressing crime but also identifying high-crime areas in an effort to prevent it. Where did they look first? The Black and Brown neighborhoods that War on Poverty programs had also targeted.[17]

The Vietnam War only further accelerated the growing conflict between Black communities and the American government. The Cold War–era battle had been raging since 1955. But by the height of the Black Power Movement, the military was drafting Black men at higher rates, offering them fewer deferment opportunities, and placing them on the front lines more often than their white counterparts.[18] The

Black wing of the antiwar movement soon ramped up to meet the moment, with activist and SNCC worker Gwen Patton founding the National Black Anti-War Anti-Draft Union (NBAWADU). Whereas the white-led peace movement was content with ending the war and leaving American racism and imperialism intact, Patton sought to center Black people's unique struggles during wartime.[19] NBAWADU was among a growing number of young Black activist groups that openly questioned America's purported role as a global emancipator.

As this new wave of activism washed over the country, Moore noticed a trend. There were echoes everywhere of the "de-Negroization" philosophy she had coined so many years earlier, the idea that *true* liberation for Black folk required a paradigm shift, a fundamental redefining of their identities outside the values of white America.[20] Much to her delight, this younger generation began to reject the word "Negro," instead asserting the beauty and boldness of being Black. Moreover, this revolution of the mind was taking on distinctly diasporic dimensions, in large part due to the successful African decolonization struggles unfolding throughout the 1960s.

Audley Moore watched with wonder as more and more young Black activists began to identify with African cultures to assert their race pride.[21] Now, when she stopped by rallies, she met organizers sporting Afros and donning colorful dashikis. Taking stock of the world around her, Moore began to wonder if it was time that she wore her Africa-oriented politics on her sleeve, too.

Adopting a new, bold, and pro-Black persona was trickier for women than it was for men during the Black Power Movement. Black Americans had long charted a course toward liberation through Black manhood and male leadership, whether that man carried a message of unity like Dr. King or of militancy like Malcolm X. But this hypermasculine rhetoric reached a fever pitch after white sociologist and Assistant Secretary of Labor Daniel Patrick Moynihan released his 1965 report on the ongoing crisis of American race relations and Black poverty, *The Negro Family: The Case for National Action.* Moynihan had ostensibly intended the study to ameliorate racial inequality in America. But he did more harm than good, pointing to a lack of Black male leadership in the home—and, in turn, the allegedly high proportion of Black women-led households, or "black matriarchy"—as the primary source of America's racial ills.[22]

Black activists soon adopted this position in droves, claiming women who took on prominent leadership roles were "emasculating" and "castrating" their men and undermining the liberation struggle. Black women were quick to point out these arguments relied on the same paternalistic, white supremacist ideas the movement railed against—never mind that they had been dictated by a white man on the government's payroll. But still, a Moynihan-shaped shadow hung over the movement. As she watched young leaders battle over the gender politics of liberation, Moore found her place within the fray. This was the same minefield she had been tiptoeing through since her days as a Garveyite, after all. And for a woman who had joined the Black Nationalist cause in the early twentieth century, her ideas of gender and leadership were as clear as they were predictable.

A Black woman "has to understand that her man has been demeaned, emasculated," Moore often lectured. "Her role is to support, to understand first of all what has happened to her black men, that they have been singled out for destruction."[23] A life spent witnessing lynchings, visiting Black men on death row, and leading protests in memory of boys killed by police had left its mark on Moore. She was convinced Black men were the primary targets of the genocidal American project, and she had long made them the focus of her reparations campaigns. Thus, she could imagine no "greater role" for a Black woman "than to protect her black man" and "build him up."[24]

Moore was especially concerned that the contemporaneous Women's Liberation Movement was undermining Black liberation. As white women witnessed Black people sit in, stand up, and boycott for their rights, they began to wonder whether they, too, were second-class citizens. By the mid-1960s, many white women had begun to openly chafe at being relegated to homemaking and child-rearing, despite attending college and putting in time in the workforce. And when they did somehow manage to forge a path into the workplace, men corralled them into low-paying, gendered jobs as secretaries and waitresses.

Right as Black Power organizers were finding their voice, women started marching for equal rights, too, and all amid the mainstream media's increasing attention to gender discrepancies in employment and education. A bevy of books, manifestos, and anthologies dedicated to defining feminism, eradicating patriarchy, and advocating for reproductive rights started to circulate throughout bookstores and at street-corner rallies.[25] And much to Moore's chagrin, both Black and white women began investing in separate, feminist organizations dedicated to ending sexism.[26] Moore was especially stunned to find that some of the most radical Black women organizers in her midst, like New York–based lawyer and activist Florynce Kennedy, had joined these feminist ranks.[27]

Moore had heard this story before, or so she believed. And she knew how it ended. She had endured decades defined by Black bodies swinging from a lyncher's rope or burning atop a pyre—and most often because a white woman had lied to protect her reputation. Moore didn't trust the white-led feminist movement; she refused to collaborate with it, and she advised other Black women to do the same. There were no "special problems for the black woman as apart from her people," she asserted. Black women had "no part in the fight that white women find necessary, to fight their oppressive white men."[28]

Her reluctance to lock arms with white feminists was easy enough to understand. But around this same time, Moore's vision for the growing Black Power Movement took a turn toward the unconventional. She argued white women's maligning of Black men had created such a "vast shortage" of them it was becoming a chronic problem.[29] Her solution, at least in terms of what Black women could do to address the crisis, was to embrace polygamy. Polygamy, she argued, was a remedy to a social problem and "the antithesis of the individualism taught" in American society. Not only would it help Black communities pool economic resources and familial labor, but it would also allow Black women—who she believed outnumbered men in society because of incarceration rates—to have the intimate relationships and families they desired. Even as she argued that "male chauvinism would be countered by women's increased involvement in leadership," Moore still believed Black liberation needed a man as head of both household and movement.[30]

For whatever it's worth, Moore never actually practiced what she preached. She was ever secretive on matters of the heart, and she rarely spoke about her three marriages. If she had any lovers later in life, she kept everyone in the dark about it. What she did clearly relish, though, was the male attention that her patriarchal, pro-polygamy position garnered. Young Black men across the country heralded Moore as a movement leader, in part because her support of polygamy helped satisfy their "black nationalist yearning for a romanticized African past" where polygamy was a part of precolonial life—which isn't to say that the contemporary American compulsion wasn't for a man to have as many women as he could get.[31] Adopting this position gave Moore a wide berth within the Black Power Movement. Whereas younger women had to contend with their youth—their viability as wives and mothers would be continually pitted against their prowess as thinkers and leaders—Moore seemed to occupy a special place. Queen Mother, as she had now embraced calling herself, was above the politics of sex and desire. Cultures and societies across Africa used the title. It connoted an elder woman's political and social centrality, her undeniable influence in her community.[32] As Queen Mother, Moore was a matriarch. She could interrupt, engage, correct, and chastise a man and yet never be accused of making a play for his position or sexual attention.

Even if they chafed at Moore's politics, the younger Black women of the movement were reluctant to rebuke its Queen Mother. Moore had always commanded respect. But it was even harder now that she looked the part. By the mid-1960s, Moore left the house clad exclusively in colorful African-print fabric. It looked as though she floated down the streets, skirts billowing. She always donned a matching head wrap, covering a full head of hair gone completely gray. The headdress was a crown, of sorts. It pulled her hair back to reveal her wrinkled neck, adorned with gold or beaded necklaces and framed by dangling earrings. Her stacks of matching brass and beaded bangles clinked as she went about her way. They announced Moore's arrival before she entered a room.

Beneath her robes and wraps, the skin on Moore's arms and face had loosened with age. But her mind was sharp as ever. Moore commanded street corners and stages with the same old orator's magnetism that had made her a household name in decades past. If anyone who met Moore in the mid-1960s found the origins of her stately title murky, the power it afforded her was clear as day. As Queen Mother, Audley Moore was beyond reproach.

Though Malcolm and others were early adopters of Moore's "Queen Mother" honorific, they were hardly the first. "I'd heard that two African students died after getting their Ph.D., from malnutrition," Moore would open whenever anyone asked about the origins of her title. While living and working in Harlem and the Bronx in the 1950s, Moore had met several students who came from Africa to the city's colleges and were struggling just to survive. It haunted her: "So terrible to think that right here in the United States, we had an African student hungry." Harking back to Eloise's makeshift recreation center for Black soldiers during World War I, Moore found an empty storefront in Harlem and opened up a soup kitchen of sorts—a place for African students to eat and study after classes. "I'd put on a pot of stew, or beans, every day, and they'd come," she recalled. "I also bought, in an old secondhand store, an old raggedy mimeograph machine and a piece of typewriter where they could do their work."[33]

Those students, like so many others, saw Moore as a kind of maternal figure. They started calling her "Queen Mother" in homage to her work, caring for members of the Diaspora from both sides of the Atlantic.[34] At the time, the honorific sat uneasily on Moore's shoulders. But a decade later, and amid the flourishing of the Black Nationalist Movement in the 1960s, she finally felt worthy of it.

For Moore, becoming a Queen Mother was more than a power play. It was a political transformation. Although she had course corrected and recommitted to nationalism after her years in the Communist Party, Moore was still hard on herself. She kept a running tally of all the times she believed she had operated with a "Negro Mind": everything from giving her son a Western name, to praying to a white god for decades, to all the years she had spent organizing for token integration. "Sometimes it takes a long time to come out of being that made thing—that Negro," she later reflected.[35] Embracing her role as a Queen Mother was like shedding old skin. She was now her true self, her African self—Queen Mother, in all her glory, of a people who were fighting to reclaim a heritage that had been torn from them.

In the afterglow of this transformation, everything began to look different. Moore had long ago abandoned any attachment to the idea of American citizenship. But she had never questioned the valid-ity of what Reconstruction had hoped to be. That enslaved people should become Americans once they were freed had always felt like a given. Now, reflecting on decades of hard-won victories and crushing defeats, she saw what should have been obvious from the start: the U.S. government had never actually asked Black people if they *wanted* to be Americans.[36]

In her estimation, a real conferral of rights during Reconstruction would have been to give Black people the right to *choose*: become an American citizen, or return to their home country. Moore now saw the Fourteenth Amendment as less an act of liberation and more an act of coercion. "We were made citizens in the United States without our consent," she said plainly.

It was no longer enough, she felt, to simply reject the Negro mind-set or to tout the race pride chants of the day: "Black Is Beautiful" and "Say It Loud, I'm Black and I'm Proud." Black people needed to fundamentally redefine their relationship to America and reconnect with Africa on a deeper, ancestral level. She implored her community to abandon any allegiance to the idea of being Americans, and even of being Black. They were "captive Africans born inside the USA."[37]

As captive Africans, Black people had to orient themselves around a new set of cultural, political, and spiritual values. Moore was determined to prove it was possible, to walk the walk herself. And religion would be her starting point. She had long ago lapsed on her family's Catholic faith; her parents' deaths saw to that, exposing her to the vapid culture and classism of the church. And her political awakening had only further stoked this spiritual discontent. Reading about the Crusades and the Spanish Inquisition, Moore discovered a long tradition of the church mistreating Black people. "I wondered how we could have ever been Catholics," she said. "Roman Catholics that is."[38]

But even after joining the Ethiopian Coptic Church, she struggled to reconcile her own humanity as a Black woman with the Christian church's racist dictates. She longed for a genuine African religious practice. She found it in the Yoruba Temple in the heart of Harlem.

Here, Moore joined a community that was centuries in the making. The Yoruba people first came to North American shores through the Transatlantic Slave Trade. Hailing from present-day Nigeria and Benin, the West African community transformed the Americas through food and culture, and most notably through melding with the traditions of Candomblé in Brazil, Santería in Cuba, and vodou in Haiti, among others.[39]

These practices had largely died out in the United States until Nana Oseijeman Adefunmi I (Walter Eugene King) revitalized them by connecting the African-based religion with the surging Black Nationalist Movement in the late 1950s. The Detroit-born religious leader studied the Yoruba religious practice in its many forms before creating a uniquely Black American iteration of it.[40]

Situating oneself in the "wider world of Africa, ancient deities, and ancestors" felt like second nature to many Black Americans—nowhere more so than in Harlem, where Black folk had been recovering their relationship to Africa for decades. But the movement got a jolt when Adefunmi established the Order of Damballah Hwedo, Ancestor Priests and positioned its headquarters in Harlem in 1959. While Moore was heading the Universal Association of Ethiopian Women in New Orleans, a handful of Black folk started gathering on Sunday evenings in Harlem to learn about continental cultures and try to master African languages.[41]

When Adefunmi met Cristobal Oliana, a Cuban priest who introduced him to Santería, he broke away from his old order and established the Shango Temple on East 125th Street. A year later, that outfit morphed into the Yoruba Temple on West 116th Street.[42]

By the time Moore returned to Harlem, the Yoruba Temple was a thriving "center of African culture."[43] She soon became part of a core group of members including women such as Mama Keke, a Barbadian woman who had been a part of the Order of Damballah Hwedo; Afro-Cuban and Afro–Puerto Rican practitioners; and local Black Nationalists who could still recall the days when Garvey ruled Harlem.[44]

On any given day, Moore could be found attending an Africa-centered festival to honor the Yoruba river goddess, Oshun, on the Hudson River; learning more about African languages and customs at the temple's headquarters; or following Adefunmi, Mama Keke, and other temple members down 125th Street in a parade to promote the temple and its classes.[45] "I've always felt a special kinship with the Yoruba," Moore observed as she became more entrenched in temple life. While she knew it was no panacea, she believed that joining the temple was an important step in reconnecting with her lost African heritage more broadly.[46]

Even still, "re-Africanization" wasn't an instantaneous shift. There were pieces of Moore's old life that she struggled to relinquish. Case in point: her name. Yoruba Temple members furthered Moore's belief in the power of naming, bolstering her claim that slave masters had stripped enslaved Africans of their ancestral names in an effort to sever them from their homeland. As such, they bestowed on Moore the name Iyaluwa—a fitting moniker, because it meant the mother of the people.[47] But even for someone as dedicated as Moore, the shift was tough.

"I don't use them," she once admitted, sheepishly, of the African names this and other Africa-oriented groups had bestowed upon her. "I'm very ashamed of that. . . . It's a growing process."[48] For Moore, it was hard to fully abandon her given name, one of the last remaining threads connecting her to generations past in Louisiana. Never lacking in guile, she began to claim her familial name actually had African roots—to the Moors, an admittedly European term used to describe sixteenth- and seventeenth-century North African Muslims. It might not have convinced her naysayers. But if anyone had the gall to question her reasoning, her reproach was simple. "People don't know me by Audley Moore," she would say. "They know me by the name Queen Mother Moore."[49] Regardless of the surname she chose, the matriarch of the movement had been crowned.

CHAPTER 17

We Refuse to Be Programmed Anymore

S tand up in front of the class, introduce yourself, and tell us how much cotton you can pick," a white teacher once told Moore's comrade Mae Mallory when she was younger.

In the 1930s, Mae's mother had moved her and her brother from Georgia to New York in hopes of eking out a better life. It all seemed possible when she woke Mae up and got her dressed for her first day at an integrated school in Brooklyn. But Mae's mother's dream was dashed as quickly as she had divined it.

"I never picked cotton," Mae replied, indignant even at such a young age.

"Well, all Negroes pick cotton in the South, so tell the kids about picking cotton."

"You're a liar," Mae retorted. Aghast at her impudence, Mae's teacher sent her home and told her not to return until her mother had taught her how to act.[1] Mae would return to school in due time, where she learned such interactions were par for the course.[2]

Although officials began integrating schools in the Big Apple in 1883, separate and unequal remained the norm for the city's Black youth well into the twentieth century. Residential segregation and restrictive covenants enforced racialized zoning, sorting Black and white children into separate schools with wildly different resources. And in those rare cases where geography alone couldn't preserve racist schooling, teachers and principals were known to take up the cause themselves.[3]

As early as the 1920s, communities in Manhattan and Brooklyn had begun launching litigation, forming parent committees, and developing Black-centered curricula to be adopted, hoping to purge racism from their local schools.[4] Yet even as groups like the NAACP worked toward integration, some members—including its co-founder W. E. B. Du Bois—questioned whether it was worth the toil. Black children undeniably deserved to learn in integrated, equal schools. But Du Bois could see the cost of the integration movement, plain as day. It left many Black schools underfunded and others shut down entirely. Some Black teachers were jobless, unable to find work in white schools. And those few Black students who did make it into predominantly white schools had to suffer through racist insults and frequent violence just to get their education.[5]

Black Nationalists were resolute: the cost of integration was too high a price. Instead, they spent the 1920s and 1930s building independent Black schools. Moore watched as in New York and across the nation, UNIA divisions founded night schools offering literacy and history classes.[6] The Nation of Islam pursued a similar strategy, establishing parochial schools. By the late 1930s, even some non-NOI parents opted to enroll their children in the Nation's schools rather than force them to endure the dehumanization of public schools.[7]

As an organizer with little formal schooling, Moore had always sought out alternative means of learning: street-corner lecturers, local bookstores, and cultural centers. She had seen firsthand how important these spaces could be to a community when she managed the Harlem People's Bookshop in the 1930s, and as a visitor to bibliophile and civil rights activist Lewis Michaux's National Memorial African Bookstore on Seventh Avenue and 125th Street in the 1940s. Ceiling-to-floor bookcases bowing with Black history books enveloped Moore as soon as she stepped into Michaux's shop. And when she sat down and cracked one open, she found herself in fine company. Portraits of Marcus Garvey, Harriet Tubman, and Sojourner Truth, among so many other legends, looked out from their frames as she studied. Michaux's bookshop had been one of the sole centers of learning for Harlemites for years until Richard Moore opened the Frederick Douglass Book Center in the 1950s.[8] It was in these spaces that Moore and her sisters discovered that a self-guided study of Black history, politics, and culture could be just as illuminating as what any public school could offer, if not more so.

After the *Brown v. Board* decision, she found that Black parents were still fighting the local boards of education. New York's schools were still hypersegregated. And yet conversations about public education were suffused with an ethos of "color blindness": the smug sense that racism couldn't possibly exist in the North, and that all students had the same chance at success regardless of race. Moore, in the middle of her post-communist political awakening, began to see the public school system as a cornerstone of the "Negroizing" process. But her calls for Black New Yorkers to create separate, Black-centered places of learning went largely unanswered.

Seasoned political strategist and organizer Ella Baker led the local NAACP's widespread desegregation campaign after *Brown,* but it suffered fits and starts.[9] It wasn't until Mae Mallory, now a mother in her late twenties, and her daughter, Patricia, appeared in *The New York Times* in 1957, beside the headline NEGRO SUES CITY ON SCHOOL ZONING, that the conversation around school segregation shifted in New York.[10]

Twelve-year-old Patricia was a bright girl with big dreams. She wanted to go to college and become a dietitian. Mallory knew the segregated school her daughter was zoned for in Harlem could never adequately prepare her for it. So she enrolled Patricia at PS 118 on the Upper West Side, a wealthier, mostly white neighborhood. When the school board blocked Patricia's enrollment, Mallory sued with the help of a young Black lawyer named Paul Zuber. They filed a lawsuit claiming that despite the *Brown* ruling, de facto segregation was still alive and well in New York City public schools.[11]

Eight other Harlem mothers joined Mallory in her lawsuit. And as the case wound its way through the courts, they attacked school segregation on all fronts. They joined other parents in calling for Black history to be added to public school curricula, and they demanded an "open transfer" policy so their kids could attend schools outside their zoned districts, just as Mallory had tried to do with Patricia.[12]

Next up, the "Harlem Nine," as the press dubbed them, refused to send their kids to their designated junior high schools. The boycott was a stress test. Zuber suspected the city would charge the moms with violating New York's compulsory student attendance law, thus forcing a judge to make a ruling on their pending suit.[13] He was right. In December 1958, Domestic Relations Court judge Justine Polier sided with the Harlem Nine, stating, "These parents have the constitutionally guaranteed right to elect no education for their children rather than to subject them to discriminatory, inferior education."[14] The community lauded Mae Mallory for her boldness—as did Moore, who followed the story closely. But she also knew these isolated lawsuits and modest protests weren't enough. They needed a bona fide grassroots movement.

Five years later, as Queen Mother Moore barreled down the Bronx sidewalk in her burly coat on a cold January day, she wondered if the moment had finally come. Everywhere she looked, on lampposts and in storefront windows, she saw flyers featuring a photograph of a frowning Black boy peering through a dirty, broken window. "I Don't Have a Good Integrated School," read the bold text. In the middle of the flyer was a call to action: that all of New York turn out for a citywide "Freedom Day" boycott on February 3, 1964.[15] Milton Galamison, a Brooklyn minister and activist, had partnered with March on Washington mastermind Bayard Rustin to coordinate the massive, five-borough boycott of New York City schools.

It was a blistering-cold, twenty-three-degree day. But more than 460,000 students and parents bundled up and headed out to join the picket lines in front of their three hundred respective schools, their gloved hands carrying signs declaring, JIM CROW MUST GO! and WE DEMAND QUALITY EDUCATION. Thousands of others attended Freedom Schools, pop-up independent schools across the five boroughs, established to combat their racist public counterparts.[16] Rustin declared it the "largest civil rights protest in the nation's history," and he was right.[17] It was a tremendous spectacle. But just as Moore suspected, it barely moved the needle.

For many in New York City, this was the final straw. The failures of the Freedom Day boycott foregrounded the futility of integration and the dire need for a separate, Black-centered education system. Moore had long served as a foot soldier in this very struggle. Now she was prepared to lead the charge.

Intermediate School 201 would be the staging ground for Moore's first campaign. After years of pressure, the New York Board of Education had finally built a new, state-of-the-art school on East 125th Street, between Central and East Harlem. It was an attempt to assuage accusations that the board only ever funded white schools. IS 201 was strikingly different from any other public school in Harlem. Although the three-story structure had a modern look and up-to-date amenities like air-conditioning, it more resembled a fortress than a place of learning with its brick walls, few windows, and slender metal fences encasing the building.[18]

But its baffling design was the least of the community's worries. The board of education declared that when it opened in the fall of 1966, IS 201 would have equal numbers of white, Black, and Puerto Rican students—supposed proof that New York's schools really were color-blind. Black parents knew all too well the school's success depended on white student enrollment; the city always gave more funding and resources to schools with a significant number of white kids. And so, the very same summer that Stokely Carmichael was calling for Black Power in the South, Harlem parents were pressuring school officials to deliver on their promises of equal schooling in the North. But by September, officials had managed to register only nine white students. In a school of nearly eighteen hundred, it wasn't nearly enough.[19]

"Either they bring white children in to integrate 201 or they let the community run the school—let us pick the teachers, let us set the educational standards, and make sure they are met," Harlem Parents Committee spokesperson Helen Testamark told the *Times*.[20] When school officials did neither, the committee called for a boycott. On September 12, 1966, only half the students enrolled at IS 201 entered the building for the first day of school. The rest joined Mae Mallory, Queen Mother Moore, and many others outside on the picket line.[21]

During the first three weeks of the protest, the cabal of Black parents and activists won key concessions. They forced the school's white principal, Stanley Lisser, to resign, though he was later reinstated with some help from the powerful teachers' union. They persuaded the school to hire a Black administrator, and they got Black history lessons added to the curriculum.[22] But most important, IS 201 caught the attention of one key power broker.

Once a family-based philanthropic juggernaut, in the 1960s the Ford Foundation shifted its focus to promoting potential solutions to the racialized civil unrest spreading across cities like Los Angeles, Newark, New York, and Philadelphia—what liberals had begun calling the urban crisis. Under the leadership of McGeorge Bundy, the foundation shifted toward supporting Black education.[23] As the battle raged on, the Ford Foundation stepped in to fund three schools: one in Brooklyn, one on the Lower East Side, and IS 201 in East Harlem. These three schools would be test cases, of sorts, to see whether New York's Black neighborhoods could run their own schools.[24]

The cause garnered widespread support and made for some strange bedfellows in the early to mid-1960s. Queen Mother Moore, not known to be a friend to white authority figures, found herself joining New York City's mayor, John Lindsay, in rallying behind the program, along with the African American Teachers Association and a large swath of Black parents and activists. But others, notably the United Federation of Teachers (UFT), saw the Ford funding as a threat.[25]

The UFT was a group of young, scrappy, white liberal teachers who sought to represent educators all across the city. Formed in March 1960, the upstart organization was just as idealistic as the decade that birthed it. It bargained for raises across the board, duty-free lunch periods, increased paid sick leave, and more.[26] After a successful strike for higher wages that same year, union membership skyrocketed. By the mid-1960s, the UFT was such a force it was effectively co-managing the New York City public school system.[27]

The UFT wasn't always antagonistic toward Black school organizers. That wouldn't come until 1964, when Albert Shanker, a slim man with a swooped side part and angular glasses, became its president. Under Shanker's leadership, the group changed tack, forsaking its social justice roots and lobbying against Black demonstration districts like IS 201 because they didn't employ union members.[28] Not long after it had gained Ford Foundation funding, IS 201 was once again sporting a picket line—only this time, it was the UFT hoisting the signs.

Moore did not take kindly to it, to say the least. "You better not ever show your faces at the school again," she hurled at the picketing teachers from the corner of Madison Avenue. "If any one of you ever dare return to this school to teach our children we will take you apart."[29] Her onslaught continued as she accused the white teachers of practicing "mental genocide" against the Black children of New York.

Next, Moore fixed her gaze on a blue-eyed, blond teacher in the picket line with a JOIN OUR FIGHT FOR EXCELLENCE IN EDUCATION sign hanging around her neck. "Look at you in your little mini skirt," she shot at the woman. "You are unfit to be a teacher of my child or anyone's child, you with your ugly little old skinny legs.... Some of you little young teachers wonder why our boys are so fresh and step out of place with you. Well, you're the one who asks for it.... You're a disgrace to the teaching profession."[30]

Moore's idiosyncratic politics and fiery personality were on full display amid the IS 201 fray. Some young organizers loved her haranguing. But others cringed at her attack-dog tactics, which seemed to especially target and degrade the white women of the opposition. At sixty-eight years old, Queen Mother Moore had no shame. She was steadfast in her belief that the only way to liberate young Black minds was to completely oust white teachers from Black schools, and she refused to back down. Amid pressure from Moore and her supporters, the UFT caved and ceded the school grounds.

Black parents and activists wasted no time taking over IS 201, remaking its staff, administration, and curriculum in the image of its students and surrounding community. Their reasoning, as educator and community organizer Preston Wilcox put it, was simple: "If one believes that a segregated white school can be a 'good' school, then one must believe that a segregated Negro and Puerto Rican school, like I.S. 201, can be a 'good' school," too.[31] With his blueprints in hand, the governing board, which included Harlem education activists such as Babette Edwards and Isaiah Robinson, got to work remaking the embattled school. They developed extensive programming, including a community center, college prep programs, bilingual courses, a dual-language newspaper called *Kweli,* and an Afrocentric curriculum, all under the banner of the Schomburg Complex—the new name they gave the school as a tribute to Afro-Latino bibliophile and Harlem resident Arturo Schomburg, who had kept the flame of Black literacy and education alive for years.[32]

The next few years at IS 201 were a beautiful but messy experiment in Black education and self-rule. The school's all-Black governing body had the unenviable job of navigating the board of education, community members, movement politics, and local teachers to keep the school functioning and thriving.[33] Nevertheless, Harlemites had gotten a taste of "quality education, segregated style," and they liked it.[34] Black organizers, parents, and teachers kept struggling to make IS 201 a shining example of what community-controlled education could truly be.

What's more, they pushed Mayor Lindsay and the board to divide the city into twenty-nine school districts—each with its own school board that controlled teachers' assignments, curricula, and texts. Passing the control of schools to the communities, they argued, would better equip schools to meet students' needs. It would take a few years, but the New York Education Act that decentralized schools eventually became law in 1969.[35] In the meantime, Queen Mother Moore, now almost seventy years old, was more resolved than ever to wrest back control of Black schools once and for all.

On a blustery day in December 1966, the New York City Board of Education held an open school budget meeting. Though its members couldn't have known it, their boardroom was destined to be Audley Moore's next battleground. The place was packed with parents, students, and protesters—some of whom had already gone toe-to-toe with the board over control of IS 201 in the years before. The meeting droned on as usual, until a Black woman in an aqua dress and maroon stockings stepped up to the microphone.

She'd like "five minutes to express my views," said Lillian Wagner, a mother from the predominantly Black and Puerto Rican neighborhood of Ocean Hill–Brownsville in Brooklyn. She was there to talk about her local public schools, which were underfunded and in total disrepair. But since she wasn't on the list of sanctioned speakers, the board denied her request to speak. Wagner, however, had been silent for too long, and she refused to sit back down.

"Let her speak! Let her speak!" the crowd behind Wagner chanted, rising from their seats. The board's vice president, Alfred Giardino, banged his gavel, hoping to restore order, but it was too little, too late. "The voice of the people is with me," Wagner roared over the crowd. "I don't want my child to grow up in the same ghetto as I did." When the crowd refused to quiet down, the board members gave up. Gathering their papers, they filed out of the chamber in disgust.[36]

With the board in retreat, parents and protesters—including Milton Galamison and Babette Edwards, who had kept up the fight since the Freedom Day boycotts and IS 201—scrambled over the tables and commandeered the board's red-cushioned chairs. The group offered the superintendent's chair to Wagner and declared themselves the "Ad Hoc Board of Education of the People of the City of New York." They sent a telegram to Mayor Lindsay, alerting him of their takeover, before settling in to occupy the chambers overnight.[37]

When the organizers realized that they were gearing up for a multi-day fight, they called in reinforcements. It was almost midnight when Moore was startled from her sleep by a loud, blaring ring. She took a minute to come to, shuffled over to the wall, picked up the phone, and listened intently as the protesters relayed the events of that day's takeover. She knew she had to be there. Moore hung up, threw on a head wrap and a kaftan, and headed downtown.

"Run them out," she boomed, charging into the chamber later that night. "They're perpetuating idiot factories among us." Protesters cheered her on as she rallied her people, and called white board of ed officials evil "czars in our communities."[38]

After riling up the crowd, Moore ceded the floor and took a seat among the audience. She knew she was witnessing a shift in the struggle over New York's Black schools. There, among her compatriots new and old, poetic inspiration struck once more. Setting pen to paper, Black Nationalism's poet laureate documented the moment for posterity:

From the stately halls of the Board of Ed,
I received a telephone call while sleeping in my bed,
It was very cold on this December night,
But the people carried on their legal fight
For education was their greatest need
Since most of their children couldn't even read.
I arrived there just about midnight
And shall never forget the magnificent sight—
A young black man was seated in Donovan's chair
And parents surrounded him everywhere.
To think that I had lived to witness this—
The kind of struggle no one should miss.
It was a people's Parliament if there ever was one
And each vowed to remain until the rising sun.
They talked curriculum, budgets and such

And nobody missed the Donovans much.
There were several white priests and then a black preacher came—
And just for the record, Galamison was his name.[39]

Three days into the protest, activists scrambled to their feet as the assistant superintendent of schools stormed in. "Clear the room, so it [can] be made ready for a scheduled board meeting at 8 P.M.," he ordered.

"We will have to be placed under arrest," Galamison replied. The board was more than willing to oblige. As police marched the hand-cuffed people's board out of the building, supporters greeted them with cheers. The community had been keeping vigil outside the building, too, and they kept the picket going long after, carrying signs that read, FREE THE REAL BOARD OF EDUCATION and WILL JAIL HELP MY CHILD READ?[40]

The people's board protest was a watershed moment. Moore watched as Black neighborhoods across the city began singling out those who had neglected Black and Brown school districts. Gone were the days of Black organizers begging for integration—for a chance at sending their kids to a school that would never serve them. From now on, they would demand no less than total control of their schools.

When she wasn't protesting in schoolyards or at education board meetings, Moore dedicated her time to cultivating independent Black houses of learning. In those days, she frequented the Black Arts Repertory Theatre and School (BARTS), a community-driven artistic center smack in the heart of Harlem. The brainchild of writer and activist Amiri Baraka, BARTS was a school for Black dramatic and creative arts, and a play at making the arts accessible to the city's masses. Starting in May 1965, Black New Yorkers of all ages could file into a brownstone on West 130th Street for acting, writing, directing, set design, and production management classes, as well as courses in African American literature and other subjects. The idea of a freestanding, Black-centered art school and collective attracted up-and-coming musicians and artists like Sun Ra and Larry Neal, all of whom were part of the nationwide Black Arts Movement, to teach about making art that reflected Black life.[41] Moore took the proverbial podium as a guest lecturer at BARTS frequently, and others, including poet and teacher Sonia Sanchez, would pack the Harlem house to hear Queen Mother speak on African culture and the role of Black women in the nationalist struggle.[42]

On Saturday mornings, Moore journeyed just a few blocks farther south to the Hotel Theresa and into Malcolm X's Organization of Afro-American Unity headquarters and Liberation School. Since 1964, Harlemites had crammed into the small, makeshift classroom where students, including Japanese American activist Yuri Kochiyama, learned the ins and outs of Black history, African philosophy, and political organizing while parsing books like Frantz Fanon's *Wretched of the Earth* and Herbert Aptheker's *American Negro Slave Revolts*. When Malcolm died, Harlem's leading educators and activists stepped in to continue his educational legacy. Queen Mother Moore was part of this cohort. She taught Liberation School courses on multiple occasions, hoping a new generation of Black visionaries would pick up where Malcolm had left off.[43]

Moore was happy to serve as a substitute teacher and a guest speaker. But deep down, she was beginning to nurture bigger educational dreams. Since their sister's death, she and Loretta had been steadily gathering funds for the Eloise Moore Memorial College of African History and Research at Mount Addis Ababa, imagining a place "where people could come to us from all over the world to be de-negroized and de-colonized."[44] But they had quickly been swamped with the everyday work of the movement, and thus far had managed to put up only a few trailers and outhouses on the property. It wasn't much. But with a few books and a place for students to rest their heads, it was enough to get the school started.

Amid the sweltering heat of summer, the remaining Moore sisters hosted several busloads of New York City schoolchildren in Parksville, offering crash courses in basic agricultural skills like gardening, landscaping, and food preservation. Moore had envisioned these sessions as lessons in service of global Black liberation. "Africa needs those skills," she said, imagining a world where her students would one day journey to the continent and teach others. The summer camp classes were not meant to be a solution for the myriad challenges Afri-

can countries faced. Rather, Moore saw them as "a token of our kinship and the very least that we can do" as members of the Diaspora.[45]

Shaping young Black minds and showing them their value and connection to Africa was a way for Moore to keep Eloise's ideas alive.
These summer camps became a staple for Black kids in the city—
a place where they were free to explore nature and the idea of African
liberation. But as much as Moore loved the idea of building a school
in the Catskills, she knew it could provide only a small respite from
the real battle for the soul of the city's schools.

By the late 1960s, Ocean Hill–Brownsville was ground zero for this
fight.[46] With a $44,000 grant from the Ford Foundation in hand, and in
a rare moment of cross-neighborhood and cross-cultural cooperation,
Black and Puerto Rican parents took over their newly decentralized
district. They wasted no time setting up their own governing board,
hiring policies, and school budgets.[47] Their first move, of course, was
to oust the white folk. On May 9, 1968, the school board fired nineteen
UFT-backed white teachers. The union rebuffed this decision, and
white teachers everywhere walked off the job. Queen Mother Moore
joined with other Black Nationalists on the front lines of what is now
known as the 1968 New York City teachers' strike.[48]

Fifty thousand teachers from all across the city went on strike for
thirty-seven days, disrupting education entirely and further sour-
ing Black-white relations. The local school boards were powerless
to stop it all.[49] New York City students of all stripes lost out when
their education was interrupted, but the Black community was the
ultimate loser. In the end, UFT's white teachers were reinstated, the
Black school boards invalidated, and the school system reorganized
to ensure that Black control over community schools would never
flourish. Moore and her fellow activists put up a valiant fight, but the
strike had made it clear they were on the losing side.

Battered and bruised from their IS 201 and Ocean Hill–Brownsville
fights, Moore and her fellow organizers gathered for a postmortem at
the Priorities in Urban Education Conference at Cornell University
as the school year ended, alongside a smattering of Ivy League professors, teachers, and education activists. For a boots-on-the-ground
perspective on the fight for Black-controlled schools in New York

City, they tapped none other than the "highly personal and spellbinding speaker" Audley Moore.[50]

"The whole system is rotten to the core," Moore said. By her measure, the "Board of Mis-Education" couldn't even serve the white schools it was funneling all its money into, let alone the Black schools it openly neglected.[51] She punctuated the speech with a clarion call: "We are no longer looking to the white people or to the power structure, to solve the educational problem for us.... We refuse to be programmed anymore."[52]

In Moore's eyes, the constant sabotage of Black schools was just one more check on her long list of reasons for a separate Black nation. There could be no more capitulation, no more toiling to work within a fractured system. There could only be total, unquestioned self-determination for Black folk or nothing at all.

Some members of her audience were on board. Everyone there had experienced the disappointments of integration, after all. But Moore's audience contained just as many moderates, who likely felt as if her off-script haranguing was at best counterproductive, at worst hurting their cause.

Then, in a striking departure from her previous speeches, Moore argued there was actually space for white people—in particular, white teachers—in her Black Nationalist vision. Addressing them directly, she explained, "You killed us mentally, now the best thing you can do, those of you who want to help restore us, is to help us restore ourselves, in preparation for self-determination." Arguing that Black Nationalists were "race-conscious" rather than "racist," she envisioned a place for white people and educators in the Black republic: "To the white people who live under *our* domination, we're going to give them civil rights ... and justice for the first time in their lives. They'll see just what a government can do."

Her remarks no doubt caused a stir. Any white teacher or organizer there surely fancied themselves committed to righting racist wrongs. Still, Moore's claims they had "killed" Black children's minds, or that they needed to embrace Black dominion, were a far cry from what they expected from a discussion about the city's public schools. Others in the crowd must have perked up and smiled. This was classic Moore, wandering off script and riling up a crowd.

To drive home her point, Queen Mother took a tack few could

have anticipated: she burst into song. Jaws dropped and legs shifted uncomfortably as Moore broke into an off-key, a cappella rendition of "My Country 'Tis of Thee," though with her own special twist:

> This country 'tis for thee,
> A sweet land of liberty,
> For which you sing,
> A land that you stole with pride,
> For which your fathers died.
> But from every mountainside,
> Justice fails to ring.
>
> Black fathers died here, too
> To make it safe for you.
> Black mothers suckled your young,
> In this land where we hung from trees,
> For refusing to bend our knees,
> But now we've mastered Master's master keys,
> So our liberty will be rung.[53]

CHAPTER 18

The Revolution Has Come

The Unofficial Mayoress of Harlem," as some had cheekily dubbed her, had come a long way from her days speaking on street-corner soapboxes.[1] Now, when Moore wasn't on the ground fighting to remake New York City schools, she could often be found attending lively summits where Black leaders from across the country—and the political spectrum—gathered to reconcile calls for Black autonomy with the mainstream push for integration.[2]

Moore's old friend Adam Clayton Powell Jr. planted the seed for these meetings back in September 1966. With some help from the Capitol Police, the long-reigning Harlem congressman snuck nearly a hundred Black activists into the Rayburn House Office Building on Capitol Hill to debate the future of Black organizing. Always one to reach across constituencies, Powell invited both moderate and radical leaders to attend. But none of the "old civil rights leaders," as he called them, took him up on the invitation.[3] It was the younger, nationalist-leaning organizers who ultimately answered the call: activists like Maulana Karenga, Florynce Kennedy, and theologian and scholar Nathan Wright. At the meeting's end, Powell handed this young cohort the reins, urging them to gather the greatest Black minds they knew and chart a new course toward Black liberation. They left the capital galvanized, deciding to reconvene in Newark the following summer for the Second Black Power Conference.[4]

But the city erupted in violence on July 12, 1967, just eight days before the conference was slated to begin. At dusk that day, two white police officers stopped a Black taxi driver, John Smith, after he drove his car past a police car and double-parked. As it so often does, the traffic stop turned into a beating and an arrest. When the city's residents turned out to protest, Newark police turned their ire on the crowds. The backlash ignited a five-day rebellion, during which twenty-four Black people and two white people were killed. Police arrested more than a thousand others and expended more than thirteen thousand rounds of ammunition—all in the name of restoring order.[5]

When thousands of activists gathered in the smoldering city a week later, the evidence of its battered Black community was on full display. Newark native Amiri Baraka showed up bruised and hastily bandaged from the police beating he had endured just a few days before.[6] Some questioned whether it was prudent to gather in the wake of the violence. But many, including the conference planners, believed holding the conference amid the "ashes of Newark's scorched black community would represent a phoenix of tomorrow's black power for all black communities."[7] Queen Mother Moore agreed.

When she arrived at Newark's Episcopal Cathedral House on July 20, 1967, Moore was delighted to see the previous week's bloodshed hadn't scared attendees away. Organizers had expected a crowd of maybe two hundred. But nearly five times that many, from forty states, had descended on Newark amid the rash of police aggression. Moore was among the "civil rights militants and armed revolutionaries, scholars, laborers, housewives, corporation executives, teachers, ministers, ghetto organizers, and students" who all came together to hash out a concrete political agenda for the future.[8]

Moore's bracelets clanked on the metal banister she gripped as she gingerly climbed the stairs up to the old church. She nodded to the helmeted members of the Harlem Mau Mau Society—the security guards for the conference—and shuffled into the sanctuary.[9]

Directly in front of her was a pop-up registration booth that looked more like a reunion of her old comrades from Harlem, Philadelphia, and California than a conference check-in center.[10] Moore chatted animatedly with her old friends and promised they'd have the chance to reconnect after the keynote, where comedian and civil rights ally Dick Gregory and the newly elected chairman of SNCC, H. Rap Brown, were slated to speak.[11] Moore also mingled with new acquaintances amid coffee breaks, and even delighted in the spectacle of an argument turned shoving match between a white *New York Times* reporter and conference officials. Leadership had made it clear there were to be no white people allowed inside save for the daily press briefing at 3:00 p.m. When the reporter didn't comply, conference goers shoved him right out the ground-floor window and got back to the day's programming.[12]

Moore also did her part to hold the line. On the second day, she wandered into the Black Arts, Craftsman, and Communications Personnel workshop, featuring Florynce Kennedy and actors and activists Carol Green and Ossie Davis. Black people had long lamented the lack of a Black presence on major TV networks, in front of and behind the cameras. The trio was there to discuss how to pressure mainstream media to diversify. But workshop members got an unexpected show of their own when Queen Mother swept into the room.

Moore greeted old friends and new ones on her way to her seat. She shuffled in between a row of chairs, but just as she was about to sit down, Moore stopped dead in her tracks. Out of the corner of her eye, she saw two strangers sitting in the back of the room.[13] "These white women have to get out!" she yelled before the session could get under way. "This meeting is for blacks only!" The crowd went stiff, then turned in unison to gawk at the outburst.

Flo Kennedy quickly jumped to the white women's defense. They were Ti-Grace Atkinson and Peg Brennan, two New York–based feminist activists whom Kennedy had worked with before. Kennedy invited them because she wanted her friends and fellow organizers to see Black self-determination in action. But Moore didn't care. Sure, she had made room for white people in Black-controlled spaces in the past. But this Black Power Conference was meant to be the first large-scale, all-Black meeting of its kind. Moore's mandate was clear: no white spectators, no exceptions.

"I don't invite people some place and then tell them to leave," Kennedy said, doubling down. At this, even more attendees rose from their seats. They joined Moore in shouting Kennedy down, and some even reportedly threatened her life. "Do what you have to do," Kennedy replied coolly, according to the FBI agents who were embedded among the crowd. Brennan made a break for it. She wanted no part in the battle. "Stay where you are!" Kennedy yelled at Atkinson as the woman moved to follow suit. She stood there, rooted to the floor, as the shouting match played out. In a surprising turn of events, Moore relented and let Atkinson stay. Flo Kennedy was a formidable opponent, the rare case of a young woman who refused to genuflect.

Though Moore must have been miffed about losing the skirmish, perhaps she admired Kennedy's assertiveness—and saw a little bit of herself in the younger activist.[14]

Queen Mother Moore understood the power of causing a scene. These days, her outbursts were frequent, and to the untrained eye they often seemed unmeasured—an eccentric elder of the movement shooting from the hip. But for Moore, it was important to publicly stand by her separatist principles. In the context of the mid-1960s, when the mainstream push for integration was gaining considerable steam, the Black Left needed to hold the line.

She said as much at the workshop for Black women, the only part of the conference dedicated to debating women's rights and gender politics in the Black Power Movement, which Moore led.[15] She was still a force to be reckoned with. Even as she drew in new recruits by the thousands—and a bright, young cohort of leaders among them—Queen Mother Moore was still in charge.

In part because of incidents like these, the Second Black Power Conference garnered far more attention than anticipated. Journalist Chuck Stone called the Newark meeting one of the most diverse gatherings of "black people ever assembled . . . conceived and organized by black people for black people to talk to black people on what black people must do to empower black communities." But others claimed it was an exclusionary and "bourgeois affair" because of high registration costs and white corporate funding.[16] After it convened, reports tended to spotlight the clash of ideas and characters among attendees.

But all this post hoc analysis missed a key point. The Second Black Power Conference saw an unprecedented groundswell of support. The spirit of the 1960s had taken hold, and it was clear that Black America—as diverse as it was—had developed a taste for the radical. For Moore, this meant real momentum.[17] Back in New York, she dove headlong into helping plan the third annual conference. As fate would have it, the next year's summit would bring her back to her old stomping grounds.[18]

Queen Mother Moore stopped to gaze at the street art before her on a muggy Thursday morning in August 1968. The stenciled block

letters on the sidewalk read, BLACK SURVIVAL MEANS BLACK PEOPLE
WORKING TOGETHER, a message the Third Black Power Conference
hoped to hammer into its attendees, who flocked en masse to the
City of Brotherly Love. Queen Mother approached the gray-stoned
Church of the Advocate and entered the lobby, where the conference
had much the same look and feel of its predecessor. There were Black
guards patrolling the entrances and a list of Black male speakers slated
to headline. Another holdover from the previous year: the FBI infor-
mants who milled about, trying to disappear amid the thousands.[19]

Seeing as the Newark conference had fallen far short of total political unity, conference leaders—who now counted Maulana Karenga,
Amiri Baraka, Stokely Carmichael, and Muhammad Ahmad among
their ranks—had a more modest goal in mind this time. Reflecting on
the lessons from past Black Power convenings, organizers planned to
promote "black survival and empowerment through black operational
harmony," a wonky way of saying: fewer ideological fault lines and
more practical collaboration.

In Newark, Moore had spent her days shuffling between rooms
and attending workshops. This time, she stayed put. For three days
straight, conference goers hunkered down in working groups headed
up by a designated movement leader. The idea was that each workshop
would develop an actionable position paper, then present it for the
wider conference to ponder.[20] Politics, culture, and education were
all topics up for discussion. But Moore had her eye on the economics
workshop. In the fifteen years since she had jump-started the modern
reparations movement, Moore's demands had gained some real traction. She hoped this conference, with its collegial mission in mind,
could be a space where her calls for repayment finally made it into
the mainstream.

She was right to be hopeful. For several days, the economics workshop hammered out a "Resolution on Reparations." The paper was
ostensibly a group effort, but the final draft had Moore's fingerprints
all over it. "We the captive, non-self governing Africans born in the
U.S. have endured slavery for centuries under indescribable, inhuman, barbaric cruelties," it read, as if lifted from a draft of a Moore
speech. It laid out the many atrocities Black folk had faced: from "violence, torture, rape, [and] lynchings" to "outright theft of our inven-

tions, properties, and national identity," all while the United States "imposed a quasi citizenship" on Black Americans "without our knowledge, without our consent, and without even a plebiscite."[21]

The resolution followed Moore's lead, too, on how distributing the resources might work. Moore believed redistribution of funds should be a grassroots effort. It should have everyday activists and organizers at the helm, people on the ground who knew how their communities could benefit most. Of course, groups that were committed to helping Black people reconnect with their African ancestry got priority in Moore's eyes.[22] She suggested that repayments go to organizations like the World Federation of African People, a collective dedicated to developing "people-to-people program[s] for the benefit of all peoples of African descent"—notably, a group headquartered in New York City that Moore headed herself.[23] As ever, she had a way of adding a dash of nationalism.

Queen Mother Moore was proud of the workshop's final resolution. But when her group took the stage to present it to the wider conference, she was frustrated—if not a little embarrassed—by how little the room seemed to respond. She was worried the annual meeting would come to an end without any real reckoning with her life's work and the impact that reparations could have on Black folk. She begged her Philadelphia-based protégé Muhammad Ahmad to cede his time at the closing proceedings to her so she might raise the issue once more.[24]

"We have had five workshops report and her[e] we have not dealt with what I consider the most basic question before us. That is the question of reparations, of what the white man owes us," she admonished. "I can assure you that reparations is the crux of our problems here," and "the crux of our solution to our problems," too.

Reparations was the linchpin of every other policy, every other strategy the conference's workshops had laid out, she argued. "This colonialistic nation owes us for the damages committed against our families, our homes and our people... the injuries, how they stole from us, and how they worked us for centuries free of charge, for the rape of our women, how they changed our names, how they destroyed our inheritance." The more impassioned Moore became, the more explicit she got about a separate Black nation as her endgame: "We are talking about setting up a government, a nation within this country. What are you going to do for your heavy industry and all of your means of production if you don't have reparations?" Some at the conference were behind Moore and her bravado. Others wanted to quickly move on to what they believed were bread-and-butter issues of the conference, like the state of the Black family and Black political goals.

"Yes, they changed us from the African into the Negro," she continued. "We give our children white dolls. We got a white Jesus. We got white saints. We got a white Santa Claus." The audience gave her the floor, and many concurred at least in theory. But her fiery sermon failed to persuade the crowd to take unified action. Moore returned to her seat and watched despondently as they took up her cause "in spirit" but not in deed.[25]

In the end, attendees found enough common ground to champion a few other timely causes: the "unilateral and immediate withdrawal of the United States from the war in Vietnam" and opposition to Black participation in the draft. There was even widespread support for "the creation of a black urban army for the protection of black communities." Despite broad consensus, attendees still struggled to carry out these ideas.[26]

The Philadelphia conference was the largest U.S.-based Black Power gathering of its kind to date. But its attendees found there were limits to imagining Black liberation within the confines of America. By 1968, Black folk across numerous colonized nations were pushing for independence, and some had even succeeded. Maybe the wisdom of the Diaspora could point the way to true Black liberation.

"As-salaam alaikum." A young man spoke above the din as conference goers milled about during the closing proceedings. The crowd quieted down, and anticolonial activist Pauulu Kamarakafego (Roosevelt Brown) introduced himself and offered a suggestion that would change the course of Black protest history: the next big Black Power conference should be held on his home island of Bermuda.[27]

Often called the South Africa of the West Indies, the twenty-one-square-mile island of Bermuda was a British colonial stronghold where a white minority ruled the Black masses. When the tidal wave of Black Power swept across the world, it crashed over Bermuda especially hard. Gone was the complacent Black working class. Galvanized, many across the island were now making a concerted push to overthrow colonial rule.[28] Moore was among those who recognized this new, fomenting militancy. Bermuda was a powder keg, and in July 1969, Black activists from across the globe descended on the island, prepared to light the fuse.[29]

Colonial officials and U.S. surveillance agencies also recognized the shift. The CIA feared what it called "a real and growing … interest in the potential of black power as a political and social force in the Caribbean."[30] To head off a strengthening alliance between U.S. and Caribbean activists, the British and Bermudan governments worked together to ban foreign Black activists from setting foot on the island. It worked for some, but not for all. That summer, Flo Kennedy, Trinidadian leader and intellectual C. L. R. James, Queen Mother Moore, and a handful of others slipped past border control.[31]

A thousand activists and thinkers had already assembled for the conference when Moore arrived on July 10. As she strode into a white colonial-style building, with its wood paneling, enormous crystal chandeliers, and portrait of Queen Elizabeth II, Moore turned heads as much for her regality as for her boisterous reputation. A new generation of organizers had gotten word there was a famous activist in their midst. Some stopped and stared as she drifted past. Others rushed forward to say hello.[32] Moore greeted anyone and everyone she met graciously. She loved basking in her renown.

But she was in Bermuda on business. Moore held an audience of nearly seven hundred rapt when she headlined a session: "Black Women in the Liberation Struggle."[33] Because of what the typical Moore lecture on women in the movement entailed, those present likely heard her vouch that the "black woman has a great role to play. … She has got to get a hold of herself and stop, stop completely imitating white women," and remember that she is "an African Woman. … She's got to be about her business of establishing nationhood for herself, her people."[34]

The CIA and MI6 feared that the conference would foster dangerous "relationships between US and Caribbean area black militants." They were right.[35] The fifteen-hundred-person gathering riled up the island's radical spirit. A whole new generation of Black organizers was able to meet the veterans who had carried the movement for decades. And those veterans, in turn, welcomed in new perspectives from the

Diaspora, Black folk who were still living under the crushing weight of colonial British rule.

What's more, this International Black Power Conference had caught the attention of liberation fighters from the African continent. When Kwame Nkrumah, now the former president of Ghana, got word of the meeting, he sensed "the world rebellion of the oppressed against the oppressor" was entering a new stage. He couldn't attend in person, but he did send a message to be read on his behalf. It included an open invitation: Africa welcomed the next major Black Power summit back to the motherland.[36] To bring the next year's conference over to the continent would be a herculean feat. But if they were successful, Moore believed, it would be the culmination of more than fifty years of struggle for the cause of an autonomous Black nation.[37] Queen Mother, for one, wasn't daunted. She left Bermuda with a promise on her lips: that whenever and wherever Black people were organizing for their freedom, she would be there.

CHAPTER 19

Mother of the Republic of New Afrika

Anyone standing on the corner of Fourteenth Street and Warren Avenue must have stopped and stared when they saw Moore and her African-clothed compatriots crossing the street. On Sunday, March 31, 1968, just a handful of months before she would return to Philadelphia for the third Black Power summit, Queen Mother Moore filed into Detroit's 20 Grand Motel. Others at the intersection were headed to the neighboring club of the same name, with plans to grab a cocktail before visiting its bowling alley or hearing Ella Fitzgerald in the Gold Room. Dressed in their Sunday evening best and looking for a good time, club goers couldn't have known about the insurrection taking place next door.

Moore found her seat among Black folk milling about the Black-owned motel's meeting room, where more than five hundred radicals and thinkers from across the Black Left had spent the past three days hunkered down at the Black Government Convention, debating the next steps in the Black Liberation Movement. Suddenly a group pressed to the front of the room and unfurled a document. "We, Black People in America, declare ourselves free and independent of this jurisdiction of the United States of America," it began.[1]

The crowd was stunned as the group pressed on. Some shifted in their seats. It was all well and good to talk about the failures of the American government or to daydream about a Black utopia. But renouncing U.S. citizenship and supporting Black secession—these were serious, even treasonous acts. An uneasiness started to grow among the conference goers; were they truly willing to risk their lives and livelihoods for this cause? Moore, for one, knew where she fell.

"Hallelujah," she called out above the murmurs of the crowd. "Hallelujah, I've lived to see the day." The aged activist rose from her seat, lifted her hands to the heavens, and strode to the front of the room as if leading a procession. Grabbing the pen, Moore bent down, signed her name in loopy cursive, and then turned to see who, if any, would follow. Numerous young men and women rushed to the front, lining up to join her. If a seventy-year-old grandmother could risk her hide for liberation, surely they could, too.[2]

Detroit was a fitting host for the day's events. When Moore returned to the Motor City—a full twenty-four years after she had left it, still a card-carrying communist, to move back to New York—she could see how long-held discontent had fomented a surge of Black Nationalism in her absence. To be sure, there had been some wins since she had been gone. The local NAACP had championed housing and school desegregation. Alongside a coalition of Black liberal workers in the Trade Union Leadership Council, they propelled white liberal politician Jerome Cavanagh into the mayorship in 1962 and got a taste of what political power could do.[3]

Intent on making the city an exemplar of the Great Society—the Johnson administration's name for its sweeping domestic antipoverty and racial equality programs—Cavanagh ushered in funding for housing and education reform. What's more, Black Detroiters battled to have a say in how this funding would be doled out to their communities.[4]

By 1965, Black Detroiters had elected ten Black state legislators and two Black members of Congress, and now they even had Black judges like George Crockett. And by the late 1960s, Black homeownership had increased.[5] If Moore happened upon any communist or trade union organizers from the old days, she would have surely learned there were now more Black people in skilled trades than ever before. Her people were getting an education, too. Wayne State University, a large public university in Midtown Detroit, now had thousands of Black students enrolled, more than ever before.[6]

Yet all this progress was no match for the suburbanization and deindustrialization that laid waste to Black Detroit.[7] Despite their hard-won footholds in the auto industry and unions, Black men and women remained trapped under a wage ceiling, underemployed, or on welfare.[8] Highway construction had accelerated white flight and an industrial exodus, leaving Black neighborhoods overcrowded, underfunded, and constantly under threat of being razed.[9] If these issues were not enough, police surveillance and brutality were constant features of Black life. Everyone had a story—a friend, family member, or neighbor whom the local police had beaten, arrested, framed, or killed.[10] These years of roiling discontent had made Detroit ripe for the late twentieth century's spike in Black Nationalist activity.

The philosophy had deep roots in the city. Detroit was home to a vibrant UNIA chapter during Garvey's heyday. But the true gem in the city's radical crown was its claim to fame as the birthplace of the Nation of Islam. The NOI sprung up in the city in 1930, when the organization's founder, Wallace Fard Muhammad, started Temple No. 1. Nationalism continued to flower throughout Detroit and all across the Midwest in the 1940s as NOI temples proliferated, and the UNIA moved its headquarters to nearby Cleveland.[11]

By the 1960s, Detroit was a lightning rod for radicalism. When Malcolm X wasn't in Harlem or Philadelphia rousing support for the cause, he headlined events like the 1963 Grassroots Leadership Conference, a gathering hosted by a contingent of Detroit radicals who had been booted from the more moderate Detroit Council on Human Rights' Leadership Conference.[12] "The only revolution based on loving your enemy is the Negro revolution," Malcolm told his rapt audience crowded inside King Solomon Baptist Church that November. "The only revolution in which the goal is a desegregated lunch counter, a desegregated theater, a desegregated park, and a desegregated public toilet; you can sit down next to white folks on the toilet. That's no revolution."[13]

Local organizers, including James and Grace Lee Boggs, heard the firebrand loud and clear. Soon after his "Message to the Grassroots" speech, the interracial activist couple helped create the Freedom Now Party, the first all-Black political party to run Black residents for citywide office.[14] The party sparked newfound interest in the working-class Black electorate and spurred the creation of the League of Revolutionary Black Workers, a Marxist-Leninist coalition that jockeyed for political and economic power across the city.[15]

Queen Mother Moore wasn't without influence, either. The Revolutionary Action Movement, which she had mentored in Philadelphia, created a Detroit chapter. And a handful of leaders from across all these groups also created a chapter of the Black Panther Party for

Self-Defense—a Midwestern iteration of the group that Huey Newton and Bobby Seale had started in Oakland.[16]

Looking to get in on the action, brothers Milton and Richard
Henry created the Group on Advanced Leadership (GOAL). At first,
the pair of forty-something-year-old organizers thought their group
might function as an auxiliary of sorts—a way to boost the signals of
other civil rights groups by lending extra support to their causes. But
years of struggle had changed their minds. The cycles of maddeningly
incremental racial progress, followed by extreme violent backlash,
made the Henry brothers realize integration was "almost as dangerous as it [was] desirable." GOAL, which had ballooned to hundreds
of members and affiliates by the mid-1960s, shifted course and began
supporting more militant causes.[17]

Their fervor caught Malcolm X's attention. "The Henry brothers . . .
are very progressive young men," he told his audience when he came
back to Detroit on February 14, 1965. "I would advise all of you to get
with them in every way that you can to try and create some kind of
united effort toward common goals, common objectives." This would
be the last time the Henry brothers, or anyone else in Detroit, saw
the young leader.[18] One week later, Malcolm was dead. Just as Moore
interpreted Malcolm's assassination as a sign to embrace her role as
Queen Mother, the Henry brothers treated his death as a call to hoist
the banner of a fledgling Black nation. Milton and Richard changed
their names to Gaidi and Imari Obadele and formed the Malcolm X
Society. Their core pursuit was "land and power" for Black people.[19]

They weren't alone in changing course. While some gathered at
Black Power conferences in the Northeast, a new Black militancy
was brewing in the Midwest. In the early morning hours of July 23,
1967, Detroit police raided a party at the United Community League
for Civic Action, housed at Twelfth Street and Clairmount Avenue, a
well-known "blind pig," or illegal bar. Twelve officers broke into the
building, expecting to find a handful of partygoers at most. Instead,
they happened upon close to eighty Black people drinking, gambling,
and listening to an old jukebox, celebrating the safe return of two
Vietnam War vets. The officers sensed their chance; they'd be heroes
back at the station. They began a mass arrest, marching droves of
handcuffed partiers out the door. But outside, they already had an
audience. At the sight of multiple squad cars, Black folk in the area

gathered round to see what the police were up to. And as the arrests continued—squad car after squad car turning up to seize the well-meaning revelers—the crowd grew increasingly angry. Epithets flew first, and empty glass bottles followed. The police responded, in turn, as the police were wont to: with violence.[20]

The rebellion had started.

Over the next five days, the National Guard and the Eighty-Second Airborne descended to quell the uprising. When the smoke finally cleared, forty-three people had died in the tumult; thirty-three of them were Black Detroiters. More than a thousand were injured, and police arrested more than seven thousand locals in the end.[21]

While many saw the 1967 Detroit rebellion as the end of the Great Society in the city, the Obadele brothers saw in it a new beginning. It was time to rally the troops.

Back in New York, Queen Mother Moore got the invitation to the Black Government Convention just as she was coming home from a long day of work in the community. The Obadele brothers invited hundreds of activists to attend, to imagine what the future of Black governance might entail. It was an exciting prospect, to be sure, but Moore had her hesitations. At seventy years old and with little money to her name—all while mired in annual Black Power conferences and near-constant fights with local school districts—making it back to the Midwest was a tall order. She also had her suspicions about what the meeting could achieve. Over the last ten years, Moore had watched plenty of young Black men take her ideas of an autonomous Black nation and run away with them, only to find they were both "ill-prepared" and "ill-equipped" to make the dream a reality.[22] She admired the Obadele brothers' ambition, but she questioned their organizing chops. Still, Moore couldn't resist. The tenor of the country had changed in the late 1960s. Maybe this time would be *the* time her nationalist dreams would come true.

Many of the Black radicals she had worked with over the last decade felt the same. When Moore arrived, she found all the usual suspects there: Maulana Karenga and Amiri Baraka; Mae Mallory and Malcolm X's widow, Betty Shabazz; and RAM organizers Muhammad Ahmad and John Bracey had all come. Even some more moderate organizers like local Mississippi SNCC worker Lawrence Guyot showed up, tentatively interested in what the Obadele brothers were selling.[23] While some attendees were stalwart supporters of founding a separate Black nation, others were skeptical. Some came just to see if it was all real—were people genuinely planning to renounce American citizenship? For three days, they shuffled between the Shrine of the Black Madonna Church, Wayne State University, and the 20 Grand Motel to debate everything from religion to culture, sexism to politics, and, of course, government repression.

Moore was right to come. For years now, she had been saying the only viable solution for Black people was secession. But even some of the most radical, self-proclaimed militants around her had balked at putting the idea into practice. After a decade driven by urban rebellion and defined by toothless civil rights legislation—juxtaposed to real, meaningful revolution among the African nations, to boot—people were coming around. Moore could sense the radicals in her midst were on the verge of a bold new approach; they just needed a push.

With her longtime friend and fellow activist Virginia Collins, who had also gathered what little money and energy she had to make the trek, Moore shared the "Draft Resolution for the Establishment of an Independent Black Republic" she and the women of the UAEW had worked on nearly a decade earlier in New Orleans—a sort of blueprint for building a new Black nation.[24] The fact that the UAEW women had proposed such an idea years before only emboldened the younger crowd of organizers, who were already toying with the concept. On the second day of the conference, leaders announced their plans to establish an independent Black nation, marching through the 20 Grand Motel with their declaration that would soon gain its first signature: one Audley Moore.

With their formal declaration set out and signed, conference attendees wasted no time establishing their new government. Similar to Moore's previous nationalist efforts, the Republic of New Afrika's (RNA) founders emulated America's hierarchy. They elected Gaidi Obadele as the first vice president and Betty Shabazz as the second vice president. Imari Obadele would serve as the minister of interior; Amiri Baraka and Maulana Karenga as ministers of culture; Muhammad Ahmad as a special ambassador; and Herman Ferguson, the leader of the OAAU's Liberation School, as the RNA's first minister of education.[25]

When it came time to select a president, only Robert F. Williams would do. Moore had been a friend and supporter of Williams since the late 1950s, when he had joined her and her sisters in supporting African liberation on the Hearts of Africa Committee. And she had stayed in contact with him when he fled to Cuba after his and Mallory's run-in with the North Carolina KKK in August 1961.[26]

Now in political exile, Williams moved in and out of communist nations, gaining some powerful international allies along the way. His defiance had made him a pariah at home and an ally of anticapitalists and critics of America everywhere. So when the RNA elected him as president of their newfangled Black nation almost a decade later, the symbolic weight was clear. There was also a practical angle to the move. The newly minted RNA hoped to claim territory for their new nation in the southeastern United States, and the surest way to do so was by resurrecting the Communist Party's long-lapsed Black Belt Thesis—their claims that Black people constituted a "nation within a nation." To do so, they would undoubtedly need backing from the international community—especially the communists who harbored Williams.[27] Electing him as president in exile was their best shot.[28]

The group selected Queen Mother Moore as the minister of health and welfare and New York–based activist Joan Franklin as the minister of justice. They named Virginia Collins, who had been heading the nationalist movement in New Orleans since Moore left, vice president of the South.[29] The collective also established several RNA consulates in places like New York and placed seasoned nationalists like Mae Mallory at their helms. It was a small sign that women's roles in nationalist organizing were shifting slightly.[30]

RNA declared its citizens New Afrikans, a people united by their heritage, belief in self-determination, and the shared desire to separate from the American nation-state.[31] Moore's fingerprints—especially her ideas about "de-Negroization"—were all over the moniker. "I named the Republic of New Afrika, which I helped found," Moore claimed of that monumental day, beaming. Her community of captive Africans had declared themselves free.[32]

The RNA's first members left Detroit soon after, bonded in their lofty aspirations. But the work ahead, of building a Black republic on Louisiana, Mississippi, Alabama, Georgia, and South Carolina soil, was considerable. As they parted, Moore reminded the cohort that nation building was slow, arduous, and dangerous work. "You have the idea and you work toward it," she told them. "Agitation, preparation, and organization."[33] That was the way.

The RNA fanned its members out across the country, holding rallies and political education classes while jumping headlong into community struggles for Black self-determination wherever it could. Its government might have been provisional, but its members were committed. The first step was to build a groundswell of support.[34]

In between lectures at independent schools and trips to Mount Addis Ababa, Moore did her part as one of the RNA's chief advocates and officers.[35] At the New York consulate's first public event in July 1968, she appeared alongside Mae Mallory and Joan Franklin to pitch the Republic of New Afrika to her local community. Before a crowd of three hundred, Moore cheered as Mallory shared a letter of support from the still-exiled Williams and listened stoically as Franklin recited Frederick Douglass's "What to the Slave Is the Fourth of July?" speech. The Black founding father's words were a reminder that, for Black people, the spoils of American citizenship had never truly been within reach.[36]

Propelled by the success of that event, over the next few months Moore arranged an array of RNA-focused affairs across the city, tapping into every possible school, community organization, nationalist-minded acquaintance, and cultural or religious group she had ever worked with. Her FBI detail noted this newfound gusto. Soon the RNA began to appear in its reports on her comings and goings.[37]

Some days she could be found stumping for the new nation, delivering speeches in between musical breaks at the Yoruba Temple. Other times, she seeded support among her brethren in the school districts. Moore understood her separatism could get only so far. Black New Yorkers, after all, were fighting to found autonomous school districts *in the city,* not to secede and build anew in the South. Even still, Moore knew an opening when she saw one. And her life bore witness to the power of a full broadside.[38]

———

"We got guys with rifles out here, Linwood and Euclid," two white Detroit police offers radioed in from their squad car. They had "happened" to drive by the New Bethel Baptist Church on that corner on March 29, 1969, around 8:00 p.m. as New Afrikans from across the country reconvened for their first annual conference and Nation Day Celebration.[39]

It was a frigid night in Detroit, thirty degrees at the most, and Moore had bundled up to hoof it briskly into the modern-looking church. New Bethel looked like the kind of place where dreams of Black liberation might take hold. The local reverend C. L. Franklin became head pastor in 1946 and grew both the congregation and the church's reputation through a gospel choir featuring his daughter: Aretha Franklin. By the time Moore set foot in the sanctuary, New Bethel's membership had ballooned so much that Franklin moved the congregation into the old Oriole Theatre building after an all-Black architectural and construction team renovated it. Its brick facade, angled edges, rows of glass doors, and modern signage blared to passersby that New Bethel was a new kind of Black church—one where Black people could both worship the Lord and praise new ideas of freedom.[40]

The first night of the conference was all celebration. Against all odds, this group of ragtag Black separatists had survived a year. African-robed and suited supporters alike streamed into the church, gleefully greeting one another before settling into the pews. Later, there would be plenty of work to do—Supreme Court justices to elect, a legal code to develop, and some hard facts to face about finances.[41]

When Moore arrived, she joined a throng of men, women, and children. She hugged old friends and chatted up the new recruits. Meanwhile, trouble was brewing just beyond the church doors. Though the anniversary was a peaceful event, the New Afrikans knew better than to assume law enforcement would just let them be. They stationed Black Legionnaires outside to stand guard against intruders: cops, reporters, and interlopers of all kinds.

When a pair of police officers exited their car, their hackles were raised. They approached the RNA's security force, and the conversation got heated. Minutes later, shots rang out into the night. One police officer lay dead, and his partner was wounded. Bleeding badly, he stumbled to his squad car and radioed for backup, then started to drive off before losing consciousness and crashing into a storefront.

It took only five minutes for squad cars filled with officers to come streaming onto the scene. They were out for blood.

At least a dozen officers stormed into the church, firing indiscriminately. Men and women dropped to the floor, wrapping themselves around the children among them as glass shattered and bullets flew. A hundred rounds of ammunition later, the New Afrikans slowly rose to their feet, only to find the Detroit police ready to arrest them for conspiracy to commit murder.[42]

Moore escaped the shoot-out and the arrests that followed. By her own account to FBI agents who interviewed her a week later in New York, she had left New Bethel before it all started. The agents found that, suddenly, Moore couldn't seem to recall whom she had left the church with, or how she got back to her hotel that night; memory, so fussy in old age! When they showed her photographs of suspects, she claimed they were "unknown to her"—certainly, they couldn't be members of the RNA. Frustrated, the agents reminded Moore that lying to law enforcement and harboring criminals were serious crimes. Deadpan, she explained that violence had never been on the day's agenda, and "whatever trouble did take place must have been started by the DPD [Detroit Police Department]."[43]

Queen Mother Moore might have left New Bethel unscathed that day, but the RNA did not. It was a turning point for leadership. The Obadele brothers had always disagreed as to when the group should begin its plans to build a Black nation on U.S. soil in earnest. For Gaidi, the shoot-out proved that a "calculated educational organizing process in the North" was the "safest way." Imari read the altercation as a sign it was time to move south and dig in to the hard work of nation building.[44] A year into the RNA's existence, and as factions formed around the feuding brothers, several of its members—including its instrumental president, Robert F. Williams—resigned.[45]

Moore pressed onward amid the turmoil. Throughout 1969, she still proselytized for the Republic when she wasn't at Black Power conferences or reparations conventions.[46] In early 1970, she agreed to another three-month stint as a leader in the floundering RNA, even as its members struggled to sort out their personal and political disputes.

But she couldn't mask her frustration with the Obadele brothers, who she felt were more interested in fighting with each other than furthering the cause. By August of that year, Moore had renounced her formal position as a cabinet minister. But on her way out the door, she chose a side. Moore threw her support behind Imari. Her reasoning was simple: "He had the guts to go ahead and establish the RNA on land in Mississippi."[47]

Imari Obadele believed Mississippi, with its majority-Black population and rich tradition of grassroots activism, was an ideal space to begin building. After a successful conference in Jackson in 1971, his contingent of the RNA decided to stay and set up shop in the state.[48] Two months later, Imari Obadele and his followers purchased a stretch of land from local Black folk near Bolton, Mississippi, renamed it El Malik, and designated it as their capital. Later that year, they established a presidential residence and government headquarters in Jackson—a couple of houses near Jackson State University. Adorned with the Pan-African black, red, and green flag and photos of Malcolm X and other movement icons, the fledgling nationalist stronghold was a humble operation.[49]

This small group of RNA diehards soon got to work. Henry Hatches and his wife, Mary Alice, activists who were already involved in local Black Power politics, joined Obadele in Bolton, as did Kele Nyaga Simba, a mother of seven.[50] A young Black Panther Party member from Boston, Fulani Sunni Ali, Detroit-born organizer Chokwe Lumumba, and dozens of other organizers relocated to Jackson, all committed to the hard labor of achieving their nationalist dreams.[51]

Most days were fairly mundane. They began by reciting the Republic of New Afrika Oath:

For the fruition of black power,
For the triumph of black nationhood,
I pledge to the Republic of New Africa
and to the building of a better people
and a better world, my total devotion,
my total resources and the total power
of my immortal life.[52]

Then they took to the quotidian tasks of the day: hosting meetings, mingling with locals, and selling RNA newspapers to anyone willing to read. Some New Afrikans planted crops; others trained for combat.[53] No matter how menial the task, it was serious work for a people who planned to secede from the Union.

Queen Mother Moore watched from afar as New Afrika took shape. Now seventy-two years old, she was living with her sister Loretta in the Bronx and battling the typical ailments of old age. It's possible she thought she was just too old to start anew down south, or that she believed she was of more help whipping up support for the RNA in the Big Apple. Or maybe Moore wanted to see how the young guns fared before she joined them. The reports trickling up to New York City from Jackson left her cautiously optimistic. What's more, she could see how her years of political theory had shaped the budding nationalist site.

Back in 1968, at the RNA's founding conference in Detroit, Moore had reiterated her age-old declaration: any serious attempt at building a new nation would need a level of funding only the U.S. government could provide. RNA architects took her words to heart. Their founding document had included a claim for reparations to Black people "for the grievous injuries sustained by our ancestors and ourselves."[54]

By the early 1970s, Mississippi-based RNA members had doubled down on their demands for repayment. Imari's loyalists proclaimed the "minimum dollar cost for starting a New Community of 500 families (or approximately 2500 people) is seven-and-a-half million dollars," and that it was only right and just that the bulk of this money would come from a penitent U.S. government.[55] They believed these payments should be dispersed directly to the families roughing it on New Afrikan land, to provide the "five essentials of decent human life: food, housing, clothing, health services, and education" and "to provide for the nation as a whole sufficient surplus wealth to achieve our world freedom."[56] A bold claim, to be sure, and one to which government officials paid little mind.

Money was a chief concern, but winning converts to the cause was even more crucial. The RNA spent much of its time proselytizing to Black people in neighboring communities, encouraging them to consider the identity, politics, and way of life that defined the New

Afrikans. For many, that started with the simple step of the name change ceremony.

"El Hajj Malik El-Shabazz," Imari Obadele would chant before pouring out a bit of water in homage to the ancestor more commonly known as Malcolm X. The RNA leader then proclaimed the names of other "powerful predecessors" with his community gathered round. If ever it seemed he forgot a name, his fellow elders interjected to exalt the nationalist greats. Ancestor, water, ancestor, water, the ritual went as Imari moved from one New Afrika inductee to the next, bestowing on each new member the name chosen for them. Recruits like Richard Trice left the ceremony Bokeba Wantu Enjuenti, or "one that struggled for a beautiful nation."

"Harambee!" the newly minted New Afrikans shouted in unison before they sipped from a unity cup. The Swahili chant "Let's pull together" was a sign they had all accepted new names, new lives, and a new commitment to the Afrikan struggle.[57] This was the first, bold step. But there was much more personal and political reorienting ahead.[58]

Some RNA members envisioned the New Afrikan nuclear family as a small, traditional pod. But with a new nation came the chance to explore new social and sexual values, too. Breaking ranks with many other radical Black organizations at the time, the RNA asserted the equality of women in its new country. And much to Moore's delight, members advocated for polygamous relationships across gender lines: in this new nation, both men and women would be allowed to have multiple partners of the opposite sex.[59]

Where and how these New Afrikan families would worship was another core question. Black Americans came from a diverse and diasporic array of religious traditions. Moore was one such case, and at the RNA's founding conference she had used her own spiritual journey—first a Catholic, then a convert to the Ethiopian Coptic Church, and finally a member of the Yoruba Temple—as a plea for a more capacious understanding of Afrikan faith, all while Gaidi Obadele and Yoruba Temple leader Oseijeman Adefunmi debated which religion would best nurture the New Afrikans.[60] Ultimately, the RNA followed Moore's lead, settling on a loose understanding of spirituality that didn't restrict members to a singular set of teachings.

They found the divine in the ritual of nation building itself, rather than in a singular deity.

In this and many more ways, Moore's values and life experience served as the blueprint that built the RNA's new world. As a twenty-year-old, she had sworn her own oath of "total devotion" to the "triumph of Black nationhood." She had renounced her religion, her commitment to capitalism, and her U.S. citizenship, all in the name of "building a better people" and a "better world." Some fifty years later, these young Black radicals were following the same path she had forged. For the first time in quite a while, Queen Mother didn't feel as if she carried the banner of a free Black nation alone. But, as was so often the case, her euphoria was short-lived.

Around 6:30 a.m. on August 18, 1971, wildlife scattered from the sound of crunching gravel as a battalion of police cars, fifteen cops with just as many FBI agents crammed inside, rolled up to 1148 Lewis Street in Jackson. The FBI had ratcheted up its surveillance of the RNA for months with help from Mississippi law enforcement, staking out the group's headquarters in the South and infiltrating meetings across the North. A group of Black radicals gathering in a Detroit church to discuss the mere *idea* of a Black nation was enough to draw the FBI's ire. But when the New Afrikans established a government headquarters in Jackson, it sent J. Edgar Hoover's G-men into a frenzy.

The agents and officers exited their cars, drew their weapons, and got into position. Once he got the silent signal, Agent James Sammon grabbed his bullhorn. They had the house surrounded and warrants of arrest in hand. "Come out with your hands up," he yelled.

The deafening voice startled the New Afrikans out of their beds. They scrambled to wake up, get dressed, and get out. But there was no time. Seventy-five seconds later, tear gas canisters shattered windows, and bullets punched through walls.[61] There was no way out, so the New Afrikans dug in. The men grabbed their guns and returned fire, while the women hurried groggy and frightened children into a makeshift bunker—a hole dug into the ground inside a closet. The RNA and law enforcement exchanged more than three hundred rounds of ammunition. When the smoke cleared, everyone inside the house had survived and one officer lay dead. Another agent and an officer were wounded.

But the siege wasn't over. Just like at the New Bethel shoot-out, agents and officers donned bulletproof vests, riot guns, and helmets and stormed the house to arrest seven men and women inside. They arrested four more—including Imari Obadele—at another RNA residence on Lynch Street a few blocks away.[62] The media soon dubbed the New Afrikans they captured the RNA-11.

Back in New York City, Moore was horrified to hear of the shoot-out and arrests. She anxiously awaited word of her captured compatriots' fates—especially after she had heard that one, Njeri Quddus, was pregnant at the time of the attack and that the police had paraded the men half-dressed and in chains through the Jackson city streets like slaves. The state charged all eleven with assault, murder, and sedition. The RNA, the police claimed, had waged war on the state of Mississippi.[63]

Other RNA members responded just as quickly, hiring lawyers to defend their fellow New Afrikans and starting a national defense campaign to free them from prison. But the legal fees were costly, so much so that they bankrupted the group.[64] After a lengthy battle, a judge ultimately ordered eight of the eleven to stand trial on weapons possession, conspiracy, murder, and assault charges. Juries convicted all of them—even teenager Karim Njabafudi.[65]

The Mississippi contingent, tasked with rebuilding from the wreckage of their bullet-riddled compound, never recovered. The Republic of New Afrika, or at least this iteration of it, dissolved. But these and other RNA members scattered across the country, creating a bevy of new organizations wherever they landed—the New Afrikan People's Organization, the Afrikan People's Party, the New Afrikan Women's Organization, and the New Afrikan Prisoners Organization—all paying homage to that plot of land in Jackson where, for so brief a moment, Moore's dreams of a bold new Black nation had felt within reach.[66]

CHAPTER 20

Nationtime!

As the 1960s ended, it was clear the Black Power Movement was going mainstream. Black America had been energized by activists' calls for race pride, cultural revolution, and Black political power. Activists like Black Panther leader Elaine Brown and SNCC's Julian Bond ran for office, with Bond winning a seat in the Georgia House of Representatives. Meanwhile, Black students battled to get Black history, literature, and political science classes in their schools, and they scored some victories, too. Black studies programs proliferated in colleges and universities across the country. And after classes, students gathered in their common rooms to watch *Soul!*, a Black variety show featuring everyone from singer Bill Withers to writer James Baldwin on national television.[1]

The newly elected president, Richard Nixon, could see the rising tide. As soon as he came into office in January 1969, he asked his aides what to do about Black people's growing calls of "Power to the People." Daniel Patrick Moynihan—now the assistant to the president for domestic policy after demonizing Black mothers just a few years before—suggested Nixon adopt a policy of "benign neglect."[2]

When the proposal leaked (a common occurrence for Moynihan's reports, it seemed), the president tried to pivot. His administration established the Office of Minority Business Enterprise in 1969, in a half-hearted attempt to reframe Black entrepreneurship as a form of community control and self-determination. A few ambitious businessmen took the administration's funds. But most Black organizers and politicians rejected such state-sponsored distortions of Black Power.[3]

Nixon's rise to power, in part, pushed Michigan congressman Charles Diggs to start developing the Congressional Black Caucus

(CBC) in 1969. Once political outliers and outsiders, newly elected representatives and senators Shirley Chisholm (New York), Charles Diggs (Detroit), Adam Clayton Powell Jr. (Harlem), and William Dawson (Chicago), among others, were now a formidable congressional conglomerate. And thanks to the Voting Rights Act, they had constituencies devoted to keeping them in office.[4]

It was time to marshal this newfound political power. In just a few short years, the CBC became an unignorable political bloc. It gained national attention after boycotting Nixon's State of the Union address, instead presenting him with a set of sixty-one policy recommendations for Black America. But the president had a playbook of his own. After posing for a photo op with the CBC, Nixon trashed the document and added some of its members to his FBI-surveilled "enemies list."[5] It was this very dissonance—between the lip service the administration paid to Black politicians and the real political power afforded to them—that made the CBC start to wonder if the far left was correct: maybe working within the establishment was futile.[6]

While the CBC was looking to the Left for guidance, Black Nationalists were pondering the potential of the political establishment. This was especially the case for Amiri Baraka, whose Newark-based organization CFUN had popularized cultural nationalism while also engaging in a citywide voter registration campaign that helped Kenneth Gibson become the first Black mayor of Newark in 1970.[7]

"My view was that Newark should be a model for the country," Baraka recalled.[8] He was still a nationalist, through and through. But Baraka felt the movement needed unity and a permanent organization "whose function would be to struggle for Black Power wherever black people were in the world."[9]

But Baraka knew he couldn't forge these kinds of bonds on his own. Believing Moore to be a "primary inspiration for the Black movement," he asked her and other luminaries for guidance.[10] Queen Mother was thrilled to oblige.

The elder activist joined a committee tasked with planning a 1970 Labor Day weekend meeting in Atlanta to discuss the creation of the Congress of African People (CAP), which would bring radical Black activists and Black elected officials under one big tent. If the Black Power conferences over the last five years had taught Moore anything, it was that nationalist sympathies were on the rise. But any attempt to make those ideas manifest had failed to fly. As they converged in Atlanta, Moore and her compatriots hoped to make some concrete progress. The theme of the three-day event was to be "Nationtime."[11]

As August came to an end, thousands packed onto the campuses of Spelman, Morehouse, and Morris Brown Colleges, a conglomerate of historically Black schools, in the lingering Georgia heat. When Queen Mother Moore arrived on Thursday, September 3, she hustled to her seat to hear Atlanta's vice-mayor, Maynard Jackson, deliver the opening address before she joined the throng in the auditorium for the evening's entertainment: African singers, musicians, and poets.[12]

First thing Friday morning, Moore rose early and donned her royal regalia. As soon as she stepped out, she could feel the energy. Passing in and out of old brick buildings, Moore was greeted by Black organizers as far as the eye could see. To her left she could find Mississippi voting rights organizer Fannie Lou Hamer and Harlem school advocate Preston Wilcox. Down the hall, she could likely spot Detroit-based Black Nationalist preacher Albert Cleage and New York writer and cultural critic Larry Neal.[13] The crème de la crème of Black leadership from across the political spectrum had come to the Black Mecca of the South. But Moore still had her doubts. This was the fourth major conference she'd attended in as many years aimed at effecting real political change. As she wandered in and out of college classrooms, she must have wondered if and when Nationtime would actually arrive.

Huddled elsewhere in one of those hot college classrooms, a group of young women excitedly prepared to make a bold case before the larger conference. Whereas in the past women had been relegated to the margins of the movement, leading only the gender-specific initiatives, these women wanted no less than the full pie. They wanted combat training, for one, to help protect their families and to join the larger Black defense forces if need be. And they wanted childcare centers so new mothers could still carry on their good work.[14] When they presented their ideas to the larger congress, however, they found themselves at the center of a tug-of-war. On one side were the Black feminists, who rallied behind their cause. On the other was a sea of Black men, who claimed the women were using "European concepts of family to solve Black problems." Queen Mother Moore was on the boys' side. On matters of gender and sexual politics, Moore seemed more like a relic than a revolutionary. Even as she pioneered the nationalist boom, Moore saw Black men as the lead actors in her free Black nation, and she continually cast Black women in supporting roles. She believed the Black woman had a "responsibility to establish values. A value system based on her own heritage, not an emulation of that of her oppressors." The younger women of the movement often rolled their eyes behind her back after such lectures.[15] It was lost on no one—least of all Moore, in all likelihood—that Queen Mother lived in defiance of the very same standards she held other women to.

Settling into her seat that day for the evening program, Moore paid those women little mind. She was simply there to savor the show. Though Moore loved the arts, she had little money with which to enjoy them. So the cultural component of these conferences was always an added treat. She nodded along when poet and music critic A. B. Spellman spoke about the importance of art and liberation. And she tapped her toes—she liked to slip out of her shoes when she sat down—to the music during the dance numbers.

When the lights came up, Moore looked around for someone to help her get up from her seat. But the program, it seemed, wasn't over. Instead, her old friend Preston Wilcox took the stage. The Harlem activist unveiled a commemorative portrait of Moore—a tribute to her years of struggle that had laid the groundwork for the Atlanta gathering. The conference rose to its feet in a standing ovation.[16] Moore swelled with pride.

Queen Mother had much to be proud of by the end of the conference. The meeting was proof that Black Nationalism was alive and well across the United States and that there was common ground to be found with the political establishment.[17] Most important, the CAP gathering showed that Black Nationalists were a force to be reckoned with in Black American politics. It was Nationtime indeed.

Ten months later, in June 1971, Baraka led CAP members in gathering a group at Howard University to meet about a "Strategy for Unity: '72 and Beyond." Both radicals and Black politicians had made an earnest effort to reach across the aisle during the previous fall in Atlanta. But a united Black political front had been slow to materialize. With the presidential election around the corner, and Nixon running for another term, the stakes were too high not to try to close the gap between the two groups. Nationalists, Baraka asserted, had to be willing to "risk a bit of [their] own ideological security" to create an organization that Black Americans could "relate to" and engage with.[18] Yet many of them, Queen Mother Moore included, questioned whether such political compromises, as well as the cult of personality that had developed around some activists, would undermine the radical thrust of their work.[19]

Black Nationalists including RNA leader Imari Obadele and members of the Malcolm X Liberation University—a Durham-based independent school and organization headed by local activist Owusu Sadaukai (Howard Fuller)—came out to Baraka's Black Leadership Unity Conference. Newark's mayor, Kenneth Gibson, showed up, too. But there was nothing but radio silence from most Black politicos. Baraka soon learned why. Forty-eight hours before the Howard gathering was set to begin, he got word that another meeting had been called around the same time. This one was to be held in Cleveland, at the home of Mayor Carl Stokes. Its goal was the same: "What kind of strategy, what kind of movement, could be put together to deal with the 1972 election year?" But the invite list included establishment leaders only. Black power brokers like Jesse Jackson went to Cleveland rather than Washington. As a result, Baraka's meeting had hope in spades, but no cross-ideological harmony. What the nationalists did have was a problem on their hands.[20] By the summer of 1971, it was clear that two camps were vying for the leadership of Black America. The question was, could Baraka, Moore, and the nationalists win?

As he watched it all unfold over the summer and early fall, the mayor of Gary, Indiana, Richard Hatcher, devised a plan. In September 1971, he secretly summoned a smaller group of sixty leaders, including Amiri Baraka, Julian Bond, Texas congresswoman and CBC member Barbara Jordan, and Coretta Scott King, to a secluded conference room in Northlake, Illinois—a Chicago suburb.[21] Absent the fanfare, crowds, and big egos of the previous meetings, Hatcher hoped they might find common ground. But it wouldn't be as easy as he'd once thought, now that Shirley Chisholm was gaining ground.

Born in Brooklyn but raised by her grandmother on a farm in Barbados, Chisholm had boldly proclaimed she was steeped in "strength, dignity, and love" from an early age, and that she "didn't need a Black revolution" to convince her of her worth.[22] She burst onto the political scene back in 1964, when Brooklynites elected her to a newly created assembly seat. She toiled away as a member of the education committee, pushing through bills that helped diversify the local student body and support teachers—particularly when they went out on maternity leave.[23] With a few years in Albany under her belt, Chisholm set her eyes on becoming the first Black woman in Congress, and she succeeded in 1968.

"We have had a lot of speakers here, and none of them have dealt with the issues the way you have. We need someone who will do that," southern college kids told Congresswoman Chisholm when she visited their campuses on her speaking tour. They encouraged her to run for president. The congresswoman understood their perspective. Sixties radicals, she reasoned, had "failed to capture the Democratic Party in 1968," and the "party's traditional liberals" had kept up the status quo. "As 1972 came closer," Chisholm explained, disenchanted young people "strongly suspected" the change they sought wasn't coming.[24] And so, when Congressman John Conyers suggested that Black folk put forth their own candidate for president, Chisholm was at the top of many lists.[25]

Reactions were mixed. Some, like her fellow CBC member Ron Dellums, claimed Chisholm could develop a new power base. He believed if Black elected officials supported her campaign, then the Black masses would, too.[26] But others were suspicious of her establishment ties and the fact that she had forged relationships with white feminists—would she be a candidate for women or for Black people? Still, Chisholm felt she was the right person for the job, and she began to build up support for her presidential bid in the summer of 1971.

At Northlake, Mayor Hatcher hoped the smaller collective could at least come to a consensus on whether or not to support Chisholm (who was invited but declined to come), to leverage the Black vote from within the Democratic Party, or to listen to Baraka's repeated calls for a national Black political convention. Ultimately, organizers couldn't settle on any one tack. But at the very least, it was clear the idea of a mass convention was gaining steam among radicals and moderates alike.[27]

Two months later, the CBC held the Conference of Black Elected Officials. The goal: to create a plan of legislative action for the caucus to rally behind. Even still, the politicos invited three hundred others, including Baraka and other Black leftist activists, to the Sheraton-Park Hotel in Washington, D.C., in November 1971. Baraka braved the chilly weather and the even icier relationships between Chisholm and her colleagues in Congress. If Queen Mother Moore had gone, she would have remarked at how similar the meeting looked to the CAP conference the year before. Attendees met in fourteen different workshops focusing on the challenges Black America faced, everything from Black Vietnam vets and the war to health and aging. The plan was to create an agenda that any presidential candidate would need to adopt to get the CBC's support.[28]

They didn't get far. Chisholm quickly figured out that the organizers asked her to chair a session on childhood education at the exact same time as the panel on Black political power in the 1970s. She and her supporters saw it for what it was: a ploy to undermine her presidential campaign. Chisholm stormed the room and launched into a ten-minute tirade against her male colleagues in the CBC, calling them out for their "insecure egos" and "plotting and planning" against her. When it was all said and done, any hope she had of gaining the CBC's endorsement died. But Baraka, who watched the whole thing transpire, was seeing the seeds of his idea for a Black political convention start to sprout.[29]

"Why not? ... What other plan had been arrived at?" he asked the crowd after the dust had settled over Chisholm's stunt.[30] At this point, a national conference gathering Black minds from across the political spectrum was the only path forward. And if present company couldn't get behind the cause, then Black Nationalists would do it on their own. Chastened, the CBC stepped up to act. After dinner that night, Congressman Diggs made a bold declaration.

"For 300 years Black People have been the victims and pawns of the American political process," he began. "Tonight the Congressional Black Caucus issues a call to the Black people of the United States for a national political convention ... for the purpose of developing a national Black agenda and the crystallization of a national Black strategy for the 1972 elections and beyond."[31]

The prospect of bringing moderates and nationalists all under one roof in the name of unity was a tall order. But ultimately, both sides could see a tenuous alliance was their best bet for keeping Nixon at bay. A month later, they agreed to hold a collective meeting in Gary, Indiana—a city with a Black mayor, Black men on the police

force, and some Black-owned hotels and businesses that could support the affair. The group tasked Mayor Hatcher, Amiri Baraka, and
Congressman Diggs with heading the convention.[32] The only question
was whether they could pull it off in just a few months.

Queen Mother Moore arrived at the Westside High School gym for
the National Black Political Convention early on the morning of
March 10, 1972. She stepped out of the car and gazed up at the red,
black, and green flags flapping against parking lot lampposts before
joining the lines of Black people streaming through the double doors.
Inside felt like a Black Nationalist bazaar. Vendors sold T-shirts, Afro
combs, balloons, and Africa-shaped jewelry. Moore walked past poets
offering spoken word on the Black struggle and a bevy of books about
Marcus Garvey and Malcolm X out on display. The scent of soul
food filled the air as caterers careered by with their carts full of fried
chicken and red beans and rice. Moore was full of excitement as she
greeted RNA members sporting their leopard-print military uniforms
and black-suited political brokers mingling among student activists
and journalists.[33]

The atrium was packed, but the crowd parted as the seventy-
three-year-old, clad in African fabric and stacks of beads and bangles,
ambled by. "Queen Mother! Queen Mother!" those who approached
her exclaimed. "My dear, it's nice to see you," Moore would reply,
cupping their hand between hers. The surrogate mother of the movement's memory wasn't as sharp as it once was, and names didn't come
so easily to her anymore. Not that it mattered. To Queen Mother, all
captive Africans were her children.

When she opened the doors to the gym floor, Moore saw hundreds
of silver folding chairs in neat rows across the basketball court, punctuated by white signs featuring the names of all fifty states. As she
made her way to the New York delegation's seating area, she surveyed
the raised stage—set up with more chairs and a wooden podium that
looked as if it might collapse under the weight of the dozens of silver-
wired microphones attached to it.[34]

The energy in the room was electrifying, but Moore and the others in the crowd quieted as the speeches started. Mayor Hatcher took

the stage to open the National Black Political Convention, which had swelled to become the largest and most diverse gathering of Black thinkers, politicians, radicals, and leaders of the twentieth century. Beneath Westside High sports pennants and the school's growling cougar, the bespectacled politician peered out over the microphones and proclaimed the convention was a warning shot to "both American parties." The 1972 election was "their last clear chance" to court the Black vote with commitment to meaningful change. If they failed to do so, a third party was the only reasonable solution. If it wasn't yet clear, the crowd's roaring response made it so: the future of American democracy depended on what happened there in Gary.

When Moore was just starting out as a young organizer, she had tried to work within the two-party political system. But she soon found that Democrats and Republicans pandered to Black people during election years, only to abandon them once political office was secured. After two world wars, the Cold War, and the tumultuous 1960s, she had learned the price Black Americans, the Diaspora, and other non-white countries paid to keep the United States in power. At every turn, her activism confirmed this. America, as it was conceived, was a failed project. And the white ruling class, whether liberal or conservative, was either unable or unwilling to redesign it. The only solution was for Black people to work independently, to champion their own interests. She was happy to hear other Black folk finally felt the same.

The crowd quieted down after Hatcher's prophetic announcements. But they were soon roused back into a frenzy when a thirty-year-old Afroed and sideburned Jesse Jackson, clad in a quintessentially 1970s periwinkle shirt and leather vest, took the stage.

"Brothers and Sisters, what time is it?" Jackson bellowed.

"Nationtime!" the crowd responded in unison. The gymnasium walls rumbled.

"For Black Democrats, Black Republicans, Black Panthers, Black Muslims, Black Independents, Black laborers, Black businessmen, Black professionals, Black mothers on welfare, what time is it?"

"Nationtime!"

"When we form our own political party, what time is it?"

"Nationtime!"

Moore stood and cheered, her kaftan sleeves billowing. Right before her eyes, a crowd of thousands had been brought to its feet in the name of Black Nationalism.

Jackson concluded by reminding the audience of the luminaries who had forged this political moment. Standing together in Gary, they were in fact standing on the shoulders of giants. "Muhammad Ali, Imamu (Amiri) Baraka, Ralph Abernathy, and Angela Davis," he called out. Then he added another name to the list: "Queen Mother Moore."[35]

Moore beamed. The mother of Black Nationalism was witnessing her children come of age.

Organizers planned to address seven key areas that they believed portended the future of Black America. Political empowerment, economic empowerment, and human development were on the docket to be discussed, as were attendees' ideas about foreign policy, environmental protection, communications, and rural development. Groups of organizers, politicians, and artists from across the country— everyone from local housing activists and NAACP leaders to Betty Shabazz, Bobby Seale, and the world's most famous Black actors and singers—came together to create detailed and exhaustive reports and resolutions for each topic. Their goal was to walk out of the Westside's doors with a comprehensive political program. Of course, such a heterogeneous collective was destined to disagree.[36]

Moore was never one to let her voice go unheard. "I'm demanding reparations," she hollered, shoving her pamphlets into hands as hundreds filed past her in and out of the gym. "That's the answer for our people . . . and this document tells you why the Man owes you reparations." Among the throng of students, scholars, and squads of roving plainclothes police officers, Moore stood out. She was draped in a silver, purple, and pink silk head wrap and kaftan, paired with matching silver earrings and necklaces.[37]

"This is how you've been injured. This is how you've been destroyed," she continued. "You was changed from an African into a Negro . . . you've been damaged. Injured, took your name, took your color. I don't have my pretty black color no more. . . . I want an Afro [but] I can't even wear one. The Man messed it up." A small crowd had started to gather around the gesticulating nationalist, laughing and nodding along. Some had by now heard of her and her reparations campaign, and they were delighted to see it in action. Others

Audley Moore as a young child. *(Courtesy of the Warner family)*

Audley Moore's father, St. Cyr Moore. *(Courtesy of the Warner family)*

Audley Moore's mother, Ella Moore. *(Courtesy of the Warner family)*

Audley (right), Eloise (left), and Loretta Moore (center). *(Courtesy of the Warner family)*

Audley Moore as a teenager.
(Courtesy of the Warner family)

Audley Moore speaking in
New York City. *(Courtesy
of the Warner family)*

Queen Mother Moore with members of the Republic of New Afrika, late 1960s. *(Courtesy of Emily Moore)*

Queen Mother Moore in Ghana. *(Photographs and Prints Division, Schomburg Center for Research in Black Culture, New York Public Library)*

Queen Mother Moore pictured with schoolchildren.
(Courtesy of Emily Moore)

Queen Mother Moore on a tarmac in Nigeria.
(Courtesy of Marilyn Nance / Artists Rights Society, New York)

Queen Mother Moore speaking at the U.S. Embassy in Nigeria.
(Courtesy of Marilyn Nance / Artists Rights Society, New York)

Queen Mother Moore
journaling during a visit to
Africa. *(Courtesy of Emily Moore)*

Audley Moore (left) and her sister Loretta (center) with a young student at Mount Addis Ababa. *(Courtesy of Emily Moore)*

The school grounds at Mount Addis Ababa. *(Courtesy of Emily Moore)*

Queen Mother Moore at the Women's Encampment
for a Future Peace and Justice in Seneca Falls, 1980s.
(Courtesy of Collette Fournier)

Queen Mother Moore with Julius Garvey (first on left), Marcus Garvey Jr. (fourth from left), and others at the 1987 Garvey Centennial Celebration. *(Photographs and Prints Division, Schomburg Center for Research in Black Culture, New York Public Library)*

In front, from left, Rosa Parks, Dr. Delois Blakely, Queen Mother Moore (seated), and Elaine Steele in Washington, D.C., for the Million Man March. (*Courtesy of Mark Kerrin and the Library of Congress*)

were enchanted to hear the venerated Queen Mother speak for the first time.

Their reaction emboldened Moore. "You understand? Or maybe you don't. I know your name is Jones, or Johnson, or Williams, huh?" she said, singling out a young man who had been milling about the atrium. "And you know darn well you have no business with English names."[38]

Moore riled up the crowds with a humor only she could land. But her agenda was serious. The idea of reparations was finding a wider berth across the Black Left, and she hoped to make it a central part of the agenda that organizers developed at Gary that weekend.

That all hinged on the decisions of the Platform Committee, a small collective charged with coming together and drawing up the political plan that would, henceforth, lead Black Americans to liberation. When the time finally came for the convention leaders to read what is now known as the Gary Declaration, Moore was delighted.

"We come to Gary in an hour of great crisis and tremendous promise for Black America. While the white nation hovers on the brink of chaos, while its politicians offer no hope of real change, we stand on the edge of history and are faced with an amazing and frightening choice," the declaration opened. "We may choose in 1972 to slip back into the decadent white politics of American life, or we may press forward, moving relentlessly from Gary to the creation of our own Black life." This wasn't the typical lip service Moore had come to expect from the politicos and integrationists. Something was shifting in the room. For the first time in her life, she watched as thousands of Black folk seriously considered the question of whether to sideline Black liberation to join forces with the white political establishment or to once and for all break ties with the two-party system and forge their own path.

"[The] American system does not work for the masses of our people, and it cannot be made to work without radical fundamental change," the committee continued. "Like all white institutions in America, [the system] was designed to operate for the benefit of the white race: It was never meant to do anything else." Thus, the Gary Declaration and the larger meeting began with a simple question, "What Time Is It?" and ended with an answer that was music to Moore's ears: it was Nationtime.[39]

Queen Mother Moore had much to be proud of. But deep down, she must have wondered whether she was witnessing a new wave of Black Nationalism or simply its co-opting. She was still an avid Garveyite, and when she led the UAEW in drafting a declaration for an independent Black republic all those years ago, she meant just that: a separate Black state, standing as an equal among those around the globe. Yet as she listened to leaders and state delegations debate the direction of the movement, it seemed as if many were reluctant to go all the way. When she witnessed thousands proclaim it was Nationtime, Moore likely had a nagging feeling: nationalism had been the convention's rallying cry, but not its final solution. Still, it was something.

During the last hours of the conference, delegates proposed resolutions on a range of topics. It felt as if unity, just maybe, was within reach—and without the typical tax of ideological compromise. But two points of contention remained. The first was busing. The nationalists in attendance were predictably opposed to busing as a means of desegregation. They argued that neither students, teachers, nor parents—white or Black—wanted Black children bused into majority-white school districts.[40] But the liberal wing in attendance, organizations like the NAACP among it, supported the strategy. And for the moderates there, standing against the civil rights juggernaut was a daunting prospect.[41]

The second issue was the looming question of Palestine. In the waning hours of the conference, Reverend Douglas Moore (no relation) introduced a bill calling for an end to U.S. support of Israel and recognition of a Palestinian state. By and large, Moore's nationalist compatriots viewed Palestine as an internal colony, and believed the people there to be living under apartheid rule.[42] In the end, the resolution passed, much to the dismay of Black elected officials and their Jewish supporters—many of whom felt it was a slap in the face, given their support of civil rights. This was the last order of business before the convention ended at 9:30 p.m., but it would be a source of contention for months to come.[43]

Moore was among the nationalists who came to the meeting with the express goal of forming a third political party by and for Black people. They jockeyed for it at breakfasts, during breaks, and even between events, hoping the idea would gain traction. And yet Hatcher's offer of one last chance for the two ruling parties won out. For the radicals in attendance, convincing those who clung to the mainstream that they had the power to create a separate political bloc was too high an order. Instead, they compromised by creating the National Black Political Assembly, which organizers hoped would function as a body that would endorse and support candidates, lobby for Black interests, and amplify Black voter registration efforts.[44]

Even still, Moore was able to add a couple victories to her personal scorecard. She persuaded a then-nineteen-year-old Charles Ogletree to join her reparations fight. Though Moore could hardly have known it then, Ogletree would become a civil rights legal luminary and lead some of the most successful litigations for reparations in the twentieth century.[45] And she was equally gratified when organizers in Gary resolved to create a commission to demand and develop the infrastructure for reparations.[46] After fifteen years of agitation, she had made real progress on this front.

The convention planned to publish a summary of its ratified resolutions as the "National Black Political Agenda" on May 19— Malcolm X's birthday. The treatise included calls for statehood for the District of Columbia, for tuition-free college education for all Black Americans, and for federal funds to be funneled to agricultural laborers in the South. It also affirmed support for anticolonial struggles across Africa, committed to counteracting climate change, and called for an end to the Vietnam War and the FBI's COINTELPRO program.[47] With the backing of delegates from a wide array of religious and political affiliations, it was a striking moment of unity after decades of factionalism. But the sentiment wouldn't last.

Before convention leaders could publish its bold agenda, the NAACP revoked its support because of the busing and Palestine resolutions.[48] In June 1972, the CBC broke ranks and issued its own "Black Declaration of Independence" and a "Black Bill of Rights," each similar in scope and form to the "National Black Political Agenda" but lacking "the fiery rhetoric and nationalist orientation."[49] What's more, the CBC made no mention of Gary during the press conference it held to announce its declaration. There would be no hope of unity henceforth. Just power grabs. The "shotgun wedding" between Black Nationalists and the establishment ended in a bitter divorce.[50]

CHAPTER 21

Queen Mother Visits the Motherland

M other, you have been to Africa, tell us about Africa." It was a
common request, something Moore heard countless times over
the years from those who came to learn at her feet.

"I have not been," she would inevitably reply.[1] Since her youth,
Moore had fantasized about a world where Africans, not Europeans, led African nations. She had always spoken of Africa as a homeland, and she had spent the past fifty years fighting for its freedom
from afar. How, then, could the Queen Mother of captive Africans
in America have not yet witnessed Black liberation on African soil?

Opportunities to visit had come and gone. But Moore had always
refused. "I couldn't see myself going to Africa as a tourist," she explained.[2] If she was going to set foot on the continent, it had to be as
either emigrant or emissary. In the years following the Gary Convention, however, the ache to see her mother country grew even stron-
ger. Moore was getting older: she was less mobile, and she now needed
help getting most places. She must have known her traveling days
would soon be over, and Moore was determined to make the trip—at
least once—before her body finally gave out.

By the early 1970s, Africa was still ablaze with the independence
struggles that had caught fire over the previous thirty years. When
Moore first began her African liberation advocacy in the 1920s and
1930s, Ethiopia and Liberia were just the first, faint embers. But they
had made total liberation feel distantly possible. World Wars I and II
were true turning points. Allied forces established military bases in
African nations, and in some cases these countries were even theaters
of war. Europeans expected the men in their colonial strongholds
to fight on their behalf, albeit in segregated regiments. Those lucky

enough to return home came back to war-torn communities crumbling under the oppressive weight of the very same Western powers they had just fought to uphold. By mid-century, it was simply too much to bear.[3]

While Europeans marked the triumph of democracy over fascism with World War II victory celebrations, Africans staged parades of a different kind. In French-controlled Algeria, for example, civilians and soldiers alike dutifully placed wreaths at their local war memorials and hoisted a precursor to the Algerian flag as they marched in honor of their fallen. They intended to test the integrity of the West's lofty claims of universal and sovereign rights for all.[4] It took less than a decade for leaders such as Kwame Nkrumah of Ghana to become new, more permanent symbols of freedom. In March 1957, Nkrumah transformed Ghana, the African continent, and indeed the world by leading his country to a largely peaceful declaration of independence.[5] Ghana was just the beginning of a domino effect; soon, many more empires would fall. In 1960 alone, no fewer than seventeen countries gained independence. The global press dubbed it the Year of Africa.

"I was very active, on every level that I could [be], for the [sic] African liberation," Queen Mother Moore remarked of this period of rapid decolonization.[6] Moore devoured newspaper articles about Tanganyika and Zanzibar uniting, becoming the independent republic of Tanzania under President Julius Nyerere.[7] She joined fellow New Yorkers in supporting the decades-long nationalist movement in Nigeria, culminating in postwar independence on October 1, 1960.[8] Two years later almost to the day, it was Uganda's turn to free itself from the British Crown. Milton Obote became prime minister of the embattled nation in the months before it declared independence on October 9, 1962.[9]

Yet liberation would not come so easily to others. France, Britain, and Portugal clung tightly to their anachronistic, imperialist fantasies in a rapidly modernizing world. And they had backup, too. When the United States emerged as a postwar global superpower, it propped up its war-torn Western allies in a desperate attempt to keep the Soviet Union from gaining control of the continent. Bolstered by American military might, South African apartheid raged on, and Angolans endured an equally brutal Portuguese regime. But they fought back.

It started small. On January 4, 1961, a group of Angolan workers staged a protest against their harsh working conditions on a Portuguese-run cotton plantation in Baixa do Cassange. They burned their identification cards and attacked Portuguese traders and officials. Their rage spread throughout the local village, and the Portuguese authorities responded in kind. The next day, Angolans across twenty villages woke up to air raids killing hundreds if not thousands. A month later, a small group stormed the São Paulo fortress—a prison in the Angolan capital of Luanda—to free a group of political prisoners. Forty died at the hands of the Portuguese in the wake of the attack. But the uprising had begun.[10] As the resistance spread across the country, multiple nationalist groups developed to try to lead the embattled country to independence.

It would cost thousands of lives, and the splintering of the nationalist liberation forces between the socialist National Front for the Liberation of Angola and the National Union for the Total Independence of Angola, before the country finally achieved independence.[11] Other Portuguese colonies soon followed suit. Engineer and Marxist Amílcar Cabral led Guinea-Bissau and Cape Verde in driving out colonial forces through the African Party for the Independence of Guinea and Cape Verde—until party rivals assassinated him to seize power, an all-too-common fate for African nationalist visionaries.[12]

Mozambique was the next to take on its Portuguese oppressors. A long history of colonial rule and recent massacres of protesters had stoked nationalist sentiment in the colony. In 1962, disparate revolutionary groups coalesced into the Mozambique Liberation Front (FRELIMO) and began a guerrilla war against Portugal. FRELIMO quickly won international support, but victory and independence wouldn't come until 1975.[13]

Across these nearly two decades of African liberation fights, the continent's nationalist leaders had held on to power by courting one of the most powerful groups in the global Diaspora: Black Americans. To be sure, African freedom fighters and heads of state—everyone from Nkrumah to Cabral—believed Black folk's battles against white supremacy around the world were intertwined. But they also saw Black American backing as a sort of pocket ace. Garnering their support, many African leaders believed, was their best shot at getting the most powerful government in the world to turn its gaze toward their cause. Queen Mother Moore was a sought-after prize in this international game: a heralded leader headquartered in Harlem, the Black Mecca of the United States.

As this new generation of state leaders sent their diplomats and emissaries abroad, they tasked them with meeting Moore. Queen Mother always obliged. She donned her full regalia whenever ambassadors from Ghana, Zambia, Tanzania, and other countries called on her in New York.[14] These meetings helped solidify Moore's status as a global liberation leader. But they also left her with a longing. She wanted to meet these vaunted African heads of state herself, and on their own soil. In 1972, she finally got her chance.

Dr. Kwame Nkrumah passed away just one month after the Gary Convention convened. There was much to mourn and celebrate in equal measure. Although many, including Moore, had admired Nkrumah's leadership during Ghana's liberation movement, they knew his real test would come when Ghanaians chose him to be president of their newly independent nation.

Moore watched with great interest as Nkrumah carefully tried to balance his fulcrum of power. At times, he was immersed in the domestic, feverishly trying to engage in nation-building projects to strengthen his newly liberated country. In other moments, he was laser focused on his lofty dream of unifying Africa and once and for all chasing European powers from the continent. It was a tough balance, and Nkrumah was uncompromising in his political vision, if not inflexible. The Ghanaian leader made a series of grave missteps in navigating his country's tribal groups—namely the Asante tribe, who believed him to be insensitive to their long-standing political and cultural importance. Nkrumah fought to bring all the different kingdoms and tribal groups under one struggling governmental body and ally it with other nations across the continent.[15] With detractors on all sides, Nkrumah grew suspicious of the leaders, elites, and government workers around him. Fearing a coup, he began imprisoning his opponents without trial, ultimately increasing dissent and tanking his popularity after just a few short years on the job.[16]

Nkrumah knew his opposition was plotting. But he was still stunned when he got word on February 24, 1966, that six hundred soldiers were headed toward Accra to disband his government and arrest his supporters. And they had chosen an opportune time: he was on a diplomatic visit to China and then on to war-torn Vietnam at the invitation of its leader, Ho Chi Minh.[17] Nkrumah was powerless to stop the coup, and the opposition was barred from returning home once it was done. Instead, his friend and fellow president, Sékou Touré, welcomed him in Guinea and appointed him honorary co-president. Nkrumah resided there and processed the loss of his position until he succumbed to cancer in 1972.

The intervening six years between the coup and Nkrumah's death had proven to be difficult for Ghana, too, with various political parties looking to unite the country amid regional, tribal, and political conflict. There was no doubt Nkrumah's critics had been sound. But political and physical distance had revealed that the governing struggles he faced were not so easily solved. As the United States and the Soviets continued to jockey for power over African countries, Nkrumah's call for unity across the continent became all the more resonant. And so, when Ghanaians heard the news of his death, a new fervor for "all things Nkrumah" took hold. Nkrumah had ended his life a paranoiac and a pariah.[18] But in death, he had become global Black Nationalist royalty. It was only fitting that Queen Mother Moore attend his funeral.[19]

This proved to be more complicated than the activist had originally thought. Still smarting at the treatment of his friend before his death, Sékou Touré initially refused to return Nkrumah's body to his homeland without the restoration of his reputation and the release of his imprisoned supporters.[20] The countries compromised and agreed to hold a state funeral in Conakry, Guinea, before returning Nkrumah to Ghana to lie in state in Accra and be buried in his hometown of Nkroful.[21] Queen Mother Moore's first trip to Africa followed the same route.

"I felt that we should be represented," she later said of the funeral plans. "I didn't have the money. But I felt we just had to go." Moore gathered seven or eight of her fellow nationalists together at The East, a community center and school for Black folk in Brooklyn, to plan how they might make the trip.[22] The East got its start when teacher and activist Jitu Weusi (Les Campbell) opened up an independent school in a three-story building in Bed-Stuy to serve local children caught up in the tumult of the 1960s New York City school struggles.

The collective grew quickly, eventually filling four more buildings and adding an Africa-centered bookstore, a boutique, primary and secondary schools, and a small publishing house on the side.[23] Moore had eagerly supported the group in any way she could.[24] Now it was time for the brothers and sisters of The East to return the favor.[25]

As her plane began its initial descent, Moore looked out the window and marveled at the city of Conakry, which sat on a slender peninsula jutting out into the Atlantic. By the time they touched down, she was overcome. "When the plane landed, such a thrill came over me," Moore recalled. "All the years I had suffered, all of the separation, all of the whips on our backs, all of the rapes, all the everything [that] came before me." The typically stoic Moore fell into total hysterics. She wept as she deboarded.

A caravan of soldiers flanked the plane as Moore walked out and allowed the heat of the African summer to dry her tears. As soon as her feet hit the ground, Guinean troopers ushered her and the other members of the American delegation into a motorcade and off to their hotel. "Lord, look at what they've robbed us of," she remarked as her car wound through the Conakry streets.[26] Moore was moved by the beauty of the motherland and devastated that Black Americans had nothing like it that they could call their own.

The elder organizer was even more overcome when she joined the throngs of Africans entering the Palace of the People, a Western-style, five-story white building, where Nkrumah lay. Queen Mother took her seat and watched in silence as state leaders dutifully approached Nkrumah's casket—fittingly draped in Ghana's red, gold, and green flag—to lay tall funeral wreaths before him. And she stood, unflinching, during the earsplitting 103-cannon salute. Sékou Touré himself eulogized his fallen friend: "Nkrumah is not a Ghanaian; he's an African" who "will never die" in the hearts and minds of the people. It was an admittedly hagiographic tribute in death to a man who had led a complicated life.[27]

"Sékou Touré came up and kissed me," Moore remembered fondly. Indeed, the Guinean president made a pointed effort to seek out Moore and the American contingent after the rites. They had traveled a long way, after all. And it would only bolster his own country's reputation if they enjoyed their stay. The activist basked in the fact that Touré had treated them "like VIPs," presenting Moore with gifts and inviting the group to dine with him at his palace during their stay. "Each evening, at the people's palace," he "would acknowledge me," Moore recounted whenever anyone asked her about the trip. "Oh, I felt so proud. Just to feel that he knew I was there."[28]

The Guinean president also gave Moore a tour of the countryside, where she found joy in the mundane materiality of West African life. "I was taken all over, all over, [to] these plants where they made cloth, the beautiful cloths," she recollected. "I ate so much in the pineapple factory . . . I paid for it later, but I sure enjoyed the sweetest pineapple in the world."[29] Anyone listening could tell this was more than the seventy-three-year-old activist satisfying her ever-present sweet tooth. For most of her life, Moore had dreamed of savoring the fruits of the continent. And now she had.

The delegation left Guinea with full stomachs and hearts alike as they followed Nkrumah's body back to his homeland. But Moore soon found the former president wasn't the only one making news. Word had gotten out: another international leader had come home, too.

Queen Mother Moore rose one morning to find an emissary at her door. An elder chief of the Asante tribe was requesting an audience. She didn't have a firm grasp of all the different Ghanaian tribes and factions, but Moore was well versed enough to know this was a prestigious invitation. Considered the most dominant ethnic group in all of Ghana, the modern-day Asante traced their lineage back to the seventeenth and eighteenth centuries. For Black Americans like Moore, they were a symbol of African power—a people who had survived the slave trade and colonialism with their culture and society still intact.

Moore heard the drums before she could see them. Her face lit up as she joined the throng of people in their vibrant fabrics and elaborate headdresses dancing to the rhythmic thrum as they guided her down a dirt road to their chief, who was holding a roll of fabric in his hand. The drumming slowed and the people stilled. He gestured for Moore to step up and unrolled the cloth to reveal "gobs and gobs of gold jewels," she recalled, "big bracelets, bracelets with roses and leaves of gold." He unfurled his arms in front of her—a sign for her to do the same. Then one by one he slid the bracelets over Moore's wrinkled hands and up her arms. Next came the rings. Moore must have marveled at the treasures adorning her fingers and forearms; Ghana wasn't called the Gold Coast for nothing, after all. The chief then picked up "ropes of gold" and gingerly placed them around her neck, followed by a crown for Queen Mother's regal head.[30]

In the Asante culture, Queen Mothers sit upon a wooden stool, a seat of power akin to a throne in European monarchies.[31] As Moore lowered herself onto the ceremonial chair, a U-shaped seat with four sturdy legs, tribe members held above her the customary umbrella: colorful, long-stemmed, and lined with fringe. And with that, she had been initiated as a Queen Mother of the Asante people.[32]

Of course, Moore had been using the title for more than a decade by this point. She interpreted the ceremony in Ghana as a recognition of her devotion to Black liberation and a validation of her right to the title. "I was Queen Mother long before that," she explained. This was simply "an honor bestowed upon me by people who knew of my work."[33]

The honor was indeed all Moore's as she concluded her tour. Her journey was a joyous one. It exceeded her wildest dreams and fantasies. But it was also disorienting. Coming face-to-face with cultures, traditions, labor, ceremonies, and celebrations of the Asante people, among others, Moore realized how oblivious she and other Black Americans were of the realities of continental life. She had bought into African independence wholesale, without understanding the consequences that changing regimes and political upheavals had on the lives of her African brethren.[34] She returned to America ambivalent about her relationship with the continent. But at least one thing was certain. Now, when her children asked her what Africa was like, she had a resolute answer.[35]

To her total surprise, Moore had an invitation to return to Africa just a few months later. Back in Conakry that April, she happened to meet Madame Jeanne Martin Cissé, a Guinean nationalist and secretary-general of the All-Africa Women's Conference (AAWC). The AAWC was a leader in the growing network of women's organizations developing across the continent, Cissé had likely told Moore when they met at a state dinner one night.[36] She was now in the final throes of planning the group's 1972 gathering in Dar es Salaam—a meeting that would reflect the growing size and influence of the ten-year-old organization.[37] Moore should come if she could, Cissé offered, though she recognized it was a tall order given the conference was slated to take place in just a few months. It would be historic if she could make it, though. Moore's presence at the July 1972 meeting would mark the first time a Black American woman would participate in the conference.[38]

Returning to Africa just a few months after Nkrumah's funeral was no easy task for the debt-ridden activist. But Moore was determined to go. She couldn't miss the opportunity to meet many of the African women leaders she had long idolized, nor the chance to take her grandchildren—her *actual* grandchildren—to Africa for the first time. Her son, Tom, now forty-two, was a father of four: Thomas Jr., Audley, Christine, and Judith. After much cajoling, he agreed to let his mother take his oldest two children, Thomas Jr. and her namesake, Audley, with her for the summer vacation of a lifetime.[39] But first Moore needed the money.

Queen Mother Moore had never been shy about the economic realities of an activist's life, and she wasn't about to start now. Reaching out to reporters at the *New York Amsterdam News*, Moore spread the word of her plight far and wide. "Harlem's—and the world's—adored and adoring Queen Mother Moore needs help," local reports said, to attend the Dar es Salaam conference. "The very limited money she has buys her one meal a day and pays her rent. Queen Mother doesn't have the plane fare or hotel funds" to attend. Donations were to be sent directly to Moore's apartment on Stebbins Avenue in the Bronx. And in return, she invited any able and willing Black women to join her in making the trip. Her plan worked. Moore raised the money she needed, and she wrangled a handful of organizers to join her, too.[40]

On July 22, 1972, the mother of America's captive Africans touched down in Africa for a second time. It was close to midnight when Moore, Thomas Jr., and young Audley groggily made their way to the Hotel Kilimanjaro, a nine-story, modern, Western-style hotel in Dar es Salaam. Despite being jet-lagged, Moore wasted no time. The next morning, she appointed someone to look after her grandchildren so she could go meet up with Alberta Hill, an activist from The East in New York, and New York–based SNCC activist Emily Moore (no relation). With her young chaperones in tow, Moore first went to visit a community of Black American expats.[41] A Queen Mother, after all, had to tend to all her children, both at home and abroad. Moore was curious to see how they were faring, and to get a firsthand account of Africa's struggles on the ground.

After a few days of informal meetings, Moore climbed into a car headed to the Diamond Jubilee Hall. Melodic singing and drumming from the crowd of women who lined the entranceway enveloped her as soon as she stepped out of the car and into the conference site. Everywhere she looked, she saw women decked out in their national dress, clapping and stepping in time to the rhythm of drums ricocheting off the building. She likely joined the crowd's cheers at the arrival of Tanzania's women leaders. The country's first lady, Maria Nyerere, glided into the conference. Sofia Kawawa, leader of the Tanzania Women's Union, was close behind her.[42]

Inside, Moore maneuvered around brown wooden tables arranged in a semicircle, adorned with placards designating the different delegations' seating assignments.[43] She took her seat and dutifully listened through her headphones as a translator relayed the impassioned speeches of women from across the continent about how to best contribute to global Black liberation.[44]

These frank discussions laid some of African women's problems bare for Moore. The gathering confirmed the enduring effects of patriarchy across African cultures, as well as the fraught relationships that African countries had with the West. Moore faced a reckoning. She had underestimated the challenges of wholesale African unity, and she realized banding Black women together across oceans and borders was much easier said than done. Still, she wanted to do her part.

The next day, it was Queen Mother Moore's turn to speak. After a brief introduction and rousing applause, Moore stood up and inched her way to the front of the room. She fingered through the strands of beads around her neck until she found the one connected to her reading glasses, then sat the square-frame spectacles on her nose and unfolded her papers. One final pause; she looked up just to take the moment in. Then she began.[45]

"I have the honor to convey sisterly greetings to you from thousands of your sisters in the United States of America," she opened in her loud, Louisiana drawl. "Your invitation to us across the Atlantic Ocean will do more to cement our relationship than any occurrence since the terrible days of slavery which so ruthlessly severed us from you." It was a somber salutation, but Moore soon caught fire. Speaking on behalf of the U.S. delegation, she recounted how Black American women had witnessed Africa's freedom struggles from afar and how it had "awakened in us a new inspiration to fight our most common enemies, United States imperialism and racism, the most deadly enemies of the liberation forces in Africa today." And she extolled the power that Africans had to chart their own course to a free future: "We cannot rely on the morality of the world.... What is needed is a total mental revolution. The form that our revolution takes will depend first on a common goal—African Unity."

Whether they be native-born Africans fighting for independence or captive Africans born under the dominion of America, the endgame was the same: "retake what was originally ours (our land, our wealth, and our natural resources) and... demand reparations for all these years of inhuman treatment."

Moore devoted the rest of her speech to assuring her audience that Black American women were ready and willing to take up the cause. "My dear sisters," she continued, "we in the United States are in the most strategic position to help wage a struggle against the most powerful and awesome enemy of Africa—the imperialism of the United States. We are in the belly of the beast and in a position to crush its ugly head with our heels."

To be sure, there was no love lost between Queen Mother and her nation-state: "We Africans living in the United States, are disinherited from our motherland, and are striving for restoration.... We are treated as sub-humans with little or no protection under the law. We have the same status in American society as do our brothers and sisters in Southern Africa.... We have no political power. We have no control over a single economic institution."

She conceded that while some Black folk had achieved "the appearance of affluence and equality" through high-powered jobs or cultural clout, the tokenism of a few vaunted Black faces among the sea of struggling, everyday Black folk only drove the knife deeper. "Our men have been the victims of lynchings, unfair imprisonment, and disproportionate slaughter in wars, and the mind-killing ravages of dope and alcohol," she boomed. "Our women have suffered untold misery because of the impact of these deterrents to wholesome family life."

Even still, all was not lost in Moore's eyes. "Today, as never before, there is a large degree of conscious development toward Africanization on the part of Black people in the United States," she said. "The dawn has broken. The sun of freedom is rising gloriously over the horizon of our Motherland, Africa. With work and cooperation on both sides of the Atlantic among all of our people, we shall achieve a united and independent Africa." Here, Moore paused. It was time for her big crescendo, and she would reach it the only way she knew how.

"For we are Africans too, regardless of being born in the U.S.A. Just as if a cat had kittens in an oven"—it was an age-old Moore-ism, but she relished the chance to bust it out for a new, rapt audience—"you wouldn't call them biscuits." A sly little grin crept across the aged activist's face; her audience responded in kind with chuckles. "No matter where an African is born, he is still an African."

Applause replaced laughter as Moore proclaimed, "Long live the unity of African People! Long live African Women wherever they are! Long live the All-Africa Women's Conference! Long live our Motherland, Africa!"[46]

The conference was a rare chance to forge Black solidarity outside the confines of Moore's typical American, male-led spaces, and she made the most of it. If there had ever been any doubt, now there was none: Black American women were willing, ready, and able to fight.

Moore opened her eyes the following morning officially one year older. Later that night, she donned one of her more festive outfits for the conference reception and sauntered into the Hotel Kilimanjaro ballroom. She expected to find a sea of well-dressed women, wandering from group to group, mingling with drinks in hand. But when she opened the doors, Moore was stunned to find the room staring back at her and a massive cake frosted with her name before them. Not to be outdone, First Lady Nyerere and the local workers unions feted Moore even further. "They all gave me wonderful presents," she recalled. "It was the most magnificent thing you ever saw in your life."[47]

The festive air wafted into the closing proceedings, where delegates voted on final resolutions, many of which echoed the mandates of Moore's speech. The AAWC vowed to support women's full involvement in African liberation struggles, to actively fund liberation movements, and to work toward reinstating African languages in schools where colonial regimes had tried to stamp them out. Attendees also vowed to return to their homelands and "drop ancient prejudices they had about themselves," and to "take their rightful place as liberators and moulders of the future of Africa." The women of the African Diaspora, they vowed, would henceforth "march forward as one people, with one identity."[48]

Once the conference had ended, Moore made the transition from global activist to grandma. She, Tom Jr., and young Audley spent several more weeks in Tanzania as special guests of President Nyerere, using his private plane to tour the countryside. As the plane angled down toward the dusty runways, Moore saw the small dots in the distance transform into figures holding signs reading, WELCOME QUEEN MOTHER. At each stop in the ten provinces she visited, Moore stayed in their finest hotels and awoke to breathtaking views of the Tanzanian countryside. She and the grandkids ate and drank to their hearts' delight.[49]

Moore relished this time abroad. It was a notable respite from the fraught financial realities of an activist's life in America, for one. But more crucially, it was a rare opportunity to have unmediated access to an esteemed African state leader. When President Nyerere suggested they extend their stay a few more days, Moore readily took him up on the offer and relocated to his more secluded home on the Indian Ocean coast.

There, Moore and Nyerere spent their extra time together deep in spirited policy talk. She was among the many Black Americans who had become enraptured by the idea of *Ujamaa*, the Swahili word many use to describe cooperative economics and the catchall term for Nyerere's ambitious domestic policy. In addition to nationalizing banks and industry, the president hoped to counter colonial urbanization by creating government-funded countryside cooperatives. Nyerere envisioned these Ujamaa villages, as they were called, as spaces where Tanzanians could re-create traditional, precolonial family and social structures while harnessing the country's natural resources through technological innovation. Moore wanted to see the process in action. But she had her own motives, too. The aging activist was desperate to gain international support for her reparations campaign, and she hoped leaders like Nyerere might bring Black Americans' plight before the Organization of African Unity, the manifestation of Kwame

Nkrumah's Pan-African dreams and an international conglomerate of African nations founded in May 1963.[50]

Perhaps because they wanted to talk politics in peace, the pair conspired to get the children out from underfoot; they sent Nyerere's son and Moore's grandchildren on long walks on the beach for some much-needed space.[51] Nyerere's Ujamaa plan, the president revealed, wasn't without its setbacks. Started in 1964, it was as ambitious as it was arduous for the Tanzanian people. By the time Moore arrived, Nyerere had resorted to forcing reluctant citizens into leaving their individual farms and joining communal ones when too few had volunteered to do so—a sign that betting on socialism might be getting the better of him.[52] Queen Mother Moore was feeling the sting of defeat, too. She began traveling to Africa only seven months after the attack on the RNA's Jackson headquarters. As she watched the fledgling Black republic unravel, she too was pondering the cost of realizing Black Nationalist ideals.

When it was time to go, Moore left with a clearer understanding of the limits of American-centered ideas of African nationalism and a sobering sense of the costs of wresting African economies back from Western countries.[53] She promised to return to Tanzania in due time, and to keep forging bonds between African and American activists. But even if she never made it back, she had accomplished two lifelong dreams. Moore had finally felt African soil between her toes. And she had given the same gift to her grandchildren, who by their own accounts now saw "how vast and beautiful and how wonderful the world was." From that day forward, they associated Africa with "being with Queen Mother and being free."[54]

CHAPTER 22

Tanzania Redux

President Julius Nyerere's charisma propelled him to near-mythological status among Black activists and nationalists. A prolific writer, he penned treatises on Black culture, identity, and community development that made Tanzania a beacon of hope for a liberated and thriving Africa.[1]

In response, a sizable Black expat community developed in the port city of Dar es Salaam throughout the mid-1970s, comprising activists, teachers, and artists looking to reconnect the threads that slavery had long since severed.[2] Whether it was Moore's old comrade Mae Mallory or more moderate organizers like Boston's Muriel Snowden, Black Americans flocked to Dar es Salaam in the 1970s to witness the Ujamaa philosophy in action.[3]

At Moore's age, relocating to Tanzania was implausible at best. But that wouldn't keep her from visiting again. She got her chance sooner than she imagined with the advent of the Sixth Pan-African Congress (PAC), a June 1974 meeting in Dar es Salaam. The goal was the same as that of many of the previous meetings of this kind she had attended. But the constituency was decidedly different. This would be the biggest and most diverse gathering of the Diaspora to date, and it would finally fulfill the Pan-African Congress founders' dream of gathering on the African continent.

The meeting sprouted from a seed planted back in 1969 at the International Black Power Conference in Bermuda, where Moore and so many others had delighted in receiving an invitation from Kwame Nkrumah to host an international summit on the African continent.[4] Back then, such a gathering seemed as implausible as it was thrilling. Radical Black activists inside and outside the United States had to navigate a labyrinthine web of government surveillance, not to mention ideological divides among their own ranks, real and imagined, to bring such an idea to fruition. These challenges, coupled with the financial and logistical hurdles of transporting thousands of Black folk to Africa, had stoked Moore's doubts.

But then again, Black people had done more with less. And so, while Queen Mother Moore was attending the funerals and lavish dinners of African state leaders in 1972, Pauulu Kamarakafego, SNCC organizer James Garrett, writer Liz Gant, and Tanzania's high commissioner to Canada, Abbas Sykes, went to Europe to do some international politicking of their own.[5]

At first, Kamarakafego, Garrett, Gant, and Sykes were met with plenty of questions but little buy-in. Some scoffed at the idea that such a congress could even take place, let alone that it could be cohesive enough to yield real results. Others questioned who should be allowed to make the cut—to be considered "Black" or "African" enough to be included—and how they planned to fundraise for the conference without acquiescing to donor demands.[6] By the time they returned home, one thing was clear: if the quartet thought it would be easier to organize a Pan-African Congress during the height of African decolonization, they were sadly mistaken.

Yet they did make headway on one front: the location. Tanzania had long served as a home base and haven for South African and Portuguese anticolonial fighters and as a model of African liberation in action thanks to Nyerere's leadership. Although organizers had considered Nigeria, Guinea, and Algeria potential sites for the conference, Tanzania, most agreed, was the ideal place to meet.

Back home, American organizers got some help from the grassroots. SNCC organizers Judy Richardson, Charlie Cobb, Courtland Cox, and Curtis Hayes founded the Drum and Spear Bookstore in Washington, D.C., shortly after Dr. King's assassination in 1968. They hoped the shop would act as an "alternative source of communication between Africa and the Diaspora" by publishing texts extolling global Black liberation, especially Tanzanian Ujamaa. In time, Drum and Spear expanded into a printing press under the same name, as well as a community school that they called the Center for Black Education. By the early 1970s, it was the largest bookstore in the country dedicated to the African Diaspora. And it soon went global. Store runners set up a headquarters in Dar es Salaam to better work with a local press there: the Tanzanian Publishing Company.[7]

In 1972, Drum and Spear took up the Sixth PAC cause. Activists such as Courtland Cox set up an office in the Center for Black Education in D.C., while others, including JoAnn Favors and Geri Augusto, established an international headquarters in Tanzania, where they negotiated the logistics of getting their fellow Black Americans to soon follow.[8]

Organizers on both sides of the Atlantic shared the "Call to Congress," a document that Geri Augusto drafted with guidance from Trinidadian theorist C. L. R. James.[9] "The 20th century is the century of Black Power," Augusto wrote. Black people around the world were taking it upon themselves to "solve the problems that threaten to overwhelm human society," and the Sixth Pan-African Congress was to be "part of that movement."

Organizers made the stakes clear as day. They called on all "Africans everywhere," no matter their "political attitudes," to "draw a line of steel against those, Africans included, who hide behind the slogans and paraphernalia of national independence" while excusing capitalist domination of the continent, and to give their "total support to fighters who engage the enemies of Africa in day-to-day struggle." They hoped that the Sixth PAC would unite the entire African Diaspora under the banner of Black self-determination and economic self-reliance, free from white intervention.[10]

By the end of 1973, Sixth PAC missives were flying back and forth across the Atlantic. Telegrams from U.S.-based activists like Sylvia Hill indicated that organizing Black people across the North American continent had begun in earnest. And dispatches from Tanzania spoke to making inroads with African liberation leaders, who were committing to attend.[11] The next task was to determine who, from a wide "cross-section of political and economic organizations, community groups, and members of the scientific and technical community," would be selected to join North America's delegation.[12]

The second that Moore saw the "Call to Congress," she knew she had to attend. Whatever doubts she might have had about the organizers' capabilities, she believed—if they could pull it off—the Sixth PAC would be the "most historic occasion that has happened in the world as far as the African people [were] concerned."[13] Moreover, it had been more than a year since the Black Left had declared it "Nationtime!" in Indiana. And yet no independent Black political party had ever materialized. The Jackson RNA raid had brutally suppressed Black people's boldest attempt at nation building. And Moore could count only a handful of cases where a struggle for Black control of their own communities had succeeded. The children were losing their way, she believed. An international meeting of the minds as ambitious as the Sixth PAC could set them straight—but only if the North American delegation came prepared.

Moore spent a significant part of 1973 attending Sixth PAC planning meetings to help shape the delegation's platform and roster. Her first stop was Kent State University, where 175 activists representing forty-five organizations assembled to hash out their differing visions of what the North American delegation to the PAC would champion during the meeting.[14]

As one of the most senior and experienced organizers in the room, Queen Mother Moore was unafraid to question the group's agenda and the male leaders who had set it. Was the theme of the congress "unity" or "liberation"? she asked.[15] It was a crucial question. Goodwill and warm wishes weren't enough. Before the North American delegation set foot on PAC grounds, it needed to have a steely-eyed vision of how Black freedom might be achieved. Without it, they were destined to squander this chance to parley with Africa's emerging Black nations.[16]

Moore was dancing around her *actual* question, and the organizers around her could tell. A central point of contention at the Kent State meeting—and in the Black Power Movement writ large those days— was whether racism or capitalism was the primary animator of global white supremacy and Black oppression. This question had been on Black radicals' minds for decades, of course—Garveyites and communists had sparred over it for much of the 1920s and 1930s.[17] Moore had tried to walk the line between these dueling ideologies all her career. As a Garveyite, she believed racism preceded the creation of Western capitalism and therefore should be the focus of the Black struggle. But her time in the party showed her that class analysis was valuable. It could be the key to galvanizing the Black masses.

The two-line struggle, as many organizers called the race versus class debate, took on new life in the 1970s as Black organizers from Amiri Baraka to the Black Panther Party began to widen their ideological frame. They were still wholeheartedly nationalists. However, a decade of Black Power organizing had helped them see that white supremacy, while important, was only part of the problem; they needed to also fight against class oppression. Leaders like Baraka began to embrace a broader conception of nationalism, one that was more internationalist and class-conscious.[18] Or, as the Panthers put it, they became "nationalists who want[ed] revolutionary changes in everything, including the economic system that the oppressor inflicts upon us."[19]

Contemporaneous African liberation struggles had also put the limits of stalwart nationalism in sharp relief. Although Tanzanians, Kenyans, and Ugandans, among others, had achieved independence, they still struggled to survive as Western powers circled the wagons, excluding them from the global marketplace. As a result, the anticolonial movement turned to socialism, forging a new ideology that combined African nationalist traditions with economic reform that aimed to address inequality and wrest back control of their industries. The more Black American organizers learned about these struggles, the more they wondered if they, too, had been too narrow in their political focus.[20]

As the debate raged on, Moore had tried to keep her finger on the nationalist side of the scales. On May 27, 1972, for example, Queen Mother donned her regalia and led thousands—many also dressed in African clothing and carrying signs declaring, AFRICA FOR THE AFRICANS—through the streets of D.C. for African Liberation Day. The demonstrators paraded through Embassy Row, stopping only to denounce the South African, Rhodesian, and Portuguese governments represented there before reaching their rallying point at the Washington Monument, which they rechristened Lumumba Square for the protest.[21]

"I've waited 45 years for this day!" Moore exclaimed to the sea of people waving black, green, and red flags in the square.[22] The crowd erupted in cheers for her and other speakers like Black Panther leader Elaine Brown. The Washington, D.C., march reached its zenith when Owusu Sadaukai led the throng of protesters in chanting "We are an African People."[23] Similar demonstrations took place across the

Americas, with Black people rallying in places like Pittsburgh, San Francisco, and Montreal.[24]

But the euphoria Moore had felt that day quickly dissolved when leaders like Sadaukai reversed course. After a monthlong stint working with the Mozambique Liberation Front in 1971, the Durham-based organizer began to question his strictly nationalist lens. Black Americans were complicit in America's imperialism in Africa, he realized. And Black leadership of a capitalist Black nation would never bring about true liberation.[25] Not long after African Liberation Day, he began to embrace Marxism.

This sent shock waves through the Black Left.[26] The Student Organization for Black Unity, a major player in student-led Black struggles in the 1970s, adopted a Marxist position and changed its name to the Youth Organization for Black Unity, indicating their advocacy for *all* members of the Black community, rather than mostly middle-class students. And as Amiri Baraka mingled with Sadaukai and studied the writings of African liberation leaders, he officially shifted CAP's position, eventually declaring it a Marxist-Leninist organization.[27]

In the wake of this defection, Moore and her compatriots doubled down. Whether it was in raucous organizing meetings or in magazines like *Black Scholar*, they vehemently denounced Marxist turncoats.[28] A student of Marxism since her Communist Party days, Moore could not deny that a class analysis was an integral part of any assessment of the Black condition. But violent white supremacy had defined as much of her life as poverty had. She was skeptical of the idea that economic revolution was the silver bullet destined to slay racism. These debates raged on as Sixth PAC plans developed. Entire organizations crumbled under the weight of activists' infighting and mudslinging.[29]

Still, Moore remained obstinate. The North American delegation had to be firmly nationalist. Six months after the Kent State meeting, she and her sister Loretta joined Black Studies professors, Pan-African student activists, and members of The East to pen a letter to North America's Sixth PAC leaders.

The group emphasized that Black Americans "were taken [from] our land involuntarily, not willfully," and they wanted their African "inheritance rights to be recognized by the existing independent African states." They also argued that the American government had denied Black Americans "the basic human right to choose [their] governor," a point Moore had continually made when arguing for Black sovereignty. "We recommend that the delegation to the Sixth PAC emphasize the importance of choice through a plebiscite, therefore giving African Americans the opportunity to choose between assuming American citizenship, returning to Africa or establishing a nation state" on American soil, they wrote. Last of all, they called on the delegation to push for the creation of an embassy system among African countries, where "representatives of the currently stateless African" could find both refuge and a political voice.[30]

"There appears to be some opposition to the Congress on the parts of old-time Nationalists and Pan-African groups in the city," Julian Ellison of the Black Economic Research Center think tank wrote to Sixth PAC leadership after hearing Moore's criticism. The Moore sisters were particularly miffed that they had not been called upon to lead the North American delegation.[31] The pair had a long history of Pan-African organizing, and Queen Mother Moore had just returned from a series of meetings with African leaders. Who better to help guide the group headed to the Sixth PAC, the sisters reasoned, than those who had been on the ground since organizers issued the first Call to Congress more than seventy years ago?

Moore's dissatisfaction with Sixth PAC planning reflected her growing sense of marginalization, both personally and politically. As Queen Mother of the movement, she expected younger activists to genuflect to her. But more important, she wanted them to keep her nationalist vision alive and carry it forward after she was gone. As she watched these young, mostly male organizers host meetings without her, often to debate the centrality of class consciousness to the cause, she could sense her influence slipping.

But the final straw was when these young guns made her *apply* to join the delegation sent to the Sixth PAC. Congress organizers asked all interested individuals to fill out an application detailing their previous movement work and their "commitment to the betterment of African People." Space and funds were limited, after all. And they needed to whittle down the bunch to a cool two hundred Canadians and Americans.[32]

"For 55 years I have worked assiduously in the Black communities of these United States of America, organizing and bringing knowledge to Black people of the African identity denied to them," Moore scribbled in her loopy cursive on the bottom of the first page. "I consider this application demeaning to my integrity and reputation as a revolutionary."³³ Still, leadership wouldn't budge. Even movement royalty had to follow standard procedure.

Ultimately, Sixth PAC organizers accepted her application. With the help of the Council of Churches of the City of New York's Task Force Against Racism, which paid for her trip in full, Moore prepared to once more travel to Tanzania, as part of the North American delegation.³⁴ But there was a caveat. She was to be a special guest to the PAC's proceedings, rather than a voting member of the group. Young organizers framed this choice as an honor, commemorating Moore's "years of commitment to the Pan-African struggle."³⁵ But Moore must have seen it as yet another slight—a ceremonial post at best. It was a sign the tides were changing for the mother of the movement. Perhaps Moore's vision of Black Nationalist liberation, if not the activist herself, was past its prime.

The flight would depart from JFK, Sylvia Hill wrote to Moore and the other artists and activists awaiting word on their travel plans. "Be there at 8:00 a.m."³⁶ In addition to curating the delegation, Hill was responsible for getting them all to Tanzania.³⁷ She'd done her due diligence, contracting with an Atlanta-based Black travel agency, Henderson Travel, to get the cohort to Dar es Salaam. But all the while, the FBI was sending correspondence of its own.

When President Nixon and his FBI director, Clarence M. Kelley, learned that several hundred Black teachers, activists, lawyers, and politicians planned to travel to Tanzania to commune with African liberation leaders, they got spooked. The feds informed Henderson Travel it was doing business with "questionable characters" and demanded a full passenger list. The agency obliged, then canceled Hill's contract just two days before the delegation was set to depart.

Nearly three years of planning would soon be for naught if Hill and her compatriots couldn't figure out an alternative, and fast. But at this point, the tired and panicked Hill had two seemingly insurmountable problems: the FAA and the State Department both required them to file a passenger manifest at least thirty days before departure. And

even if they could somehow circumvent this rule, Sixth PAC participants still needed an airline willing to ferry them to Africa. As she
pleaded with Henderson Travel to reconsider, Hill got word about a
loophole. If a foreign president personally requested that a group be
permitted to travel to their homeland, it negated the thirty-day rule.
Finding a small group of African presidents and prime ministers willing to make the ask was simple enough. But what airline would defy
the U.S. government and transport a cadre of Black organizers? To
Hill's surprise, an Indian airline agreed to fly the delegation across
the Atlantic, so long as she could get from Atlanta to New York in
time to pay their fee.

Apprehension hung in the air as Moore and the other delegates
milled about the airport. They had arrived the morning of June 17,
just as Hill requested, but no plane had come. Finally, the group got
word they'd be leaving, but they wouldn't make it to Tanzania all at
once. They'd have to fly to London and then wait for another plane to
take them on to Kenya and then to Tanzania the following morning.
It was less than ideal, but it worked. Twelve hours after she had first
arrived at JFK, Moore dutifully filed out of the terminal, across the
tarmac, and onto the flight that would spirit her back to Africa for the
third time.[38]

Perched on a hill on the west side, with beautiful views of downtown,
the University of Dar es Salaam was a sight to behold. Moore took in
the rounded buildings ensconced in lush vegetation and palm trees
as she climbed the campus's peaks and valleys in the summer heat.
Perhaps she stopped at one of the vendors to snag a soda or something
sweet, or listened as a "brass band, in full uniform, played old British
martial music," while making her way to the two-story, dome-shaped
conference center for the opening ceremonies.[39]

Moore tried to take in the moment—the fact that organizers had
pulled off the Sixth PAC was remarkable. But the tension between
the Marxists and the nationalists was palpable from day one. President Nyerere opened an event by proclaiming that the growing
"Pan-African movement was a reaction to racialism" and that white
supremacy had yet to be "completely defeated." But then he cau-

tioned his audience that seeing the world in black and white forced the Diaspora to "defend our position as black men regarding ourselves as different from the rest of mankind."

"Yet in economic matters," he continued, "the real problem is not color. . . . We are neither poor, nor are we kept poor, because we are Black," but because of global capitalism's suppression of the Third World.[40] Moore was no doubt glad to witness her old friend in action again. But between his speech that day and his widespread embrace of Ujamaa socialism, she must have recognized the gap in their perspectives.

If Nyerere's speech made her uneasy, Moore's stomach must have dropped when Owusu Sadaukai took the stage. Just two years before, she had joined him in celebrating their ties with Africa. Now, in the motherland, she listened as Sadaukai invoked Marxist thinkers and leaders—Black and white—before proclaiming, "No longer could the world be viewed as Black people versus white people," and that it was now "necessary to see the very essence of imperialist domination was its capacity to use persons of all races to suppress" the masses. Black folk wouldn't reach freedom by ending capitalism alone, he conceded. But its destruction "set the conditions conducive for a victorious struggle to end racism" in America and around the world.[41] By the time the African Liberation Day leader stepped offstage, it was clear where his allegiances lay.

Baraka's speech was more of the same. Stateside, Moore had gotten word that he was abandoning some of the culturally restorative elements of Karenga's Kawaida philosophy. He now believed cultural nationalism to be a "reactionary" philosophy and a form of "racial chauvinism."[42] And she had watched as the Congress of African People, once the shining example of Black Nationalist influence, transformed into a Marxist organization. Gone were the days of organizing around Black people's shared African culture and heritage. Here to stay were the CAP leader's claim that "Africans all over the world must be dedicated to the liberation and unification of the African continent under socialism." She saw this on full display at the congress. Baraka spoke at length about nationalists' "backward" reliance on race-based cultural organizing, before ultimately proclaiming, "Pan-Africanism . . . is a commitment to struggle for socialism for the world."[43] Outside the auditorium, it was more of the same. No matter where Moore went—meeting rooms, bathrooms, or dormitory rooms—the debate over race and class raged on.[44]

Amid the turmoil, congress goers devoted the next seven days to a dizzying array of meetings dedicated to topics such as "Political and Material Support for the Liberation Movements" and "Technology and the Development of Natural Resources." Moore was particularly interested in discussions about culture, education, and political organizing. And she likely attended the sessions on "Women's Contribution to Pan-African Struggle."[45] As a special guest of the congress and not a voting delegate, Moore could move freely in and out of sessions, sampling all on offer. Whatever luxury it afforded her, though, it kept her from having a say in any final resolutions the North American delegation put forth. There can be little doubt that she was miffed over the slight. But there was one upside: it gave her plenty of time to roam the university grounds and poll the people on her own measures.

The stuffy lecture halls weren't really Moore's scene, anyway. She preferred being among the myriad people eating, drinking, passing out pamphlets, and standing on soapboxes to state their positions on congress causes.[46] It felt like Africa's answer to her old stomping grounds on 125th Street, and Moore was completely in her element. As delegates exited university buildings, they'd often find her lecturing about reparations and nationalist pride, her dangling gold earrings and stacked bracelets clanking as she shouted.[47]

But her words fell on deaf ears. When the congress presented its final resolutions from the weeklong summit, Moore discovered leaders from all across the African Diaspora had resolved to "completely restore the dignity of African people through the building of socialism," and to "exclude all racial, tribal, ethnic, and religious considerations in the development of Pan Africanism."[48] Many of the African liberation groups Moore had supported for years now fell in line, fervently rejecting her brand of Black Nationalism as a "superficial and emotional" ideology. They called for the "liquidation of colonialism," which in their view "had no colour."[49]

Moore was devastated. At both the CAP conference and the Gary Convention, she had beamed with pride as Black Nationalism and Pan-Africanism had finally gained broad support. Now many of these same leaders were forsaking this ideological position. She witnessed the first Pan-African Congress on African soil, only to watch the discussion move away from race-centered approaches to nation building—it could not have been more disappointing to a dyed-in-the-wool Garveyite.

What's more, the congress ended with few plans for concrete action. Attendees left with no clear path to create a permanent Pan-African headquarters, no talks of allowing Black Americans citizenship in Africa, and no embassies. They didn't even settle on a date and place for the next meeting. The lack of tangible resolutions disappointed many attendees, no matter their political bent. Reporters covering the week largely deemed it a failure.[50] Moore believed that, as the biggest and most politically influential delegation, the North Americans were to blame.

She had tried to warn them early on. They were veering off course, and before they left for Dar es Salaam she had pushed for all the "intellectuals to come together" to "come up with something to present before the world."[51] Her fellow activists had squandered the moment and caved to outside voices, Moore believed, because they had not hammered out their positions beforehand. She had been around long enough to know that without a clear "line" for organizers to follow, gatherings like the Sixth PAC were dead on arrival. From here on out, and for better or worse, she would travel to Africa and liaise with its state leaders on her own terms.

CHAPTER 23

Diaspora and Dictators

It was early 1975, and Queen Mother Moore had a spring in her step as she hoofed it down her Bronx block to the train station. No sooner had she hopped off in Harlem than she ran into one of Tom's oldest and dearest friends, Charles Turner. Reaching into her purse, Moore pulled out a letter and showed it off with pride. It was an invitation from Ugandan president Idi Amin to attend the next Organization of African Unity meeting in Kampala. If that wasn't exciting enough, Amin wanted Moore to come a week before the summit and spend some time touring his country, to "visit different places of interest as well as meet and know the people of Uganda," the note read. Amin, Moore excitedly explained, believed her visit would "contribute greatly to the strengthening of brotherly ties which unite the Black people" of America and Africa.[1]

Charles was puzzled. He knew Moore was "no stranger to Africa." And yet she seemed to not acknowledge the obvious: in recent years, Amin had gained an international reputation as a murderous despot and the head of a violently corrupt regime. How could Moore be so excited to meet someone who had killed so many Africans on his own soil?

"I could use a press secretary," Moore blurted out, unfazed, before Charles could inquire any further. "I'm going to deputize you." She then proceeded to drag him downtown to the Ugandan consulate, right then and there, to get him credentialed.[2]

"The total liberation of Africa must be put into practice," Idi Amin declared as he opened the Organization of African Unity's twelfth summit. Moore was both perplexed and excited, taking it all in. She was well acquainted with the reports. Uganda's world-famous turmoil had been fueled by its president's devilish nature, so they said: his unpredictable temper, his penchant for human rights abuses, and his reliance on violent political repression. But this moment felt different—momentous, even. Standing inside the Nile Conference Center, a brutalist building built especially for this occasion, the Ugandan leader looked nothing like the caricatures of him she saw in newspapers back home. He had donned a blue business suit accentuated with an orange-and-white African-print scarf, and he looked every bit the levelheaded leader as he spoke to continental delegates seated in rows of red-felt chairs.[3]

It wasn't just seeing Amin that thrilled Moore. She had been around long enough to know the OAU was historic. Moore had kept her eye trained on Africa throughout the 1960s, and she could remember first hearing reports that Kwame Nkrumah was calling for African nations to unify and stave off Western influence.[4] "No independent African State" had "a chance to follow an independent course of economic development," or cultural or political development, for that matter, the Ghanaian leader had often explained. And this would not change until African nations banded together.[5] He implored his fellow heads of state to reject the idea that national sovereignty should come before continental unity. For the good of Africa, differences had to be set aside.

While Moore was establishing the movement for reparations in America, reports trickled in that Ethiopian emperor Haile Selassie had invited the leaders of thirty-two independent African nations to convene in Addis Ababa (the capital city whose name Moore had snagged for her land upstate) in May 1963. In the wee hours of May 25, these leaders signed a "single Charter for the whole Continent," transforming the face and pace of African liberation. Their newly formed alliance, the OAU, aimed to promote unity and solidarity among the African states through the sharing of weapons and military training and mediating boundary disputes.[6] Moore was filled with pride at the news. Back in 1935, she had gotten her start as an activist advocating for a free and sovereign Ethiopia. Twenty-eight years later, the same country that had sparked her foundational sense of race pride had become ground zero for a new era of liberation.

As the OAU was finding its footing, Idi Amin was climbing to power in Uganda. Born in the 1920s, Amin came of age under British rule. He joined the King's African Rifles (KAR), an East African regiment of the British army, in 1946. Whereas other future African leaders, Tanzania's Julius Nyerere and Kenya's Jomo Kenyatta among them, saw World War II as a chance to break colonialism's vise grip, Amin sought to tighten the stranglehold.[7] He gained a merciless reputation in the early 1950s, fighting on behalf of Great Britain to subdue the Mau Mau rebellion in Kenya. The British admired Amin's willingness to quell an uprising that many—including Audley Moore, at the time—had hailed as one of the first major nationalist fights on the continent.[8]

But Moore wasn't the only one who believed the Mau Mau rebellion was a turning point. Former head of the British army Lord Carver later recalled it had "a profound effect in persuading Conservative political figures in Britain to bow to the winds of change in Africa."[9] By the end of the decade, both politicians in London and British boots on the ground had come to accept the end of their empire in Kenya and Uganda. When they finally ceded control of the latter in 1962, Amin remained to lead the army they left behind.[10]

Amin rode the wave of Ugandan independence from this martial perch. By 1965, he had gained the rank of colonel and was widely regarded as the second most powerful official in Uganda behind President Milton Obote.[11] With Amin as his headman, Obote dismembered Uganda's ethnic and religious kingdoms and ruthlessly consolidated his rule over the country.[12] As astute as he was merciless, Obote saw Amin as both a powerful ally and a formidable threat.[13] By 1969, he knew a coup was coming. The only question was when it would strike.[14]

On January 25, 1971, men, women, and children across the country turned on their radios and heard, "The men of the Uganda Armed Forces have this day decided to take over power from Obote and hand it to our fellow soldier Major-General Idi Amin."[15] Many celebrated Amin's rise to power, only to realize it soon would be their downfall. The newly installed leader could only rest once he had eliminated any semblance of dissent. He turned the East African country into a vicious police state, massacred thousands of soldiers for fear of disloyalty, and disappeared even more civilians, judges, bishops, and politicians. In less than a year, his name became synonymous with murder, despotism, and the expulsion of non-Africans—especially Uganda's sizable South Asian population.[16]

To counter his tyrannical reputation at home and abroad, Amin sought support from the OAU. Now a dozen years old, the continental collective had suffered political rivalries, bleak economic realities, and resilient colonial regimes. But it remained intact.[17] In hosting the OAU's 1975 meeting in Uganda, Amin would have the chance to show off the city of Kampala to other African leaders, the international press, and Black supporters outside Africa. Most crucially, it gave him the chance to refute reports of his unpredictable behavior and bloody rampages. But to do so would require a carefully choreographed dance. Foreign visitors could come into contact only with the *right* Ugandans, in the *right* circumstances.

Amin was gunning for the esteemed title of OAU chairman, a position customarily bestowed on the leader of that year's host country. Amin coveted the title; whoever held it became the de facto spokesman for Black Africa for the year. And by right, it was his.[18] But the specter of his crimes cast a long shadow, and many of his fellow heads of state feared he would either humiliate or utterly discredit the OAU, and Africa writ large, on the global stage. Tanzania, Botswana, and Zambia boycotted the meeting in protest, and others tried backroom meetings to thwart his appointment. In the end, Amin succeeded. "I want to assure you that I will be very faithful, loyal and frank," he told the OAU officials after winning out against their protestations, "and I will not embarrass you."[19]

Aside from placating his fellow African leaders, a large part of Amin's rehabilitation scheme involved courting Black Americans, many of whom learned of his reign from the white press. By the 1970s, it was not uncommon for Moore and those in her circles to open a newspaper and find apelike caricatures of Amin, his enlarged stomach folded over his too-tight, medal-spangled military uniform above captions like "Dr. Idi Amin Dada. President for Life."[20]

Black Americans were all too familiar with these stereotypical depictions and the racist ideas undergirding them. Some began to wonder if white folk were defaming Amin to undermine the rising tide of Black Power on the continent. The Ugandan leader, meanwhile, cultivated this curiosity. He made a habit of hosting Black American leaders, thinkers, and activists to tour his home country. Enter: Queen Mother Moore.

Around the time she and her compatriots were returning from the Sixth PAC, Amin made contact with several members of The East for one of these guided visits. He had sent a private jet to whisk them away to his beleaguered land, planned a spate of elaborate dinners, and set up tours of African-run textile mills. But it was all a smoke screen, a ploy to cover the brutal truth of his 1972 expulsion of South Asians and their businesses as part of his plan to re-Africanize Uganda. It was a "heavy experience" for many in the group. Some couldn't reconcile Amin's vision of political and economic independence with the atrocities he had committed to achieve it. Still, others in the group found it "refreshing to see Africans in control" and to witness Black Nationalism made manifest.[21]

Back in New York, Moore eagerly awaited news of the visit. She was among those willing to overlook Amin's British military background in the KAR, his odd alliances with European powers, and his mass killings—the latter of which she and like-minded organizers thought had been exaggerated by Western media. His race-first approach to nation building, his open critique of the United States, and his hard line on foreigners had won her over from afar. And so, when a personal invitation to visit Uganda arrived from its dubious president the next year, she was more than willing to oblige. It was only right, after all. She was a matriarch of the American Black Nationalist Movement, and he was an African visionary who was just as loyal to the cause.

As their motorcade wound its way through the hills of Kampala on a hot July day, Queen Mother Moore and Charles Turner gawked at the newly finished buildings adorned with flags and banners promoting Pan-African unity. Their hotel had all of the Western trappings to which they were accustomed, sparkling new with plush carpets and fresh paint for the occasion. When Moore looked out her window, she saw large crowds gathering and heard cheers wafting over the rooftops. Some of the applause was for President Amin himself, who made public appearances to kick off OAU-sponsored festivities like the International Motor Rally.

And yet Amin's quest for complete control spoiled some of the fantasy. Kampala was no Pan-African Neverland. If Moore wanted to get out and wander through the well-stocked shops displaying OAU flags, see the beauty pageant, or attend state dinners, she had to do so under the watchful eyes of Amin's men. As Queen Mother explored Uganda, she took note of the armed militiamen who always seemed to be following her. It must have felt eerily reminiscent of being back home, with FBI agents constantly on her tail.[22]

Still, it was worth it just to see Amin in action. When the summit opened, the Ugandan leader delivered an hour-long speech hailed as "one of the toughest ever delivered to a meeting of the organization." Amin demanded an end to South African apartheid and called for a single African army to be raised to fight white-minority colonial regimes.[23] Moore was thrilled to see an African leader stand up so forcefully against the Western establishment. "All praise due to President Amin," she offered to OAU delegates and observers as she greeted them.[24]

"I don't know how President Amin knew me," she later said of the trip. "But I do know that I didn't take the invitation personally, I took it on behalf of my people, and I took it as an attempt on their part to reach out to us through me." Moore had spent her entire life working with organizations that could serve as vehicles for her nationalist politics. She didn't always need to align with them in lockstep. And she believed Amin was doing just the same: using her as a conduit to forge relations between their two embattled Black nations.[25]

"My attendance at this gathering demonstrates to the world that the children of Africa who were kidnapped centuries ago and scattered throughout the western hemisphere are linked by the bonds of common origin, common struggle, and common aspirations," Moore said when given the floor. She also used this moment to deliver a communique on behalf of the African People's Party (APP).

The APP, like many collectives during this time, developed out of the 1968 Black Power Conference in Philadelphia. It comprised activists from RAM, SNCC, Malcolm X's OAAU, and other militant groups, many of whom Moore had mentored herself. As was the trend, the APP had rebranded as Revolutionary Nationalists and Pan-Africanists, linking racism with capitalism and a class consciousness. But it also still cleaved to a Moore-esque vision of Black sovereignty.

The cadre called for the creation of a separate Black nation just as she did. But this free and independent Black country would be socialist.[26]

Thus, it came as no surprise that as Moore shared the APP's ten-point plan, it sounded like something lifted straight from one of her old lectures. The first point: "We want self-determination and independent nationhood," she read aloud. She had always framed Black people as "African captives" and demanded a separate government and territory. The second: "We want an independent self-governing economy," both money and land to serve as "partial repayment for [America's] crimes of genocide against our people." And last, the communiqué echoed Moore's claim that Black Americans were actually "colonial captives," having never been given the right to choose or reject American citizenship. The group's aim, like that of the woman who had inspired it, was to gain state power.

"We call upon our African brothers and sisters to support us in our just demands for reparations [and] self-determination," Moore concluded. "[And we] ask that you bring the United States before the United Nations General Assembly for violating the Universal Declaration of Human Rights and support our just demand for a United Nations convened plebiscite."[27] This was a new step forward in Moore's lifelong fight. She hoped that in presenting the idea of reparations and Black American statehood to such a powerful, international audience, she might tip the scales back in her political favor after so many recent setbacks.

Moore paired her formal duties with sightseeing on the arm of Amin. She left Charles behind in Kampala while she attended a dizzying spate of state dinners and shows in the city and across the countryside. She even dined on the dictator's yacht with his wives.[28] Lavish gifts aside, Moore would later claim it was the everyday Ugandan's alleged support of Amin that solidified her own. "President Amin was loved by the people, loved by his people.... [A]ll along the way, they lined in the roads where he was going to pass" just to see him. He was "out there in the open among his people," she recalled, not hidden away in palaces or behind a phalanx of armed guards.[29]

What Moore didn't see, or refused to acknowledge, was that Amin had staged these moments specially for her and other foreigners. Only barely hidden from view were the mass graves, the torture chambers, and the agents of the Uganda State Research Bureau, a secret intelligence and police agency that surveilled, abducted, and tortured Amin's enemies.

All Moore seemed to know was that Amin treated her like a queen, and she began to talk of him as if he were her king. Whereas others viewed Amin as an erratic and reckless leader, Moore saw a Black man standing up for Black Africa. When Black American activists called Amin's overtures disingenuous, Moore argued he was connecting the captive Africans of America with their homeland. As people decried Amin's ethnic purges, Moore claimed he was fulfilling Garvey's dream of "Africa for the Africans." And when the world denounced his gruesome mass killings, Moore saw them as a commitment to liberating Africa at all costs. When her family members and fellow organizers questioned her support of Amin's genocidal reign, Queen Mother responded icily, "A king's got to do what a king's got to do."[30]

This cold and calculated approach to Black Nationalism came as a surprise to many who knew Moore and who had watched her advocate for the dignity and rights of Africans all over the world for years. But there certainly were clues as to how and why Moore could endorse a man like Amin. Queen Mother Moore's introduction to Black Nationalism was through a strong-willed Garvey, who donned military regalia and, at times, an authoritarian approach to organizing. Moore had remained steadfastly loyal to Garvey and his causes, even when he mistreated followers and his business dealings went awry. And it was through Garvey that Moore became a stalwart advocate for Black self-defense, which she saw as the antidote to the white vigilante violence she experienced in the Deep South. Was it any surprise she was inured to brutality?

Moore wasn't the only one who felt Amin's use of violence in the name of reclaiming Uganda for Ugandans was admirable. Perhaps a kind of groupthink had helped her somehow justify the mass casualties. Whatever the cause, the mental gymnastics she performed to endorse Amin gave her community pause. Did she envision a similar path for her sovereign Black nation in the American South?

Moore wasn't just an Amin admirer. She was besotted with the man. Queen Mother had garnered plenty of admiration from young and old men alike since she'd left Jose. But she didn't have much of a romantic life, it seemed. It's possible Amin was the exact kind of man she had been looking for all her life—one whom she enjoyed spending time with, in private, and whom she admired as an uncompromising nationalist leader, in public. He was a true partner in the Africanization of their people, someone who would go to the hilt for Black Nationalism, just like her.

Queen Mother Moore quelled none of her loved ones' concerns. Instead, when she came back, she implored those around her to see Amin through her eyes. He was never "mean Amin" to her. She maintained that in their shared car rides and private asides the Ugandan president had let her see behind his strongman persona and revealed a softer, gentler side.[31] "He's warm, he's beautiful, and he's sweet," she would say. "And I love him."[32]

Amin continued to cultivate Moore's adoration for him Stateside three months later. In October 1975, he made the controversial decision to visit New York to attend a meeting of the UN General Assembly.[33] Once again, he made sure to look the part. Clad in his blue, red, and gold field marshal's uniform, his war medals gleaming, Amin climbed to the podium and held world leaders rapt for a ninety-seven-minute diatribe. He criticized France for refusing to free its final colonial strongholds and Britain for its oppression of Northern Ireland. When the East African leader expressed solidarity with Black organizers, proclaiming "the black American has done as much, if not more, than other races in the construction of his country," he garnered light applause. But decorum soon gave way to chaos when Amin called for Israel's expulsion from the UN, a stance that coincided with the OAU's support of Palestine against what it saw as Israeli settler colonial rule.

The controversy spilled into the reception Amin held at the Hilton Hotel in midtown later that evening. Despite protestations from friends, family, and fellow activists who feared her attendance would only further associate Moore with his murderous reign, Queen Mother put on one of her favorite dresses and headed downtown. She took a tour of the ballroom when she arrived, marveling at the multiple well-stocked bars and the lavish buffets of continental cuisine.[34] Moore then went in search of a seat in the back of the room; her hips didn't hold her up the way they used to. She clapped politely between bites as Amin presented awards to Ugandans and UN diplomats.

"And now for the most prominent African woman in the United

States," he declared as the applause died down, "Queen Mother Moore." He beckoned her to join him onstage. Stunned and a little smitten, Moore hurriedly slipped her feet back into her shoes and shuffled to the stage. There, Amin honored Black America's Queen Mother with a gift fit for royalty. Later that week, Moore could be seen sashaying down 125th Street sporting a lavish zebra-skin bag.[35]

For those closest to Moore, it was both a shock and a heartbreak to witness her devotion to such an unquestionable despot. Just a few years before, Moore had opened her granddaughter's eyes to Africa: all the beauty, diversity, and cultural richness of the continent. Now the college-aged Audley found herself questioning her grandmother's judgment and politics. Others were aghast as they watched Moore's love for Amin evolve from political admiration into romantic obsession, further deadening her to the realities of his dictatorial reign. After the UN event, Moore began to talk about Amin even more salaciously, as if he were her lover or husband. It was clear to those around her, however, that Amin's interest in Moore was entirely political.[36]

A few prominent nationalists followed her in supporting Amin. Neither Stokely Carmichael, who by 1973 lived in Guinea full-time and headed up the All-African People's Revolutionary Party, nor CORE leader Roy Innis believed that Amin was the monster that the West had made him out to be, and they took Amin up on his invitation to visit Uganda.[37] But Moore lost the support of friends and followers—and most important, some of the admiration of her own family. "I started to see my grandmother as a flawed individual, rather than the infallible figure that I idolized," Audley Warner recalled, watching Queen Mother become enraptured with the dictator.[38] For so many like the younger Audley, sovereignty could never be won through tyranny.

Perhaps Moore wondered if she would soon see Amin again as she sat on the small, hard plastic seats in JFK airport two years later, in January 1977, once again waiting for a plane that promised to spirit her back to Africa. This time, she was headed to Nigeria to attend the Second World Black and African Festival of Arts and Culture (FESTAC), a monthlong international celebration of art, music, literature, drama, and dance from across the Diaspora. The festival would be the biggest event devoted to African culture the world had ever seen, with more than fifteen thousand participants from fifty-six countries. And Moore was determined to attend. For years now, she had been admonishing her fellow Black Americans for their idolatry of white culture—everything from deities to dolls.[39] But FESTAC sparked a hope that a shared celebration of Black culture could unite Africans all over the world.

Once again, it wasn't at first clear whether an airline would agree to fly a group of Black folk, many of whom, like Moore, were still on the FBI's subversives list. And as she and her fellow activists waited in JFK, they worried their ride wouldn't show. But this wasn't the only thing on Moore's mind.

While on the picket lines at New York City schools, Moore had caught wind of the challenges some activists had faced when they tried to attend the initial iteration of this type of gathering: the First World Festival of Black Arts (FESMAN). Hosted by Senegalese poet turned president Léopold Senghor, the 1966 gathering in Dakar promised Black people the opportunity to redefine African identity, albeit under Senghor's concept of Negritude—the Afro-francophone cultural and literary tradition aimed at elevating Black consciousness and culture.[40]

In Black Americans' eyes, FESMAN had been marred first and foremost by Senghor's appointment of Virginia Inness-Brown, a white woman and head of the American National Theatre and Academy (ANTA), as the chairperson of the U.S. committee to the festival. Congress created the ANTA in 1935 to support theater projects across the United States, but during the Cold War, it morphed into a "propaganda outfit," sponsoring productions that bolstered America's reputation abroad. Through the theater company, Inness-Brown had become a de facto State Department consultant. And the feds, ultimately, had the final say in whom she allowed to participate in FESMAN.[41]

Still, a handful of Black Americans managed to join the crowds of dancers, writers, sculptors, and playwrights in Dakar. Whether it was the nightly performances from the Black dancers of Manhattan's Alvin Ailey school or Senghor's classical African art exhibit, thousands across the Diaspora converged on the "glittering little cosmopolitan city on the western-most bulge" of the continent to engage in "a series of exhibitions, performances and conferences designed to illustrate the genius, the culture and the glory of Africa."[42]

If Moore had any misgivings about attending the second conference of this kind a decade later, she found reassurance in writer, educator, and cultural critic Hoyt Fuller's sound planning. By now, Black Americans had learned some hard lessons about the perils of interracial U.S. delegations and the strings attached to state funding. This time around, Fuller hoped to arrange for Black Americans to participate in FESTAC without their government's oversight. They were a nation within a nation, after all. And they were more than capable of representing their own culture and interests abroad.[43] Moore was delighted by the idea of an all-Black delegation operating on its own terms, even if it did create significant fundraising challenges—and raise the hackles of the surveillance state.[44]

Moore was a member of the first contingent of Americans to make the trip to the cultural convention. Once aboard the Pan Am flight, she let out a deep sigh of relief, settled into her seat, and steadied herself for the first leg: New York to Madrid. Soon, the captain announced they were now free to move about the cabin. This was Queen Mother Moore's cue. She unbuckled her seat belt and started striding down the plane rows, her bangles clanking and her kaftan dragging behind her as she went. There were plenty of new, up-and-coming artists to meet—everyone from writer and activist Audre Lorde to Chicago-based director, actress, and producer Val Gray Ward. In no time at all, Moore had set up shop among a group of travelers whom she soon had in fits and "tears of laughter," cracking jokes about her old days in activism. Queen Mother had yet to find a court she couldn't command.[45] When the plane finally landed in Lagos, and Moore felt it shift back into park, she hopped up and proclaimed, "Children, Welcome Home! The mother is waiting for you."[46]

Queen Mother Moore arrived in Lagos on January 13, two days before the start of FESTAC. She was happy to be back on African soil, even if her body was not. Sitting crunched in a plane for twenty hours had made for stiff joints and more aches and pains than Moore cared to acknowledge. But she took it in stride as she climbed into a cramped minibus and sped off.

WELCOME TO FESTAC TOWN, she read as the bus rolled up to the massive new district the Nigerian government had built to house the tens of thousands descending on their country. They were still putting the finishing touches on the village (adding plumbing, building kiosks, and bringing in food) when Moore arrived that night. But she could see the potential. It was a self-sufficient mini-city for African people from all over the world, with public transportation, medical care, and housing—a Pan-African nation within a nation, created specially for the festival.[47]

"The Nigerian government" should be "highly commended for the manner in which it received everybody [from] all over the world," she remarked of the meeting site. Moore marveled at "the village with modern houses for all of the different people" they built. When she arrived at USA Street, the space designated for the American delegation, she found "a row of houses on both sides," three-story structures with two- and three-bedroom apartments, shared parlors, and modern amenities.[48] Moore viewed the village as a central part of the Nigerian nation-making project, one aspect of President Olusegun Obasanjo's goal of moving "everything toward freedom, toward the liberation of the people."[49] She was right; although FESTAC Town initially welcomed international guests, the government intended to use it to house locals when the festivities ended.

Perhaps Moore sampled the different foods at one of its twelve restaurants. Or maybe she meandered the streets where musicians from Guinea, Cuba, and Brazil practiced as dancers moved in time. Queen Mother Moore was notorious for her street-corner speeches, and in FESTAC Town she was in great company. She might have joined in talks with Gambians as they lamented how Europe had created false boundaries and needless enemies when it carved up Africa during the height of colonialism, or pontificated about the possibilities of leaving colonial languages, government structures, and cultural practices behind. A full day of eating, dancing, and politicking behind her, she would have likely stayed in as the young folk headed to Lagos for a night out.[50]

The next day, Moore got up and joined a group headed to the National Theatre, a multimillion-naira performance hall that resembled a crown cresting up from the horizon. It was time for the opening ceremonies. Organizers helped Moore to her seat on the stadium risers as a voice overhead announced the festival was about to begin.

Turning her head toward one of the stadium's many tunnels, she saw a man dressed in dark pants and shoes, a white dress shirt with a flap collar, and a white Dixie cup hat emerging. In his hands was a sign announcing the Algerian delegation, and following behind him were men in flowy white gandouras and women in colorful, long-sleeved velvet jackets adorned with silver and gold threads.[51] Representatives from the other fifty-five countries followed in alphabetical order, each with a FESTAC officer walking in front of them and carrying a sign proclaiming their arrival. For Moore, the display was both magnificent and overwhelming. It was the first time she'd ever seen so many Black people in their traditional cultural clothing gathered in one place.[52]

For the next few days, Moore bounced between the National Stadium, Tafawa Balewa Square, Ikoyi Island, and the National Theatre, taking in the paintings, performances, and poetry of Africans from around the world. During an event that felt like "the Olympics, plus a Biennial, plus Woodstock . . . but Africa Style," she could listen to the soothing beats of Nigerian composer and singer Fela Kuti and the sweet sounds of South African singer Miriam Makeba, or take in the words of Wole Soyinka, Nigeria's famed writer who would go on to win the Nobel Prize.[53]

"Many of the African tribes way in the backwoods . . . came out with their dances and performed with their feathers all down their backs, with their beads, beaded cloth, [and] skin attire made out of animal skin, all beaded and so on," she recalled. As she sat and watched these resplendent performances, Moore was reminded of cultural practices she had witnessed among Indigenous peoples and African-oriented communities Stateside. The elder activist recognized the symbolism and symmetry immediately. The performances were "just fantastic and they're similar to what you find" in the Americas, she explained to her friends and family once she returned.[54] Queen Mother Moore had spent nearly twenty years arguing the American government owed Black people reparations for systematically decimating their culture. FESTAC showed her that despite white supremacists' best efforts Black culture in the Americas was very much alive.

But amid it all, Moore couldn't help but feel the American delegation came up short. Moore believed Black Americans "had beautiful things to present" at FESTAC, homegrown traditions that harked back to roots in Africa. They just hadn't brought the right people. The delegation was too star-studded, in her sober eyes, as performers like Stevie Wonder took top billing over grassroots groups. "What we had in FESTAC was demeaning," she offered in her final, post hoc assessment of the festival.[55]

That disappointment aside, FESTAC had been a true show of African unity and pride amid decolonization. And it showed Moore what Pan-Africanism could look like in action. FESTAC organizers had wrapped the festival in the trappings of nationalism, creating a distinct emblem, stamp, flag, and even passports for entry into the many different neighborhoods in FESTAC Town—"nations" of sorts, in and of themselves.[56] There, Moore had been a citizen of the modern Black world, a liberated space where everyone celebrated Black culture and where Africans—captive and free alike—convened with little regard for white-constructed borders. For nearly eighty years, Moore had dreamed of a place where Africans at home and abroad could be one. For a brief and imperfect moment in Nigeria, she had found it.

CHAPTER 24

Last Decade, Lasting Resources

Queen Mother Moore was restive.

Her last few trips to Africa had put both the promise and the perils of Black nation building in sharp relief. By her own admission, she had been ignorant of many of the challenges Africans across the continent faced. But if anyone thought attending cultural festivals or keeping company with state leaders—some less savory than others—would make Moore widen her political frame, they were wrong. When asked about her politics at the end of the 1970s, Moore's answer was clear: "I'm a hard nationalist."[1]

Even still, Moore was approaching nearly half a century in the struggle. And by now, she had learned that being hard-nosed wasn't going to bring about her dream of "Africa for the Africans—at home and abroad." To be sure, there were signs that colonial regimes like South African apartheid were finally crumbling. The Soweto Uprising back in 1976, during which police had killed hundreds of South African schoolchildren protesting their colonial education, sparked a new wave of anticolonial outrage. American activists pressured their local politicians and companies to divest from the murderous government, while South Africans formed the United Democratic Front, a mass movement with close ties to the left-wing African National Congress (ANC). When the world got word that ANC leader Nelson Mandela was languishing in prison, the global anti-apartheid movement reached a fever pitch.[2]

But even Moore knew international support for a free Africa could only go so far when its rulers were at odds. Her beloved Idi Amin was a case in point. In April 1979, she learned that the dictator had fled Kampala; the Tanzanian troops and Uganda National Liberation

Front forces, long intent on ousting the brutal leader, had closed in. Perhaps she took heart in hearing he had vowed to keep up the fight, even while on the run.[3] Or maybe she felt conflicted. She admired Nyerere and Amin both, and the fact that the two leaders had become enemies must have been a source of dissonance. Whatever the case, she likely felt a sense of relief when Amin finally escaped to Libya, taken in by his fellow dictator Muammar al-Gaddafi.[4]

The picture wasn't much rosier in America. The past decade's Black Power Movement had splintered over the issue of class politics, and since the Sixth PAC the discord had only accelerated. And there were other shake-ups within the coalition, too. Women from the Congress of African People had created the Black Women's United Front (BWUF), dedicated to liberating working-class Black women from capitalism, sexism, and racism in the 1970s.[5] It was as clear an expression as any that, among the radical Black Left, Marxism and feminism were here to stay. For what it's worth, Queen Mother Moore appreciated the BWUF's approach to organizing more than she did other Black feminist groups'. The BWUF was committed to working within Black Power organizations like CAP, rather than fragmenting off and taking key members with it. Even still, she was frustrated by these young women's adoption of the mainstream feminist ideals she abhorred.

The younger generation was losing its focus, she felt. And as a veteran organizer, Queen Mother Moore believed it was up to her to set them right. In the late 1970s, she rededicated her days to speaking with students across the nation. "I find myself giving lectures in the colleges," she recalled. "I even went to Meharry and gave a lecture to young doctors; I've been to Tufts University; I've been to Brandeis University. I've been to Cal State University, Berkeley, and throughout the West Coast." It didn't really matter to the movement matriarch where she spoke. "I only know my children are there and that they want to hear from Mama."[6]

College campuses were fertile ground and full of friendly faces. A good number of the activists from her heyday who had survived the previous decade's COINTELPRO-spurred repression had found refuge in higher education. Poet Sonia Sanchez, RAM activist John Bracey, and SNCC organizer Ivanhoe Donaldson, among others, could now be found ensconced in the hard-won, newly minted Black

Studies programs across the country, where they taught classes that concretized the pillars of Black radical thought and invited movement legends to campus to commemorate the struggle.

Queen Mother Moore was a sought-after guest. She headlined the 1975 Black Women's Conference at the University of Massachusetts Amherst, and she teamed up with her old comrades at Tufts University for the National Black Students Solidarity Conference a year later.[7] Alongside Robert F. Williams, now back from political exile; RNA president Imari Obadele; and Philadelphia activist Playthell Benjamin, Moore called for college students to "revive their active participation in the struggle" rather than coast on the coattails of their predecessors.[8] As the children of the early civil rights generation, they had a responsibility, Moore told them, to keep their forebears' work alive. When disaffected students asked Moore what they should be fighting for, exactly, her answer was always the same: community control, reparations, and Black statehood.[9]

Moore relished any opportunity she got to speak to Black youth. But it wasn't just a labor of love. At nearly eighty, she toured the country in part because she desperately needed the money. By the late 1970s, she had relocated to Brooklyn, opting to share an apartment with her little sister. She and Loretta lived on Greene Avenue until a fire ripped through their home on October 27, 1978. Local organizers scrambled to help Moore after the fire destroyed "an estimated $15,000 in clothes, furniture and mementos of her life": some of the most precious objects from her travels, so many books and papers, all lost to history.[10] Some suggested taking Moore to Mount Addis Ababa as a temporary refuge. But others pointed out that a fire had recently ripped through Moore's upstate dwelling, too, and many believed that local white supremacists had started it.[11]

Moore's friends mobilized and put the elder activist up in a hotel in Coney Island while they worked feverishly to find her a new home. They hoped to get her a room in the Fort Greene Senior Citizens Center; it would be nice for Moore to stay in the neighborhood, near her sister. But they soon found that a lengthy waiting list, inadequate staffing, a lack of funds, and a wall of bureaucratic red tape stood in their way.[12] And as the 1980s dawned, any hope Moore might have had of relying on social services to live out her days was quickly vanishing.

Moore moved back uptown to the Mary McLeod Bethune

Houses—a public housing development for senior citizens in Harlem. As young men carried her boxes into the building named after her old organizing friend, it must have weighed on Moore how much their paths had diverged. She was grateful for the flood of donations that had helped her stay afloat, to be sure. But she couldn't deny how far she had fallen from the comforts she had tried to keep all her life—not to mention the grandeur she had momentarily tasted in Africa. It was now dawning on her just how precarious life had become. She had little money, few possessions, and no family close by save Loretta, who was dealing with her own housing and health challenges. Queen Mother needed a young, loyal subject: someone devoted to the same causes Moore had championed all her life—but most important, someone who would stick by her side in her twilight years. As she sat in her cramped new apartment, ensconced among the few salvaged books, photos, and plaques from her decades in the movement, one young woman came to mind.

When Delois Blakely opened her fifth-floor apartment door, she was stunned to find Moore's friend and fellow organizer Thelma Moore (no relation) standing outside. Blakely invited her in, and the small-statured, elderly woman wasted no time getting to the point. "She wanted to know when I could call on Queen Mother Moore," Blakely remembered.[13] It was the third time Moore had asked for her. She couldn't refuse again.

Born in Florida, Blakely first moved to New York City in the 1960s to become a nun, right as the spirit of Black Power was taking hold. As the movement swelled around her, Blakely began to question whether the church could ever truly make space for Black liberation. She eventually left the cloth and opted for a covenant with her community instead, making significant inroads in helping Black folk in Harlem and the Bronx through her nonprofit: New Future Foundation Inc.[14]

"Now this is what I want to see. You know what it means to be an African woman," Moore had told Blakely the first time she laid eyes on the young woman back in the fall of 1973. They were both at a dinner hosted by the United Nations General Assembly. As the night wound down, Moore—whose colorful African gown and array of jewels made her stand out among the crowd—approached the young Blakely. Moore introduced herself briefly before staff members swept the Harlem royal away to meet the other UN delegates.

Surely, "she must be a prominent U.N. figure," Blakely thought to herself as she pushed her way through the throng of people surrounding Moore later. She wanted to have another look.

Queen Mother of what country? she inquired once they were face-to-face again.

"Harlem," Moore replied confidently. "All my life I've been in the struggle for African people. Honey, you must join the movement."

Blakely was taken aback. She had just made two of the biggest moves of her life: the first when she relocated to the Big Apple, the second when she left the church. What's more, she had just taken on the enormous task of trying to renovate the run-down building where she and her daughter lived. Barely getting by with her caregiving and organizing responsibilities, Blakely couldn't commit to Moore's cause. "Queen Mother sent me off with a knowledgeable, pensive look," she recalled of their first parting, "which translated, without saying a word, that we would meet again."[15]

Moore made the ask again a few years later in 1980, in Atlanta, over a breakfast of hominy grits, eggs, and biscuits drenched in syrup—Moore's sweet tooth needed tending to first thing in the morning. She shared her life story with Blakely, who responded in kind. Moore realized Blakely shared her love of Africa and Black institution building, as well as her firsthand knowledge of how hard it was to balance motherhood and activism. "We could use a bright young woman like you in the movement," Moore proffered once again. Yet Blakely had her own designs. She told Moore of her plans to visit Tanzania and Nigeria on a Fulbright Scholarship to better understand the liberation struggles taking place there. "Queen Mother was disappointed that I was not at a point to join her and be by her side," the young activist recalled, "but at the same time gratified to know that I was working diligently on another front and that there was still hope for my future involvement."[16]

When Blakely finally returned from her stint in Africa, Moore dispatched her friend Thelma to ask after the young activist one last time. Two days later, Blakely visited Moore, cramming into her small

Harlem apartment with Thelma, Loretta, and Queen Mother herself. Blakely took in the small abode. She stepped around the "rare and cultural literature strewn about the tiny apartment" until she found a spot in the living room and turned to face the three women. The elders got to work. For hours on end, the trio spoke about Black people, their suffering, and the "toiling and atrocities imposed upon generations of African descendants."

"After listening to these dynamic and colorful women for the entire afternoon," Blakely recalled, "I knew that I couldn't leave there without letting them know that I would do my best to help carry on the struggle."[17] But that was only half the job.

Moore needed help getting her message out to the Black masses, yes. But more crucially, she needed help simply getting around town. She was looking for a protégée who could do both: serve as a loyal caretaker for the activist in her final years and carry on her work long after she passed. Tom had never wanted to be a movement king. But in Blakely, Moore had found a surrogate daughter ready and willing to take up the Queen Mother mantle. And so, Moore welcomed the young woman into nearly every aspect of her life. To her family's surprise, she listed Blakely as her legal guardian and transferred the deed to her Parksville land to her. For the next twelve years, Blakely played the role of the loyal lady-in-waiting. She accompanied the stately activist everywhere she went, from trips abroad to meet dignitaries to trips down the block to the doctor's office.[18]

Queen Mother Moore needed all the help she could get. After Hollywood actor turned politician Ronald Reagan ascended to the presidency in 1981, he wasted no time instituting tax breaks for the wealthy, rolling back civil rights gains, and attacking affirmative action policies. Reagan also "swung his budget axe at Great Society programs," scapegoating Black people as he cut federal funding for programs that served all poor and working-class Americans. Moore watched the TV in the senior citizens' center with dismay as newscasters reified the Reagan-promulgated stereotype of the "welfare queen": the allegedly lazy and promiscuous Black woman who cheated the government out of benefits to support her extravagant lifestyle. Reagan often invoked the caricature to justify his spending cuts and increased surveillance of Black communities.[19] When Moore stepped out, she saw his special brand of "law and order" in action. If the spike in police officers patrolling Harlem was any sign, the next four years would be a continuation of the surveillance and bullying Nixon had started—if not an escalation.[20]

It was "Morning in America," Reagan proclaimed as he instituted his new economic agenda, now known as Reaganomics. But for Black Americans, the sun never rose. And with the financial instability of the 1980s came a reliance on substances to ease the aches. South American countries began developing cocaine as a cash crop in the 1960s to fuel American demand. At first, it was largely confined to port cities in the Caribbean and Miami, but a glut of product and a burgeoning American market was a potent combination for international cartels.

With very little money, cocaine could be turned into crack and sold for a quick profit—perfect for ambitious hustlers and everyday Black folk looking for an escape from poverty, pain, and prejudice. Crowded into inner cities, with shoddy housing, impoverished schools, and few job prospects, many Black people found selling crack to be a viable way to put food on the table. And using it helped dull the pain of daily life.[21]

Calls for treatment centers and employment programs to mitigate the crack epidemic dovetailed with activists' attempts to curtail the spread of AIDS. Not long after *The New York Times* had documented a "rare cancer" among gay men in 1981, organizers started creating the first community programs to support patients—white ones, to be specific. Black health-care providers and community organizers, including the NOI, rallied to meet the moment, developing their own Black-centered responses to the health crisis that was ripping through Black neighborhoods.[22]

Queen Mother Moore supported these efforts. But she also believed the Black community's drug use stemmed from cultural degradation. Her people had made huge strides in the last two decades alone, never mind the last two centuries. But under Reagan's regime, they were in danger of forgetting all that Black Power had promised. And they were at risk of forgetting her, too. In her eighties and hampered by a bad hip that needed replacing, Moore couldn't shake the feeling that both she and her legacy might soon be buried, never to be found again. And so, with the help of Delois Blakely, in the early 1980s, Moore turned to two projects that she hoped might last, regardless of the roiling political seas: the Queen Mother Moore Institute and a monument to the Middle Passage.

"Many of you may already know of the marvelous work that was done at Mount Addis Ababa in the past," she began, explaining to anyone who would listen. Though she had long been spiriting eager young Black thinkers up to her plot of land, she now envisioned an institute bearing her name to "teach, define, and preserve our African lineage" and "focus on the African diaspora and the ramifications of colonialism on the African worldwide."[23] Decades earlier, she had hoped to galvanize Black folk to donate money for a school in her sister Eloise's name, but she hadn't had much luck. Perhaps the notoriety that she brought as the Queen Mother of the movement would turn a few more heads at home and abroad.

In early 1980, a group of young Black British organizers in London huddled around a tape deck. Their eyebrows shot up in surprise as the crackle of the recorder gave way to a voice, an older woman with a Southern American accent speaking about "her mentor Marcus Garvey, whom she helped defend with a gun as a teenager," and other liberation leaders like Haile Selassie and Malcolm X.

Makeda Coaston, an American activist and expat, had interviewed Queen Mother Moore during a trip to New York, and she brought the recording back to her friends at the Tree of Life, a London-based Rastafarian organization. As social and political outsiders searching for a culture to call their own, the group was stunned to come across this woman: a "powerful example of evolved African consciousness" who had met Garvey, their political idol. They had to know more. And so the Tree of Life members invited Moore to England to speak.[24]

Moore took a leap of faith when she accepted the invitation in 1981. The activist hadn't been back on English shores since the 1940s, when she had taken a stand against segregated lodgings for Coast Guard stewardesses. When she deplaned in London nearly forty years later, she found that, just like in America, race relations in England had remained much the same. Despite the country's attempt at creating a multiracial Commonwealth in the mid-twentieth century, by and large Britons still treated non-white folk as outsiders.[25] Moore wasn't surprised. She had read enough about England to know that its racist ideals were as old as the empire itself.

Africans, she had learned, had served as intermediaries and translators for the first English expeditions of the seventeenth century to the continent, and they had a small but significant presence in Tudor and Stuart England.[26] The Black British community morphed as Black Loyalists sailed to Canada and the metropole after the American Revolution, and during the nineteenth century when white racists and abolitionists found common ground over their desire to resettle Black people from England to Africa.[27] Some Black Britons did embrace the idea of immigration to British colonies like Sierra Leone. But they didn't pin all their dreams of freedom on resettling in a foreign land.

Spurred on by rebellions in the West Indies, world antislavery meetings, and testimonials from former slaves such as Frederick Douglass, white abolitionists eventually joined their Black counterparts in pushing the metropole to end slavery throughout the empire in 1834. By the mid-nineteenth century, London was home to a small but resilient Black community made up of students, preachers, fugitive slaves from America, and even some families who had been free for generations.[28]

These Black Britons navigated a complicated sense of belonging and alienation as colonialism replaced slavery as the primary global oppressive system in the early twentieth century. After two world wars, a new generation of Black organizers, many from British colonial strongholds, convened the Fifth Pan-African Congress in Manchester. They were searching for a way to collectively unlock the shackles of empire. But ultimately, it was a ship full of workers, rather than a summit of international leaders, that was the key.

When the HMT *Empire Windrush* docked at the Port of Tilbury in Essex in June 1948, hundreds of West Indians walked down the gangway and into a new world. Most had never intended to immigrate to the empire that had ruled their lives from afar for more than two hundred years. But rumor had it England needed workers to help rebuild after World War II.[29]

No matter what part of the Commonwealth they came from, it was clear to the first wave of the *Windrush* generation that they were not welcome. As soon as they set foot on the dock, British officials ushered them into dilapidated, overcrowded housing in impoverished neighborhoods and did nothing as they faced severe discrimination in the labor market. *Windrush* passengers' arrival coincided with the Nationality Act of 1948, which conferred citizenship rights to all subjects of the Commonwealth, including the right to work in the U.K. But to many English people, the influx of West Indians was a threat to the racially homogeneous society they felt was exclusively theirs.[30]

Resentment metastasized into outright violence in Notting Hill, a working-class borough known for its immigrant enclaves. The Teddy Boys, members of a turbulent, white supremacist subculture, had been relentlessly harassing Black residents there for years. As the sun set on August 29, 1958, they persuaded other locals to join in.

Their first target was a young Black man named Seymour Manning. When Manning found refuge in a local grocery store, the white mob, now numbering in the hundreds, moved in a phalanx down Notting Hill's streets, hurling glass bottles and homemade petrol bombs. Black residents barricaded themselves in their homes for days and fashioned homemade weapons to defend themselves against the brazen attack.[31] Britain had its first modern race riot.

The following year, mourners gathered to pay their respects to Antigua-born Kelso Cochrane, whom a white mob stabbed to death in the same neighborhood. Moore's old friend and comrade Claudia Jones joined others to create "We Mourn Cochrane" memorials. Cochrane's death became a rallying point for Black British civil rights organizing. Activists circulated his photo around the world.[32] Britain now had its own Emmett Till.[33]

In response, the state only further entrenched anti-immigrant racism. Parliament passed the 1962 Commonwealth Immigrants Act, restricting entry into the U.K. to only those with work permits— a direct response to the Caribbean migrants who had continued to arrive in England in the decades after the *Windrush* first docked.[34] Local Black activists fought valiantly against these laws and widespread racial retrenchment. Their movement even got a boost in 1964, when Dr. King paid Parliament a visit during a stopover on his way to Oslo to receive the Nobel Peace Prize. Soon after, progressive organizers formed the Campaign Against Racial Discrimination (CARD), a conglomerate of West Indians, South Asians, Africans, and white supporters who lobbied for more equitable race-related legislation.[35]

Those who felt CARD was too conciliatory had Malcolm X and Stokely Carmichael to look up to. Of Grenadian and Trinidadian descent, respectively, both men had an acute understanding of British rule. Malcolm X spoke out fervently against British racism in the small town of Smethwick just nine days before he was killed in New York City.[36] Carmichael came two years later, in 1967, just as a host of Black Power–oriented organizations was emerging, including the Black Power Party, the Black Panther Movement, and the Brixton Black Women's Group.[37]

As in America, these organizations found that after a decade of progress their movement had stalled. Margaret Thatcher rode into power as prime minister in 1979 with an agenda to match her future presidential counterpart across the Atlantic. The Conservative government's opposition to immigration, along with a recession, high unemployment, and inflation, fueled white resentment of those who called themselves both Black and British. And all this came to a head in 1981, the very same year that Moore returned to the U.K.

On January 17, 1981, Mrs. Gee Ruddock was hosting a sixteenth birthday party for her daughter, Yvonne, in their three-story family town house at 439 New Cross Road in South London. The festivities had started in the early evening, but Ruddock's friends kept streaming in well after midnight, and the teenagers kept partying into the early hours of the next morning. Dozens were singing and dancing in a second-floor bedroom when the DJ suddenly stopped spinning and told everyone to quiet down. Someone downstairs was shouting.

"Fire! Fire!" was all they heard a woman yell from the bottom of the stairwell before the whole house went dark with choking smoke. Kids and adults screamed and groped around for any way out as flames engulfed the second and third floors, but there were too many people and too few exits. When the sun came up, the neighborhood counted the casualties. Thirteen teenagers were dead, and twenty-seven more suffered horrific injuries.[38]

Ruddock maintained it was a bomb attack. After all, New Cross was a South London area that many called "the race hate capital of Britain." Police agreed, but they made no arrests. Even worse, Margaret Thatcher and Queen Elizabeth showed no sympathy. Their lack of public acknowledgment was made all the more painful when, just one month later, they showed public support for the victims of the

Stardust discotheque fire in Ireland.[39] In response, local Black activists Darcus Howe and John La Rose started the New Cross Massacre Action Committee, which mobilized an estimated twenty thousand people for the March 1981 Black People's Day of Action to demand justice for the fire victims—and for victims of British racism writ large.[40]

For the Tree of Life members who had invited Moore to speak, New Cross was just another example of the perils of "Babylon," the term Rastafarians used to describe the corrupt, capitalist, and colonialist white world.[41] An import from Jamaica, and largely comprising the disaffected children of the *Windrush* generation, the English Rastafarian movement adhered to the same core principles as their island forebears had. Chief among them was the belief that Prince Regent Ras Tafari, who became Ethiopian emperor Haile Selassie I in 1930, was a god in human form.[42] Selassie would deliver his loyal followers from Babylon, it was said, and return them to their utopian cradle of humanity in Africa, which they called Zion.

Until then, Rastas combated daily injustices by reconnecting with their African roots and shedding their political and cultural fidelity to white society.[43] They adopted a culture that Jamaican singer Bob Marley largely introduced to Black Britons, including wearing dreadlocks, becoming vegetarians, and speaking in Jamaican patois.[44] Britain-based Rastas also supported reparations, called for African liberation, and rejected British cultural assimilation.

Their common refrain was as effective as it was pithy: "Africa yes, England no."[45]

This was a message Moore could get behind. Queen Mother stepped off the plane and onto the stage of a Rasta rally as soon as she arrived in London. Moore spoke in her unabashed, warm style for more than an hour, moving seamlessly from "the psychology of oppression to the politics of liberation," while peppering in humorous anecdotes and vivid stories from her activist career.

Yet it wasn't necessarily what Moore said that made her an icon among Britain's disaffected Black youth. It was how she made them feel. "You see some of us, our mother cast we out because we grow our dread," rally organizer J. Sagladalla explained. "Our parents run us out the yard cause we don't eat the pork.... So when Queen Mother Moore came, all those who didn't have a mother, them with a living mother who don't want to know them, them was glad cause here was somebody to feel as a mother."[46] The Rasta community had simply hoped Moore would validate their cause. But they got so much more from her.

The feeling was mutual. Moore was "simply amazed" by the welcome she received. She had only ever heard "the wrong derogatory things about Rastas," and she wasn't the only one. As was now her custom, Moore had conscripted one of her grandkids into joining her—this time it was sixteen-year-old Christine—to expose them to the Diaspora and to help her travel. During their five-day stay, Christine came down with a bad ear infection. But Moore had a list of speaking engagements to complete. Never one to stay at home and tend to children when there was work to do, the activist left her granddaughter in the care of the Tree of Life members. They took such good care of Christine that she later claimed the London Rastas were the "kindest people [she'd] ever met."[47]

Moore was grateful for their care, but she didn't let their kindness paper over politics. "The Rastas have a philosophy of returning to the motherland, but I say that you should go with your reparations. You don't need to start from scratch, you have to claim what is yours," she admonished during her visit.[48] "You look at the jewels Elizabeth wears on her crown, and you don't know those jewels belong to you.... We must have our wealth back in our hands where it belongs."[49]

For Moore, the fall 1981 trip was a chance to build the reparations movement across the ocean. And for Christine, seeing her grandmother outside a familial context was a revelation. "When they approached Queen Mother, they bowed down to her," she recalled. "It hit me that my grandmother mean[t] something to people."[50]

Moore's visit proved so generative that organizers in the U.K. begged her to come back the next year. Queen Mother was happy to oblige, but her health threatened to keep her away. In March 1982, just months before her second planned trip to England, Moore suffered a stroke. Doctors demanded the eighty-three-year-old stay on bed rest, but Moore had a different type of medicine in mind. That week alone, she was scheduled to speak alongside Nation of Islam leader Louis Farrakhan in Chicago, then fly to Boston, and then speak at a conference at the University of Louisville after that. In Moore's eyes, getting back on her feet and fulfilling her obligations was the only true cure. Her medical team watched in amazement as she gripped a pen and, in her characteristic looping letters, signed her name on the waiver line discharging herself from the hospital.

She barely made it forty-eight hours before she was back in. Queen Mother had pneumonia. This time, the medical staff forced her to stay for a few days until her fever broke and her strength improved. But as soon as her doctors gave the okay, Moore was gone again. She stopped by her apartment for a few things before boarding a flight to Kentucky.[51] She might have missed out on her other engagements that week, but she meant to keep her promise to speak at the National Conference on the Black Family.

Moore's eyelids drooped as she lowered her head, bracing herself against the coughs that shook her body as she waited to take the podium. She was just as decked out as ever in her head wrap and silver bracelets. But a thick blanket now covered her colorful kaftan. Even queens had to find ways to keep out the cold.

"My dear brothers and sisters. I'm here today against my doctor's advice," Moore opened. Both her body and her mind were putting up a fight—against exhaustion, against the cough she couldn't shake, and against the medications doctors had given her to keep it all at bay.

Moore went on to recite her well-worn stump speech, a free-ranging diatribe against the American government that always began with a chastening—we Black people have "not yet demanded our just due"—and ended with a joke: "A group of us were going to Africa. Some said they were going to find their family roots. Some said they were going to see what it felt like to sleep in a hut. And there were others who mentioned what it was that they were going to see. Because when I was there, what I was going to do, I told them that I was going to check on my real estate," she added, eliciting laughter.[52]

To the amazement of Blakely, and students and activists all around her, Moore continued to speak to crowds across the country until it was time to return to England just two months later.[53] Still ailing from the stroke and pneumonia one-two punch, Moore did not have the strength to muster her usual aplomb.[54] Yet even in her weakened state, Queen Mother still garnered a strong police presence.

Just as locals were gathering in Stonebridge Park in London on

May 29, for no apparent reason a set of police cars sped across the grass and through the nearby playground, forcing the crowd to dive out of the way.[55] Moore likely smirked to herself, once she was sure everyone was okay. America might have severed ties with Britain long ago, but the two countries were still bound together by their unimaginative repression tactics.

Despite her health setbacks, Moore kept up the grueling pace during her second stay in England. She stopped by Bulmershe College in Reading and the offices of the *Caribbean Times,* a newly minted anticolonial newspaper by and for local Caribbean, African, and Asian communities. But the Africa Centre was the locus of her visit. In the meeting hall dedicated to African life and culture on King Street, Queen Mother Moore made the purpose of her visit known. "Specifically I have come to England for two reasons: To help establish a permanent channel of communication between our people" and to "urge our Brothers and Sisters to join in the development of a great monument in memory of our lost ancestors and freedom fighters."[56]

College students, activists, and reporters alike sat in stunned silence as Moore laid out her rationale for the Middle Passage monument. She lectured about the slave trade, renaming what some called the African Holocaust the "Hell-of-a-Cost." African slaves' harrowing voyage to the Americas was the "most inhumane journey that has taken place in modern times," and "there's never been a memorial to the hundred million who perished," she lamented. So many Africans died during the Atlantic crossing that "the sharks followed the ships."[57]

"They are crying out to us from the depth of the seas," she exclaimed. "Millions lost their lives even prior to reaching so-called America. They were thrown overboard for resistance to slavery, sickness acquired from their captives, and just for sport."[58]

In an era when Black history was only just beginning to be included in school curricula, many in the audience stood in horror as they heard details about the slave trade for the first time. Moved by Moore's urgency, local activists, including Len Garrison, who had already heeded Moore's call to continue her work by creating the Black Cultural Archive in Brixton, established the African People's Historical Monument Foundation while she was there.[59]

Moore excitedly explained to the group that she hoped that the structure would be more than a static sculpture. She envisioned a "living monument in the form of a facility that would serve as a focal point for research and cultural development of African people—all with the aim of embracing our 'right mind' and uniting in our common struggle."[60]

When she and her sisters bought the property of Mount Addis Ababa nearly forty years before, they dreamed of making it a center of African-centered organizing and culture. Yet many around them had been slow to see their vision. For the first time in a long time, Queen Mother Moore had hope she might see a monument built to their ancestors before she inevitably became one.

At the behest of a local Black activist, Amelda Inyang, Moore made one last stop, in the southwest London suburb of Clapham. Now in the second week of her trip, she had slowed down significantly. But tired as she was, she couldn't possibly miss the opportunity to see Britain's supplementary school movement in action.

Talking to educators and parents, Moore learned that Black children were at the epicenter of a contentious battle over education in Britain. Black Caribbean migration to England had peaked between 1955 and 1962. As they reached a critical mass on the island, Afro-Caribbeans began to see themselves less as fair-weather migrants and more as settled-in immigrants putting down roots. Now permanent residents, *Windrush*-generation parents believed education was the best path to advancement, and they trusted U.K. schools to do it.[61] But their confidence was misplaced. White families worried about having Black children in state-supported schools and started busing Black students to separate schools outside their local districts.

Black parents and community leaders resented this. But they soon found they had a bigger problem. School officials were tracking their children into educationally subnormal (ESN) schools. A product of Britain's 1944 Education Act, the classification was originally to support disabled students or those with learning differences. But as was so often the case, the law became a weapon. White teachers pushed Black immigrant kids into ESNs, often without informing them or their parents that these schools had no curricula or testing, and that their kids had no hope of gaining useful jobs or skills training. What they had in droves was abuse. By the time Moore visited England for the second time, thousands of Black children had endured these soul-crushing schools, only to find the ESN label followed them for the rest of their lives, limiting their job prospects and their self-confidence in equal measure.[62]

Black activist and bookshop owner John La Rose led groups like the North London West Indian Association and the Caribbean Education and Community Workers Association (CECWA) in amplifying parents' concerns about ESN schools and educational racism.[63] But any illusions parents might have had of improving their children's education were shattered when CECWA-appointed educator Bernard Coard published his findings in *How the West Indian Child Is Made Educationally Subnormal in the British School System.*

Coard came to the same conclusion that Queen Mother Moore had in America: the U.K. was, in Moore's words, "perpetuating idiot factories" for Black youth.[64] Subnormal schools were horrific by all accounts. But it had to be said, most public schools in Clapham were hardly better. He recommended that Black parents develop supplementary schools to counter this subpar education and cultivate their children's identity, pride, and political consciousness.[65]

Clapham-based community activist Reverend Hewlett "Hewie" Andrew heard Coard loud and clear. On a cold Sunday night in January 1982, he and La Rose asked local parents to come to Clapham Methodist Church to discuss Coard's findings.[66] It didn't take long for La Rose and Andrew to convince them that they needed a supplementary school.

Andrew, they decided, should be the headmaster. A Dominica-born man with deep brown skin, a full beard, and a toothy smile, he preached African-centered expressions of Christianity from the pulpit and put Black people's liberation at the center of his ministry.[67] He brought this same ethos to this educational endeavor. The core value of his curriculum was also one of Queen Mother Moore's most sacred principles: "Blacks are an African people."[68]

Andrew's and Moore's shared love of African history was on full display when Queen Mother walked into the Methodist church's makeshift school in May 1982. Moore was aptly dressed. She had donned a black dress and matching head wrap with light *sankofas* printed across them—birds facing forward with their necks craned backward. In the Twi language of Ghana, *sankofa* translated to "go back and fetch it."

It was her subtle call for those at the school to learn from the past to build a prosperous future. Teachers quickly offered Moore a seat at the front of the room. From there, she could get a good look at the church turned classroom with its bulletin boards featuring photos of Black Nationalist heroes like Marcus Garvey and Haile Selassie. At their teachers' urging, a group of Black children approached Moore, each holding out their hand to greet the aged activist.[69]

"Queen Mother Moore gave a soul-searching address on the education of the Black child" during her visit, Andrew remembered. And the staff was both "inspired and challenged" by her message. They unanimously agreed to name the school after her.[70] "It's the first time a school has been named in my honour," Moore replied as she accepted the accolade. "I am overwhelmed."[71]

The school honored Moore in more ways than one. Andrew and his fellow educators developed an extensive curriculum that taught local Black children as young as three about African and Black British history and culture. They did not "solely project ourselves as victims and the oppressed," the headmaster explained. Rather, the staff at the Queen Mother Moore School dedicated their lives to helping their students understand their history and how Black people's "strength and knowledge of our selves have helped us survive and will help us to progress."[72]

These Saturday morning sessions served as a respite for young Black kids who faced racial alienation in their day schools and as a bulwark against claims they were "subnormal." In the heat of the struggles for the soul of New York City schools, Moore had boldly proclaimed that Black parents and kids refused to be programmed anymore. Fifteen years later and an ocean away, the educators at the Queen Mother Moore School were doing the same.

Queen Mother herself was justly proud. "My greatest ambition," the activist declared as she left the city, "is to be worthy of the children of the Queen Mother Moore School."[73]

CHAPTER 25

The End of Queen Mother Moore's Reign

W hen Moore returned to the States, she found Black Nationalism on the ropes. It had taken decades since the dawn of the
modern civil rights fight, but a small segment of the Black population
was starting to taste true American success. The Black press, in turn,
had taken these token wins and run with them. When Blakely took
Moore down to the corner store, they saw magazines featuring honey-
brown-skinned men and women dressed in business attire and holding
brick-sized cell phones above headlines detailing the best corporate
jobs for young Black professionals. If Queen Mother Moore happened
to pick up an issue of *Black Enterprise* and flip through it while Blakely
bought her something sweet, she'd have read reports that more than
half of its readership believed Black employment opportunities and
wealth had increased as a result of civil rights fights.[1]

The promise of Black advancement was just as strong on the TV
and the big screen. On Thursdays in the mid-1980s, millions tuned in
to watch a Black doctor and lawyer raise five kids in a big, beautiful
Brooklyn brownstone on *The Cosby Show*. On Fridays, they made plans
to head to the theater and see Eddie Murphy's smash hit *Coming to
America*, a comedic tale of a middle-class Black woman from Queens
who unwittingly falls in love with a rich African prince in disguise.
Moore saw through it all. Pretending a precious few Black people
were better off in America couldn't soothe the heartbreak that so many
have-nots felt. In a moment when many were falling for the seduction
of mainstream comforts, Moore knew she would have to work harder
to keep her nationalist ideals alive.

Black faces in high places made the fight even more arduous. Once
a team of outsiders punching above their weight, by the mid-1980s

the Congressional Black Caucus had landed a few political knock-outs. Though it had failed to thwart Reagan's budget cuts, the caucus succeeded in introducing key pieces of affirmative action and anti-apartheid legislation in Congress.[2] Many took this as a sign of real Black political progress.

On the local level, there was just as much momentum. The Voting Rights Act had created Black districts and constituencies in the 1970s, and the white flight that defined the mid-1980s further solidified Black urban political power. Tom Bradley became the first Black mayor of Los Angeles. Maynard Jackson manned Atlanta, the Black Mecca of the South. Coleman Young ruled Detroit. But just like their congressional counterparts, Black leaders on the state and city levels spent much of their time scrambling to mitigate the consequences of Reagan's brutal economic plan.

Surveying this critical mass of Black voters and legislators, Jesse Jackson—now a seasoned organizer in his forties—decided it was time to make a run for the top job. Jackson campaigned for the Democratic presidential nomination in both 1984 and 1988, seeking to unite America's marginalized groups in the "Rainbow Coalition."[3]

Moore had her misgivings when she first got wind of Jackson's ambitions. A Black president of the United States wasn't what she had in mind when she'd heard him shout "Nationtime!" all those years ago. Even still, she supported his candidacy in hopes of helping rekindle some of that nationalist energy—and her own political relevancy, too.

Both she and Jackson got a boost from a young man born in the Bronx and raised in Boston. Louis Farrakhan was a talented musician who had had a moderately successful music career before putting down his calypso drum at twenty-two years old and picking up the Koran. He joined the Nation of Islam back in 1955. And in the 1960s and 1970s, he followed a similar trajectory as Malcolm X, first worshipping in and then leading some of the same temples as Elijah Muhammad's once-favored son. The similarities didn't end there. Like Malcolm, Farrakhan was a dynamic and charismatic speaker with a clear political vision. Many inside and outside the NOI saw him as Muhammad's new heir apparent.

But when the embattled NOI leader passed away in 1975, a different plan unfurled. He had chosen one of his actual heirs, his son Warith Deen Mohammed, to lead the group. Warith forged a different racial and religious path for the NOI, converting it to orthodox Sunni Islam and ridding it of his father's separatist teachings. Farrakhan couldn't abide by the betrayal; he soon broke ties with Warith and created a new iteration of the Nation headquartered in Chicago, along with a new paper as its mouthpiece, *The Final Call.* What began as a separate sect with a few thousand followers increased tenfold in 1984 when Farrakhan became a household name, thanks in part to his support of Jackson's first presidential campaign.[4]

Queen Mother Moore recognized a historic moment when she saw one. Not only did Jackson have the opportunity to get closer than any other Black person ever had to the pinnacle of American political power, but Black Nationalism was poised to move back into the country's consciousness by virtue of Farrakhan's endorsement. When Black America saw the two men standing side by side, it gave many hope that the 1980s might be the decade when the age-old divide between integration and separation could at last be bridged.[5]

Queen Mother Moore resolved to unite the two camps, and she lent her status as a movement elder to both men's political projects. In the mid- to late 1980s, she appeared alongside Jackson at campaign stops and onstage with Farrakhan at NOI events at Madison Square Garden.[6] If the nationalist movement was moving toward mainstream partnerships, then Moore wanted to make sure she was still a top power broker.

She also wanted to make sure that it didn't lose its internationalist edge. This is likely why, despite a heap of health problems, including a breast cancer scare, Moore accepted Zambian president Kenneth Kaunda's invitation to attend the OAU's Extraordinary Summit in November 1987 in Ethiopia—a special meeting called to address the current debt crisis on the continent.

When the eighty-nine-year-old touched down in Africa's ever-free nation, she found the tenor of the talks to be quite different from those she had witnessed twelve years before. Whether at summit proceedings or state dinners, African leaders were now mired in technocratic matters like economic stagnation rather than decolonization.[7]

To be sure, Moore had heard reports about the continent's money troubles in the Western press. But the summit crystallized the seemingly insurmountable obstacles many African leaders faced. Rising oil prices in the 1970s had led them to borrow more money to import goods into their countries, while the prices for the commodities they produced decreased. This, coupled with high-interest loans from other nations, made it nearly impossible for many African countries to stay afloat. No matter which Western power they borrowed the money from, the continent's leaders found entering the world stage was a devil's bargain.[8]

The OAU must either "find effective and lasting solutions to the debt crisis" or consign Africa to "wallow in abject mass poverty," Kaunda proclaimed at the proceedings.[9] Burkina Faso's leader, Thomas Sankara, had a more radical idea: don't pay the debt back at all. "We cannot repay the debt because we have nothing to pay it with," and "those who led us into debt were gambling, as if they were in a casino," he told his fellow leaders. "As long as they were winning there was no problem. Now that they're losing their bets, they demand repayment."[10] Moore was on Sankara's side. She supported his call for African leaders to form a united front against the predatory lending of Western countries.[11]

She said as much in her speech on the final day of the summit. That day, she dressed herself in a colorfully patterned kaftan and headdress. A lanyard with her name on it replaced the usual strings of beads around her neck. Moore summoned all her strength to make what she knew might be her last appeal before the African governing body. Whereas once she could go for an hour or longer, now she had just enough in her to speak for close to two minutes. But in that short time, she made such an impassioned plea to refocus on the "struggle to free African people everywhere" that it brought the heads of state to their feet for a just-as-lengthy standing ovation.[12]

The real privilege came afterward, though, when Moore had the chance to explore Addis Ababa and meet Ethiopian president Mengistu Haile Mariam. Ethiopia had taken on a mythical quality for Moore ever since her young Garveyite days. It was one of the few African nations that could boast never having been colonized, and the gleam of that history had never worn off. In the 1930s, Moore fought against its Italian occupation. She named many of her grassroots organizations after it in the 1950s, and by the 1960s she had joined the Ethiopian Coptic Church. Now the mother of the Black Nationalist Movement had finally made it back to the promised land. What's more, the Ethiopian president had made time to speak with her directly about how they might work together.[13] As she surveyed the city, a collage of North African architecture largely untouched by colonialism, Moore made a promise to herself that she would be back. She would in fact return to the continent soon enough, but not to the Garveyite mecca.

Three years later, Moore trekked across the ocean again, this time to meet the newly freed Nelson Mandela in Zambia. Nestled in the heart of southern Africa and bordering Angola, Namibia, Botswana, Zimbabwe, and Mozambique, the butterfly-shaped country was a frequent destination for South African political refugees and liberation leaders. Queen Mother Moore knew the African National Congress had used Zambia as a home base during their anti-apartheid struggle.[14] Thus, she was delighted but unsurprised when she learned it would be Mandela's first stop after South Africa's president, F. W. de Klerk, finally released him from prison.[15]

Moore likely gathered with others to watch the footage of Mandela's arrival on February 27, 1990. Black people on both sides of the Atlantic cheered when the former political prisoner emerged in a black business suit from a red-black-and-green-striped plane at Lusaka International Airport, waving to a throng of well-wishers nearly fifty thousand strong. "It was clear that this was no ordinary visit," reporters noted of this historic moment in global Black history. "It was a visit of a recognized African and world leader whose stature had not been diminished by nearly three decades behind prison walls."[16]

Two months later, Queen Mother Moore and Delois Blakely landed in Lusaka, too. Mandela had granted her an audience, one lifelong freedom fighter to another. Moore used what precious time she had with him to extol the connection between their two communities, asking that Mandela make "Harlem a priority" when he came to visit the States in a few months' time. The people of Harlem would be grateful, she said, if he could "lay a wreath and plant a tree to memorialize the Children of Soweto," a gesture of solidarity with the captive Africans in New York who had long supported the fight against apartheid.[17]

Mandela made good on his promise that June when he and his wife, Winnie, visited New York City. Queen Mother Moore could hardly contain her excitement when, on the second day of their stay in the Big Apple, the South African couple came to Harlem.[18] As she made her way to the rally on 125th Street and Adam Clayton Powell

Boulevard, Black folk were spilling out onto the streets and craning their necks from rooftops, balconies, and fire escapes to get a glimpse of the world-famous freedom fighter.

"Amandla!" the masses shouted in unison with raised fists as the Mandelas took the stage. The Zulu word for "power" had become a rallying cry. Mandela thrust his right fist skyward and returned the chant.

"[I] have followed closely your own struggle against the injustices of racial discrimination and economic inequality," Mandela told Harlemites. "We continue to be inspired by your indomitable fighting spirit. To our people, Harlem symbolized strength and beauty in resistance."[19]

Moore lit up. Here was a leader who understood her message. After the rally, Moore remarked on how good it felt to hear Mandela acknowledge "the capitals of Black America and Africa are kin."[20]

Over the next few days, the elder freedom fighters met for a series of photo ops and solidarity sessions. Queen Mother Moore could be found posing with Mandela in front of New York landmarks and among the crowds as Winnie told thousands in Brooklyn she was "skeptical about the 'change of heart' now being showed by the 'white racist regime'" who had imprisoned and then freed her husband.[21]

Moore was also there at the Adam Clayton Powell Office Building on 125th Street, part of Africa Square in Harlem, for the tree planting ceremony Mandela had promised her. She arrived with some soil that she had collected during her trip two months earlier. When asked how she circumvented customs to bring the sacred earth back to Harlem's Little Africa, Moore replied slyly: "They asked us about fruit" at the declaration point. "They didn't ask us about dirt."[22]

The Mandelas could see the neighborhood was in flux as their motorcade rolled through Harlem. The fight for Black community control and self-determination, coupled with entrenched residential segregation, had kept a white takeover of housing and businesses at bay in the 1960s and 1970s. But the dam couldn't hold forever. By 1990, a new wave of neoliberal law and order, largely stemming from Mayor Ed Koch's office at city hall, was rushing through Harlem's streets. The Black unemployment rate was twice that of white America, and Reagan's laissez-faire approach to the economy and gutting of social services in the previous decade had catalyzed both the AIDS epidemic and rampant poverty, which now wreaked havoc on the Black men and women who called Harlem home.[23] Touring Moore's neighborhood, the Mandelas saw it all. On the one hand, a cataclysmic combination of violence, surveillance, and repression; on the other, severe government neglect. Winnie Mandela encapsulated this cognitive dissidence, and Harlemites' fighting spirit, when she took the stage at the Harlem rally and proclaimed, "I greet you here in the Soweto of America, the capital of the revolution throughout the world."[24]

Meanwhile, Moore kept a steady schedule of nationalist events, hoping Harlem would continue to live up to its radical reputation. She presented gifts to Guyanese president Hugh Desmond Hoyte, who visited Harlem seeking Black American investment in his country, and she attended a Martin Luther King Day celebration featuring the Ghanaian ambassador to the United Nations, where four hundred people gathered to call for the "salvation of Africa" by Africans all over the world.[25] She kept the dream of the Queen Mother Moore Institute and a Middle Passage monument alive by holding fundraisers and benefits with the Ethiopian Coptic Church. She even found support from Marcus Garvey Jr., who rallied the community to Moore's cause.[26]

Queen Mother returned the favor to Garvey's children by keeping aloft the banner of the UNIA. She and Loretta worked alongside John Henrik Clarke, Professor Robert Hill, and Marcus Garvey Jr. to posthumously clear the UNIA leader of his old mail fraud conviction. Harlem's Charles Rangel, known as the Lion of Lenox Avenue, helped to bring the issue before the House of Representatives. The Congressional Black Caucus member knew Garvey's exoneration was near and dear to his constituents like Moore.[27] Queen Mother Moore was also a regular at the Marcus Garvey Centennial Committee's events and took every opportunity she could to spread Garvey's message. She still corralled the crowds when she headlined community rallies such as "Black Nationhood, Pan-Africanism, African Liberation: By Any Means Necessary."[28]

As she headed home from these kinds of gatherings, Moore saw her neighborhood's growing pains on full display. She and Blakely passed by burned-out and boarded-up buildings, and people begging for spare change. On one block she'd see a stately old brownstone that a white family had bought at a bargain-basement price, and on another, young Black men in Malcolm X T-shirts talking shop. "Hold up the peace sign, *as-salaam alaikum!*" kids yelled as Big Daddy Kane's "Ain't No Half Steppin'" bumped from their radios. Others sat on stoops simmering to the sounds of rapper Lakim Shabazz's "Black Is Back": "I know the ledge, over the edge, I won't fall / This rhyme was designed for *The Final Call*." Moore might not have known what to make of her transitioning neighborhood, but one thing was clear: hip-hop was introducing a new generation to the icons she had helped raise—Malcolm X and his Nation of Islam, first among them—and to the nationalism that had energized them.[29]

The Nation of Islam had become *the* vehicle through which to reassert nationalist ideas in the 1990s. Farrakhan had focused his movement on building Black economic power and two-parent Black family units, drawing in a new generation of supporters coming of age in overpoliced and drug-ravaged cities.[30] Farrakhan's claims that Black people were plagued by "drugs, crime, teenage pregnancy, unemployment" and "divorce, disease and disunity" might not have thrilled Queen Mother, who still believed the focus should be separation and reparations. But there could be no denying he was the top game in town.

Thus, Moore agreed to headline events such as the NOI's Black Family Day, where thousands packed into the Harlem Armory to celebrate the best parts of Black life and culture. Here, locals heard from Farrakhan, local Mosque No. 7 leader Conrad Muhammad, civil rights attorney Alton Maddox, and Harlem doctor Barbara Justice. Performances from rappers Chuck D and Public Enemy were the prize for enduring the harangues and calls to action.[31]

Moore was no stranger to sharing the stage with organizers and artists. But now she found herself sitting next to the newest members of the Black elite. Women like Dr. Justice, a Howard-educated physician and the first Black woman resident in general surgery at Columbia University, came to symbolize a new generation of Black Americans who had broken through the racial barriers in education and employment thanks to the civil rights and affirmative action policies of the last thirty years. Queen Mother cheered as Justice called out the crack and AIDS "genocides" ravaging Harlem and seconded her demands for more funding and treatment centers.[32] She was thrilled the young doctor was using her newfound status to give back to her community. Others took a different route.

Some among the Black middle class believed their successes were the fruits of their labor alone. The Reagan administration welcomed this attitude as it looked for Black faces to be the front men for its conservatism. Reagan initially nominated an inexperienced Black businessman, William Bell, to replace Eleanor Holmes Norton, a Black lawyer and chair of the Equal Employment Opportunity Commission (EEOC). The president followed the same playbook when he targeted the Commission on Civil Rights, supplanting white progressive Arthur S. Flemming with a Black conservative, Clarence Pendleton.[33] Bell and Pendleton peddled a different approach to racial progress, whereby Black people, not the U.S. government, were to blame for the community's poverty, among other ills.

This unholy trinity of issues—AIDS, crack, and poverty—helped politicians like George H. W. Bush spin a narrative that framed Black people as diseased and criminal, and helped propel him into office in the early 1990s. Bush called for a "kinder, gentler America," but his administration was methodically brutal in its anti-Blackness.[34] The president made it clear he planned to continue the cuts to taxes and social services his predecessor had started, all while pretending to care about Black progress through targeted, token government appointments like nominating Clarence Thomas for the Supreme Court in 1991.

Everyone had something to say about Thomas once his confirmation hearing started. But the nation was stunned when a thirty-five-year-old Black lawyer stared head-on into blinding lights, raised her right hand, and vowed to tell the whole truth about her former boss's abuse to an all-white, all-male Senate Judiciary Committee. With astounding aplomb, Anita Hill recounted the lurid sexual harassment she had endured while Thomas was her supervisor at the Department of Education and the EEOC.[35] But Hill's testimony was no match for Thomas's story of pulling himself up by his bootstraps and climbing to the highest echelons of government, like something straight from a Horatio Alger story. He framed Hill's testimony as a "high-tech lynching," and the media ate it up.

Still, Black women came out in force to support Hill, with more than fifteen hundred signing "African American Women in Defense of Ourselves," a full-page ad in *The New York Times* that protested her treatment and the harassment that so many other Black women faced.[36] Disappointingly, if not predictably, Queen Mother Moore's name was nowhere to be found. She had always passed off men's lewd behavior as little more than carnal instinct. "[If the] last woman on earth disappeared, a man will do it with a hole in the wall," she would often quip.[37] Nationalist or not, she abhorred the idea of a Black woman "attacking" a Black man so openly, for all of white America to see.

In Moore's opinion, Black people had more pressing matters to address. Back in March 1991, headlines were awash once again with the name King. Rodney King, a Black man who led police on a high-speed chase through the streets of Los Angeles. When King finally pulled over and climbed out of the car, four officers beat him mercilessly. Moore, like the rest of America, watched in horror as national news aired the grainy black-and-white footage of the attack.

She could barely catch her breath before another video surfaced two weeks later, this time of Korean convenience store owner Soon Ja Du shooting a sixteen-year-old Black girl, Latasha Harlins, in the back of the head. Du thought Harlins was stealing a bottle of orange juice. When police stepped into the shop, they found $2 crumpled in her left hand as she lay lifeless on the ground.[38]

Both cases came to a head in 1992 when one jury acquitted King's assailants and another convicted Du of manslaughter but recommended a fine rather than jail time. The City of Angels went up in flames in the rebellion that followed, protesters making good on their mantra of "no justice, no peace."[39] Queen Mother Moore likely echoed their cries in Harlem, alongside protesters carrying signs with TODAY RODNEY KING, TOMORROW ME scrawled across them.[40]

Those days, Moore was rallying what little strength she had to protect Harlem from the same fate that had brought L.A. to its knees. She could be found at meetings aimed at fighting AIDS, building alternative schools for children, supporting single mothers, or educating the community about their African heritage. Queen Mother received top billing at events like the Rally Against Crack, where a conglomeration of Muslim mosques and community groups tried to develop strategies to quell drug use and crime in their neighborhoods before the police deployed methods of their own.[41]

Still, these were just temporary solutions for Moore. Even in her nineties, she maintained that the ills plaguing Harlem and other Black enclaves throughout the country could be solved only through a nationalist agenda and reparations. But much to Moore's delight, others had seen the light. She was happy to hand over the reins of the reparations movement to a new generation who had vowed to carry on her cause.

Throughout the 1970s and 1980s, Black lawyers and activists had heeded Moore's call and created a host of repayment-focused groups. There was the Black Reparations Committee, headquartered in Maryland, and the African National Reparations Organization (ANRO) in New York, and many more.[42] But by the late 1980s, these many disparate groups had coalesced into the most recognizable, "energetic, independent unifying national movement for reparations" the country had ever seen.[43]

In August 1987, RNA leader Imari Obadele issued a call for "more than twenty-five organizations to come to Washington, D.C., and discuss the armed struggle in Namibia, South Africa, Angola, and Mozambique," and the "development of a definitive campaign for reparations."[44] It was an enticing prospect for Black Nationalists, Pan-Africanists, integrationists, and legal analysts alike. Word was Congress was pushing through a bill that included a formal apology for Japanese internment camps and funds to repay those whom the government interned, and that Reagan planned to sign it in the next year. Many across Moore's nationalist camp wondered if a promising new precedent was about to be set.[45]

Their timing was prescient in more ways than one. A few weeks later, the National Conference of Black Lawyers, what many considered the legal arm of the Black Liberation Movement, held its annual meeting in the nation's capital. Here, a collection of the best and brightest Black legal minds gathered to imagine a world where the U.S. Constitution had been written with the "material needs of enslaved Africans and their descendants in mind."

The Black Freedom Movement had always looked more like a Venn diagram than discrete political circles. Thus, it was only natural that there were activists who attended both events. According to reparations activist and director of the lawyers' guild Adjoa Aiyetoro, the National Conference of Black Lawyers realized if the group truly planned to champion Black liberation, it had to make reparations a central tenet. A month later, in September 1987, the National Coalition of Blacks for Reparations in America (N'COBRA) was born.[46]

N'COBRA began an ambitious campaign to advance the reparations movement from its headquarters in Washington, D.C. And Moore, though aged and ailing, loved seeing it take shape. She gathered all her money and strength to attend the group's town hall meetings and conferences over the next few years, including its second annual convention in Cleveland in 1990, where she shared her expertise as the matriarch of the movement.[47]

Four years later, in 1994, she needed significantly more help to move, travel, and speak. Yet Queen Mother Moore still made it a point to meet with N'COBRA organizers again, this time in Detroit just days before her ninety-sixth birthday. It was summer, but Moore couldn't shake the chills. She wore a white shawl over her signature head wrap and kaftan as the group's leaders welcomed the wheelchair-bound activist to the opening day of the conference.

As she scanned the room, Moore was stunned to see so few familiar faces. In the six short years since its founding, N'COBRA had spread like wildfire. Its annual conferences now drew in several hundred people from across the political spectrum, most of them new to reparations activism. Still, Moore picked out some old friends in the crowd. As soon as they spotted her, Jesse Jackson and Preston Wilcox rushed to Moore's side, bent down to meet her eye, and clasped the wrinkled hand she offered from under her blanket. "It's good to see you again, Queen Mother," they said. "We are here because of you."[48]

As the day continued, Moore listened as reparations advocates old and new offered their two cents on how repayment might work. She also added her own, wading into the debate over N'COBRA's support of H.R. 40, the bill Michigan congressman John Conyers put forth that, if passed, would establish a commission to study and develop proposals for reparations for Black Americans.[49] Forty years before, Moore was the lone voice calling for reparations. She couldn't have imagined that, one day, a bill debating the merits of her movement might make it to the congressional floor.

"Queen Mother Moore wants to see you," was all the group of women were told when they answered a knock at their hotel door that evening. When they peered inside Moore's door a while later, the young activists found Queen Mother dressed in white, lying so still on her bed that she blended in with her bedsheets. "Come in, come in," she rasped. The women pushed inside the room, shut the door, and gathered around Moore's bedside.[50]

Surrounded by some of the most radical sisters in the reparations struggle, Moore once again held court. And the women, in turn, leaned in close to hear her speak. There's no definitive account of Moore's lesson that night. In all likelihood, it included many of her classics: how reparations was "more than a paycheck and an apology"; how repayment was just one more step toward Black sovereignty.[51] Perhaps they shot each other glances when Moore peppered her message with a bit of patriarchy. At this stage in her life, she was still extolling the virtues of polygamy and the need to support Black men as leaders in the movement.[52] These were the quirks and contradictions that had come to define Queen Mother Moore. But for those willing to humor her eccentricities, there was a lifetime of hard-won knowledge to be found in her words.

The next day, Moore mustered up the energy to address N'COBRA for the last time. Organizers quieted and cleared out of the way as her supporters wheeled her to the stage. Looking out onto the sea of faces, Moore was overcome. So many now believed in her cause—believed that reparations for the sins of slavery were possible. Yet even still, a sinking feeling told her she wouldn't live to see it fulfilled. Queen Mother Moore steadied herself. She pushed the thought down as tears welled up. "Reparations. Reparations," she began. But her voice betrayed her. She sat silent for several seconds. "Keep on. Keep on. We've got to win." It was all she could muster. For maybe the first time ever, Audley Moore was at a loss for words.[53]

For some conference goers, keeping on meant forcing the Clinton administration to acknowledge reparations were due.[54] This goal seemed more possible than ever, given the politician's special relationship with the Black community. Black Americans were skeptical of the Arkansas governor when he first announced his plan to pursue the presidency. But his June 1992 appearance on Black comedian Arsenio Hall's late-night show won them over.

As soon as the nightly news ended, Black folk across the country watched with rapt attention as the camera panned to Clinton, clad in a black suit and sunglasses, playing a saxophone in front of Hall's house band as the show opened. He wowed audiences again a few minutes later with a solo rendition of "Heartbreak Hotel," before chatting with the infamous Hall. And when it came time to vote, Black Americans took Clinton up on his cool affect and his campaign promises.[55]

Just like his television stunt, Clinton's support of Black America was more showmanship than substance. He appointed more Black people to federal posts than any other president before him. But he also paired these high-profile appointments with brutal policy reversals. When Clinton became president, 33 percent of Black Americans—Queen Mother Moore among them—lived in poverty while hanging on to the perpetual hope his pledge to reform the welfare system would improve their daily lives. Instead, his presidency dredged up old shibboleths about Black pathology. Clinton's first term came and went with few legislative gains and a lot of neglect of the Black masses who had rocketed him into office.[56]

Moore, who had never put much faith in presidents, was still focused on international administrations. In 1995, the activist announced her plan to attend the Fourth World Conference on Women in Beijing and asked for funds for her "Last Will and Testament Journey to Africa" the next year. If anyone questioned whether a woman her age should be traveling, Moore quashed their reservations with an indefatigable spirit: "I feel good, I feel young. My work isn't complete."[57] Though she couldn't have known, it was only a half-truth.

Moore didn't make it to Beijing, but she did make one last major trip. Washington, D.C., was overflowing by the time Queen Mother arrived at the National Mall on October 16, 1995, for the Nation of Islam–led Million Man March. Months of organizing and backroom brokering had given way to an auspicious event, during which hordes of Black men engulfed monuments commemorating a freedom they had never truly felt. The crowd included celebrities and common folk alike: Cornel West, Will Smith, Stevie Wonder, and others came by the busload, as did Black men and boys from colleges, churches, and community centers from across the country.

"Good morning, brother. Thank you for coming," NOI members said amid backslapping hugs as participants trickled onto the Mall before sunrise.[58] By midday, the crowd had swelled to the biggest gathering of Black men the country had ever seen. Hidden from view were complaints from Black women organizers in the National Council of Negro Women, Bethune's group that Moore had joined more than fifty years before, who had helped organize the event yet received no recognition. Also buried under the spectacle: the battle between Farrakhan and D.C. mayor Marion Barry's wife, Cora Barry, over who would lead voter registration efforts before and during the march.[59]

But on that cool October morning, when Delois Blakely wheeled Moore onto the stage, all Queen Mother could see was a sea of Black men that would have made Garvey proud. At 6:00 a.m., the Muslim call to prayer began, followed by calls to action, greetings from across the African Diaspora, and performances by dancers, poets, and singers. The subsequent speeches were powerful, but the sound system was not. Men across the Mall strained to hear speakers like NAACP leader Ben Chavis or the Million Man March chorus. Fathers hoisted their sons on their shoulders to help them get a glimpse of Marion Barry, Reverend Jeremiah Wright, and Jesse Jackson. The program went on for hours, but few dared leave as the day wore on. They were waiting for one man only: Louis Farrakhan.

But first: the "Mothers in the Struggle."[60]

"Rosa! Rosa!" Her name echoed through the National Mall as the civil rights icon walked to the podium. Standing amid a sea of young Black men in suits, Rosa Parks looked both diminutive and different from the woman whom many had first encountered in a buttoned-up blouse, skirt, and glasses during the Montgomery Bus Boycott. Now eighty-two, she sported a baggy shirt and pants, a black hat with FREEDOM stitched across it in white block letters, and a kente cloth—the traditional handwoven Ghanaian scarf that had become a fashionable symbol of Afrocentric politics in the 1990s.

"I am very happy to be here," Parks offered in her drawl. "I honor my late husband, Raymond Parks, other freedom fighters, men of good will who could not be here. I am also honored that young men respect me and invited me as an elder."

"I am here because you are here," Dorothy Height, leader of the National Council of Negro Women, said when she took the podium next. Clad in her signature purple dress and church hat and introduced to the audience as "one of the treasures of our family," Height had earned one of the few coveted spots for women on the program due to her tireless work on behalf of promoting Black education and voter registration.

Height reminded the men of the contributions Black women had made to the struggle while praising their efforts to fight the most derelict stereotypes about them. Both Parks and Height had been at the last great gathering on the Mall: the 1963 March on Washington, where, as Height noted, no women made major speeches. Surely the irony was not lost on her as she stood at the microphone to speak at a gathering dedicated to Black men almost three decades later.[61]

"Alright now, brothers...I need you to just step back and be very quiet," the emcee announced. "We're gonna bring to the microphone a sister, an elder who is dear to us all. Would you welcome Queen Mother Moore." The clump of men onstage parted to reveal her. Hunched in her wheelchair, unmistakable in her gold-and-black headdress and matching jewelry, it was Queen Mother's turn to take the stage. Amid murmurs from the restless crowd, Moore began to speak. But her voice was too weak. Delois Blakely stepped up on her mentor's behalf. Taking Moore's papers into her own hands, Blakely leaned down to the microphone to recite Queen Mother's remarks.

"My sons and grandsons," she began in her best, booming impression of her mentor and friend. "I am your mother and your grandmother in the liberation struggle of all African people. I am ninety-seven years old, and I have been in this struggle for all of my people for seventy-five years. Struggle is my life."

Blakely continued, offering one last benediction from the woman who had seen it all. She called on the crowd to "bond in love for each other and to unify a force that will mend and heal our broken families." "Straighten out your backs and stand on your feet with the strong determination to reclaim your rightful place in this world in righteousness and divine order," she told the men in her midst. After a short pause, she concluded: "I was born in a world full of bigotry and hate. A world that raped, lynched, and murdered the spirit and bodies of many Black men, women, and children. My sons, I ask you to remember: Reparations! Reparations! Reparations! My sons, bond together, straighten out your backs. Up, you mighty people! You can conquer what you will."

Blakely sent Garvey's age-old mantra soaring through the speakers before delivering Moore's final line: "One God, One Aim, One Destiny."[62] Moore was too weak to raise her arm as the crowd clapped for her. Instead, Blakely lifted it up herself and swirled a flourish of valediction: one final, regal wave from Black America's Queen Mother.

After the march, Moore returned to her nursing home on the edge of Harlem. These days, she only ever left to attend ceremonies around the city, where Blakely would push her in front of an adoring crowd for a quick wave. If she was feeling good that day, she might offer a few words. But her ears perked up when she heard Blakely had invited Winnie Mandela back to Harlem.[63] Queen Mother had one last request for her most loyal subject: she wanted to pass her title on to the South African leader before it was too late.

On April 18, 1996, men from the NOI hustled Winnie Mandela and Moore into the Victoria Theater on 125th Street. For an impromptu event, it was well attended. A sea of local teachers and elders were there, as well as Stokely Carmichael, who now went by Kwame Ture. A handful of UN representatives made their way uptown, as did ambassadors from Ghana, South Africa, Sierra Leone, and Nigeria, who happened to be in the city. Everyday Harlemites wanted a chance to witness the meeting of the two movement mothers, too. A crowd formed outside the door as the dignitaries made their way into the event.

The ceremony was short and sweet. Everyone took their seats in Harlem's lesser-known theater as a Yoruba priest opened the ceremony, offering a libation and a blessing to all in attendance. The two leaders sat together, their colorful clothing peeking out above the circle of NOI security members that surrounded them to keep the throng of spectators at bay. Knowing her body was giving out on her, as Blakely told reporters, Queen Mother Moore "desperately wanted to make this gesture now." Moore was lucid but used a wheelchair and was physically weak. But some were equally concerned about Winnie Mandela, who had been rushed to Harlem Hospital the night before; her supporters were worried about her heart. They offered prayers for the South African hero before NOI security stepped aside. Then a circle of women formed around "Mandela as she embraced Queen Mother Moore in a passing on ceremony." And with that, the Queen Mother of Harlem had passed on her title to a freedom fighter who was well worth the honor. The festivities ended as quickly as they had begun, with NOI leaders hustling both Queen Mothers—old and new—out the side door.[64]

Their timing couldn't have been more apt. Moore was clearly on the decline. The following February, she suffered another stroke. At the intensive care unit at St. Luke's Hospital in upper Manhattan, her visitor list was surprisingly spartan given how decorated an activist she was. Moore could have counted on one regal hand the number of visitors—like Asantewaa Gail Harris, a local Black activist and wellness worker—who came to see her.

Once released, Moore relocated to Linroc Nursing Home in Brooklyn, a facility that could better accommodate her post-stroke health challenges.[65] She lived out the last few weeks of her life there with little more than a framed photo of Marcus Garvey and article clippings about her activist career keeping vigil over her.

It's impossible to know what Moore felt as she lay there, facing her own death. "If I die in Atlanta my work shall then only begin, but I shall live, in the physical or spiritual to see the day of Africa's glory," her idol Garvey once wrote from his Georgia jail cell in 1925. "Look for me in the whirlwind or the storm, look for me all around you, for with God's grace, I shall come and bring with me countless millions of black slaves who have died in America and the West Indies and the millions in Africa to aid you in the fight for Liberty, Freedom, and Life."[66] It's nice to imagine that she was lucid enough to contemplate her idol's words as she prepared to enter the storm herself.

Queen Mother Audley Moore—Garveyite, near-century-long champion of the Black millions in Africa, the West Indies, and America, and indefatigable supporter of Black people's right to self-determination—died on May 2, 1997.[67]

———

Seven days later, it looked as though the skies might open up as Tom Warner and his children donned their black and steadied themselves for the long day ahead. As their limousine wound its way through Harlem on May 9, they were stunned to see throngs of people lining the streets for blocks, jockeying to reach the sidewalk's edge. When the car crept to a stop, the quiet, somber air inside the car gave way to the roar of the crowd outside, trying to catch a glimpse of the dignitaries, politicians, and poets mourning Queen Mother. The Nation of Islam security force had to clear a path for the grief-stricken family to step out of the car.[68]

Ethiopian Coptic Church members greeted them when they arrived. Harkening back to Moore's funeral march for her spiritual son Malcolm some thirty-one years earlier, supporters and drummers led Moore's family members and mourners as they stoically walked the few blocks toward Harlem's Mount Olivet Baptist Church.[69]

It was already packed when they arrived. Professors, actresses, activists, African priests, poets, and politicians came en masse to mourn the mother of the movement. They clasped one another's hands and passed around tissues under a sea of red, black, and green flags rippling from the balconies.

"Queen Mother lived her life dedicated to the freedom of her people," Louis Farrakhan said as he began the hours-long homegoing celebration. "She lived her life for those who did not know that she lived.... She is the eternal mother of the historical struggle, so let the body rest from that labor.... For when we mention Sojourner Truth, Mary McLeod Bethune, Fannie Lou Hamer, Mary, Moses, Jesus and Muhammad," went the NOI leader's solemn conclusion, "Queen Mother Moore will be mentioned," too.[70] Farrakhan then solemnly walked off the stage, stooped down in front of Moore's family, and wiped away the tear streaming down young Christine's cheek.[71]

"She didn't bake cakes, she made gumbo—Louisiana style," the younger Audley said in a stirring speech. "She didn't take us on trips to the zoo, instead she took us to Africa.... When we were young everyone else was going to the museum, our grandmother took us to the U.N." And Moore was never afraid of "a good old fashion motherly spanking," her other grandchildren recalled, choosing to remember the matriarch they knew just as much as the freedom fighter she had been.

Poet Sonia Sanchez—one of the few women to speak that day—praised Moore for "working from morning to midnight [for] a new and better country." Another mourner read a poem of Moore's called "The Watchman," a lyrical account of watching and waiting for the day reparations would come.[72]

"Don't trust a tree by the bark it wears, trust it by the fruit that it bears," Al Sharpton counseled as he eulogized his friend and mentor. "For 98 years she bore great fruit—all over the Diaspora the seeds are planted.... So rest now, Queen Mother," Sharpton offered by way of a final message to the departed movement legend. "Thank you for being the Queen of all the Mothers."

Somber music played as six pallbearers—some in black suits, others in African garb—carried Moore out of the church and into the hearse that would take her out of Harlem one last time. Her funeral procession headed to Ferncliff Cemetery in Hartsdale, New York, to lower Moore into her final resting place, in the same hallowed ground as her friend and fellow icon Malcolm X.[73]

"Many people are discouraged these days," a young organizer told Moore when they sat down for what would be one of her last interviews. "They do not know where to go from here."[74]

In life, Moore had always looked to the past for strength to continue her fight. And though she's been gone for decades now, it's not hard to imagine what she might say today. The wily Queen Mother would likely point to her near century of struggle as proof that against all odds we must remain doggedly committed to the freedom dreams that inspire us the most, no matter how out of reach they may seem.

At times, the life of an activist can look like barely organized chaos—a series of small fights, some wins and others losses, and a hope that when it's all over, it amounts to some kind of a better world. Indeed, it's only when you take a step back and look at Audley Moore's life in its entirety that her rich mosaic of activism—and its global impact—comes into focus.

Though she is gone, her indomitable spirit lives on in the whirlwind of Black life and thought around us. Traces of her booming voice echo with demands to "run them out" as Black parents fight for a say in their children's schooling today; her whispers of "keep on, keep on, we've got to win" are in the wind as reparations campaigns across the country gain steam.

We see her nation-building schemas everywhere—in the Saturday morning programs Black communities create to counter the harmful stereotypes they endure, in the way we take care of one another when the state has failed us, through GoFundMe campaigns, donations, and myriad other forms of mutual aid. We even conjure up her visions of a free and sovereign Black nation-state, however far-fetched, when we cross our arms across our chests and utter "Wakanda Forever."

Still, other parts of Moore's message have found less purchase. Queen Mother Moore believed there could be no true voting rights until Black folk decided whether we really want to be part of the American polity. There could be no "Africa for the Africans" if Black Americans didn't first fight to rip neocolonialism up from its foundations. And there could be no full integration without reparations—no true self-determination until Black people had built a nation of their own, for themselves. Queen Mother Moore spent her life calling out the contradictions inherent in Black American citizenship and cajoling Black people, and all Americans, for that matter, to focus their attention on building a new world rather than trying to reseal the cracks in the foundation of American democracy.

As we face what some now call a Third Reconstruction—an ongoing period of racial struggle defined by Barack Obama's presidency and the Black Lives Matter Movement as much as by the racial violence and virulent anti-Black laws that have followed—Queen Mother Moore's life is an inciting invitation to all of us to rethink our vision for America.[75] To ask ourselves: What exactly are we reconstructing? Why are we rehabilitating it? And are the former iterations of the nation-state really worth returning to? It's not easy to answer these questions and even harder to face our complicity in the state of the world today. But Queen Mother Moore would surely tell us, in her sharp-witted way, that facing the past is the only way to imagine a different future.

"In spite of the weaknesses" in the movement, "and there is much of that," Moore told the interviewer in response to their comment about the palpable despair many felt, "you have brothers and sisters that are striving, who are holding on, who are developing themselves the best way they can." No matter how bleak the circumstances, Moore always believed that her children and grandchildren, that you and I, were worth fighting for. And she, in turn, only ever hoped to be worthy of the fight. "Yes, I have done my best to measure up," she offered as a parting word. "I have done my best."[76]

She did indeed. The next century of striving is up to us.

Acknowledgments

I first began dreaming of writing about Moore in 2008. I was a graduate student who had just dipped her toes into the waters of academia, and I was stunned to discover that, amid the vast scholarship on Black women, virtually no work existed on Moore. When I raised the possibility of writing about her, many cautioned against it, fearing there was not "enough" material for a viable project. Reluctantly, I set aside the idea of a book on Moore and pursued "safer" intellectual endeavors. But the idea of writing *Queen Mother* still swam around in my mind for years. Ten years later, I decided to dive in once more. This time buoyed by a community of thinkers, archivists, friends, family, and loved ones without whom Moore's story might never have surfaced.

Her son, Tom Warner, and his wife, Nikena, welcomed me into their home and have generously shared their memories and love of Queen Mother Moore with me over the years. Moore's grandchildren—Audley, Christine, and Judy—sometimes joined us around the kitchen table, where we created lasting memories listening to old recordings of their grandmother singing and mining through what few artifacts they had of her life. Our relationship has grown over the years, mainly during our multiple trips to Moore's hometown of New Iberia, where we celebrated the installation of a historical marker to honor her life. During the time that it has taken to complete this book, we all have grown to appreciate Queen Mother Moore and one another even more. Thank you to the entire Warner family for sharing her with me and allowing me to share Moore's life with the world.

I am indebted to a range of wonderful researchers and archivists who helped locate many of Moore's artifacts. These include collectors and archivists at the Schomburg Center for Research on Black Culture, the Black Cultural Archive, the Archdiocese of New Orleans, the Stuart A. Rose Library, the Tamiment Library, and many others who were especially helpful during the COVID-19 pandemic. I was also able to uncover pieces of Moore's life thanks to the many community collectors who carefully cared for her ideas and artifacts—recognizing their significance even when others didn't. I'd like to thank Erik McDuffie, Emily Moore, Earl Pinto, Muhammad Ahmad, and Roderick Jenkins for opening their personal collections to me. Thank you to Sonia Sanchez, Jimmy Garrett, Akinyele Umoja, Charles Turner, Conrad Warren, Delois Blakely, Earl Pinto, Hanif Khalifah, Jenna Knights, John Bracey, Marylin Nance, Nkrumah Olinga, Playthell Benjamin, Val Gray Ward, Shafeah M'Balia, Saladin Muhammad, Emily Moore, Roderick Jenkins, Daedria Farmer-Pallemann, Muhammad Ahmad, Komozi Woodard, Asantewaa Gail Harris, and many others I met along the way for sharing their memories of Moore.

A remarkable cohort of researchers across multiple universities contributed their time and talents to this book. They include Mirielle Wright, Jordan Villegas, and Kyrah March, who were vital to the beginning stages of this project. Signe Fourmy, Magdalena Augustine, Sarah Porter, and Jon Buchleiter, along with Mary Elizabeth Marquardt, mined records, located long-lost files, sorted through endless documents, and went on fact-finding missions to make this book possible.

Uncovering a life of this length and magnitude requires time and space to think. Several granting agencies afforded me the time to dig into this work, including the National Endowment for the Humanities, the Radcliffe Institute for Advanced Study, the Gilder Lehrman Institute, and the New Orleans Center for the Gulf South at Tulane University. I am also indebted to the Whiting Foundation's Creative Nonfiction Grant for helping to get this project over the finish line.

This book would not have been possible without a slew of intellectual interlocutors who engaged in thoughtful dialogue with me about Moore for years. They include Russell Rickford, Ed Onaci, Quito Swan, Garrett Felber, Charisse Burden-Stelly, Minkah Makalani, and others who generously shared their thoughts and resources about Moore. I am also grateful to the "Masterminds" group and myriad other thinkers and scholars who read drafts, shared their research, and pondered questions about the authenticity and intellectual influence of Moore's life. I have been very fortunate to think alongside other Black women writing about Black women's lives, loves, and labors. I am especially grateful to our Black Women's Biography Collective for their support and guidance as I completed this book and to my co-organizer and dreamer Tanisha Ford, a brilliant life writer in her own right. A host of scholars, including Daina Ramey Berry, Talitha LeFlouria, Anastasia Curwood, Brooke Blower, Robyn Spencer, Rhonda Williams, Donna Murch, Keisha Blain, and Jeanne Theoharis, supported this book in countless ways. It's been a joy to be on this journey with each of you.

I am particularly blessed that some of my closest friends are also stellar scholars. I am grateful to members of the Austin, Texas, "Turn Up Crew": Monica Jimenez, Ana Schwartz, Amira Rose Davis, Chelsi West-Ohueri, Ashley Coleman Taylor, Bedour Alagraa, Nicole Borrows, Marisol LeBrón, Snehal Patel, Khytie Brown, and Pavithra Vasudevan. Your community and counsel made the process of weaving Moore's life together feel possible.

I am eternally grateful to Monica Huerta, who for nearly ten years and through multiple writing projects and phases of life has regularly greeted me online most mornings to write, with care, encouragement, and a timely GIF to begin the day. Ashanté Reese is the best team player I have ever met. She not only sees the good and potential in people everywhere but also helps people see it in themselves. Her daily check-ins, reminders to take care of myself, and life-giving strategy sessions helped create the best version of this book and myself. I am also thankful to Roger Reeves, who believed I could be a different kind of writer and storyteller long before I could see this in myself.

I am deeply appreciative of my agent, Eric Simonoff, for seeing the potential of this book and for connecting me to my amazing team at Pantheon: Lisa Lucas, Zach Phillips, and Beatrice Chaudoin in editorial, Ciara Tomlinson in publicity and Bianca Ducasse in marketing, Kathleen Cook in production editorial, and Janet Hansen for the beautiful cover. I also want to thank Grey Osterud, Brandon Proia, and Kristin Thiel for their incredible attention to detail and support of the earliest iterations of *Queen Mother,* as well as Kima Jones and Gretchen Gary for helping this book shine once it was out in the world. These folks took my very rough draft and a dream for what this book could be and made it into a beautiful reality.

"When is the next book party?" my friends of more than twenty years ask whenever we get together. Every author should be fortunate enough to have friends like Bridget Billups, Brandy Canady, April Farley, Jokae Ingram, Amissa Miller, Linda Chavers, Peter Geller, and Tonya Taylor, who are always ready to celebrate you when you cross the finish line. Such support reminds you that there is a light at the end of the tunnel and that your friends will be there to celebrate you no matter how long it takes to get there.

My parents were the first history teachers and archivists I encountered. With a dogged persistence that rivaled Queen Mother's, my mother, Madeline Farmer, enthusiastically shared the stories of Black women—past and present—with me as I was growing up in Nashville, Tennessee, while also fighting to make history on her own. The first time I ever had to do historical research, my father, Absolom Farmer, took me to the Fisk University archives. Little did he know that this experience planted the seed for the central idea that undergirds this book: Black women's archives *do* exist everywhere—you just have to know where and how to look for them. He, along with my sister and brother-in-law, Sylvia and Keith Wright, and my niece Madeline Wright, have not only kept my mother's memory alive; they have also created a loving space from which to teach and write Black women's history for years. It has been nothing less than life-sustaining.

Ade Adamson has lived with Queen Mother Moore as long as I have. We joined our lives together around the time that I became enamored with writing about Moore. To find someone who takes your work seriously enough to regularly and rigorously engage with it is a treat. To find it in someone you love deeply is a godsend. Ade has given me the space—both literally and figuratively—to help this book take shape, doing everything from taking over our shared childcare responsibilities to poring over drafts. There is no other way to say it: this book would simply not have been possible without him.

Finally, I became a mother while writing *Queen Mother,* and it changed my relationship to work and the world. My daughter, Ella, is a rainbow baby, and she has connected me to this history in a way that books and artifacts never could. She has helped me understand Moore's desperate desire for a new world and the choices she made so that "her children," or all Black people, might see it one day. I hope that when she is old enough to pick up *Queen Mother,* Ella will take heart in the fact that there are people all around her who are fighting for a better world every day. But above all, I hope that she will see this book as a delicious invitation to join them.

Notes

Key to Abbreviations

AAC Alli Aweusi Collection, Briscoe Center

AM-BWOHP Interview with Audley Moore, Schlesinger Library

AM-Naison Audley Moore, Interview by Mark Naison, Oral History of the American Left, Tamiment Library

AM-Prago Audley Moore, Interview by Ruth Prago, Oral History of the American Left, Tamiment Library

APM American People's Mobilization Collected Records, Swarthmore College

BP Papers of Amiri Baraka, Gale Primary Sources Unbound

BARTS Collection of Material Relating to the Black Arts Repertory Theatre & School, Beinecke Library

BEC Babette Edwards Collection, Schomburg Center

CBR Charles B. Roussève Papers, Amistad Research Center

CFP Campbell Family Papers, Wilson Library, University of North Carolina at Chapel Hill

CPUSA Papers Communist Party of the United States of America Papers, Tamiment Library

CRC Civil Rights Congress Records, Schomburg Center

IPCC Iberia Parish County, La., Clerk Office

JFK Papers of John F. Kennedy, Kennedy Presidential Library

JHC John Henrik Clarke Papers, Schomburg Center

JRC John E. Rousseau Collection, Amistad Research Center

KLR Kim Lacy Rogers Collection, Amistad Research Center

LAMR Louis A. Martinet Records, Orleans Parish Clerk of Court

LNP Larry Neal Papers, Schomburg Center

LTP Louise Thompson Patterson Papers, Rose Library, Emory University

MOSP Muriel S. and Otto P. Snowden Papers, Northeastern University

MXC Malcolm X Collection, Schomburg Center

NAAC Newark African Americans Collections, Charles F. Cummings New Jersey Information Center

NASSC National Association of Supplementary Schools Collection, Padmore Institute

NNC National Negro Congress Records, Schomburg Center

NOPVR New Orleans Parish Vital
  Records
OAAU Organization of Afro-American
  Unity Collection, Schomburg Center
PJP Philip J. Jaffe Papers, Rose Library
PWP Preston Wilcox Papers,
  Schomburg Center
RAM Papers Papers of the
  Revolutionary Action Movement,
  ProQuest History Vault
RBP Robert S. Browne Papers,
  Schomburg Center
RFW Robert F. Williams Papers,
  ProQuest History Vault
RFW-Bentley Robert F. Williams
  Papers, Bentley Historical Library
RNA-MDAH Republic of New Africa
  Collection, Mississippi Department of
  Archives and History
RNAWC Records of the National
  Association of Women's Clubs,
  Microfilm

RPP Rosa Parks Papers, Library of
  Congress
6PAC Records Sixth Pan-African
  Congress Records, Moorland-
  Spingarn Research Center
SKR St. Katharine's Church Records,
  Archdiocese of New Orleans Archives
  and Records
SPA Socialist Party of America Papers,
  ProQuest History Vault
SPC Social Protest Collection, Bancroft
  Library
TDR Theodore Draper Research Files,
  Rose Library
TW-Payne Thomas O. Warner,
  Oral History, Bronx County
  Archives
UNIA-EMORY Universal Negro
  Improvement Association Records,
  Rose Library
VHP Vincent Harding Papers, Rose
  Library

Introduction

1. "Lanker Salutes 'Black Women Who
   Changed America,'" *Chicago Tribune,*
   Aug. 23, 1991, N53–54; "Black
   Women Share Tears and Laughter,"
   The News Journal (Wilmington),
   Feb. 21, 1989, 29.
2. Hurston, *Their Eyes Were Watching
   God,* 20.
3. Lanker, preface to *I Dream a World,* 10.
4. "Queen Mother Audley Moore," in
   Lanker, *I Dream a World,* 102.
5. Warner family, interview by author;
   Sonia Sanchez, interview by author;
   Delois Blakely, correspondence with
   author.
6. "Queen Mother Audley Moore," 103.
7. Joseph, "Black Power Movement," 752.
8. Blakely, "40 Acres and a Mule," 131.
9. Ford, *Liberated Threads,* 4.

10. Moore and others recall her
    mentorship of Malcolm. AM-
    BWOHP, 35; Playthell Benjamin,
    phone conversation with author;
    Muhammad Ahmad, interview
    by author. Moore's New Orleans
    address also appears in Malcolm X's
    address book. reel 1, box 1, MXC.
11. Blouin and Rosenberg, *Processing the
    Past,* 7, 16–17.
12. Farmer, "Disorderly Distribution," 6.
13. Notable exceptions include
    McDuffie, "'I Wanted a Communist
    Philosophy'"; Blain, "'To Keep Alive
    the Teaching of Garvey and the Work
    of the UNIA'"; Harley, "'I Don't Pay
    Those Borders No Mind at All.'"
14. Sawyer, *Black Minded,* 10–13, 17. Moore
    was not alone in this approach; for

more on how Black women operated as organic intellectuals, see Taylor, "Street Strollers."

15. Naison, *Communists in Harlem During the Depression,* 72.
16. AM-BWOHP, 16.

Chapter 1: MY PEOPLE HAD PRIDE IN THEMSELVES

1. AM-BWOHP, 7; "Portrait of a Revolutionary," *Black American* 22, no. 1, Queen Mother Moore Vertical File; "Queen Mother Moore as the Struggle Intensifies," *Black News,* Oct. 1, 1978, 14.
2. Certificate of Baptism, Audley Moore, St. Peter's Catholic Church, vol. 6, p. 324, no. 237, New Iberia, La.
3. No formal birth record for St. Cyr exists. However, the ages listed on his multiple marriage licenses put his birth date between 1853 and 1855 and list his parents as Anderson and Arsene Moore. Marriage Certificate, St. Cyr Moore and Rose Edgar, April 18, 1892, St. John the Evangelist Catholic Church, vol. 1, p. 105, no. 209, Jeanerette, La.; Marriage Certificate, St. Cyr Moore and Ella Johnson, June 23, 1897, NOPVR.
4. Bernard, *Teche,* 4.
5. Follett, *Sugar Masters,* 24–25, 37.
6. AM-BWOHP, 4.
7. Follett, *Sugar Masters,* 180–82.
8. Coen, *Exploring Cajun Country,* 59–60; Bonin, *Where the Bayou Runs Straight,* 35.
9. Richardson, "Teche Country Fifty Years Ago."
10. Nystrom, *New Orleans After the Civil War,* 7.
11. Winters, *Civil War in Louisiana,* 14–20; Bonin, *Where the Bayou Runs Straight,* 72.
12. Hebert and Perrin, *Iberia Parish,* 8.
13. Bonin, *Where the Bayou Runs Straight,* 165–67.

14. Hollandsworth, *Pretense of Glory,* 116.
15. For more on these refugee or contraband camps, see Manning, *Troubled Refuge.*
16. Bonin, *Where the Bayou Runs Straight,* 76–84.
17. For more on Louisiana's bureau, see Conway, *Freedman of Louisiana.*
18. England, "Historical Overview of Afro-Americans in New Iberia," 433, 442.
19. Bryant, "Reminiscences of the '60s and '70s," 171.
20. Conrad, *New Iberia,* 289–90. Although McIlhenny is credited with developing Tabasco, there is some question as to whether he was the creator of the pepper sauce. He certainly conferred with ex-slaves on how to make the mixture. Nevertheless, it became the city's claim to fame. Rothfeder, *McIlhenny's Gold,* 3–4.
21. Conrad, *New Iberia,* 9.
22. Vandal, "Politics and Violence in Bourbon Louisiana," 28.
23. For a national overview of this era in American history, see Foner, *Short History of Reconstruction.*
24. Thompson, *Exiles at Home,* 14–15.
25. AM-BWOHP, 4.
26. There are multiple and, at times, conflicting reports about the office St. Cyr Moore held in New Iberia. Audley Moore claims he was a deputy sheriff. However, newspaper reports list him as a constable. See AM-BWOHP, 1; "Audley Moore,

Born in Poverty, Raised in Toil, and Steeled in Struggle, Typified Delegates to Parlay on Jobs for Negro Women," *Daily Worker,* June 30, 1941, 3; "First City Criminal Court," *Times-Picayune,* Jan. 3, 1900, 6.

27. The exact date of Rebecca and St. Cyr's marriage is difficult to ascertain. However, they were listed as married on the 1880 census. St. Cyr Moore, 1880 Federal Census, Iberia Parish, Louisiana, sheet 38.

28. Birth of Henry Junior Moore, March 4, 1880, vol. 1, p. 21, no. 100; Birth of George Clarence Moore, July 31, 1889, vol. 1, p. 47, no. 221, St. John the Evangelist Church, Jeanerette, La. Also see "Succession of St. Cyr Moore and Rebecca Kelley Moore," IPCC.

29. For an overview of Rebecca and St. Cyr's neighborhood, see the 1880 Federal Census, Iberia Parish, Louisiana, sheet 26.

30. Christensen, "1868 St. Landry Massacre," 5–6.

31. Sandoz, "Brief History of St. Landry Parish," 226–27.

32. Sandoz, "Brief History of St. Landry Parish," 228. Pelagie Johnson, 1870 Federal Census, St. Martin Parish, Louisiana, sheet 51; Honora Johnson, 1880 Federal Census, Iberia Parish, Louisiana, sheet 19.

33. Christensen, "1868 St. Landry Massacre," 6.

34. Brasseaux, "Creoles of Color in Louisiana's Bayou," 67–69.

35. Brasseaux, "Creoles of Color in Louisiana's Bayou," 67–69.

36. Brasseaux, "Creoles of Color in Louisiana's Bayou," 72–74.

37. Christensen, "1868 St. Landry Massacre," 229.

38. 08-ORAL-30-8-Side-01, Queen Mother Moore Tapes.

39. Brasseaux, Fontenot, and Oubre, *Creoles of Color in the Bayou Country,* 95–96.

40. Secession Record, Estate of Alphonse Dubourdieu, Oct. 5, 1868, St. Landry Parish Clerk of Court, Opelousas, La.; Death Certificate, Alphonsine Springfield, Texas, Orange County, No. 507, July 10, 1935, Texas Death Index, 1903–2000.

41. Christensen, "1868 St. Landry Massacre," 40–41.

42. Christensen, "1868 St. Landry Massacre," 53, 55; Boissoneault, "Deadliest Massacre in Reconstruction-Era Louisiana Happened 150 Years Ago"; DeLatte, "St. Landry Riot."

43. Secession Record, Estate of Alphonse Dubourdieu.

44. For evidence of Honora's first set of children residing with Phillip and Pelagie Johnson, see 1870 Federal Census, St. Martin Parish, Louisiana, sheet 51.

45. Phillip Johnson v. Oneziphore Delahoussaye Jr., No. 6608, Sept. 7, 1871, St. Martin Parish Clerk Office, St. Martinville, La.

46. AM-BWOHP, 5; "Audley Moore, Born in Poverty."

47. For Ella's approximate birth date, see Ella Johnson 1880 U.S. Federal Census, Iberia Parish, Louisiana, sheet 36; 1900 Federal Census, New Orleans, Louisiana, sheet 11.

48. Marriage Certificate, Honora Johnson and William Henry, St. Peter's Catholic Church, Dec. 20, 1878, vol. 3, p. 80, no. 303, New Iberia, La.

49. William Henry, 1880 Federal Census, Iberia Parish, Louisiana, sheet 19.

50. See, for example, Mortgage Bank Sale from John M. Hensham to William Henry, Jan. 13, 1880, IPCC.

51. Land Sale, Edgar Cockson to St. Cyr Moore, Jan. 29, 1880, IPCC.

52. See, for example, Land Sale, Edgar Cockson to St. Cyr Moore, Jan. 29, 1880; Land Sale, W. J. Hudson to St. Cyr Moore, March 14, 1884; Land Sale, A. L. Monnot to St. Cyr Moore, March 27, 1890, IPCC.

53. See, for example, Mortgage of Property, St. Cyr Moore to Louis Romagosa, Nov. 18, 1884; Mortgage of Property, St. Cyr Moore to John C. Bussey, Feb. 3, 1887; Mortgage of Property, St. Cyr Moore to Felix Loeb Brothers, March 18, 1889; Lease of Property, William Roberson to St. Cyr Moore, Oct. 11, 1886, IPCC.

54. Coldon J. Darce, "A True Story of Jeanerette," *Attakapas Gazette* 13, no. 3 (1978): 137.

55. Bonin, *Where the Bayou Runs Straight*, 145.

56. For more on the sugar mills and New Iberia writ large, see Hebert and Perrin, *Iberia Parish*.

57. Bonin, *Where the Bayou Runs Straight*, 145, 273.

58. For an overview of Black advancement during Radical Reconstruction, see Foner, *Reconstruction*.

59. For more on the backlash against Black folk during and after Reconstruction, see Litwack, *Been in the Storm So Long;* Williams, *I Saw Death Coming;* Sinha, *Rise and Fall of the Second Republic*.

60. Conrad, *New Iberia*, 146.

61. "The Iberia Outrages," *Weekly Pelican,* Feb. 2, 1889, 1, 3; "Black Men Shot Down," *Summit County Beacon,* Feb. 13, 1889, 5; "The Irrepressible Conflict," *Kingston Daily Freeman,* May 6, 1889, 2; "Frightened Negroes: Bad Louisiana Negroes Made to Leave by White Citizens," *Chattanooga Daily Times,* Jan. 28, 1889, 1.

62. Death Certificate, Rebecca Keller, Aug. 5, 1890, St. John the Evangelist Church, vol. 1, p. 61, no. 266, Jeanerette, La.

63. Marriage License of St. Cyr Moore and Rose Edgar, St. John the Evangelist Church, vol. 1, p. 105, no. 207, Jeanerette, La.; AM-BWOHP, 4.

64. 08-ORAL-30-8-Side-01, Queen Mother Moore Tapes; AM-BWOHP, 4.

65. 08-ORAL-30-8-Side-01, Queen Mother Moore Tapes.

66. "Police Board," *Times-Democrat,* Aug. 27, 1896, 2; city directories list Cenance's residence in New Orleans and occupation as a police officer. See, for example, U.S. City Directory 1891, Louisiana, New Orleans, 226.

67. "Police Board."

68. AM-BWOHP, 5.

69. St. Cyr Moore v. Rose Edgar, His Wife, State of Louisiana, City of New Orleans Civil District Court, Case No. 52413, Feb. 15, 1897, New Orleans Public Library.

70. Marriage License of Evelina Dubourdieu and Baptiste Senegal, St. John the Evangelist Church, vol. 1, p. 67, no. 133, New Iberia, La.

71. Marriage Certificate, J. Manuel Springfield and Alphonsine Diebordier [*sic*], March 7, 1887, St. Peter's Catholic Church, vol. 3, p. 260, no. 2, New Iberia, La. The 1900 and 1910 census list John Springfield as a commercial traveler and picture agent, respectively. 1900 U.S. Federal Census, Iberia Parish, Louisiana,

sheet 30; 1910 Federal Census,
New Orleans, Louisiana, sheet 20.

72. See, for example, Mortgage of
Property, John M. Springfield to

William Henry, Sept. 21, 1896,
IPCC.

73. Land Sale, J. M. Springfield to Ella
Johnson, Nov. 10, 1896, IPCC.

Chapter 2: LITTLE BOURGEOIS STINKER

1. Marriage Certificate, St. Cyr Moore
and Ella M. Johnson, June 22, 1897,
New Orleans Parish Record of Bills,
Marriages, and Deaths. New Orleans
Public Library.

2. Photograph of Ella Johnson, in
author's possession; AM-BWOHP, 4.

3. Certificate of Baptism, Audley
Moore.

4. Certificate of Baptism, Charles
St. Cyr Moore, Nov. 14, 1899; Death
Sacrament, Charles St. Cyr Moore,
June 17, 1900, SKR.

5. Certificate of Baptism, Loretta A.
Moore, June 28, 1902, SKR. This
certificate lists Loretta's birth date as
June 10, 1902; Certificate of Baptism,
Eloise Agnes Moore, April 14, 1901,
SKR. This certificate lists Eloise's
birth date as March 20, 1901.

6. St. Cyr Moore, 1900 Federal Census,
New Orleans, Louisiana, sheet 11.

7. Medley, *Black Life in New Orleans,*
88–90.

8. Campanella, "Ethnic Geography
of New Orleans," 709; Ross, *Great
New Orleans Kidnapping Case,* 9, 144.
Howard Street became LaSalle
Street in 1924. For occupants of
the Moore household in 1900 New
Orleans, see St. Cyr Moore, 1900
Federal Census, New Orleans,
Louisiana, sheet 11.

9. Campanella, *Bienville's Dilemma,*
325–26.

10. Ross, *Great New Orleans Kidnapping
Case,* 6.

11. Nystrom, *New Orleans After the Civil
War,* 82–87.

12. Ross, *Great New Orleans Kidnapping
Case,* 11, 16–17.

13. Dray, *Capitol Men,* 111–14; Mitchell,
"Oscar James Dunn," 101–2.

14. Campbell to his daughter Katherine,
April 9, 1871, box 1, folder 11, CFP.

15. Nystrom, *New Orleans After the Civil
War,* 215.

16. For more on the Separate Car Act,
see Medley, *We as Freemen.*

17. Citizen's Committee, "The Violation
of a Constitutional Right," box 1,
folder 12, CBR.

18. AM-Naison.

19. For examples of their collective
property holdings in New Iberia, see
Land Sale, Mrs. William Henry to
Ella M. Johnson, Aug. 14, 1899, IPCC.

20. AM-Naison.

21. Campanella, *Lost New Orleans,* 23;
AM-BWOHP, 5.

22. AM-BWOHP, 14.

23. AM-BWOHP, 14.

24. "Constitution and By-Laws of Les
Jeunes Amis: Société de Bienfaissance
Mutuelle," box 3, folder 4, CBR.
For more information on Black
benevolent societies in New Orleans
and the United States writ large,
see Harris, "Early Black Benevolent
Societies"; Jacobs, "Benevolent
Societies of New Orleans Blacks
During the Late Nineteenth and
Early Twentieth Centuries."

25. "Amended Charter of the Jeunes

Amis Benevolent Association of New Orleans, LA," Nov. 23, 1899, vol. 3, act 38, 1899, LAMR; Barthé, *Becoming American in Creole New Orleans,* 83–84.

26. For St. Cyr's induction into the organization, see Minutes, Dec. 9, 1901, meeting, container 25-12. For St. Cyr's membership and habitual payment of dues, see Ledgers (of membership assessments), 1902; Feb. 13, 1905–Oct. 14, 1907; Jan. 13, 1908–Jan. 8, 1912; Feb. 12, 1912–Aug. 14, 1916; Sept. 11, 1916–July 12, 1920. For evidence of bills paid by the organization on behalf of the Moore family, see Ledgers, Feb. 10, 1902, and Jan. 12, 1903, container 25-11, Société des Jeunes Amis Collection.

27. Barthé, *Becoming American in Creole New Orleans,* 80.

28. "Société des Jeunes Amis," *New Orleans Republican,* Feb. 15, 1874, 5; "Announcements, Saturday April 23, 1881," *Louisianan,* April 23, 1881, 3.

29. AM-BWOHP, 6.

30. "Watchman Schroeder Game, and Runs Down a Black Man Who Has Evidently Been Stealing Railroad Property," *Times-Picayune,* Dec. 31, 1899, 9.

31. "Water Works Case Resumed in Court," *Times-Picayune,* Jan. 3, 1900, 6.

32. "Convicted," *Times-Picayune,* March 15, 1900, 16.

33. "Lawyers Grow Hot, Jury Keeps Cool," *Times-Picayune,* March 17, 1900, 11; "Criminal District Court," *Times-Picayune,* April 11, 1900, 13; "The Courts," *Times-Picayune,* July 13, 1900, 11; "Royal Street Too Much for Courts," *Times-Picayune,* July 19, 1900, 3; "Sentenced,"

Times-Picayune, July 24, 1900, 3. For a full account of the witnesses and testimony, see St. Cyr Moore Arrest Record, No. 29534, First City Criminal Court of New Orleans, New Orleans Public Library.

34. DeVore, *Defying Jim Crow,* 159, 109; "Phillis Wheatley Training School," *Times-Picayune,* Nov. 1, 1896, 10.

35. Medley, *Black Life in Old New Orleans,* 106; DeVore, *Defying Jim Crow,* 169; Alice Ruth Moore, "Louisiana," *Women's Era,* June 1896, 8.

36. Medley, *Black Life in Old New Orleans,* 107–9. For more on the second line, see Turner, *Jazz, Religion, the Second Line.*

37. For more on St. Joseph's congregation, see St. Joseph's Church, N.O. (Tulane Ave.), Annual Reports (1860–1927), 12:50 [AR/00507], Archdiocese of New Orleans Archives; Slawson, "Segregated Catholicism," 142–43; Bennett, *Religion and the Rise of Jim Crow in New Orleans,* 146.

38. AM-BWOHP, 6; Blassingame, *Black New Orleans,* 16.

39. AM-BWOHP, 6. To be sure, Moore would have been young when she witnessed this incident. Yet secondary sources indicate that this practice was becoming increasingly common at the turn of the century. See Slawson, "Segregated Catholicism," 152.

40. Slawson, "Segregated Catholicism," 150–52. For more information on Drexel, see Hughes, *Mother Katharine Drexel.*

41. "Negro Church, Protest Against Building Colored Missions, 1888–1894," 2:37 [AR/00741], Archdiocese of New Orleans.

42. Bennett, *Religion and the Rise of Jim Crow,* 181–86. For examples of Comité articles, see "Prejudice in the Catholic Church," *Crusader,* June 1891, folder 4, box 2; "A Separate Church," *Crusader,* n.d., folder 5, box 2, CBR.

43. Alice Ruth Moore, "Louisiana."

44. Bennett, *Religion and the Rise of Jim Crow,* 162.

45. "A Church Devoted to Colored Catholics," *Times-Picayune,* May 20, 1895, 10.

46. Marriage Contract, Henry Moore and Celestine Houston, Sept. 24, 1900; Certificate of Baptism, Charles St. Cyr Moore, Jan. 7, 1900; Certificate of Baptism, Eloise Agnes Moore; Certificate of Baptism, Loretta A. Moore, SKR.

47. For an overview of New Orleans schools, see DeVore and Logsdon, *Crescent City Schools.*

48. "St. Katherine's School," *Times-Picayune,* June 1, 1900, 10.

49. For St. Katharine's enrollment numbers in the late 1890s and early twentieth century, see St. Katharine's Church, N.O.—Parish Visitation Reports (1912–1934), 13:21 [AR/00508], Archdiocese of New Orleans.

50. AM-BWOHP, 6.

51. AM-BWOHP, 6.

52. Death Certificate, Ella Moore, NOPVR, Louisiana; Certificate of Burial, Ella Moore, Feb. 17, 1904, SKR.

53. AM-BWOHP, 52.

54. AM-BWOHP, 14.

55. AM-BWOHP, 14. Moore states that they stayed in "the country" for ten years; see 08-ORAL-30-8-Side-01, Queen Mother Moore Tapes. But census reports indicate it was likely a shorter amount of time.

56. Bennett, *Religion and the Rise of Jim Crow,* 154. For more information on the order, see Deggs, Gould, and Nolan, *No Cross, No Crown.*

57. "Alleged Horse Thief," *Times-Picayune,* July 23, 1908, 5. The 1910 census lists St. Cyr as "Sam" Moore; however, the three children listed in the home are "Audly" Moore, aged eleven, Eloise Moore, aged nine, and Lorita Moore, aged seven. The head of the household is also listed as single. This entry lists his occupation as the owner of a wood and coal business, which other sources indicate St. Cyr operated at this time. See 1910 U.S. Federal Census, Louisiana, New Orleans, sheet 30.

58. John and Alphonsine's older children were Bertha, born around 1887, and Alice, born around 1890. John Springfield, 1910 Federal Census, Louisiana, New Orleans, sheet 20B.

59. 5-ORAL-30-5-Side-1, Queen Mother Moore Tapes.

60. "Negro Pythian Temple," *Times-Democrat,* Aug. 19, 1909, 6; Medley, *Black Life in Old New Orleans,* 86.

61. Washington to O. G. Villard, May 28, 1909, quoted in Harlan, *Booker T. Washington,* 360–61. For more on these turn-of-the-century leaders and their liberation philosophies, see Gaines, *Uplifting the Race.*

62. For more on women's organizing during this period, see White, *Too Heavy a Load.*

63. Salvaggio, *New Orleans' Charity Hospital,* 99–102; Campanella, *Lost New Orleans,* 52–53.

64. Act of Sale, John Adam Lautenschlaeger Jr. unto Henry J.

Moore, Aug. 7, 1915, New Orleans
Conveyance Office; "Wood and
Coal," in Woods, ed., *Woods Directory,*
1914, 91.

65. AM-BWOHP, 13–14; AM-Naison;
Death Certificate, St. Cyr Moore,
Oct. 25, 1917, NOPVR.

66. AM-BWOHP, 13; AM-Prago.

Chapter 3: WARTIME DISRUPTIONS

1. "Audley Moore, Born in Poverty."
2. AM-BWOHP, 1.
3. Census reports indicate that Nora
was back in New Iberia by 1920 and
that Alphonsine was in Texas. See
Alphonsine Springfield, 1920 Federal
Census, Orange, Texas, sheet 13B;
Nora Henry, 1920 Federal Census,
Iberia Parish, Louisiana, sheet 13A.
Although Narceas was older, he still
had a draft card: Narceas Joseph
Henry, 1917–1918, Louisiana County,
Orleans, roll 1684819, Draft Board 02,
U.S. World War I Draft Registration
Cards, National Archives and
Records Administration; Lentz-
Smith, *Freedom Struggles,* 42; Williams,
Torchbearers for Democracy, 52.
4. "Audley Moore, Born in Poverty."
5. AM-BWOHP, 3; AM-Prago; Hunter,
To Joy My Freedom, 26–27.
6. "Audley Moore, Born in Poverty."
7. Baker and Cooke, "Bronx Slave
Market," 330.
8. For more on turn-of-the-century
domestic work, see Nadasen,
Household Workers Unite.
9. "Crescent Hairdressing College,"
in Woods, *Woods Directory, 1914;*
"Crescent Hairdressing College,"
Town Talk, June 14, 1913, 2; AM-
BWOHP, 1. Moore only mentions
attending the Poro hairdressing
college. She did indeed attend this
school, but in New York, not New
Orleans.
10. For more information on Black

beauty culture and economic
autonomy, see Gill, *Beauty Shop*
Politics.
11. This explanation of the rationale for
Loretta's first marriage comes from
Moore's remaining family. Audley
Warner, correspondence with author.
12. Registration Card, Charles A. Bazile,
Louisiana; Registration, Orleans
Parish, roll 1684924, Draft Board
02, National Archives and Records
Administration.
13. Certificate of Marriage, Charles A.
Bazile to Loretta Moore, April 22,
1918, NOPVR.
14. "Of Emancipation Relieving the
Minor from the Time Prescribed
by Law for Attaining the Age of
Majority," in *The Revised Civil Code*
of the State of Louisiana, 1910 (New
Advocate Official Journal, 1910), 61.
15. "Emancipation of Audley Moore
and Loretta Moore, Wife of Charles
Bazile," No. 123847; "Emancipation
of Eloise A. Moore," Civil District
Court, Parish of New Orleans, No.
123951, New Orleans Public Library.
16. Lentz-Smith, *Freedom Struggles,*
42; Williams, *Torchbearers for*
Democracy, 52.
17. "World War I Liberty Bond Parade,
1917," Charles L. Franck Studio
Collection; "Camp Martin, New
Orleans," Permanent Collection,
Historic New Orleans Collection.
18. Nelson, "Negro Women in War
Work," 375; Breen, "Black Women

and the Great War," 422; Brown, *Private Politics and Public Voices,* 31–32.

19. Brown, *Private Politics and Public Voices,* 31–32.

20. Brown, *Private Politics and Public Voices,* 6.

21. Sartain, *Invisible Activists,* 52.

22. AM-BWOHP 2; AM-Prago; "Eloise Moore: A Woman Dedicated to Liberate [*sic*] Afro-Americans from Mental Slavery," *Atlanta Daily World,* Feb. 9, 1986, 4.

23. AM-BWOHP, 2; "Negro Troops Are Coming to Camp," *Anniston Star,* Aug. 31, 1917, 1.

24. AM-Prago.

25. AM-BWOHP, 2.

26. Lentz-Smith, *Freedom Struggles,* 171.

27. Newton, "'Tenting Tonight on the Old Camp Grounds,'" 54–56.

28. Williams, *Torchbearers for Democracy,* 111–12. Robert Gilbert to W. E. B. Du Bois, Dec. 12, 1918, Part 9, Discrimination in the U.S. Armed Forces, Series A: General Office Files on Armed Forces' Affairs, 1918–1955, Folder 001535-001-0020, Papers of the NAACP.

29. AM-Prago; AM-BWOHP, 2.

30. Brown, *Private Politics and Public Voices,* 58; *War Camp Community Service and the Negro Soldier* (West Camp Community Service, 1920), 2–3.

31. AM-BWOHP, 2.

32. Brown, *Private Politics and Public Voices,* 77; Brandimarte, "Women on the Home Front," 201–2.

33. "Eight Hostess Houses Established for Colored Soldiers," *Emancipator,* Nov. 2, 1918, 3.

34. AM-BWOHP, 2; Brown, *Private Politics and Public Voices,* 32, 38.

35. Harris, *Sex Workers, Psychics, and Numbers Runners,* 2.

36. Lentz-Smith, *Freedom Struggles,* 208.

37. For more on Eloise's influence on Audley, see McDuffie, "'We Owe a Debt to Her, She Taught Us How to Think.'"

38. Widmer, *New Orleans in the Twenties,* 27; Berry, *City of a Million Dreams,* 184–90.

39. Adler, *Murder in New Orleans,* 3.

40. Brown, *Private Politics and Public Voices,* 108.

41. *Chicago Defender,* May 24, 1919, 1.

42. McWhirter, *Red Summer,* 41.

43. "Report Six Killed in Negro-Sailor Riot," *New York Times,* May 11, 1919, 3; "Six Killed in Charleston Riot," *Knoxville Journal and Tribune,* May 11, 1919, 1.

44. McWhirter, *Red Summer,* 128–29.

45. Brown, *Private Politics and Public Voices,* 113–14.

46. Jones, *Vanguard,* 178–80.

47. The 1920 census indicates that Charles Bazile was stationed overseas in 1920. Charley [*sic*] A. Bazile, 1920 U.S. Census, Military and Naval Forces, Fort Stotsenburg, Philippines, sheet 19B; Van Ells, *America and World War I,* 225.

48. Audley Bazile, 1930 Federal Census, New Orleans, Louisiana, sheet 21B.

Chapter 4: FOLLOWING GARVEY

1. "Queen Mother Moore Recalls Historic UNIA Meeting," *City Sun,* July 1987, 6. For details on Spraggs, see Registration Card, Josiah Spraggs, Louisiana, Orleans Parish, roll 1684922; Draft Board 09, U.S. World War I Draft Registration Cards, National Archives

and Records Administration; "Declaration of Intention," Josiah Spraggs, No. 53978, Eastern District Court, Michigan Federal Naturalization Records, Detroit.

2. For more information on this type of work, see Echeverri-Gent, "Forgotten Workers."

3. Chapman, *Bananas,* 44–45.

4. Chapman, *Bananas,* 8, 13, 74.

5. Echeverri-Gent, "Forgotten Workers," 279. For more on UFCO tourism and Jamaican workers, see Chambers, *From the Banana Zones to the Big Easy,* 73, 84; Cocks, *Tropical Whites.*

6. United Fruit Company, *A Short History of the Banana and a Few Recipes for Its Use* (United Fruit Company, 1904), 31.

7. For evidence of Spraggs's work on ships, see "S.S. Saramacca Manifest List," Arriving in New Orleans on Nov. 16, 1918, from Puerto Barrios, Guatemala; "S.S. Saramacca Manifest List," Arriving in New Orleans on Dec. 27, 1918, from Puerto Limon, Costa Rica; "S.S. Jamaica Manifest List," Arriving in New Orleans on March 17, 1920, from Kingston, Jamaica; "Norwegian Steamship Ellis Manifest List," Arriving in New Orleans on Nov. 2, 1918, from Omoa, Honduras, in *Crew Lists of Vessels Arriving at New Orleans, Louisiana, 1910–1945,* National Archives and Records Administration.

8. Echeverri-Gent, "Forgotten Workers," 276, 283; Sullivan, "'Forging Ahead' in Banes Cuba."

9. For an overview of the world Garvey stepped into, see Chomsky, "Afro-Jamaican Traditions and Labor Organizing on United Fruit Company Plantations in Costa Rica."

10. Grant, *Negro with a Hat,* 26–32.

11. Harpelle, "Cross Currents in the Western Caribbean," 49.

12. Martin, *Race First,* 6. For more on Ashwood's role in developing the UNIA, see Blain, *Set the World on Fire;* Martin, *Amy Ashwood Garvey;* Duncan, *Efficient Womanhood.*

13. Harpelle, "Cross Currents in the Western Caribbean," 53.

14. Hill, *Marcus Garvey and Universal Negro Improvement Association Papers,* 4:lxxxvi. For more information on Caribbean migrants, literacy, and the circulation of migrants, see Putnam, *Radical Moves.*

15. Spraggs's World War I draft registration card indicates that he was registered with the British West Indian Regiment.

16. Harpelle, "Cross Currents in the Western Caribbean," 50; Echeverri-Gent, "Forgotten Workers," 292; Smith, *Jamaican Volunteers in the First World War,* 63–66; Olusoga, *Black and British,* 434–35.

17. Records indicate that he was "discharged" in 1920. Moreover, Spraggs begins to appear in New Orleans city directories after 1920. See "S.S. Jamaica Ship Manifest," Arriving in New Orleans on March 17, 1920, from Kingston, Jamaica, in *Crew Lists of Vessels Arriving at New Orleans, Louisiana, 1910–1945.*

18. "Spraggs, Josiah," *U.S. City Directories, New Orleans, Louisiana, 1921,* 1396.

19. Kein, *Creole,* 204.

20. Marriage Certificate, Audley Moore and Josiah Spraggs, July 26, 1920, NOPVR.

21. The city directory for 1923 lists Spraggs as a grocer on Erato Street in New Orleans. Moore also said

that she and Spraggs did well in business during the early years of their marriage. AM-Prago; "Spraggs, Josiah," *U.S. City Directories, New Orleans, Louisiana, 1923,* 1423.

22. 5-ORAL-30-5-Side-01, Queen Mother Moore Tapes.

23. AM-BWOHP, 9.

24. For Moore's various recountings of this story, see AM-BWOHP, 9; AM-Prago; "*Black Scholar* Interviews Queen Mother Moore"; "A Witness to the History," *Daily News,* Feb. 3, 1995; Audley Moore, interview by Earl Menelik Pinto, in *Queen Mother Moore: Witness to a Century of Injustice* (Reparations for Education Fund, 1985), DVD.

25. For more on this tradition of self-defense, see Johnson, *Negroes and the Gun;* and Jackson, *We Refuse.*

26. AM-BWOHP, 9; AM-Prago; "*Black Scholar* Interviews Queen Mother Moore"; "A Witness to the History," *Daily News;* Audley Moore, interview by Earl Menelik Pinto, in *Queen Mother Moore: Witness to a Century of Injustice.*

27. "Police Prevent Promised Speech by Negro 'Moses,'" *Times-Picayune,* June 24, 1922; "Four Thousand Persons Welcome Hon. Marcus Garvey Back to Liberty Hall After an Absence of Two Months," *Negro World,* July 15, 1922, 3; "Attempt to Stop Garvey Lecture Fails," *Negro World,* July 1, 1922, 8. For Moore's recollection of the delegation, see "The Black and the Red," produced by Beth Friend and Charles Potter, narrated by Jill Eikenberg, Pacifica Radio Archive, North Hollywood, Calif.

28. "Threatened with Arrest," in Hill,

Marcus Garvey and Universal Negro Improvement Association Papers, 4:694.

29. A careful combing through of the donation rolls in *The Negro World* indicates that Spraggs donated to the UNIA starting in August 1922. "Convention Fund of the Universal Negro Improvement Association," *Negro World,* Aug. 19, 1922, 10. This is the best "evidence" of Moore's formal membership in the organization.

30. Hall, *Africans in Colonial Louisiana,* 52. For information on emigration and nationalist projects in Louisiana, see Issa, "Universal Negro Improvement Association in Louisiana."

31. AM-Prago.

32. Rolinson, *Grassroots Garveyism,* 20.

33. Rolinson, *Grassroots Garveyism,* 49.

34. For descriptions of NOD meetings, see "Col. Adrian Johnson Speaks in New Orleans," *Negro World,* April 2, 1921, 8; "New Orleans, LA," *Negro World,* Dec. 5, 1925, 6; "Hymn for Opening Meeting," reel 1, UNIA Central Division Records.

35. "New Orleans, LA," *Negro World,* May 30, 1925, 8.

36. AM-BWOHP, 34.

37. AM-BWOHP, 7.

38. AM-Prago.

39. For foundational texts on the role of Ethiopia in Black Nationalism, see Drake, *Redemption of Africa and Black Religion;* Shepperson, "Ethiopianism and African Nationalism."

40. Burkett, *Garveyism as a Religious Movement,* 34.

41. Grant, *Negro with a Hat,* 168–69; Nurhussein, *Black Land,* 7.

42. AM-Naison.

43. Ewing, *Age of Garvey,* 146.

44. Garvey, "Speech Delivered at

Carnegie Hall," 101–2. For more on Garveyite sexual politics and nation building, see Mitchell, *Righteous Propagation.* For examples of articles in *The Negro World,* see "Children and the Race," Oct. 22, 1921, 6; "Birth Control Condemned as Heinous, Corrupted, Inhuman," Jan. 14, 1922, 7.

45. Mehta, "Images of Exile and the Female Condition in Nawal El Saadawi's *The Fall of the Imam* and *Memories from the Women's Prison,*" 35–36.

46. Harold, *Rise and Fall of the Garvey Movement in the Urban South,* 30.

47. Bair, "True Women, Real Men," 156–57; "Provisional Ladies of the Royal Court of Ethiopia of U.N.I.A. Who Tended the Reception to the Potentate," *Negro World,* Nov. 18, 1922, 8.

48. For more on gender roles in the UNIA, see Bair, "True Women, Real Men"; Blain, *Set the World on Fire;* Duncan, *Efficient Womanhood;* Bair, "'Ethiopia Shall Stretch Forth Her Hands unto God.'"

49. Blain, *Set the World on Fire,* 16; Duncan, *Efficient Woman,* 27–31, 34. For excellent biographies on Garvey's wives, see Taylor, *Veiled Garvey;* Martin, *Amy Ashwood Garvey.*

50. For more on de Mena, see Morris, "Becoming Creole, Becoming Black." For more on Vinton Davis, see Duncan, "'If Our Men Hesitate Then the Women of the Race Must Come Forward'"; Duncan, *Efficient Womanhood,* chap. 3.

51. Bourbonnais, "Our Joan of Arc," 141, 149; Ewing, *Age of Garvey,* 139.

52. "Articles in the Negro World," in Hill, *Marcus Garvey and Universal Negro Improvement Association Papers,* 4:781–82.

53. "The Unity of Our Women," in Hill, *Marcus Garvey and Universal Negro Improvement Association Papers,* 4:1037–38.

54. "Unity of Our Women."

55. For more on the role of Garveyite women and how they navigated the gender politics of the organization, see Blain, "'To Keep Alive the Teaching of Garvey and the Work of the UNIA'"; Taylor, *Veiled Garvey;* Duncan, *Efficient Womanhood.*

56. "Unity of Our Women." Some call this approach "community feminism," a term coined by Ula Taylor. Taylor, *Veiled Garvey,* 2.

57. "Unity of Our Women."

58. "African President Held: Head of Black Star Line Accused of Illegally Using Mails," *New York Times,* Jan. 13, 1922, 9.

59. Bandele, "Understanding African Diaspora Political Activism," 749.

60. Bandele, *Black Star,* 140.

61. "Garvey Pleads Not Guilty," *Washington Post,* Feb. 21, 1922, 19; "Garvey Convicted in Black Line Fraud," *New York Times,* June 19, 1923, 21.

62. "The Enthusiasm of the New Orleans Division, No. 149, U.N.I.A.," *Negro World,* Feb. 18, 1922, 3; "Louisiana Firmly Behind Marcus Garvey," *Negro World,* March 4, 1922, 9. For evidence of the NOD support of Garvey's Defense Fund, see "Marcus Garvey Defense Fund," *Negro World,* Nov. 25, 1922, 10.

63. Issa, "Universal Negro Improvement Association in Louisiana," 122.

64. "Cable by Marcus Garvey to Chairman, Liberty Hall," June 25,

1922, in Hill, *Marcus Garvey and Universal Negro Improvement Association*, 4:679.

65. "Eason Trial," in Hill, *Marcus Garvey and Universal Negro Improvement Association*, 4:954, 988.

66. Stein, *World of Marcus Garvey*, 174.

67. Martin, *Race First*, 318.

68. "Commissioner Smyers Pushing Things in the New Orleans, LA, Div.," *Negro World*, Oct. 28, 1922, 7.

69. Marcus Garvey to William Phillips, November 9, 1922, in Hill, *Marcus Garvey and Universal Negro Improvement Association*, 5: 133. For subsequent correspondence between Garvey and Phillips about Eason and a UNIA-backed secret service unit, see 141–42, 153, 161.

70. "Negro Preacher Is Shot in Back," *Times-Picayune*, Jan. 2, 1923, 23.

71. Stein, *World of Marcus Garvey*, 171–85; "Eason, at One Time Connected with the U.N.I.A., Shot and Killed in New Orleans," *Negro World*, Jan. 13, 1923, 10.

72. "The Rape of the New Orleans Division," *Negro World*, March 10, 1923, 7; "The Principles of the U.N.I.A. Vindicated in the City of New Orleans," *Negro World*, April 24, 1923, 2; "Police at New Orleans, Arrest Eight Negroes," *Town Talk*, Feb. 12, 1923, 1; Harold, *Rise and Fall of the Garvey Movement in the Urban South*, 43.

73. "Defense Fund for the New Orleans Division of the U.N.I.A. and Dyer and Shakespeare, Innocent Men Charged with the Death of J. W. H. Eason," *Negro World*, Jan. 27, 1923, 3.

74. "Defense Fund for the New Orleans Division," *Negro World*, Feb. 3, 1923, 8; "New Orleans Defense Fund; Everybody Must Subscribe," *Negro World*, March 3, 1923, 9.

75. Harold, *Rise and Fall of the Garvey Movement in the Urban South*, 45.

76. "Garvey Sentenced to Five Years in Jail," *New York Times*, June 22, 1923, 19.

77. Ewing, *Age of Garvey*, 1.

78. Grant, *Negro with a Hat*, 268–75; Thomas, "Exodus and Colonization." For more on these early colonization attempts, see Clegg, *Price of Liberty*.

79. Ewing, *Age of Garvey*, 83–84.

80. Grant, *Negro with a Hat*, 276.

81. "Universal Negro Improvement Assn. Sending Delegation to Africa," *Negro World*, Nov. 24, 1923, 5. For NOD contributions, see "The Black Cross Navigation and Trading Company: Bonds Issued 1924," box 1, folder 2, United Negro Improvement Association Records, Western Reserve Historical Society.

82. AM-BWOHP, 10; AM-Prago.

83. Grant, *Negro with a Hat*, 371–76.

84. "New Orleans, LA," *Negro World*, Jan. 30, 1926, 5.

85. "New Orleans, LA," *Negro World*, May 23, 1925, 8; "New Orleans, LA," *Negro World*, Sept. 19, 1925, 6; "New Orleans, LA," *Negro World*, Sept. 25, 1925, 6. For more on Sherrill, see Jolly, *By Our Own Strength*.

Chapter 5: FROM MIGRANT TO MILITANT

1. AM-BWOHP, 10; "Portrait of a Revolutionary."

2. Robinson, "Race, Space, and the Evolution of Black Los Angeles," 38; Wilkerson, *Warmth of Other Suns*, 178, 231.

3. The *Green Book* refers to *The Negro Motorist Green Book*, which directed Black travelers to Black-owned and Black-serving restaurants, businesses, and hotels.

4. Sorin, *Driving While Black*, 23. For more on how Black people navigated travel during Jim Crow, see Loewen, *Sundown Towns*; Bay, *Traveling Black*; Taylor, *Overground Railroad*.

5. Sorin, *Driving While Black*, 23; Wilkerson, *Warmth of Other Suns*, 391.

6. Flamming, *Bound for Freedom*, 262–63.

7. Bryant et al., *Central Avenue Sounds*, 8.

8. Chapple, "From Central Avenue to Leimert Park," 60–63; Campbell, *Making Black Los Angeles*, 81, 95–98, 105, 107; Tolbert, *UNIA and Black Los Angeles*, 51.

9. Bryant et al., *Central Avenue Sounds*, 5.

10. *California Eagle*, Aug. 28, 1931, 10.

11. Campbell, *Making Black Los Angeles*, 103; Tolbert, *UNIA and Black Los Angeles*, 34; Gordon, *Second Coming of the KKK*, 68.

12. AM-BWOHP, 10; AM-Prago; Lanker, *I Dream a World*, 103; 2-ORAL-30-12-Side-01, Queen Mother Moore Tapes.

13. Wilkerson, *The Warmth of Other Suns*, 11.

14. Baldwin, *Chicago's New Negroes*, 28–30; Schafer, "Yesterday's City."

15. AM-BWOHP, 11; AM-Prago.

16. Wilkerson, *Warmth of Other Suns*, 261.

17. Moore indicates that she did have more money than the average Black woman at this time in large part thanks to the money Spraggs made in the store and his other business dealings. AM-BWOHP, 12.

18. AM-BWOHP, 10.

19. This description draws from Gill, *Harlem*, 226–28; Lewis, *When Harlem Was in Vogue*.

20. *New York Amsterdam News*, July 8, 1931.

21. AM-BWOHP, 10; Wilkerson, *Warmth of Other Suns*, 249.

22. For more on Moore's first days in Harlem, see AM-Naison. On Sugar Hill, see Lewis, *When Harlem Was in Vogue*, 217; Gill, *Harlem*, 285.

23. Wilkerson, *Warmth of Other Suns*, 251.

24. AM-BWOHP, 15.

25. AM-BWOHP, 15; FBI, SAC, New York, May 15, 1943, File No. 100-13205, Audley Moore.

26. "List of Graduates, New York Branch of Poro College," *New York Age*, Nov. 8, 1930, 3. For more on Malone's influence on Walker, see Bundles, *On Her Own Ground*.

27. Spraggs is listed as a boarder in a different house in Harlem. Josiah Spraggs, 1930 Federal Census, Manhattan, New York, sheet 12A.

28. "Eloise Moore: A Woman Dedicated to Liberate [*sic*] Afro-Americans from Mental Slavery," AM-BWOHP, 15.

29. "Queen Mother Moore Recalls Historic UNIA Meeting," 6.

30. Grant, *Negro with a Hat*, 411–12.

31. Blain, *Set the World on Fire*, 42–43. For evidence of internal strife, see letters and correspondence from Garvey, Uriah Gittens, and Toote, box 1, folders 8 and 9, Universal Negro Improvement Association Miscellaneous Collection.

32. Gill, *Harlem*, 282.

33. Greenberg, *To Ask for an Equal Chance*, 27–29.

34. Greenberg, *"Or Does It Explode?,"* 42; Wilkerson, *Warmth of Other Suns*, 249; Gill, *Harlem*, 284.

35. AM-BWOHP, 11.

36. For more on McKay, Savage, and this program overall, see Butts, *Dark Mirror*.

37. Trotter, *From a Raw Deal to a New Deal*, 10.

38. Greenberg, *"Or Does It Explode?,"* 44–45; Gill, *Harlem*, 283; Opdycke, *WPA*, 58–59.

39. AM-BWOHP, 11. Moore described what her fellow activists called the Bronx Slave Market, where Black women lined the streets for "housewives to buy their strength and energy for an hour, two hours, or even a day." See Baker and Cooke, "Bronx Slave Market."

40. AM-BWOHP, 11–12.

41. "6,000 Gotham Elks Will Go to Richmond," *Chicago Defender*, Aug. 22, 1925, 2; "Manhattan Lodge of Elks Votes $6,000 Donation to Presbyterian Hospital," *Pittsburgh Courier*, June 6, 1925, 7; "J. Dalmus Steele Harlem's 'Mayor,'" *Chicago Defender*, Sept. 4, 1932, 13.

42. "Candidates Address Voters at Forum at Abyssinian Church," *New York Age*, Oct. 14, 1933, 2.

43. "Harlem Committee Gives Out 153 Baskets for Thanksgiving Day," *New York Age*, Dec. 6, 1930, 10; "Elks of N.Y. State Plan Monster Unemployment Mass Meeting," *New York Age*, Nov. 15, 1930, 7.

44. For 1933, see "Steele to Sue if Votes Are Thrown Out," *Daily Citizen*, Nov. 8, 1933, 2; "Election Afterthoughts," *Daily Citizen*, Nov. 9, 1933, 4; "J. Dalmus Steele to Contest Opponent's Seat," *Daily Citizen*, Nov. 21, 1933, 3, 4. Steele also ran and lost in 1934; see "Harlem Primary Designations," *New York Age*, Sept. 1, 1934, 6; "Win Important Political Victories in New York," *Chicago Defender*, Sept. 22, 1934, 5.

45. AM-BWOHP, 15; AM-Prago.

46. AM-Naison.

47. Horne, *Black Liberation/Red Scare*, 22–23; Franklin, *From Slavery to Freedom*, 423; Rigueur, *Loneliness of the Black Republican*, 14; Farrington, *Black Republicans and the Transformation of the GOP*, 13–14.

48. AM-BWOHP, 15.

49. Martin, "International Labor Defense and Black America," 171. For an overview of the case, see Carter, *Scottsboro*.

50. AM-Naison.

51. Solomon, *Cry Was Unity*, 25–28; Naison, *Communists in Harlem*, 5; Makalani, *In the Cause of Freedom*, 45.

52. Naison, *Communists in Harlem*, 5; Makalani, *In the Cause of Freedom*, 45; Solomon, *Cry Was Unity*, 9–15.

53. Makalani, *In the Cause of Freedom*, 89.

54. For a great overview of Black Americans who journeyed to the Soviet Union, see Carew, *Blacks, Reds, and Russians*.

55. "Draft Resolution on the Negro Question in the United States," box 15, folder 8, TDR; Adi, "Negro Question," 158; Makalani, *In the Cause of Freedom*, 133–34; Kelley, *Hammer and Hoe*, 1.

56. Smethurst, *New Red Negro*, 18–23; Solomon, *Cry Was Unity*, 33; Burden-Stelly, *Black Scare/Red Scare*, 88–89.

57. AM-BWOHP, 15–16; AM-Prago; Moore in "The Black and the Red." It is difficult to ascertain exactly which Scottsboro protest Moore attended because there were many between 1930 and 1933. Since James Ford was in the Soviet Union until 1932, however, this protest likely took place after this date. See Naison, *Communists in Harlem*, 57–62.

58. AM-BWOHP, 16.

59. Martin, "International Labor Defense and Black America," 167–68.

60. AM-BWOHP, 16; AM-Prago; "Peace Picketer Stays in White House Line," *Afro-American,* June 21, 1941, 23; Solomon, *Cry Was Unity,* 254.

61. Martin, "International Labor Defense and Black America," 167; *What the I.L.D. Does for Labor: Civil Rights, Defense, Relief, Legislation, Education* (International Labor Defense, 1940), Widener Library, Harvard University.

62. See, for example, "Parade August 13 for Jobs and Bread," *Hunger Defender,* July 25, 1932; "A Call to All Activists in the Unemployed Movement," *Hunger Defender,* Aug. 6, 1932, 1. The ILD's newspapers, *Labor Defender* and *Equal Justice,* offered continual updates and calls to action for Herndon, Mooney, and others. Reels 1 and 2, International Labor Defense Records.

63. "Denmark Vesey—a Lesson in Self Defense," *Labor Defender,* Feb. 1934.

64. Solomon, *Cry Was Unity,* 271; "Negroes Assail Italy," *New York Times,* Feb. 16, 1935, 6; "2,000 Parade in Harlem's Protest to Ethiopia Invasion," *Afro-American,* May 11, 1935, 12. Also see flyers for meetings and parades in support of Ethiopia found in reels 4 and 5, Universal Negro Improvement Association Central Division, New York Records.

65. "150 Here Rally to Help Africa," *Record,* Oct. 18, 1935, 1; Naison, *Communists in Harlem,* 175.

66. Moore in "The Black and the Red."

67. "Harlemites Pay Tribute to J. W. Ford," *Chicago Defender,* April 11, 1936, 4; Harlem Division of the Communist Party, *A Political Manual for Harlem* (New York, 1939), 15–16, Courtesy of Robin D. G. Kelly.

68. For an assessment of the party's

Harlem branches and Black women's roles within them, see George Blake, "The Party in Harlem, New York," *Party Organizer,* June 1938, 14–15.

69. Harris, "Running with the Reds," 23–26; Naison, *Communists in Harlem,* 40.

70. AM-Prago.

71. Kraditor, "*Jimmy Higgins,*" 2.

72. Moore in "The Black and the Red."

73. Rudolph Langley, Application for Seaman's Protection Certificates, Records of the Bureau of Marine Inspection and Navigation, Record Group 41, box 061; "S.S. Jamaica Ship Manifest," Arriving in New Orleans on March 17, 1920, from Kingston, Jamaica, in *Crew Lists of Vessels Arriving at New Orleans, Louisiana, 1910–1945.*

74. For evidence of Langley's travels, see Passenger Manifest, Vessel: *Ellis,* arriving at Truxell, S.H., June 23, 1921; Passenger Manifest, Vessel: *Munmar,* arriving at New Orleans on Dec. 22, 1927, from Havana, Cuba; Passenger Manifest, Vessel: *Munplace,* arriving at New Orleans, Oct. 1, 1932, from Progresso, Mexico, in *Crew Lists of Vessels Arriving at New Orleans, Louisiana, 1910–1945.*

75. Loretta Langley, 1940 Federal Census, Manhattan, New York, sheet 12B; Audley Moore, 1940 Federal Census, Manhattan, New York, sheet 12B; Eloise Moore, 1940 Federal Census, Manhattan, New York, sheet 6A.

76. Naison, "From Eviction Resistance to Rent Control," 97–98; King, *Whose Harlem Is It Anyway?,* 112–14.

77. "Women Picket Harlem House," *Daily Worker,* Nov. 17, 1936, 1, 4.

78. AM-BWOHP, 18, 8, 16.

79. "Harlem Gets Its Bookshop," *Daily*

Worker, Jan. 1936, 7; "About Books," *New York Amsterdam News,* Dec. 28, 1935, 9.

80. "Scottsboro Fight Renewed at Conference," *Daily Worker,* Oct. 28, 1937, 3; "A Call for the Harlem Scottsboro Defense Conference," Part 6, The Scottsboro Case, 1931–

1950, Folder 001524-020-0485, Papers of the NAACP; "Scottsboro Parley in Harlem Tonight," *Daily Worker,* Oct. 25, 1937, 4.

81. "Call for the Harlem Scottsboro Defense Conference"; Frank Warner, 1940 Federal Census, Manhattan, New York, sheet 12B.

Chapter 6: PULLING WEIGHT IN THE POPULAR FRONT

1. This description comes from a photo of Moore in her mid-forties, in the author's possession.

2. This description is drawn from Schamberg, "Midwestern Study of the Foods and Foodways of the Great Depression"; Greenberg, *To Ask for an Equal Chance,* 44.

3. This composite picture of Harlem during the Depression comes from images in Blair, *Harlem's Crossroads.*

4. Greenberg, *To Ask for an Equal Chance,* 44.

5. Von Eschen, *Race Against Empire,* 19; Solomon, *Cry Was Unity,* 170.

6. Naison, *Communists in Harlem,* 126–27; Biondi, *To Stand and Fight,* 6.

7. "New Women Party Members: Official Blank from Districts from May–June 1937," box 7, folder 12, New York District of the Communist Party, CPUSA Papers; "The Women's Fight for Equality, Maternity, and Childhood Protection," folder 20, box 33, TDR.

8. "Baby Carriage Parade to Protest Milk Gouge," *Daily Worker,* Nov. 20, 1937, 1; "'Give Us Milk,' Mothers Plead in Mass Protest at N.Y. Price," *Washington Post,* Nov. 21, 1937, 4.

9. "Death-Birth in Huge Blaze: Death on Seventh Avenue Hero," *New York Amsterdam News,* Dec. 11, 1937, 1.

10. "Women C.P. Leaders Honor Mother Bloor," *Daily Worker,* Jan. 6, 1938, 3; Triece, *On the Picket Line,* 46–50; Brown, "'Savagely Fathered and Unmothered World' of the Communist Party, U.S.A."

11. For Flynn's own account of her activism, see Flynn, *Rebel Girl.*

12. "Women's Day Rallies Spur Unity Actions," *Daily Worker,* March 25, 1939, 6.

13. "It'll Be a Mothers' Day for Peace," *Daily Worker,* May 6, 1938, 5; "Cheer Mother Bloor After Her Plea for Aid to Boys in Spain," *Daily Worker,* May 31, 1938, 4; "Mother Bloor, Gurley Flynn Will Speak," *Daily Worker,* Nov. 29, 1938, 5; "Rally Today to Perfect Drive," *Daily Worker,* Dec. 1, 1938, 4; "Stop the Nazi Massacre of Women and Children," protest flyer, Dec. 1, 1938, box 141, folder 2, CPUSA Papers.

14. "Labor Day Heroines," *Daily Worker,* Sept. 4, 1938, 8.

15. "Harlem to Hit Filibuster at Demonstration," *Daily Worker,* Feb. 2, 1938, 3; "Don't Give Up the Lynch Fight, Harlemites Say," *Afro-American,* Feb. 12, 1938, 7; "Harlem C.P. Shows How to Lead Anti-lynch Drive," *Daily Worker,* May 4, 1939, 3; "Admit Ban on Race Workers by Utilities," *Chicago Defender,* April 16, 1938, 7;

"New Yorkers Seek Opportunity in Utility Field," *New Journal and Guide* (Norfolk, Va.), April 16, 1938, 4; "Telephone Co. Admits Policy to Not Give Negroes Jobs," *Cleveland Call and Post* (Cleveland), April 21, 1938, 8; "Negro Tenants Defeat Landlord as Court Backs Housing Bill," *Daily Worker*, Dec. 4, 1938, 3; "Whalen Office to Be Picketed for Race Bias," *Daily Worker*, April 13, 1939, 4; "Invite Whalen to Harlem Job Rally for Fair," *Daily Worker*, April 22, 1939, 3.

16. "Harlem Love Girls Get 25 Cents, Whites $5," *Afro-American*, Jan. 29, 1938, 22.

17. Naison, *Communists in Harlem*, 42.

18. Audley Moore, "Women's Commission Report," in *Proceedings 10th Convention, Communist Party New York State* (New York State Committee, 1938), 288–91.

19. Moore, "Women's Commission Report."

20. Frank Warner's early life remains nebulous. His son, Tom Warner, states that his father told him he was from Haiti. The FBI listed him as born in 1906, of West Indian origin, and not a naturalized citizen. Warner family, interview by author; FBI, SAC Report, Albany, Feb. 14, 1955, File No. AL-100-12069, Audley Moore.

21. Warner family, interview by author; "Call for the Harlem Scottsboro Defense Conference."

22. Charles Turner, interview by author.

23. Frank Warner, 1940 Federal Census, Manhattan, New York, sheet 12B.

24. Blakely, "40 Acres and a Mule," 132; TW-Payne.

25. For Tom's thoughts on his childhood, see Warner,

"Recollections and Reflections," 160–62.

26. Isserman, *Which Side Were You On?*, 46, 33–35.

27. Horne, *Black Liberation/Red Scare*, 79; "Anti-war Unit Hears Senator Gerald P. Nye," *Chicago Defender*, April 5, 1941, 8.

28. "Harlem Section Running Four Candidates," *Harlem Pointer*, Aug. 30, 1940, 3; "New York State C.P. to Place 60 Candidates on Ballot in Fight for Peace and Jobs," *Daily Worker*, Aug. 5, 1940, 5; Naison, *Communists in Harlem*, 244.

29. "Tragic Death of Two Year Old Arouses Harlem," *Harlem Pointer*, Aug. 30, 1940, 5.

30. Gellman, *Death Blow to Jim Crow*, 1, 13.

31. Isserman, *Which Side Were You On?*, 21.

32. Gellman, *Death Blow to Jim Crow*, 166. For more on Dale and Esther Cooper Jackson, see Gore, *Radicalism at the Crossroads*; McDuffie, *Sojourning for Freedom*; McDuffie, " 'No Small Amount of Change Could Do,' " 25–46.

33. "Minutes, National Board Meeting of the National Negro Congress," Nov. 16, 1941, box 26, folder 54, reel 13, NNC.

34. "First New York State Conference of the National Negro Congress," Nov. 16 and 17, 1940, box 20, folder 34, reel 10; Manhattan Council of the National Negro Congress, press release, n.d., box 27, folder 68, reel 14, NNC.

35. Horne, *Black Liberation/Red Scare*, 74.

36. "Thousands at City Hall on TWU Issue," *Daily Worker*, March 14, 1941, 1; Naison, *Communists in Harlem*, 306.

37. "Negroes Open Job Fight on Bus Lines," *Daily Worker*, March 26, 1941, 3; "Harlemites Win Bus Fight, Get

500 Jobs," *Chicago Defender,* April 26, 1941; New York National Negro Congress, "A Victory for the Negro People," box 27, folder 68, reel 14, NNC.

38. "Negroes Open Job Fight on Bus Lines."

39. Vaughn-Roberson, "Fascism with a Jim Crow Face," 192; "New Organization Votes to Sponsor Peace Units and to Fight Conscription," *Courier-Journal,* Sept. 2, 1940, 2.

40. "Officers of the American Peace Mobilization," *Daily Worker,* Sept. 3, 1940, 4; "Peace Mobilization Calls Rally to Block Draft Bill," *Washington Post,* Sept. 14, 1940, 2.

41. "What Is APM?," box 1, Folder: History and Goals, APM.

42. "Peace Organization Tendered Luncheon," *New York Age,* June 14, 1941, 5.

43. "Negro Women Firm in Support of APM," *APM Memo,* April 5, 1941, box 1, Folder: American People's Meeting, New York, APM.

44. American Peace Mobilization, press release, May 13, 1941, box 1, Folder: Perpetual Peace Vigil [at White House], Washington (D.C.), 1941 (May–June 21), APM.

45. "Peace Picketer Stays in White House Line," *Afro-American,* June 21, 1941, 23; "Peace Mobilization Group Flays Roosevelt's Policy," *Pittsburgh Courier,* Oct. 26, 1940, 1; "Clergymen Greet APM's Peace Vigil," *Daily Worker,* May 27, 1941, 2.

46. Schmidt, *Red Scare,* 349–50.

47. Isserman, *Which Side Were You On?,* 68.

48. "Dies Agents Charge APM Exploiting Race Issues," *Afro-American,* May 31, 1941, 8; "Dies to Probe Source of Funding for 'Peace' Group," *Baltimore Sun,* March 2, 1941, 1.

49. "Statement of Mrs. Sarah V. Montgomery Before the Dies Committee, March 4, 1941," box 18, folder 7, reel 9, NNC; "APM Calls New Hearings by Dies 'Smear' on Peace," *Daily Worker,* May 22, 1941, 1.

50. Isserman, *Which Side Were You On?,* 47–50.

51. Ryan, *Earl Browder,* 182–83.

52. Ryan, *Earl Browder,* 204–5.

53. "New York Browder Campaign Launched," *Daily Worker,* Jan. 24, 1942, 1, 2.

54. "City Rallies for Earl Browder," *Daily Worker,* Feb. 25, 1942, 3; "For the Freedom of Earl Browder...," *People's Voice,* March 21, 1942, 11; "Negro Parley on Browder to Be Held Wednesday," *Daily Worker,* Nov. 21, 1941, 1; "Harlem Conference Tonight to Push Aid for Earl Browder," *Daily Worker,* Nov. 26, 1941, 1; "Harlemites Ask Browder Release," *New Journal and Guide,* Dec. 13, 1941, 11.

55. "Browder to Talk in Harlem Next Sunday," *Daily Worker,* Oct. 11, 1942, 4; "Harlem Rally Says Free Earl Browder, Cheer His Fights for Negro People," *Daily Worker,* Feb. 28, 1943, 3; "Browder to Speak Sunday at Meeting of Communist Party," *Boston Globe,* Dec. 10, 1942, 10; "Browder Rally to Get Governor's Message," *Daily Worker,* Dec. 11, 1942, 1.

Chapter 7: NEGRO WOMAN·LEADER

1. AM-Naison.

2. "Should I Sacrifice to Live 'Half-American'?," *Pittsburgh Courier,* Jan. 31, 1942, 3.

3. Washburn, "Pittsburgh *Courier's* Double V Campaign in 1942"; Wynn, *African American Experience during World War II*, 46.

4. Lucander, *Winning the War for Democracy*, 24, 33–34.

5. Lucander, *Winning the War for Democracy*, 7–38; Gellman, *Death Blow to Jim Crow*, 160; Weiner, *Enemies*, 70; Franklin D. Roosevelt, Executive Order 8802, "Prohibition of Discrimination in the Defense Industry," in *1941 Supplement to the Code of Federal Regulations* (1942), 234.

6. Naison, *Communists in Harlem*, 310–11; Gellman, *Death Blow to Jim Crow*, 161; Isserman, *Which Side Were You On?*, 118.

7. World Peace Ways Broadcast, "Questions and Answers with Earl Browder," July 11, 1943, box 3, folder 27, TDR.

8. AM-BWOHP, 8.

9. For the most complete overview of Jones's life, see Davies, *Left of Karl Marx*.

10. Claudia Jones, "Quiz," *Weekly Review*, Dec. 9, 1941, 14. For an overview of Jones's World War II–era journalism, see Mislan, "Imperial 'We.'"

11. Naison, *Communists in Harlem*, 287–91.

12. Isserman, *Which Side Were You On?*, 145–48.

13. Isserman, *Which Side Were You On?*, 149–50.

14. For this statistic as well as composition of neighborhood, see Logan, Zhang, and Chunyu, "Emergent Ghettos."

15. *Complete Report of Mayor LaGuardia's Commission on the Harlem Riot, March 19, 1935* (New York, 1935), Western Washington University Archives, Bellingham; Abu-Lughod, *Race, Space, and Riots in Chicago, New York, and Los Angeles*, 140–42.

16. "Minutes of Harlem Defense Conference," Jan. 17, 1942, box 25, folder 37, reel 13, NNC.

17. "Much Ado About Something...," *Daily Worker*, Feb. 8, 1942, 6; Donelan J. Phillips (president of Consolidated Tenants League) to Harlem Labor Victory Committee, March 29, 1944, box 78, folder 88, reel 37, NNC.

18. "City Rallies for Earl Browder," *Daily Worker*, Feb. 23, 1942, 3.

19. "Rally May Day Smash Hitler in '42," *People's Voice*, May 2, 1942, 8; "Harlem Stirred by Great Rally, Hopes United Action Will Follow," *Daily Worker*, June 10, 1943, 4; "Second Front Rally to Hear Powell," *Daily Worker*, April 15, 1943, 4.

20. For more on Miller, see Cutrer and Parrish, *Doris Miller, Pearl Harbor, and the Birth of the Civil Rights Movement*.

21. "Negro Achievement Day to Be Observed Here Tomorrow," *Daily Worker*, June 26, 1942, 1; "'Negro Day' Honors for Dorie's Mother," *People's Voice*, June 27, 1942, 2; "Leaders Gather for Negro Day," *People's Voice*, July 4, 1942, 4; "Achievement Day Is Set for June 27," *Chicago Defender*, May 30, 1942, 7.

22. "Werner Heads High Rent Fight," *People's Voice*, Oct. 31, 1942, 14. For evidence of Moore's role on the executive board of the Coordinating Committee for Employment, see Joseph E. Ford to Dr. Channing Tobias, April 16, 1945, Folder: Discrimination in the Armed Forces, Camp Livingston, Louisiana, 1941–1945, African Americans in the Military Part 1, RNAWC. For CP wartime activities, see "Gift for Mother Bloor: 50 New Recruits,"

Daily Worker, Sept. 15, 1942, 3; "Negro Servicemen 'Captured' by Mother Bloor at Birthday Fete," *Daily Worker,* Sept. 28, 1942; "Lecture Series on Women's Role Opens," *Daily Worker,* Sept. 23, 1942, 5; "Exhibition: 'The Role of Women in America,'" *People's Voice,* Oct. 3, 1942, 8.

23. "Harlem House of Horrors Cries Out for Gov't Action," *Daily Worker,* Oct. 17, 1942, 4.

24. "Harlem Needs Child Centers Not Surveys," *Daily Worker,* Dec. 7, 1942, 4; "Browder Rally to Get Governor's Message," *Daily Worker,* Dec. 11, 1942, 1.

25. For more on Bethune's incredible life, see Rooks, *Passionate Mind in Relentless Pursuit.*

26. White, *Too Heavy a Load,* 70.

27. White, *Too Heavy a Load,* 155; Tuuri, *Strategic Sisterhood,* 13–14; Hanson, *Mary McLeod Bethune and Black Women's Political Activism,* 165–68.

28. Tuuri, *Strategic Sisterhood,* 19–20.

29. "Women Hold Defense Confab at Howard University," *Chicago Defender,* July 5, 1941, 6.

30. AM-BWOHP, 23.

31. "Programme," Twenty-Second Biennial Convention of the National Association of Colored Women, July 26–Aug. 1, 1941, Mary McLeod Bethune Papers, Bethune-Cookman College Archives; "Partial List of Delegates to N.A.C.W.," *Black Dispatch,* Aug. 1, 1941, 9.

32. "Convention Minutes, 1941," Minutes of the National Conventions, Publications, and President's Office Correspondence, RNAWC; "Prominent Women of Pittsburgh Honor Audley Moore," *New York Age,* Sept. 6, 1941, 4; Isserman, *Which Side Were You On?,* 110.

33. "Addenda…," *Pittsburgh Courier,* Dec. 4, 1943, 11; "A Symposium on Women and National Unity," box 1, folder 1, Bessye B. Bearden Papers. For evidence of Moore's role as the New York representative of the executive committee at large, see Jeanetta Welch Brown to Dean Edward K. Weaver, April 25, 1944, Folder: NCNW Correspondence, 1941–1944, Mary McLeod Bethune Papers, Bethune-Cookman College Archives.

34. Tuuri, *Strategic Sisterhood,* 16; "Women in the National Picture," *Chicago Defender,* Jan. 1, 1944, 14.

35. "Permanent Headquarters Is a Step in the Right Direction, President Claims," *Pittsburgh Courier,* Jan. 1, 1944, 11; "Women in the National Picture"; "Women's Council Plans for Political Action," *Chicago Defender,* Jan. 1, 1944, 5; "They Authorized the NCNW Purchase," *Afro-American,* Jan. 8, 1944, 12.

36. Horne, *Black Liberation/Red Scare,* 40–43.

37. Horne, *Black Liberation/Red Scare,* 86–88; Naison, *Communists in Harlem,* 109–10.

38. "Delegation Gets Macy to Stop 'Mugging Stick' Sale," *Daily Worker,* April 29, 1943, 1, 2.

39. "Delegation Gets Macy to Stop 'Mugging Stick' Sale."

40. "Now It's 'Mugging Night Sticks,'" *New York Age,* May 8, 1943, 9.

41. Powell, *Adam by Adam,* 68.

42. Powell, *Adam by Adam,* 68; Naison, *Communists in Harlem,* 312.

43. "Mark 1 for Benjamin J. Davis Jr.," *New York Age,* Oct. 30, 1942, 2; "Powell Backs Communist," *New York Herald Tribune,* Oct. 7, 1943, 19.

44. AM-BWOHP, 20–21; AM-Naison.

45. "5 Prominent Women Join Davis Sponsors," *Daily Worker,* Oct. 12, 1943,

3; "Big Group Supporting Davis in Council Race," *People's Voice,* Oct. 2, 1943, 13.

46. AM-Naison; "5 Prominent Women Join Davis Sponsors."

47. AM-BWOHP, 20; AM-Prago.

48. "The Low Down—the Great Hours After Ben Davis Was Elected to the Council," *Daily Worker,* Nov. 11, 1943, 5; "Davis Wins Seat on Gotham's Council," *New Journal and Guide,* Nov. 20, 1943, 1.

49. Horne, *Black Liberation/Red Scare,* 117; "Davis Wins Seat on Gotham's Council."

50. Horne, *Black Liberation/Red Scare,* 119, 134; "Wilkins; Harlem Paper, Hails Davis Election," *Daily Worker,* Nov. 23, 1943, 3; "Ben Davis Sr.— GOP Stalwart; Ben Davis Jr.—C.P. Radical," *New York Amsterdam News,* Nov. 20, 1943, 7.

51. "Letters to the Editor," *People's Voice,* Nov. 13, 1943; "Letters from Our Readers," *Daily Worker,* Nov. 14, 1943, 8.

52. "Davis Supporters Will Long Tell of Audley Moore's Work," *Daily Worker,* Nov. 20, 1943, 3; "Successful Campaign Manager," *New York Age,* Nov. 27, 1943, 4; "Miss Moore Feted," *Afro-American,* Dec. 25, 1943, 12; "People Like These Helped Elect Davis," *Daily Worker,* Nov. 11, 1943, 4.

53. "Teddy Wilson Presents…All Star Victory Show," *People's Voice,* Oct. 16, 1943, 9; "Showlife's Top Artists in Million Dollar Show for Ben Davis, Jr., at Golden Gate Ballroom," *New York Amsterdam News,* Oct. 16, 1943, 7B; AM-BWOHP, 20.

54. AM-BWOHP, 20.

55. AM-Naison.

56. AM-Prago.

Chapter 8: BURNING QUESTIONS

1. This description is drawn from Strahan, *Lost Springfield, Massachusetts.*

2. "Foster to Talk at Buffalo Lenin-'Daily' Meeting," *Daily Worker,* Jan. 5, 1944, 4; "Audley Moore Gets 9 of 25 to Sign," *Daily Worker,* April 24, 1944, 3.

3. "Audley Moore Gets 9 of 25 to Sign."

4. Ryan, *Earl Browder,* 209–10; Isserman, *Which Side Were You On?,* 145–48.

5. Ryan, *Earl Browder,* 217.

6. "CP Adopts Unity Program for 1944, Post-war; Proposes Change of Name," *Daily Worker,* Jan. 10, 1944, 1–2.

7. "CP Adopts Unity Program for 1944, Post-war; Proposes Change of Name"; "Communist Party in U.S. Disbanded," *Detroit Free Press,* May 21, 1944, 1; Ryan, *Earl Browder,* 222–23.

8. For more on civil rights during and after World War II, see Kruse and Tuck, *Fog of War.*

9. Isserman, *Which Side Were You On?,* 197–98.

10. Earl Browder, "On the Negroes and the Right of Self-Determination," *Communist* 23 (Jan. 1944): 83–85.

11. "Negro Women Hit 'Equal Rights' Bill," *Daily Worker,* Feb. 15, 1944, 1; "Fire Dept. Probes Burned Negro Home," *Daily Worker,* March 2, 1944, 1.

12. Isserman, *Which Side Were You On?,* 203; "Browder Heads Reds Again in the New Set-Up," *New York Herald Tribune,* May 23, 1944, 15A; "Communist Party Ends; Fourth Term," *Daily News,* May 21, 1944, 6.

13. Isserman, *Which Side Were You On?*, 204; "Constitution of the Communist Political Association," Series IV, Part J, Section 8, SPA.

14. Isserman, *Which Side Were You On?*, 203–4.

15. "Browder Heads Reds Again in the New Set-Up."

16. Communist Political Association, press release, May 22, 1944, Series IV, Part J, Section 8, SPA.

17. Communist Political Association, press release, May 22, 1944; "Browder Heads Reds Again in the New Set-Up"; "Officers Elected by the CPA," *Daily Worker*, May 28, 1944, 4.

18. AM-Nasion.

19. AM-Naison; AM-Prago; FBI, Letter to FBI Director, June 1, 1944, File No. 100-13205, Audley Moore.

20. AM-BWOHP, 19.

21. AM-Naison; AM-Prago.

22. Warner, "Recollections and Reflections," 160; TW-Payne.

23. Thomas Warner, phone conversation with author.

24. This description comes from Austin, *Lost Detroit*, 101–10; "Passenger Station of Michigan Central Credit to Detroit," *Detroit Free Press*, Dec. 31, 1913, 1, 9.

25. "Passenger Station of Michigan Central Credit to Detroit."

26. For more on the Black experience in Detroit in wartime, see Boyd, *Black Detroit*; Shockley, *"We Too Are Americans."*

27. Pettengill, "Communists and Community," 11; Ward, *In Love and Struggle*, 52–54.

28. Pettengill, "Communists and Community," 30–32, 40, 57; "4 Dead, 23 Wounded Is Ford's Answer to the Demand for Work, Bread," *Daily Worker*, March 9, 1932; "Ford Victim to Be Buried Today," *Daily Worker*, Aug. 13, 1932, 1.

29. "Detroit Has a Race Riot as Whites Bar Negroes from Homes in U.S. Housing Unit," *Life*, March 16, 1942, 40; "Eye Witness Account of 'Race Riot,'" *Michigan Chronicle*, March 7, 1942, 1; "Biddle Orders KKK Probe for Attacks upon Detroit Negroes," *Daily Worker*, March 10, 1942, 1; Boyd, *Black Detroit*, 140–41. For more on the Sojourner Truth Housing Project and the race riot that ensued because of it, see Van Dusen, *Detroit's Sojourner Truth Housing Riot of 1942.*

30. "Michigan CPA Is Formed," *Daily Worker*, June 11, 1944, 12; "Michigan Communists Re-organize," *Detroit Free Press*, June 10, 1944, 1; FBI, Letter from R. A. Guerin, SAC, to FBI Director, Aug. 18, 1944, File No. 100-12344, Audley Moore.

31. FBI, SAC Report, Detroit, Oct. 9, 1944, File No. 100-12344, Audley Moore.

32. "Daily Worker Picnic in Detroit Sunday," *Daily Worker*, Sept. 6, 1944, 2; "Reception for Audley Moore," *Michigan Chronicle*, Aug. 26, 1944, 3; "Paul Robeson Guest of the Tolans," *Michigan Chronicle*, Oct. 10, 1944, 5.

33. FBI, SAC Report, Detroit, Feb. 3, 1945, File No. 100-12344, Audley Moore; "Detroit Negroes Are Eager to Register," *Daily Worker*, Sept. 12, 1944, 7.

34. FBI, SAC Report, Detroit, Feb. 3, 1945, File No. 100-12344, Audley Moore; "Detroit Rally Friday," *Daily Worker*, Oct. 22, 1944, 3; "23,000 Cheer Wallace in Detroit Rally," *Daily Worker*, Oct. 31, 1944, 4; "Notables to Attend 'Roosevelt Rally,'" *Detroit Free Press*, Oct. 15, 1944, 6.

35. FBI, SAC Report, Detroit, Feb. 3, 1945, File No. 100-12344, Audley Moore.

36. FBI, SAC Report, Detroit, Feb. 3, 1945, File No. 100-12344, Audley Moore; FBI, Letter from SAC Detroit to Director, Nov. 30, 1944, File No. 100-12344, Audley Moore.

37. Marriage License, Audley A. Moore and Frank Warner, vol. 3, no. 1836, Jan. 22, 1945, New York County Clerk, New York.

38. "The Allerton Coops and Black Women's Liberation: Virtual Roundtable Discussion," March 6, 2024, www.youtube.com/watch ?v=N9C1NAUGw0Q&t=240s.

39. TW-Payne.

40. Charles Turner, interview by author.

41. "Allerton Coops and Black Women's Liberation."

42. TW-Payne; Warner, "Recollections and Reflections," 160; FBI, Letter from Special Agent in Charge E. E. Conroy to Director, Feb. 21, 1945, File No. 100-13205, Audley Moore.

43. "Fluctuating Negro Membership in CPA," *Daily Worker*, Jan. 21, 1945, 12; "Wilford E. Lewis Outlines Year's Program of Henry Lincoln Johnson Lodge No. 636," *New York Age*, Feb. 10, 1945, 4; "Plan Lincoln-Lenin Memorial in Newark," *Daily Worker*, Feb. 16, 1945, 4; "New Haven War Worker Has 48-Yr. Service Record," *Afro-American*, March 17, 1945, 6; "Negro Women Inc. Honor Two Members," *New York Amsterdam News*, March 31, 1945, 13; "FDR Memorial Incorporated," *People's Voice*, April 23, 1945, 4; "Seen at Lovelace Recital," *New York Age*, Sept. 22, 1945, 4; "Organizations Tender Farewell Reception for Mrs. Amy A. Garvey," *New York Age*, Aug. 19, 1945, 4; "Holds

36th Annual Convention," *New York Age*, July 1, 1944.

44. FBI, Report from SAC Baltimore, April 26, 1945, File No. 100-11631, Audley Moore; "Baltimore— Gateway to the New South," *Daily Worker*, March 22, 1945, 7.

45. FBI, Report by Oscar J. Keep, May 19, 1945, File No. 3100-17241, Audley Moore.

46. For Foster's side of this debate, see Barrett, *William Z. Foster*, chap. 10.

47. Isserman, *Which Side Were You On?*, 216–21; Ryan, *Earl Browder*, 250–53.

48. Barrett, *William Z. Foster*, 218–19; Isserman, *Which Side Were You On?*, 227.

49. Isserman, *Which Side Were You On?*, 233; Audley Moore, National Committee Meeting, June 20, 1945, box 36, folder 4e, PJP.

50. Audley Moore, National Committee Meeting, June 20, 1945.

51. Isserman, *Which Side Were You On?*, 227–28; Howe and Coser, *American Communist Party*, 430; AM-Naison.

52. Peter V. Cacchione, National Committee Meeting, June 18, 1945, box 36, folder 4a, PJP.

53. I. Amter, National Committee Meeting, June 19, 1945, box 36, folder 4c, PJP.

54. Rose Gaulden, National Committee Meeting, June 18, 1945, box 36, folder 4b, PJP.

55. Wm. Patterson, National Committee Meeting, June 19, 1945, box 36, folder 4c, PJP.

56. Audley Moore, National Committee Meeting, June 20, 1945.

57. Barrett, *William Z. Foster*, 218; Horne, *Black Liberation/Red Scare*, 140.

58. Isserman, *Which Side Were You On?*, 234.

59. Isserman, *Which Side Were You On?*,

233–35; Barrett, *William Z. Foster,* 223–24.

60. AM-BWOHP, 19; AM-Prago.

61. Solomon, *Cry Was Unity,* 179–80; "George Padmore Is Expelled by Communist International," *Daily Worker,* April 25, 1934, 6. Padmore's views on Garvey shifted over the course of his lifetime. For more on his political evolution, see Worrell, *George Padmore's Black Internationalism,* 58–59.

62. Turner and Turner, *Richard B. Moore,* 67.

63. AM-BWOHP, 22.

64. FBI, Report from Joseph H. Phelan, July 6, 1945, File No. 100-13205, Audley Moore.

65. Horne, *Black Liberation/Red Scare,* 140–43.

66. "Tammany Supports Davis, Communist," *New York Times,* July 21, 1945, 1.

67. "Kennedy Calls on Tammany to Disavow Davis," *New York Herald Tribune,* July 22, 1945, 16; "Negroes Fear Davis Case Will Split Their Vote," *New York Herald Tribune,* July 26, 1945, 13.

68. "Women Honor Councilman Benjamin J. Davis, Jr.," *New York Age,* Sept. 15, 1945, 4; "'Let's Reelect Ourselves to the City Council,'" *People's Voice,* Sept. 8, 1945, 2; "All-Star Victory Show to Re-elect Benjamin J. Davis, Jr.," box 49, folder 37, reel 24, NNC; "Harlem Banks Jimcro[w]," *People's Voice,* June 9, 1945, 4.

69. "Furniture Workers Demand Elimination of Ban Against Negro Players in Majors," *Pittsburgh Courier,* Aug. 28, 1943, 18.

70. "'Jimcro[w] in Baseball' Draws 7th Ave. Crowd," *People's Voice,* Aug. 25, 1945, 2; AM-BWOHP, 18.

71. Horne, *Black Liberation/Red Scare,* 164–65; "Official Count Shows Davis Re-elected by 63,000 Votes," *Jackson Advocate,* Nov. 24, 1945, 1; "Across the Desk," *New York Age,* Nov. 24, 1945, 6.

72. See, for example, "Quick-Trigger Cop in Harlem Slays 14-Year-Old Negro Boy," *Daily Worker,* Nov. 3, 1945, 2; "Case of Wilbert Cohen Re-opened," *Daily Worker,* Dec. 31, 1945, 2.

Chapter 9: POSTWAR BLUES

1. Wynn, *African American Experience during World War II,* 83–84; Gaddis, *Cold War,* 10–11.

2. Wynn, *African American Experience during World War II,* 83–84; Woods, *Black Struggle, Red Scare,* 26–27.

3. Horne, *Red Seas,* 18–19, 81–85.

4. "Mrs. Moore Says War Brides Shun Racial Biases," *Afro-American,* Jan. 18, 1947, 13; "Woman Makes 10 Trips from Europe to Escort War Brides," *Chicago Defender,* Jan. 25, 1947, 12; "Negro Women in the News,"

Arizona Sun, April 4, 1947, 5; Horne, *Red Seas,* 78; "Personal Touch," *People's Voice,* June 1, 1946, 20.

5. AM-BWOHP, 8.

6. For more on how the uneven distribution of GI Bill benefits shaped Black America, see Humes, *Over Here.*

7. AM-BWOHP, 81–82.

8. "Woman Makes 10 Trips"; Warner, "Recollections and Reflections," 160; "Royal Jewel Club Will Have Anniversary Banquet," *Middletown*

Times Herald, April 22, 1946, 3. For Moore's trips, see Ship Manifest, Vessel: *Zebulon B. Vance,* Sailing from Port of New York, Aug. 28, 1946; Ship Manifest, Vessel: *Zebulon B. Vance,* Sailing from Port Le Havre, May 11, 1946; Ship Manifest, Vessel: *T. Jarrett Muddleton,* Sailing from New York, in Passenger and Crew Lists (including Castle Garden and Ellis Island), 1820–1957, National Archives and Records Administration.

9. Warner family, interview by author; AM-BWHOP, 74–75.

10. This debate was published in *Political Affairs.* See Claudia Jones, "On the Right to Self-Determination for the Negro People in the Black Belt"; Doxey Wilkerson, "The Negro and the Nation"; William Z. Foster, "On Self-Determination for the Negro People," *Political Affairs* 25 (July 1946).

11. Starobin, *American Communism in Crisis,* 131–32.

12. "Resolution on the Question of Negro Rights and Self-Determination," in *The Communist Position on the Negro Question* (New Century, 1947), 9–13.

13. Gellman, *Death Blow to Jim Crow,* 257–59.

14. Gore, "From Communist Politics to Black Power," 71–94.

15. Letter from Vicki Best, Audley Moore, and Edward E. Strong, Jan. 29, 1947, box 68, folder 40, reel 32, NNC. For more on Bilbo, see Fleegler, "Theodore G. Bilbo and the Decline of Public Racism."

16. "Bias in Bronx Tax Bureau Charged by Employes [*sic*]," *Daily Worker,* Jan. 23, 1947, 8; "Tenants Declare 'War' on Negligent Landlords,"

People's Voice, Jan. 25, 1947, 15; "NNC Blasts Unfair Labor Practices," *New York Age,* Feb. 8, 1947, 3; "Harlem Marchers Blast Dewey's Gestapo Tactics," *People's Voice,* March 1, 1947, 6.

17. "NNC to Picket Walt Disney Film," *People's Voice,* Feb. 8, 1947, 3.

18. For more on the rise in anticolonial activism in the postwar era, see Von Eschen, *Race Against Empire;* Meriwether, *Proudly We Can Be Africans.*

19. Adi, *Pan-Africanism,* 123–25.

20. For a history of Black folk internationalizing their struggle, see Kelley, "'But a Local Phase of a World Problem.'" For an example of the NNC's internationalizing of the Black American struggle, see "San Francisco," *Congress View,* March 1945, 4.

21. National Negro Congress, "Program (1944)," reel 20, NNC.

22. UN General Assembly, Resolution 217 A(III), Universal Declaration of Human Rights, Dec. 10, 1948.

23. "Voiceless in Congress," *Pittsburgh Courier,* Jan. 10, 1942, 6.

24. "Demand United Nations Probe U.S. Race Prejudice," *Chicago Defender,* June 8, 1946, 1. For texts that examine this "Cold War, Civil Rights" strategy, see Anderson, *Eyes off the Prize;* Duziak, *Cold War, Civil Rights.*

25. "The Oppression of the American Negro: The Facts," box 59, folder 98, reel 29, NNC; Anderson, "From Hope to Disillusion," 544–46.

26. "Continuations Committee on the Problems of Minorities and the United Nations," Meeting Minutes, Feb. 22, 1947, box 62, folder 186, reel 30, NNC.

27. "UN Commission Seeks More Data on Negroes," *People's Voice,* July 6, 1946, 1; Memorandum, "On the Organization of Community People's Tribunals," box 18, folder 15, reel 9, NNC. For examples of newspaper petitions, see box 63, folder 202, reel 30, NNC.

28. Woods, *Black Struggle, Red Scare,* 26–28; National Negro Congress, "National Executive Board Meeting," June 1947, box 70, folder 27, reel 33, NNC; Anderson, *Eyes off the Prize,* 91–92; Gellman, *Death Blow to Jim Crow,* 255–65.

29. Anderson, "From Hope to Disillusion," 553.

30. Anderson, "From Hope to Disillusion," 556–57.

31. Harry S. Truman, Executive Order 9835, "Prescribing Procedures for the Administration of an Employees Loyalty Program in the Executive Branch of the Government," *1947 Supplement to the Code of Federal Regulations,* Title 3 (1948), 129; Storrs, "Revisiting Truman's Federal Employee Loyalty Program," 70.

32. For more on what many have come to call the Lavender Scare, or the mid-century moral panic over gay people in the U.S. government, see Johnson, *Lavender Scare;* Charles, *Hoover's War on Gays.*

33. "Call Truman Doctrine Threat to Negro People," *Daily Worker,* April 4, 1947, 3.

34. "Community Leaders Fight Red Scare," *People's Voice,* March 29, 1947, 4.

35. Weigand, *Red Feminism,* 46–47.

36. Weigand, *Red Feminism,* 60; Castledine, *Cold War Progressives,* 45.

37. "Boro CAW Unit Honors Civil War Heroine," *Brooklyn Daily Eagle,* March 10, 1947, 18; Weigand, *Red Feminism,* 153.

38. *Afro-American,* April 5, 1947, 9.

39. "The Feminine Front," *Afro-American,* April 5, 1947, 8.

40. Alonso, "Mayhem and Moderation," 145–56.

41. Committee on Un-American Activities, U.S. House of Representatives, *Report on the Congress of American Women,* Oct. 23, 1949; "Plans Meet on Harlemites and May Day," *New York Amsterdam News,* April 5, 1947, 4; "May Day Plans Formed Expect 80,000 Marchers," *People's Voice,* April 12, 1947, 4; "All-Out for the Big May Day Parade," *People's Voice,* April 19, 1947, 9.

42. "Arrest of Red Seen as Racial Attack," *Afro-American,* Jan. 31, 1948, 1; "Harlem Parley Tonight to Defend Claudia Jones," *Daily Worker,* Jan. 23, 1948, 4; Davies, *Left of Karl Marx,* 71; Commissioner, Immigration and Naturalization Service, "Claudia Vera Scholnick, with Aliases, May 22, 1947," folder 4, box 1, Claudia Jones Research Collection.

43. "Harlem Parley Tonight"; "Harlem Acts to Help Free Claudia Jones," *Daily Worker,* Jan. 26, 1948, 3.

44. "Life of the Party: A Women's Meeting of Vital Importance," *Daily Worker,* Feb. 9, 1948, 11.

45. "Foster Recalls Past Frame-Ups," *Daily Worker,* Feb. 6, 1948, 10.

46. "Press Release, Dec. 8, 1947," folder m316, box 78; "Summary of Proceedings: Congress on Civil Rights, April 27–28th, Detroit Michigan," folder n67, box 64, CRC; Horne, *Communist Front?,* 30.

47. "Minutes of the Continuations Committee Meeting, Civil Rights

Congress," folder n102, box 66, CRC.

48. Horne, *Communist Front?*, 40; Martin, "Civil Rights Congress and Southern Black Defendants," 29.

49. Martin, "Civil Rights Congress and Southern Black Defendants," 26.

50. Horne, *Communist Front?*, 56.

51. Horne, *Communist Front?*, 57; Martin, "Civil Rights Congress and Southern Black Defendants," 34.

52. Martin, "Civil Rights Congress and Southern Black Defendants," 30.

53. "Grant Execution Stay to Mother, Two Sons," *Chicago Defender*, Feb. 28, 1948.

54. Martin, "Race, Gender, and Southern Justice"; Gore, *Radicalism at the Crossroads*, 78–79; "Mother, Teenage Sons to Die in Electric Chair," *Chicago Defender*, Feb. 7, 1948, 1.

55. Audley Moore to Dear Friends, March 11, 1948; "Rosa Lee Ingram, Mass Defense," box 8, folder a151, CRC; "Harlem Women to Take Ingram Case to Capital," *Daily Worker*, March 11, 1948, 7; "Women's Group in Fight for Ingram Family," *People's Voice*, March 27, 1948, 14; Gore, *Radicalism at the Crossroads*, 79.

56. "Harlem Women to Take Ingram Case to Capital."

57. "Harlem Women to Take Ingram Case to Capital"; "Save Mrs. Ingram Delegation," *Daily Worker*, March 18, 1948, 2.

58. "As We See it: Truman Was Too Busy to Discuss Civil Rights and Aid to the Ingrams," *Daily Worker*, March 22, 1948, 9.

59. "3 Ingram Kids Stricken by Flu," *Daily Worker*, Jan. 28, 1949, 6.

60. "Charges of Ingram Children Neglected Denied by NAACP," *New Journal and Guide*, Feb. 19, 1949, 1; "Claims Persist That Ingram Family Is Suffering Despite Contributions," *Call and Post* (Cleveland), March 12, 1949, 1B.

61. "Claims Persist That Ingram Family Is Suffering Despite Contributions"; "Care of Ingram Children Still Open to Question," *New Journal and Guide*, March 12, 1949, 20; "Feud Rages over Welfare of Mrs. Ingram's Family," *Afro-American*, March 12, 1949, C3A.

62. For more on Moore's CRC work, see "Audley Moore Speaks on Civil Rights Thurs.," *Daily Worker*, July 21, 1948, 13; "Arrest Connolly, 5 Others at Anti–Mundt Bill Rally," *Daily Worker*, June 11, 1948, 3; Daniel Benjamin to Ralph Powe, Aug. 17, 1948, box 16, folder a324, CRC. For other efforts, see "At New Party Convention," *Afro-American*, July 31, 1948, A1; "2 Negro Unionists Bid for Harlem's Votes on ALP Line," *Daily Worker*, Oct. 7, 1948, 5; "1000 at Harlem Rally Rap Cop's Beating of Woman," *Daily Worker*, May 18, 1948, 6; "Golden Gate Rally to Hit Harlem Police Brutality," *Daily Worker*, May 21, 1948, 5.

63. Thelma Dale to Matt Crawford, n.d. [Jan.–Feb. 1946], item 60, box 2, Matt N. and Evelyn Graves Crawford Papers.

Chapter 10: HEARTBREAK

1. Herman, *Joseph McCarthy*, 275–77.

2. Storrs, *Second Red Scare and the Unmaking of the New Deal Left*, 91; "Communism and the Youth of America," Mandel interview, ABC,

Nov. 27, 1948, box 692, J. B. Matthews Papers.

3. Lundberg and Farnham, *Modern Woman*, 166.

4. Lieberman and Lang, *Anti-communism and the African American Freedom Movement*, xiv.

5. Lieberman and Lang, *Anti-communism and the African American Freedom Movement*, xiv. For more on the toll McCarthyism took on the Black Left, see Washington, *Other Blacklist*; Morgan, *Reds*; Horne, *Black Liberation / Red Scare*; Isserman, *Which Side Were You On?*; Burden-Stelly, *Black Scare / Red Scare*.

6. "Red Forgot Answer, Now Forgets Them All," *Daily News*, June 7, 1949, 1; "Length of Trail Believed Record," *New York Times*, Oct. 15, 1949, 4.

7. "Claudia Jones to Be Deported as Communist," *New York Herald Tribune*, Dec. 22, 1950, 6; "Claudia Jones to Be Deported," *Afro-American*, Nov. 15, 1955, 14.

8. McDuffie, "March of Young Southern Black Women," 93–94.

9. For more on Du Bois's activism during this period, see Marable, "Peace and Black Liberation"; Sinitiere, *Citizen of the World*.

10. AM-Naison.

11. AM-BWOHP, 34.

12. AM-Prago.

13. AM-Prago.

14. Thomas Warner, phone conversation with author; Warner family, interview by author; Frank Warner and Audley Moore, Bronx County New York Divorce Case and Civil Records, April 24, 1951, New York.

15. AM-BWOHP, 22.

16. AM-Naison.

17. FBI, Report: New York, Dec. 9, 1953, File No. 100-13205, Audley Moore.

18. For more on this report, see Lawson, *To Secure These Rights*. For more on Executive Order 9981, see Taylor, *Freedom to Serve*.

19. Warner family, interview by author; AM-BWOHP, 75–76; Warner, "Recollections and Reflections," 161.

20. Smallwood, *Reform, Red Scare, and Ruin*, 129–30; Lieberman, *Strangest Dream*, 33; "65 Notables Call for Great Peace Pilgrimage to Capital," *Daily Worker*, Feb. 1, 1951, 2.

21. "65 Notables Call for Great Peace Pilgrimage"; "Robeson, Mann Join New 'Peace Crusade,'" *New York Times*, Feb. 15, 1951, 11; "Thousands in Capital Today for Great Peace Pilgrimage," *Daily Worker*, March 15, 1951, 3.

22. "Women, Kids, to Rally at UN Tomorrow," *Daily Worker*, July 23, 1951, 3; "UN Head Tells Peace Group That He May Soon Act for Truce," *Daily Worker*, Aug. 10, 1951, 1.

23. "Peace Crusade a 'Front' for Reds, Bowker Charges," *Boston Globe*, Feb. 17, 1951, 15; "Report Rules That Peace Group Is Red Front," *Washington Post*, Jan. 26, 1957, A4.

24. Lieberman, *Strangest Dream*, 106.

25. Thomas Warner, phone conversation with author; Warner family, interview by author.

26. TW-Payne; Blakely, "40 Acres and a Mule," 131.

27. Gilyard, *Louise Thompson Patterson*, 171; McDuffie, "'New Freedom Movement of Negro Women,'" 85–86.

28. McDuffie, "'New Freedom Movement of Negro Women,'" 86.

29. "A Call to Negro Women," box 12, folder 18, LTP.

30. "Call to Negro Women"; B. Richardson to the President,

Sept. 25, 1951, B. Richardson to Alexander Pace (secretary of war), Sept. 25, 1951; B. Richardson to Dean Acheson (secretary of state), Sept. 25, 1951, box 12, folder 17, LTP.

31. FBI, Memo from Washington and Washington Field from New York to Director and SAC, Sept. 26, 1951, File No. 100-384225, Sojourners for Truth and Justice.

32. "Digest of Proceedings," box 12, folder 17, LTP.

33. Parker, *Unceasing Militant,* 286.

34. "Call to Negro Women"; "Digest of Proceedings."

35. "Digest of Proceedings"; Richardson to Alexander Pace (secretary of war), box 12, folder 17, LTP.

36. "Digest of Proceedings"; Louise Thompson Patterson interview, March 16, 1988, regarding Sojourners for Truth and Justice, box AV1, LTP.

37. "Digest of Proceedings."

38. "New National Club to Be Described," *Daily Independent Journal,* Nov. 15, 1951, 9; "Announcement for the Eastern Seaboard Conference of the Sojourners for Truth and Justice," box 12, folder 18, LTP.

39. For more information on the Moores, see Green, *Before His Time.*

40. "Our Cup Runneth Over" and "5,000 Negro Women Wanted," box 12, folder 18, LTP.

41. Louise Thompson Patterson interview, March 16, 1988.

42. Gilyard, *Louise Thompson Patterson,* 176.

43. McDuffie, "'New Freedom Movement of Negro Women,'" 82; Louise Thompson Patterson interview, March 16, 1988.

44. FBI, Washington Field to Director

and SAC, Sept. 21, 1951, File No. 100-3842252, Sojourners for Truth and Justice.

45. FBI, Memo from A. E. Belmont to D. M. Ladd, Sept. 27, 1951, File No. 100-3842252, Sojourners for Truth and Justice.

46. FBI, Memo to the Attorney General, Director, FBI, Nov. 2, 1951, File No. 100-384225-12, Sojourners for Truth and Justice.

47. "Mothers' Day Delegation for Mrs. Ingram Mapped," *Daily Worker,* March 25, 1953, 3; Gore, *Radicalism at the Crossroads,* 88; McDuffie, "'New Freedom Movement of Negro Women,'" 96.

48. FBI, Memo from H. Howard McGrath (attorney general) to Mr. Hoover (director), Nov. 24, 1951, File No. 100-384225-14, Sojourners for Truth and Justice.

49. FBI, Office Memorandum, To: Director, FBI, From: SAC, Savannah, May 2, 1952, File No. 100-38422, Sojourners for Truth and Justice.

50. FBI, Teletype from FBI, Savannah, To: Director, FBI, Dec. 25, 1952, File No. 100-384235-86, Sojourners for Truth and Justice; "Georgia Cops Break Word, Stop Ingram Delegation," *Daily Worker,* Dec. 26, 1952.

51. FBI, Report of Anthony E. Constantino, Dec. 18, 1953, File No. 100-384225, Sojourners for Truth and Justice.

52. McDuffie, "March of Young Southern Black Women," 86, 96–98.

53. Davies, *Left of Karl Marx,* 141–44; Davies, *Claudia Jones Beyond Containment,* xv.

54. Herbert Brownell Jr., Attorney General of the United States,

petitioner, v. United May Day
Committee, respondent. Cecil R.
Heflin [and others] for petitioner.
Reuben Terris and John J. Abt for
Louis Weinstock. Report and order
of the Board decided April 27, 1956,
University of Michigan Library,

Docket No. 111-53, United States
Subversive Board, 1956.

55. Transcript of Hearing in Case of
Mr. Samuel Leroy Brown, Held at
the Pentagon, Jan. 12, 1955, Folder:
Papers, Jan. 12, 1955, Arthur W.
Mitchell Papers.

Chapter 11: NOT YOUR NEGRO

1. AM-BWOHP, 22.

2. "African National Group Names a
New Organizer," *New York Amsterdam
News,* Sept. 28, 1946, 8; Harris, Harris,
and Harris, *Carlos Cooks and Black
Nationalism,* xi–xii; Rivera, "Carlos
Cooks and Garveyism," 24, 32.

3. Harris, Harris, and Harris, *Carlos
Cooks and Black Nationalism,* xii–xiii.

4. Harris, Harris, and Harris, *Carlos
Cooks and Black Nationalism,* 3.

5. Harris, Harris, and Harris, *Carlos
Cooks and Black Nationalism,* xiv;
Rivera, "Carlos Cooks and
Garveyism," 4, 67.

6. "Marcus Garvey Day Is Observed,"
New York Amsterdam News, Aug. 28,
1954, 1.

7. "What We Know," *Street Speaker* 1,
no. 1 (1955).

8. W. A. Domingo, "What Are We,
Negroes or Colored People?,"
Messenger, May–June 1919, 23–25.

9. "The Term 'Negro,'" *Chicago
Defender,* Nov. 17, 1934, A2.

10. "Reorganization U.N.I.A.," box 15,
folder 15.6, UNIA-EMORY.

11. See, for example, "Eliminate the
Term 'Negro,'" *Afro-American,* Oct. 7,
1939, 12; "The Term 'Negro' Has
Two Meanings or Applications,"
Afro-American, May 23, 1921, 6.

12. Carlos Cooks, "Hair Conking,
Buying Black," in Harris, Harris,

and Harris, *Carlos Cooks and Black
Nationalism,* 63–71.

13. "No Longer Majority Black, Harlem
Is in Transition," *New York Times,*
June 5, 2010.

14. Turner and Turner, *Richard B. Moore,*
69; "Harlem Bookshops Have a
Wealth of Material by and About
Negroes," *Chicago Defender,* Feb. 14,
1953, 10; "In and Out of Books," *New
York Times,* June 11, 1961, 8.

15. W. Burghardt Turner and Joyce
Moore Turner, introduction to *The
Name "Negro,"* by Richard B. Moore,
14–15.

16. Turner and Turner, *Richard B. Moore,*
57–58. For evidence of Richard
Moore's organizing, see "Tenants
Campaign for Rent Law Extension,"
New York Amsterdam News, Feb. 8,
1928, 4; "Tenants League Meets,"
Afro-American, Feb. 18, 1928, 5;
"A.N.L.C. Leaders Cheered by
Brooklyn Citizens," *Pittsburgh
Courier,* Sept. 1, 1928, 4; "Rent Strike
Is Proposed," *New York Amsterdam
News,* Dec. 12, 1928, 1; "Many Attend
'Harlem Revels': Hear Richard B.
Moore of A.N.L.C.," *Pittsburgh
Courier,* Feb. 2, 1929, 2.

17. "Scottsboro Fight Renewed at
Conference," *Daily Worker,* Oct. 28,
1937, 3; "Call for the Harlem
Scottsboro Defense Conference."

18. Turner and Turner, *Richard B. Moore,* 52; Naison, *Communists in Harlem,* 136; "Street Speakers Muzzled," *New York Amsterdam News,* Sept. 29, 1926, 1.

19. Turner and Turner, *Richard B. Moore,* 67–68.

20. Ricard J. [*sic*] Moore, interview by Theodore Draper, Jan. 15, 1958, box 21, folder 20, TDR; "Harlem Bookshops Have a Wealth of Material"; AM-BWOHP, 23–24; Frederick Douglass Book Center advertisement, *New York Amsterdam News,* July 28, 1945, 3; Frederick Douglass Book Center advertisement, *New York Amsterdam News,* Dec. 4, 1943, 2A.

21. Turner, "Richard B. Moore Collection and Its Collector," 135–36.

22. Turner and Turner, *Richard B. Moore,* 88.

23. "*Black Scholar* Interviews Audley Moore," 51.

24. AM-BWOHP, 22.

25. "The Committee to Present the Truth About the Name 'Negro' Invites You to Attend a Lecture-Discussion," box 8, folder 4, JHC.

26. Richard B. Moore, *The Name "Negro,"* 36–37.

27. Moore, *The Name "Negro,"* 46–50.

28. "*Black Scholar* Interviews Audley Moore," 54.

29. "*Black Scholar* Interviews Audley Moore," 53.

30. AM-BWOHP, 18.

31. AM-Naison.

32. Sawyer, *Black Minded,* 31.

33. Du Bois, *Souls of Black Folk,* 11.

34. See, for example, "Message to the Grassroots" in Malcolm X, *Malcolm X Speaks,* 1–17.

35. Muhammad, *What Every American So-Called Negro Should Know About;* Sawyer, *Black Minded,* 64.

36. Sawyer, *Black Minded,* 38.

37. Fanon, *Black Skin, White Masks,* 2.

38. Fanon, *Black Skin, White Masks,* 2, 21.

39. "*Black Scholar* Interviews Audley Moore," 52.

40. AM-Naison.

41. AM-BWOHP, 84.

Chapter 12: ARISE, ETHIOPIAN WOMEN!

1. Act of Sale, John Adam Lautenschlaeger Jr. unto Henry J. Moore, Aug. 7, 1915, "Judge Orders Inventory of Moore Estate," *Louisiana Weekly,* Aug. 20, 1955, 1; "Deaths—Moore," *Times-Picayune,* Aug. 6, 1955, 2.

2. "Judge Orders Inventory of Moore Estate"; "Succession in Moore Estate Awarded to Kin," *Louisiana Weekly,* Feb. 4, 1956, 1. Patterson claimed that he left the will in "olographic" form. An olographic will was Louisiana's version of a holographic will that is handwritten, signed, and dated by the testator alone and is not witnessed by a third party to establish authenticity.

3. "Succession in Moore Estate Awarded to Kin."

4. Firven, "From Paternalism to Black Power," 68.

5. "NAACP Moves Forward on All Fronts," *Louisiana Weekly,* Jan. 21, 1956, 10; Rogers, *Righteous Lives,* 199–200.

6. Fairclough, *Race and Democracy,* 106.

7. Fairclough, *Race and Democracy,* 106; "Negro Vote Surpasses 150,000 Mark," *Louisiana Weekly,* Jan. 14, 1956, 1.

8. Fairclough, *Race and Democracy*, 154–55; Emanuel and Tureaud, *More Noble Cause*, 132–36.

9. For more on Citizens' Councils in New Orleans and around the country, see Rolph, *Resisting Equality*, 43–44. For the rise of councils in New Orleans, see *Resisting Equality*, 53

10. "Suit to Ban NAACP to Be Heard Thursday," *Louisiana Weekly*, March 31, 1956, 1; "Defers Action on NAACP Suit," *Louisiana Weekly*, April 7, 1956, 1; "Judge Puts NAACP out of Business in State," *Louisiana Weekly*, April 28, 1956, 1.

11. Fairclough, *Race and Democracy*, 196, 225.

12. "Plans Mass Purge of Negro Voters in La.," *Louisiana Weekly*, Dec. 22, 1956, 1; "NAACP Loses Another Round in Louisiana Fight for Its Life," *Louisiana Weekly*, April 14, 1956, 1; Bosworth, "Black New Orleans," 75.

13. "Urban League Booted Out of Agency," *Louisiana Weekly*, May 25, 1957, 1; "The Evidence Is Quite Clear," *Louisiana Weekly*, May 26, 1956, 1.

14. "Report of Membership Drive in the New Orleans Division, #400," box 17, folder 22; Monthly Report of Local Division, April 1954; Monthly Report of Local Division, July 1955; Monthly Report of Local Division, April 1957, box 17, folder 23, UNIA-EMORY.

15. Harold, *Rise and Fall of the Garvey Movement in the Urban South*, 48–49.

16. "Call Mass Meet to Discuss 'One Sided' Rape Law in La.," *Louisiana Weekly*, June 29, 1957, 2; "Mass Meeting to Discuss La. Rape Law," *Louisiana Weekly*, Aug. 3, 1957, 2.

17. "Michel in Last Ditch Fight to Escape Chair," *Louisiana Weekly*, June 1, 1957, 1.

18. "Victim of 'Southern Justice,' Michel Goes to the Chair Calmly," *Louisiana Weekly*, June 8, 1957, 1, 2.

19. "Mardi Gras Slayer Is Ruled Sane," *Louisiana Weekly*, May 25, 1957, 1–2; "Jenkins Is Sane Enough for 'Chair,'" *Louisiana Weekly*, July 6, 1957, 1; "Maintains Jenkins 'Insane,'" *Louisiana Weekly*, July 13, 1957, 1–2; "Mardi Gras Slayer Loses Appeal, to Die," *Louisiana Weekly*, Dec. 20, 1958, 1.

20. "Mass Meeting to Discuss La. Rape Law"; "Ethiopian Group Will Hold Meeting," *Times-Picayune*, Aug. 4, 1957, 22; "Ask Gov. Long to Review One Sided Rape Convictions," *Louisiana Weekly*, Aug. 17, 1957, 3; "Jenkins Sentenced to 'Chair,'" *Louisiana Weekly*, Nov. 20, 1957, 1, 6.

21. Hermann, "Specters of Freedom," 269, 314.

22. Angola switched to sugar cultivation after the boll weevil infestation of 1907. Hermann, "Specters of Freedom," 362; "State Farm Work Well Under Way," *Times-Democrat*, Feb. 23, 1913, 6; Butler and Henderson, *Angola*, 34–55.

23. "Angola: Long Way to Go," *Daily World*, Jan. 8, 1953, 4; "Danger Seen in Use of Prisoners as Guards at State Penitentiary," *Town Talk*, Dec. 14, 1953, 25.

24. AM-BWOHP, 29.

25. AM-BWOHP, 27; Jackson-Issa, "Her Own Book," 40; Earl Pinto, interview by author; "Ethiopian Churchmen Welcomed to America," *California Eagle*, June 12, 1952, 6.

26. "Protest Meet Is Called," *Louisiana Weekly*, Sept. 14, 1957, 1.

27. For an overview of Collins's life and activism, see Farmer, "Mothers of Pan-Africanism."

28. "Ethiopian Women Seek Funds for African Confab," *Louisiana Weekly*, Aug. 16, 1958, 3.

29. "Appeal to U.N. to Stop Race Violence," *Louisiana Weekly*, May 9, 1959, 1; "Urges Mass Appeal to Save 'Accused' Rapist," *Louisiana Weekly*, April 2, 1960, 1.

30. Edgar M. Labat, "My Arrest & Tortures," *Louisiana Weekly*, Jan. 1, 1966, 1, 8.

31. Labat, "My Arrest & Tortures."

32. Edgar Labat and Clifton Alton Poret v. Robert B. Bennett, Acting Warden, Louisiana State Penitentiary, U.S. Court of Appeals for the Fifth Circuit, No. 2218, box 1, folder, 15, JRC.

33. "High Court Denies New Trial for Negroes in Rape Cases," *Montgomery Advertiser*, Dec. 6, 1955, 7.

34. "Consider Plea of Labat, Poret Court Is Told," *Louisiana Weekly*, Nov. 23, 1957, 1; Friedman, *Champion of Civil Rights*, 112–13. For details of the writ, see State of Louisiana et rel., Clifton Alton Poret and Edgar Labat v. Maurice Sigler, Warden of the Louisiana State Penitentiary, Angola, Louisiana, box 2, folder 13, JRC.

35. "Women's Group Seeks to Save 2 from 'Hot Seat,'" *Louisiana Weekly*, Sept. 14, 1957, 1.

36. "A Memorial for Mercy," Sept. 29, 1957, Erik S. McDuffie Collection; "Press Efforts to Save 2 From Electric Chair," *Louisiana Weekly*, Sept. 28, 1957, 1.

37. "On the Way," *Daily Worker*, Dec. 3, 1957, 2.

38. Theoharis, *Rebellious Life of Mrs. Rosa Parks*, 23.

39. "Moore, Audley, 1957," box 4, General Correspondence, 1928–2006, RPP.

40. Weiner, *Enemies*, 196–201. For more on how COINTELPRO affected Black people specifically, see O'Reilly, *Racial Matters;* Churchill and Vander Wall, *Agents of Repression;* Maxwell, *F.B. Eyes;* Perrusquia, *Spy in Canaan.*

41. See, for example, FBI, Report from J. Woodrow Gilmore, Dec. 9, 1957. File No. 100-3751, Audley Moore.

42. "New Evidence May Save 2 from Chair," *Louisiana Weekly*, Sept. 21, 1957, 1, 6.

43. "Women's Group Seeks to Save 2 from 'Hot Seat,'" 1.

44. "New Evidence Uncovered Is 'Startling,'" *Louisiana Weekly*, Sept. 28, 1957, 1, 8.

45. "Press Efforts to Save 2 from Chair," 1; Friedman, *Champion of Civil Rights*, 114.

46. "Poret, Labat Win Stay of Execution," *Louisiana Weekly*, Oct. 5, 1957, 1; "Negroes Cheat Death Row, Swedish Woman Happy," *Jet*, Sept. 1, 1966, 49.

47. "A Miracle," *Los Angeles Times*, Oct. 5, 2007; "In the Shadow of the Chair," *Time*, Aug. 26, 1966, 80.

48. "Negroes Cheat Death Row, Swedish Woman Happy," 49.

49. "A Norwegian Newspaper Asks Clemency for Negro," *New York Times*, Dec. 5, 1965, 26.

50. "2 Battling for Life After 7 Years on La. 'Death Row,'" *Louisiana Weekly*, July 9, 1960, 1.

51. "Louisianan, Freed from 'Death Row,' Is Arrested Again," *New York Times*, May 6, 1967, 19; "Another Trial Set for Labat, Poret," *Afro-American*, Oct. 14, 1967, 16; "2 Convicts Freed

After 14 Years on Death Row," *New York Times,* Dec. 30, 1969, 14.

52. "New Evidence Uncovered Is 'Startling'"; "Poret, Labat Interviewed at Angola," *Louisiana Weekly,* Oct. 12, 1957, 1, 2.

53. "Moore, Audley, 1957."

54. "Insufficient Evidence Is Reply to Negro Girl's Charge," *Louisiana Weekly,* July 12, 1958, 1; "Freed Rape Suspect Tries to Kill Self," *Louisiana Weekly,* Aug. 2, 1958, 1. For more on the history of how Black women in New Orleans navigated the continual threat of white sexual violence, see Simmons, *Crescent City Girls.*

55. "Freeing of Rape Suspect Hit by Clergy," *Louisiana Weekly,* July 19, 1958, 1.

56. "Protest Freeing of Rape Suspect to the FBI," *Louisiana Weekly,* Aug. 16, 1958, 8.

57. "Ask Gov. Long to Review One Sided Rape Convictions," 3; "Mass Meeting Slated for Sun., Feb. 22," *Louisiana Weekly,* Feb. 21, 1958, 6; "Ethiopian Women Blast 'Rape' Law," *Louisiana Weekly,* Feb. 28, 1959, 1, 7.

58. "The Twain Has Met," *Louisiana Weekly,* June 27, 1959, 11, 12.

59. Lawinski, *Living on the Edge of Suburbia,* 23–26.

60. "23,000 Children Cut Off La. Welfare Roll," *Louisiana Weekly,* Aug. 13, 1960, 3; "1270 Families Cut Off Welfare Rolls," *Louisiana Weekly,* July 23, 1960, 1, 7; "The Relief Roles for Unwed Mothers," *Indianapolis Recorder,* Oct. 1, 1960, 10; Neubeck and Cazenave, *Welfare Racism,* 72; Germany, *New Orleans After the Promises,* 220.

61. "Ethiopian Women Make Plea for Hungry Children," *Louisiana Weekly,* Aug. 27, 1960, 3; "Plight of Hungry Children Aired at NUL Convention," *Louisiana Weekly,* Sept. 10, 1960, 6; "No Emergency Relief in Sight for Hungry Babies," *Louisiana Weekly,* Sept. 17, 1960, 1, 7; "Government Studying La. Welfare Situation," *Pittsburgh Courier,* Sept. 17, 1960, 16B; "Food Sought for Welfare 'Cutoffs,'" *Louisiana Weekly,* Aug. 13, 1960, 1, 5.

62. "Will Bias Cause Louisiana to Sacrifice $21,000,000?," *Pittsburgh Courier,* Nov. 5, 1960, 6.

63. "Appeal to U.S. Agency, Red Cross to Aid Hungry Babies," *Louisiana Weekly,* Sept. 3, 1960, 1.

64. "Appeal to U.S. Agency, Red Cross to Aid Hungry Babies."

65. "Ethiopian Women Group Founder Makes a Speech," *Atlanta Daily World,* Dec. 6, 1960, 2; "Buffalo Group Joins 'Starving Babies' Fite," *Afro-American,* Dec. 3, 1960, 12; "Appeal Made in Elmira to Aid Louisiana Tots," *Star-Gazette,* Nov. 22, 1960, 9; "Spirit of Giving Reigns at Yuletide," *Chicago Defender,* Dec. 20, 1960, 14.

66. "Terrorized by Bigots Bullets in Tennessee," *Louisiana Weekly,* Jan. 14, 1961, 1.

67. "Charges Gov. Davis Welfare Aid Remarks 'Irresponsible,'" *Louisiana Weekly,* Oct. 1, 1960, 1, 7.

68. "Louisiana Welfare Laws Are Attacked," *Arizona Republic,* Sept. 13, 1960, 4; "Kennon, US Officials in Welfare Fund Clash," *The Times* (Shreveport, LA), Nov. 15, 1960, 23; "Child Welfare League Asks for Probe of La. Welfare Laws," *Louisiana Weekly,* Oct. 1, 1960, 2; "U.S. Takes Long Look at La. Welfare Laws," *Louisiana Weekly,* Nov. 26, 1960, 1, 7.

69. Germany, *New Orleans After the Promises,* 229; Lindhorst and Leighninger, "'Ending Welfare as We Know It' in 1960"; "We Are Our Brothers' Keepers," box 2, folder 4, Mae Mallory Papers.

70. "Charges Gov. Davis Welfare Aid Remarks 'Irresponsible.'"

Chapter 13: THE UNITED NATIONS AND REPARATIONS

1. United States ex rel. Jose Cuevas v. Alfred T. Rundle, Superintendent, U.S. District Court for the Eastern District of Pennsylvania, Sept. 19, 1966. For more on the conditions in early twentieth-century Angola, see Butler and Henderson, *Angola.*

2. Jose Angel Cuevas y Pitre, 1930 Federal Census, San Sebastián, Puerto Rico, sheet 5B.

3. United States ex rel. Jose Cuevas v. Alfred T. Rundle.

4. United States ex rel. Jose Cuevas v. Alfred T. Rundle; Playthell Benjamin, phone conversation with author.

5. Duany, *Puerto Rican Nation on the Move,* 246–60.

6. United States ex rel. Jose Cuevas v. Alfred T. Rundle.

7. Warner family, interview by author; Playthell Benjamin, interview by author.

8. Duany, *Puerto Rican Nation on the Move,* 122.

9. Duany, *Puerto Rican Nation on the Move,* 4, 24.

10. "The Universal Association of Ethiopian Women, Inc.—a Brief History," box 4, folder 7, Vicki Garvin Papers.

11. For more on the rise of nuclear warfare and the Truman and Eisenhower presidencies, see Spalding, *First Cold Warrior,* McClenahan Jr. and Becker, *Eisenhower and the Cold War Economy.*

12. "Hearts of Africa Committee Fundraising Letter," box 3, folder 7, UNIA- EMORY; "Queen Picketed at U.N. by Kenya Protest Group," *Tampa Tribune,* Oct. 22, 1957, 37.

13. Tyson, *Radio Free Dixie,* 108; International Committee in Defense of Africa, "Robert F. Williams: Anti-lynch Fighter, a Man and a Cause for Unity, Freedom, and Justice," box 2, folder 9, Committee to Combat Racial Injustice Records.

14. Kwame Nkrumah, "Independence Speech," in Konadu and Campbell, *Ghana Reader,* 133–34.

15. For more on Black Americans in Nkrumah's Ghana, see Gaines, *American Africans in Ghana.*

16. Meriwether, *Proudly We Can Be Africans,* 133.

17. "Ethiopian Women Ask African's Aid," *Louisiana Weekly,* May 2, 1959, 2.

18. Snyder, *From Selma to Moscow,* 6.

19. Snyder, *From Selma to Moscow,* 3, 9.

20. *We Charge Genocide: The Historic Petition to the United Nations for Relief from a Crime of the United States Government Against the Negro People* (International Publishers, 1951). For more on Patterson's life and activism, see Horne, *Black Revolutionary.*

21. "Appeal to UN to Stop Racial Violence," *Louisiana Weekly,* May 9, 1959, 1; Universal Association of Ethiopian Women to Hammarskjöld, May 1, 1959, reprinted in "The Universal Association of Ethiopian

Women—a Brief History," Roderick Jenkins Collection.

22. Wynn, *African American Experience during World War II*, 91. For more on U.S. domination of the UN, see Anderson, "From Hope to Disillusion."

23. UAEW, "Draft Resolution for the Establishment of an Independent Black Republic." Copies found in UAEW's FBI file and Folder: African Descendants Nationalist Independence Partition (AD-NIP) Party, Folder: 009051-025-0181, RFW.

24. Virginia Collins interview, part 5, box 3, May 10, 1975, item 23, side 1, Kim Lacy Rogers Collection.

25. UAEW, "Draft Resolution for the Establishment of an Independent Black Republic."

26. Virginia Collins interview, part 5, box 3, May 10, 1975.

27. Berry, *My Face Is Black Is True*, 21–22, 28–29. For more on how Black women engaged in politics in the post-emancipation South, see Brimmer, *Claiming Union Widowhood*.

28. Berry, *My Face Is Black Is True*, 33. For an example of how these ads would have appeared in Tennessee, see "To Pension Ex-slaves," *Memphis Appeal-Avalanche*, Nov. 24, 1890, 4.

29. Carey and Plank, *Quakers and Abolition*, 113–14. For more on this subject, see Jackson and Kozel, *Quakers and Their Allies in the Abolitionist Cause*.

30. "Petition of an African slave to the Legislature of Massachusetts," in Carretta, *Unchained Voices*, 142–44.

31. Vaughan, *Vaughan's "Freedmen's Pension Bill*," 56–57; Berry, *My Face Is Black Is True*, 34–35.

32. Vaughan, *Vaughan's "Freedmen's Pension Bill*," 30.

33. Vaughan, *Vaughan's "Freedmen's Pension Bill*," 39, 58, 178; Perry, "Prospect of Justice," 59–60.

34. For evidence of chapters of the association developing in various cities, see "They All Want Pensions," *Kansas City Times*, Nov. 22, 1899, 8; "The Ex-slaves' Bounty," *Indianapolis Journal*, Sept. 16, 1899, 8; "North Carolina," *Baltimore Sun*, Dec. 30, 1899, 9; Berry, *My Face Is Black Is True*, 116.

35. "Fraud Order Issued," *Evening Star*, Oct. 29, 1903, 1.

36. Berry, *My Face Is Black Is True*, 60, 116–17.

37. "Act of Incorporation of the Ex. Slave Mutual Relief, Bounty, and Pension Association of Louisiana," vol. 3, act 20, LAMR; Berry, *My Face Is Black Is True*, 169, 200.

38. Berry, *My Face Is Black Is True*, 236.

39. Marcus Garvey, "The Sign by Which We Conquer," in Hill, *Marcus Garvey and the Universal Negro Improvement Association Papers*, 5:461.

40. Farmer, "'Somebody Has to Pay'"; Martin, *Race First*, 6; Harris, "Political Autonomy as a Form of Reparations to African Americans," 33.

41. Araujo, *Reparations for Slavery and the Slave Trade*, 127.

42. Araujo, *Reparations for Slavery and the Slave Trade*, 128–29. For more information on this aspect of reparations, see Pross, *Paying for the Past*.

43. Newton, "Indian Claims for Reparations, Compensation, and Restitution in the United States Legal System," 262–63.

44. Daniels, "Relocation, Redress, and the Report," 183–84.

45. "*Black Scholar* Interviews Queen Mother Moore," 51.

46. "*Black Scholar* Interviews Queen Mother Moore," 51. Scholars have struggled to locate this clause for verification. Nevertheless, Moore stood by this as a primary impetus for her reparations activism.

47. Virginia Collins interview, part 5, box 3, May 10, 1975.

Chapter 14: SOMEBODY HAS TO PAY

1. Ahmad, *We Will Return in the Whirlwind*, 112–13; Ahmad, "Queen Mother Moore," 169; Playthell Benjamin, interview by author; Muhammad Ahmad, interview by author; FBI, Memo from SAC, Philadelphia, to Director, FBI, July 27, 1962, File No. 110-61122-76, Audley Moore.

2. Playthell Benjamin, interview by author; Muhammad Ahmad, interview by author.

3. For an overview of civil rights struggles in the City of Brotherly Love, see Countryman, *Up South*.

4. Jose Cuevas and Audley A. Moore, Certificate of Marriage Registration, License No. 9590, May 15, 1961, City Clerk, Bureau of Manhattan, New York.

5. United States ex rel. Jose Cuevas v. Alfred T. Rundle.

6. Levenstein, *Movement Without Marches*, 10.

7. AM-BWOHP, 73–74.

8. Tom Warner stated in interviews with the author that the reason his mother moved to Philadelphia was to be closer to him.

9. Tom Warner, interview by author; TW-Payne.

10. Countryman, *Up South,* 50; Philadelphia Charter Commission, "Philadelphia Home Rule Charter, 1951"; Pedro Regalado, "Fair Housing," in *Encyclopedia of Greater Philadelphia* (Mid-Atlantic Center for the Humanities, 2014), philadelphiaencyclopedia.org.

11. Playthell Benjamin, interview by author.

12. Levenstein, *Movement Without Marches,* 10.

13. Vázquez-Hernández, "From Pan-Latino Enclaves to a Community," 104.

14. Primitive Cuevas y Rodriguez, 1930 Federal Census, San Sebastián, Puerto Rico, sheet 5A; Birth Certificate, Jose Angel Cuebas [Cuevas] y Pitre, San Sebastián, March 17, 1929, Puerto Rico Civil Registraciones, 1885–2001; Jose Cuevas, 1930 Federal Census, San Sebastián, Puerto Rico, sheet 5B.

15. Denis, *War Against All Puerto Ricans,* 29–30; Alamo-Pastrana, *Seams of Empire,* 39–40.

16. Duany, *Puerto Rican Nation on the Move,* 21.

17. Dennis, *War Against All Puerto Ricans,* 37–39.

18. Census reports indicate that Jose could not read or write as a young child. Court reports indicate that he had limited fluency in English and his formal schooling ended in the seventh grade. United States ex rel. Jose Cuevas v. Alfred T. Rundle.

19. Bosque-Pérez and Morera, *Puerto Rico Under Colonial Rule,* 24.

20. Whalen, "Colonialism, Citizenship,

and the Making of the Puerto Rican Diaspora," 27–28; Duany, *Puerto Rican Nation on the Move,* 13; Perez, *Near Northwest Side Story,* 10.

21. "African American Groups— Voluntary Organizations Among Philadelphia Afro-Americans," in Toll and Gillam, *Invisible Philadelphia.*

22. Haley and Malcolm X, *Autobiography of Malcolm X,* 210; Countryman, *Up South,* 89.

23. Arnau, "Evolution of Leadership Within the Puerto Rican Community of Philadelphia"; Ribeiro, " 'Asking Them and Protesting.' "

24. For evidence of Cecil Moore's support of local Black residents, see "Contempt Case Is Dismissed," *Philadelphia Inquirer,* April 18, 1962, 4; "Juvenile Court Jurisdiction Urged for Boy Accused of Murder at 14," *York Daily Record,* May 4, 1962, 4.

25. Countryman, *Up South,* 123; "Philadelphia's Labor-Racial Row Settled," *Record,* May 31, 1963, 5.

26. Countryman, *Up South,* 124–25.

27. Schmidt, *Sit-Ins,* 13; Carson, *In Struggle,* 9.

28. Arsenault, *Freedom Riders,* 141–45.

29. Arsenault, *Freedom Riders,* 184.

30. For more on JFK's and RFK's responses to the Freedom Rides and resistance to supporting Black Americans' civil rights struggles more broadly, see Niven, *Politics of Injustice.*

31. Ahmad, *We Will Return in the Whirlwind,* 95–96; Ho and Mullen, *Afro Asia,* 107–8.

32. Countryman, *Up South,* 110, 139.

33. Ahmad, *We Will Return in the Whirlwind,* 98–99.

34. Kelley, *Freedom Dreams,* 76–78.

35. Muhammad Ahmad, "People's Organizing: How Ella Baker and Mothers of the Movement Influenced My Philosophy on Organizing." In author's possession.

36. Ahmad, "Queen Mother Moore," 169. For more on Mallory's upbringing, imprisonment, and trial, see Farmer, " 'All the Progress to Be Made Will Be Made by Maladjusted Negroes' "; Seniors, *Mae Mallory, the Monroe Defense Committee, and World Revolutions.*

37. Playthell Benjamin, interview by author; Muhammad Ahmad, interview by author.

38. Ahmad, *We Will Return in the Whirlwind,* 111.

39. Ahmad, "People's Organizing."

40. Ahmad, *We Will Return in the Whirlwind,* 113.

41. Ahmad, *We Will Return in the Whirlwind,* 112–14.

42. Ahmad, *We Will Return in the Whirlwind,* 108.

43. Summers, *Manliness and Its Discontents,* 96–98.

44. Moore in Lanker, *I Dream a World,* 103.

45. For more on the implications of this meeting and their relationship more broadly, see McDuffie and Woodard, " 'If You're in a Country That's Progressive, the Woman Is Progressive.' "

46. Address Books, 1958–1961, reel 1, MXC.

47. Playthell Benjamin, interview by author; Ahmad, *We Will Return in the Whirlwind,* 98, 100.

48. "JFK to Be Given Chance to Finish Lincoln's Work," *Afro-American,* Jan. 27, 1962, 5.

49. "JFK to Be Given Chance to Finish

Lincoln's Work." For list of initiating organizations, see "NEPCOC-Press Release," in FBI, Memo from SAC (100-new) to SAC [Redacted], April 20, 1962, FBI File No. 100-46312, National Emancipation Proclamation Centennial Observance Committee (NEPCOC).

50. "NEPCOC-Press Release."

51. "JFK to Be Given Chance to Finish Lincoln's Work"; "Afros Demand Indemnity; JFK Ignores Their Request," *Herald Dispatch,* April 7, 1962, 10.

52. "Freedom Day Fete," *Philadelphia Tribune,* April 14, 1962, 13.

53. "Afros Demand Reparations," *Herald Dispatch,* April 12, 1962, 10.

54. Telegram from Audley Moore and Rabbi Eliezer to White House, Jan. 10, 1962, Folder: 001349-002-0643 HU2 10-26-61-2-19-62, Civil Rights During the Kennedy Administration, 1961–1963, Part 1: The White House Central Files and Staff Files and the President's Office Files, JFK.

55. NEPCOC, press release, Feb. 6, 1962, Rodrick Jenkins Collection; "Rabbi Starts Reparations Campaign," *Herald Dispatch,* April 2, 1962, 10; Telegram from Audley Moore and Rabbi Eliezer to White House.

56. See, for example, "Public Forum, Subject: $500 Reparations due Each Descendant of U.S. Slaves," May 25, 1962, in FBI, File No. 100-46312-1A-4, NEPCOC. The FBI tracked Moore traveling to speak about reparations. FBI, Memo from Special Agent Erling W. Harbo, To: SAC, Seattle, July 26, 1962, FBI File No. 100-46312-30, NEPCOC.

57. "African American Emancipation Proclamation Centennial Conference Souvenir Journal," in FBI, File No. 100-46312, NEPCOC; Audley Moore, "Address to the National Emancipation Proclamation Centennial Observance Committee Conference," Oct. 12, 1962, carton 4, reel 35, SPC.

58. Audley Moore, "Address to the National Emancipation Proclamation Centennial Observance Committee Conference."

59. Moore, "Address to the National Emancipation Proclamation Centennial Observance Committee Conference."

60. "Resolution on Reparations," in "African American Emancipation Proclamation Centennial Conference Souvenir Journal."

61. Moore, "Address to the National Emancipation Proclamation Centennial Observance Committee Conference."

62. "African-Descendant Centennial and Reparations Conference Resolutions," carton 4, reel 5, folder 35, SPC.

63. For more on AD NIP and founding documents, see "African-Descendant Centennial and Reparations Conference Resolutions," carton 4, reel 5, folder 35, SPC.

64. "The Members of the Politburo Held the Following Portfolios," carton 4, reel 5, folder 25, SPC. Loretta also joined the organization as the minister of finance. AD NIP leaders to Robert F. Williams, June 7, 1963; Audley Moore to *The Crusader,* Oct. 1, 1963; Audley Moore to Robert F. Williams, May 12,

1964, Audley Moore to Williams, April 12, 1964, box 12, folder AD NIP, RFW-Bentley.

65. McDuffie, "'I Wanted a Communist Philosophy,'" 190; "*Black Scholar* Interviews Queen Mother Moore," 47.

66. "Suspect Arrested in Slaying over $3," *Philadelphia Daily News,* Oct. 8, 1962, 5.

67. United States ex rel. Jose Cuevas v. Alfred T. Rundle.

68. 5-ORAL-30-5-Side-02, Queen Mother Moore Tapes.

Chapter 15: THE REPARATIONS COMMITTEE INC.

1. For more on the planning and execution of the march, see Jones, *March on Washington.* For women's roles in the march, see Scanlon, *Until There Is Justice;* Height, "We Wanted the Voice of a Woman to Be Heard," 83–91.

2. Davis and Wiener, *Set the Night on Fire,* 13.

3. Robinson, "Race, Space, and the Evolution of Black Los Angeles," 43.

4. Marable, *Malcolm X,* 148–49.

5. Davis and Wiener, *Set the Night on Fire,* 64; Plummer, *In Search of Power,* 44; "Nationalist Speaker Lays It on the 'Rev,'" *California Eagle,* Dec. 13, 1962, 1.

6. The author located these flyers at Locus Solus Rare Books, Los Angeles.

7. Garibaldi, *Impermanent Blackness,* 148.

8. "Grand Opening Africa House," *Los Angeles Sentinel,* July 9, 1959, C1; "Africa House Meets Challenge," *Herald-Dispatch,* Oct. 26, 1973, 10; "Africa House Inc. Stresses African Americans' Heritage," *Herald-Dispatch,* Dec. 16, 1967, 1. For more on the Alexanders, see Elizabeth Pat Alexander, interview by R. Donald Brown, Topic: *The Herald Dispatch,* April 8, 1967, Black Oral History of California Project, Lawrence de Graff Center for Oral and Public History, California State University–Fullerton; "Sanford Alexander," Negro Who's Who of California, 1948 ed., California State Library, Sacramento; "Muslim Hatred Called Threat to Community," *Los Angeles Times,* May 7, 1962, 32.

9. Lincoln, *Black Muslims in America,* 124; Felber, *Those Who Know Don't Say,* 125–26; Davis and Wiener, *Set the Night on Fire,* 65–66.

10. The FBI file on the NEPCOC states that the organization employed the civil rights lawyer Conrad Lynn to help transform the NEPCOC into the Reparations Committee. FBI, Memo from SAC to Unknown SAC, May 3, 1962, FBI File No. 100-46312, NEPCOC.

11. For the committee's ongoing activities, see "Reparations P.R. Man Seeks Legal Talent," *Herald-Dispatch,* May 20, 1964, 1; "Reparations: An Economic Necessity," *Herald-Dispatch,* Oct. 1, 1964, 8; "Stop $100 'Billion Swindle' Pay Negroes Reparations," *Herald-Dispatch,* Jan. 7, 1967, 1, 9; "Calendar of Events: Reparations Committee Pink and White Tea," *Los Angeles Sentinel,* April 5, 1963, C5.

12. Moore, *Why Reparations?* For evidence of the committee's efforts to sell and circulate *Why Reparations?,* see *Herald-Dispatch,* July 23, 1964, 8.

13. Moore, *Why Reparations?*, emphasis in original.

14. Moore, *Why Reparations?*

15. "*Black Scholar* Interviews Queen Mother Moore," 51.

16. "Reparations Committee to Meet Sunday," *Herald-Dispatch,* June 4, 1964, 3; "Reparations Committee Charges U.S. Genocide," *Herald-Dispatch,* Dec. 10, 1964, 1, 6.

17. "Reparations P.R. Man Seeks Legal Talent."

18. "Reparations Comm. Not a Part of Ad Nip Party," *Herald-Dispatch,* Jan. 20, 1968, 1, 8.

19. Moore, *Why Reparations?*

20. "U.S. Failure to Appropriate Emancipation Centennial Celebration Money Causing Embarrassment for Kennedy Administration," *Black Dispatch,* Jan. 18, 1963, 3; "TV Previews," *Post Standard,* Sept. 22, 1962, 17.

21. Remarks Recorded for Emancipation Proclamation Centennial Ceremony, Lincoln Memorial, Sept. 22, 1962, President's Office Files, JFK.

22. "Emancipation Proclamation Centennial," *Birmingham Mirror,* Dec. 8, 1962, 18; "Emancipation Celebration Set," *St. Louis Globe-Democrat,* Jan. 3, 1963, 33.

23. "Emancipation Event Scheduled December 30th," *Columbia Daily Tribune,* Dec. 22, 1962, 1; "Brochure Proofs," box 1, folder 4, Emancipation Centennial Committee Records.

24. Moore to Randolph, Aug. 11, 1963, box 28, Folder: March on Washington, General Correspondence, Aug. 8–12, 1963, Bayard Rustin Papers.

25. Moore, *Why Reparations?*

26. Haley and Malcolm X, *Autobiography of Malcolm X,* 295.

27. AM-BWOHP, 35; AM-Naison; Lanker, *I Dream a World,* 103; "Nationhood, Queen Mother Moore, 1966," box 96-129/6, No. 0117, AAC; McDuffie and Woodard, "'If You're in a Country That's Progressive, the Woman Is Progressive,'" 522.

28. Playthell Benjamin, interview by author.

29. Payne, *Dead Are Arising;* Haley and Malcolm X, *Autobiography of Malcolm X,* 295, 303.

30. Malcolm X, "The Race Problem," African Students Association and NAACP Campus Chapter, Michigan State University, East Lansing, Jan. 23, 1963, ccnmtl.columbia.edu.

31. King, *Why We Can't Wait,* 12–13.

32. King, *Why We Can't Wait,* 165, 170.

33. King, *Why We Can't Wait,* 160–61. For more on King's reparations advocacy, see Coates, "Martin Luther King Makes the Case for Reparations"; Balfour, "Living 'in the Red,'" 237–39; Eig, *King: A Life,* 358–59.

34. "Women to Build Library in Mrs. Moore's Name," *New York Amsterdam News,* Feb. 15, 1964, 4; "Birthday Celebration," *Kweli,* May 1970, 12.

35. McDuffie, "'We Owe a Debt to Her, She Taught Us How to Think,'" 151; Warner family, interview by author.

36. "Nationhood, Queen Mother Moore, 1966."

37. "Women to Build Library in Mrs. Moore's Name"; "Build College in Memory of Eloise Moore"; "Resolution in Memory of Eloise Moore," box 24, folder 36, RBP.

38. "The Eloise Moore Memorial College of African History and Research," Erik S. McDuffie Collection. This poem was also reprinted in "Queen Mother Moore:

Poem of Eloise," *Black Scholar* 1, no. 8 (1970): 50–52.

39. Warner family, interview by author; "Build College in Memory of Eloise Moore."

40. Payne, *Dead Are Arising*, 477–78.

41. "Statement to the Press by Malcolm X, March 8, 1964," folder 1, reel 13, MXC.

42. Haley and Malcolm X, *Autobiography of Malcolm X*, 345.

43. Playthell Benjamin recalls discussions that offered some of the central ideas of what would become the OAAU. William Sales argues that Muhammad Ahmad and other activists in Philadelphia played an important role in helping Malcolm separate from the NOI and form the OAAU. Benjamin, interview by author; Sales, *From Civil Rights to Black Liberation*.

44. "Burying Malcolm X," *Village Voice*, March 4, 1965, 1, 10.

Chapter 16: BECOMING QUEEN MOTHER

1. "Who Mourns Malcolm X?," *New York Herald Tribune*, Feb. 21, 1966, 3; "March for Malcolm X Is Small and Lonely," *Star Tribune*, Feb. 21, 1966, 2; "75 March to Mark Malcolm X's Death," *New York Times*, Feb. 21, 1966, 45.

2. FBI, "Memorial Tribute to Malcolm X," May 19, 1966, File No. NY 105-8999, Malcolm X.

3. Moore, "The Princely Malcolm X," Erik S. McDuffie Collection.

4. For an excellent history of the Lowndes County freedom struggle, see Jeffries, *Bloody Lowndes*.

5. Joseph, *Stokely*, 87–88; Patton, *My Race to Freedom*, 224–26; "Lowndes County Freedom Organization Founded," SNCC Digital Gateway, snccdigital.org.

6. "New Leaders and New Course for 'Snick,'" *New York Times*, May 22, 1966, 208; William A. Price, "SNCC Charts a Course: An Interview with Stokely Carmichael, Chairman, Student Nonviolent Coordinating Committee," *National Guardian*, June 4, 1966, Civil Rights Movement Veterans website, https://www.crmvet.org/info/6605_stokely.pdf.

7. For a concise history of the Meredith March Against Fear, see Goudsouzian, *Down to the Crossroads*.

8. Joseph, *Stokely*, 102–3.

9. Howard quoted in Jeffries, *Bloody Lowndes*, 152–53.

10. On the founding of the Oakland-based Black Panther Party, see "Carmichael Hits U.S. Policies at Berkeley Rally," *Los Angeles Times*, Oct. 30, 1966, C1; Bloom and Martin, *Black Against Empire*, 39–42; Newton, *Revolutionary Suicide*, 119.

11. For a comprehensive overview of the US organization, see Brown, *Fighting for US*.

12. "Kawaida Philosophy and Practice: Questions for a Life of Struggle," *Los Angeles Sentinel*, Aug. 8, 2007, A7.

13. For the spread of Kawaida and its cultural impact during the 1960s, see "Holiday for Malcolm X Asked Here," *Los Angeles Times*, May 18, 1967, 29; "Observance Set for Malcolm X," *Los Angeles Sentinel*, Feb. 3, 1966, A1. For an overview of how Kwanzaa has evolved in the United States, see Mayes, *Kwanzaa*.

14. Baraka, *Autobiography of LeRoi Jones*,

350–58; Simanga, *Amiri Baraka and the Congress of African People*, 79–84.

15. For more on Black Power–era politicians and their political brokering with Black Power organizers, see Woodard, *Nation Within a Nation;* Johnson, *Revolutionaries to Race Leaders;* Moore, *Carl B. Stokes and the Rise of Black Political Power.*

16. Lyndon B. Johnson, "Special Message to the Congress on Law Enforcement and the Administration of Justice," March 8, 1965.

17. Elizabeth Hinton has done the painstaking work of showing this connection. See Hinton, *From the War on Poverty to the War on Crime;* Hinton, *America on Fire.*

18. Westheider, *African American Experience in Vietnam*, 49.

19. Gwen Patton, "Black Militants and the War," *Student Mobilizer,* Jan. 1968, 1–2.

20. Farmer, *Remaking Black Power,* 4–5.

21. Butler, "Africa and the Reinvention of the Nineteenth Century Afro-Bahian Identity," 149–51.

22. For more on the Moynihan report, and its effect on the Black community, see Patterson, *Freedom Is Not Enough;* Massey and Sampson, *Moynihan Report Revisited;* Greenbaum, *Blaming the Poor.*

23. AM-BWOHP, 60.

24. AM-BWOHP, 61.

25. Hesford, *Feeling Women's Liberation*, 3.

26. For an analysis of the political differences between Black and white women, see Roth, *Separate Roads to Feminism;* Brines, *Trouble Between Us.* For a comprehensive study of Black feminist organizing in the late 1960s, see Springer, *Living for the Revolution.*

27. For more on Kennedy's role in the feminist movement, see Randolph, *Florynce "Flo" Kennedy.*

28. AM-BWOHP, 60; "*Black Scholar* Interviews Queen Mother Moore," 48.

29. "*Black Scholar* Interviews Queen Mother Moore," 49.

30. M'Balia, "Remembering Queen Mother Moore," 175.

31. Nelson, *Straight, No Chaser,* 116.

32. For an overview of the Queen Mother role in historical context, see Stoeltje, "Asante Queen Mothers."

33. AM-BWOHP, 21.

34. Jackson-Issa, "In Her Own Book," 42; Blakely, "40 Acres and a Mule," 133; Sonia Sanchez, interview by author.

35. Audley Moore, "The Queen Mother on That Negro Mind, on Birth Control, and the Ethiopian Woman," Roderick Jenkins Collection.

36. Moore, "Queen Mother on That Negro Mind."

37. Moore, "Queen Mother on That Negro Mind."

38. AM-BWOHP, 28–29.

39. Dionne Ford, "Overlooked No More: Adefunmi I, Who Introduced African Americans to Yoruba," *New York Times,* Oct. 27, 2023; Curry, *Making the Gods,* 46, 51; Olupona and Rey, *Òrìṣà Devotion as World Religion,* 8.

40. Ford, "Overlooked No More"; Hucks, *Yoruba Traditions,* 3.

41. Hucks, *Yoruba Traditions,* 41, 74.

42. Hucks, *Yoruba Traditions,* 99.

43. "Temple Center for African Culture," *New York Amsterdam News,* Aug. 12, 1961, 8.

44. Hucks, *Yoruba Traditions,* 106–7.

45. Hucks, *Yoruba Traditions*, 101; Ford, "Overlooked No More." Photo of Moore in these parades in Hucks, *Yoruba Traditions*, 115.

46. Hucks, *Yoruba Traditions*, 116; AM-BWOHP, 59.

47. AM-BWOHP, 59; Hucks, *Yoruba Traditions*, 106; Olademo, *Women in Yoruba Religions*, 110–11.

48. AM-BWOHP, 59.

49. Nkrumah Olinga, interview by author.

Chapter 17: WE REFUSE TO BE PROGRAMMED ANYMORE

1. Mallory, interview by Malaika Lumumba, Feb. 27, 1970, Ralph J. Bunche Collection Oral History Project.

2. Douglas, *Jim Crow Moves North*, 143–45.

3. Douglas, *Jim Crow Moves North*, 154.

4. Douglas, *Jim Crow Moves North*, 167, 208, 216–17; Rabin and Kridel, "Cinema for Social Change," 103–18; Burrell, "Black Women as Activist Intellectuals," 89–112.

5. Douglas, *Jim Crow Moves North*, 197–201; W. E. B. Du Bois, "Postscript," *Crisis*, May 1934, 147–49.

6. Hill and Bair, *Marcus Garvey*, 263–65; Bair, "Garveyism and Contested Political Terrain in 1920s Virginia," 229–30; Rickford, *We Are an African People*, 76.

7. Rickford, *We Are an African People*, 76; Taylor, *Promise of Patriarchy*, 28.

8. Rickford, "Black Power as Educational Renaissance," 214; Lawrence Neal, "Black Power/Liberation," MS, n.d., box 6, folder 15, LNP.

9. Burrell, "Black Women as Activist Intellectuals," 91–94; Ransby, *Ella Baker and the Black Freedom Struggle*, 153.

10. Burrell, "Black Women as Activist Intellectuals," 100.

11. "Negro Sues City on School Zoning," *New York Times*, July 18, 1957, 1.

12. "JHS Committee Lists Demands," *New York Amsterdam News*, Feb. 8, 1958, 25.

13. Back, "'Exposing the Whole Segregation Myth,'" 74.

14. "Judge Polier Won't Convict," *New York Amsterdam News*, Dec. 20, 1958, 1; "Rip Curtain Off Unequal Treatment," *New York Amsterdam News*, Nov. 15, 1958, 1.

15. City Wide Committee for Integrated Schools, "School Boycott!" flyer, box 1, folder 8, Elliot Linzer Collection.

16. Taylor, *Knocking at Our Own Door*, 27, 133–35; Franklin, *Young Crusaders*, 137–39.

17. "Boycott Cripples City Schools," *New York Times*, Feb. 4, 1964, 1, 20; Delmont, *Why Busing Failed*, 43.

18. James Bailey, "Harlem's Besieged Showpiece," *Architectural Forum* 125, no. 4 (1966): 50.

19. Gutman, "Intermediate School 201," 184–89; Rickford, *We Are an African People*, 26.

20. "Showcase School Sets Off Dispute," *New York Times*, Sept. 2, 1966, 28.

21. "Unite for Black Power" flyer and "Unite for School Boycott" flyer, Black Panther Party Harlem Branch Files; "A Brick Concentration Camp," *Jet*, Oct. 14, 1966, 17; "Schools in City Open Smoothly Despite Protests," *New York Times*, Sept. 13, 1966, 1; "Schedule of Action to Keep IS 201 Closed," box 2, folder 5, BEC.

22. "Teachers Revolt in Harlem School as Boycott Ends," *New York Times*, Sept. 20, 1966, 1, 36; "Showcase School Sets Off Dispute," 28, 38; Gutman, "Intermediate School 201," 186.

23. Ferguson, *Top Down*, 5, 89.

24. "News from the Ford Foundation," July 6, 1967, box 4, folder 7, BEC.

25. Podair, *Strike That Changed New York*, 42.

26. Gaffney, *Teachers United*, 23–25.

27. Podair, *Strike That Changed New York*, 42–43; O'Neil, "Rise and Fall of the UFT," 177.

28. For Moore's opinions on Shanker, see Queen Mother Moore, "Band-Aid for a Cancer"; "Shanker Assailed in I.S. 201 Dispute," *New York Times*, Nov. 5, 1967, 42.

29. "Parents Bitter at 201," *New York Amsterdam News*, Sept. 16, 1967, 1, 38; "Pupils Find 4th R Is Teacher's Resignation," *New York Daily News*, Sept. 12, 1967, 3–4.

30. "Parents Bitter at 201," 1; Edgell, *Movement for Community Control of New York City's Schools*, 40.

31. Preston Wilcox, "The Controversy over I.S. 201: One View and a Proposal," box 24, folder 1, PWP.

32. "Demands of Parents and Community to Make I.S. 201 a Model School," box 13, folder 3, BEC; Gutman, "Intermediate School 201," 199; Rickford, "Black Power as Educational Renaissance," 222–23. For *Kweli*, see box 6, folder 9, BEC.

33. Lewis, *New York City Public Schools from Brownsville to Bloomberg*, 62–64.

34. Rickford, *We Are an African People*, 28.

35. Rickford, *We Are an African People*, 29; Lewis, *New York City Public Schools from Brownsville to Bloomberg*, 58.

36. "Parents Disrupt School Hearing, Then Start Sit-In," *New York Times*, Dec. 20, 1966, 1; Podair, *Strike That Changed New York*, 71–72; Taylor, *Knocking at Our Own Door*, 182.

37. "Parents Disrupt School Hearing," 1; Taylor, *Knocking at Our Own Door*, 183; "Harlem Parents Stage All Night Sit-In," *Chicago Defender*, Dec. 21, 1966, 11.

38. "Brooklyn Sit-In Bars 2D Hearing by School Board," *New York Times*, Dec. 21, 1966, 1; "Say Bd. of Ed 'Must Go,'" *New York Amsterdam News*, Dec. 24, 1966, 1, 46.

39. Queen Mother Audley Moore, box 35, folder 5, BEC.

40. "Galamison and 11 Seized in Sit-In at School Board," *New York Times*, Dec. 22, 1966, 1.

41. For in-depth assessments of the Black Arts Movement, see Smethurst, *Black Arts Movement*; Clarke, *After Mecca*.

42. Black Arts Repertory Theatre/ School, "Schedule of Events," folder 7, BARTS.

43. Felber, "'Harlem Is the Black World,'" 210–11; Ferguson, *Unlikely Warrior*, 132; "OAAU Liberation School Graduation" flyer, box 1, folder 1, OAAU.

44. Warner family, interview by author; AM-BWOHP, 83.

45. "*Black Scholar* Interviews Queen Mother Moore," 50.

46. Ferguson, *Top Down*, 135–36.

47. Lee, *Building a Latino Civil Rights Movement*, 185–86.

48. Edgell, *Movement for Control of New York City's Schools*, 175.

49. For a complete overview, see Podair, *Strike That Changed New York City*.

50. "The Queen Mother at Work: Harlem 'Mayoress' Blasts Whites,"

Cornell Daily Sun, May 9, 1968, 14; "Demands for Local Control Grow," *New York Times,* Jan. 12, 1968, 49; "Harlem Hearing Defends Demonstration Schools," *Daily World,* Dec. 23, 1969, 11.

51. Queen Mother Moore, "We Refuse to Be Programed Anymore," 19–20.

52. Moore, "We Refuse to Be Programed Anymore," 19.

53. Moore, "We Refuse to Be Programed Anymore," 23.

Chapter 18: THE REVOLUTION HAS COME

1. "Queen Mother at Work," 14; "Priorities in Urban Education," *Cornell Daily Sun,* April 30, 1968, 7.

2. Woodard, *Nation Within a Nation,* 202–3.

3. Moore, *Defeat of Black Power,* 4; "Powell to Hold Planning Talks on Black Power," *Washington Post,* Aug. 29, 1966, A2; "Powell Confers on Black Power," *New York Times,* Sept. 4, 1966, 50.

4. Randolph, *Florynce "Flo" Kennedy,* 110; "Black Power Continuation Committee Minutes," April 1, 1967, box 7, folder 4, PWP.

5. "Newark Mayor Calls in Guard as Riots Spread," *Los Angeles Times,* July 14, 1967, 11; "New Violence in Newark: Stores Burned and Looted," *Newark Star Ledger,* July 14, 1967, 1; Woodard, *Nation Within a Nation,* 79–80; Mumford, *Newark,* 125.

6. "Newark Meeting on Black Power Attended by 400," *New York Times,* July 21, 1967, 1; Woodard, *Nation Within a Nation,* 85.

7. Stone, "National Conferences on Black Power," 190.

8. "Conference Projects New Directions," press release, July 24, 1967, box: NWK AFAM, Folder: Black Power Conference, NAAC.

9. *News,* July 24, 1967, 8.

10. "Conference Description 1967" and "Registration," box: NWK AFAM, Folder: Black Power Conference, NAAC.

11. "Black Power Parley Opens in Newark: Farmer Calls Place and Time Proper for Such Conferences," *Washington Post,* July 21, 1967, A1.

12. "Black Power Parley Opens in Newark."

13. Randolph, *Florynce "Flo" Kennedy,* 116; "Absolute Equality Demanded by Negroes," *Washington Post,* July 22, 1967, A1.

14. Randolph, *Florynce "Flo" Kennedy,* 116.

15. Wright, *Let's Work Together,* 148.

16. Stone, "National Conference on Black Power," 191.

17. "Black Power Manifesto from the National Conference on Black Power," box 18, folder 6, RBP.

18. Woodard, *Nation Within a Nation,* 107; "2000 Expected to Attend 3d Annual Black Power Parley Here," *Philadelphia Inquirer,* Aug. 29, 1968, 44; "Black Power Groups Meet Here to 'Save Nation from Whites,'" *Philadelphia Inquirer,* Aug. 30, 1968, 7; "Advisory Committees" and "To the Leadership of the July 20–23 National Conference on Black Power, Subject: Continued Leadership and Planning, August 18, 1967," box 8, folder 6, RBP; "Minutes, National Conference on Black Power Advisory Committee, February 3, 1968, Newark, N.J."; "Minutes, National Conference on Black Power Advisory Committee,

February 24, 1968, Washington D.C.," box 18, folder 7, RBP.

19. Black Power Conference, "Background and Purpose," box 7, folder 5, PWP; "Survival Is Topic at Black Power Conference," *New York Times,* Aug. 30, 1968, 24.

20. Welcome Address, Dr. Nation Wright, Chairman, box 7, folder 5, PWP.

21. Economics Workshop, "Resolution on Reparations," box 7, folder 5, PWP.

22. Economics Workshop, "Resolution on Reparations."

23. For more on the World Federation of African People, see "African People's Federation Sets First '66 Meet," *Herald-Dispatch,* Jan. 6, 1966, 10; Letter from Officers and Members of the UNIA, Dec. 14, 1973, box 12, folder 9, UNIA-EMORY.

24. Ahmad, interview by author.

25. Queen Mother Moore, "Reparations," box 7, folder 5, PWP.

26. "Black Parley OKs Drive for Own Party," *Philadelphia Inquirer,* Sept. 2, 1968, 1.

27. Swan, *Pauulu's Diaspora,* 111.

28. Swan, "I & I Shot the Sheriff," 198–201.

29. "Members of the 1969 Advisory Planning Committee of the National Conference on Black Power," Komozi Woodard's Office Files, 1956–1986: Miscellaneous Materials, Komozi Woodard Amiri Baraka Collection.

30. CIA, "Intelligence Memorandum: Black Radicalism in the Caribbean," July 6, 1970, File 0524/70, Black Power Conference.

31. Swan, "I & I Shot the Sheriff," 202; "Bermuda Is Quiet as Blacks Meet," *New York Times,* July 12, 1969, 15.

32. Jeanna Knights, interview by author.

33. Swan, *Black Power in Bermuda,* 79; Jimmy Garrett, interview by author.

34. AM-BWOHP, 62.

35. CIA, "Intelligence Memorandum: Black Radicalism in the Caribbean."

36. Swan, *Black Power in Bermuda,* 81; James Garrett, "A Historical Sketch: The Sixth Pan-African Congress," *Black World,* March 1975, 5.

37. Swan, *Black Power in Bermuda,* 89. Wilkins, "'Line of Steel,'" 97–114.

Chapter 19: MOTHER OF THE REPUBLIC OF NEW AFRIKA

1. Onaci, *Free the Land,* 1–2; "For Black Entertainers, Fans, Hotel Was Place to Mingle," *Detroit Free Press,* Feb. 26, 1989, 22; Hearing Before the Permanent Subcommittee on Investigations of the Committee on Government Operations, U.S. Senate, 91st Cong., 1st Sess. (June 26 and 30, 1969), Part 20 (U.S. Government Printing Office, 1969), 4178.

2. Onaci, *Free the Land,* 1–2; Umoja, *We Will Shoot Back,* 188; John Bracey,

interview by author; Akineyele Umoja, interview by author.

3. Jay and Conklin, *People's History of Detroit,* 132.

4. Thompson, *Whose Detroit?,* 20–21, 31–33.

5. Dillard, *Faith in the City,* 200.

6. Dillard, *Faith in the City,* 199; Jay and Conklin, *People's History of Detroit,* 133.

7. Dillard, *Faith in the City,* 197.

8. Thompson, *Whose Detroit?,* 36–37.

9. Dillard, *Faith in the City,* 200–201.

10. Thompson, *Whose Detroit?,* 39–41.

11. For more on mid-century and midwestern Garveyism, see McDuffie, "'New Day Has Dawned for the UNIA'"; Stephens, "Garveyism in Idlewild"; McDuffie, *Second Battle for Africa*, 150–52.

12. Malcolm X, *Malcolm X Speaks*, 3.

13. Malcolm X, "Message to the Grassroots," in *Malcolm X Speaks*, 3–17.

14. Ali, *In the Balance of Power*, 149. On James and Grace Lee Boggs, see Ward, *In Love and Struggle*.

15. For more on the League of Revolutionary Black Workers, see Georgakas and Surkin, *Detroit*; Geshwender and Jeffries, "League of Revolutionary Black Workers," 135–62.

16. Onaci, *Free the Land*, 20–21; Rhodes and Jeffries, "Motor City Panthers," 126.

17. Onaci, *Free the Land*, 22.

18. Malcolm X, "After the Bombing, February 14, 1965, Detroit," in *Malcolm X Speaks*, 177.

19. Brother Imari, *War in America: The Malcolm X Doctrine* (Malcolm X Society, 1968), 6.

20. Stone, "Steel Meets Flint," 142–43.

21. Rhodes and Jeffries, "Motor City," 129; Locke, *Detroit 1967 Rebellion*, 36.

22. AM-BWOHP, 47.

23. "Negro Group Asks End of Ties to U.S.," *New York Times*, March 31, 1968, 2; Umoja, *We Will Shoot Back*, 188.

24. Collins, interview by Kim Lacey Rodgers, box 3, item 23, side 1, KLR.

25. Onaci, *Free the Land*, 27.

26. For Moore's correspondence with Williams, see African Descendants Nationalist Independence Partition (AD-NIP) Party, Folder: 009051-025-0181, RFW.

27. For an overview of Williams's life in exile and his allies, see Mares, "Exile Is Hell."

28. "RNA Chief Fights Extradition," *Detroit Free Press*, Sept. 13, 1969, 1, 2A.

29. "The Background of the Republic of New Africa," box 1, folder 5, RNA-MDAH.

30. See, for example, "Republic of New Africa–New York Consulate," rally flyer, Folder: 009051-101-0104, RFW.

31. Lumumba, *Roots of the New African Independence Movement*, 42; Berger, "'Malcolm X Doctrine,'" 53.

32. Umoja, *We Will Shoot Back*, 188; AM-BWOHP, 17.

33. AM-BWOHP, 47.

34. Onaci, *Free the Land*, 30–31; "Petition Drive on for Black Republic," *Jet*, Sept. 12, 1968, 5.

35. Robert Sherrill, "We Also Want Four Hundred Billion Dollars Back Pay," *Esquire*, Jan. 1969, 73.

36. "N.Y. Rally Crowded, 350 Attend," *New African*, July 20, 1968, 2.

37. See, for example, FBI, Urgent Teletype from FBI New York to Director and Detroit, Dec. 3, 1968, FBI No. NY 157-2290, RNA.

38. Davenport, *How Social Movements Die*, 195–97; FBI, Dec. 16, 1968, File No. 157-3390; FBI, Feb. 6, 1969, File No. 157-3390, RNA.

39. "The Linwood Incident: A Detailed Report," *Detroit Free Press*, March 31, 1969, 1.

40. "New Glory for Old Theatre," *Detroit Free Press*, March 11, 1963, 3. For more on C. L. Franklin and his role in civil rights, see Salvatore, *Singing in a Strange Land*.

41. Davenport, *How Social Movements Die*, 223.

42. Onaci, *Free the Land*, 15; "1969 Church Arrests Spawned Political Power Change in the City," *Detroit Free*

Press, March 28, 1989, 1, 14; "Detroit
Policeman Killed in Separatist
Shootout," *Lansing State Journal*,
March 31, 1969, 10; "Detroit Police
Battle Blacks; 135 Arrested," *Tampa
Bay Times*, March 31, 1969, 10;
"Two Are Jailed After Slaying in
Police Shoot Out," *Detroit Free Press*,
March 31, 1969, 1A, 4.

43. FBI, New York, to Director and
Detroit, April 18, 1969, File No. 157-
9079-499, RNA.

44. Onaci, *Free the Land*, 34; Umoja, *We
Will Shoot Back*, 191.

45. Onaci, *Free the Land*, 167–68;
"Background of the Republic of New
Africa."

46. FBI, SAC, New York, to Director,
Sept. 9, 1969, File No. 157-9079-653,
RNA.

47. Onaci, *Free the Land*, 27; Moore quoted
in "Detroit Police Department to
Commanding Officer, Intelligence
Division, August 21, 1970," Folder:
009051-022-0399, RFW.

48. "What Is the Republic of New
Africa?," box 1, folder 1, RNA-
MADH; Umoja, *We Will Shoot Back*,
189; Onaci, *Free the Land*, 37.

49. "Jackson Tragedy: The RNA
Revisited," *Jackson Free Press*,
March 5, 2014; "Black Separatists
Raided in Jackson, Miss.," *New York
Times*, Aug. 19, 1971, 27.

50. Onaci, *Free the Land*, 37; Umoja, *We
Will Shoot Back*, 173; "Republic of
New Africa: Yes, Separation—No,
Integration!," *Close Up*, March–
April 1971, 12–17, box 1, folder 1,
RNA-MADH.

51. Gaines, "I Am a Revolutionary Black
Female Nationalist," 116.

52. Republic of New Africa, "Short
Official Basic Documents," box 1,
folder 1, RNA-MDAH.

53. Gaines, "I Am a Revolutionary
Black Female Nationalist," 116,
153; "Republic of New Africa: Yes,
Separation—No, Integration!"

54. Onaci, *Free the Land*, 26–27; "Short
Official Basic Documents."

55. "What Is the Republic of New
Africa?"

56. "New African Ujamaa: The
Economics of the Republic of
New Africa," Joseph A. Labadie
Collection.

57. This description draws from Onaci,
Free the Land, 79.

58. "Names," Republic of New Africa
Collection; Shakur, *Assata*, 183–85.

59. Onaci, *Free the Land*, 145–47; Republic
of New Africa conference 1974;
Oscar Brown Jr., Sister of Motivation,
AAC.

60. Onaci, *Free the Land*, 156; John Bracey,
interview by author.

61. Davenport, *How Social Movements Die*,
282; FBI Agent William J. Crumley
Interview, Supplementary Offence
Report, Aug. 19, 1971, Jackson Police
Department; Wright, "'Free the
Land!,'" 65.

62. Wright, "'Free the Land!,'" 66–68;
"FBI Agent Tells Jury of Gunfire
from RNA," *Clarion-Ledger*, April 27,
1972, Republic of New Africa Subject
Files, 1971–1972, RNA-MDAH.

63. Gaines, "I Am a Revolutionary Black
Female Nationalist," 155; Davenport,
How Social Movements Die, 285;
Republic of New Africa, "Transcript
of Preliminary Hearing for the
RNA-11," box 1, folder 4, RNA-
MDAH; Lumumba, "Short History
of the U.S. War on the R.N.A.,"
73–74.

64. For examples of this work, see
"RNA National Solidarity Day
Rally," Aug. 18, 1972; "International

Day of Solidarity with New African Prisoners of War," box 1, folder 4, RNA-MDAH.

65. Lumumba, "Short History of the U.S. War on the R.N.A.," 73–74.

66. Onaci, *Free the Land,* 190, 194.

Chapter 20: NATIONTIME!

1. Rickford, *We Are an African People,* 168–75; Wald, *It's Been Beautiful,* 1. For a synthesis of how the white power structure engaged with Black Power, see Davies, *Mainstreaming Black Power.*

2. Kotlowski, *Nixon's Civil Rights,* 173–74; Moore, *Defeat of Black Power,* 14.

3. Kotlowski, *Nixon's Civil Rights,* 133–40; Hill and Rabig, *Business of Black Power,* 5.

4. Moore, *Defeat of Black Power,* 16–21.

5. Musgrove, *Rumor, Repression, and Racial Politics,* 65–67.

6. Moore, *Defeat of Black Power,* 16.

7. Moore, *Defeat of Black Power,* 28; Watts, *Amiri Baraka,* 367.

8. Baraka, *Autobiography of LeRoi Jones,* 403.

9. Amiri Baraka, "Gary and Miami— Before and After," *Black World,* Oct. 1972, 55; Moore, *Defeat of Black Power,* 28.

10. Congress of African People, "Black Power Conference Set in Atlanta, Georgia," press release; "Black Leaders Hold Unity Conference," *Nationtime News,* July 1971, 2, box 8, folder 1, PWP.

11. "Young to Address African Congress," *Chicago Defender,* Sept. 3, 1970, 10; "Gains Recounted by Black Muslim," *New York Times,* Sept. 7, 1970, 13.

12. "Congress of African People Program and Workshop Schedule," box 35, folder 19, JHC; "Tentative Workshop Breakdown," box 33, folder 1, LNP.

13. "Tentative Workshop Breakdown."

14. "Social Organization: New Black Family, New Marital Institutions [and] Black Women & the Revolution," box 35, folder 19, JHC.

15. AM-BWOHP, 60; "*Black Scholar* Interviews Queen Mother Moore," 47; M'Balia, "Remembering Queen Mother Moore," 176.

16. "Congress of African People Program and Workshop Schedule."

17. Moore, *Defeat of Black Power,* 29.

18. "Black Leaders Hold Unity Conference"; Johnson, *Revolutionaries to Race Leaders,* 89–90.

19. Amiri Baraka, "Toward the Creation of Political Institutions for All African Peoples," *Black World,* Oct. 1972, 56; Baraka, "Gary and Miami," 56.

20. Baraka, "Gary and Miami," 56; Moore, *Defeat of Black Power,* 32–33.

21. "Black Politicians Keep Parley Secret," *Chicago Defender,* Sept. 27, 1971, 1, 3; "Top Blacks Deciding Strategy," *Austin Statesmen,* Sept. 26, 1971, A5.

22. "The Short, Unhappy Life of Black Presidential Politics: 1972," *New York Times,* June 25, 1972, 15.

23. Curwood, *Shirley Chisholm,* 79.

24. Chisholm, *Good Fight,* 15, 22–23.

25. Conyers, "Black Political Strategy for 1972," 130.

26. Moore, *Defeat of Black Power,* 44.

27. Baraka, "Toward the Creation," 56; "Chisholm's Candidacy Gains: Meeting in Illinois," *Washington Post,*

Oct. 4, 1971, A9; Moore, *Defeat of Black Power,* 39–47; Johnson, *Revolutionaries to Race Leaders,* 91–93.

28. Moore, *Defeat of Black Power,* 56.
29. "13 Hill Blacks Call National Convention," *Washington Post,* Nov. 21, 1971, A3; "Mrs. Chisholm Chides Black Caucus," *New York Times,* Nov. 20, 1971, 18.
30. Baraka, "Gary and Miami," 64.
31. "A Call for a National Black Political Convention," box 35, folder 1, VHP; Moore, *Defeat of Black Power,* 60–62.
32. Baraka, "Gary and Miami," 64.
33. "Gary: Odd Place for a Convention," *Washington Post,* March 11, 1972, A2; "Hatcher Calls for Blacks to Unite Politically," *Washington Post,* March 12, 1972, A2; Clay, *Just Permanent Interests,* 203.
34. William Greaves, dir., *Nationtime* (Kino Lorber, 2021).
35. Greaves, *Nationtime.*
36. Moore, *Defeat of Black Power,* 113–14.
37. "Black Meet Without Incident Bodyguards, Police Vigilant," *Times* (Hammond, Ind.), March 12, 1972, 12A; Greaves, *Nationtime.*
38. Greaves, *Nationtime.*
39. "National Black Political Agenda," box 1, folder 35, VHP.
40. "Black Parley Comes Out Against Busing," *Chicago Tribune,* March 13, 1972, 1, 2.
41. "NAACP Differs with Assembly; Quits," *Milwaukee Star,* May 25, 1972, 1.
42. For an overview of Black-Palestinian solidarity during this period, see Fischbach, *Black Power and Palestine.*
43. Moore, *Defeat of Black Power,* 135; "Black Caucus Praised for Israel Support," *Milwaukee Star,* April 5, 1972, 2; "Hatcher Reviews Parlay of Blacks," *New York Times,* March 16, 1972, 34.
44. "Blacks Vote to Organize: Political Arm Established at Gary Session," *Washington Post,* March 13, 1972, A1; Daniels, "National Black Political Assembly"; "Our National Assembly," *New York Amsterdam News,* March 25, 1972, A1.
45. Ogletree, *All Deliberate Speed,* 280–81.
46. "Agenda Urges Plan for U.S. Reparations," *Washington Post,* March 12, 1972, A2; Berger, "'Malcolm X Doctrine,'" 50.
47. Moore, *Defeat of Black Power,* 114–21; "National Black Political Agenda," box 1, folder 35, VHP.
48. "Black Convention Eases Busing and Israeli Stands," *New York Times,* May 20, 1972, 14.
49. Baraka, "Toward the Creation," 69; Moore, *Defeat of Black Power,* 142–43.
50. Johnson, *Revolutionaries to Race Leaders,* 129.

Chapter 21: QUEEN MOTHER VISITS THE MOTHERLAND

1. AM-BWOHP, 48.
2. "*Black Scholar* Interviews Queen Mother Moore," 50.
3. Zuberi, *African Independence,* 25.
4. Vince, *Algerian War,* 47.
5. Adi, *Pan-Africanism,* 122–24; Zuberi, *African Independence,* 58–60.
6. AM-BWOHP, 48.
7. Examples include "Tanganyika White Rule to Be Ended by Britain," *Washington Post,* Dec. 16, 1959, A6; "The Key to Tanganyika: Julius Kambarage Nyerere," *New York Times,* Feb. 11, 1960; AM-BWOHP, 48.

8. Falola and Heaton, *History of Nigeria,* 137, 156.

9. Mutibwa, *Uganda Since Independence,* 19–20.

10. Wright, *Destruction of a Nation,* 5–6.

11. Tomás, *Amílcar Cabral,* 71–73; Isaacman and Isaacman, *Mozambique,* 79–84.

12. Tomás, *Amílcar Cabral,* 192–95.

13. Marcum, *Conceiving Mozambique,* 20–21.

14. "Ambassador Cisse Gets Farewell from Harlem," *New York Amsterdam News,* April 24, 1976, A2; "African Journey: Guest of President Kenneth Kaunda and the Citizens of the Republic of Zambia," *New York Amsterdam News,* June 5, 1971, 2.

15. Allman, "The Youngmen and the Porcupine," 265. For more on Nkrumah's nation making and Pan-Africanism, see Fuller, *Building the Ghanaian Nation-State;* Kaba, *Kwame Nkrumah and the Dream of African Unity.*

16. Davidson, *Black Star,* 84; Birmingham, *Kwame Nkrumah,* 86.

17. Kandeh, *Coups from Below,* 66.

18. Fuller, *Building the Ghanaian Nation-State,* 201.

19. Blakely, "40 Acres and a Mule," 132; AM-BWOHP, 49; "Resent the Scant Notice Given Nkrumah Death," *New York Amsterdam News,* May 6, 1972, C1; "Brooklynites Spearhead Tribute to Nkrumah," *New York Amsterdam News,* May 13, 1972, C1.

20. Davidson, *Black Star,* 205; "Nkrumah Hailed in Guinea Rites," *New York Times,* May 14, 1972, 8; "Nkrumah's Burial in Ghana Unsure," *New York Times,* May 7, 1972, 5; "Nkrumah's Mother Awaits Return of Son's Body," *New York Times,* July 5, 1972, 10; "Tears as Body of Nkrumah Arrives in Exile Home of Guinea," *Daily Nation,* May 1, 1972, 24.

21. "Nkrumah Goes Home to Ghana," *New York Times,* July 16, 1972, E3.

22. "*Black Scholar* Interviews Queen Mother Moore," 50.

23. "The East, a Black Culture and Education Center, Brings a Bit of Africa to Brooklyn," *New York Times,* Aug. 17, 1975, 87; Konadu, *View from the East,* xx, xxiii.

24. Konadu, *View from the East,* 34, 49; Alberta Hill, "All-Africa Women's Conference, Dar-es-Salaam, Tanzania," *Black News,* Nov. 1, 1972, 22; "Interview with Queen Mother Moore," *Black News,* Oct. 1978, 14.

25. "*Black Scholar* Interviews Queen Mother Moore," 50.

26. "*Black Scholar* Interviews Queen Mother Moore," 50; Blakely, "40 Acres and a Mule," 132.

27. "Nkrumah Hailed in Guinea Rites," *New York Times,* May 14, 1972, 8; "Driver Dies... Linda Page Lives!," Sara Speaking, *New York Amsterdam News,* June 3, 1972, B1.

28. AM-BWOHP, 49; "*Black Scholar* Interviews Queen Mother Moore," 50.

29. AM-BWOHP, 49.

30. AM-BWOHP, 49; AM-Prago.

31. Stoeltje, "Asante Queen Mothers," 51. For an overview about the importance of these stools in Asante culture, see *Ashanti Stool Histories* (Institute of African Studies, University of Ghana, 1976).

32. AM-BWOHP, 49; Stoeltje, "Asante Queen Mothers," 41.

33. AM-Prago; 08-ORAL-30-8-Side-01, Queen Mother Moore Tapes.

34. "*Black Scholar* Interviews Queen Mother Moore," 49.

35. "Driver Dies... Linda Page Lives!"

36. "A Look at Ten Years of an African Women's Organization," *Daily News* (Tanzania), July 24, 1972, 7.

37. "Delegates Ready for Conference," *Daily News* (Tanzania), July 22, 1972, 1.

38. "African Women's Confab: Africa for the Africans at Home and Abroad," *Herald Dispatch,* Sept. 7, 1972, 1; "*Black Scholar* Interviews Queen Mother Moore," 49–50.

39. Audley Warner, interview by author.

40. "*Black Scholar* Interviews Queen Mother Moore," 49; "Queen Mother Needs Help," *New York Amsterdam News,* July 15, 1972, B8.

41. Hill, "All-Africa Women's Conference, Dar-es-Salaam, Tanzania," 22; "The Historical Journey of Dr. Emily Moore: Educator, Civil & Human Rights Activist," Emily Moore Collection.

42. "Africa Women's Conference Opens Today," *Daily News* (Tanzania), July 24, 1972, 1.

43. "Focus on All-Africa Women's Conference," *Daily News* (Tanzania), July 29, 1972, 6. This description also draws from photos from the Emily Moore Collection, in author's possession.

44. "Look at Ten Years of African Women's Organization."

45. "Letters," *Black News,* Jan. 1, 1973, 30–32; Emily Moore, "Queen Mother Moore in Tanzania, Africa, 1972," Emily Moore Collection; photos found in Emily Moore Collection.

46. Audley Moore, "Speech to All-Africa Women's Conference," box 39, folder 2, PWP; "Women Told to Rally Around One Cause," *Daily News* (Tanzania), July 27, 1972, 1.

47. "*Black Scholar* Interviews Queen Mother Moore," 49.

48. "Women Urged to Forget Prejudices," *Daily News* (Tanzania), Aug. 1, 1972, 1; "Women End Talks Today," *Daily News* (Tanzania), July 31, 1972, 5.

49. "*Black Scholar* Interviews Queen Mother Moore," 49–50.

50. Tate, "Power of Pan Africanism," 8; Kaba, *Kwame Nkrumah and the Dream of Pan-African Unity,* 105–7.

51. Audley Warner, interview by author.

52. For more on Nyerere and the promise and perils of Ujamaa, see Sheikheldin, "Ujamaa"; Lal, "Militants, Mothers, and the National Family."

53. "*Black Scholar* Interviews Queen Mother Moore," 49–50.

54. Audley Warner, interview by author.

Chapter 22: TANZANIA REDUX

1. Walters, *Pan-Africanism in the African Diaspora,* 66. For examples of Nyerere's writings, see Nyerere, *Ujamaa;* Nyerere, *Freedom and Socialism.*

2. For more on this community, see Kalamu ya Salaam, "The Realities of Living and Working in Afrika," *Black Collegian* 5, no. 1 (1974): 28, 66–67; Markle, *Motorcycle on Hell Run.*

3. Farmer, "'All the Progress to Be Made Will Be Made by Maladjusted Negroes,'" 15; Farmer, "Working Toward Community Is Our Full-Time Focus," 23; Seniors, *Mae Mallory,* 225–32.

4. Garrett, "Historical Sketch," 4.

5. Garrett, "Historical Sketch," 17; Wilkins, "'Line of Steel,'" 100.

6. Wilkins, "'Line of Steel,'" 100–102.

7. Markle, "'Book Publishers for a Pan-African World,'" 16; Wilkins, "'Line of Steel,'" 104; "Drum and Spear Books Founded," SNCC Digital Gateway, snccdigital.org.

8. Markle, "'We Are Not Tourists,'" 259; Publicity release, Jan. 17, 1974, box 3, folder 85, 6PAC Records.

9. Augusto, interview by Charles Cobb, in *No Easy Victories*, www .noeasyvictories.org; Farmer, *Remaking Black Power*, 139.

10. "The Call to the Sixth Pan African Congress," in *Resolutions and Selected Speeches from the Sixth Pan African Congress* (Tanzania Publishing House, 1976), 219–22.

11. Levy, "Remembering Sixth-PAC," 40.

12. Hill, "Progress Report on Congress Organizing," 35–36.

13. "Sixth PAC: North American Women," *Daily News* (Tanzania), June 26, 1974, 4.

14. Julian Ellison to Courtland Cox, July 23, 1973, box 4, folder 3; "The North American Region Planning Conference General Report, May 11–13, 1973," box 4, folder 8, 6PAC Records; Markle, "'We Are Not Tourists,'" 150.

15. New England District Committee, "Conference Proceedings and Positions," box 3, folder 21, 6PAC Records.

16. New England District Committee, "Conference Proceedings and Positions."

17. For more on this battle in the early twentieth century, see Bush, *We Are Not What We Seem*; Makalani, *In the Cause of Freedom*.

18. Watts, *Amiri Baraka*, 424–26.

19. Newton, "'Intercommunalism,'" 28.

20. Adi, *Pan-Africanism*, 180; Lal, *African Socialism in Postcolonial Tanzania*, 41.

21. "12,000 Blacks March to Support Africa," *Washington Post*, May 28, 1972, A1.

22. "ALD: Mass Expression to Learn and Support," *African World*, June 10, 1972, 12; "African Liberation Day Speakers," *African World*, June 10, 1972, 11; Rickford, *We Are an African People*, 185.

23. Woodard, *Nation Within a Nation*, 179; Rickford, *We Are an African People*, 185.

24. "Locals Back African Liberation Day Rallies," *New Pittsburgh Courier*, April 1, 1972, 8; "Liberation Day Planned in Bay Area," *Los Angeles Sentinel*, May 25, 1972, A12.

25. Owusu Sadaukai, "Inside Liberated Mozambique with the FRELIMO Guerillas: Part 1," *African World*, Feb. 5, 1972, 8.

26. Kalamu ya Salaam, "Tell No Lies, Claim No Easy Victories," *Black World*, Oct. 1974, 18–34.

27. Marable, *Reform, Race, and Rebellion*, 134. For more on Baraka's ideological shift, see Simanga, *Amiri Baraka and the Congress of African People*.

28. Examples include Thomas, "Black Nationalism and Confused Marxists"; Madhubuti, "Latest Purge."

29. Marable, *Reform, Race, and Rebellion*, 135–36.

30. New England District Committee, "Conference Proceedings and Positions."

31. Ellison to Courtland Cox, box 3, folder 20, 6PAC Records.

32. "Memo from Sylvia Hill, Secretary-General, to State/District Contact Person Responsible for Distribution of This Application and Questionnaire," Dec. 19, 1973, box 6, folder 21, 6PAC Records.

33. "Audley Moore North American

Region Delegate Information Questionnaire," box 2, folder 142, 6PAC Records.

34. Rev. Franklin D. Graham to Sylvia Hill, April 3, 1974, box 2, folder 142, 6PAC Records.

35. James Turner (chairman) to Queen Mother Moore, March 13, 1974, box 2, folder 142, 6PAC Records.

36. Hill, interview by William Minter, in *No Easy Victories,* www.noeasyvictories.org.

37. Levy, "Remembering Sixth-PAC," 41; Claude, "Some Personal Reflections on the Sixth Pan-African Congress."

38. Tate, "Power of Pan Africanism," 206; "Alien-Radical Tie Disputed by CIA," *New York Times,* May 25, 1973, 73; Hill, interview by Minter, in *No Easy Victories;* Levy, "Remembering Sixth-PAC," 47.

39. Sixth Pan-African Congress Program, box 1, folder 22a, MOSP; Hoyt W. Fuller, "Notes from a Sixth-Pan-African Journal," *Black World,* Oct. 1974, 73–74; "Nyerere Opens PAC Talks Today," *Daily News* (Tanzania), June 19, 1974, 1.

40. "President Mwalimu Julius K. Nyerere's Opening Speech," in *Resolutions and Selected Speeches,* 6–7; Markle, *Motorcycle on Hell Run,* 165, 168.

41. Owusu Sadaukai, "Politics and Material Support for the Liberation Movements," in *Resolutions and Selected Speeches,* 138–44.

42. Amiri Baraka, "The Meaning and Development of Revolutionary Kawaida"; Amiri Baraka, "Revolutionary Party; Revolutionary Ideology," BP.

43. Imamu Baraka, "Revolutionary Culture and Future of Pan African Culture," in *Resolutions and Selected Speeches,* 171–79.

44. Fuller, "Notes from a Sixth-Pan-African Journal," 73–74; Wilkins, "'Line of Steel,'" 108.

45. Sixth Pan-African Congress Program; "Immigration Form for Special Guests: Audley Moore," box 2, folder 142, 6PAC Records.

46. Markle, *Motorcycle on Hell Run,* 165.

47. Fuller, "Notes from a Sixth-Pan-African Journal," 75–80.

48. "PAC Must Be Dynamic—Plea," *Daily News* (Tanzania), June 28, 1974, 1.

49. See, for example, FRELIMO, "On the Liberation of Mozambique," in *Resolutions and Selected Speeches,* 100–106.

50. "'Failures' Mar 6th Pan African Congress," *Afro-American,* July 27, 1974, 16; "Pilgrimage Reflections, II: 6th Pan African Congress," *Los Angeles Sentinel,* July 18, 1974, A7; "Pan-African Congress Falls Short in Action and Policy," *Chicago Defender,* July 18, 1974, 12.

51. AM-BWOHP, 52.

Chapter 23: DIASPORA AND DICTATORS

1. "Amin Extends Historic Invitation," *Jihad News* (1974): 9, Folder: Jihad News (Jihad News Service), 1974–1975, RAM Papers.

2. Charles Turner, interview by author.

3. "President Amin Addresses Opening Session of OAU," Associated Press, July 27, 1975.

4. For a more comprehensive overview of Nkrumah's vision for the OAU, see Kaba, *Kwame Nkrumah and the Dream of African Unity.*

5. Nkrumah, *Revolutionary Path*, 3, 240–43.
6. "Summit Conference Ends in Success, One Charter for All Africa Signed Here," *Ethiopian Herald*, May 26, 1963, 1, 8.
7. Leopold, *Idi Amin*, 38, 53, 68.
8. Meriwether, "African Americans and the Mau Mau Rebellion"; Bennett, *Fighting the Mau Mau*, 22.
9. Quoted in Page, *King's African Rifles*, 210.
10. Leopold, *Idi Amin*, 73, 91–92.
11. Leopold, *Idi Amin*, 121; Decker, *Idi Amin's Shadow*, 3, 6, 30–31.
12. Kyemba, *State of Blood*, 27–28. For more on Obote's rule, see Ingham, *Obote*.
13. Peterson and Vokes, *Unseen Archive of Idi Amin*, 25–26.
14. Kyemba, *State of Blood*, 28.
15. Leopold, *Idi Amin*, 180–81; Peterson and Vokes, *Unseen Archive of Idi Amin*, 35; Uganda Ministry of Information Broadcasting, "Soldier's Voice on Radio Uganda" (Kampala: Ministry of Information and Broadcasting, 1972), 1.
16. For an insider's perspective on Amin's reign, see Kyemba, *State of Blood*. For more on how Amin's regime and propaganda affected Ugandans, see Decker, *Idi Amin's Shadow*; Peterson and Vokes, *Unseen Archive of Idi Amin*.
17. For an assessment of the first years of the OAU, see Sesay, Ojo, and Fasehun, *OAU After Twenty Years*; "The OAU Consensus and Conflict," *New York Times*, Aug. 3, 1975, 144.
18. "Africans Thwart Amin's OAU Goal," *Chicago Defender*, July 14, 1975, 2.
19. "Somalia Suggests: Chairmanship of OAU to Be Given to Machel," *Ethiopian Herald*, July 5, 1975, 1; "Prospect of New Role for Amin Stirs Misgivings Among Africans," *New York Times*, July 21, 1975, 3; "Amin Named Chairman of African Unity Group," *Washington Post*, July 29, 1975, A10.
20. See, for example, "Dr. Idi Amin Dada," *Fort-Worth Star Telegram*, March 7, 1979, 24.
21. Rickford, *We Are an African People*, 239; "Ugandan Experience," *Black News*, Aug. 1974, 32–33.
22. Charles Turner, interview by author; "Kampala Puts On a Festive Facade for Big Meeting," *New York Times*, July 29, 1975, 3; "A 'Clean Sweep' for Amin at O.A.U. Conference," *Daily Nation*, July 22, 1975, 24.
23. "Appeals for Joint Army at OAU; Amin Says Destroy S.A.," *Chicago Defender*, July 21, 1975, 24; "Africa Must Be Free, Says Amin," *Daily Nation*, July 29, 1975, 1.
24. AM-BWOHP, 73.
25. AM-BWOHP, 49.
26. Saladin Muhammad, interview by author. For an overview of this organization, including its ideological philosophy and organizing documents, see Folder: African People's Party: Basic Documents, RAM Papers.
27. "African People's Party Reaches Out To: The Organization of African Unity," July 28, 1975, Folder: African People's Party, 1975, RAM Papers.
28. AM-BWOHP, 55; Charles Turner, interview by author.
29. AM-BWOHP, 56.
30. Audley Warner, interview by author; Warner family, interview by author.
31. Charles Turner, interview by author; Audley Warner, interview by author.
32. AM-BWOHP, 57.
33. "UN Awaits Ugandan Chief," *Chicago Defender*, Sept. 30, 1975, 2; "Ugandan

Leader Off to the UN," *Los Angeles Sentinel,* Sept. 25, 1975, A2.

34. "He Came, He Saw, He Conquered," *Black News,* Nov. 1, 1975, 3–4.

35. AM-BWOHP, 57; "Cathy's Column," *New York Amsterdam News,* Oct. 22, 1975, B5.

36. Audley Warner, interview by author; Delois Blakely, conversation with author.

37. "Uganda Adopts Carmichael," *New York Times,* June 27, 1973, 65; Joseph, *Stokely,* 300–301; Monotooth, "'Bridges to Human Dignity,'" 51–54; "Roy Innis on Africa," *New York Amsterdam News,* June 23, 1973, A14.

38. Audley Warner, interview by author.

39. "Reparations," Third International Black Power Conference.

40. Fenderson, *Building the Black Arts Movement,* 96.

41. Fenderson, *Building the Black Arts Movement,* 96–99; Donaldson, "FESTAC '77 Documemoir"; "United States Committee Formed to Participate in First World Festival of Negro Arts in 1966," box 33, folder 20, LNP.

42. Hoyt Fuller, "Festival Postscripts," *Negro Digest,* June 1966, 91.

43. Fenderson, *Building the Black Arts Movement,* 110–11; Donaldson,

"FESTAC '77 Documemoir"; Falola and Heaton, *History of Nigeria,* 158–209; "No New Date Set for Festival in Nigeria," *New York Amsterdam News,* Oct. 22, 1975, D14; "Nigeria's Mohammed Delays FESTAC '75 Indefinitely," *Afro-American,* Aug. 23, 1975, 16.

44. Fenderson, *Building the Black Arts Movement,* 111.

45. Val Gray Ward, interview by author; De Vaux, *Warrior Poet,* 172.

46. Val Gray Ward, interview by author; Conrad Worrill, interview by author; Twa, "Great Congress of the Black Spirit," 79.

47. Nance, *Last Days in Lagos,* 49.

48. Lecomote, "In Excess of the Brief"; "Life in the Village," in Soyinka, *FESTAC '77;* AM-BWOHP, 54.

49. AM-BWOHP, 51–52.

50. "Life in the Village."

51. This and the other descriptions of FESTAC come from photos found in Nance, *Last Days in Lagos.*

52. AM-BWOHP, 51.

53. Miss Rosen, "Revisiting FESTAC '77, the Landmark Pan-African Festival," *Blind Magazine,* Jan. 11, 2023.

54. AM-BWOHP, 8, 54.

55. AM-BWOHP, 52–53.

56. Murphy, "Performing Global African Culture and Citizenship."

Chapter 24: LAST DECADE, LASTING RESOURCES

1. K. G. Coaston, "Queen Mother Moore: A Lifetime of Liberation," 125-Queen Mother Moore, 1-Black History Resources, 5-Collections Management, Queen Mother Moore, 1990s.

2. Louw, *Rise, Fall, and Legacy of Apartheid,* 131–33.

3. "Amin, Still Wobbly, Denies End

Is Near," *Afro-American,* March 17, 1979, 16; "How Amin Was Defeated," *Philadelphia Tribune,* July 20, 1979, 15.

4. "Amin's Days Numbered as Ruler of Uganda," *Afro-American,* March 10, 1979, 16; "Libyan Leader 'Has Hidden Amin Away,'" *Afro-American,* May 26, 1979, 16; Leopold, *Idi Amin,* 285–91.

5. For the history of the BWUF, see Farmer, "'Abolition of Every Possibility of Oppression.'"

6. AM-BWOHP, 14–15.

7. "Black Women's Conference," *Daily Collegian* (UMass Amherst), May 6, 1975, 14; "Queen Mother Moore," *Daily Collegian,* May 8, 1975, 6; Nkrumah Olinga, interview by author; John Bracey, interview by author.

8. "Crossroads of Survival: Black Student Conference at Tufts U.," *Grassroots,* March 8, 1978, 8.

9. For Moore's lectures, see "Rep. Chisholm to Open Black History Week," *Atlanta Constitution,* Feb. 5, 1972, 15; "Black Men, Women 'Have to Work Together,'" *Atlanta Constitution,* Feb. 8, 1972, 4B; "Black Teachers Hold 3-Day Meeting Here," *New York Amsterdam News,* April 22, 1972, C1; "Program to Feature Black Arts," *Morning Call,* May 2, 1972, 28; "Which Way Black Woman," *Chicago Metro News,* Jan. 20, 1973, 20; "The Sharp Tongue of Queen Mother Moore," *Sun Reporter,* Dec. 6, 1975, 3; "Black Queen Coming to Bay Area," *Sun Reporter,* Feb. 24, 1973, 5; "Queen Mother Moore to Speak," *Tri-state Defender,* July 1, 1978, 8; "Words of Wisdom," *New York Amsterdam News,* Nov. 9, 1985, 11.

10. "Press Release," *Black News,* Nov. 22, 1978, 33; "Fire Destroys Mother Moore's Home," *New York Amsterdam News,* Dec. 2, 1978, B1.

11. "Queen Mother Moore Interview for Black History Month," box 15, Black Mass Communications Project, University of Massachusetts Amherst Special Collections; Nkrumah Olinga, interview by author.

12. "Press Release"; "Fire Destroys Mother Moore's Home," B1.

13. Blakely, "40 Acres and a Mule," 131.

14. "Former Nun Praised for Youth Work," *Daily News,* April 14, 1973, 167; "She's Bringing the Good Works Home," *Miami Herald,* Aug. 29, 1978, 136.

15. Blakely, "40 Acres and a Mule," 131.

16. Blakely, "40 Acres and a Mule," 131. For an overview of Blakely's life, see Blakely, *Harlem Street Nun.*

17. Blakely, "40 Acres and a Mule," 131.

18. Blakely, "40 Acres and a Mule," 131; "Kenya Conference New Perspective for Senator," *New York Amsterdam News,* Aug. 25, 1985, 48; "Queen Mother Moore's Appeal," *New York Amsterdam News,* June 29, 1985, 45.

19. Davis, *Mainstreaming Black Power,* 49–51; George, *Post-soul Nation,* 291; Lucks, *Reconsidering Reagan,* 122; Kohlman-Hausman, "Welfare Crises, Penal Solutions, and the Origins of the 'Welfare Queen.'"

20. Lucks, *Reconsidering Reagan,* 158–60, 164–65, 177; "Poverty Rate 14%, Termed Highest Since '67," *New York Times,* July 20, 1982, A1, A18.

21. Farber, *Crack,* 2–5. For a vivid account of the Black experience during the crack epidemic, see Ramsey, *When Crack Was King.*

22. "Rare Cancer Seen in 41 Homosexuals," *New York Times,* July 3, 1981, A20. For more on how Black Americans experienced the AIDS crisis, see Royals, *To Make the Wounded Whole.*

23. Queen Mother Moore, "To All My People," Erik S. McDuffie Collection.

24. Coaston, "Queen Mother Moore"; Makeda Coaston, interview by Hayley Reid, 10-Interview with Makeda Coaston, Oral Histories

of the Black Women's Movement: The Heart of the Race; "Back to Africa: Two London Rastafarian Groups Speak Out," *Caribbean Times*, April 3–9, 1981, 18; Kathi Coaston, "A Family Reunion: Queen Mother Moore and Tree of Life," 1-Black History Resources, 5-Collections Management, Queen Mother Moore, 1990s.

25. For more on race relations at this moment in Britain, see Barker, *New Racism*.

26. Olusoga, *Black and British*, 46, 58, 84, 120–21.

27. Olusoga, *Black and British*, 161.

28. Olusoga, *Black and British*, 276–77, 230–33, 344, 401; Coaston, "Queen Mother Moore."

29. Perry, *London Is the Place for Me*, 59, 66, 73; Hall, "Reconstruction Work," 78–94.

30. Perry, *London Is the Place for Me*, 54, 84.

31. Perry, *London Is the Place for Me*, 89–91; "'Bombs' in Race Riot," *Daily Mail* (London), Sept. 2, 1958, 1, 7; Blagrove, *Frontline*, 68.

32. Perry, *London Is the Place for Me*, 130, 139; "West Indian Chiefs Will Be at Rally," *Daily Worker*, Sept. 9, 1958, 1.

33. Perry, *London Is the Place for Me*, 128, 139, 142–46.

34. Perry, *London Is the Place for Me*, 155, 160.

35. Waters, *Thinking Black*, 21.

36. Waters, *Thinking Black*, 34–35; Street, "Malcolm X, Smethwick, and the Influence of the African American Freedom Struggle on British Race Relations in the 1960s."

37. Waters, *Thinking Black*, 35–38; Gilroy, *Ain't No Black in the Union Jack*, 45.

38. For a heart-wrenching account of the fire and its aftermath, see Steve McQueen, dir., *Uprising*, documentary film (Rogan Productions, 2021).

39. Bunce and Field, *Darcus Howe*, 189–90, 195–96.

40. Bunce and Field, *Darcus Howe*, 198–200; "Blacks Marching Forward in Britain," *Caribbean Times*, March 20–26, 1981, 12–13.

41. For a contemporaneous assessment of the Rasta movement, see Len Garrison, *Black Youth, Rastafarianism, and the Identity Crisis in Britain* (ACER Project Publication, 1979).

42. Cashmore, *Rastaman*, 22.

43. Cashmore, *Rastaman*, 129, 131.

44. Cashmore, *Rastaman*, 57, 126.

45. Cashmore, *Rastaman*, 34, 147; Bedasse, *Jah Kingdom*, 110; "Rastas and Repatriation," *Caribbean Times*, Jan. 8, 1982, 20–21.

46. Coaston, "Family Reunion."

47. "Queen Mother Moore: Her Life and Ideas," *West Indian Digest*, Sept. 1982, 30; Christine Warner Rivers, interview by author.

48. "Queen Mother Moore: Her Life and Ideas," 30.

49. "Queen Mother Moore," *Caribbean Times*, Sept. 11–17, 1981, 11.

50. Christine Warner Rivers, interview by author.

51. 1-ORAL-30-1-Side-01, Queen Mother Moore Tapes.

52. 1-ORAL-30-1-Side-01, Queen Mother Moore Tapes; "Blacks in America Settle for Too Little, Says Self-Styled Queen," *Courier-Journal*, March 14, 1982, 21.

53. 1-ORAL-30-1-Side-01, Queen Mother Moore Tapes.

54. "Queen Mother Moore: Her Life and Ideas," 28.

55. "Police Upset Queen Mother Moore Visit," *Caribbean Times*, June 11–17, 1982, 3.

56. "Black History: Queen Mother Moore," 1-Papers Relating to Black Cultural Archives Mission, ca. 1980s–1999, 7-Policy, 1980s–2006, 6-Governance, 1980s–2006, Papers Relating to the Black Cultural Archives Mission; "A Statement from Queen Mother Moore," 125-Queen Mother Moore, 1990s, 1-Black History Resources, 1833–2001, 5-Collections Management, 1833–2005, Queen Mother Moore, 1990s.

57. "Queen Mother Moore Interview for Black History Month."

58. "Queen Mother Moore: To All My People."

59. Garrison, in Zhana, *Black Success Stories,* 77–78, 81–82; Len Garrison, "Where Are Our Monuments," 125-Queen Mother Moore, 1990s, 1-Black History Resources, 1833–2001, 5-Collections Management, 1833–2005, Queen Mother Moore, 1990s.

60. "Reparations and Monuments," *West Indian Digest,* Sept. 1982, 32.

61. Andrews, *Resisting Racism,* 3–4; Ishmael, "Development of Black-Led Archives in London," 107–8.

62. For more information, see Jackson, "Ties That Bind," 121–24.

63. Warrington, *Black British Intellectuals and Education,* 46–53.

64. "Say Bd. of Ed 'Must Go.'"

65. Andrews, *Resisting Racism,* 6; Waters, *Thinking Black,* 129–31; Jackson, "Ties That Bind," 121–22.

66. "This Is Queen Mother Moore School," Schomburg Center for Research in Black Culture.

67. Reddie, *Black Theology in Transatlantic Dialogue,* 26–27.

68. "This Is Queen Mother Moore School."

69. "Queen Mother Moore Opens School," *South London Press,* June 4, 1982, 11.

70. "This Is Queen Mother Moore School."

71. "Queen Mother Moore Opens School."

72. "Curriculum," "Syllabi," and "Proposed Curriculum for QMMS," NAS/02/02/01, Queen Mother Moore School, NASSC.

73. Queen Mother Moore School Annual Report 1985/1986, LRA/01/0650, Personal Papers of John La Rose.

Chapter 25: THE END OF QUEEN MOTHER MOORE'S REIGN

1. "Black Americans Speak Out: A Self Portrait," *Black Enterprise,* Aug. 1980, 47–52.

2. Nelson, *Congressional Black Caucus,* 118–24.

3. For an excellent overview of Jessie Jackson's Operation PUSH, which is now the Rainbow PUSH Coalition, see Deppe, *Operation Breadbasket.*

4. Singh, *Farrakhan Phenomenon,* 83–85, 94–106.

5. Kitwana, "Hip-Hop Generation," 357; George, *Post-Soul Nation,* 83–85; "Candidacy of Jackson Highlights Split Among Black Muslims," *New York Times,* Feb. 27, 1984, 10.

6. "That's a Good One," *Pittsburg Press,* July 16, 1984, A3; "Predict 'Super' Win for Rev. Jesse Jackson," *Chicago Defender,* Oct. 12, 1987, 3–4; "Jesse Takes Over the Big Apple," *New York Amsterdam News,* Sept. 5, 1987, 1; "In

This Arena, You've Got to Play to Win," *Democrat and Chronicle,* Oct. 14, 1985, 6.

7. Buckoke, "Assessing the OAU Summit."

8. Smith, *Where Credit Is Due,* 74–80.

9. "African Group Blames $200 Billion Debt on Industrialized Nations," *Philadelphia Tribune,* Dec. 8, 1987, 14B.

10. Harsch, *Thomas Sankara,* 61, 65–66.

11. Sawadogo, *Africans in Harlem,* 43–44.

12. Blakely, "40 Acres and a Mule," 132; Playthell Benjamin, interview by author; "Leaders Honored at Garvey Centennial Gala," *New York Amsterdam News,* March 26, 1988, 18; "Africa Maps Out a Common Strategy on Mounting External Debt," *Ethiopian Herald,* Dec. 2, 1987, 1, 5.

13. "President Mengistu Holds Talks with Leaders," *Ethiopian Herald,* Dec. 2, 1987, 1, 6.

14. Macmillan, *Lusaka Years,* 20–21.

15. "Mandela Arrives in Zambia, Appeals for International Aid," *Pittsburgh Courier,* March 10, 1990, 1.

16. "Zambia Declares Mandela Holiday," *Chicago Defender,* Feb. 24, 1990, 5; "Free Africa Welcomes Mandela's Return," *Sechaba,* April 1990, 3.

17. "Concern Voiced for Conserving Mandela's Health," *New York Amsterdam News,* June 23, 1990, 34; "The Proposed Visit to Harlem by Nelson Mandela, ANC," box 39, folder 2, PWP.

18. "Mandela! Apple Blossom Time in New York City," *New York Amsterdam News,* June 30, 1990, 38; "Mandela's Message to the U.S.: 'Keep the Pressure on S. Africa,'" *Chicago Defender,* June 28, 1990, 5.

19. "For Mandela: He's Toast of the Town," *New York Daily News,* June 22, 1990, 3; "Harlem Gives Mandela a Tumultuous Welcome," UPI Archives, June 22, 1990.

20. "For Mandela: He's Toast of the Town."

21. *New York Amsterdam News,* June 30, 1990, 24; "Be Ready to Fight, Winnie Cries," *Daily News,* June 23, 1990, 6; "Winnie Says Women Are Source of Hope," *New York Amsterdam News,* June 30, 1990, 40.

22. "Mother Earth," *Daily News,* June 21, 1990, 38; "Thousands to Salute Nelson Mandela," *New York Amsterdam News,* June 23, 1990, 39.

23. Marable, *Race, Reform, and Rebellion,* 226–27; Whitaker, *Peace Be Still,* 170–71.

24. "Harlem Rocks with Amandla," *New York Amsterdam News,* June 30, 1990, 1.

25. "Guyanese Prez Woos Investors," *New York Amsterdam News,* Sept. 17, 1988, 2; "Envoy Urges Unity for Africa's Salvation," *New York Amsterdam News,* May 13, 1989, 2.

26. "Mother Moore Center Needs Contributions," *New York Amsterdam News,* Aug. 17, 1991, 33; "Middle Passage Holocaust Commemoration," box 28, folder 2, PWP.

27. Mail Fraud Charges Against Marcus Garvey: Hearing Before the Subcommittee on Criminal Justice of the Committee on the Judiciary, House of Representatives, 100th Cong., 1st Sess., July 28, 1987 (U.S. Government Printing Office, 1988); "Rangel: Back Garvey Bill," *New York Amsterdam News,* Aug. 8, 1987, 4.

28. "Pan-Africanism, African Liberation Convention at CCNY in Harlem,"

New York Amsterdam News, Dec. 14, 1991, 4; "Effort to Erect Memorial over Negro Burial Ground Gains Support," *New York Amsterdam News,* March 28, 1992, 1; "News Brief: Henrik Clarke Cited," *New York Amsterdam News,* Feb. 13, 1988, 4; "Uganda Prez Attacks White Rape of Africa," *New York Amsterdam News,* Oct. 31, 1987, 2.

29. Jackson, *Harlemworld,* 20; Ahmad, "Brief History of Islam and Hip-Hop from DJ Kool Herc to Alia Sharrief."

30. Walker, "Revived Nation of Islam and America's Western System in the 1990s," 449, 465.

31. "Muslims Hold Black Family Day to Celebrate Life and Survival," *New York Amsterdam News,* July 31, 1993, 34.

32. "Dr. Justice, Doc with a Mission," *New York Amsterdam News,* Nov. 30, 1985, 4; Carmichael, *Ready for Revolution,* 736.

33. Whitaker, *Peace Be Still,* 172–74; Lewis, *Conservatism in the Black Community,* 45.

34. Busa, *Creative Destruction of New York City,* 30.

35. For Hill's accounting of this moment and Thomas's behavior, see Hill, *Speaking Truth to Power.*

36. *New York Times,* Nov. 17, 1991, 52.

37. Audley Warner, interview by author; Judith Warner, interview by author.

38. Stevenson, *Contested Murder of Latasha Harlins,* xv–xix.

39. Stevenson, *Contested Murder of Latasha Harlins,* xviii.

40. "Harlem Businesses Shut Down Early as Demonstrators Took to the Streets," *New York Amsterdam News,* May 9, 1992, 8.

41. "Emergency Summit on the African Family," *New York Amsterdam News,* April 16, 1988, 24; "Rally Against Crack," *New York Amsterdam News,* Sept. 24, 1988, 35.

42. Aiyetoro and Davis, "Historic and Modern Social Movements for Reparations," 729; "Reparations: Compensation Sought for Slavery," *Atlanta Constitution,* Oct. 24, 1993, 90. For ANRO's activities, see "ANRO Sponsors National Black History Essay Contest," *Atlanta Voice,* Jan. 21, 1984, 21; "Walk Against Genocide," *Oakland Tribune,* June 15, 1984, 48; "Farrakhan Brings Black-Power Message Here Today," *Baltimore Sun,* Sept. 26, 1985, 6C; "MOVE Supports Conduct Vigil," *Lebanon (Pa.) Daily News,* May 13, 1986, 5.

43. Khalifah, *Brief History of N'COBRA,* 28.

44. Aiyetoro, "National Coalition of Blacks for Reparations in America (N'COBRA)," 211–12.

45. For more on Japanese Americans' fight for reparations, see Tateishi, *Redress.*

46. Aiyetoro and Davis, "Historic and Modern Social Movements for Reparations," 730–31; Aiyetoro, "N'COBRA and the Reparations Movement," 40.

47. "Queen Mother Visits N'COBRA Conference," *Call and Post* (Cleveland), Sept. 13, 1990, 1B.

48. "N'COBRA Sessions Open Here July 22 at Cobo," *Michigan Chronicle,* July 13, 1994, 2A; "Reparations Demanded for Slavery," *Philadelphia Tribune,* Aug. 2, 1994, 5B; Khalifah, *Brief History of N'COBRA,* 60–61.

49. Aiyetoro, "National Coalition of Blacks for Reparations in America (N'COBRA)," 207–25; Kelley, "'Day of Reckoning,'" 217.

50. Khalifah, *Brief History of N'COBRA,* 63–64.

51. Kelley, "'Day of Reckoning,'" 216; Biondi, "Rise of the Reparations Movement"; Khalifah, *Brief History of N'COBRA*, 30–31, 38.

52. Farmer, "'Somebody Has to Pay,'" 125–26.

53. "Reparations Debate Heats Up in Courts, Black Communities," *Los Angeles Sentinel*, July 28, 1994, A1.

54. "Reparations Debate Heats Up in Courts, Black Communities."

55. Whitaker, *Peace Be Still*, 203.

56. Whitaker, *Peace Be Still*, 208; Carter, *Brother Bill*, 64–66.

57. "The Queen Mother," *Lansing State Journal*, Aug. 29, 1995, 32; "Nation of Islam Give Praise to Queen Mother Moore," *Final Call*, Jan. 4, 1995, 11.

58. Selwyn Seyfu Hinds, "Black Monday," in Madhubuti and Karenga, *Million Man March*, 64–65.

59. "The Women Behind the Million Man March," *New York Times*, Oct. 17, 2020; Davis, "Organizing Process in the Discourse of the Million Man March," 89.

60. "Million Man March Official Program," in Madhubuti and Karenga, *Million Man March*, 159–66.

61. "Speeches at the Million Man March, a Gathering of Social Activists, En Masse, Held on and Around the National Mall in Washington, D.C.," CNN, Oct. 16, 1995; Height, "We Wanted the Voice of a Woman to Be Heard," 83–92; "Women Play a Major Role in the March," *Final Call*, Nov. 8, 1995, 2.

62. "Speeches at the Million Man March."

63. "Queen Mother Continues Life as Activist," *Wisconsin State Journal*, July 15, 1996, 18; "The Mandela Ticker," *Philadelphia Inquirer*, Nov. 6, 1994, 12.

64. "Queen Mother Title Passed on to Winnie," *New York Amsterdam News*, April 27, 1996, 5.

65. Asantewaa Gail Harris, interview by author; "Gravely Ill," *New York Amsterdam News*, Feb. 8, 1997, 11.

66. Garvey, "First Message to the Negroes of the World from Atlanta Prison," 183.

67. "Queen Mother Moore, Activist, Dies at 98," *Philadelphia Tribune*, May 9, 1997, 4D; Asantewaa Gail Harris, interview by author.

68. "Farrakhan Eulogizes Movement's Legendary 'Queen Mother' Moore," *Los Angeles Sentinel*, May 15, 1997, A3; Audley Warner, interview by author.

69. "Fit for a Queen: Life of Queen Mother Moore Celebrated as She Is Laid to Rest," *Daily Challenge*, May 12, 1997, 3.

70. "Fit for a Queen."

71. Christine Rivers, interview by author; "Farrakhan Eulogizes."

72. Sanchez, interview by author. For the complete text of this poem, see Sanchez, "Poem for Queen Mother Moore."

73. "Fit for a Queen."

74. "*Black Scholar* Interviews Queen Mother Moore," 55.

75. For more evidence of organizers' ideas about a Third Reconstruction, see Poor People's Campaign, *Third Reconstruction Agenda to Heal the Nation: End Poverty and Wages from the Bottom Up*. For a scholarly approach, see Joseph, *Third Reconstruction*.

76. "*Black Scholar* Interviews Queen Mother Moore," 55.

Selected Bibliography

Archival Collections

ABAKANOWICZ RESEARCH CENTER, CHICAGO HISTORY MUSEUM

Arthur W. Mitchell Papers

AMISTAD RESEARCH CENTER, TULANE UNIVERSITY

Kim Lacy Rogers Collection
John E. Rousseau Collection
Charles B. Roussève Papers

ARCHDIOCESE OF NEW ORLEANS ARCHIVES AND RECORDS

Archdiocese of New Orleans Records
St. Joseph's Church Records
St. Katharine's Church Records

ARCHIVES AND SPECIAL COLLECTIONS, NORTHEASTERN UNIVERSITY

Muriel S. and Otto P. Snowden Papers

AUBURN AVENUE RESEARCH LIBRARY ON AFRICAN AMERICAN CULTURE
AND HISTORY, FULTON COUNTY LIBRARY SYSTEM, ATLANTA

Komozi Woodard Amiri Baraka Collection

AUTHOR'S POSSESSION

Roderick Jenkins Collection
Erik S. McDuffie Collection
Emily Moore Collection

BANCROFT LIBRARY, UNIVERSITY OF CALIFORNIA, BERKELEY

Social Protest Collection

BEINECKE RARE BOOK AND MANUSCRIPT LIBRARY, YALE UNIVERSITY

Collection of Material Relating to the Black Arts Repertory Theatre & School

BENTLEY HISTORICAL LIBRARY, UNIVERSITY OF MICHIGAN, ANN ARBOR

Joseph A. Labadie Collection
Robert F. Williams Papers

BLACK CULTURAL ARCHIVES, LONDON

Oral Histories of the Black Women's Movement: The Heart of the Race
Papers Relating to the Black Cultural Archives Mission
Queen Mother Moore, 1990s
Queen Mother Moore Tapes

DOLPH BRISCOE CENTER FOR AMERICAN HISTORY, UNIVERSITY OF TEXAS, AUSTIN

Alli Aweusi Collection, 1969–1995

BRONX COUNTY ARCHIVES, BRONX COUNTY HISTORICAL SOCIETY AND RESEARCH LIBRARY, NEW YORK

Thomas O. Warner, Oral History, Sept. 15, 2020, Interview by Steven Payne

CHARLES F. CUMMINGS NEW JERSEY INFORMATION CENTER, NEWARK

Newark African Americans Collections

DAVID M. RUBENSTEIN RARE BOOK & MANUSCRIPT LIBRARY, DUKE UNIVERSITY

J. B. Matthews Papers

GALE PRIMARY SOURCES UNBOUND

Papers of Amiri Baraka, Poet Laureate of the Black Power Movement

IBERIA PARISH COUNTY, LA., CLERK OFFICE

St. John the Evangelist Catholic Church
St. Peter's Catholic Church

JOHN F. KENNEDY PRESIDENTIAL LIBRARY, BOSTON

Papers of John F. Kennedy

LIBRARY OF CONGRESS, WASHINGTON, D.C.

Rosa Parks Papers
Bayard Rustin Papers

EARL K. LONG LIBRARY, UNIVERSITY OF NEW ORLEANS

Société des Jeunes Amis Collection

MICROFILM

Mary McLeod Bethune Papers, Bethune-Cookman College Archives
Records of the National Association of Women's Clubs, 1985–1992

MISSISSIPPI DEPARTMENT OF ARCHIVES AND HISTORY, JACKSON

Republic of New Africa Collection

MOORLAND-SPINGARN RESEARCH CENTER, HOWARD UNIVERSITY

Ralph J. Bunche Collection Oral History Project
Sixth Pan-African Congress Records

NEW ORLEANS PARISH VITAL RECORDS

Historic New Orleans Collection
Permanent Collection

ORLEANS PARISH CLERK OF COURT, NEW ORLEANS

Louis A. Martinet Records

GEORGE PADMORE INSTITUTE, LONDON

National Association of Supplementary Schools Collection
Personal Papers of John La Rose

PROQUEST HISTORY VAULT

Papers of the NAACP
Papers of the Revolutionary Action Movement
Socialist Party of America Papers
Robert F. Williams Papers, Black Freedom Struggle in the 20th Century: Organizational Records and Personal Papers, Part 2

QUEENS COLLEGE DEPARTMENT OF SPECIAL COLLECTIONS
AND ARCHIVES, NEW YORK

Elliot Linzer Collection

WALTER P. REUTHER LIBRARY, WAYNE STATE UNIVERSITY, DETROIT

Emancipation Centennial Committee Records
Mae Mallory Papers

STUART A. ROSE MANUSCRIPT, ARCHIVES,
AND RARE BOOK LIBRARY, EMORY UNIVERSITY, ATLANTA

Matt N. and Evelyn Graves Crawford Papers
Theodore Draper Research Files
Vincent Harding Papers
Philip J. Jaffe Papers
Louise Thompson Patterson Papers
Universal Negro Improvement Association Records

SCHLESINGER LIBRARY, RADCLIFFE, CAMBRIDGE, MASS.

Interview with Audley Moore (Queen Mother Moore), Black Women Oral History
Project, Interviews, 1976–1981

SCHOMBURG CENTER FOR RESEARCH IN BLACK CULTURE, NEW YORK

Bessye B. Bearden Papers
Black Panther Party Harlem Branch Files
Robert S. Browne Papers
Civil Rights Congress Records
John Henrik Clarke Papers
Babette Edwards Collection
Vicki Garvin Papers
International Labor Defense Records
Claudia Jones Research Collection
Queen Mother Moore Vertical File
Richard B. Moore Papers
National Negro Congress Records
Larry Neal Papers
Organization of Afro-American Unity Collection
Republic of New Africa Collection
Universal Negro Improvement Association Central Division, New York Records
Universal Negro Improvement Association Miscellaneous Collection
Preston Wilcox Papers
Malcolm X Collection

SPECIAL COLLECTIONS, TULANE UNIVERSITY

Kim Lacey Roberts Collection

ST. LANDRY PARISH, LA., CLERK OFFICE

ST. MARTIN PARISH, LA., CLERK OFFICE

SWARTHMORE COLLEGE PEACE COLLECTION

American People's Mobilization Collected Records, 1940–1941

TAMIMENT LIBRARY AND ROBERT F. WAGNER LABOR ARCHIVES,
NEW YORK UNIVERSITY

Communist Party of the United States of America Papers
Audley Moore, Interview by Mark Naison
Audley Moore, Interview by Ruth Prago
Oral History of the American Left Collection

WILSON SPECIAL COLLECTIONS LIBRARY,
UNIVERSITY OF NORTH CAROLINA AT CHAPEL HILL

Campbell Family Papers, Southern History Collection

WESTERN RESERVE HISTORICAL SOCIETY, CLEVELAND

Universal Negro Improvement Association Records

WISCONSIN HISTORICAL SOCIETY, MADISON

Committee to Combat Racial Injustice Records

Newspapers

African World
Afro-American (Baltimore)
Anniston Star
Arizona Republic
Atlanta Constitution
Atlanta Daily World
Atlanta Voice
Attakapas Gazette (St. Martinville, La.)
Austin American-Statesmen
Baltimore Sun
Birmingham Mirror
Black Dispatch (Oklahoma City)
Black News
Boston Globe
Brooklyn Daily Eagle
California Eagle
Call and Post (Cleveland)
Chattanooga Daily Times
Chicago Defender

Chicago Metro News
Chicago Tribune
City Sun
Clarion-Ledger (Jackson, Miss.)
Columbia (Mo.) Daily Tribune
Congress View
Cornell Daily Sun
Courier-Journal (Louisville, Ky.)
Daily Challenge
Daily Citizen (New York City)
Daily Independent Journal (San Rafael,
   Calif.)
Daily Mail (London)
Daily Nation (Kenya)
Daily News (New York City)
Daily News (Tanzania)
Daily Worker (New York City)
Daily World (Opelousas, La.)
Detroit Free Press

Emancipator (Montgomery, Ala.)

Ethiopian Herald

Evening Star (Washington, D.C.)

Final Call

Fort Worth (Tex.) Star-Telegram

Harlem Pointer

Herald-Dispatch (Los Angeles)

Hunger Defender

Indianapolis Journal

Indianapolis Recorder

Jackson (Miss.) Advocate

Kansas City (Mo.) Times

Kingston (N.Y.) Daily Freeman

Knoxville (Tenn.) Journal and Tribune

Labor Defender

Lansing (Mich.) State Journal

Los Angeles Sentinel

Los Angeles Times

Louisiana Weekly (New Orleans)

Louisianian

Memphis Appeal-Avalanche

Messenger

Miami Herald

Michigan Chronicle

Middletown (N.Y.) Times Herald

Milwaukee Star

Montgomery (Ala.) Advertiser

Morning Call (Allentown, Pa.)

Negro World

New African

Newark Star Ledger

New Journal and Guide (Norfolk, Va.)

New Orleans Republican

News (Paterson, N.J.)

News Journal (Wilmington, Del.)

New York Age

New York Amsterdam News

New York Herald Tribune

New York Times

Oakland Tribune

People's Voice (Harlem, N.Y.)

Philadelphia Daily News

Philadelphia Inquirer

Philadelphia Tribune

Pittsburgh Courier

Pittsburg Press

Post Standard (Syracuse, N.Y.)

Record (Hackensack, N.J.)

South London Press

Star-Gazette (Elmira, N.Y.)

Star Tribune (Minneapolis)

St. Louis Globe-Democrat

Street Speaker

Student Mobilizer (New York City)

Summit County Beacon (Akron, Ohio)

Sun Reporter (San Francisco)

Tampa Tribune

Times (Hammond, Ind.)

Times (Munster, Ind.)

Times (Shreveport, La.)

Times-Democrat (New Orleans)

Times-Picayune (New Orleans)

Town Talk (Alexandria, La.)

Tri-State Defender (Memphis)

Village Voice

Washington Post

Weekly Pelican (New Iberia, La.)

Weekly Review (New York City)

Wisconsin State Journal

Women's Era

York (Pa.) Daily Record

Published Interviews

"The Black and the Red." Produced by Beth Friend and Charles Potter. Narrated by Jill Eikenberg. Pacifica Radio Archive, 1983. www.pacificaradioarchives.org /recording/sz0162.

"*The Black Scholar* Interviews Queen Mother Moore." *Black Scholar* 4, no. 6/7 (1973): 47–55.

"Queen Mother Moore as the Struggle Intensifies." *Black News,* Oct. 1, 1978, 14.

Sources

Abu-Lughod, Janet. *Race, Space, and Riots in Chicago, New York, and Los Angeles.* Oxford University Press, 2007.

Adi, Hakim. "The Negro Question: The Communist International and Black Liberation in the Interwar Years." In *From Toussaint to Tupac: The Black International Since the Age of Revolution,* edited by Michael O. West and Fanon Che Wilkins. University of North Carolina Press, 2009.

———. *Pan-Africanism: A History.* Bloomsbury Academic, 2018.

Adler, Jeffrey S. *Murder in New Orleans: The Creation of Jim Crow Policing.* University of Chicago Press, 2019.

Ahmad, Muhammad. "Queen Mother Moore: Mentor and Teacher." *Palimpsest: A Journal on Women, Gender, and the Black International* 7, no. 2 (2018): 169–72.

———. *We Will Return in the Whirlwind: Black Radical Organizations, 1966–1975.* Charles H. Kerr, 2007.

Ahmad, Muna. "A Brief History of Islam and Hip-Hop from DJ Kool Herc to Alia Sharrief." *Gal-Dem,* Dec. 11, 2020.

Aiyetoro, Adjoa A. "The National Coalition of Blacks for Reparations in America (N'COBRA): Its Creation and Contribution to the Reparations Movement." In *Should America Pay? Slavery and the Raging Debate on Reparations,* edited by Roy A. Winbush. Amistad, 2003.

———. "N'COBRA and the Reparations Movement." *Guild Practitioner* 60, no. 1 (2003): 40.

Aiyetoro, Adjoa A., and Adrienne D. Davis. "Historic and Modern Social Movements for Reparations: The National Coalition of Blacks for Reparations in America (N'COBRA) and Its Antecedents." *Texas Wesleyan Law Review* 16, no. 4 (2010): 687–766.

Alamo-Pastrana, Carlos. *Seams of Empire: Race and Radicalism in Puerto Rico and the United States.* University Press of Florida, 2016.

Ali, Omar H. *In the Balance of Power: Independent Black Politics and Third Party Movements in the United States.* Ohio University Press, 2008.

Allman, Jean Marie. "The Youngmen and the Porcupine: Class, Nationalism, and Asante's Struggle for Self-Determination, 1954–57." *Journal of African History* 31, no. 2 (1990): 151–79.

Alonso, Harriet Hyman. "Mayhem and Moderation: Women Peace Activists During the McCarthy Era." In *Not June Cleaver: Gender and Postwar America, 1945–1960,* edited by Joanne Meyerowitz. Temple University Press, 1994.

Anderson, Carol. *Eyes off the Prize: The United Nations and the African American Struggle for Human Rights, 1944–1955.* Cambridge University Press, 2003.

———. "From Hope to Disillusion: African Americans, the United Nations, and the Struggle for Human Rights, 1944–1947." *Diplomatic History* 20, no. 4 (1996): 531–63.

Andrews, Kehinde. *Resisting Racism: Race, Inequality, and the Black Supplementary School Movement.* IOE Press/Trentham Books, 2013.

Araujo, Ana Lucia. *Reparations for Slavery and the Slave Trade: A Transnational and Comparative History.* Bloomsbury, 2017.

Arnau, Ariel. "The Evolution of Leadership Within the Puerto Rican Community of

Philadelphia, 1950s–1970s." *Pennsylvania Magazine of History and Biography* 136, no. 1 (2012): 53–81.

Arsenault, Raymond. *The Freedom Riders: 1961 and the Struggle for Racial Justice.* Oxford University Press, 2011.

Austin, Dan. *Lost Detroit: Stories Behind the Motor City's Majestic Ruins.* History Press, 2010.

Back, Adina. "'Exposing the Whole Segregation Myth': The Harlem Nine and New York City's School Desegregation Battles." In *Freedom North: Black Freedom Struggles Outside the South, 1940–1980,* edited by Jeanne Theoharis and Komozi Woodard. Palgrave Macmillan, 2003.

Bair, Barbara. "'Ethiopia Shall Stretch Forth Her Hands unto God': Laura Kofey and the Gendered Vision of Redemption in the Garvey Movement." In *A Mighty Baptism: Race, Gender, and the Creation of American Protestantism,* edited by Susan Juster and Lisa MacFarlane. Cornell University Press, 1996.

———. "Garveyism and Contested Political Terrain in 1920s Virginia." In *Afro-Virginian History and Culture,* edited by John Saillant. Taylor and Francis, 1999.

———. "True Women, Real Men: Gender, Ideology, and Social Roles in the Garvey Movement." In *Gendered Domains: Rethinking Public and Private in Women's History,* edited by Dorothy O. Helly and Susan M. Reverby. Cornell University Press, 1992.

Baker, Ella, and Marvel Cooke. "The Bronx Slave Market." *Crisis* 42 (1935): 330–32.

Baldwin, Davarian. *Chicago's New Negroes: Modernity, the Great Migration, and Black Urban Life.* University of North Carolina Press, 2007.

Balfour, Lawrie. "Living 'in the Red': Time, Debt, and Justice." In *To Shape a New World: Essays on the Political Philosophy of Martin Luther King Jr.,* edited by Tommie Shelby and Brandon Terry. Harvard University Press, 2018.

Bandele, Ramla. *Black Star: African American Activism in the International Political Economy.* University of Illinois Press, 2008.

———. "Understanding African Diaspora Political Activism: The Rise and Fall of the Black Star Line." *Journal of Black Studies* 40, no. 4 (2010): 745–61.

Baraka, Amiri. *The Autobiography of LeRoi Jones.* Lawrence Hill Books, 1997.

Barker, Martin. *The New Racism.* Junction Books, 1982.

Barrett, James R. *William Z. Foster and the Tragedy of American Radicalism.* University of Illinois Press, 1999.

Barthé, Darryl. *Becoming American in Creole New Orleans, 1896–1949.* Louisiana State University Press, 2021.

Bay, Mia. *Traveling Black: A Story of Race and Resistance.* Harvard University Press, 2021.

Bedasse, Monique A. *Jah Kingdom: Rastafarians, Tanzania, and Pan-Africanism in the Age of Decolonization.* University of North Carolina Press, 2017.

Bennett, Huw. *Fighting the Mau Mau: The British Army and Counter-Insurgency in the Kenya Emergency.* Cambridge University Press, 2013.

Bennett, James B. *Religion and the Rise of Jim Crow in New Orleans.* Princeton University Press, 2005.

Berger, Dan. "'The Malcolm X Doctrine': The Republic of New Afrika and National Liberation on U.S. Soil." In *New World Coming: The Sixties and the Shaping of Global Consciousness,* edited by Karen Dubinsky, Catherine Krull, Susan Lord, Sean Mills, and Scott Rutherford. Between the Lines, 2009.

Bernard, Shane K. *Teche: A History of Louisiana's Most Famous Bayou.* University Press of Mississippi, 2016.

Berry, Jason. *City of a Million Dreams: New Orleans at Year 300.* University of North Carolina Press, 2018.

Berry, Mary Frances. *My Face Is Black Is True: Callie House and the Struggle for Ex-Slave Reparations.* Vintage Books, 2005.

Biondi, Martha. "The Rise of the Reparations Movement." *Radical Historical Review* 87, no. 1 (2003): 5–18.

———. *To Stand and Fight: The Struggle for Rights in Postwar New York City.* Harvard University Press, 2003.

Birmingham, David. *Kwame Nkrumah: The Father of African Nationalism.* University of Ohio Press, 1998.

Blagrove, Ishmahil, Jr., ed. *The Frontline: A Story of Struggle, Race, and Black Identity in Notting Hill.* Rice and Peas, 2022.

Blain, Keisha N. *Set the World on Fire: Black Nationalist Women and the Global Struggle for Freedom.* University of Pennsylvania Press, 2018.

———. " 'To Keep Alive the Teaching of Garvey and the Work of the UNIA': Audley Moore, Black Women's Activism, and Nationalist Politics During the Twentieth Century." *Palimpsest: A Journal on Women, Gender, and the Black International* 7, no. 2 (2018): 83–107.

Blair, Sara. *Harlem's Crossroads: Black Writers and the Photograph in the Twentieth Century.* Princeton University Press, 2008.

Blakely, Delois. "40 Acres and a Mule: Queen Mother Moore." *Harlem Magazine* (1994): 130–33.

———. *The Harlem Street Nun: Autobiography of Queen Mother Dr. Delois Blakely Known as Sister Noelita Marie.* Create Space Independent Publishing Platform, 2013.

Blassingame, John W. *Black New Orleans, 1860–1880.* University of Chicago Press, 1973.

Bloom, Joshua, and Waldo E. Martin Jr. *Black Against Empire: The History and Politics of the Black Panther Party.* University of California Press, 2013.

Blouin, Francis X., Jr., and William G. Rosenberg. *Processing the Past: Contesting Authority and History in the Archives.* Oxford University Press, 2011.

Boissoneault, Lorraine. "The Deadliest Massacre in Reconstruction-Era Louisiana Happened 150 Years Ago." *Smithsonian Magazine,* Sept. 28, 2018.

Bonin, Blair. *Where the Bayou Runs Straight: The History of Jeanerette.* P. Rampey, 1982.

Bosque-Pérez, Ramón, and José Javier Colón Morera, eds. *Puerto Rico Under Colonial Rule: Political Persecution and the Quest for Human Rights.* State University of New York Press, 2006.

Bosworth, Gary Lamont. "Black New Orleans, 1955–1985: The Rise of a Southern Black Metropolis out of the Ashes of Jim Crow." PhD diss., Howard University, 2009.

Bourbonnais, Nicole. "Our Joan of Arc: Women, Gender, and Authority in the Harmony Division of the UNIA." In *Global Garveyism,* edited by Ronald Jemal Stephens and Adam Ewing. University Press of Florida, 2019.

Boyd, Herb. *Black Detroit: A People's History of Self-Determination.* Amistad, 2017.

Brandimarte, Cynthia. "Women on the Home Front: Hostess Houses During World War I." *Winterthur Portfolio* 42, no. 2 (2008): 201–22.

Brasseaux, Carl A. "Creoles of Color in Louisiana's Bayou, 1766–1877." In *Creoles of Color in the Gulf South*, edited by James H. Dormon. University of Tennessee Press, 1996.

Brasseaux, Carl A., Keith P. Fontenot, and Claude F. Oubre, eds. *Creoles of Color in the Bayou Country*. University Press of Mississippi, 1994.

Breen, William J. "Black Women and the Great War: Mobilization and Reform in the South." *Journal of Southern History* 44, no. 3 (1978): 421–40.

Breines, Winifred. *The Trouble Between Us: An Uneasy History of White and Black Women in the Feminist Movement*. Oxford University Press, 2006.

Brimmer, Brandi Clay. *Claiming Union Widowhood: Race, Respectability, and Poverty in the Post-Emancipation South*. Duke University Press, 2020.

Brown, Kathleen A. "The 'Savagely Fathered and Un-Mothered World' of the Communist Party, U.S.A.: Feminism, Maternalism, and 'Mother Bloor.'" *Feminist Studies* 25, no. 3 (1999): 537–70.

Brown, Nikki L. M. *Private Politics and Public Voices: Black Women's Activism from World War I to the New Deal*. Indiana University Press, 2006.

Brown, Scot. *Fighting for US: Maulana Karenga, the US Organization, and Black Cultural Nationalism*. New York University Press, 2003.

Bryant, Clora, et al. *Central Avenue Sounds: Jazz in Los Angeles*. University of California Press, 1998.

Bryant, Louis Paul. "Reminiscences of the '60s and '70s." In Conrad, *New Iberia*.

Buckoke, Andrew. "Assessing the OAU Summit." *Africa Report*, Sept.–Oct. 1987, 28–30.

Bunce, Robin, and Paul Field. *Darcus Howe: A Political Biography*. Bloomsbury, 2014.

Bundles, A'Lelia. *On Her Own Ground: The Life and Times of Madam C. J. Walker*. Scribner, 2002.

Burden-Stelly, Charisse. *Black Scare / Red Scare: Theorizing Capitalist Racism in the United States*. University of Chicago Press, 2023.

Burkett, Randall K. *Garveyism as a Religious Movement*. Scarecrow Press, 1978.

Burrell, Christopher Bryan. "Black Women as Activist Intellectuals: Ella Baker and Mae Mallory Combat Northern Jim Crow in New York City's Public Schools During the 1950s." In *The Strange Careers of the Jim Crow North: Segregation and Struggle Outside of the South*, edited by Brian Purnell, Jeanne Theoharis, and Komozi Woodard. New York University Press, 2019.

Busa, Alessandro. *The Creative Destruction of New York City: Engineering the City for the Elite*. Oxford University Press, 2017.

Bush, Roderick. *We Are Not What We Seem: Black Nationalism and Class Struggle in the American Century*. New York University Press, 1999.

Butler, Anne, and C. Murray Henderson. *Angola: Louisiana State Penitentiary, a Half-Century of Rage and Reform*. University of Louisiana at Lafayette Press, 1990.

Butler, Kim D. "Africa and the Reinvention of the Nineteenth Century Afro-Bahian Identity." In *Rethinking the African Diaspora: The Making of the Black Atlantic World in the Bight of Benin and Brazil*, edited by Kristin Mann and Edna G. Bay. Routledge, 2001.

Butts, J. J. *Dark Mirror: African Americans and the Federal Writers Project*. Ohio State University Press, 2021.

Campanella, Richard. *Bienville's Dilemma: A Historical Geography of New Orleans*. University of Louisiana at Lafayette / Garrett County Press, 2010.

———. "An Ethnic Geography of New Orleans." *Journal of American History* 94, no. 3 (2007): 704–15.

———. *Lost New Orleans.* Pavilion Books, 2015.

Campbell, Marne L. *Making Black Los Angeles: Class, Gender, and Community, 1850–1917.* Chapel Hill: University of North Carolina Press, 2016.

Carew, Joy Gleason. *Blacks, Reds, and Russians: Sojourners in Search of the Soviet Promise.* Rutgers University Press, 2010.

Carey, Brycchan, and Geoffrey Plank, eds. *Quakers and Abolition.* University of Illinois Press, 2014.

Carmichael, Stokely (Kwame Ture). *Ready for Revolution: The Life and Struggles of Stokely Carmichael.* With Ekwueme Michael Thelwell. Scribner, 2003.

Carretta, Vincent, ed. *Unchained Voices: An Anthology of Black Authors in the English Speaking World of the Eighteenth Century.* University Press of Kentucky, 1996.

Carson, Clayborne. *In Struggle: SNCC and the Black Awakening of the 1960s.* Harvard University Press, 1995.

Carter, Dan T. *Scottsboro: A Tragedy of the American South.* Louisiana State University Press, 2007.

Carter, Daryl A. *Brother Bill: President Clinton and the Politics of Race and Class.* University of Arkansas Press, 2016.

Cashmore, Ellis. *Rastaman: The Rastafari Movement in England.* 2nd ed. Routledge, 2013.

Castledine, Jacqueline. *Cold War Progressives: Women's Interracial Organizing for Peace and Freedom.* University of Illinois Press, 2012.

Chambers, Glen Anthony. *From the Banana Zones to the Big Easy: West Indian and Central American Immigration to New Orleans.* Louisiana State University Press, 2019.

Chapman, Peter. *Bananas: How the United Fruit Company Shaped the World.* Canongate, 2007.

Chapple, Reginald. "From Central Avenue to Leimert Park: The Shifting Center of Black Los Angeles." In *Black Los Angeles: American Dreams and Racial Realities,* edited by Darnell Hunt and Ana-Christina Ramón. New York University Press, 2010.

Charles, Douglas M. *Hoover's War on Gays: Exposing the FBI's "Sex Deviates."* University Press of Kansas, 2016.

Chisholm, Shirley. *The Good Fight.* Harper and Row, 1973.

Chomsky, Avi. "Afro-Jamaican Traditions and Labor Organizing on United Fruit Company Plantations in Costa Rica, 1910." *Journal of Social History* 28, no. 4 (1995): 837–55.

Christensen, Matthew. "The 1868 St. Landry Massacre: Reconstruction's Deadliest Episode of Violence." Master's thesis, University of Wisconsin–Milwaukee, 2012.

Churchill, Ward, and Jim Vander Wall. *Agents of Repression: The FBI's Secret Wars Against the Black Panther Party and the American Indian Movement.* South End Press, 1990.

Clarke, Cheryl. *After Mecca: Women Poets and the Black Arts Movement.* Rutgers University Press, 2005.

Claude, Judy. "Some Personal Reflections on the Sixth Pan-African Congress." *Black Scholar* 37, no. 4 (2008): 48–49.

Clay, William. *Just Permanent Interests: Black Americans in Congress, 1870–1991.* Amistad Press, 1992.

Clegg, Claude. *The Price of Liberty: African Americans and the Making of Liberia.* University of North Carolina Press, 2004.

Coates, Ta-Nehisi. "Martin Luther King Makes the Case for Reparations." *Atlantic,* June 12, 2014.

Cocks, Catherine. *Tropical Whites: The Rise of the Tourist South in the Americas.* University of Pennsylvania Press, 2013.

Coen, Cheré Dastugue. *Exploring Cajun Country: A Tour of Historic Acadiana.* History Press, 2011.

Conrad, Glenn R., ed. *New Iberia: Essays on the Town and Its People.* University of Southern Louisiana Press, 1979.

Conway, Thomas. *The Freedman of Louisiana: Final Report of the Bureau of Labor.* New Orleans Times Book and Jobs Office, 1865.

Conyers, John. "A Black Political Strategy for 1972." In *What Black Politicians Are Saying,* edited by Nathan Wright Jr. Hawthorne Books, 1972.

Countryman, Matthew. *Up South: Civil Rights and Black Power in Philadelphia.* University of Pennsylvania Press, 2006.

Curry, Mary Cuthrell. *Making the Gods: The Yoruba Religion in the African American Community.* Garland, 1997.

Curwood, Anastasia C. *Shirley Chisholm: Champion of Black Feminist Power Politics.* University of North Carolina Press, 2023.

Cutrer, Thomas W., and T. Michael Parrish. *Doris Miller, Pearl Harbor, and the Birth of the Civil Rights Movement.* A&M Press, 2018.

Daniels, Roger. "Relocation, Redress, and the Report: A Historical Appraisal." In *When Sorry Isn't Enough: The Controversy over Reparations for Human Injustice,* edited by Roy L. Brooks. New York University Press, 1999.

Daniels, Ron. "The National Black Political Assembly: Building Independent Black Politics in the 1980s." *Black Scholar,* July/Aug. 1984, 33–44.

Davenport, Christian. *How Social Movements Die: Repression and Demobilization of the Republic of New Africa.* Cambridge University Press, 2015.

Davidson, Basil. *Black Star: A View of the Life and Times of Kwame Nkrumah.* Reprint. Routledge, 2007.

Davies, Carole Boyce. *Claudia Jones Beyond Containment: Autobiographical Reflections, Essays, and Poems.* Ayebia Clarke, 2011.

———. *Left of Karl Marx: The Political Life of Black Communist Claudia Jones.* Duke University Press, 2008.

Davies, Tom A. *Mainstreaming Black Power.* University of California Press, 2017.

Davis, Joanna Maria. "The Organizing Process in the Discourse of the Million Man March." PhD diss., Howard University, 1998.

Davis, Mike, and Jon Wiener. *Set the Night on Fire: L.A. in the Sixties.* Verso Books, 2020.

Decker, Alicia C. *Idi Amin's Shadow: Women, Gender, and Militarism in Uganda.* Ohio University Press, 2014.

Deggs, Mary Bernard, Virginia Meacham Gould, and Charles E. Nolan. *No Cross, No Crown: Black Nuns in Nineteenth-Century New Orleans.* Indiana University Press, 2002.

DeLatte, Carolyn E. "The St. Landry Riot: A Forgotten Incident of Reconstruction Violence." *Louisiana History* 17, no. 1 (1976): 41–49.

Delmont, Matthew F. *Why Busing Failed: Race, Media, and National Resistance to School Desegregation.* University of California Press, 2016.

Denis, Nelson A. *War Against All Puerto Ricans: Revolution and Terror in America's Colony*. Bold Type Books, 2015.

Deppe, Martin L. *Operation Breadbasket: An Untold Story of Civil Rights in Chicago, 1966–1971*. University of Georgia Press, 2017.

De Vaux, Alex. *Warrior Poet: A Biography of Audre Lorde*. W. W. Norton, 2004.

DeVore, Donald E. *Defying Jim Crow: African American Community Development and the Struggle for Racial Equality in New Orleans, 1900–1960*. Louisiana State University Press, 2015.

DeVore, Donald E., and Joseph Logsdon. *Crescent City Schools: Public Education in New Orleans, 1841–1991*. University of Louisiana at Lafayette Press, 2012.

Dillard, Angela D. *Faith in the City: Radical Social Change in Detroit*. University of Michigan Press, 2007.

Donaldson, Jeff. "FESTAC '77 Documemoir." In Soyinka, *FESTAC '77*.

Douglas, Davison M. *Jim Crow Moves North: The Battle over Northern School Segregation, 1865–1954*. Cambridge University Press, 2005.

Drake, St. Clair. *The Redemption of Africa and Black Religion*. Third World Press, 1970.

Dray, Philip. *Capitol Men: The Epic Story of Reconstruction Through the Lives of the First Black Congressmen*. Houghton Mifflin, 2008.

Duany, Jorge. *The Puerto Rican Nation on the Move: Identities on the Island and in the United States*. University of North Carolina Press, 2002.

Du Bois, W. E. B. *The Souls of Black Folk*. Norton, 1999.

Duncan, Natanya. *An Efficient Womanhood: Women and the Making of the Universal Negro Improvement Association*. University of North Carolina Press, 2025.

———. "'If Our Men Hesitate Then the Women of the Race Must Come Forward': Henrietta Vinton Davis and the UNIA in New York." *New York History* 95, no. 4 (2014): 558–83.

Duziak, Mary. *Cold War, Civil Rights: Race and the Image of American Democracy*. Princeton University Press, 2002.

Echeverri-Gent, Elisavinda. "Forgotten Workers: British West Indians and the Early Days of the Banana Industry in Costa Rica and Honduras." *Journal of Latin American Studies* 24, no. 2 (1992): 275–308.

Edgell, Derek. *The Movement for Community Control of New York City's Schools, 1966–1970*. Edwin Mellen Press, 1998.

Eig, Jonathan. *King: A Life*. Farrar, Straus and Giroux, 2023.

Emanuel, Rachel L., and Alexander P. Tureaud Jr. *A More Noble Cause: A. P. Tureaud and the Struggle for Civil Rights in Louisiana: A Personal Biography*. Louisiana State University Press, 2011.

England, Sandra E. "A Historical Overview of Afro-Americans in New Iberia, 1865–1960." In Conrad, *New Iberia*.

Ewing, Adam. *Age of Garvey*. Princeton University Press, 2016.

Fairclough, Adam. *Race and Democracy: The Civil Rights Struggle in Louisiana, 1915–1972*. University of Georgia Press, 1995.

Falola, Toyin, and Matthew M. Heaton. *A History of Nigeria*. Cambridge University Press, 2008.

Fanon, Frantz. *Black Skin, White Masks*. New ed. Grove Press, 2008.

Farber, David. *Crack: Rock Cocaine, Street Capitalism, and the Decade of Greed.* Cambridge University Press, 2019.

Farmer, Ashley D. "'Abolition of Every Possibility of Oppression': Black Women, Black Power, and the Black Women's United Front, 1970–1976." *Journal of Women's History* 32, no. 3 (2020): 89–114.

———. "'All the Progress to Be Made Will Be Made by Maladjusted Negroes': Mae Mallory, Black Women's Activism, and the Making of the Black Radical Tradition." *Journal of Social History* 53, no. 2 (2019): 508–30.

———. "Disorderly Distribution: The Dispersal of Archives and the Illegibility of Black Women Intellectuals." *Black Scholar* 52, no. 4 (2022): 5–15.

———. "Mothers of Pan-Africanism: Audley Moore and Dara Abubakari." *Women, Gender, and Families of Color* 4, no. 2 (2016): 274–95.

———. *Remaking Black Power: How Black Women Transformed an Era.* University of North Carolina Press, 2017.

———. "'Somebody Has to Pay': Audley Moore and the Modern Reparations Movement." *Palimpsest: A Journal on Women, Gender, and the Black International* 7, no. 2 (2018): 108–34.

———. "Working Toward Community Is Our Full-Time Focus: Muriel Snowden, Black Power, and the Freedom House, Roxbury, MA." *Black Scholar* 41, no. 3 (2011): 17–25.

Farrington, Joshua D. *Black Republicans and the Transformation of the GOP.* University of Pennsylvania Press, 2016.

Felber, Garrett. "'Harlem Is the Black World': The Organization of Afro-American Unity at the Grassroots." *Journal of African American History* 100, no. 2 (2015): 199–215.

———. *Those Who Know Don't Say: The Nation of Islam, the Black Freedom Movement, and the Carceral State.* University of North Carolina Press, 2020.

Fenderson, Jonathan. *Building the Black Arts Movement: Hoyt Fuller and the Cultural Politics of the 1960s.* University of Illinois Press, 2009.

Ferguson, Iyaluua. *An Unlikely Warrior: Herman Ferguson, the Evolution of a Black Nationalist Revolutionary.* With Herman Ferguson. Ferguson-Swan Publications, 2011.

Ferguson, Karen. *Top Down: The Ford Foundation, Black Power, and the Reinvention of Racial Liberalism.* University of Pennsylvania Press, 2013.

Firven, Michael Shane, Jr. "From Paternalism to Black Power: Civil Rights, the Black Panther Party, and the Evolution of Black Leadership in New Orleans, Louisiana." PhD diss., Howard University, 2008.

Fischbach, Michael. *Black Power and Palestine.* Stanford University Press, 2018.

Flamming, Douglas. *Bound for Freedom: Black Los Angeles in Jim Crow America.* University of California Press, 2015.

Fleegler, Robert L. "Theodore G. Bilbo and the Decline of Public Racism, 1938–1947." *Journal of Mississippi History* 68, no. 1 (2006): 1–27.

Flynn, Elizabeth Gurley. *Rebel Girl: An Autobiography of My First Life.* International Publishers, 1973.

Follett, Richard. *The Sugar Masters: Planters and Slaves in Louisiana's Cane World, 1820–1860.* Louisiana State University Press, 2005.

Foner, Eric. *Reconstruction: America's Unfinished Revolution.* Harper Perennial, 2014.

———. *A Short History of Reconstruction, 1863–1877.* Harper Perennial Modern Classics, 2015.

Ford, Tanisha. *Liberated Threads: Black Women, Style, and the Global Politics of Soul.* University of North Carolina Press, 2015.

Franklin, John Hope. *From Slavery to Freedom: A History of African Americans.* 8th ed. Knopf, 2000.

Franklin, V. P. *The Young Crusaders: The Untold Story of the Children and Teenagers Who Galvanized the Civil Rights Movement.* Beacon Press, 2021.

Friedman, Joel William. *Champion of Civil Rights: Judge John Minor Wisdom.* Louisiana State University Press, 2009.

Fuller, Harcourt. *Building the Ghanaian Nation-State: Kwame Nkrumah's Symbolic Nationalism.* Palgrave Macmillan, 2014.

Gaddis, John Lewis. *The Cold War: A New History.* Penguin Press, 2005.

Gaffney, Dennis. *Teachers United: The Rise of New York State United Teachers.* State University of New York Press, 2007.

Gaines, Kevin K. *American Africans in Ghana: Black Expatriates and the Civil Rights Era.* University of North Carolina Press, 2006.

———. *Uplifting the Race: Black Leadership, Politics, and Culture in the Twentieth Century.* University of North Carolina Press, 1995.

Gaines, Rondee. "I Am a Revolutionary Black Female Nationalist: A Womanist Analysis of Fulani Sunni Ali's Role as a New African Citizen and Minister of Information in the Provisional Government of the Republic of New Africa." PhD diss., Georgia State University, 2013.

Garibaldi, Korey. *Impermanent Blackness: The Making and Unmaking of Interracial Literary Culture in Modern America.* Princeton University Press, 2024.

Garvey, Marcus. "First Message to the Negroes of the World from Atlanta Prison." In *Selected Writings and Speeches of Marcus Garvey,* edited by Bob Blaisdell. Dover, 2004.

———. "Speech Delivered at Carnegie Hall." In *The Philosophy and Opinions of Marcus Garvey: Africa for the Africans,* edited by Marcus Garvey and Amy Jacques Garvey. Cass, 1977.

Gellman, Erik S. *Death Blow to Jim Crow: The National Negro Congress and the Rise of Militant Civil Rights.* University of North Carolina Press, 2012.

Georgakas, Dan, and Marvin Surkin. *Detroit: Do I Mind Dying: A Study in Urban Revolution.* Haymarket Books, 2012.

George, Nelson. *Post-Soul Nation: The Explosive, Contradictory, Triumphant, and Tragic 1980s as Experienced by African Americans (Previously Known as Blacks and Before That Negroes).* Viking, 2004.

Germany, Kent B. *New Orleans After the Promises: Poverty, Citizenship, and the Search for the Great Society.* University of Georgia Press, 2007.

Geshwender, James A., and Judson L. Jeffries. "The League of Revolutionary Black Workers." In *Black Power in the Belly of the Beast,* edited by Judson L. Jeffries. University of Illinois Press, 2006.

Gill, Jonathan. *Harlem: The Four Hundred Year History from Dutch Village to Capital of Black America.* Grove Press, 2012.

Gill, Tiffany M. *Beauty Shop Politics: African American Activism in the Beauty Industry.* University of Illinois Press, 2010.

Gilroy, Paul. *Ain't No Black in the Union Jack: The Cultural Politics of Race and Nation.* University of Chicago Press, 1991.

Gilyard, Keith. *Louise Thompson Patterson: A Life of Struggle for Justice.* Duke University Press, 2017.

Gordon, Linda. *The Second Coming of the KKK: The Ku Klux Klan of the 1920s and the American Political Tradition.* Liveright, 2017.

Gore, Dayo F. "From Communist Politics to Black Power: The Visionary Politics and Transnational Solidarities of Victoria 'Vicki' Ama Garvin." In *Want to Start a Revolution? Radical Women in the Black Freedom Struggle,* edited by Dayo Gore, Jeanne Theoharis, and Komozi Woodard. New York University Press, 2009.

———. *Radicalism at the Crossroads: African American Women in the Cold War.* New York University Press, 2011.

Goudsouzian, Aram. *Down to the Crossroads: Civil Rights, Black Power, and the Meredith March Against Fear.* Farrar, Straus and Giroux, 2014.

Grant, Colin. *A Negro with a Hat: The Rise and Fall of Marcus Garvey.* Oxford University Press, 2008.

Green, Ben. *Before His Time: The Untold Story of Harry T. Moore, America's First Civil Rights Martyr.* Free Press, 1999.

Greenbaum, Susan D. *Blaming the Poor: The Long Shadow of the Moynihan Report on Cruel Images About Poverty.* Rutgers University Press, 2015.

Greenberg, Cheryl Lynn. *"Or Does It Explode?": Black Harlem in the Great Depression.* Oxford University Press, 1991.

———. *To Ask for an Equal Chance: African Americans in the Great Depression.* Rowman & Littlefield, 2009.

Gutman, Marta. "Intermediate School 201: Race, Space, and Modern Architecture in Harlem." In *Educating Harlem: A Century of Schooling and Resistance in the Black Community,* edited by Ansley T. Erickson and Ernest Morrell. Columbia University Press, 2019.

Haley, Alex, and Malcolm X. *The Autobiography of Malcolm X.* Ballantine Books, 1965.

Hall, Gwendolyn Midlo. *Africans in Colonial Louisiana: The Development of Afro-Creole Culture in the Eighteenth Century.* Louisiana State University Press, 1992.

Hall, Stuart. "Reconstruction Work: Images of Post-war Black Settlement." In *Writings on Media: History of the Present,* edited by Charlotte Burnsdon. Duke University Press, 2021.

Hanson, Joyce A. *Mary McLeod Bethune and Black Women's Political Activism.* University of Missouri Press, 2003.

Harlan, Louis R. *Booker T. Washington: The Wizard of Tuskegee, 1901–1915.* Vol. 2. Oxford University Press, 1983.

Harley, Sharon. "'I Don't Pay Those Borders No Mind at All': Audley E. Moore ('Queen' Mother Moore)—Grassroots Global Traveler and Activist." In *Women and Migration: Responses in Art and History,* edited by Deborah Willis, Ellyn Toscano, and Kalila Brooks Nelson. Global Institute for Advanced Study, 2019.

Harold, Claudrena N. *The Rise and Fall of the Garvey Movement in the Urban South, 1918–1943*. Routledge, 2007.

Harpelle, Ronald. "Cross Currents in the Western Caribbean: Marcus Garvey and the UNIA in Central America." *Caribbean Studies* 31, no. 1 (2003): 35–73.

Harris, LaShawn. "Running with the Reds: African American Women and the Communist Party in the Great Depression." *Journal of African American History* 94, no. 1 (2009): 21–43.

———. *Sex Workers, Psychics, and Numbers Runners: Black Women in New York City's Underground Economy*. University of Illinois Press, 2016.

Harris, Lee A. "Political Autonomy as a Form of Reparations to African Americans." *Southern University Law Review* 29, no. 1 (2001): 25–56.

Harris, Robert L. "Early Black Benevolent Societies, 1780–1830." *Massachusetts Review* 20, no. 3 (1979): 603–25.

Harris, Robert, Nyota Harris, and Grandassa Harris, eds. *Carlos Cooks and Black Nationalism: From Garvey to Malcolm*. Majority Press, 1992.

Harsch, Ernest. *Thomas Sankara: An African Revolutionary*. Ohio University Press, 2014.

Hebert, Nelwyn, and Warren A. Perrin. *Iberia Parish*. Arcadia, 2012.

Height, Dorothy. "We Wanted the Voice of a Woman to Be Heard." In *Sisters in the Struggle: African American Women in the Civil Rights–Black Power Movement*, edited by Bettye Collier-Thomas and V. P. Franklin. New York University Press, 2001.

Herman, Arthur. *Joseph McCarthy: Reexamining the Life and Legacy of America's Most Hated Senator*. Free Press, 2000.

Hermann, Christina Pruett. "Specters of Freedom: Forced Labor, Struggle, and the Louisiana State Penitentiary System, 1835–1935." PhD diss., Michigan State University, 2015.

Hesford, Victoria. *Feeling Women's Liberation*. Duke University Press, 2013.

Hill, Anita. *Speaking Truth to Power*. New York: Anchor Books, 1997.

Hill, Lauren Warren, and Julia Rabig, eds. *The Business of Black Power: Community Development, Capitalism, and Corporate Responsibility in Postwar America*. University of Rochester Press, 2012.

Hill, Robert A., ed. *The Marcus Garvey and Universal Negro Improvement Association Papers*. Vol. 4. University of California Press, 1985.

———. *The Marcus Garvey and Universal Negro Improvement Association Papers*. Vol. 5. University of California Press, 1987.

Hill, Robert A., and Barbara Bair. *Marcus Garvey: Life and Lessons*. University of California Press, 1987.

Hill, Sylvia. "Progress Report on Congress Organizing." *Black Scholar* 5 (April 1974): 35–39.

Hinton, Elizabeth. *America on Fire: The Untold History of Police Violence and Black Rebellion Since the 1960s*. W. W. Norton, 2021.

———. *From the War on Poverty to the War on Crime: The Making of Mass Incarceration in America*. Harvard University Press, 2017.

Ho, Fred, and Bill Mullen. *Afro Asia: Revolutionary Political and Cultural Connections Between African Americans and Asian Americans*. Duke University Press, 2008.

Hollandsworth, James G., Jr. *Pretense of Glory: The Life of General Nathaniel P. Banks.* Louisiana State University Press, 1998.

Horne, Gerald. *Black Liberation/Red Scare: Ben Davis and the Communist Party.* University of Delaware Press, 1993.

———. *Black Revolutionary: William Patterson and the Globalization of the African American Freedom Struggle.* University of Illinois Press, 2013.

———. *Communist Front? The Civil Rights Congress, 1946–1956.* Associated University Presses, 1988.

———. *Red Seas: Ferdinand Smith and Radical Black Sailors in the United States and Jamaica.* New York: New York University Press, 2005.

Howe, Irving, and Lewis Coser. *The American Communist Party: A Critical History.* Praeger, 1962.

Hucks, Tracey E. *Yoruba Traditions and African American Nationalism.* University of New Mexico Press, 2012.

Hughes, Cheryl D. *Mother Katharine Drexel: The Riches-to-Rags Life Story of an American Catholic Saint.* William B. Eerdmans, 2014.

Humes, Edward. *Over Here: How the GI Bill Transformed the American Dream.* Diversion Books, 2014.

Hunter, Tera. *To 'Joy My Freedom: Southern Black Women's Lives and Labors After the Civil War.* Harvard University Press, 1997.

Hurston, Zora Neale. *Their Eyes Were Watching God.* 1937; University of Illinois Press, 1991.

Ingham, Kenneth. *Obote: A Political Biography.* Routledge, 1994.

Isaacman, Allen, and Barbara Isaacman. *Mozambique: From Colonialism to Revolution, 1900–1982.* Gower, 1983.

Ishmael, Hannah. "The Development of Black-Led Archives in London." PhD diss., University College London, 2020.

Issa, Jahi U. "The Universal Negro Improvement Association in Louisiana: Creating a Provisional Government in Exile." PhD diss., Howard University, 2005.

Isserman, Maurice. *Which Side Were You On? The American Communist Party During the Second World War.* University of Illinois Press, 1993.

Jackson, John L., Jr. *Harlemworld: Doing Race and Class in Contemporary America.* University of Chicago Press, 2001.

Jackson, Kellie Carter. *We Refuse: A Forceful History of Black Resistance.* Seal Press, 2024.

Jackson, Maurice, and Susan Kozel, eds. *Quakers and Their Allies in the Abolitionist Cause, 1754–1808.* Routledge, 2015.

Jackson, Nicole M. "The Ties That Bind: Questions of Empire and Belonging in Black British Educational Activism." In *Blackness in Britain,* edited by Kehinde Andrews and Lisa Amanda Palmer. Routledge, 2016.

Jackson-Issa, Kai. "In Her Own Book: Autobiographical Practice in the Oral Narratives of Queen Mother Audley Moore." PhD diss., Emory University, 1999.

Jacobs, Claude F. "Benevolent Societies of New Orleans Blacks During the Late Nineteenth and Early Twentieth Centuries." *Louisiana History* 29, no. 1 (1988): 21–33.

Jay, Mark, and Philip Conklin. *A People's History of Detroit.* Duke University Press, 2020.

Jeffries, Hasan Kwame. *Bloody Lowndes: Civil Rights and Black Power in Alabama's Black Belt.* New York University Press, 2009.

Johnson, Cedric. *Revolutionaries to Race Leaders: Black Power and the Making of African American Politics*. University of Minnesota Press, 2007.

Johnson, David K. *The Lavender Scare: The Cold War Persecution of Gays and Lesbians in the Federal Government*. University of Chicago Press, 2004.

Johnson, Nicholas. *Negroes and the Gun: The Black Tradition of Arms*. Prometheus Books, 2014.

Jolly, Kenneth S. *"By Our Own Strength": William Sherrill, the UNIA, and the Fight for African American Self-Determination in Detroit*. Peter Lang, 2013.

Jones, Martha. *Vanguard: How Black Women Broke Barriers, Won the Vote, and Insisted on Equality for All*. Basic Books, 2020.

Jones, William P. *The March on Washington: Jobs, Freedom, and the Forgotten History of Civil Rights*. W. W. Norton, 2013.

Joseph, Peniel E. "The Black Power Movement: A State of the Field." *Journal of American History* 96, no. 3 (2009): 751–76.

———. *Stokely: A Life*. Basic Books, 2014.

———. *The Third Reconstruction: America's Struggle for Racial Justice in the Twenty-First Century*. Basic Books, 2022.

Kaba, Lansine. *Kwame Nkrumah and the Dream of African Unity*. Diaspora African Press, 2017.

Kandeh, Jimmy D. *Coups from Below: Armed Subalterns and State Power in West Africa*. Palgrave Macmillan, 2004.

Kein, Sybil. *Creole: The History and Legacy of Louisiana's Free People of Color*. Louisiana State University Press, 2000.

Kelley, Robin D. G. "'But a Local Phase of a World Problem': Black History's Global Vision, 1883–1950." *Journal of American History* 86, no. 3 (1999): 1045–77.

———. "'A Day of Reckoning': Dreams of Reparations." In *Redress for Historical Injustices in the United States: On Reparations for Slavery, Jim Crow, and Their Legacies*, edited by Michael T. Martin and Marilyn Yaquinto. Duke University Press, 2007.

———. *Freedom Dreams: The Black Radical Imagination*. Beacon Press, 2002.

———. *Hammer and Hoe: Alabama Communists During the Great Depression*. University of North Carolina Press, 1990.

Khalifah, Hanif. *A Brief History of N'COBRA and the Reparations Movement*. KHA Books, 2005.

King, Martin Luther, Jr. *Why We Can't Wait*. Signet Classics, 2000.

King, Shannon. *Whose Harlem Is It Anyway? Community Politics and Grassroots Activism During the New Negro Era*. New York University Press, 2015.

Kirkendall, Richard S., ed. *Civil Liberties and the Legacy of Harry S. Truman*. Truman State University Press, 2013.

Kitwana, Bakari. "The Hip-Hop Generation." In *Four Hundred Souls: A Community History of African America, 1619–2019*, edited by Ibram X. Kendi and Keisha N. Blain. One World, 2021.

Kohlman-Hausman, Julilly. "Welfare Crises, Penal Solutions, and the Origins of the 'Welfare Queen.'" *Journal of Urban History* 41, no. 2 (2015): 756–71.

Konadu, Kwasi. *A View from the East: Cultural Nationalism and Education in New York City*. Syracuse University Press, 2009.

Konadu, Kwasi, and Clifford C. Campbell, eds. *The Ghana Reader: History, Culture, Politics.* Duke University Press, 2016.

Kotlowski, Dean J. *Nixon's Civil Rights: Politics, Principles, and Policy.* Harvard University Press, 2001.

Kraditor, Aileen S. *"Jimmy Higgins": The Mental World of the American Rank-and-File Communist, 1930–1958.* Greenwood Press, 1988.

Kruse, Kevin M., and Stephen Tuck, eds. *Fog of War: The Second World War and the Civil Rights Movement.* Oxford University Press, 2012.

Kyemba, Henry. *A State of Blood: The Inside Story of Idi Amin.* Paddington Press, 1997.

Lal, Priya. *African Socialism in Postcolonial Tanzania.* Cambridge University Press, 2015.

———. "Militants, Mothers, and the National Family: *Ujamaa,* Gender, and Rural Development in Postcolonial Tanzania." *Journal of African History* 51, no. 1 (2010): 1–20.

Lanker, Brian. *I Dream a World: Portraits of Black Women Who Changed America.* Stewart, Tabori & Chang, 1989.

Lawinski, Terese. *Living on the Edge of Suburbia: From Welfare to Workfare.* Vanderbilt University Press, 2010.

Lawson, Steven F., ed. *To Secure These Rights: The Report of President Harry S. Truman's Committee on Civil Rights.* St. Martin's Press, 2004.

Lecomote, Jeremy. "In Excess of the Brief: The Project Behind FESTAC Town." In Soyinka, *FESTAC '77.*

Lee, Sonia Song-Ha. *Building a Latino Civil Rights Movement: Puerto Ricans, African Americans, and the Pursuit of Racial Justice in New York City.* University of North Carolina Press, 2014.

Lentz-Smith, Adriane. *Freedom Struggles: African Americans and World War I.* Harvard University Press, 2011.

Leopold, Mark. *Idi Amin: The Story of Africa's Icon of Evil.* Yale University Press, 2021.

Levenstein, Lisa. *A Movement Without Marches: African American Women and the Politics of Poverty in Postwar Philadelphia.* University of North Carolina Press, 2009.

Levy, LaTaSha. "Remembering Sixth-PAC: Interviews with Sylvia Hill and Judy Claude, Organizers of the Sixth Pan-African Congress." *Black Scholar* 37, no. 4 (2008): 39–47.

Lewis, Angela K. *Conservatism in the Black Community: To the Right and Misunderstood.* Routledge, 2013.

Lewis, David Levering. *When Harlem Was in Vogue.* Penguin Books, 1997.

Lewis, Heather. *New York City Public Schools from Brownsville to Bloomberg: Community Control and Its Legacy.* Teachers College Press, 2013.

Lieberman, Robbie. *The Strangest Dream: Communism, Anticommunism, and the U.S. Peace Movement, 1945–1963.* Syracuse University Press, 2000.

Lieberman, Robbie, and Clarence Lang, eds. *Anticommunism and the African American Freedom Movement: Another Side of the Story.* Palgrave Macmillan, 2009.

Lincoln, Eric. *The Black Muslims in America.* Beacon Press, 1970.

Lindhorst, Taryn, and Leslie Leighninger. "'Ending Welfare as We Know It' in 1960: Louisiana's Suitable Home Law." *Social Service Review* 77, no. 4 (2013): 564–84.

Litwack, Leon F. *Been in the Storm So Long: The Aftermath of Slavery.* Random House, 1981.

Locke, Hubert G. *The Detroit 1967 Rebellion.* Wayne State University Press, 2017.

Loewen, James W. *Sundown Towns: A Hidden Dimension of American Racism.* New Press, 2018.

Logan, John R., Weiwei Zhang, and Miao Chunyu. "Emergent Ghettos: Black Neighborhoods in New York and Chicago, 1880–1940." *AJS: American Journal of Sociology* 120, no. 4 (2015): 1055–94.

Louw, P. Eric. *The Rise, Fall, and Legacy of Apartheid.* Praeger, 2004.

Lucander, David. *Winning the War for Democracy: The March on Washington Movement, 1941–1946.* University of Illinois Press, 2014.

Lucks, Daniel S. *Reconsidering Reagan: Racism, Republicans, and the Road to Trump.* Beacon Press, 2020.

Lúmumba, Chokwe. *The Roots of the New African Independence Movement: A Response to the Inaccurate and Politically Immature Attacks on the New Afrikan Independence Movement by the African People's Socialist Party.* New African Productions, n.d.

———. "Short History of the U.S. War on the R.N.A." *Black Scholar* 12, no. 1 (1981): 72–81.

Lundberg, Ferdinand, and Marynia Farnham. *Modern Woman: The Lost Sex.* Harper and Brothers, 1974.

Macmillan, Hugh. *The Lusaka Years: The ANC in Exile in Zambia.* Jacana Media, 2013.

Madhubuti, Haki R. "The Latest Purge: The Attack on Black Nationalism and Pan-Afrikanism by the New Left, the Sons and Daughters of the Old Left." *Black Scholar* 6, no. 1 (1975): 43–56.

Madhubuti, Haki R., and Maulana Karenga, eds. *Million Man March/Day of Absence: A Commemorative Anthology, Speeches, Commentary, Photography, Poetry, Illustrations.* Third World Press, 1996.

Makalani, Minkah. *In the Cause of Freedom: Radical Black Internationalism from Harlem to London, 1917–1939.* University of North Carolina Press, 2011.

Manning, Chandra. *Troubled Refuge: Struggling for Freedom During the Civil War.* Knopf, 2016.

Marable, Manning. *Malcolm X: A Life of Reinvention.* Viking, 2011.

———. "Peace and Black Liberation: The Contributions of W. E. B. Du Bois." *Science and Society* 47, no. 4 (1983): 385–405.

———. *Reform, Race, and Rebellion: The Second Reconstruction in Black America, 1945–2006.* University Press of Mississippi, 1991.

Marcum, John A. *Conceiving Mozambique.* Palgrave Macmillan, 2018.

Mares, Richard M. "'Exile is Hell': Black Internationalism and Robert F. Williams's Activist Network in the Cold War, 1950–1969." PhD diss., Michigan State University, 2019.

Markle, Seth. "'Book Publishers for a Pan-African World': Drum and Spear Press and Tanzania's *Ujamaa* Ideology." *Black Scholar* 37, no. 4 (2008): 16–26.

———. *A Motorcycle on Hell Run: Tanzania, Black Power, and the Uncertain Future of Pan-Africanism, 1964–1974.* Michigan State University Press, 2017.

———. "'We Are Not Tourists': The Black Power Movement and the Making of Socialist Tanzania, 1960–1974." PhD diss., New York University, 2010.

Martin, Charles H. "The Civil Rights Congress and Southern Black Defendants." *Georgia Historical Quarterly* 1, no. 1 (1987): 25–52.

———. "The International Labor Defense and Black America." *Labor History* 26, no. 2 (1985): 165–74.

———. "Race, Gender, and Southern Justice: The Rosa Lee Ingram Case." *American Journal of Legal History* 29, no. 2 (1985): 251–68.

Martin, Tony. *Amy Ashwood Garvey: Pan-Africanist, Feminist, and Mrs. Marcus Garvey No. 1, or, A Tale of Two Amies.* Majority Press, 2007.

———. *Race First: The Ideological and Organizational Struggles of Marcus Garvey and the Universal Negro Improvement Association.* Majority Press, 1986.

Massey, Douglas S., and Robert J. Sampson, eds. *The Moynihan Report Revisited: Lessons and Reflections After Four Decades.* SAGE, 2009.

Maxwell, William J. *F.B. Eyes: How J. Edgar Hoover's Ghostreaders Framed African American Literature.* Princeton University Press, 2015.

Mayes, Keith A. *Kwanzaa: Black Power and the Making of the African American Holiday Tradition.* Routledge, 2009.

M'Balia, Shafeah. "Remembering Queen Mother Moore." *Palimpsest: A Journal on Women, Gender, and the Black International* 7, no. 2 (2018): 173–76.

McClenahan, William M., Jr., and William H. Becker, *Eisenhower and the Cold War.* Johns Hopkins Press, 2011.

McDuffie, Erik S. "'I Wanted a Communist Philosophy, but I Wanted Us to Have a Chance to Organize Our People': The Diasporic Radicalism of Queen Mother Audley Moore and the Origins of Black Power." *African and Black Diaspora: An International Journal* 3, no. 2 (2010): 181–95.

———. "The March of Young Southern Black Women: Esther Cooper Jackson, Black Left Feminism, and the Personal and Political Costs of Cold War Repression." In *Anticommunism and the African American Freedom Movement,* edited by Robbie Lieberman and Clarence Lang. Palgrave Macmillan, 2011.

———. "'A New Day Has Dawned for the UNIA': Garveyism, the Diasporic Midwest, and West Africa, 1920–80." *Journal of West African History* 2, no. 3 (2016): 73–114.

———. "'A New Freedom Movement of Negro Women': Sojourning for Truth, Justice, and Human Rights During the Early Cold War." *Radical Historical Review* 101 (2008): 81–106.

———. "'No Small Amount of Change Could Do': Esther Cooper Jackson and the Making of a Black Left Feminist." In *Want to Start a Revolution? Radical Women in the Black Freedom Struggle,* edited by Dayo Gore, Jeanne Theoharis, and Komozi Woodard. New York University Press, 2009.

———. *The Second Battle for Africa: Garveyism, the US Heartland, and Global Black Freedom.* Duke University Press, 2024.

———. *Sojourning for Freedom: Black Women, American Communism, and the Making of Black Left Feminism.* Duke University Press, 2011.

———. "'We Owe a Debt to Her, She Taught Us How to Think': Eloise Moore and Her Impact on Queen Mother Moore and Twentieth Century Black Nationalism." *Palimpsest: A Journal on Women, Gender, and the Black International* 7, no. 2 (2018): 135–58.

McDuffie, Erik S., and Komozi Woodard. "'If You're in a Country That's Progressive, the Woman Is Progressive': Black Women Radicals and the Making of the Politics and Legacy of Malcolm X." *Biography* 36, no. 3 (2013): 507–39.

McWhirter, Cameron. *Red Summer: The Summer of 1919 and the Awakening of Black America.* Griffin, 2011.

Medley, Keith Weldon. *Black Life in New Orleans.* Pelican, 2014.

———. *We as Freemen: Plessy v. Ferguson.* Pelican, 2012.

Mehta, Brinda. "'Images of Exile and the Female Condition in Nawal El Saadawi's *The Fall of the Imam* and *Memoirs from the Women's Prison.*" In *Migration Words and Worlds: Pan-Africanism,* edited by E. Anthony Hurley, Renée Larrier, and Joseph McLaren. African World Press, 1999.

Meriwether, James H. "African Americans and the Mau Mau Rebellion: Militancy, Violence, and the Struggle for Freedom." *Journal of Ethnic History* 17, no. 4 (1998): 63–86.

———. *Proudly We Can Be Africans: Black Americans and Africa, 1935–1961.* University of North Carolina Press, 2002.

Mislan, Christina. "The Imperial 'We': Racial Justice, Nationhood, and Global War in Claudia Jones' *Weekly Review* Editorials, 1938–1943." *Journalism* 18, no. 10 (2016): 1415–30.

Mitchell, Brian Keith. "Oscar James Dunn: A Case Study in Race & Politics in Reconstruction Louisiana." PhD diss., University of New Orleans, 2011.

Mitchell, Michele. *Righteous Propagation: African Americans and the Politics of Racial Destiny After Reconstruction.* University of North Carolina Press, 2004.

Monotooth, Jennifer. "'Bridges to Human Dignity': Roy Innis, Conservative Black Power, and the Transformation of CORE, 1968–1998." PhD diss., University of Maryland–Baltimore County, 2017.

Moore, Audley A. *Why Reparations? Reparations Is the Battle Cry for the Economic and Social Freedom of More Than 25 Million Descendants of American Slaves.* Los Angeles, 1963.

Moore, Leonard. *Carl B. Stokes and the Rise of Black Political Power.* University of Illinois Press, 2002.

———. *The Defeat of Black Power: Civil Rights and the National Black Political Convention of 1972.* Louisiana State University Press, 2008.

Moore, Queen Mother. "A Band-Aid for a Cancer." *Harvard Graduate School of Education Association Bulletin* 7, no. 2 (1967): 29–32.

———. "We Refuse to Be Programmed Anymore." In Wanat and Cohen, *Before the Fall.*

Moore, Richard B. *The Name "Negro": Its Origin and Evil Use.* Reprint. Black Classic Press, 1992.

Morgan, Ted. *Reds: McCarthyism in Twentieth Century America.* Random House, 2004.

Morris, Courtney Desiree. "Becoming Creole, Becoming Black: Migration, Diasporic Self-Making, and the Many Lives of Madame Maymie Leona Turpeau de Mena." *Women, Gender, and Families of Color* 4, no. 2 (2016): 171–95.

Muhammad, Elijah. *The Supreme Wisdom.* Vol. 2, *What Every American So-Called Negro Should Know About.* Secretarius Publications, 1957.

Mumford, Kevin J. *Newark: A History of Race, Rights, and Riots in America.* New York University Press, 2007.

Murphy, David. "Performing Global African Culture and Citizenship: Major Pan-African Cultural Festivals from Dakar 1966 to FESTAC 1977." *Tate Papers,* no. 30 (Autumn 2018). www.tate.org.uk.

Musgrove, George Derek. *Rumor, Repression, and Racial Politics: How Harassment of Black Elected Officials Shaped Post–Civil Rights America.* University of Georgia Press, 2012.

Mutibwa, Phares. *Uganda Since Independence: A Story of Unfulfilled Hopes.* Africa World Press, 1992.

Nadasen, Premilla. *Household Workers Unite: The Untold Story of African American Women Who Started a Movement.* Beacon Press, 2015.

Naison, Mark. *Communists in Harlem During the Depression.* University of Illinois Press, 2005.

———. "From Eviction Resistance to Rent Control: Tenant Activism in the Great Depression." In *The Tenant Movement in New York City, 1904–1984,* edited by Ronald Lawson. Rutgers University Press, 1986.

Nance, Marilyn. *Last Days in Lagos.* Fourthwall Books, 2022.

Nelson, Alice Dunbar. "Negro Women in War Work." In *Scott's Official History of the American Negro in the World War,* edited by Emmett J. Scott. Arno Press, 1919.

Nelson, Jill. *Straight, No Chaser: How I Became a Grown-Up Black Woman.* G. P. Putnam's Sons, 1997.

Nelson, Sherice Janaye. *The Congressional Black Caucus: Fifty Years of Fighting for Equality.* Archway, 2021.

Neubeck, Kenneth J., and Noel A. Cazenave, eds. *Welfare Racism: Playing the Race Card Against America's Poor.* Routledge, 2001.

Newton, Huey. "'Intercommunalism': A Statement by Huey P. Newton." In *In Search of Common Ground: Conversations with Erik H. Erikson and Huey P. Newton,* edited by Kai T. Erikson. W. W. Norton, 1973.

———. *Revolutionary Suicide.* Penguin, 2009.

Newton, Nell Jessup. "Indian Claims for Reparations, Compensation, and Restitution in the United States Legal System." In *When Sorry Isn't Enough: The Controversy over Reparations for Human Injustice,* edited by Roy L. Brooks. New York University Press, 1999.

Newton, Wesley Phillips. "'Tenting Tonight on the Old Camp Grounds': Alabama's Military Bases in World War I." In *The Great War in the Heart of Dixie,* edited by Martin T. Olliff. University of Alabama Press, 2008.

Niven, David. *The Politics of Injustice: The Kennedys, the Freedom Rides, and the Electoral Consequences of a Moral Compromise.* University of Tennessee Press, 2003.

Nkrumah, Kwame. *Revolutionary Path.* International Publishers, 1973.

Nurhussein, Naida. *Black Land: Imperial Ethiopia and Black African America.* Princeton University Press, 2019.

Nyerere, Julius K. *Freedom and Socialism.* Oxford University Press, 1974.

———. *Ujamaa: Essays on Socialism.* Oxford University Press, 1968.

Nystrom, Justin A. *New Orleans After the Civil War: Race, Politics, and a New Birth of Freedom.* Johns Hopkins University Press, 2010.

Ogletree, Charles. *All Deliberate Speed: Reflections on the First Half-Century of Brown v. Board of Education.* W. W. Norton, 2004.

Olademo, Oyeronke. *Women in Yoruba Religions.* New York University Press, 2002.

Olupona, Jacob K., and Terry Rey, eds. *Òrìṣà Devotion as World Religion: The Globalization of Yoruba Religious Culture.* University of Wisconsin Press, 2008.

Olusoga, David. *Black and British: A Forgotten History.* Pan Books, 2017.

Onaci, Edward. *Free the Land: The Republic of New Africa and the Pursuit of a Black Nation-State*. University of North Carolina Press, 2020.

O'Neil, John. "The Rise and Fall of the UFT." In *Schools Against Children: The Case for Community Control*, edited by Annette T. Rubenstein. Monthly Review Press, 1970.

Opdycke, Sandra. *The WPA: Creating Jobs and Hope in the Great Depression*. Routledge, 2016.

O'Reilly, Kenneth. *Racial Matters: The FBI's Secret File on Black America, 1960–1972*. Free Press, 1991.

Page, Malcolm. *King's African Rifles: A History*. Barnsley Pen and Sword Military, 2010.

Pan-African Congress. *Resolutions and Selected Speeches from the Sixth Pan African Congress*. Tanzania Publishing House, 1976.

Parker, Alison M. *Unceasing Militant: The Life of Mary Church Terrell*. University of North Carolina Press, 2020.

Patterson, James T. *Freedom Is Not Enough: The Moynihan Report and America's Struggle over Black Family Life from LBJ to Obama*. Basic Books, 2010.

Patton, Gwen. *My Race to Freedom: A Life in the Civil Rights Movement*. New South Books, 2020.

Payne, Les. *The Dead Are Arising: The Life of Malcolm X*. Liveright, 2020.

Perez, Gina. *The Near Northwest Side Story: Migration, Displacement, and Puerto Rican Families*. University of California Press, 2004.

Perrusquia, Marc. *A Spy in Canaan: How the FBI Used a Famous Photographer to Infiltrate the Civil Rights Movement*. Melville House, 2018.

Perry, Kennetta Hammond. *London Is the Place for Me: Black Britons, Citizenship, and the Politics of Race*. Oxford University Press, 2015.

Perry, Miranda Booker. "The Prospect of Justice: African American Redress and the Ex-Slave Pension Movement, 1865–1937." PhD diss., Howard University, 2012.

Peterson, Derek R., and Richard Vokes. *The Unseen Archive of Idi Amin: Photographs from the Uganda Broadcasting Corporation*. Prestel, 2021.

Pettengill, Ryan S. "Communists and Community: Unionism and the Rise and Fall of Community Activism in Detroit, 1932–1968." PhD diss., Michigan State University, 2009.

Plummer, Brenda Gayle. *In Search of Power: African Americans in the Era of Decolonization*. Cambridge University Press, 2013.

Podair, Jerald E. *The Strike That Changed New York: Blacks, Whites, and the Ocean Hill–Brownsville Crisis*. Yale University Press, 2001.

Powell, Adam Clayton, Jr. *Adam by Adam: The Autobiography of Adam Clayton Powell Jr.* Dafina Books, 2002.

Pross, Christian. *Paying for the Past: The Struggle over Reparations for Surviving Victims of Nazi Terror*. Johns Hopkins University Press, 1998.

Putnam, Laura. *Radical Moves: Caribbean Migrants and the Politics of Race in the Jazz Age*. University of North Carolina Press, 2013.

Rabin, Lisa, and Craig Kridel. "Cinema for Social Change: The Human Relations Film Series of the Harlem Committee of the Teachers Union, 1936–1950." In *Educating Harlem: A Century of Schooling and Resistance in the Black Community*, edited by Ansley T. Erickson and Ernest Morrell. Columbia University Press, 2019.

Ramsey, Donovan X. *When Crack Was King: A People's History of a Misunderstood Era.* One World, 2023.

Randolph, Sherie M. *Florynce "Flo" Kennedy: The Life of a Black Feminist Radical.* University of North Carolina Press, 2018.

Ransby, Barbara. *Ella Baker and the Black Freedom Struggle: A Radical Democratic Vision.* University of North Carolina Press, 2010.

Reddie, Anthony G. *Black Theology in Transatlantic Dialogue.* Palgrave Macmillan, 2016.

Rhodes, Joel P., and Judson L. Jeffries. "Motor City Panthers." In *On the Ground: The Black Panther Party in Communities Across America,* edited by Judson L. Jeffries. University Press of Mississippi, 2010.

Ribeiro, Alyssa. "'Asking Them and Protesting': Black and Puerto Rican Civic Leadership in Philadelphia Neighborhoods, 1960s–1970s." *Pennsylvania History: A Journal of Mid-Atlantic Studies* 86, no. 3 (2019): 359–82.

Richardson, Francis. "The Teche Country Fifty Years Ago." *Southern Bivouac* 1, no. 10 (1886): 593–98.

Rickford, Russell. "Black Power as Educational Renaissance: The Harlem Landscape." In *Educating Harlem: A Century of Schooling and Resistance in the Black Community,* edited by Ansley T. Erickson and Ernest Morrell. Columbia University Press, 2019.

———. *We Are an African People: Independent Education, Black Power, and the Radical Imagination.* Oxford University Press, 2016.

Rigueur, Leah Wright. *The Loneliness of the Black Republican: Pragmatic Politics and the Pursuit of Power.* Princeton University Press, 2014.

Rivera, Pedro R. "Carlos Cooks and Garveyism: Bridging Two Eras of Black Nationalism." PhD diss., Howard University, 2012.

Robinson, Paul. "Race, Space, and the Evolution of Black Los Angeles." In *Black Los Angeles: American Dreams and Racial Realities,* edited by Darnell Hunt and Ana-Christina Ramón. New York University Press, 2010.

Rogers, Kim Lacey. *Righteous Lives: Narratives of the New Orleans Civil Rights Movement.* New York University Press, 1994.

Rolinson, Mary G. *Grassroots Garveyism: The Universal Negro Improvement Association in the Rural South, 1920–1927.* University of North Carolina Press, 2007.

Rolph, Stephanie R. *Resisting Equality: The Citizens' Council, 1954–1989.* Louisiana State University Press, 2018.

Rooks, Noliwe. *A Passionate Mind in Relentless Pursuit: The Vision of Mary McLeod Bethune.* Penguin Press, 2024.

Ross, Michael A. *The Great New Orleans Kidnapping Case: Race, Law, and Justice in the Reconstruction Era.* Oxford University Press, 2015.

Roth, Benita. *Separate Roads to Feminism: Black, Chicana, and White Feminist Movements in America's Second Wave.* Cambridge University Press, 2004.

Rothfeder, Jeffrey. *McIlhenny's Gold: How a Louisiana Family Built the Tabasco Empire.* Collins, 2007.

Royals, Dan. *To Make the Wounded Whole: The African American Struggle Against HIV/AIDS.* University of North Carolina Press, 2020.

Ryan, James G. *Earl Browder: The Failure of American Communism.* University of Alabama Press, 1997.

Salaam, Kalamu ya. "The Realities of Living and Working in Afrika." *Black Collegian* 5, no. 1 (1974): 28, 66–67.

Sales, William W., Jr. *From Civil Rights to Black Liberation: Malcolm X and the Organization of Afro-American Unity.* South End Press, 1999.

Salvaggio, John E. *New Orleans' Charity Hospital: A Story of Physicians, Politics, and Poverty.* Louisiana State University Press, 1992.

Salvatore, Nick. *Singing in a Strange Land: C. L. Franklin, the Black Church, and the Transformation of America.* Little, Brown, 2007.

Sanchez, Sonia. "Poem for Queen Mother Moore." *Palimpsest: A Journal on Women, Gender, and the Black International* 7, no. 2 (2018): 163–68.

Sandoz, William J. "A Brief History of St. Landry Parish." *Louisiana Historical Quarterly* 8, no. 2 (1925): 221–39.

Sartain, Lee. *Invisible Activists: Women of the Louisiana NAACP and the Struggle for Civil Rights, 1915–1945.* Louisiana State University Press, 2007.

Sawadogo, Boukary. *Africans in Harlem: An Untold New York Story.* Fordham University Press, 2022.

Sawyer, Michael. *Black Minded: The Political Philosophy of Malcolm X.* Pluto Press, 2020.

Scanlon, Jennifer. *Until There Is Justice: The Life of Anna Arnold Hedgeman.* Oxford University Press, 2016.

Schafer, Louis S. "Yesterday's City: Chicago's Horseless Carriages." *Chicago History* 23, no. 3 (1994–95): 52–64.

Schamberg, Anne. "A Midwestern Study of the Foods and Foodways of the Great Depression." *Milwaukee Journal Sentinel,* May 5, 2011.

Schmidt, Christopher W. *The Sit-Ins: Protest & Legal Change in the Civil Rights Era.* University of Chicago Press, 2018.

Schmidt, Regin. *Red Scare: FBI and the Origins of Anticommunism in the United States, 1919–1943.* Museum Tusculanum Press, University of Copenhagen, 2000.

Seniors, Paula Marie. *Mae Mallory, the Monroe Defense Committee, and World Revolutions.* University of Georgia Press, 2024.

Sesay, Amadu, Olusola Ojo, and Orobola Fasehun. *The OAU After Twenty Years.* Westview Press, 1984.

Shakur, Assata. *Assata: The Autobiography of a Revolutionary.* Lawrence Hill, 1987.

Sheikheldin, Gussai H. "Ujamaa: Planning and Managing Development Schemes in Africa, Tanzania as a Case Study." *Journal of Pan African Studies* 8, no. 1 (2014): 78–96.

Shepperson, George. "Ethiopianism and African Nationalism." *Phylon* 14, no. 1 (1953): 9–18.

Shockley, Megan Taylor. *"We Too Are Americans": African American Women in Detroit and Richmond, 1940–1954.* University of Illinois Press, 2004.

Simanga, Michael. *Amiri Baraka and the Congress of African People.* Palgrave Macmillan, 2015.

Simmons, LaKisha Michelle. *Crescent City Girls: The Lives of Young Black Women in Segregated New Orleans.* University of North Carolina Press, 2015.

Singh, Robert. *The Farrakhan Phenomenon: Race, Reaction, and the Paranoid Style in American Politics.* Georgetown University Press, 1997.

Sinha, Manisha. *The Rise and Fall of the Second Republic.* Liveright, 2024.

Sinitiere, Phillip Luke, ed. *Citizen of the World: The Late Career and Legacy of W. E. B. Du Bois.* Northwestern University Press, 2019.

Slawson, Douglas. "Segregated Catholicism: The Origins of St. Katharine's Parish, New Orleans." *Vincentian Heritage Journal* 17, no. 3 (1996): 141–84.

Smallwood, James. *Reform, Red Scare, and Ruin: Virginia Durr, Prophet of the New South.* Xlibris, 2008.

Smethurst, James. *The Black Arts Movement: Literary Nationalism in the 1960s and 1970s.* University of North Carolina Press, 2005.

———. *The New Red Negro: The Literary Left and African American Poetry, 1930–1946.* Oxford University Press, 1999.

Smith, Gregory. *Where Credit Is Due: How Africa's Debt Can Be a Benefit, Not a Burden.* Oxford University Press, 2021.

Smith, Richard. *Jamaican Volunteers in the First World War: Race, Masculinity, and the Development of National Consciousness.* Palgrave Macmillan, 2004.

Snyder, Sarah B. *From Selma to Moscow: How Human Rights Transformed U.S. Foreign Policy.* Columbia University Press, 2018.

Solomon, Mark. *The Cry Was Unity: Communists and African Americans, 1917–1936.* University Press of Mississippi, 1998.

Sorin, Gretchen. *Driving While Black: African American Travel and the Road to Civil Rights.* Liveright, 2020.

Soyinka, Wole. *FESTAC '77: 2nd World Festival of Black and African Arts and Culture.* Walther Konig, 2019.

Spalding, Elizabeth Edwards. *The First Cold Warrior: Harry Truman, Containment, and the Remaking of Liberal Internationalism.* University Press of Kentucky, 2006.

Springer, Kimberly. *Living for the Revolution: Black Feminist Organizations, 1968–1980.* Duke University Press, 2005.

Starobin, Joseph. *American Communism in Crisis, 1943–1957.* Harvard University Press, 1973.

Stein, Judith. *The World of Marcus Garvey: Race and Class in Modern Society.* Louisiana State University Press, 1986.

Stephens, Ronald J. "Garveyism in Idlewild, 1927 to 1936." *Journal of Black Studies* 34, no. 3 (2004): 462–88.

Stevenson, Brenda. *The Contested Murder of Latasha Harlins: Justice, Gender, and the Origins of the LA Riots.* Oxford University Press, 2013.

Stoeltje, Beverly J. "Asante Queen Mothers: A Study in Female Authority." *Annals of the New York Academy of Sciences* 810, no. 1 (1997): 41–71.

Stone, Chuck. "The National Conferences on Black Power." In *The Black Power Revolt: A Collection of Essays,* edited by Floyd Barbour. Porter Sargent, 1968.

Stone, Joel. "Steel Meets Flint: How to Start a Riot." In *Detroit 1967: Origins, Impacts, Legacies,* edited by Joel Stone. Wayne State University Press, 2017.

Storrs, Landon R. Y. "Revisiting Truman's Federal Employee Loyalty Program." In *Civil Liberties and the Legacy of Harry S. Truman,* edited by Richard S. Kirkendall. Truman State University Press, 2013.

———. *The Second Red Scare and the Unmaking of the New Deal Left.* Princeton University Press, 2013.

Strahan, Derek. *Lost Springfield, Massachusetts.* History Press, 2017.

Street, Joe. "Malcolm X, Smethwick, and the Influence of the African American Freedom Struggle on British Race Relations in the 1960s." *Journal of Black Studies* 38, no. 6 (2008): 932–50.

Sullivan, Frances Peace. "'Forging Ahead' in Banes, Cuba: Garveyism in a United Fruit Company Town." *New West Indian Guide* 88, no. 3–4 (2014): 231–61.

Summers, Martin Anthony. *Manliness and Its Discontents: The Black Middle Class and the Transformation of Black Masculinity, 1900–1930*. University of North Carolina Press, 2004.

Swan, Quito. *Black Power in Bermuda: The Struggle for Decolonization*. Palgrave Macmillan, 2010.

———. "I & I Shot the Sheriff: Black Power and Decolonization in Bermuda, 1968–1977." In *Black Power in the Caribbean*, edited by Kate Quinn. University Press of Florida, 2014.

———. *Pauulu's Diaspora: Black Internationalism and Environmental Justice*. University Press of Florida, 2020.

Tate, Lessie B. "The Power of Pan Africanism: African American/Tanzanian Linkages, 1947–1997." PhD diss., University of Illinois–Urbana Champaign, 2015.

Tateishi, John. *Redress: The Inside Story of the Successful Campaign for Japanese American Reparations*. Heyday, 2020.

Taylor, Candacy. *Overground Railroad: The Green Book and the Roots of Black Travel in America*. Abrams Press, 2020.

Taylor, Clarence. *Knocking at Our Own Door: Milton A. Galamison and the Struggle to Integrate New York City Schools*. Lexington Books, 2001.

Taylor, Jon E. *Freedom to Serve: Truman, Civil Rights, and Executive Order 9981*. Routledge, 2013.

Taylor, Ula. *The Promise of Patriarchy: Women and the Nation of Islam*. University of North Carolina Press, 2017.

———. "Street Strollers: Grounding the Theory of Black Women Intellectuals." *Afro-Americans in New York Life and History* 30, no. 2 (2006): 153–71.

———. *The Veiled Garvey: The Life and Times of Amy Jacques Garvey*. University of North Carolina Press, 2003.

Theoharis, Jeanne. *The Rebellious Life of Mrs. Rosa Parks*. Beacon Press, 2013.

Thomas, Rhondda R. "Exodus and Colonization: Charting the Journey in the Journals of Daniel Coker, a Descendant of Africa." *African American Review* 41, no. 3 (2007): 507–19.

Thomas, Tony. "Black Nationalism and Confused Marxists." *Black Scholar* 4, no. 1 (1972): 47–52.

Thompson, Heather. *Whose Detroit? Politics, Labor, and Race in a Modern American City*. Cornell University Press, 2001.

Thompson, Shirley Elizabeth. *Exiles at Home: The Struggle to Become American Creole in New Orleans*. Harvard University Press, 2009.

Tolbert, Emory J. *The UNIA and Black Los Angeles: Ideology and Community in the American Garvey Movement*. Center for Afro-American Studies, 1980.

Toll, Jean Barth, and Mildred S. Gillam, eds. *Invisible Philadelphia: Community Through Voluntary Organizations*. Atwater Kent Museum, 1995.

Tomás, António. *Amílcar Cabral: The Life of a Reluctant Nationalist*. Oxford University Press, 2021.

Triece, Mary Eleanor. *On the Picket Line: Strategies of Working Class Women During the Depression*. University of Illinois Press, 2007.

Trotter, Joe William, Jr. *From a Raw Deal to a New Deal: African Americans, 1929–1945*. Oxford University Press, 1996.

Turner, Richard Brent. *Jazz, Religion, the Second Line, and Black New Orleans After Hurricane Katrina*. Indiana University Press, 2009.

Turner, W. Burghardt. "The Richard B. Moore Collection and Its Collector." *Caribbean Studies* 15, no. 1 (1975): 135–45.

Turner, W. Burghardt, and Joyce Turner, eds. *Richard B. Moore: Caribbean Militant in Harlem*. Indiana University Press, 1988.

Tuuri, Rebecca. *Strategic Sisterhood: The National Council of Negro Women in the Black Freedom Struggle*. University of North Carolina Press, 2018.

Twa, Linda J. "The Great Congress of the Black Spirit: Artist Reflections on FESTAC '77." *Nka: Journal of Contemporary African Art* 50 (May 2022): 76–89.

Tyson, Timothy. *Radio Free Dixie: Robert F. Williams and the Roots of Black Power*. University of North Carolina Press, 2009.

Umoja, Akinyele Omaowale. *We Will Shoot Back: Armed Resistance in the Mississippi Freedom Movement*. New York University Press, 2013.

Vandal, Gilles. "Politics and Violence in Bourbon Louisiana: The Loreauville Riot of 1884 as a Case Study." *Louisiana History* 30, no. 1 (1989): 23–42.

Van Dusen, Gerald. *Detroit's Sojourner Truth Housing Riot of 1942*. History Press, 2020.

Van Ells, Mark D. *America and World War I: A Traveler's Guide*. Interlink, 2015.

Vaughan, Walter Raleigh. *Vaughan's "Freedmen's Pension Bill": Being an Appeal on Behalf of Men Released from Slavery: A Plea for American Freedmen and a Rational Proposition to Grant Permissions to Persons of Color Emancipated from Slavery*. Reprint. Wentworth Press, 2016.

Vaughn-Roberson, Clayton. "Fascism with a Jim Crow Face: The National Negro Congress and the Global Popular Front." PhD diss., Carnegie Mellon University, 2019.

Vázquez-Hernández, Víctor. "From Pan-Latino Enclaves to a Community: Puerto Ricans in Philadelphia, 1910–2000." In *The Puerto Rican Diaspora: Historical Perspectives*, edited by Carmen Teresa Whalen and Víctor Vázquez-Hernández. Temple University Press, 2003.

Vince, Natalya. *The Algerian War, the Algerian Revolution*. Palgrave Macmillan, 2020.

Von Eschen, Penny. *Race Against Empire: Black Americans and Anticolonialism, 1937–1957*. Cornell University Press, 1997.

Wald, Gayle. *It's Been Beautiful: "Soul!" and Black Power Television*. Duke University Press, 2015.

Walker, Dennis. "The Revived Nation of Islam and America's Western System in the 1990s: Ambiguous Protest and the New Black Elite." *Islamic Studies* 37, no. 4 (1999): 445–78.

Walters, Ronald. *Pan-Africanism in the African Diaspora: An Analysis of Afrocentric Political Movements*. Wayne State University Press, 1993.

Wanat, Stanley, and Michael Cohen, eds. *Before the Fall: A Discussion of Schools in Conflict with Community.* Cornell University, 1969.

Ward, Stephen. *In Love and Struggle: The Revolutionary Lives of James and Grace Lee Boggs.* University of North Carolina Press, 2016.

Warner, Thomas O. "Recollections and Reflections." *Palimpsest: A Journal on Women, Gender, and the Black International* 7, no. 2 (2018): 159–62.

Warrington, Paul. *Black British Intellectuals and Education: Multiculturalism's Hidden History.* Routledge, 2014.

Washburn, Patrick S. "The *Pittsburgh Courier*'s Double V Campaign in 1942." *American Journalism* 3, no. 2 (1986): 73–86.

Washington, Mary Helen. *The Other Blacklist: The African American Literary and Cultural Left of the 1950s.* Columbia University Press, 2014.

Waters, Rob. *Thinking Black: Britain, 1964–1985.* University of California Press, 2019.

Watts, Jerry. *Amiri Baraka: The Politics and Art of a Black Intellectual.* New York University Press, 2001.

Weigand, Kate. *Red Feminism: American Communism and the Making of Women's Liberation.* Johns Hopkins University Press, 2002.

Weiner, Tim. *Enemies: A History of the FBI.* Random House, 2012.

Westheider, James E. *The African American Experience in Vietnam: Brothers in Arms.* Rowman & Littlefield, 2008.

Whalen, Carmen Teresa. "Colonialism, Citizenship, and the Making of the Puerto Rican Diaspora: An Introduction." In *The Puerto Rican Diaspora: Historical Perspectives,* edited by Carmen Teresa Whalen and Víctor Vázquez-Hernández. Temple University Press, 2003.

Whitaker, Matthew C. *Peace Be Still: Modern Black America from World War II to Barack Obama.* University of Nebraska Press, 2013.

White, Deborah Gray. *Too Heavy a Load: Black Women in Defense of Themselves, 1894–1994.* W. W. Norton, 1999.

Widmer, Mary Lou. *New Orleans in the Twenties.* Pelican, 1993.

Wilkerson, Isabel. *The Warmth of Other Suns: The Epic Story of America's Great Migration.* Vintage Books, 2010.

Wilkins, Fanon Che. "'A Line of Steel': The Organization of the Sixth Pan-African Congress and the Struggle for International Black Power, 1969–1974." In *The Hidden 1970s: Histories of Radicalism,* edited by Dan Berger. Rutgers University Press, 2010.

Williams, Chad. *Torchbearers for Democracy: African American Soldiers in the World War I Era.* University of North Carolina Press, 2010.

Williams, Kidada. *I Saw Death Coming: A History of Terror and Survival in the War Against Reconstruction.* Bloomsbury, 2023.

Winters, John David. *The Civil War in Louisiana.* Louisiana State University Press, 1991.

Woodard, Komozi. *A Nation Within a Nation: Amiri Baraka and Black Power Politics.* University of North Carolina Press, 1999.

Woods, Allen T., ed. *Woods Directory: Being a Colored Business, Professional and Trades Directory of New Orleans, Louisiana.* 1914.

Woods, Jeff. *Black Struggle, Red Scare: Segregation and Communism in the American South, 1948–1968*. Louisiana State University Press, 2004.

Worrell, Rodney. *George Padmore's Black Internationalism*. University of the West Indies Press, 2020.

Wright, George. *The Destruction of a Nation: United States Policy Toward Angola Since 1945*. Pluto Press, 1997.

Wright, Nathan, Jr. *Let's Work Together*. Hawthorne Books, 1968.

Wright, Willie Jamal. "'Free the Land!': Exploring the Spatial and Political Legacies of the Republic of New Afrika in Detroit and Jackson." PhD diss., University of North Carolina, 2019.

Wynn, Neil A. *The African American Experience during World War II*. Rowman & Littlefield, 2010.

X, Malcolm. *Malcolm X Speaks: Selected Speeches and Statements*. Edited by George Breitman. 2nd ed. Pathfinder, 1989.

Zhana. *Black Success Stories: Celebrating People of African Heritage*. Vol. 1. Zhana Productions, 2006.

Zuberi, Tukufu. *African Independence: How Africa Shapes the World*. Rowman & Littlefield, 2015.

Index

About the Author

Ashley D. Farmer is a historian and an associate professor of history and African Diaspora studies at the University of Texas at Austin. Her first book, *Remaking Black Power,* was short-listed for numerous awards, and she has received awards and fellowships from the National Endowment for the Humanities, the Radcliffe Institute for Advanced Study at Harvard University, and the Whiting Foundation. She has written for *Harper's Bazaar, Teen Vogue, The Washington Post,* and *The Independent,* among other outlets. Farmer holds a BA from Spelman College and an MA and a PhD from Harvard University. She lives in Austin, Texas.